Pacific Century

published in cooperation with

The Pacific Basin Institute

SECOND EDITION

Pacific Century

The Emergence of
Modern Pacific Asia

Mark Borthwick
with contributions by selected scholars

Westview Press
A Member of the Perseus Books Group

Copyright © 1992, 1998 by Westview Press, A Member of the Perseus Books Group

Published in 1998 in the United States of America by Westview Press, 5500 Central Avenue, Boulder, Colorado 80301-2877, and in the United Kingdom by Westview Press, 12 Hid's Copse Road, Cumnor Hill, Oxford OX2 9JJ

Library of Congress Cataloging-in-Publication Data
Borthwick, Mark.
   Pacific century : the emergence of modern Pacific Asia / by Mark
Borthwick with contributions by selected scholars. — 2nd ed.
     p. cm.
  Includes bibliographical references and index.
  ISBN 0-8133-3471-3 (pbk)
  1. Asia, Southeastern—Politics and government—1945–   . 2. East
Asia—Economic conditions. 3. Asia, Southeastern—Economic
conditions. [1. East Asia—Politics and government.] I. Title.
DX518.1.B64 1998
950—dc21   97-42756
                                                                   CIP

Second edition published in 1998 in Australia by
MACMILLAN EDUCATION AUSTRALIA PTY LTD
627 Chapel Street, South Yarra 3141

Associated companies and representatives throughout the world

National Library of Australia cataloguing in publication data
Borthwick, Mark.
   Pacific century : the emergence of modern Pacific Asia.
   2nd ed.
   Bibliography.
   Includes index.
   ISBN 0 7329 5066 X.
   1. East Asia – Politics and government. 2. Asia,
   Southeastern – Politics and government – 1945– . I. Title.
950

First published in 1992 in Australia by Allen & Unwin, Sydney

EBC   02 03 04 05   15 14 13 12 11 10 9 8 7

Contents

Maps

Preface

". . . it is by the professional favour of the great navigators ever present to my memory... that I have been permitted to sail through the very heart of the old Pacific mystery, a region which even in my time remained very imperfectly charted."

— Joseph Conrad, "Geography and Some Explorers," *Last Essays*.

Writing and editing this book has been a humbling experience. The immensity of the subject alone would have made anyone pause, but the invitation from Frank Gibney to produce the textbook for his PBS television series, *Pacific Century*, was more than I could resist, having long been persuaded of the need for a general guide to the Pacific Basin that is accessible to the non-specialist. At first glance, there would seem to be an abundance of such books, but none of them provides a survey of major themes in the economic and political development of the Pacific Asian region in ways that integrate the past with the present.

In 1988, the then-president of the Association of Asian Studies, Rhoads Murphey, delivered an address in which he observed that there seemed to be a diminishing number of genuine "Asianists" in the profession — people who were willing to consider "how their own specialized part or period or aspect of Asia ... fits into the larger Asian and world context." Such individuals do manage to survive. It is hoped that they and their students will find this book to be a useful tool, as will the "practitioners" who presently are or soon will be business leaders, government officials, institutional representatives, or simply the well-educated citizens of a Pacific community.

Joseph Conrad wrote a description, from which the opening quote above is taken, about a time when as a ship's captain taking on cargo in Sydney, Australia, he impulsively asked the ship's owners for permission to sail through the dangerous Torres Straits — a graveyard for generations of ships. It was, he admitted, a proposition that "ought to have received a severe rap on the knuckles," but the request was granted. Making the famous passage was, for Conrad, a kind of pilgrimage. Its perils had been charted by his heroes, the great Pacific explorers and navigators who revealed its geography and made its use possible by generations to come. This book, too, has been a navigation of the Pacific that has been made possible by great explorers: scholars whose published achievements rise like newly discovered islands above the surface of our navigation. If they have not always been perfectly sighted and described herein, it is hoped that this volume will enable the reader nevertheless to find them, go ashore, and explore their interiors.

— Mark Borthwick

Acknowledgments

A book such as this is not possible without the support of a wide network of people. Taken altogether, their contribution to the project far surpasses anything I have done by myself. The origin and inspiration for the *Pacific Century* project came from Frank Gibney whose experience and knowledge have been a mainstay of its progress. The Pacific Basin Institute staff in Santa Barbara — Laura Omi, Anne Schechter, and Melanie Zimmerman — prevailed against all odds and somehow managed to hold the sprawling enterprise together.

In Washington, Christopher Ragonese watched over the detailed preparation of this book, both informing its content and raising its quality with a commitment to accuracy and clarity. His organizational skills and knowledge of China were indispensable. The guide to pronunciation of Chinese names at the end of the book is largely his work.

Gil Latz and the staff at the International Trade Institute, Portland State University, were responsible for the critical review of all text materials and map development. They became an anchor point for the project, holding it to high standards. Andrea Asbell, Blaine Erickson, Paul Anton, and Richard H. Jones provided many substantive contributions in this process with a wide range of information and useful, perceptive analyses. With Gil Latz, Bill Loy of the University of Oregon Department of Geography oversaw the development of specialized maps.

Scholars who have contributed in one way or another go well beyond the brief list I can provide here. Many are the authors of excerpts taken with permission from previously published materials. Others have provided especially useful and insightful guidance, namely, Evelyn Colbert, Donald Emmerson, Chalmers Johnson, Roy U.T. Kim, Lawrence Krause, Charles Morrison, Michael Robinson, Frank Tatu, and Arthur Waldron. Special thanks are due to scholars who contributed original material to these chapters: Gilbert Rozman, John Stephan, and Michael Williams. However, the approach and editorial perspective taken here should be attributed to me, not to the contributors and advisors for either the textbook or the *Pacific Century* telecourse.

This book also traces its origins to mentors and friends who were not directly involved in its creation. At the University of Iowa, Mac Marshall introduced me to Pacific Studies and the necessity of multidisciplinary perspectives. Edward Palmer, former Staff Director of the House Subcommittee on Asian and Pacific Affairs, gave me both the rare opportunity to work on the Subcommittee and a window on foreign affairs politics in Washington. Similarly, Richard Sneider and Hugh Scott helped guide my early efforts in this field.

I am indebted also to the Asia Society and the East-West Center, two institutions that have done much to advance public information about Asia. The Asia Society generously gave permission for the reproduction of maps and various entries from the *Encyclopedia of Asian History.* The East-West Center in Honolulu similarly gave permission for the use of extracts from issues of its *Asia Pacific Report.* In addition, the *Far Eastern Economic Review*, an indispensable reference for current information on the region, donated several extracts.

The principal financial support for this project was provided by the Annenberg/CPB Project and by the Ford Foundation. The Henry M. Jackson

Foundation has provided support for development of the original Study Guide and Faculty Manual materials.

Page layout and design for this book was achieved by the talent and perseverance of Gary Roush from *Right Angle Graphics*.

Authors are inevitably in the debt of their families who support their efforts, beginning with their parents and ending with their spouses — or the other way around, I am not sure which. My family has patiently endured my immersion in this effort and sustained my flagging morale in the darker hours. I hope this book is worthy of their sacrifices on its behalf.

—M.B.

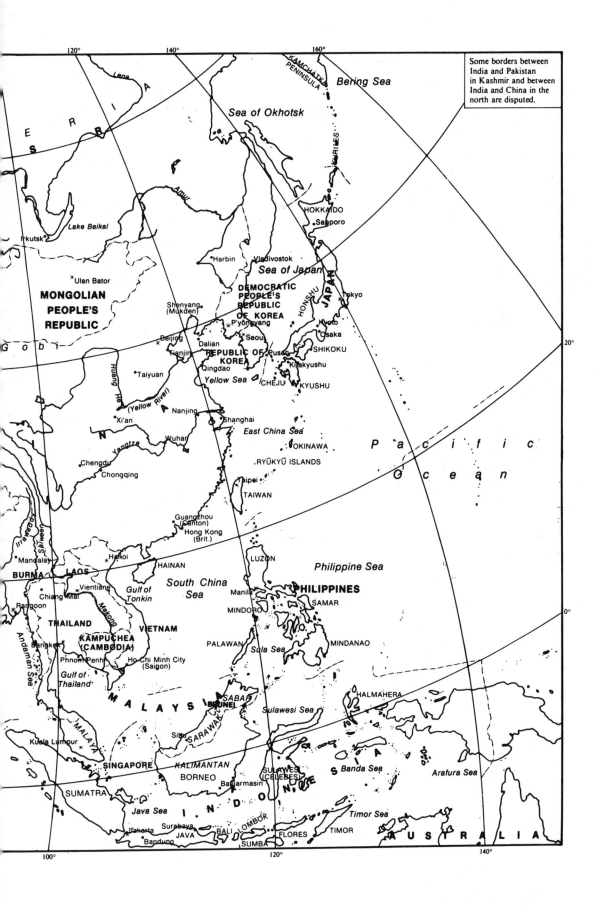

Some borders between
India and Pakistan
in Kashmir and between
India and China in the
north are disputed.

Bering Sea

Sea of Okhotsk

KAMCHATKA
PENINSULA

Lena

Amur

HOKKAIDO
•Sapporo

•Harbin   Vladivostok•   Sea of Japan

•Irkutsk   *Lake Baikal*

•Ulan Bator

MONGOLIAN
PEOPLE'S
REPUBLIC

DEMOCRATIC
PEOPLE'S
REPUBLIC
OF KOREA

HONSHU   JAPAN   •Tokyo

Shenyang
(Mukden)•   •P'yŏngyang   •Kyoto

Beijing•   •Seoul   •Osaka
•Dalian
Tianjin•   REPUBLIC OF   •Pusan   •SHIKOKU
KOREA
•Qingdao   •Kitakyushu
Yellow Sea   CHEJU   KYUSHU

Gobi

Huang He

•Taiyuan

•Xi'an   Nanjing•

(Yellow River)

Yangtze   Wuhan•   •Shanghai   East China Sea

•Chengdu   OKINAWA

Chongqing   •RYŪKYŪ ISLANDS

Taipei•

TAIWAN

Guangzhou
(Canton)•
Hong Kong
(Brit.)

•Mandalay   •Hanoi   HAINAN   LUZON   Philippine Sea

BURMA   LAOS   South China   •Manila   PHILIPPINES
Sea
Chiang Mai   •Vientiane   Gulf of   MINDORO   •SAMAR
Tonkin
•Rangoon
THAILAND   VIETNAM
KAMPUCHEA   PALAWAN   Sulu Sea   MINDANAO
(CAMBODIA)
•Bangkok   Ho Chi Minh City
•Phnom Penh   (Saigon)
Gulf of
Thailand   HALMAHERA
M A L A Y S I A   SABAH
BRUNEI   Sulawesi Sea
Sibu   SARAWAK
•Kuala Lumpur   SINGAPORE   KALIMANTAN   SULAWESI   Banda Sea   Arafura Sea
BORNEO   (CELEBES)
SUMATRA   •Banjarmasin   I N D O N E S I A

Irrawaddy   *Salween*   *Mekong*   MALAYA

Andaman Sea

Java Sea   Surabaya
•Jakarta   JAVA   BALI   LOMBOK   FLORES   TIMOR   Timor Sea
•Bandung   SUMBA

Pacific
Ocean

AUSTRALIA

120°   140°   160°

S I B E R I A

20°

0°

100°   120°   140°

Introduction

"Asian peoples no longer need think in terms of an East Asian framework. In view of the prevailing economic, defense, and political relations in the region, it would seem reasonable to take the entire Pacific Basin as the sphere of [an] emerging civilization."
—Masakazu Yamazaki, Japanese scholar and playwright

PERSPECTIVES ON A PACIFIC CENTURY

"Pacific Century" has become a catchphrase for an Asian economic renaissance. Used most frequently with reference to the future, the term more accurately reflects the past — a century of modernizing encounters with the West that have profoundly shaped the region. As the new century begins to converge with a New Asia, the term will retain its implication for the future, for many believe that the Pacific is giving rise to a new era in human history.

This book looks but tangentially at that future, being devoted primarily to understanding the present Pacific Century. If the world has experienced several, perhaps many of these "Pacific" eras, surely none has been as globally significant as the present one. The next century may bear the sobriquet of the great ocean, but it will be a product of the century that is now passing. By reviewing this past we are better able to understand why Pacific Asia, after more than a century of conflict and subjugation by the West, has revived with such force and dynamism.

The Pacific Transition

The majority of the Asia Pacific economies have passed a set of milestones which, taken together, constitute an unprecedented transformation of this broad region in a very short time. In their per capita incomes, trade and investment volumes, education levels, and numerous other indicators, many of these societies have exceeded the goals set by their most extravagant dreamers of a century ago.

The modernization period for Pacific Asia stretches back into the nineteenth century. It embraces the rise and demise of the colonial era, birth pangs of new Asian nations, calamitous wars and rebellions, the growth of great metropolises, export and investment booms and busts, and countless other landmarks of change. Yet this period in Asian history remains poorly understood in the West. Coinciding with one of the greatest worldwide economic expansions in history, it was shaped as much as in any other region by Western cultural and technological influences. Asian traditions may have exerted counter influences in artistic movements and trade relationships, but the impact from the West was proportionately greater.

This historic imbalance may be coming to an end. A transition is now underway that will place Pacific Asia on a more equal footing with the West in the coming century.

Already, this transition has altered the structure of world business and industry. Expanding as they mature, Asian industries are achieving a global reach that has displaced some industries in the West. Like all broad impacts, this one inspires exaggerated claims by pundits and alarmists, some of whom predict the "Asianization of the world" and that China will engulf the Pacific region. But just as Mandarin is not about to become the *lingua franca* of Pacific Asia — English retains that standing outside Chinese regions — it would be an exaggeration to suggest that the center of the world is returning to Asia. Rather, Asia's relationship to the world is changing and intensifying. In the process, Asia will indeed help shape the global community.

Examples abound, but to cite only a few, Korea now conducts more trade with the developing world than with all the developed nations combined. Japan has turned anew toward Asia, conducting a greater volume of trade with its Asian neighbors than with Europe and America together. Japan passed yet another milestone in 1995 by manufacturing more overseas than it exported, demonstrating how extensively its global economic activity has been dispersed. These changes imply a fundamental shift in the geographic weight of global economic activity. According to World Bank growth forecasts, the shift will have occurred decidedly toward Asia within a quarter century. This is part of a larger transition by which the so-called "developing nations" will surpass the industrial nations in aggregate percentage of world output, a change that is being driven mostly from Pacific Asia.

Barring unforeseen disasters, such as a major war or global depression, this strong economic growth will continue even if the historically fast pace gradually slows. For many, such a slowdown will be welcome and overdue. The boom of the 1980s and 1990s vaulted several Asian capitals into the ranks of the most expensive cities in the world. While living costs have soared, travelers have learned that they must book flights to these cities weeks in advance. Ports and surrounding urban regions are straining to accommodate the

Modern Western civilization has brought the world umbrella to Asia for the first time, and a dual structure of civilization is now taking shape in the region. The Asian world and Asian civilization cited so often of late have their origins not deep in the past but in modernization this century in an Asia in contact with the West.

—Masakazu Yamazaki

expansion. Not surprisingly, the environmental burdens are becoming acute as well, even if for now the remedies are being postponed in the interest of rapid, short term growth.

Modernization implies a host of real costs to societies, but in Asia the pejorative connotation of the term has lost much of its impact amid a reduction of poverty on a vast scale. We are better able to see modernization for what it is, a dynamic mix of global forces — economic, social, cultural, and technological — each having a broadly unifying effect in the Pacific Rim. The observations of playwright Masakazu Yamazaki, quoted above, summarize what is still only vaguely recognized; that modernization is shaping a "Pacific" civilization built on several levels and dividing East and West less than is commonly believed.

The first task, then, must be to define what is meant by "modern" in the Asian context. The concept of the "modern" is one that Asians have defined in a variety of ways, ranging from an economic and cultural state toward which they strive to the embodiment of influences they wish to reject. However broad the meaning, its omission from the historian's vocabulary seems unnecessary and its use in the title of a major historical work, *The Search for Modern China*, is encouraging. The author of that work, Jonathan Spence, provides us with as good a definition as any of how the term "modern" may be used in assessing China's development and, by extension, that of other nations in the Asia-Pacific region.

I understand a "modern" nation to be one that is both integrated and receptive, fairly sure of its own identity yet able to join others on equal terms in the quest for new markets, new technologies, new ideas. If it is used in this open sense, we should have no difficulty in seeing "modern" as a concept that shifts with the times as human life unfolds, instead of simply relegating the sense of "modern" to our own contemporary world while consigning the past to the "traditional" and the future to the "postmodern."[1]

PACIFIC ASIA: CONCEPTS, DEFINITIONS, RATIONALE

What Is Asia?

Asia is a concept invented by the Greeks in the fifth century BCE*. It has survived ever since as a useful construct for outsiders. For Homer, the word "Asia" meant only the region of Anatolia (modern Turkey). For the Greeks, who divided the known world into three great parts, Homer's Asia was but "Asia Minor." The real Asia to them was called "Asia Major." Evocative of a vast, rich, and powerful land that encompassed the Persian Empire, then the world's greatest empire, Asia seemed to the Greeks to stretch unendingly toward the east from Anatolia. Real and imaginary images of what we now call Asia were to haunt the dreams of Alexander the Great in his quest to unite the known world just the way they would beckon countless explorers, conquerors, traders, and wanderers in subsequent centuries.

The concept of "Asia," created by outsiders, clearly did not originate with Asians themselves, but they eventually appropriated it for their own uses and accepted a number of subdivisions established by geographers and historians. "South Asia" and "Southwest Asia" have been blocked out within the Eurasian landmass, but their boundaries remain fluid. A division of the region according to its physical features, for example, may have little bearing on political and cultural areas. Thus, Southwest Asia (or West Asia) embraces such areas as the Arabian Peninsula, Turkey, Iraq, and Iran but omits other parts of the region whose transcendent feature is the Arabic language and culture. The term "Middle East" gets us no further. It, too, is vague and strikes the inhabitants as Eurocentric, but they call it Sharqad Alwsad, which literally means "Middle East" in Arabic. Other parts of Asia confront these same dilemmas.

In short, how one defines the component parts of "Asia" are matters of time and vantage point. The terms used here may be disputed, but if it is understood that they represent concepts that have always been malleable, tolerance will prevail.

Pacific Asia

Diversity — geographic, cultural and political — is the overriding reality of the area we will call *Pacific Asia*, but the accompanying reality is one of interaction and mutual influence that makes a regional construct increasingly relevant and useful. Today more than ever, one is challenged to discern both the general and the particular when discussing trends in Pacific Asia.

This region excludes much that is traditionally embraced within the term "Asia." Omitted, for example, are "South Asia" (India, Pakistan, Afghanistan, Bangladesh, and Sri Lanka) and the countries of "Southwest Asia" noted above. Although Pacific Asia historically has had significant levels of interaction with these regions, its most recent cultural and economic orientations have been toward the Pacific littoral. Pacific Asia comprises *East Asia* and *Southeast Asia*, two major sociogeographical subsets (along with Oceania, North America, and South America) in the overarching concept of a *Pacific Basin*.[2]

A natural division can be made within this latter realm between the Western Pacific, on the one hand, and North America on the other. In spite of their being geologically connected in the north, the two halves of the region have developed throughout their histories in fundamentally different ways. Only in the past century did they begin to converge significantly, each driven by the

---

* BCE (Before the Common Era) and CE (Common Era) will be used in this text, replacing BC and AD respectively.

necessities of modern commerce. Previously, for Western Pacific societies, the Indian Ocean and the Silk Road of Inner Asia were the avenues of distant commerce. America was not part of the "known world" until the late fifteenth century.[3]

The physical barriers that have inhibited the flow of people throughout the Asia-Pacific region naturally form the boundaries around which Asian societies and cultures have coalesced. They continue to shape our understanding of how the world of the Pacific Basin is divided.

EAST ASIA

China and Inner Asia

The largest political unit of Asia has been and remains China. Its combined population and physical domain have not been equaled by any other Asian nation. Within its vast geography, stretching into "Inner Asia," are five components that make the total picture somewhat easier to comprehend:

China "proper," consists of three great river basins — the Huanghe (Yellow River) in the north, the Yangzi in central China, and the Xijiang (West River) in the South.

The first of these rivers, the Huanghe, served as "the cradle of Chinese civilization" by sustaining the earliest settlements that would become Chinese society around 3000 BCE. From there, in the area of the Wei Ho valley or "Great Bend" of the river, these settlements spread both north and south toward the natural barriers that were to establish their relative isolation from more distant lands. The Huanghe has been both bane and blessing to China for many centuries, having flooded so often with destructive results that it became known as "China's Sorrow." The flooding even led to a major change in the course of the river during the nineteenth century: Where previously it flowed southward below Shandong province it now flows north to the Gulf of Zhi Li. The possibility of its flowing southward once again cannot be ruled out.

The relatively cool climate of North China sustains bountiful harvests of millet and wheat in its river valleys. The Yangzi River Basin in central China is an area of even greater agricultural rich-ness that supports rice and cotton-growing. The great commercial cities of China — Shanghai, Nanjing (Nanking), Wuhan (Hankou), and Chongqing (Chungking) are on the Yangzi River. By far the largest proportion of China's population resides in this region which comprises about three-quarters of a million square miles.

The smallest of the three major river basins, the Xijiang, is separated from northern and central China by a mountain range known as the Nan Shan. This semitropical southern area has been physically distinct from the rest of China, a separation that has contributed to its population's reputation for being very independent-minded. Minority groups are the norm here because the Han Chinese only arrived in large numbers in the twelfth century. The key city of Guangzhou (Canton) and the colonies of Macao and Hong Kong served as important early points of contact with the West. This region of China remains the source of many Western impressions of the whole country.

Manchuria, an area in northeast China with a broad plain bordered by two mountain ranges, has attracted a massive and relatively recent inflow of Chinese from the south. Prior to the twentieth century, Manchuria was the private domain of the Manchu conquerors of China and therefore was closed to immigration by ordinary Chinese. Its immense natural resource endowments, combining soybean and wheat croplands with great forests and mineral deposits, have made it an obvious strategic-economic asset and the object of bloody contests among imperial powers in the late nineteenth and early twentieth centuries.

Mongolia is now only partially claimed by China. The present-day People's Mongolian Republic consists of what was once called "Outer Mongolia." It is bordered along the north by Russian Siberia (see below) and in this century has been allied to Russia. Next to it, "Inner Mongolia," with a slightly larger population, grew out of the traditional acceptance by the Mongols of Chinese suzerainty during the period when the Manchus controlled the imperial throne in Beijing. China has perpetuated its control in the area by creating frontier provinces whose purpose, in part, is to prevent movements toward independence and unification among the Mongol people. Another form of control has been the resettlement of Han Chinese into China's province, with the result that today more Han Chinese than Mongolians reside there. The region is bordered by the Gobi Desert in the south and is generally pastoral, supporting great herds of sheep, goats, cows, camels, and horses.

Xinjiang is one of the least-known areas of China and it defies ordinary Western notions of what China is like. Sometimes known as Chinese Turkestan, the Xinjiang region is populated by traditionally nomadic, Turkic-speaking Uigurs, most of whom are Moslems. The extreme remoteness of the area, combined with its harsh desert climate, has prevented serious exploitation of what may be extensive mineral resources.

Tibet lies to the south of Xinjiang amid a vast watershed of mountain ranges. The great river systems of both India and China flow from the deep valleys of this region, making it in popular reference the "Roof of the World." Over the centuries, China has claimed the right to control Tibet, but not until the relatively recent Manchu (or Qing) Dynasty was a close association established and then only by force. For a period in the early twentieth century Tibet became independent of China until the latter reasserted control in 1950. The inhabitants of Tibet are of Mongolian origin. Their political and religious life is centered around a Lamaist and Buddhist faith for which the focus is a spiritual leader, the Dalai Lama, and his great monastery palace at Lhasa, the Potala.

The island of *Taiwan*, with a land area of approximately 36,000 km², lies off the southern shores of China. Its mountainous terrain leaves only a quarter of the land available for intensive agriculture. The climate is subtropical. China asserted its official control over Taiwan during the Qing Dynasty. Since 1949, however, Taiwan's leaders have defied control from the mainland, treating the island as a separate economic and political entity.

Korea, Japan, and East Siberia

The *Korean Peninsula* is approximately the size of the state of Idaho. Beyond a range of high mountains in the north it is connected to the Asian landmass by the Manchurian plain. Surrounded by the Yellow Sea to the west and the Sea of Japan

to the east, it forms a natural "landbridge" to and from the Japan Islands which lie to the south. This accident of geography has made Korea a crossroad of foreign invasion from both China and Japan. Even so, passage across Korea has never been easy: Its terrain is mountainous and only 20 percent of the peninsula is available for agricultural production.

In spite of Korea's proximity to China and Japan, its people do not trace their ethnic origins to either country. The ancestors of present-day Koreans came in successive migratory waves from Siberia, Inner Mongolia and Manchuria to form, over time, a very homogenous ethnic group. The language is Altaic, that is, related to Manchurian and Mongolian tongues, and except for borrowed terms it has no relationship to Chinese or Japanese.

Japan lies off the Asian continent next to China and Korea and comprises four primary islands: Hokkaido, Honshu, Shikoku, and Kyushu. Its climate, dominated by the monsoons, is complicated by the surrounding ocean and its proximity to the Asian landmass. Winters along the coast of the Japan Sea are snowy and moderate, for example, while along the Pacific seaboard they are cold and dry. The Japanese islands are poorly endowed with natural resources but the oceans that surround them make Japan one of the major fishing nations of the world.

The islands are subject to earthquakes and occasional volcanic activity, so the population concentrates in lowland areas. The land must support the seventh highest population on earth, but only 15 percent of the area is cultivable. Thus, the appropriate uses of land, in what has become a highly industrialized society, generate ongoing controversy.

With the exception of the Ainu, a small minority ethnic group, and several hundred thousand immigrant Koreans, the Japanese population has remained remarkably homogeneous over the centuries. In ethnolinguistic terms Japan is 99 percent Japanese.

The name *"Siberia"* evokes images of vast stretches of tundra and isolated villages. In fact, there is no unitary territory officially designated by that name. Rather, Siberia refers to a region encompassing all lands within modern Russia east of the Ural Mountains. The most significant portions of this region for our purposes are "Eastern Siberia" and the "Russian Far East." The former comprises the region east of Lake Baikal and north of China and Mongolia, including its major cities Krasnoyarsk and Irkutsk. The Russian Far East consists primarily of the regions bordering the Pacific Ocean. Its major cities are Khabarovsk, Yakutsk, and Vladivostok. These two regions combined cover an area more than 10,000,000 km^2, yet the population, made up mostly of immigrants from the "European" areas of Russia, numbers little more than fourteen million.

SOUTHEAST ASIA

Mainland Southeast Asia

A major transition occurs when we move below south China into an area that is gradually losing its colonial-era label, "Indochina." For many centuries, the eastern portion of mainland Southeast Asia, principally Vietnam, fell under the nominal suzerainty of China, and the cultural attributes from that influence are still evident. Within the mainland region lie the modern states of Laos, Burma (Myanmar), Thailand, Cambodia (Kampuchea), and Vietnam.

This mainland region is divided geographically into three parts according to the north-south mountain systems that emerge from the highlands of South China. To the west of a mountain chain running down through the Malay Peninsula lies Burma. The central, lower area is Thailand and Cambodia. Laos and Vietnam are demarcated by the Annam Mountains which parallel the coast of the South China Sea. The western sections of mainland Southeast Asia are also mountainous, particularly Laos. Similarly, Burma is hemmed in by mountains on three sides which feed its triple river system: the Irrawaddy, Chindwin, and Sittang.

Cambodia and the southern area of Vietnam enjoy a thriving agriculture, mainly rice cultivation, on the great plain of the Mekong River Delta. In Burma, the Irrawaddy Delta also produces abundant rice. Thailand's main area of agricultural production, a central plain drained by the Chao Phraya River, contains both its present

capital, Bangkok, and its former capital, Ayuthya. In Vietnam, the physical geography mirrors its polarized political geography: the south's Mekong River Delta matches the Songkoi (Red River) delta in the north but is twice its size. The two are linked by a long backbone of mountains and, parallel to it, a coastal lowland region. Northern Vietnam is much more rugged than the south.

Southeast Asia's numerous ethnic groups are distributed in complex patterns. They have emerged from two sources: first, southward migrations over many centuries under pressure from the southern expansion of the Han Chinese, and second, the importation of laborers from India and China during the period of European colonization. There are broadly shared linguistic traditions in mainland Southeast Asia that include the Tai speaking peoples. The most widely-shared religious belief of the mainland area is Buddhism, although there are numerous exceptions.

Island Southeast Asia.

Geologically, the mainland of Asia juts further to the southeast than is apparent on most maps. Nearly all the great islands of Southeast Asia stand on the continental shelf of Asia known as the Sunda Shelf, covered by relatively shallow sea in the Malacca Straight, the Java Sea, and the southern part of the South China Sea. The Sunda Shelf abuts the Sahul Shelf to the south and their proximity in previous epochs has caused an upthrusting of mountain ranges alongside deep oceans, particularly near Indonesia. Much of the region is still volcanic, forming part of the geological "ring of fire" that emerges at key points elsewhere around the Pacific Rim.

In this realm lie the large nations of Indonesia, Malaysia, the Philippines, and the much smaller states of Singapore and Brunei. Climatically, most of the region is maritime equatorial, meaning that both temperatures and rainfall are consistently high. In this "watery world" of ocean and rain, a generally dense vegetation ranges from lowland swamps near the oceans to great equatorial forests covering the higher altitudes. The ratio of soils fitted for intensive agriculture

is relatively limited in comparison with the overall land area. Mineral resources, particularly oil in Indonesia and tin in Malaysia, have been mainstays of those economies. The Philippines is a strongly agricultural region with most production (especially rice) occurring on the island of Luzon. Population densities in Island Southeast Asia vary: Certain islands in both Indonesia and the Philippines (i.e., Java and Luzon) are so heavily populated that they are reaching crisis densities while in Malaysia officials are pondering ways to increase the population growth of northern Borneo.

The underlying ethnicity of Indonesia, Malaysia, and the Philippines is "Malay" with an admixture of Chinese and indigenous tribal groups. A highly fragmented geography in the region, particularly in Indonesia, which embraces thousands of islands, has contributed to this complexity. Indonesia's population speaks at least 250 languages, not counting the many local tongues in its far eastern portion of Irian Jaya. Religious beliefs are an especially important factor in social identities. Much of maritime Southeast Asia outside the Philippines professes loyalty to Islam, even though the older animistic religions continue in some areas and provide a significant underpinning to the Islamic faith. By contrast, the majority of Filipinos are Catholics. The major exception is the Muslim enclave in the southern and southwestern peripheries of the archipelago facing Malaysia, particularly on the island of Mindinao.

The most geographically diverse area in the Pacific Basin is Oceania, inclusive of Australia, New Zealand, and the Pacific Islands. The anthropologist Douglas L. Oliver summarized the diversity at the beginning of his classic survey:

Ten thousand islands lie scattered over the face of Oceania, ranging from tiny atoll islets barely visible above pounding surf to continental Australia, three million square miles large. Every conceivable kind of physical setting is to be found. Almost within sight of the snow fields which cap New Guinea's central mountains are sweltering equatorial swamps. And the traveler need not voyage from Australia's desert to rain-soaked Hawaii to compare climatic extremes: he can find nearly as great contrast on single islands.[4]

The varied and expansive area of Oceania is embraced within a single concept that derives from origins in remote geological time and from the animal, plant, and human populations that adapted in it much later. Situated on the Sunda Shelf, maritime Southeast Asia extends down almost to Australia. There it encounters "Oceania's western moat" — a deep ocean rift that has been an ancient barrier to the passage of animal and plant life. Beyond lies the Sahul Shelf containing Australia and the great continental high island of Papua New Guinea. Islands far off to the south and east are either remnants of ancient continents (such as New Zealand) or volcanoes whose crests remained above the ocean (such as Hawaii and Tahiti) or have been eroded down to sea-level coral outcrops around an ancient crater rim (such as Truk in the Caroline Islands and Kwajelein in the Marshalls). Australia and Oceania were among the last major world regions to be inhabited by humans.

NORTH AMERICA

The eastern seaboard of North America has interacted significantly with the Pacific Basin from the nineteenth century on, but now the most intensive interaction is in the American West (including western Canada, Mexico, and the United States). What follows is a sketch of the important and sometimes overlooked geographic features that have contributed to America's West Coast settlement patterns and intensifying interchange with Asia.

The Pacific coast of North America "faces" the rest of the Basin and is connected to it geologically. Two main "fold lines" cross over from Asia; one moving through the Aleutian Islands and the other coming from the Bering Strait in the heights of Northeast Asia. The first, the Aleutian fold, begins at the Alaska Mountains where it follows the curve of the Gulf of Alaska, then descends along the coast to Vancouver in the course of which it is broken by the sea into a fringe of islands. Another line of the Aleutian fold becomes the Coast Range, the Cascade Range, and the Sierras to form the western rim of a great plateau area. The second great fold descends much further to the east until it forms the eastern rim of the great plateau which is about eight hundred miles wide near San Francisco. This tableland tilts toward the Pacific, so that its rivers, breaking through the mountains, flow down to the sea.

The lowlands of the American Pacific coast run from Vancouver to the Gulf of California in an almost continuous valley lying between the ocean and the mountains of the great plateau. The three major sections are the Fraser-Columbia-Willamette valleys in the north, the Sacramento-San Joaquin valleys in the center — both rich agricultural areas — and the Gulf of California, the head of the valley, now mostly drowned by the sea and surrounded by extremely dry lowlands.

The high elevations of the great plateau are traps for the moisture coming in from the Pacific. Falling mainly as snow in the mountains, it piles up and then melts during the summer when the dry lands of California most need the water. Similar inward movement of moist air along the seaward slopes north of 40 degrees latitude creates an almost constant rainfall that nourishes the vast forest reserves of North America.

These natural endowments have greatly influenced early American commerce with the Pacific Basin. The first great attraction for settlement was gold. Then, a more diverse economy, attractive climate, and later a thriving culture have drawn millions to the American Pacific shore. Significant numbers of this still-growing immigrant population have roots that stretch, like the land itself, to Asia.

CONTINENT AND OCEAN: THE TWO FRONTIERS

Concepts of what is "Asia" have changed over time, with a fundamental shift of perspective — the "Pacific Basin" perspective — having begun as the West approached Asia from the New World. Yet an equally fundamental shift occurred in China. The nature of the change can be best visualized by holding up a globe and positioning its center at Beijing, then repositioning the globe to focus on an early maritime center such as Manila. The two worlds of Pacific Asia become readily apparent. The first is a world dominated by the continental land mass of Asia; the second by the ocean.

Over geological time, the Asian continent has been the predominant influence on the sea around it. Even though only a small part of the mainland drains into the Pacific,[5] one finds rocks, plants, animals, and inhabitants far out into the ocean that are Asiatic in character and origin. The Pacific also sends powerful currents and winds toward the continent that profoundly affect its life. These two dimensions provide a convenient analogy for the shift of perspective and new interaction that occurred between Asia's land- and ocean-centered worlds.

For many centuries, the rich treasures and innovations of China rippled outward along the maritime trade routes through Southeast Asia to India and beyond while a different flow with relatively lesser impact on China moved in the opposite direction. Then, in the sixteenth century, sea-borne Europeans began to intrude upon the oceanic commerce of Pacific Asia. Eventually, they exerted unprecedented military and economic pressures on China. The fabled overland Silk Route lost its primacy for bringing distant European influences. Central Asia ceased to be the main source of foreign threats. Just as the warming ocean in the summer causes the winds to shift, sending them rushing toward the continent, so did the great Pacific carry the gusts of change toward China and East Asia.

Until the nineteenth century, China dominated the region with its continental-centered world view. The Great Wall symbolized this overriding concern with threats, new influences, and opportunities emanating from within the Asian mainland where, from a very early time, the inhabitants of fertile river valleys competed with one another and with intruding nomadic tribes from the steppe. When at last this vision began to shift toward a recognition that the future lay at the ocean's edge, it symbolized a major turning point in Pacific-Asian history.

NOTES

1. Jonathan D. Spence, *The Search for Modern China* (New York: Norton, 1990), p. *xx*.

2. After the very early Spanish influence from the New World had diminished, only the United States in the Western Hemisphere possessed population, resources, and military power on a scale large enough to exert a major influence on the course of Pacific Basin history. Latin American and Canadian interaction with the Pacific have been significant, but like the South Pacific region, they are not discussed in detail in order to contain a topic that is already of unwieldy proportions.

3. Asians did of course cross the Bering land bridge in the late Pleistocene Epoch to begin populating the Americas around thirty thousand years ago.

4. Douglas L. Oliver, *The Pacific Islands* (Cambridge, MA: The President and Fellows of Harvard College, Natural History Libarary, 1951, 1961), p. 3.

5. The land area that drains into the Pacific Basin is approximately one-fourth the size of the area drained by the Atlantic Ocean even though the Pacific's volume is twice as large. With a globe, it is almost startling to look at the Pacific head-on, for it covers a third of the planet's surface. Its area is greater than that of all the land above sea level and, as such, constitutes a major barrier even in an era of advanced modes of communication and transportation.

TIME CHART: CHRONOLOGY AND GEOGRAPHY IN PACIFIC ASIA

Given the extraordinary diversity of Pacific Asia, an overview of the region's chronology to the nineteenth century (to accompany chapter 1) is best obtained without reference to contemporary political boundaries. The map and time chart on the following pages consolidate some of the areas described previously according to subregions whose territories have waxed and waned over the centuries. They roughly correlate with broad geographical features that have promoted their societies' interactions, but they are not intended to represent permanent "culture areas." They are best seen as physical spaces within which it is useful to trace a series of interrelated historical events.

The chart expresses these shifting boundaries and influences: The dominant political forces that occur along the horizontal paths in each region intrude occasionally on other paths. These are indicated whenever a pattern spreads across the chart or jumps briefly into other areas. Space does not permit a detailed time chart for so broad a region. This chart is meant to serve as a conceptual and mnemonic device for understanding concurrent or linked historical trends.

Eleven regions have been selected.*

1. The "Barbarian" Northern Border Region — The steppe region along the shifting northern border of China, including sometimes present-day Manchuria, presented a threat that persisted throughout China's history.

2. North China/Yellow River Region — As described in chapter one, North China comprises a distinctive cultural and geographical area based on dry-field farming, mostly wheat and millet.

3. The Yangzi River Region — Stretching from the Yangzi to as far as the Xijiang River, this is the "watery," primarily rice-growing region of China.

4. South China — The hill and forest dwellers of this region south and west of the Xijiang River spoke different dialects and had little in common with their countrymen to the north.

5. The Yalu Valley and Korea — The rugged Korean peninsula and the Yalu River valley further north have supported populations with different linguistic and ethnic origins from those of the Chinese.

6. The Japan Islands — The primary receptors of cultural influence from the mainland were the islands of Honshu, Kyushu, and Shikoku, with outlying cultural areas being Hokkaido and South Sakhalin.

7. Ryukyu Islands and Taiwan — Inhabitants of Taiwan and the Ryukyu Islands below Japan were influenced from both Japan and the mainland in their early histories.

8. Southeast Asia: The Northwest Region — Highland peoples have coalesced in the plateau area of the Irrawaddy River region, including the area of present-day Burma.

9. Southeast Asia: The West and Central Region — The region of the Chao Phraya River delta and the Great Lake, inclusive of present-day Thailand, Cambodia, and part of Laos, is bordered by the Annam mountains.

10. Southeast Asia: The Eastern Region — From the Red River delta in the north to the Mekong River delta in the south, this region, comprising present-day Vietnam and part of Laos, fringes the South China Sea.

11. Lower Malaya and Islands — Present-day Malaysia, Singapore, Brunei, Indonesia, and the Philippines together make up a vast, heterogeneous maritime region whose island groups to the east are especially distinct from those to the west in their history and interactions.

* See also *Peoples and Places of the Past* (Washington, DC: The National Geographic Society, 1983)

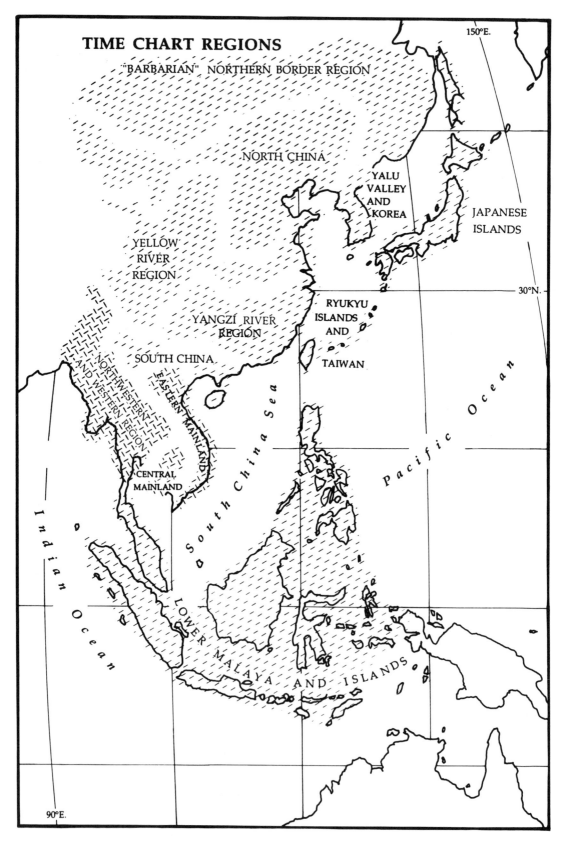

TIME CHART REGIONS

"BARBARIAN" NORTHERN BORDER REGION

NORTH CHINA

YALU
VALLEY
AND
KOREA

JAPANESE
ISLANDS

YELLOW
RIVER
REGION

YANGZI RIVER
REGION

RYUKYU
ISLANDS
AND

SOUTH CHINA

TAIWAN

NORTHWESTERN
AND WESTERN REGION

EASTERN MAINLAND

South China Sea

Pacific Ocean

CENTRAL
MAINLAND

Indian Ocean

LOWER MALAYA AND ISLANDS

150°E.

30°N.

90°E.

	800 BCE	600	400	200	BCE	0 CE	200

Northern Border Nomadic tribes attack frontier to south

Xiongnu

**North China
Yellow River**

E. Zhou, Spring & Autumn Period to 481 Warring States to 221 BCE

Former Han Dynasty

Later Han Dynasty

Yangzi River Region

Qin

Guangzhou becomes trade center

South China Dian culture flourishes in southwest

Korea & Yalu Valley Bronze casting introduced from China Chosun Kingdom

Han colonies

Iron tools Koguryo

Japan 660 BCE, according to legend, Emperor Jimmu begins reign Bronze & ironworking, wet rice agriculture are introduced from Korea.

Jomon Culture Yayoi culture emerges

Taiwan & Ryukyus Increasing trade with China reflected in style and material of ceramics

SE Asia: W. & Upper Malaysia Settlers at Ban Chiang practice wet rice cultivation with domestic water buffalo, iron tools Wet rice agriculture supports towns such as Chan Sen Buddhist artifacts made at Chan Sen

SE Asia: Central Mainland Farming culture rises in Bas-Plateaux region, southeast of the Great Lake, and continues until the 8th century CE

Funan Kingdom Mekong Delta

SE Asia: Eastern Mainland Village farming society, the Dong Son, produces sophisticated bronzes in Red River area by 800 Partial conquests by Qin (218) and Han (111) Chinese

Island SE Asia and Lower Malaya Dong Son influences island areas Iron introduced into Palawan Javanese king observes Brahmanic rites, promotes irrigation works

	800 BCE	600	400	200	BCE	CE 0	200

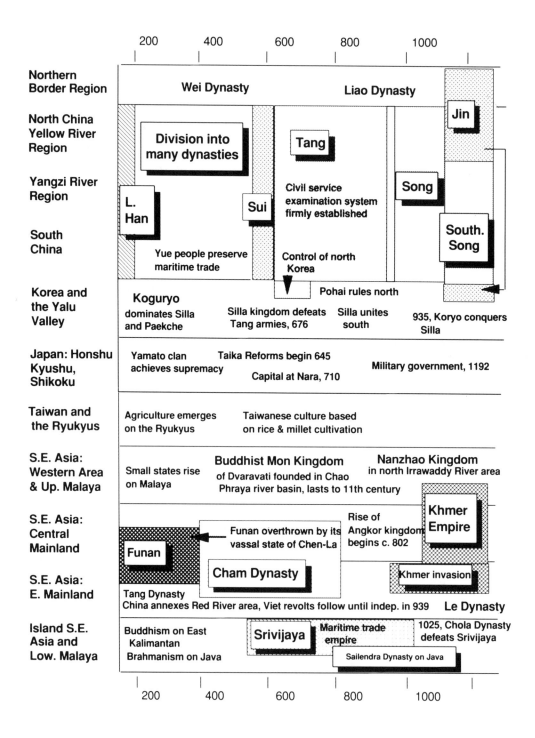

| | 200 | 400 | 600 | 800 | 1000 | |

Northern Border Region
Wei Dynasty   Liao Dynasty

North China Yellow River Region
Division into many dynasties   Tang   Jin

Yangzi River Region
L. Han   Sui   Civil service examination system firmly established   Song

South China
Yue people preserve maritime trade   Control of north Korea   South. Song

Korea and the Yalu Valley
Koguryo dominates Silla and Paekche   Silla kingdom defeats Tang armies, 676   Silla unites south   Pohai rules north   935, Koryo conquers Silla

Japan: Honshu Kyushu, Shikoku
Yamato clan achieves supremacy   Taika Reforms begin 645   Capital at Nara, 710   Military government, 1192

Taiwan and the Ryukyus
Agriculture emerges on the Ryukyus   Taiwanese culture based on rice & millet cultivation

S.E. Asia: Western Area & Up. Malaya
Small states rise on Malaya   Buddhist Mon Kingdom of Dvaravati founded in Chao Phraya river basin, lasts to 11th century   Nanzhao Kingdom in north Irrawaddy River area

S.E. Asia: Central Mainland
Funan   Funan overthrown by its vassal state of Chen-La   Rise of Angkor kingdom begins c. 802   Khmer Empire

S.E. Asia: E. Mainland
Cham Dynasty   Khmer invasion   Tang Dynasty China annexes Red River area, Viet revolts follow until indep. in 939   Le Dynasty

Island S.E. Asia and Low. Malaya
Buddhism on East Kalimantan Brahmanism on Java   Srivijaya   Maritime trade empire   1025, Chola Dynasty defeats Srivijaya   Sailendra Dynasty on Java

| | 200 | 400 | 600 | 800 | 1000 | |

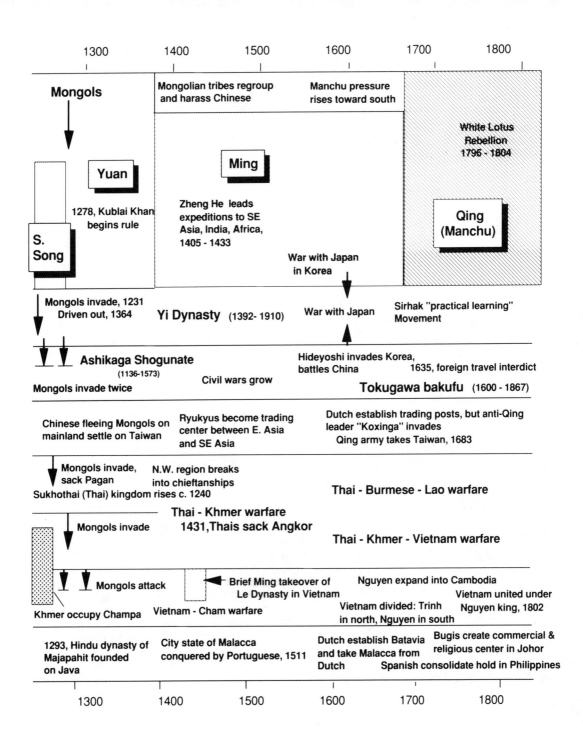

| 1300 | 1400 | 1500 | 1600 | 1700 | 1800 |

Mongols

Mongolian tribes regroup and harass Chinese

Manchu pressure rises toward south

White Lotus Rebellion 1796 - 1804

Yuan

Ming

1278, Kublai Khan begins rule

Zheng He leads expeditions to SE Asia, India, Africa, 1405 - 1433

Qing (Manchu)

S. Song

War with Japan in Korea

Mongols invade, 1231
Driven out, 1364

Yi Dynasty (1392- 1910)

War with Japan

Sirhak "practical learning" Movement

Ashikaga Shogunate
(1136-1573)

Civil wars grow

Hideyoshi invades Korea, battles China

1635, foreign travel interdict

Mongols invade twice

Tokugawa bakufu (1600 - 1867)

Chinese fleeing Mongols on mainland settle on Taiwan

Ryukyus become trading center between E. Asia and SE Asia

Dutch establish trading posts, but anti-Qing leader "Koxinga" invades
Qing army takes Taiwan, 1683

Mongols invade, sack Pagan

N.W. region breaks into chieftanships

Sukhothai (Thai) kingdom rises c. 1240

Thai - Burmese - Lao warfare

Thai - Khmer warfare
1431,Thais sack Angkor

Mongols invade

Thai - Khmer - Vietnam warfare

Mongols attack

Brief Ming takeover of Le Dynasty in Vietnam

Nguyen expand into Cambodia

Vietnam united under Nguyen king, 1802

Vietnam divided: Trinh in north, Nguyen in south

Khmer occupy Champa

Vietnam - Cham warfare

1293, Hindu dynasty of Majapahit founded on Java

City state of Malacca conquered by Portuguese, 1511

Dutch establish Batavia and take Malacca from Dutch

Bugis create commercial & religious center in Johor

Spanish consolidate hold in Philippines

| 1300 | 1400 | 1500 | 1600 | 1700 | 1800 |

1

Dynasties, Empires, and Ages of Commerce: Pacific Asia to the Nineteenth Century

QIN: THE FIRST CHINESE EMPIRE

In one of the most vivid scenes to appear in the records of ancient China, the assassin Zhong Ke enters the audience chamber of King Zheng of Qin bearing gifts from the northeastern rival state of Yan. In a box he carries the head of one of Zheng's enemies and a map showing a gift of territory. Rolled up in the map is a poison dagger with which Zhong Ke intends to kill the king.

In the midst of his presentation, he grasps the dagger and thrusts at Zheng who pulls back just in time. The panic-stricken monarch dodges behind a great pillar with the assassin in pursuit. Unarmed courtiers scatter in fright while outside the chamber door the guards hesitate at the sound of the commotion: the king's strict internal security rules forbid them to enter.

Although unforseen at the time, much more than a single life or kingdom hung in the balance in this drama. The outcome held immense consequences for the course of China's history and much of Pacific Asia. At the time, King Zheng was engaged in an effort to unite a conglomeration of feuding kingdoms. His state of Qin had become, during an earlier period of economic and legal reforms, one of the best-organized and most

powerful kingdoms among the Zhou people of the Huanghe (Yellow River) Valley, and his military successes had reached a point that caused his rivals to search for every possible means to stop him.

While the assassin lunged at him from the other side of the pillar, King Zheng struggled to draw his long, unwieldy sword. The court physician rushed forward and struck Zhong Ke with his bag. A courtier called out to the king to pull the long scabbard further back until at last the king freed his sword and wounded his assailant. Zhong Ke hurled the dagger at the king but instead struck the pillar and a few moments later the would-be murderer was slain.

Far-reaching events were to unfold with King Zheng's survival. By 221 BCE he had unified the former Zhou kingdoms and embarked on a series of changes that were to set the character of Chinese Dynasties long after his own very brief dynasty (221-206 BCE) came to an end. The region he unified and enlarged acquired the name of his own state, Qin (Ch'in)* from which its enduring name, China, is derived. The name he took for himself was Qin Shihuangdi (Ch'in Shih Huang-ti), the Qin First Emperor, a lofty title that bestowed upon him the unprecedented designation of a ruler who was superior even to the legendary sage kings.

---

* See "Representations of Foreign Words," page 555

The First Emperor was no sage, but his accomplishments warrant a special place in Chinese history. When he assumed the Qin throne in 245 BCE at the age of thirteen, much had already been achieved in the way of well-codified laws and standardized measurements, practices that he extended throughout the new empire. Aided by key advisers, he established a bureaucracy to govern China in place of a feudalistic landed aristocracy. This opened up Chinese society to greater social mobility and enabled the bureaucracy and army to draw upon the best available talent.

The First Emperor inherited and further developed an advanced Qin military force. So fundamental was his vast army to his empire's stability that an army of life-size terra cotta soldiers was buried, rank on rank, next to his great tomb at Xi'an. The living Qin army had much to defend. To the north the nomadic Xiongnu empire was rising on the Eurasian steppe, posing a constant threat. In response, the First Emperor developed fortifications that were to be extended and rebuilt in later dynasties as the Great Wall.

The Mandate of Heaven

Before his death in 210 BCE, the First Emperor survived two other assassination attempts. Both of these, like the first, assumed that the entire society he governed would be seriously weakened if its supreme leader were eliminated. A great leader in China was thought to possess the quality of *De* (Te), inherent power and virtue, which infused and made effective the rituals he performed for the continued prosperity of his people. The First Emperor made every effort to reinforce this view among the general populace.

From the time of the more primitive Shang people, predecessors to the Zhou in the period roughly from 1700 to 1100 BCE, the worship of "Heaven" had become paramount in the Chinese religious system. The Zhou called Heaven *Tian* (T'ien), which referred to "the abode of Great Spirits," the sky. In the Zhou tradition, the First Emperor bore the title *Tianzi* (T'ien Tzu) or "Son of Heaven."

Among all the supernatural forces recognized by the early Chinese, Heaven reigned supreme. It was the ultimate determinant of human affairs. Fundamental to Chinese thought down to the present century has been the view that the head of government is the supreme arbiter between Heaven and Earth. He was said to maintain stability and favorable relations between the two, much as the pillar behind which King Zheng took refuge helped hold together the roof and structure of his palace. An additional, vital notion was added, however, which is generally referred to as the "Mandate of Heaven." Whenever the beneficence of Heaven was absent (as evidenced by drought, famine, etc.) the ruler was said to have

Figure 1.1 Tomb rubbing depicting the assassination attempt against King Zheng of Qin, right, whose sleeve has been torn off. The presentation of an enemy's head (actually a renegade Qin general) lies in a box on the floor. The assassin, left, has thrown his knife which has struck the pillar.

Figure 1.2 Terracotta warrior from the tomb of the First Emperor.

lost his supernatural potency and with it his "mandate" to rule.

Upon such concepts of supreme leadership and authority the Zhou people had constructed an elaborately graded hierarchy of social ranks and land ownership within several hundred fiefdoms. The heads of these fiefs owed fealty to their emperor.

Confucius

Three centuries before the rise of Qin, the ancient Zhou system of feudatories became idealized as a model for society by an intellectual named Kong Fuzi or Kong Zhongni, otherwise known as Confucius (551-479 BCE). Because he lived during a period of dynastic decline and disorder (the so-called Spring and Autumn Annals of the late Zhou period), Confucius and other scholars of his day were concerned primarily with the means by which societal stability and order could be restored. Traveling among the various courts of warring rulers, Confucius offered his ideas and counsel but apparently was given no opportunity to put his philosophy into practice through a position of responsibility. Only after his death were his ideas collected by disciples into a single compendium, the *Analects (Lunyu)* which became a widespread influence during subsequent centuries.

Confucius longed for China to return to the era of the sage kings, rulers who were said to have presided over neatly subdivided and stable domains where each individual was sensitive to his proper station in life. In this philosophy, generally shared among the Zhou people, it was improper for ordinary men to perform rituals to the major cosmic spirits. Instead, they were to focus their sacrifices and rituals on their own ancestors and local deities. The origin of this practice, followed in every successive Chinese dynasty, lay with the ancient Shang people.

The realities of the third century BCE were something altogether different from Confucius' ideal. Amid the general dissolution of the Zhou system, differing schools of thought arose as to how to restore order to chaos. Some of them, grouped today under the term "Legalists," bade good riddance to the old feudatory system. The Confucian school, on the other hand, called for a return to the past structures and practices of ideal governance. Still others, such as the Daoist philosophers, suggested that no centralized system at all was required, only an understanding of the mysterious, ever-present force known as the *Dao* (T'ao), the Way.

The immediate consequence of this dispute, once the First Emperor had consolidated his victories, was an effort to resolve it forcibly — an altogether typical response in his case. Coming down firmly on the side of the Legalists, he ordered a massive book burning so that the countryside would be rid of all the alternative viewpoints and other "intellectual" pursuits that he deemed to have no value. His own Qin archives and books on "practical" subjects such as agriculture, medicine, and divination were spared, however. The Emperor assumed that he was eliminating a source of opposition to the founding of his new dynasty. Thus began the first documented promotion of a "party line," a pattern that was to be repeated through China's history down to the present day.

A debate between schools of philosophy and religion in ancient China may seem today like an obscure and irrelevant matter, but the intellectual duels of that time were as vital for the future of China as the thrusts and parries of the moment in which Zhong Ke sought to kill the man who would be the First Emperor. Fundamentally, the debate was over how to assert proper order in official affairs and in community and family life. For the Confucianists, the solution could be found in sincere, ethical behavior and a strict observance of traditional rules and ceremonies. Harmony, manifest in the behavior of the so-called Superior Man, was for a Confucianist an elegant balance of motives and manners. His motives were to be infused with self respect, magnanimity, sincerity, earnestness, and benevolence. These qualities may seem at first idealistic and abstract, but each was carefully observed and defined by the Confucianists. Similarly, manners were held to be a direct reflection of motives exemplified by a child's duty to the family and, above all, to the father. This principle culminated in loyalty to one's ruler. Such devotion was to be reciprocated (as in the case also of the other senior positions: father, elder brother, etc.) by benevolence, humanity, and gentility.

The political implications of this viewpoint were as potent as that of the "Mandate of Heaven" itself. The Confucianists asserted that the ethical behavior of the ruler would determine the moral and spiritual health of the entire society. Social reforms would begin at the top, not at the grassroots level.

The good life, then, was for the Confucianists a *spiritual achievement*. It depended on the notion that people are, at heart, good. Given proper leadership, goodness will blossom and harmony will prevail throughout the land.

The Rival Schools

The Legalists, whose view of human nature was grim, scoffed at Confucianist idealism. The individual responds merely to a desire for pleasure and a fear of pain, they said. Society must be

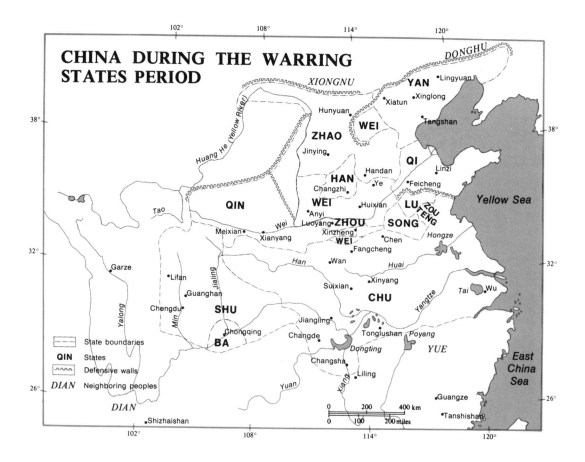

governed by strong laws that take advantage of this fact and specify a clear system of rewards and punishments. The Legalists even disdained the Confucianists' reverence for the traditional past, asserting instead that only the present should serve as guide to action. They saw the supreme ruler as someone whose influence over society should derive from his office — his stature — rather than from his moral example. Laws should be established that would reinforce that position. Once they were put in place, argued the Legalists, such laws would make the personal actions of the monarch far less relevant to the prosperity of the kingdom. Society—including its total economy—could thus be managed by an application of rigid rules that, for some of the more extreme adherents of Legalism, foresaw the creation of an essentially totalitarian state.

The original Daoist scholars heaped scorn on Confucianists and Legalists alike. Daoists were compilers and students of the *Daode jing* (Tao Te Ching) whose philosophy is derived from statements ascribed to Laozi (Lao Tzu), an older contemporary of Confucius. Whether or not Laozi actually lived in the sixth century BCE as is traditionally assumed, his disciples — particularly the sage Zhuangzi (Chuang Tzu) — popularized the teachings. These focus on the nature of the *Dao* even though it defies any simple definition. In fact, the *Dao* was acknowledged by its proponents to be indefinable. At bottom, it represents the source of all active power (*De*) in the universe.

Daoism is the second great, original Chinese tradition alongside Confucianism that survived all other traditions. Each underwent transformations over the centuries and influenced the other, but the fundamental contrast between them remained throughout: Daoism asserted that the key to all meaning was to be found in the workings of the natural world; Confucianism found such meaning in human relationships. Daoism called for a "letting go" of the *Dao* so that it and all it embraced would follow a natural course. Confucianism sought to elicit the natural harmony of things but did so by insisting on proper behavior and a far more active role by leaders if society was to be effectively governed.

The debates among these and other schools form an important philosophical base for the next two thousand years of Chinese ideas about society

The Dao that can be told
Is not the eternal Dao.
The name that can be named
Is not the eternal name.
The nameless is the beginning of heaven
  and earth;
The named is the mother of ten
  thousand things.
Ever desireless, one can see the mystery.
Ever desiring, one can see the manifestations.
These two spring from the same source
  but differ in name; thus appear as darkness.
Darkness within darkness
The gate to all mystery.

—the *Daode jing (Tao Te Ching)*

and nature. Confucianism survived the initial "book burning" assault against it by the First Emperor (which was aided and abetted by the Legalists). The Qin Dynasty itself did not survive more than a few years beyond the Emperor's death; his successor was too weak and his rule became too harsh for the society to endure without revolt. Civil war broke out and a new dynasty emerged, the Han, which was to rule China for the next four centuries (206 BCE-221 CE).

THE HAN DYNASTY AND THE CHINESE LANGUAGE

The Qin and Han empires conquered new territory that includes much of present-day China. Here began the governing structures of the Chinese state that were to hold sway for nearly two thousand years: an absolute monarch, a council of ministers, and a civil service. The only hereditary aristocracy permitted was that connected with the imperial family. Officials were recommended by an elite group of ministers and even though the imperial examination system had not yet begun, this sufficed to ensure a high quality of administration. The feudal system of land ownership was abolished, but in its place emerged a new stratification of landlord owners and peasants.

The Han Dynasty fostered the broad distribution of the Chinese language. Written Chinese became widely adopted by literate people all across East Asia who were exposed to Chinese culture. In fact, the term for "civilization" literally means "adopting writing."

Chinese is a language family within which there are several mutually unintelligible tongues (some would say dialects)[1] but its written form was less subject to such regional variations. It can be rendered in variant styles of calligraphy, some of which are beautiful products not only of the tools used but of the character and spirit of the writer. Each basic unit of meaning is normally represented by a single graph or "character" with the result that normal communications requires a knowledge of three to four thousand characters. The English language, by contrast, uses just 26 symbols in its alphabetic system to represent sounds.

The original, millennia-old system of writing in China used pictures to represent objects, but not only have the characters long since ceased to be "pictographic," they confronted from the very outset the fact that there were many abstract concepts that could not be represented by pictures. The solution was to use characters derived from words that sounded like the words used for the abstractions. Such substitutions proved confusing, however, and required the addition of special graphic elements (commonly called "radicals" but more accurately called "significs") indicating to which general category a word belonged. These and other symbols would designate changes in the overall meaning of a character.

An upheaval in the visual evolution of written Chinese came in the 3rd century BCE when the First Emperor, acting on the advice of his prime minister Li Si, had all the characters of written

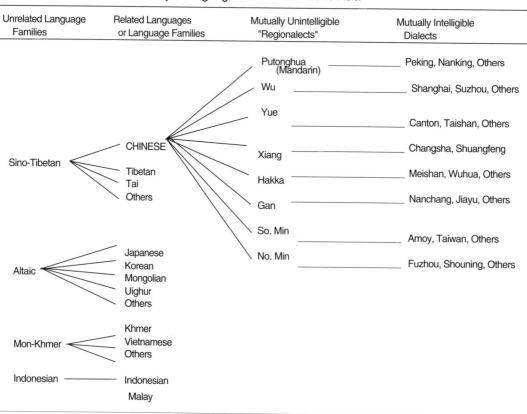

Major Language Families of Pacific Asia

Unrelated Language Families	Related Languages or Language Families	Mutually Unintelligible "Regionalects"	Mutually Intelligible Dialects
Sino-Tibetan	CHINESE	Putonghua (Mandarin)	Peking, Nanking, Others
	Tibetan	Wu	Shanghai, Suzhou, Others
	Tai	Yue	Canton, Taishan, Others
	Others	Xiang	Changsha, Shuangfeng
		Hakka	Meishan, Wuhua, Others
		Gan	Nanchang, Jiayu, Others
		So. Min	Amoy, Taiwan, Others
		No. Min	Fuzhou, Shouning, Others
Altaic	Japanese Korean Mongolian Uighur Others		
Mon-Khmer	Khmer Vietnamese Others		
Indonesian	Indonesian Malay		

Graph 1.1

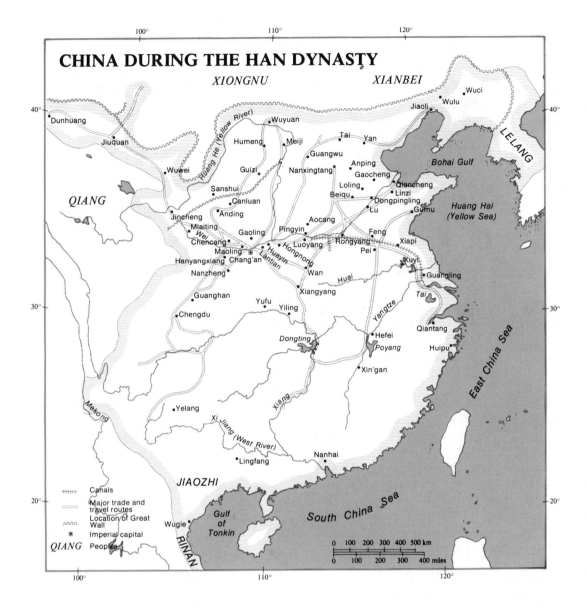

CHINA DURING THE HAN DYNASTY

XIONGNU

XIANBEI

Wuci
Wulu
Jiaoli
LELANG

Dunhuang

Jiuquan

Wuyuan

Humeng
Meiji
Tai
Yan

Guangwu

Wuwei

Guizi
Nanxingtang
Anping
Gaocheng
Bohai Gulf

Sanshui
Loling
Linzi

QIANG
Canluan
Beiqu
Qiancheng
Dongpingling

Jincheng
Anding
Lu
Gumu
*Huang Hai
(Yellow Sea)*

Miaiting
Gaoling
Pingyin
Aocang

Wei
Chencang
Huayin
Luoyang
Rongyang
Feng
Xiapi

Maoling
Hongnong
Pei

Hanyangxiang
Chang'an
Lantian
Xuyi

Nanzheng
Wan
Guangling

Guanghan
Xiangyang
Huai
Tai

Yufu
Yiling
Qiantang

Chengdu
Dongting
Hefei
Poyang
Huipu
East China Sea

Xin'gan

Yelang
Mekong
Xiang
Xi Jiang (West River)
Nanhai

Lingfang

JIAOZHI

	Canals
	Major trade and travel routes
	Location of Great Wall
	Imperial capital
QIANG	Peoples

Wugie
Gulf of Tonkin

RINAN

South China Sea

0 100 200 300 400 500 km
0 100 200 300 400 miles

Chinese reformed and standardized. Li Si changed the shapes of all characters, eliminated many, and created a great many more in the process of establishing what is known as "Small Seal" script. At the same time, Emperor Qin Shihuangdi ordered the burning of proscribed books so that history would start with him. The copying of new books in subsequent years reinforced Li Si's major alterations of the written form. After that, the written language remained relatively stable so that after centuries during which the *spoken* language diverged into many dialects, *written* Chinese could still be widely read and understood by the educated elite with reference to the terse, ancient forms of speech. After a thousand years of evolution in the spoken language, the curious result was that while the written form of a document could be easily understood regardless of the dialect of the speaker, reading such a document aloud often made no sense.

One difficulty for some cultures that sought to adapt the obvious advantages of a written language

Figure 1.3 "By order of the Emperor." This character was written by the 12th century Song dynasty emperor Hui Zong.

the last century many books were written not in the local language but in classical Chinese. The system of Chinese symbols inspired parallel systems in these other societies where its elements are recognizable today.

The Han and Its Western Contacts

It was during the early Han empire, particularly the reign of emperor Wudi (Wu Ti, 141-87 BCE) that China sent ambitious missions far to the west to make alliances with war-like societies there. An effort to forge a military pact with the people of Central Asia in present-day Afghanistan (who would later invade India and establish the Kushan Empire) proved unsuccessful as did a second mission to the Ili River Valley. These expeditions helped inform Chinese leaders of the peoples and civilizations to their west, and they signify the extent to which China, in a very early period, was probing the far reaches of the continental Asian world. The later Han forays against the Xiongnu, their long-time enemies to the north of the Gobi Desert, may have driven the latter even further toward the west where, two centuries later, they would be known as the "Huns" and begin entering central Europe.

Han society met the West through increasing maritime and overland trade with India and the

was the difference between the borrower's language and Chinese. Chinese has no "inflected" forms; i.e., words whose meanings or grammatical relationships change in accordance with slight alterations in their forms. Japan adopted Chinese script in the 7th and 8th centuries CE, but because Japanese is an inflected language the long-term result was a hybrid: Chinese graphs for basic meanings with Japanese script added for inflected words. A similar process occurred in Korea, but the native script (called *hangul*) was not invented until the 15th century.

In general, the Chinese writing system was as great an asset to the intellectual development of Pacific Asia as Latin was to Europe. It contributed to the preservation of unity within a diverse empire and supported a broad community of scholarship throughout China and in regions beyond it. For centuries the literate people of East Asia, even if they spoke mutually unintelligible dialects and languages, learned to recognize the same standard set of Chinese characters. Books written in regions far removed from one another were copied and shared and thereby reinforced a common cultural reference point even if, for many, it was not *their* culture. The writing system spread to Vietnam, Korea and Japan where until

Figure 1.4 Han Dynasty "Flying Horse." Bronze. 2nd-century CE.

Roman Orient. Occasional appearances in Chinese courts by commercial entrepreneurs claiming to have come from Rome are recorded in the annals and there is little doubt that the Mediterranean world avidly sought certain products from the East. Foremost among these was Chinese silk, for which demand grew so great that it is said to have led to a serious drain of currency from Rome. The route across Central Asia for this commerce became known as "the Silk Road," and along it caravans carried not only silk but other light, high-value products (such as glass) from the Mediterranean. Both East and West may have profoundly influenced one another intellectually during this period. Symbols are found on certain Dead Sea Scrolls, for example, that are said by some scholars to be Chinese calligraphy as copied by Central Asians, but such findings remain both mysterious and controversial.

Technologically, China had already begun to surpass the Western world by the time of the Han period. Paper and porcelain, both key commercial innovations, were invented by the Han and remained exclusively in Chinese production for more than a thousand years. China's major cities were also great metropolises that could rival the scale of Rome, albeit not necessarily its stonework.

The Early Han and the Rise of Confucianism

The early Han emperors carried forward the beliefs of their Qin predecessor in the Legalist tradition of scholarship, which, as noted above, ran counter to the Confucianist tradition. Legalist scholars held traditional "book learning" in contempt and believed that the threat of severe punishment was the only means by which a people could be ruled. Moreover, it was thought that to fail in a duty assigned by the emperor warranted only punishment, regardless of circumstances. What the ruler desired was "right," and individual rights outside this context were meaningless. Many Legalists lumped together the roles of intellectuals and merchants. Both, it was argued, were unproductive and should be eliminated altogether.

Although Confucian ideas about the role of ethics and learning gradually came to hold great influence (including in the later Han), the lasting impact of the early Han Legalist orientation cannot be overlooked. Upon its premises was based a highly centralized and authoritarian government whose arbitrariness of rule, distrust of independent merchants and occasional hostility toward intellectuals was to endure through the following two thousand years of change.

The emperor Wudi, however, was distrustful of the growing Han bureaucracy and in this sense was no Legalist. When a famous memorial was presented to him by the Confucian scholar Dong Zhongshu (Tung Chung-shu) in 136 BCE, Confucianism came to prevail over the other schools. Dong stated the case for Confucianism in terms that appealed to the Emperor's needs. National unification, he said, would never be possible if the cacophony of voices from so many schools of philosophy continued throughout the land. To build a great empire, government officials and the populace should return to the fundamentals of Confucianist thought, said Dong. It should be supported by the Emperor and all other schools should be left to drift.

The Emperor agreed. At Dong's urging, an imperial academy was set up to train Confucian officials. Even so, Confucianism was forced to take on some of the concepts and principles of its rivals, creating a complex synthesis during the Han dynasty. The Legalist influence, for example,

Figure 1.5 The Yin-Yang symbol, surrounded here by the "eight trigrams" used in divination, expresses the two complementary forces of the universe (e.g., light-dark, male-female, etc.)

prevailed in the continued growth of the large, increasingly regulated bureaucracy that was needed to operate a vast empire. Similarly, the Daoist ideas of cooperation with natural forces (which in turn incorporated the ideas of the Yin-Yang school) came to the fore in later Confucian thought, particularly in the writings of the scholar Xunzi (Hsün Tzu) (ca. 298-238 BCE). Lastly, the figure of Confucius himself became larger than life. To him were eventually ascribed the idealized qualities of the "Superior Man;" that is, the persona that Confucius had himself assigned to more ancient sages. In creating this ideal, Confucianists of later eras encouraged widespread popular belief in the idea that if more men with the character of a Confucius could be trained, the nation would be much better off.

The Rise of Koguryo and of Chinese Influence

The Emperor Wudi spread the impact of Confucianism in the course of expanding his empire.

KOREA DURING THE THREE KINGDOMS PERIOD

The most immediate effect was on the Korean peninsula, where a confederation of small kingdoms rose to challenge encroachments by the Han Chinese.

In their earliest organization, the Korean people had been no more unified politically than those of China. Their emergence as warring tribes at the end of the Bronze Age (around the fourth century BCE) in the vicinity of the Yalu River coincided with an invasion from northern China led by Wi Man (Wei Man), who founded the kingdom of Chosun in 194 BCE. Within a century the Han Dynasty invaded and established colonies, some of which survived until the fourth century CE. These Chinese colonies, particularly the one known as Lolang at the site of present-day P'yongyang, left an enduring mark on Korean social structure and technology, but several small Korean kingdoms held on to challenge the Chinese.

These kingdoms absorbed ideas of Confucianism from the Chinese intruders. By 372 CE the northernmost kingdom of Koguryo had established a National Confucian Academy on the Chinese model and a year later adopted a code of administrative law. Similar adaptations occurred in the two other rival kingdoms of Korea, Paekche in the center and southwest, and Silla in the southeast.

For Koguryo, such reforms were part of a general renewal during a time when it was threatened by invasion from both China in the north and its rivals to the south. When the Han Dynasty began to falter and decline (described below), Koguryo was able to expand northward in present-day Manchuria and consolidate its dominance throughout the northern portion of the peninsula.

Ancient Japan

During this time, the Koguryo also met and defeated a small invasion force of a people known to them only as the "Wa," who came from a great island to the south. The island, of course, was Japan, which at that time was engaged in a complex interchange of alliances and migrations with the Korean kingdoms.

However, Japanese foreign military aggression was rare during this period. Unlike the more assertive Chinese, Japan's earliest political

> ## THE TAIKA REFORMS
>
> The Taika ("great change") Reforms of 645 constitute a great divide in Japanese history comparable to the Meiji Restoration of 1868. In the former case Japan turned to China, and in the latter to the West, for institutional models as a guide in a planned program of social engineering and modernization appropriate to its time. In each case international relations played a major role in internal renovation. In the seventh century the rise of Tang China was threatening the arrangement on the Korean peninsula to which Japan had become accustomed, while in 1868 the Western imperialist advance on East Asia seemed to carry with its threats to Japanese national sovereignty. In each case an extended period of preparation made possible the changes that followed in quick order. In the nineteenth century the Tokugawa shogunate had begun the experimentation with Western forms and weapons, and in the seventh century an extended influx of Chinese culture and institutions prepared the country for transition.
>
> —Marius B. Jansen, *EAH*

leaders showed little interest in the concept of an "empire" extending beyond their shores. Until the massive incursions of the West began in the nineteenth century, some forays against Korea were the only instances of Japan breaking out of what would become a self-imposed isolation. Although it was in contact with the rest of Asia, particularly China, during much of this time (even marginally with Europe as well), Japan maintained its isolation and cultural distinctness to a degree that characterizes in some ways its behavior down to the present day.

In prehistoric times, Japan was physically joined to the Asian mainland until tectonic movement and rising sea levels separated it as an archipelago by around 18,000 BCE. The original inhabitants were probably the Ainu, a tiny minority today, who were displaced at a very early date by immigrants from the mainland and, possibly, the Pacific Islands as well. Not until the appearance of an "iron age" and expansion of wet rice agriculture from 200 BCE to 300 CE do we find evidence of what might be called a "Japanese" society.

Unlike the Koreans, these early, clannish Japanese tribes did not quickly adopt the beliefs and institutions of Confucianism in a sweeping manner, but by the seventh century they clearly were aware of and influenced by the debate between the Confucianists and other schools of thought. The Confucianist and Daoist concepts of harmony resonated strongly in Japanese traditions and appealed to aspects of their Shinto religion. Like the Chinese, the Japanese assigned the pre-eminent place in their cosmology to an impersonal "Heaven." The Japanese, however, saw Heaven to be simply the *origin* of imperial authority, not an ongoing, vital source of authority. Both the Chinese and Japanese emperors performed annual rites that were supposed to reinvigorate their earthly domains and guarantee plentitude, but Japan's ruling house was not held to a "Mandate of Heaven" standard of performance which, for example, in the event of natural disasters, might undermine its claims of legitimacy. In spite of the intrinsic appeal of Confucianism, Japanese social structure during the time of the Han Empire was especially fragmented and hierarchical, making a total embrace of Confucianism less likely.

The history of Japan during the first few centuries CE is clouded in myth, but from the late sixth century on, a picture emerges of tribal groups (*uji*) unified under the state of Yamato on the islands of Honshu, Kyushu, and Shikoku and on the southern tip of Korea. The interchange culturally and politically with Korea was probably heavy through the eighth century as migrations and alliances continued to take place between the Yamato people of Japan on the one hand and the Silla and Paekche peoples on the other. It was the Paekche who introduced Buddhism to Japan in the sixth century, from which time it was rapidly adopted alongside the traditional Shinto religion of the *uji* lineages.

By the seventh century CE, however, Japan was ripe for dramatic changes. At the initiative of the ascendant Soga clan, the Yamato sent a 600-member mission to the imperial court of China. The visit had a powerful effect on Japanese thinking and led to their adaptation of key elements of governance from the Chinese model (the so-called Taika Reforms), particularly the system of a centralized state headed by an absolute sovereign.

Following the Taika Reforms, a series of aristocrats ruled as sovereigns during what is called the Nara period (710-784), a critical early stage in the maturation of Japanese civilization that centered on the then-capital city of Heijokyo, later known as Nara. When the capital moved to modern Kyoto, the period name changes to Heian (794-1185) but the practice of rule by aristocrats remained in place alongside the titular role of the emperor. The major political shift of the time was the rise of the Fujiwara family to become the dominant power in the court. Culturally, Japan began to self-consciously define itself through literature and art as a society distinct from China. Women aristocrats provided some of the great literature of the age, such as the first novel to appear anywhere in the world, *The Tale of Genji*, by Lady Murasaki Shikibu.

At the outset of the Heian period, the sovereign was greatly bolstered by the widely shared idea that he ruled over a "public" whose production and taxes should accrue to him. Gradually, factions in the capital sought outside alliances with distant warrior groups, resulting in armed clashes between two leagues of warriors, one headed by the Minamoto clan, the other by the Taira. Eventually, the Minamoto faction prevailed, and in 1192 its leader, Minamoto Yoritomo, was appointed *sei-i tai shogun* ("barbarian-subduing generalissimo").

Silla: The Unification of Korea

Meanwhile, across the Tsushima Straits the three kingdoms of Korea had continued to vie with one another for supremacy while managing — and even using within the dynamics of their rivalry — the threat of invasion from China. Koguyro had managed to drive out the Han Chinese colonies, but it remained extremely vulnerable to alliances opposing it, particularly as a new dynasty in China, the Tang, rose to strength and allied with the Paekche people to Koguyro's south. By 668 the Koguyro kingdom had fallen. Yet Paekche did not gain in its bargain with China. Its southern neighbor, the Silla (also written Shilla), soon allied with the Tang armies and overthrew Paekche, thus bringing about the first political unification of the Korean peninsula.

These totemistic, animistic tribes of the southernmost reaches of the peninsula had been the last to succumb to Chinese penetration. The golden antler-like crowns covered with pendants found in the Silla tombs suggest not only a vigorous and distinct culture but one whose ancient origins lay in tribal regions far to the north. The Silla rise to dominance over the peninsula coincided with the consolidation of Chinese power under the Tang. However, the alliance with China that had helped make Silla victorious also confirmed its ability to resist Chinese occupation, particularly as the former Koguryo and Paekche states placed their allegiance with Silla, not China. This Silla-led alliance succeeded in defeating the Tang Chinese and preventing their control of the peninsula.

The importance of a major Silla victory over the Tang in 676 can hardly be exaggerated. Not only did it result in Tang recognition of Silla's claim to control the peninsula, it enabled Korean society and culture to develop relatively unhindered by outside aggression during a critical, formative stage. It also set the tone for Korea's "tribute" relationship to China.

Since at least the time of the Zhou, tribute-bearing missions to the Chinese monarch from outlying peoples had been required by the Chinese to reinforce their regional hegemony and their view of themselves as the center of civilization, the Middle Kingdom that resides between Heaven and the rest of Earth. In return, the foreigners were granted special trading rights with China. Korea was part of this system of relationships. In general, whenever China's internal chaos increased, Korea's peninsular power expanded; conversely, it decreased in the face of expansionary assertions from its giant neighbor. This fluctuating dynamic typified the Sino-centric East Asian world order for many centuries, but of all the so-called tributary relationships, the one between China and Korea was to prove the most enduring.

THE BUDDHIST AGE IN PACIFIC ASIA

The Han Empire began to decline from the first century CE when tax revenues became increasingly difficult to exact from the powerful landholding families. From these independent bases emerged generals who became virtual warlords. Symptomatic of the change was a militant protest around 166 CE by thousands of students in the imperial academy, supported by some of the court families, in an effort to prevent the monopolization of central authority by a few powerful eunuchs. Many of the students were killed or imprisoned. Eventually, a power-sharing arrangement emerged among three generals who commanded the north, Sichuan, and south regions respectively (each region a common locus of power throughout China's history). The empire effectively broke up, giving way to a realm known as the Three Kingdoms among which there was constant warfare. Thus the Han dynasty, representing the early, great flowering of Chinese civilization, proved unable to adjust to the structural changes and emergent centers of power that its own development had fostered.

The era that followed is called the Six Dynasties period (222-589 CE). During this time not only was China seriously divided internally, but it also faced an increased military threat from the northern nomadic peoples whom it had earlier conquered. Defeated, sinicized,[2] and incorporated at times into the Chinese military system, these tribes were quick to perceive the weaknesses of the Northern Kingdom, and by 316 they overran it. In response, the southern reaches of China became more militarized under local defensive family groups, the most powerful of which attempted to rule a "Southern Kingdom" from Nanjing.

Emergence of the Tang Dynasty

While in far-off imperial Rome the decay of empire began to accelerate, China began to reconstitute itself as a resurgent and unified society. The "barbarians" that had invaded the Northern region had gradually become absorbed into Chinese culture and little was left to distinguish them from it. By 589 a general of mixed "barbarian" and

THE TRIBUTARY SYSTEM

The Tributary System was the traditional Chinese system for managing foreign relations. By establishing the rules and controlling the means and symbolic forms by which foreign countries entered into and conducted their relations with China, the Chinese found in the tributary system an effective mechanism for exacting compliance from neighboring states and peoples on important matters of political, defensive, economic, and diplomatic concern to China.

According to the usual practice, foreign peoples would be granted permission to establish trade and contact with China on the condition that their ruler or the ruler's emissaries demonstrate their subservience to the Chinese emperor by personally bearing him tribute. On presenting the tribute, usually a largely token offering of native products or rare and precious commodities, they were also to perform an act of ritual obeisance (anglicized as "kowtow"), which consisted of three kneelings and nine prostrations or bows of the head to the floor in the presence of the emperor. In return, the Chinese ruler would formally invest the foreign ruler with the nominal status of a vassal. As proof of this status, the ruler was provided with an imperial letter of patent, a seal of rank, and the Chinese calendar, important symbols of legitimacy and acceptance into the civilized Sinocentric world order. In addition, the emissaries received lavish gifts of cloth, silks, gold, and other luxuries that often far exceeded the value of what they had brought. For as long as this relationship was maintained, the tributaries were awarded legal trading privileges and the right to render tribute in the future. Obviously, the very profitable advantages of tribute-trade, as it came to be called, served as a powerful economic inducement, perhaps the real reason why nonChinese acquiesced to the otherwise inferior status imposed on them by China.

On the Chinese side, the economic motive provided only a secondary purpose, although it did occasionally serve as a useful, if disguised, expedient for material exchange. To the Chinese, the system served constantly to reaffirm their own ethnocentric worldview that posited the Middle Kingdom (*Zhongguo*) as the source and center of civilization and the Chinese emperor as the supreme and universal ruler who governed by the will or "Mandate of Heaven" (*tianming*); [and that] beyond the bounds of China proper, there existed a vast array of culturally inferior, less civilized barbarians, who were inevitably attracted by the brilliance of China's superior civilization. Consequently, it was only natural to expect barbarians to seek its irresistible benefits, or, put another way, "to come and be transformed" (*lai hua*) by it. Thus, the system explained and accommodated this unequal relationship and erected an artificial separation between China and the outside world. The system was also in large measure an extension of the Confucian social and political order, which was hierarchical, conservative, emphasized ritual and ethical behavior, and cast the emperor as the "son of Heaven" (*tianzi*), the ultimate exemplar of virtue and patriarch of a China-centered family of nations.

The system reached its apogee during the Ming dynasty (1368-1644), when contacts with more than a hundred different tributaries were recorded as a result of the vast overseas expansion at the time of the great maritime expeditions of the early 1400s. Although these maritime ties did not long endure, at their height embassies arrived with regularity from countries in South and Southeast Asia, such as Bengal, Sri Lanka, Sumatra, and Java, and from as far away as Hormuz and the east coast of Africa. Tribute from the latter included zebras and even giraffes. During these years, Japan entered the system for the first time, but only until 1549. In the following years, the Western European trading countries of Portugal, the Netherlands, and England also began to arrive and were gradually fitted into the tributary system as well.

—Roland L. Higgins, *EAH*

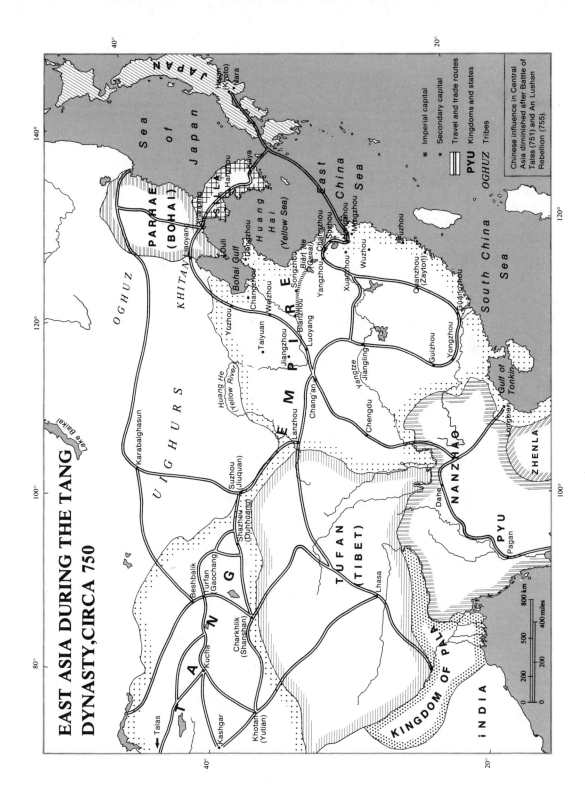

EAST ASIA DURING THE TANG DYNASTY, CIRCA 750

Imperial capital
Secondary capital
Travel and trade routes
PYU Kingdoms and states
OGHUZ Tribes

Chinese influence in Central Asia diminished after Battle of Talas (751) and An Lushan Rebellion (755).

Chinese blood, Yang Jian (Yang Chien), had reunified China and begun the rebuilding of its infrastructure, including the major canals and fortifications in the system that would become known as the Great Wall. Although he and his successor were unable to sustain their family's hold over what is called the Sui Dynasty, the succeeding Tang Dynasty (618-907 CE) was to last for nearly three centuries and inspire the second great flowering of Chinese civilization.

Europe had entered its so-called Dark Ages when the Tang Dynasty began. Pressing militarily outward to the previous borders of the Han Dynasty and beyond them, the Tang Dynasty improved upon the Han system of governance. An examination system for the civil service was to become the mainstay of quality recruitment of officials for many centuries to come. The replacement of the military aristocracy by a professional bureaucracy opened up new opportunities for talented people all over China. Arts and literature flourished once again and a detailed census, testifying to the administrative skills of the bureaucracy, was conducted in 754, showing a population of 52,880,488.

This was a period of renewed and unprecedented contact with the greater world of Asia and the West. Confident in their self-image as rulers of the Middle Kingdom, whose status soared above all others, the Tang emperors were willing to extend their contacts to the farthest possible reaches of the globe. Their courts were visited by representatives from throughout the known Asian world as far away as the Middle East. Nestorian Christians were received and permitted to not only proselytize but build several churches whose congregations were to survive in China for two centuries. Judaism and Islam were also introduced at this time, the latter taking particular root in Chinese Turkestan.

By the eighth century CE Tang society had undergone fundamental structural changes. Bureaucrats and merchants rather than soldiers came to play dominant roles. The archetypal relationship between the ruler and his Confucian advisers re-emerged during this period when the minister Wei Zheng, risking the wrath of the Emperor Tai Zong (ruled 626-49), routinely offered critical comments whenever he felt it his duty to do so. This ideal standard of critical comment and advice by the Confucian intellectual remains alive, if not always in practice, down to the present day and still creates a profound tension within Chinese political life.

Governmental influence and cultural life, meanwhile, gravitated toward the commercial centers of the South, thus adding to the loss of contact by the elite with the dangerous trends that threatened the security of the empire. Less and less attention was given to both the maintenance and control of a powerful military force. The capacity of the system to suppress rebellions in restless far-away regions began to wane at the same time that its defenses against the growing threat from northern "barbarians" were also weakening.

THE TANG INFLUENCE

Tang, as the greatest empire of its day, was assiduously imitated by many neighboring peoples. Never before or again did such a large proportion of mankind look to China not only as the paramount military power of the time but as the obvious model for government and culture.

—John K. Fairbank, et al., *East Asia: Tradition and Transformation*

Daoism and Buddhism

The Han dynasty collapse and its eventual replacement by the Tang marks the resurgence of two major religious influences: Daoism and Buddhism. Daoism had been in existence since the Zhou dynasty as a school of thought and now it began to overshadow Confucianism. Religious Daoism, as distinguished from its philosophical aspect, ranged from shamanism to divination to herbalism. The early Daoist pantheon of gods evolved into an elaborate system that was said would establish a "great equilibrium" in a utopian society.

Rivaling the Daoist resurgence, Buddhism was introduced to China from India by merchants traveling the Silk Road. Both Daoism and Buddhism were favored by the aristocratic families, but Buddhism was supported by a more systematized, monastic tradition. Born in the revelation of an Indian prince, Siddhartha, of what came to be known as the Four Noble Truths surrounding the origin and extinction of suffering, Buddhism had spread to many corners of greater Asia by the time it reached China around 100 CE.

The Buddhist faith was extensively modified in the process of its transmission from India, however. Two major divisions recognized today are Mahayana ("Universal" or "Greater" Vehicle) and Theravada — which the Mahayanas called Hinayana ("Individual" or "Lesser" Vehicle) to contrast it with their own. Mahayana spread not only to China but also Japan, Korea and Vietnam; Theravada reached (via Sri Lanka) Burma, Thailand and Cambodia. Mahayana Buddhism tolerated a greater variety of religious belief and practice than did the Theravada and this tolerance was especially important in its adaptation by the Chinese. Mahayana Buddhism considered mystical Daoism, particularly that of the Daoist founder Laozi and the *Daode jing*, to be a version of itself, albeit a more primitive one, and it absorbed the Confucian principles as being compatible with Buddhist ideals of proper behavior. Buddhism held a further advantage, in having originated in a neighboring great civilization, India. It thus brought with it a rich tradition of art and ritual, a literature containing great scriptures (sutras) which were soon translated into Chinese, and a monastic life that appealed to those who sought peace in an unstable, chaotic period of change.

Perhaps no single cultural phenomenon has unified the entire Asian continent to the extent that Buddhism did in the fourth through the ninth centuries CE, for even though it was to be supplanted in later centuries by the vicissitudes of political change and rival religious movements, it alone during this period was able to culturally unite much of Asia within the apolitical embrace of belief and discipline.

Buddhist Influences in Japan and Korea

Buddhism in China remained fundamentally a cultural import to be absorbed, transformed or extruded like all other imports. It had only a limited influence on the structure and fundamental values of the society over the long course of China's history, but its artistic impact was profound. Its adaptability, like a stream flowing onto new ground, made it the ideal vehicle to carry China's philosophy, literature and arts into societies such as Korea and Japan. In both instances, Buddhism soon became a "state religion" and enjoyed the patronage and protection of the elite families.

The encounter between Buddhist and Confucianist influences within Japanese traditions is illustrated by the so-called "Seventeen Article Constitution" attributed to the seventh century Japanese statesman, Prince Shotoku (574-622 CE).

This document became a central point of reference for the evolving Japanese government in the seventh and eighth centuries. It asserted both Buddhist and Confucian principles of religious belief and proper behavior, but without the presumptions of supreme central authority that were so characteristic of the Chinese. Instead, evidence already appears in these writings that Japanese authority will depend, as it does today, from consensus developed within a core group.[3]

The Koguryo kingdom in Korea had adopted Buddhism to be its official religion as early as 384 CE, a time of political and territorial resurgence for that state. As noted above, the Silla kingdom eventually overwhelmed Koguryo and its neighbor Paekche to unify the Korean peninsula. This unification embraced cultural elements of Buddhism (and its Chinese-influenced art forms) and Confucianism. Like the Japanese, the Koreans of both Unified Silla and the Three Kingdoms Period that preceded it preferred to blur their strictly hierarchical means of assigning authority within a consultative process. For the early Koreans, the embodiment of such a process was the *Hwabaek* council of senior aristocrats. Important decisions of state, including the official adoption of Buddhism, were made by such councils.

Korean Buddhism, infused with Confucian traditions, also served to inspire the formation of elite groups of young warriors known as the *hwarang* whose tenets of behavior (such as filial piety) were set down by a famous Korean monk named Won'gwang. Buddhism entered strongly into Korean poetry and music during this period, and influenced painting and sculpture. Some of the greatest Buddhist sculpture in Asia dates to the era of the Three Kingdoms in Korea. Later, during the Silla unification, the casting of great bronze temple bells reached its apogee. The bronze bell dedicated to King Songdok, now in the National Museum of Kyongyu, is exquisitely wrought and measures 7 feet 6 inches (2.27 meters) in diameter by 11 (3.3 meters) in height.

The Silla kingdom flourished for two centuries, but was never able to successfully resolve a fundamental contradiction that was to plague Korea for much of its history. On the one hand its initial success was based upon the warrior leadership of aristocratic lineages who thereafter were given special privileges by the Silla kings. On the

other, it attempted to utilize the Chinese model by incorporating an administrative elite through a Confucian examination system. The two traditions were irreconcilable, and by 800 CE serious feuding had erupted.

Yet the general prosperity of the population continued to grow through a flourishing commerce with Japan and China. Merchants discovered that the aristocratic feuding preoccupied and weakened the central government, leaving them free to develop their power and wealth. Meanwhile, Korea's scholars were becoming adept Confucian classicists within academies modeled on the Chinese system. Korean priests participated in the lively international Buddhist community, visiting the great monasteries of China, India and Japan. Block printing was introduced by the Korean Buddhist community around the mid-eighth century — nearly a century before its appearance in China. The studies of medicine, mathematics and astronomy all reached a high level of achievement in Korea during this period.

The rise of the merchant class paralleled the growth of great private estates in the provinces (among which must be counted the largest Buddhist monasteries). The plight of the peasant farmer on the estates deteriorated, however, for he was treated virtually as a slave by the landowners. Eventually, peasant revolts erupted which soon were taken over by discontented and feuding aristocrats. The final decades of the Silla period saw political havoc throughout the countryside and the eventual overthrow of the Silla king by the general Wang Kon. There emerged a new dynasty, the Koryo, from which the Western name for Korea is derived.

The Kingdom of Koryo

The Koryo dynasty (918-1392) built upon the ruins of the Silla while borrowing even more than before from the Chinese. A new capital was laid out at Kaesong in the northern delta of the Han River with ancillary centers located at present-day Pyongyang (the old Koguryo capital) and Seoul. From here a Tang-style central government was established based on the Confucian civil service examination system. While superficially this arrangement seemed to ensure the use of the merit principle as an avenue to top administrative posts, such was not to be the case. The old patterns of aristocratic privilege re-emerged and again the landed estates began to consolidate independent wealth and power. Koryo became overly centralized in its orientation. All significant economic, artistic an political activity took place in the capital. No one of any importance was content to live on a remote estate, however wealthy. The Korean hinterland became viewed merely as an object of taxation and received little serious infrastructural investment from either the central government or the absentee landlords. Buddhism continued to flourish during most of this period while artistic achievements languished except in the specialty of pottery-making. The manufacture of pale green celadon vases in Korea at this time achieved qualities unmatched before or since.

To protect itself from northern invasion, Koryo constructed a wall across the peninsula from the Yalu River to the coast of the Japan Sea. While this and a vigilant army managed to shelter Korea from invasion for a long period, the intrigues and rivalries among the leading aristocratic families grew worse. Unlike China, where there regularly developed a dynasty with a powerful monarch at the center, Korea's kingship remained a weak institution under constant pressure from factions of a landed, aristocratic ruling class. At the same time, the ever-present threat of invasion from the nomads of the north left little alternative to strong military cooperation.

Decline of the Tang Dynasty in China

Like the Han dynasty, the Tang began to break down when its revenue from taxes shrunk and its governing expenses ballooned. A new, more sophisticated urban class was developing whose sense of egalitarianism, secular (less Buddhist) orientations, and capacity to pass tax burdens to an oppressed peasant farmer class blinded it to the rot that had set in. The turning point came in 751 with a major Tang defeat by an Arab army at the Battle of Talas in the distant region west of the Pamir Mountains of Central Asia. Although far-removed from the court life of China, this event led to a cascading series of defeats and internal rebellions led by independent generals, the most

devastating of which was a revolt led by a powerful military governor, An Lushan. The stability of the Tang realm began to crack even while its basic infrastructure continued to function smoothly. Again in parallel with the earlier Han, powerful eunuchs and bureaucrats feuded openly until a few regional military commanders divided China into their separate domains. Three of the generals who led this subsequent "Five Dynasties" period were foreign — one was probably Iranian and the other two Turkish — reflecting the extent to which "barbarians" had once again both intruded into and been absorbed by Chinese society.

By this point in China's history, however, its preceding achievements in culture, governance and technology stood like a mountain absorbing the force of a storm. Within a few short decades the chaos subsided and a new imperial rule was restored under the stable, relatively gentle, centralized authority of the Song (Sung) Dynasty (960-1280). Yet once again, the very sun-like gentility of this regime had the double-edged effect of encouraging not only a competent civil service and flourishing arts but also of undermining the practice of a unified, ruthless defense of the northern borders. The latter, as we shall see, was to prove its undoing.

In addition to improving and extending the civil service examinations system, the Song Dynasty encouraged two other developments of long-lasting impact, one in the commercial realm, the other in intellectual matters.

THE SONG DYNASTY AND PACIFIC COMMERCE

Building upon the commercial growth of the Yangzi Valley[4] and the southern coast that had developed in the Tang dynasty, the Song commercial centers of Guangzhou (Canton) and Quanzhou expanded under the stimulus of foreign trade. Closely controlled by the Song emperors who derived significant revenues from it, foreign trade was encouraged by sending imperial embassies abroad. During this period major sea routes opened to the west, presaging the great maritime expeditions of the Ming Dynasty (see below). The Song trade placed China at the epicenter of the nascent global economy. Chinese ports were filled with Koreans, Arabs, Iranians and other foreigners who occupied special permanent enclaves set aside for them and who became as familiar with these commercial centers as are today's international businessmen with Tokyo, Osaka, Seattle and Los Angeles. China's exports were its sophisticated manufactured goods: silks, porcelains, books, paintings, and copper cash, prized in lands as far away as Zanzibar. In return, China took in raw materials, gems, spices, ivory, and horses.

The Song commercial renaissance stimulated and supported a vast maritime trading empire in Southeast Asia known as Srivijaya to which the Song sent four trade-promoting missions in the year 987 alone. In both realms, merchants served their own particular interests and those of a ruling hierarchy, but it is likely that the traditional status of trader-merchants in Southeast Asia remained higher than in China. Confucian scholars still viewed merchants as parasites and saw to it that in the social hierarchy they remained at the very bottom, below farmers. It was virtually impossible for wealthy merchants in China to gain social status without giving up commercial activities. Their status was so closely controlled that Tang Dynasty rules forbade them to ride horses.

Yet commercial talent was sorely needed and eventually had to be rewarded. By the time Marco Polo arrived in China at the end of the Southern Song dynasty, its scale of commerce in the Yangzi delta alone was greater than in all Europe. In conjunction with this growth, China began to make the transition to a paper money economy. During the Song, China's need for the commercial expertise of merchants caused the social barriers between the merchants and the upper strata to erode somewhat.

When these changes came about, the inland northwest region of China receded in commercial importance but the threat from its nomadic neighbors grew more ominous. The size of the army required to defend against this threat was a further motivation for the Song empire to seek revenues through maritime trade, primarily through licenses and taxes. Meanwhile, advanced technology from China including gunpowder and the compass began leaking back to the West via the Moslem trading world, eventually revolutionizing warfare and navigation among the emerging medieval kingdoms of Europe.

The Southern Song Dynasty and Neo-Confucianism

The Tungusic tribes known as the Jurchen, who occupied the Manchurian plain by 1127, had swept away not only their northern tribal rivals, the Liao, but also their erstwhile allies the Song Chinese whom they pushed out of northern China all the way to the Yangzi River. Their rule became a Chinese dynasty in the north known as the Jin or Ruzhen (1115-1234) while the Song rulers, relegated to hold on merely as the "Southern Song" (1127-1279), remained wealthy and powerful by world standards of the time. Moreover, the retreat to the south inspired the Song leaders to reinvigorate their seafaring and maritime trading capabilities both as a revenue base and defense against the northerners.

Southern Song society began to turn inward intellectually and to re-examine its Confucian premises. A series of contending new schools of

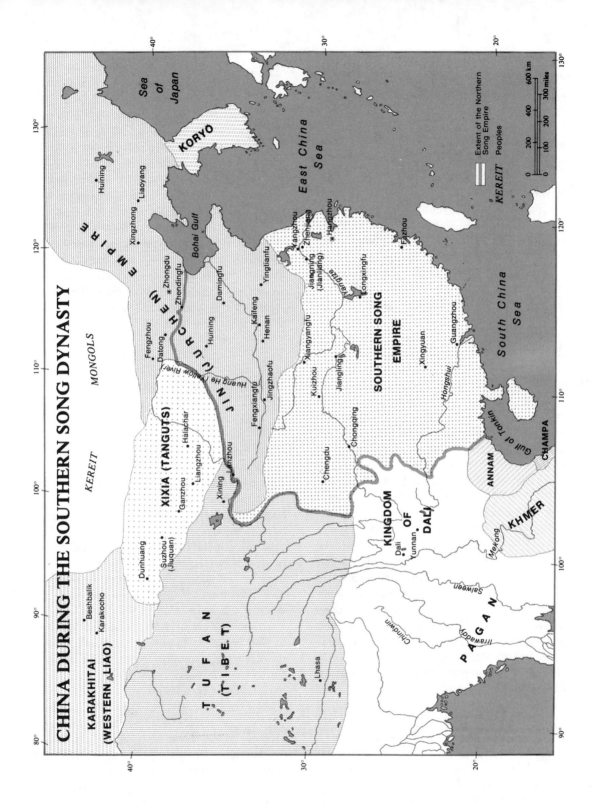

CHINA DURING THE SOUTHERN SONG DYNASTY

KARAKHITAI
(WESTERN LIAO)

• Beshbalik
• Karakocho

MONGOLS

KEREIT

TUFAN
(TIBET)

• Lhasa

• Dunhuang

XIXIA (TANGUTS)

Suzhou
(Jiuquan)

• Ganzhou
• Liangzhou

• Halachar

• Xining
• Lanzhou

KINGDOM
OF
DALI

• Dali
• Yunnan

PAGAN

Irrawaddy
Salween
Chindwin

KHMER

Mekong

ANNAM

CHAMP A

Gulf of Tonkin

Hongshui

• Xingyuan

• Chengdu

• Chongqing

• Jiangling

SOUTHERN SONG
EMPIRE

• Longxingfu

• Guangzhou

South China
Sea

• Kuizhou

• Xiangyangfu

• Jingzhaofu

• Fengxiangfu

• Henan

Huang He (Yellow River)

JIN (JURCHEN) EMPIRE

• Fengzhou
• Datong

Zhongdu •
Zhendingfu •

• Huining

• Damingfu

• Kaifeng

• Yingtianfu

Yangtze

• Yangzhou
• Zhenjiang

Jiangning
(Jianjiang)

Hangzhou •

• Fuzhou

East China
Sea

Sea
of
Japan

• Huining

Xingzhong •
Liaoyang •

Bohai Gulf

KORYO

KEREIT

Extent of the Northern
Song Empire

KEREIT Peoples

600 km
400
200
0

300 miles
200
100
0

thought emerged which today are broadly termed "Neo-Confucian." Neo-Confucianism drew heavily on Buddhism for inspiration even while Buddhism itself was falling into disfavor. Neo-Confucianism explained the world in terms of natural principles or laws and material forces. It held that human nature was essentially inclined toward goodness in accordance with such principles, but that one's feelings and emotions could disrupt one's mind and result in incorrect behavior. In succeeding centuries, Neo-Confucian thought would vary according to national experiences and influences, but in general it would lay stress on the role of the individual in maintaining societal well-being. In its more conservative manifestations, it emphasized rigid principles and social stratification.

Neo-Confucianism revived a great debate about the nature of a proper education. An influential scholar of the early Song, Hu Yuan (993-1059), sought to combine classical learning with "practical learning" such as civil administration, engineering, and mathematics. This kind of balance was sorely needed amid the increasing economic complexity of Song society. The great synthesis of all Neo-Confucianist thought came in the twelfth century in the hands of Zhuxi (Chu Hsi, 1130-1200). In spite of the fact that he lived after the Song Dynasty had retreated to the south, giving up not only territory but also efforts at broad educational and governmental reform, Zhuxi was to greatly influence the basic stock of ideas to which educated men throughout East Asia would be exposed. The timing of his strong intellectual leadership could hardly have been better, for it coincided with the advent of woodblock printing in China. This enabled Confucian ideas to be transmitted for the first time to a mass audience and greatly expanded education throughout East Asia. It also came in advance of the Mongol conquests (described below) which spread Confucian thought much more widely throughout the Asian world than the scholars would have otherwise done by themselves.

In Korea, the Neo-Confucian revival was especially vigorous and it developed in original ways. In particular, the Koreans surpassed the Chinese by more thoroughly incorporating the ideas of Neo-Confucianism into the workings of their social institutions and code of ethics. In Japan, on the other hand, the influence was notable in that it provided a rationale for new forms of "practical learning" about nature and the world.

This period of creative ferment in China died down around the end of the thirteenth century. Neo-Confucianism ceased being a creative wellspring and became a straightjacket of conservative orthodoxy. The answers in the civil service examinations had to conform to its strict guidelines. Thereafter, China's capacity for scientific and philosophical innovation began to decline. While this may have carried the considerable advantage of regularizing and stabilizing the assumptions by which society and governance would be conducted, it left China ill-prepared technologically and politically for the modern era which finally would break upon it in the nineteenth century.

THE MONGOL EMPIRE AND THE GREAT KHAN

In the year 1206 a chieftain of a northern nomadic tribe of the eastern steppe was proclaimed Genghis Khan ("universal sovereign") after a prolonged internecine conflict among warring tribes. His victorious tribe, the Mongol, became the name applied to all his subsequent tribal allies in the steppe region. The core genius of this extraordinary leader was his ability to organize and utilize elite corps of warriors and civil administrators, all derived from a central structure of linked tribal families and clans.

Although Genghis Khan's mounted army was by Chinese standards quite small (about 130,000), its discipline, mobility, tactics and toughness formed an offensive war-making machine of unprecedented capabilities.

Not only the northern Tangut tribes of the Xi Xia kingdom but also the Jurchen, who had previously driven the Song Chinese southward, quickly fell before the juggernaut of the Mongol cavalry. Yet here the invaders halted their southern drive — testimony to the compact strength of the Southern Song Dynasty — and consolidated their position in the north. Then they turned their invading forces toward the western frontiers of Asia. Genghis Khan and his successors came to rule the

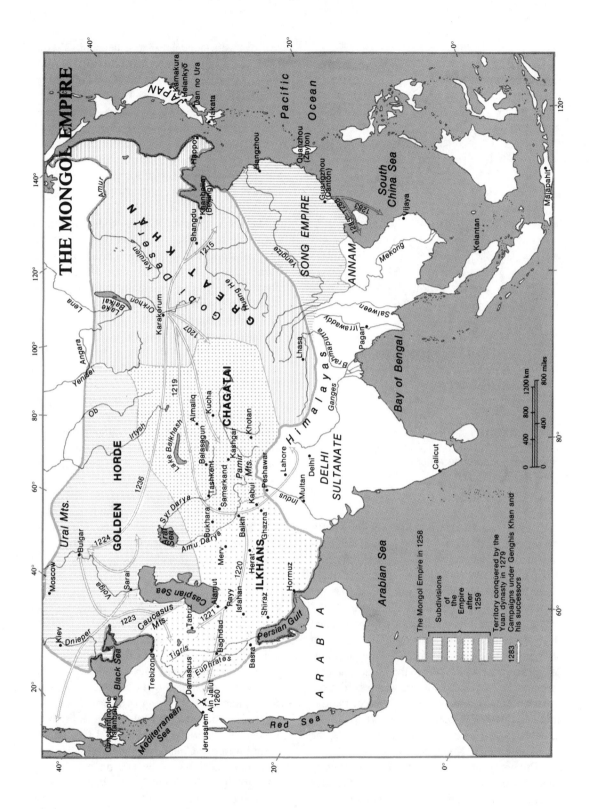

THE MONGOL EMPIRE

Pacific Asia to the Nineteenth Century • 39

Figure 1.6   A Jurchen warrior.

armadas were launched against Japan in 1274 and 1281 and against Java in 1292 but all the naval invasions were unsuccessful. Overland forces invaded Korea (the Koryo kingdom), Vietnam (the Tran kingdom) and Burma, establishing China's dominance in those areas once again.

The Mongol Invasion of Korea: Emergence of the Yi Dynasty

In Koryo Dynasty Korea, conditions for the peasants had so deteriorated that in 1176 an uprising broke out. This instability was accompanied by a series of coups by a discontented military bureaucracy, eventually stabilizing around 1196 with the takeover of the entire country by a military leader named Choe Chung-hon. However, no Korean military force was prepared to withstand the completely new phenomenon that swept down from the north in 1231: the Mongol cavalry. Korea was completely subjugated, and the Mongols exacted onerous tributes and labor from the populace in support of two attempted invasions of Japan in 1274 and 1281. The Koryo dynasty was dominated by the Mongols for another century, but when the Mongol Empire declined in influence, King Kongmin (reigned 1351-1374) attempted to reassert the authority of a strong central government. Resistance from the nobility was fierce, mainly in response to the king's efforts to redistribute land more equitably to the people, and within a few years he was assassinated.

Rejuvenation of East-West Exchanges

The Mongol khanates inflicted great human suffering when they extended their empire in the thirteenth century, but they also stabilized and unified the Asian continent to a degree that permitted another flourishing of international commercial traffic between East and West. For about a century, from around 1240 to 1340, passage from Europe to China over the long and arduous Central Asia trade routes was protected by the Mongol outposts (although local conflicts always threatened the traveler). Thereafter it closed once again when the Ottoman Turks widened their control in Asia Minor. While the opportunity lasted,

largest land empire the world has ever known. By the time of his death in 1227 his forces had consolidated his control over all of Central Asia. The empire was thereafter divided into four main "khanates" among his four sons. The East Asian portion, the "Great Khan," was initially ruled over by the son named Ogodei. The khanates continued to expand, overrunning present-day Iran, Russia (burning Moscow in the process), Poland, Hungary and probing all the way to the Danube and the Adriatic Sea. Western Europe was saved from invasion only because Batu, the khan of the formidable "Golden Horde," had to return to the east to participate in the choice of a successor after the death of the Great Khan Ogodei in 1241.

The conquest of the Southern Song dynasty finally occurred when the grandson of Genghis Khan, Kublai, became the Great Khan in 1260. Under his rule came the most ambitious contacts between China and the known world. Massive

thousands of European merchants again poured eastward, joining a few elite Mongol traders and investors, to seek their fortunes in China and other parts of Asia. Of these, the most famous is Marco Polo, who not only visited the court of Kublai Khan with his Venician merchant father, but remained for a number of years and became an administrator for the Khan.[5] Catholic missionaries were permitted to conduct baptisms in Beijing and, at the height of the Crusades, Franciscan monks could be found there exploring, on behalf of the pope, the prospects of an alliance against the Saracens. Coincidentally, around the same time (1278) a Nestorian Christian monk who was born in Beijing was meeting with the kings of France and England to suggest an alliance between the Khanate of Persia and the Crusaders against the Saracens.

A contemporary traveler during the height of the Mongol rule (approximately 1250-1350) would have found it difficult to predict which global region and polity would come to dominate commerce. The historian Abu-Lughod has noted, "No single hegemon dictated the terms of production and trade to others, no geographic entity could be said to be located at *the* center." The eventual dominance of Asia by the European powers in the nineteenth and early twentieth centuries showed no signs of emerging. Indeed, "there was no *inherent historical necessity* that shifted the system to favor the West rather than the East."[6]

Invasion of Japan: Mongols Versus the Samurai

Following the rise in Japan of the Minamoto faction in 1192 and a new shogun, Minamoto Yoritomo, the era of warrior rule over Japan began. Its central administrative structure was called the *bakufu*. Although it began as a rather simple governmental structure under Yoritomo at the site of Kamakura near present-day Tokyo, the *bakufu* eventually transformed itself into an elaborate, sophisticated bureaucracy. The shogun, formally appointed by the Emperor, became in effect the principal administrator over the domain of his family, that of his vassals, and to a lesser extent of the vassals allied to the emperor.

The shogun was charged with the security and tranquility of Japan itself, something that proved especially difficult to achieve in 1274 and 1281 when the Mongols under Kublai Khan attempted to invade Japan. Both times, the Mongols stormed ashore on the island of Kyushu, and the samurai met and fought them to an initial standstill. A more extensive struggle for survival was precluded in each instance by the arrival of a great storm, christened "divine wind" (*kamikaze*), which wrecked the Mongol fleet. From this time forward, the Japanese began to think of their land as the beneficiary of supernatural protection. Nevertheless, the great resources required to defend Japan against the Mongols seriously weakened the Kamakura shogunate.

With the exception of the Mongol invasions, the years under the Kamakura *bakufu* were relatively stable and secure. Art and culture were no longer the exclusive domain of the elegant courtiers in Kyoto. The *samurai*, with their new power and affluence, became the new patrons of the arts. (As befitted warriors, the art they favored was starkly realistic, rather than the delicate forms of the courtiers.) Buddhism also spread from the temples and became a more popular religion. The samurai themselves became devout Buddhists and were particularly drawn to the rigorous schools of Rinzai and Soto Zen, each of which was adapted from Chinese Buddhist schools.

In the fourteenth century, the Kamakura *bakufu* was succeeded by the Ashikaga shoguns who moved their headquarters to the Muromachi sector of Kyoto. The Muromachi *bakufu* reached its peak under its third Shogun, Ashikaga Yoshimitsu, who lavishly patronized the arts. However, the status and power of the shoguns began to decline when their provincial governors became more wealthy and independent. By the fifteenth century open conflict broke out between rival alliances over the succession to the position of shogun. Entering the sixteenth century, Japan had become fragmented into small domains and was mired in civil war among powerful regional lords. Paradoxically, the breakdown of central authority freed local merchants and entrepreneurs to increase their economic activities (paralleling similar cases in China and Korea), stimulating overall economic growth during the Muromachi period.

THE BUILDING OF CHINA'S GREAT WALL

The name *Great Wall* is commonly applied to a variety of Chinese border fortifications, usually taken as referring to a single structure, thought to have been created by Qin Shihuangdi and subsequently maintained and enlarged. A Great Wall of China, so understood [as a single, ancient unit], has never existed, although it is firmly entrenched in both Chinese and Western cultural mythology.

Chinese states have built "long walls" (the literal meaning of the Chinese *changcheng*) since the fourth century BCE; among the important wall-building dynasties were the Qin, Han, Northern Wei, Northern Qi, Sui, and Jin. Of simple tamped-earth construction, their works have left few traces. The Ming border defense line, whose ruins at such sites as Juyongguan, Shanhaiguan, and Jiayuguan define the concept and constitute the "Great Wall" visited today, follows a route south of most of these earlier lines.

The Ming walls were begun in the late fifteenth century with a line across the southern margin of the Ordos Desert, followed in the next century by construction in the area west of Beijing, and in the latter part of the sixteenth century in the eastern sector between the capital and the sea. Made of earth at first, portions of these walls were faced with or reconstructed in stone beginning in the mid sixteenth century.

Unaware of the recent origins of these walls, early Western visitors associated them with Qin Shihuangdi's long-vanished work, well known from historical texts and popular tradition, and transmitted to Europe an account of an ancient yet still extant Great Wall that quickly captured the Western imagination. Although its error has been repeatedly pointed out by both Chinese and Western scholars, this account remains widely accepted.

— *Arthur N. Waldron, EAH*

THE MING DYNASTY

Soon after Kublai Khan's death the Mongol khanate in China began to disintegrate. Civil war and rebellion followed from which emerged the foundation of the Ming Dynasty (1368-1644) at the hands of the commoner, Zhu Yuanzhang, who became the emperor Hongwu. There followed three centuries of orderly government, albeit one that was also despotic and rife with imperial court factionalism. This long term stability needs to be emphasized in a historical overview that identifies so many turbulent transitions. The prevalent situation in China over the millennia was not one of chaotic change but of stasis, of peace and stability. The foundations of Ming stability were several hundred thousand "officials and scholars" at the local level whose devotion to the precepts of Confucianism led them to serve a broad range of societal functions without recompense from the throne.

Convenient to the Ming emperors, this Confucian emphasis on hierarchical relationships and the duties of one rank to the other were applied to the vassal states who were expected to show homage and bring tribute to The Son of Heaven in the capital of Nanjing. The perspective was cultural condescension, not hostility, and an appreciation of the value that could be placed upon trade and contact with China. The "vassal states" did not always see things from this perspective, however, and sometimes resisted the full extent of what the Ming emperor presumed to be his authority. The Ming emperors gradually came to realize that the lavish hospitality and gift-giving required of them for the myriad foreign missions arriving in Nanjing might exceed the value of the trade with such states.

During the early Ming period the states of South and Southeast Asia were incorporated into this extensive tribute system by maritime expeditions beginning in 1405. Led mostly by the "Three-Jewel Eunuch" Zheng He, a Muslim from Yunnan, immense fleets were commissioned to sail to India, then beyond to Hormuz and eventually even the coast of Africa. In purely expeditionary terms, this was the greatest armada of the pre-modern era. The first fleet carried more than twenty-thousand men aboard an estimated 317 ships. Occasionally, these expeditions involved the use of force: Zheng He destroyed an overseas Chinese pirate fleet in Sumatra, but overall they were highly successful diplomatic missions whose size and sophistication created awe in foreign ports. It should be stressed that they were not missions of conquest and plunder but of commerce and trade. A special concern of the expeditions, in fact, was the securing of the Malacca Strait through which valuable commerce passed to and from China. They inaugurated an "age of commerce" in Pacific Asia, particularly because

they stimulated the growth and trade of pepper in Southeast Asia.

These triumphs of imperial navigation seem in retrospect to suggest that China might have been poised to become a great naval power that would dominate all of maritime Asia, but such was not to be the case. The adventurous, outward looking spirit of the Ming expeditions ran counter to the inward-turning sentiments of the Nanjing court where many capable administrators became angry over the resources required for the fleets at a time of growing domestic crisis. By 1480, when a powerful eunuch requested resources for another great expedition, he was fiercely opposed by bureaucrats who not only blocked his proposal but went so far as to destroy the records of Zheng He's achievements out of fear that they would inspire further naval initiatives. Unwittingly, China's bureaucrats had ceded to future foreign navies the control of the seas that would one day determine the fate of Asia. They did so, however, not out of xenophobic ignorance but in response to their own domestic priorities and a growing concern over the wealth and independence of the coastal merchants.

The Ming and the Founding of Korea's Yi Dynasty

As noted earlier, the reformist king of Korea, Kongmin, was assassinated in 1374 after trying to break the dominance of the powerful families over the Koryo government. A brief period of instability followed during which the Ming Emperor decided to seize the advantage and lay claim to the Koryo kingdom's northeastern territory. While his great army gathered on Korea's border, the commander of the Korean forces, general Yi Song-gye, decided against fighting a suicidal battle and instead turned against the Koryo court, dispatching it entirely. Then he negotiated with the Chinese. His regime, the Yi dynasty (termed the Chosun dynasty by the Ming court to which general Yi accepted the customary status of "younger brother"), was to endure for more than five centuries.

Chinese influence thus remained strong in virtually all aspects of Korean life even though Korean culture retained its distinctive character.

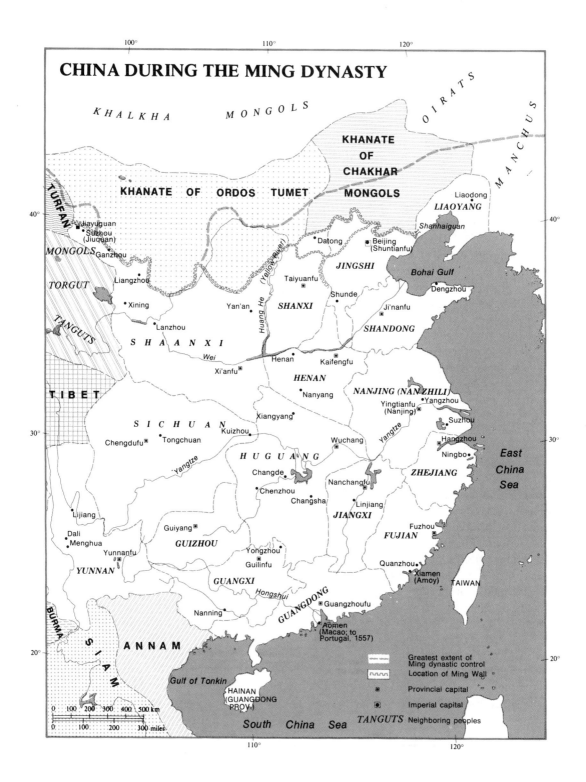

CHINA DURING THE MING DYNASTY

KHALKHA MONGOLS OIRATS

MANCHUS

KHANATE
OF
CHAKHAR
MONGOLS

KHANATE OF ORDOS TUMET

LIAOYANG

Liaodong

TURFAN

Jiayuguan
Suzhou
(Jiuquan)

Shanhaiguan

MONGOLS Ganzhou

Datong

Beijing
(Shuntianfu)

JINGSHI

Bohai Gulf

TORGUT

Liangzhou

Taiyuanfu

Dengzhou

Xining

Yan'an

SHANXI

Shunde

Ji'nanfu

Lanzhou

SHANDONG

TANGUTS

SHAANXI

Wei

Henan

Kaifengfu

Xi'anfu

HENAN

NANJING (NAN ZHILI)

Yingtianfu
(Nanjing)

Yangzhou

TIBET

Nanyang

Xiangyang

Suzhou

SICHUAN

Kuizhou

Yangtze

Hangzhou

Chengdufu

Tongchuan

Wuchang

Ningbo

East
China
Sea

HUGUANG

Changde

ZHEJIANG

Chenzhou

Nanchangfu

Lijiang

Changsha

Linjiang

Dali
Menghua

Guiyang

JIANGXI

Yunnanfu

GUIZHOU

Yongzhou

Fuzhou

FUJIAN

YUNNAN

Guilinfu

Quanzhou

BURMA

GUANGXI

Xiamen
(Amoy)

TAIWAN

Hongshui

GUANGDONG

Nanning

Guangzhoufu

SIAM

ANNAM

Aomen
(Macao; to
Portugal, 1557)

Gulf of Tonkin

HAINAN
(GUANGDONG
PROV.)

Greatest extent of
Ming dynastic control
Location of Ming Wall
Provincial capital
Imperial capital
TANGUTS Neighboring peoples

South China Sea

0 100 200 300 400 500 km
0 100 200 300 miles

CHINESE MARITIME INNOVATIONS

Critical to the success of China as a maritime power and global trader were its innovations in navigation and sailing. Among these were:

- The *magnetic compass*, in use by 1119, was probably noticed by Arab traders who subsequently introduced it to the Mediterranean world.
- An early version of the *sextant* called the "dipper-observer" was used in navigation along with the compass to track the Great Bear constellation.
- China's shipbuilders produced the *leeboard, the centerboard, the windlass, and the watertight compartment*, all of which were introduced by Arabs into the West.
- The *dry dock*— enabling extensive repair and maintenance of a great Song fleet— did not appear in Europe until centuries later.
- Warship construction included *paddle-wheel ships*, operated by treadmill, with up to eleven wheels per ship.
- *Weather forecasting*, primarily with respect to wind shifts, was based upon seasonal and weather signs.

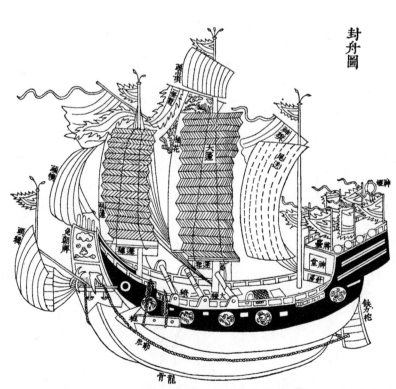

Figure 1.7   A Qing Dynasty design for an ocean-going junk. Versions used during the Ming expeditions were very similiar to this and reached perhaps 180 feet in length, dwarfing the small Portuguese caravels that were to enter the region after the Ming voyaging had ended.

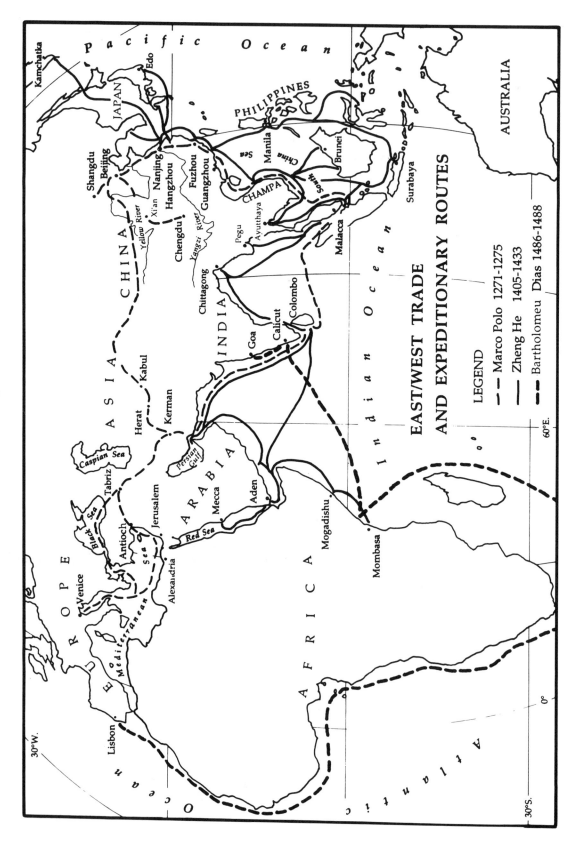

EAST/WEST TRADE
AND EXPEDITIONARY ROUTES

LEGEND

— — Marco Polo 1271-1275
—— Zheng He 1405-1433
- - - Bartholomeu Dias 1486-1488

The Yi dynasty Koreans embraced Confucianism as much or more than their predecessors but in addition they reformed the examination system, making it a genuine avenue to power and prestige.

The average Korean official's disdain for commercial affairs was perhaps linked to the Confucian Chinese legacy. Trade relations both domestically and with the outside world remained at a primitive level although, as in China, a limited amount of external commerce was conducted covertly. The infrastructure of basic housing and agriculture likewise remained underdeveloped by standards of the peasantry in China and Japan. Once again, the obsession of the aristocracy with court life in the capital led to ruthless exploitation of the farmers who nevertheless managed to increase production with improved rice strains and land reclamation. The profitability of aristocratic ownership of land probably held back the development of a commercial class, but the proliferation of the aristocracy eventually had its costs. Over many generations its numbers grew to levels that could not be supported so that many of the upper class, the so-called *yangban*, fell on hard times and turned to farming for survival.

Yi Dynasty Koreans faced the same internal contradictions as their predecessors: while the nobility espoused Chinese-style ideals of orderly, centralized Confucian governance, it willingly split into feuding factions to a degree far beyond anything witnessed in neighboring China. These factions became hereditary groupings with established bases of support in the provinces that were often associated with private Confucian academies, or *sowon*. In their rivalries they tended to offset one another, creating frequent political stalemates in the court and contributing to the growing rigidity of the overall political system.

The intellectual world of Korea during this period was by no means stagnant, however. Innovation and learning continued in mathematics and astronomy. The first extensive use of moveable type for printing anywhere in the world took place in Korea in the fifteenth century. The crowning intellectual achievement of the Yi dynasty was its innovation of a system for writing the Korean language. Until that point, only Chinese was available for the written word. The new Korean script, *hangul*, developed under the guidance of King Sejong, provided a simple, elegant means of representing spoken Korean by means of a phonetic script. Although it saw only very limited use at the time, it was revived at the end of the nineteenth century as a powerful tool for inspiring Korean national consciousness. It is in common use in Korea today, sometimes supplemented by Chinese characters.

Running counter to the empty formalism of Confucian orthodoxy there arose in the eighteenth century an intellectual movement called "Practical Learning" (*Sirhak*) which was inspired by Western science and the growing need to find new solutions to Korea's societal ills. The Sirhak scholars represented a nascent group of Koreans who wished to assert their socio-cultural identity as distinct from China and having equal value. Their solutions to social problems, couched in the context of early Confucian texts, were highly egalitarian and reformist in nature.

The Ming Decline

Meanwhile, the Ming Dynasty began a steep decline. It turned from distant maritime explorations to shore-hugging coastal defense and transport. Its loss of a sea-faring spirit deprived it of the means by which to understand the emerging, if still slight, interdependence of the global economy in the fifteenth and sixteenth centuries. Perhaps this was too much to ask of a leadership that had always gained its primary revenue from land taxes, not trade taxes. The Mongols were again resurgent, forcing a relocation of the capital from Nanjing to Beijing for a faster defensive response. The emperors, preoccupied with the constant threat from the north and the dramatic growth of coastal piracy by Chinese and Japanese, prohibited maritime trade altogether. One of most serious blows to Ming stability then came from the sea: the invasion of Korea by Japan.

Hideyoshi: Japan Looks West

By the end of the sixteenth century, Japan reunified under warrior leadership. At a time when fundamental forces were changing the Japanese economy, society and government, feudal domains increased in size through the successful warfare and diplomacy of a few family groups. New technologies, including primitive firearms, were introduced from abroad. These developments favored a new type of leader, capable of martialing large forces and deploying them ruthlessly against his enemies.

The first to make major strides toward reunification was Oda Nobunaga (1534-1582). By the time of his death (by assassination), Nobunaga had gained control of central Japan and driven the shogun into exile. His successor, Toyotomi Hideyoshi (1536-1598), further consolidated these gains but squandered them with an ill-considered invasion of the Asian mainland. Hideyoshi believed that the time was ripe for the conquest of China and the advent of a great Japanese empire in East Asia.

His natural avenue of conquest lay through the Korean peninsula, but the Koreans, permanent allies of the Chinese Emperor, resisted until a vast Ming army rushed to their aid. What ensued was above all a tragedy for Korea. While its military resistance helped repulse the Japanese, two centuries of relative peace in the Yi Dynasty and the pacifist sentiments of Neo-Confucianism had left it ill-prepared for the conflict. The Korean admiral Yi Sun-sin did make up for Ming naval weaknesses, successfully leading the attack against Japan's naval forces with his armored ships (the so-called "turtle ships") but the Japanese invasion left Korea in an economic shambles and entailed great loss of life. Amid the chaotic aftermath, as the *yangban* nobility scrambled to consolidate its land holdings even further, removing them from the base of desperately needed tax revenues, a second disaster descended from the north: the invasions by an ascendant northern tribe, the Manchus, in 1627 and 1636. The Manchus went on to establish their new Qing dynasty in China (described below) while Korea's Yi kings were forced to recognize their dominance.

While enduring these external shocks, the Yi system retained an internal stability derived from the power balances among its strong ruling families. The cost of this stability was a deeply factionalized leadership. Steeped in an inward-looking Neo-Confucian tradition, perhaps no country was so ill-prepared as Korea for the wrenching changes that were to be demanded of it and the rest of Asia in the nineteenth century.

THE RISE OF THE TOKUGAWA SHOGUNATE

Korea and China were at least fortunate in that Hideyoshi died during his continental expedition in 1598. Soon thereafter the Japanese forces retreated to their home islands, but the effects of the invasion were to be long-lasting. Not only did it engender a deep, abiding hostility and suspicion in Korea toward Japan, it seriously weakened China's Ming Dynasty and contributed to its eventual downfall. Japan itself benefited culturally. The invasion broadened the exposure of the Japanese to the Neo-Confucianism of Zhuxi, led them to acquire the technology of moveable-type printing, and permitted them to relocate a large number of Korean ceramic artists to Japan where they greatly enriched the Japanese ceramic industry with porcelain ware.

Hideyoshi's death resulted in yet another power struggle among the great feudal lords (*daimyo*) of Japan. One of them, Tokugawa Ieyasu (1542-1616), succeeding in forming an alliance of nearly half the *daimyo*, while a rival "Western Alliance" formed against him. The military contest came in 1600 at one of the most famous engagements in Japanese history, the Battle of Sekigahara, where Ieyasu defeated his rivals. With his victory, all of Japan came under his control and he set about reducing the domains of his opponents while seizing control of the major harbors and commercial centers.

Ieyasu moved his headquarters to Edo (also spelled Yedo), yet still had the imperial court in Kyoto under his strict control. The success of the Tokugawa can be judged from the fact that Edo was but a small fishing village when the Tokugawa came — and is now known as Tokyo. Those *daimyo* who had been loyal to the Tokugawa, the *fudai*, were rewarded and treated as favored vassals; the nobles that had opposed Ieyasu at the battle of Sekigahara were the "outside lords" or *tozama*. The latter remained a dangerous threat to the Shogun and, along with the favored lords, were required to rotate their residences between their domains and Yedo. The heavy expenses of moving and maintaining their households as well as undertaking public works in their domains served to keep them in a weakened state.

Tokugawa Society

What emerged was a feudal version of the modern police state. The Tokugawa Shoguns carefully monitored and dominated the rival families. The *daimyo* dominated the merchants and peasantry. The *tozama* were excluded from participation in the political life of the *bakufu* and none of the nobility were permitted to have direct communication with the imperial court so as to prevent any new political movement.

Once again borrowing from the Chinese, the Tokugawa Shoguns held that society should be divided into four broad classes: (1) warrior-bureaucrats (parallel to China's scholar-bureaucrats), (2) peasants (mostly farmers), (3) artisans, and (4) merchants.[7] The merchants were considered to be the very bottom rung of the social ladder in spite of the fact that some of them were quite wealthy. The most important social division was,

of course, that between the nobility and the peasantry. The extent to which this distinction was rigidly maintained is reflected in the fact that a samurai had the right to slay any commoner who dared to be disrespectful. Below the peasant such rigid distinctions were relatively unimportant but social mobility tended to be constrained by the hereditary nature of class categories.

Gradually, Tokugawa life became so regularized that the concerns of the samurai became less those of military skill and discipline and more those of civil administration. At the same time, the "bushido code" of the samurai was projected into the larger population through popular culture such as the *kabuki* theater. Consisting of more than just martial values, *Bushido*, the "Way of the Warrior" provided guidance for exemplary conduct that included rectitude, benevolence and politeness along with courage and honor. Yet the popular culture of Tokugawa was ebullient. Color in art and action in theater replaced the restraint of earlier periods and fiction portrayed a demimonde of profligate behavior in the licensed quarters of the cities.

Confucianism played a key role in the transformation of the samurai from warriors to bureaucrats. Neo-Confucian philosophy, which had been introduced by Zen monks from China in the fourteenth century but expanded its impact via Hideyoshi's occupation of Korea, began to find a wider audience outside the monasteries. Yet in adopting the precepts of Confucianism the samurai faced the same dilemma as their counterparts in Korea: how could hereditary, carefully ranked, aristocratic privileges co-exist within a growing bureaucracy shaped around the Confucian ideal of a status that is achieved by means of correct behavior and learning? Some have argued that the modern Japanese personality is partially the product of this tension in the Tokugawa era: that present-day pressures toward conformity to rigidly defined rules of behavior derive from an emphasis on inner discipline and societal obligation which became especially strong in the seventeenth and eighteenth centuries.

Economic Change

The Tokugawa era transformed Japan economically. Tokyo (Edo) and Osaka rose to become major urban centers. Tokyo's population rose to nearly a million by the eighteenth century. The merchant class became wealthy amid a thriving commerce among cities and districts. Its financial power became carefully balanced against the political power and rank of the *daimyo,* each depending heavily on the other for a continuation of the status quo. The merchants, however, grew steadily wealthier as suppliers of goods and services to the *daimyo* while many of the latter fell into debt. Meanwhile, the Shogun's bureaucrats, trapped by rigid concepts of governance and taxation, squelched innovative efforts to seek new sources of revenue that would have fostered foreign trade and investment in national resources. By contrast, the outlying *tozama* clans of Satsuma and Choshu grew steadily more powerful in the early nineteenth century by enacting economic reforms in their domains which exploited the talents of local merchants and drew upon their exclusive, if sometimes secret, commerce with the outside world.

Tokugawa Isolationism

That foreign commerce by the Satsuma and Choshu clans was often of a clandestine nature leads us to the other major feature of the Tokugawa era: its relative isolation from the rest of the world. An isolationist policy seemed the furthest from Ieyasu's mind when he assumed the shogunate at the beginning of the seventeenth century. At that time, he actively sought foreign commerce with China and the few European ships that were beginning to appear on his shores. More importantly for the Pacific Asian region, Japan vastly increased the output from its silver mines and sent much of it abroad, thus stimulating commerce far beyond its shores.

The newly-arrived Dutch and English were permitted to establish trading posts; Spanish Franciscan monks were allowed to proselytize. For a short time both traders and Christians flourished in Japan but the ever-suspicious Shogun soon came to accuse the latter of "subversive" activities. The tension with the Christian population came to a climax with the so-called Shimabara revolt in 1637-1638 when a samurai-led peasant tax revolt, comprising mostly Christians, inflicted

serious losses on the Shogun's army before finally being suppressed.

The Shimabara rebellion tipped the balance in what had been a growing pressure to restrict Christian and foreign activities. Suspecting the Europeans of planning to colonize Japan and the Christians of subverting his authority, the Tokugawa shogun took drastic measures to close Japan off from outside influences. He expelled the missionaries and reduced the activities of European traders to a tiny group of Dutch whom he isolated on the island of Deshima in Nagasaki harbor. Only a trickle of commerce was permitted by the Japanese themselves with Korea and China, the latter conducted via the Ryukyu Islands by the Satsuma clan.

This self-imposed isolation paralleled that which was growing in China around the same time. It arose, however, not from imitation of China but the Shogun's own unique perception that control over his domain could be guaranteed only by such a policy. He forbade the construction of large open-ocean ships and effectively marooned overseas Japanese by banning not only foreign travel by any Japanese, but the return of Japanese from abroad on the grounds that they would bring with them the corruption of foreign ideas.

Intellectual Currents

While Japan remained commercially isolated from the world in the Tokugawa period, its cultural and intellectual ties to China, Korea and Europe were far less curtailed. The Dutch outpost in Nagasaki harbor proved to be crucial in this respect, serving as narrow bridge across which could be transferred information about developments abroad. The *bakufu* had several books translated from the Dutch that were of strictly utilitarian value and independent scholars were permitted to pursue the so-called "Dutch learning" (*Rangaku*) by acquiring foreign books on medicine, science, and military technology. These scholars would be a vital element in Japan's later burst of activity to "catch up" with the industrializing world of the late nineteenth century.

A counterpoint to the intellectual trend of "Dutch learning" occurred in the so-called "national studies" (*Kokugaku*) school whose contribution was to be equally powerful during the tumultuous period of change that followed the demise of the Tokugawa *bakufu*. The *Kokugaku* scholars held up for admiration a Japanese culture that was presumed to have existed in the era prior to becoming "tainted" by cultural imports from China. From this developed a mystique about the divine blessings bestowed upon Japan and a focus on the Emperor as the symbol of all that was Japanese. Interest in the "Way of the gods" (*Shinto*) asserted a uniquely Japanese identity. By elevating the Emperor to such preeminent status, imbuing him with divine origins and supreme authority even over the *bakufu* itself, the *Kokugaku* scholars laid the foundations for the mid-nineteenth century overthrow of the *bakufu* in the name of the Emperor.

Equally contributive to the intellectual ferment and change occurring in the late Tokugawa period was the dramatic expansion of literacy among commoners. From both ends of the social spectrum people were being drawn to literature and learning. At the upper end, the samurai were becoming a scholarly class through the institution of special schools (*terakoya*) restricted to their use. At the same time, ancillary private schools to which commoners had access led to the spread of education throughout the greater population resulting in one of the highest literacy rates in the world by the mid-nineteenth century. Another result was explosive growth in the market for popular literature which was printed by woodblock and illustrated with attention-getting pictures.

Social Change and Stability

Japan under the Tokugawa *bakufu* was remarkably stable and might have remained so for some time to come had it not been for the intrusion by Western nations in the mid-nineteenth century. Yet fundamental contradictions were beginning to crack the foundations of the *bakufu*, mainly the rising wealth of the merchant class alongside the relative impoverishment of many samurai. The peasant economy was strained by the demands made upon it by the *daimyo*. Disastrous famines accompanied by riots and rebellions, racked the late Tokugawa

period. Even so, the shogunate remained firmly in control, its major "error" (in Western eyes) having been to isolate Japan from the growing technological prowess of Europe and America. From a domestic standpoint, it had prospered. The growth of intellectual competition and the spread of learning meant that Japan possessed the human resources with which to meet the challenge of the West — and eventually surpass it.

THE QING (MANCHU) DYNASTY

The beginnings of the Tokugawa period in Japan coincided with the decline and fall of the Ming Dynasty in China and its replacement by a dynasty not of Chinese origin but from a northern nomadic tribe known as the Manchu. To understand this transition, it is necessary to recall the nature of the problem that had faced the Ming.

The massive Chinese response to Hideyoshi's invasion of Korea was an immensely expensive operation. In combination with subsidies that were required to pay off the threatening Mongols and a series of grand construction projects, the cost of repelling the Japanese nearly bankrupted the Ming court in 1598.

The problem was further exacerbated by the growing dependence of Ming China on the vicissitudes of international commerce. China had begun to trade its silk and porcelain in ever greater quantities for silver originating in Japan, Peru and Mexico. When around 1610 there came a sharp downturn in world silver flows, China had no monetary reserves upon which to fall back and the result was a financial crisis that seriously undermined its capacity to maintain the northern defense. The situation was ripe for the advent of a new dynasty.

In the north there still lurked the Jurchen tribes who had founded the Jin dynasty in China before being driven back to the far reaches of the Manchurian plain by the Mongols. There they had languished in disunity until a leader named Nurhachi united them again into a powerful fighting force at the beginning of the seventeenth century. In 1618 he launched an attack against the Ming and in succeeding years his sons and grandsons extended their rule over all of China.

The Nature of Manchu Control

The Manchu ascension of the imperial throne resulted in relatively little alteration of China's social order. In fact, this very stability — some would say resistance to change — was to prove a fatal weakness to the Manchu's Qing (Ch'ing) dynasty (1644–1911). Also, whereas the Ming leadership had been indigenously Chinese, the imposition of Manchu "barbarian" control over the imperial throne created a permanent tension with the underlying Chinese population. That a thin layer of Manchu elite military and civilian government officials were able to maintain control for two and a half centuries over many millions of Chinese is testimony to their political skills. They were careful to bury the Ming emperor with honors and claimed to have entered China to restore order and suppress what had been, in fact, a serious internal Ming rebellion. In parallel with such tactics, they introduced their own uniquely Manchurian organizational modes such as the "banner" system under which Manchu tribesmen had been grouped according to one of eight colored banners. This system permitted the Emperor to mix and move units at will and to maintain maximum control over his troops ("bannermen") and officials.

The conquest of the Ming empire did not take place smoothly or all at once in spite of Manchu strength and the Ming's enfeebled state. Powerful Chinese generals at first collaborated with the Manchus but later established themselves in their own feudal territories to the south and on the prosperous Liaodong Peninsula. In the meantime the island of Taiwan, which had never been brought under Ming administration, remained a wealthy maritime outpost whose leaders commanded broad regions of the southern coast and carried on a lucrative commerce within the Western Pacific Basin. Fierce resistance led by the Taiwan-based Zheng Chenggong, whose title was pronounced "Koxinga" by the Dutch, proved especially troublesome. Two generations of determined warfare were to pass before the Qing empire was firmly established.

The Manchus were adept at using the talents of the previous Chinese system, but they also were careful to preserve their own cultural identity. This was accomplished by such means as the

---

CHRISTIANITY IN THE TAIPING REBELLION

Compliance with theocratic rule was reinforced through constant worship. Every Sabbath, Hong [Hong Xiuquan, the founder], as Heavenly King, publicly venerated the Heavenly Father at the grand Palace of Glory and Light, in the center of Nanjing. He ordered every government office and private residence to convert a room into a chapel, where a Taiping official was to lead public worship and explain the Bible. Beginning in 1854, every basic administrative unit of twenty-five families, called a "congregation," was to be under the supervision of a "sergeant." This official was responsible for leading worship and supervising the daily lessons for children, who were taught literacy through the Bible and Hong's writings. These also became the basis of the Taiping examination system.

Every Sabbath the Taiping faithful recited Christian prayers and sang hymns and the doxology to the accompaniment of gongs, drums, and firecrackers. Patriotic sermons preached loyalty to the Heavenly Father and the Taiping leadership and exhorted victory against the Manchus. Every fourth Sabbath the eucharist was celebrated. The Ten Commandments were read to assembled crowds weekly and were to be committed to memory. Adherence to them was ruthlessly enforced, most infractions resulting in summary execution. The Lord's Prayer was to be posted in every home, and grace was to be said before each meal.

—P. Richard Bohr, *EAH*

prohibition of intermarriage between Manchus and Chinese, the maintenance of a cosseted Manchu aristocracy, and a mandated physical distinction between themselves and the Chinese which required the latter to braid their hair in a queue and shave the rest of their heads — creating an image that became the stereotype of the Chinese in the eyes of westerners during the later Qing period. Such obvious impositions by the Manchus on the ordinary Chinese peasant were uncommon, however, and it is likely that the transition from the Ming to the Qing, apart from the warfare it entailed, went relatively unnoticed at the local level. A great deal of the administration of China was carried on as before in the hands of the same local Chinese gentry as had prevailed under the Ming.

Many other Confucian and imperial Chinese traditions continued under the Qing Emperors. The traditional Confucian academies were revived (the foundation for the imperial examination system), and the Imperial Court co-opted Confucian scholarship by encouraging the writing of histories of previous empires. This was a highly selective history, however; the Manchu dictates to the intellectual elite helped them to maintain "thought control" over the populace. In a 15-year literary purge, many manuscripts were destroyed by the Manchus in an effort to wipe out references derogatory to themselves or their "barbarian" predecessors.

After two centuries of rule, the usual rot of empire began to set in. Scandalously expensive military campaigns on the edge of the empire, which gained little booty and only enriched their commanders, sapped the strength of the Manchu throne. Powerful and corrupt eunuchs once again insinuated themselves into key positions. The decay became dramatically evident as popular uprisings grew in size and number. The first of these took place in the late eighteenth century in the rugged regions of Hubei, Shaanxi, and Sichuan provinces. Called the White Lotus Rebellion after the Buddhist religious sect that inspired it, the revolt was suppressed within a few years but not until it had demonstrated the weaknesses of the allegedly invincible Manchu banner forces.

In the mid-nineteenth century a far more widespread and disastrous uprising erupted: the Taiping Rebellion (1851-1864). The grievances were the same: extreme poverty amid poor civil services and local ethnic conflict (it began in a confrontation between Hakka and Cantonese in Guangdong and Guangxi, then spread north). The inspiration by a secret religious cult, this time quasi-Christian rather than Buddhist in its nature, also paralleled the earlier rebellion. What distinguished the Taipings, however, was their ability to develop ideologically, often utilizing the preachings of Christian missionaries, while gaining the support of the Chinese population in key regions. Had they been more sophisticated in matters of administration and able to engage the broad support of local scholars and gentry (the Taipings were strongly anti-Confucian), they might have successfully overthrown the Manchus. Instead, their fifteen-year civil war cost hundreds of thousands of lives and ended in defeat. It further weakened the Qing Dynasty. Other revolts within China and on its borders added to the chaos. About this time the imperial authorities became gradually aware of an even greater threat that had begun to appear on their shores: newly assertive European navies and trading fleets. The account of this phase in China's history will be taken up in the following chapter.

CHINA: NORTH AND SOUTH

North China has historically been a land of dry-field farming, mostly wheat and millet. South China has been the home of wet-field rice farming. The general nature of the soils is also different, being more alkaline in the north and more acidic in the south. Much of south China is crisscrossed with navigable rivers and canals; travel and transportation have for more than a millennium made great use of boats. Intensive coastal shipping also developed early up and down the southeastern littoral, making use of the convenient seasonal alternation of the monsoon winds. In north China, however, one went on horseback in imperial times if one was in a hurry, otherwise by two-wheeled cart or on foot. Loess does not allow the easy construction of good roads and becomes an almost impassable mud when wet. The building of railroads since the end of the 19th century has had only a limited impact on transportation in south China, but a dramatic one in north China, especially Manchuria, where the best "roads" of earlier times were the ice-bound rivers in winter.

South China is a land of Han in-migration, but once the migrants had arrived there the hilly valleys seem to have limited further mixing and to have preserved a great variety of subcultures and different dialects. By contrast, the language of the north is relatively homogeneous; almost everyone speaks some form of what is commonly, if not entirely accurately, called "Mandarin" after the former lingua franca of the imperial officials. The physical appearance of northerners and southerners is also different: the northerners are on average more than five centimeters taller, and more solidly and heavily built. In vulgar speech, northerners sometimes refer slightingly to the southerners as "monkeys" and the southerners respond in kind by calling the northerners "steamed bread." Making sweeping cultural contrasts is too hazardous, especially given the many changes over time and the extent of more local variations. It would seem, though, that the southerners have long had a stronger sense of the numinous quality of the landscape. They are the originators both of earth magic or geomancy, and of the first purely landscape poetry in the Chinese tradition, during the middle third of the first millennium AD. The southern economy has also for many centuries been richer than that of the north, and the south, especially the lower Yangzi valley, has been more inclined to extravagance, ostentation and sensuality. In recent times, but before the Communist revolution in the economic and social institutions in the countryside, south China was distinguished for its powerful lineages or "clans," and for its relatively high levels of tenancy. North China, by way of contrast, was a land of small owner-operator farmers for the most part, and strong lineages were much less in evidence.

The historic links between north and south China were the various Grand Canals. The first of these was built with conscripted labor, including many women, early in the 7th century under the Sui dynasty. As can be seen from a map, its two main arms followed the nearly level ground used by the courses of the Yellow River at various times. Its basic purpose was to bring the plentiful rice of the south to the Sui capital in the northwest at Daxingcheng (present-day Xi'an) and to the armies stationed in the northeast. When the Mongol (Yuan) dynasty located their capital at Dadu, on the site of modern Beijing, much of the canal was rebuilt on a shorter route that took it over the western spurs of the Shandong hills. This led to engineering difficulties, and use was also made of both a sea route and a combination of a sea route and a subsidiary canal cut across the middle of the Shandong peninsula, the so-called Jiao-Lai Canal.

It was only in the 15th century, under the Ming dynasty, that the problem of keeping enough water in the higher parts of the canal was solved. Although the Chinese had invented the double-gate or pound lock in the 11th

(continued on next page)

(continued from previous page)

century, they did not use it on this part of the waterway, preferring immovable solid barriers that retained water, while the boats were hauled around them on slipways. This of course limited the size of vessel that could be used. In its final form, the state grain transportation system sometimes employed up to 150,000 soldiers to man its fleet, and required compulsory labor-services of many more civilians to dredge and maintain the channels. Boats belonging to commoners were also entitled to use the Grand Canal, and it thus served as a commercial artery linking the north and the south. Its scale was stupendous for the Middle Ages, being over 1,000 kilometers in length. Canals of a comparable scale only began to be cut in Europe, notably in France, in the 18th century.

In this way there developed a sort of complementary relationship between the north and the south. The economic center of gravity was in the south, but the political center was almost always in the north. This split had not existed at the beginning of the empire. The earliest imperial capital, late in the 3rd century BC, was that of the Qin at Xianyang, near Xi'an in the area known as Guannei ("Within the Passes"). It was more fertile than it is today, and there was a local system of irrigation and transportation canals. The principal capitals of both the Han and Tang dynasties were on essentially the same site, at Chang'an, the name of which means "Everlasting Peace." Guannei was a strategically well-protected location, but its remoteness made it difficult to supply from outside. As the local economy deteriorated, probably through climatic desiccation, and the size of the capital grew, the Han and the Tang both established a secondary capital in the north China plain at Luoyang.

It was during the Tang that the south first began to challenge the north for economic supremacy, and the split of which we have spoken began to appear. The capital of the Northern Song from the late 10th to the early 12th century AD was at Kaifeng, on the last safe high ground to the east and close to the point where the Yellow River has historically shifted its course either north or south. Kaifeng was also the nearest of the northern capitals to the southern granaries, and the easiest to supply by waterway. In its heyday the official transportation brought it six million Chinese bushels of rice annually, or a quantity of the order of a third of a million tons (the exact conversion ratio is uncertain).

The Mongol (Yuan) in the 13th century had their capital near modern Beijing, deliberately straddling the divide between Inner and Outer China. They were the first dynasty to rule over both these areas. The original Ming capital was at Nanjing ("Southern Capital"), but they soon turned to a double capital system with the substantive administrative center in the north at Beijing and a more ceremonial center in the south. The reason for this shift was presumably strategic: to make the capital, in conjunction with the rebuilt Great Wall, a massive obstacle in the way of any would-be invader from Mongolia or Manchuria. Both the Manchu (Qing) and the People's Republic have kept the capital at Beijing, presumably partly out of respect for tradition, and partly because it remains close to the meeting-point of Han and non-Han domains.

There have been only two other southern capitals belonging to regimes that have had some claim to speak for China as a whole. These were the Southern Song metropolis at Hangzhou in the 12th and 13th centuries, the single seaport in imperial history to be a capital, and the Nationalist center at Nanjing from 1927 to 1937. The sole western city to be a national capital was the wartime headquarters of the Nationalist government at Chongqing on the upper Yangzi between 1937 and 1945, a time when most of eastern China was occupied by the Japanese.

— Caroline Blunden and Mark Elvin,
Cultural Atlas of China

SOUTHEAST ASIA

Introduction

Strong commercial maritime linkages developed between Northeast Asia and Southeast Asia from at least the time of the Tang Dynasty and contributed significantly to the coastal economies of both regions. These linkages waxed and waned according to historical circumstances, but in the premodern era they received perhaps their greatest single stimulus when the Ming admiral Zheng He brought his fleets into Southeast Asia. This was the advent of what historian Anthony Reid has called an "Age of Commerce" in Southeast Asia, a term that can be extended to much of Pacific Asia during the period in question, 1400-1680.

Our focus shifts, then, to Southeast Asia where great states with sophisticated cultures were building cities and trade networks. Known to ancient navigators as the "Lands Below the Winds," Southeast Asia lies south of China and east of India and is the most culturally diverse region within our purview. The challenge of integrating it into a regional Pacific Asian history derives from more than just its diversity, however: Compared to Northeast Asia, the quantity of original records in Southeast Asia is modest indeed. Not only did a record-keeping bureaucracy not work with such obsessive thoroughness as in the north, but many records that may have existed have long-since perished along with other material objects in the tropical environment. In addition, Southeast Asian historical records before the European presence contain such a mix of the factual and the fabulous as to make historical interpretation more difficult. Nevertheless, we can define broad historical trends and influences for Southeast Asia as interpreted here by two scholars.

The first, Anthony Reid, focuses primarily on the maritime regions of Southeast Asia. In doing so, he delineates the geographic areas that have been the focus of most scholarly attention, drawing a boundary at the southeastern corner so as to leave out New Guinea with its great varieties of ancient cultures and languages. The cultures of Southeast Asia are also diverse, but Reid notes that there appear to be certain ancient linguistic associations within the region. The primary unifying elements, however, have been the physical environment and commercial interaction.

◆   ◆   ◆

THE LANDS BELOW THE WINDS
— by Anthony Reid

Environment and Culture

Two factors [besides complex, often distant linguistic associations] have given this region a common character. The first is adaptation to a common physical environment; the second, a high degree of commercial intercourse within the region.

The common environment was responsible for a diet derived overwhelmingly from rice, fish, and various palms. Southeast Asia has no substantial grasslands, no pastoral tradition, and therefore a very limited intake of animal proteins. Rice is probably indigenous to Southeast Asia and has been for millennia the basic staple of the great majority of its people. In areas as far dispersed as Luzon, Sulawesi, Java, Sumatra, and parts of Siam and Vietnam, harvesting was done by women using not a sickle but a characteristic Southeast Asian finger-knife, which honoured the rice-spirit by cutting only one stalk at a time.

The dominance of rice and fish in the diet, and the small part played by meat and milk products, was characteristically Southeast Asian. So were the half-fermented fish paste which provided the major garnish to the rice, and the palm wine which constituted the favourite beverage. Palm trees provided much of the flavor of Southeast Asian diets, as of life-styles. In a few areas the sago palm was the staple source of starch, but everywhere coconut and sugar palms provided sugar and palm wine, as well as the fruit itself. The areca palm, probably also native to the region, furnished the vital ingredient of betel, which was throughout Southeast Asia not only the universal stimulant but also a vital element in social relations and ritual transactions.

The predominance of forest and water over a relatively thinly peopled region accounts for much else in the life-styles of Southeast Asians. Wood, palm, and bamboo were the favoured building materials, seemingly inexhaustibly provided by the surrounding forest. By preference Southeast Asians lived in houses elevated on poles, whether on the coastal plains, as a precaution against the annual floods, or in the most remote highland villages, where security against human and animal predators may have been the major motive. Much of the characteristic architecture, domestic pattern, and even sociopolitical structure characteristic of Southeast Asia can be derived from the ease of building and rebuilding such elevated wood-and-thatch houses.

Not all the common features of Southeast Asia, however, can be explained by a common environment. The universality of betel chewing cannot have derived from similar spontaneous responses to the existence of areca palm in the region, since the three ingredients of areca, betel leaf, and lime have to be brought together in a complicated operation before the desired effects are experienced. Similarly, the dispersal of the finger-knife, the piston bellows, and such characteristic sports as cockfighting and *takraw* (kicking a basketwork ball in the air), of musical patterns dominated by the bronze gong, or of similar patterns of body decoration and of classification has little to do with the environment. Fundamental social and cultural traits distinguish Southeast Asia as a whole from either of its vast neighbors — China and India. Central among these are the concept of spirit or "soul stuff" animating living things; the prominence of women in descent, ritual matters, marketing and agriculture; and the importance of debt as a determinant of social obligation.

In defining any region there are peripheral zones whose position is problematic. In the first place, I am consciously defining a maritime region linked by waterborne traffic, so that the hill peoples of the northern mainland will not play a large part, even though many of them were linked by culture with the Thai of the coast and the central plain. At the opposite extremity of the region, I am inclined to draw a boundary between Maluku (the Moluccas) and New Guinea, across which the level of maritime exchange and cultural similarity (although it cannot be ignored) becomes of a much lower order than that which linked Maluku with the islands to the west and north.

Vietnam, incontestably a major actor in Southeast Asia as we define it today, presents much more of a problem. Here alone one cannot say with confidence that the common Southeast Asian elements outweighed the factors which linked Vietnam to China, and particularly to the southernmost provinces of China. In their diet and many of their pleasures — betel chewing, cockfighting, a type of *takraw* — the Vietnamese clearly shared in a common Southeast Asian culture, as indeed did some of their neighbors in South China. Their women were markedly freer, their manufacturing less developed, than was the case in China. Yet the political and intellectual life of Vietnam, and even such basic habits as the manner of eating (with chopsticks), had already borrowed deeply from China by the fifteenth century. Moreover, the population of the Red River delta was already closer to China's dense pattern than Southeast Asia's dispersed one.

The role of Vietnam is as a frontier between Southeast Asia and China, and a critical one. Had Vietnam not learned so well the lessons of Chinese bureaucratic and military practice, and fought so hard to maintain its equality and independence from the Middle Kingdom, Chinese political influence would certainly have spread further south, using land as well as sea routes. As it was,

Figure 1.8 Southeast Asian sailing vessels using complex rigging and outriggers were active in the region by the ninth century CE. This image of such a ship appears in a frieze on the great temple of Borobudur in central Java.

Vietnam forced the Chinese to reach the *Nanyang* only by sea, and almost exclusively as peaceful traders. In some important respects Vietnam will appear as part of the Southeast Asian maritime world. In most it will not.[8]

♦   ♦   ♦

THE CLASSICAL WORLD

— by Milton Osborne

The Maritime and Mainland Worlds

It is necessary to try and provide a brief picture of the pattern of states that had emerged in Southeast Asia by the ninth century CE, but there is much of Southeast Asia at that time that we simply cannot describe either in terms of the location of states or in terms of populations living away from the centres of kingly power. Most of the Philippines remains outside our knowledge at that period, as do other sections of the Southeast Asian maritime world. But once our gaze shifts to the west of the Indonesian Archipelago the forms are easier to discern. Recognizable kingdoms or states had already emerged in Java by the ninth century and these states had demonstrated considerable artistic capacity in the temples and shrines they erected an in the forms they chose to decorate them. Moving further west and north to the island of Sumatra, we know of the existence of a trading empire, Srivijaya, that had risen to power in the sixth and seventh centuries and, despite setbacks along the way, continued to dominate trade between the West (India) and the East (China), as well as more local trade in the Archipelago itself. While the existence of Srivijaya seems certain, however, no physical trace of its capital remains and scholarly argument continues as to where the actual location of that city, or series of cities, might have been.

If we risk a broad summary of the situation in the *maritime* Southeast Asian world in the ninth century CE, it might be in the following terms. Whatever the petty states that existed elsewhere, the truly significant centers of power that had emerged were linked with coastal Sumatra and inland Java. These centers of power were to remain important in the following centuries, until the end of the classical period.

The situation on the *mainland* is clearer. During the ninth century there was still no independent Vietnamese state since Imperial China occupied the Red River delta region and administered it as one of the most remote Chinese provinces. Stretched along the modern Vietnamese coast was the state of Champa, populated by the Chams, a people linguistically linked with the inhabitants of Indonesia. To the west was the growing state of Cambodia, which was just beginning its rise to greatness and dominance over much of mainland Southeast Asia. Although we know today that greatness lay ahead for Cambodia, this was far from clearly the case in the ninth century. The first Cambodian kings to rule in the Angkor region had already begun to develop techniques for mastering the environment that were, eventually, to provide the economic base for military expansion and a programme of great temple-building. In the ninth century, however, they were only a little more clearly masters of their quite limited world than were the petty rulers scattered throughout the lowland regions of modern Thailand and along the great river valleys of modern Burma.

The Influence of India

Wherever recognizable states existed in this uncertainly defined Southeast Asian region of the ninth century the rulers and their courts were followers of imported religions, of Hinduism and Buddhism. These Indian religions were one of the most important features of a development that took place in the Southeast Asian region over many centuries, beginning early in the Christian era. The development has been given the name "Indianization", though once again there is continuing disagreement among scholars as to just what the term means. Broad agreement does exist, however, about certain features of the Indianization process.

Beginning in the second and third centuries CE there was a slow expansion of Indian cultural contacts with the Southeast Asian region. It was an uneven process, with some areas receiving

Indian influence much later than others, and with the degree of cultural impact varying from century to century. In the case of the Vietnamese, who were in this early period living under Chinese rule, the process of Indianization never took place. For different reasons — distant geographical location — the Philippines, too, did not participate in this process. Indianization did *not* mean that there was a mass migration of Indian populations into Southeast Asia. Rather, a relatively limited number of traders and priest-scholars brought Indian culture in its various forms to Southeast Asia where much, but not all, of this culture was absorbed by the local population and joined to their existing cultural patterns.

Several cautionary remarks are immediately necessary. Because Indian culture "came" to Southeast Asia, one must not think of Southeast Asians as lacking a culture of their own. Indeed, the most generally accepted view is that Indian culture made such an impact on Southeast Asia because it fitted easily with existing cultural patterns and religious beliefs present among populations that had already moved a considerable distance along the path of civilisation. Just because this was the case, the process of Indianization should not be seen as simply involving a Southeast Asian acceptance of Indian cultural values. Indian culture was absorbed in much of Southeast Asia and its theories of government came to be of the greatest importance. But these various cultural gifts from India became Southeast Asian and in doing so changed their character. In some cases, moreover, quite fundamental features of Indian culture and society were not adopted. The caste system of India did not, for instance, accompany the practice of Hinduism in Southeast Asia, however much early Southeast Asian kings might have felt that they were modelling themselves on Indian rulers and making use of caste terminology to describe themselves and their court. Southeast Asian art drew upon Indian artistic models, but then developed its own forms. Indian languages were used in government and religion. Yet while the inscriptions written in Sanskrit remain one of our most important sources for early Southeast Asian history, the use of this language ultimately lapsed as Southeast Asians came to use Indian scripts to render their own languages.

Southeast Asians, to summarize the point, borrowed but they also adapted. In some very important cases they did not need to borrow at all. The techniques of wet rice cultivation seem to have been indigenous to Southeast Asia and not a technological import from another area. In addition, if there was borrowing and adaptation that justifies the term Indianization, one must realise that our view of this process tends to be shaped by the evidence with which historians must work. We know infinitely more about the world of kings, courts, and priests than we do about the world of the peasantry. The anonymous worker in the rice fields was probably little affected by Indianization. The complex features of Hinduism and Mahayana Buddhism — the form of Buddhism that first had an impact in Southeast Asia — were the concerns of his masters as he retained his fear and respect for the spirits that he believed were associated with both the animate and inanimate beings and objects that surrounded him.

In the Indianised Southeast Asia of the ninth century, two states existed that have probably attracted more historical attention than any others. These states, the inland state based at Angkor in Cambodia and the maritime state of Srivijaya with a centre somewhere in Sumatra, are seen as typifying the two very different kinds of states that can be identified in the early or classical period. They were also, in contrast to a number of other examples, states that preserved their existence over a long historical period. As such, an examination of their history can suggest some of the reasons that led to the success and development of kingdoms and empires in the early history of Southeast Asia, and finally some of the factors that brought decay and collapse.

The Khmer Empire

Angkor rose to a dominating position in much of mainland Southeast Asia as a result of a notable combination of human genius, religious belief, and geographical location. In order to survive and then to develop more than a bare subsistence civilisation in Cambodia it was and is necessary to master the problem of water, or rather the lack of it. Despite the torrential rains of Cambodia's wet season, the land dries rapidly once the rains

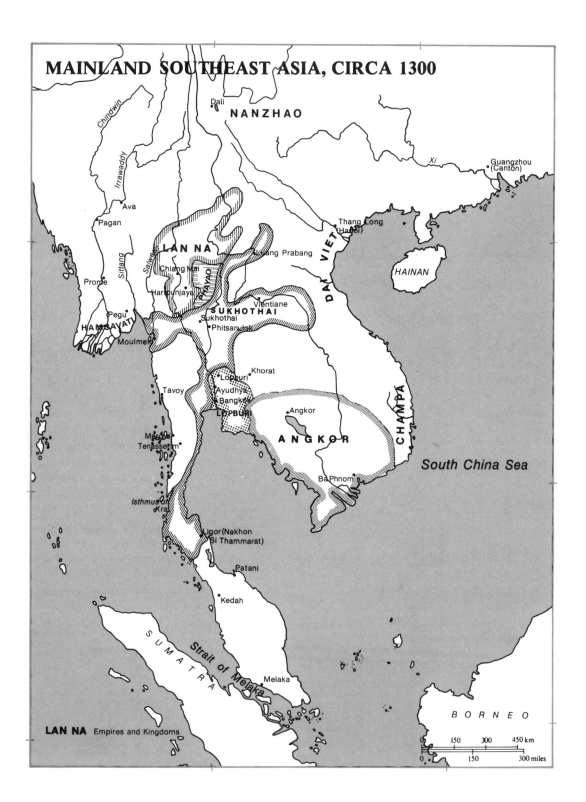

MAINLAND SOUTHEAST ASIA, CIRCA 1300

Chindwin

Irrawaddy

Dali

NANZHAO

Xi

Guangzhou
(Canton)

Ava

Pagan

Salween

Sittang

LAN NA

Chiang Mai

Haripunjaya

PHAYAO

Thang Long
(Hanoi)

DAI VIET

HAINAN

Luang Prabang

Prome

Vientiane

SUKHOTHAI

Pegu

Sukhothai

HAMSAVATI

Phitsanulok

Moulmein

Khorat

Lopburi

Tavoy

Ayudhya

Bangkok

LOPBURI

Angkor

Mergui

Tenasserim

ANGKOR

CHAMPA

South China Sea

Ba Phnom

Isthmus of
Kra

Ligor (Nakhon
Si Thammarat)

Patani

Kedah

S U M A T R A

Strait of Melaka

Melaka

BORNEO

LAN NA Empires and Kingdoms

150   300   450 km

0

150   300 miles

cease and nearly six months of rainless weather follows. Settlement is possible along the banks of the rivers, but the further one moves away from these sources of water the more acute the problem becomes. The Cambodian answer, increasingly refined over the centuries, was to develop reservoirs that could trap rain during the wet season for use during the subsequent dry period.

So skillful were the Cambodians, or Khmers to use the other word that describes the inhabitants of Cambodia, in their hydraulic engineering that they turned the once unproductive region around Angkor into a stupendously successful rice-growing area where three crops a year were grown to support a population in excess of one million. This was the agricultural economic base that permitted the Angkorian state to maintain a population able to build the great temples that remain as a reminder of Khmer achievements in the past. Angkorian Cambodia's wealth was in people and in water. Without the right combination of these two assets there could not have been an Angkor Wat, the most famous of the great temples and the largest single religious building in the world. Wealth, it is true, came into the city in the form of captured booty and prisoners of war who were put to work as slaves. But in the broadest sense Angkorian Cambodia was not a state that depended on trade for its existence. The temples built by Angkor's rulers, and on occasion by their great officials, enshrined the religious ideals of the state. The wealth needed to build and maintain them and to feed and clothe the priestly communities associated with them came from the productive rice fields that spread about the temples.

The size of the Cambodian achievement during the years between the ninth and the fifteenth centuries is vividly apparent. Temples great and small spread over hundreds of square miles. Scholars are still discovering new and important facts about the society that could bring these magnificent buildings into being. One of the latest discoveries to fascinate historians is the possibility that the great temple of Angkor Wat was built in such a way as to aid astronomical observations. The investigations that have led to this suggestion have shown that the architects and builders who worked on the temple were able to achieve building feats of a quite remarkable character. Accuracy in construction was so great that variations from a theoretically exact line in the height or direction of walls built over great distances was less than 0.1 per cent.

This evidence of technological capacity linked with the knowledge we have of the skilful control of water underlines the existence during Angkorian times of a highly developed society. Its achievements in aesthetic terms matched its capacities in technology. The statues, the carvings in both high and low relief, the architectural forms that were increasingly refined over the centuries of the Angkorian empire's existence all give eloquent testimony to the richness of Cambodian culture during the classical period of Southeast Asian history. There is other evidence to emphasise the richness of the culture. Even though his visit came at a time when the Khmers of Angkor were losing their grip on the empire they had built up over four centuries, the Chinese envoy, Chou Ta-kuan, who saw Angkor in 1296, was convinced that the city was the richest in Southeast Asia. Despite his Chinese reserve towards the culture and customs of a non-Chinese society, Chou Ta-kuan was clearly impressed by the wealth of the Angkorian ruler and by the dimensions of the city in which he lived.

Yet if Angkor could impress even a sceptical Chinese civil servant, its economic foundations were highly fragile. Cambodian power had extended from its base in Angkor to incorporate within its empire large sections of modern Thailand, Laos, and Vietnam. This was not a trading empire, though some exchange of goods took place. The really important unifying feature for the Angkorian empire was something quite different from commerce. It was the acceptance by many lesser rulers and governors that the king at Angkor was their supreme lord, their suzerein to use a European term once again. When some of these lesser rulers no longer accepted this situation and chose to fight for their independence from the Angkorian ruler they did more than shatter a political relationship. In addition they threatened and eventually damaged the remarkable irrigation system upon which Angkor's very existence depended. The final abandonment of Angkor some time in the fifteenth century was an event of the deepest importance for mainland Southeast Asia, though quite unknown in Europe. A great empire had come to an end and with its end other states began their rise to greatness. The Thais were the people who brought Angkor down and their history from that time onwards was marked by a slow but sure progress towards the achievement of control over the territories that comprise modern Thailand.

The state of Vietnam, which had gained independence from China in 939 AD, did not contribute directly to Angkor's fall. Nevertheless, in the longer-term historical perspective we can see that the collapse of Cambodian power was vital for Vietnam's subsequent expansion into areas of modern southern Vietnam that once had been part of the Angkorian empire. In the west of mainland Southeast Asia, events in Cambodia had had little direct importance for the early Burmese state. A great Burmese city had been built at Pagan between the eleventh and thirteenth centuries, only to be sacked in 1287 by the invading Mongols who at that time ruled China. While these events and efforts made by later Burmese leaders to found a stable state had no direct links with the decline of Cambodia, once again the end of Pagan forms part of a broader pattern in which we can by the fifteenth century discern the emergence of a new pattern of states and power in the mainland region.

To think in terms of a changing pattern rather than in terms of decline and fall is much more rewarding. Angkor collapsed, in large part, because its economic structure could not be maintained under the pressure exerted by the newly powerful Thais. But Angkorian culture did not disappear. The successful Thais absorbed much from those who had once been their rulers. Thai architecture, the written form of the Thai language, concepts of administration, even dance forms owe much to Khmer inspiration. Moreover, if Angkor and Pagan fell, new states arose and other existing states increased their power so that an approach that concentrates on the decline of the most successful of the states in the early or classical period is historically one-sided.

The Srivijayan Empire and Relations with China

So far, our concern has been with the mainland and more particularly with the Angkorian empire. As important in its own fashion but cast in a very different mould was the sea-borne empire of Srivijaya. Just as Angkor enshrined the achievements of a land-based, non-trading Southeast Asian state during the classical period, so did Srivijaya represent the greatest achievement among maritime trading powers during this early phase of the Southeast Asian region's history.

Srivijaya's rise to power depended upon trade and upon China's sponsorship. Put in a rather simplified form, the international trade pattern that was of greatest importance in the early period of Southeast Asian history was the east-west trade between China and the region including India but stretching further west to Persia and beyond. Precious Western goods, including forest products believed to have medicinal qualities, were exchanged in China for silks and porcelain, lacqueurs and other manufactured items. By the seventh century control of much of this trade, at least for the trade passing backwards and forwards between the Indonesian islands, was in the hands of Malays whose chief centre of power was somewhere in southern Sumatra, on the eastern coast of that island.

How this came about is still uncertain, as, too, is the explanation as to how the sailors who manned the ships that carried the trade goods to China came to master the navigational difficulties of a long voyage with few intermediate landfalls. Some aspects of these historical developments are fairly clear, however, and these throw much light on the emergence of a state that was very different in character to the land-based kingdoms of both the mainland and the maritime Southeast Asian world. One of the most clearly important factors in Srivijaya's rise to power was its political relationship with China. In briefly surveying this relationship the whole question of China's role in Southeast Asia is broached so that some general observations are necessary.

Whether strong or weak, the successive rulers of China regarded their country as the central world state — the "Middle Kingdom" of popular usage. This did not mean that away from China's land borders its emperors thought in terms of the existence of a Chinese empire, certainly not in any normal use of that term. The Chinese view of the relationship with Southeast Asia was both more

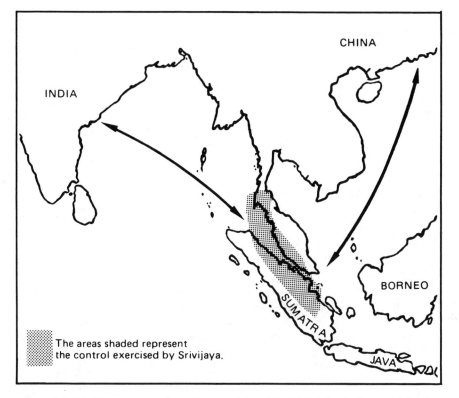

The areas shaded represent
the control exercised by Srivijaya.

Figure 1.9   Scholars argue over the exact location of Srivijaya, the great trading empire that dominated maritime trade through Southeast Asia and between India and China during the seventh to the thirteenth centuries. Srivijaya probably had a number of capitals, with the most important in southern Sumatra. As indicated in this map, Srivijaya maintained its power by controlling the ports and waters of the Malacca Straights.

subtle and more complex, and for a maritime trading state such as Srivijaya vitally important.

For China, over a long historical period, the area described today as Southeast Asia was the *Nanyang* region, the region of the "southern seas". Only Vietnam was ever directly ruled by China and only during one dynasty, the foreign Mongol or Yuan dynasty that ruled China from 1280 to 1368 AD, did Chinese emperors seek to impose their will on Southeast Asian countries other than Vietnam by force. The countries of the southern seas were, in Chinese eyes, lacking in discipline and order, and sadly without the proper Confucian state apparatus that permitted the Chinese state and Chinese culture to survive and progress despite foreign threat and internal political upheaval.

Such a region, in the Chinese view, could only function in a satisfactory fashion if the various Southeast Asian states were in a proper tributary

relationship with China. Here is yet another instance in which the limits of vocabulary impede easy understanding. To be a tributary state of China did not mean that an individual Southeast Asian kingdom was ruled by the Chinese as part of some ill-defined Chinese empire. Rather, the tributary relationship was one that involved a considerable degree of give and take. The fact of being a tributary certainly involved agreement not to act contrary to Chinese interests, but the relationship also implied that China would protect its tributary's interests against those who might challenge them. Most importantly for a trading state such as Srivijaya, the recognition that went with being granted tributary status was linked to the right to trade with China. Once China had granted this status to Srivijaya, the maritime trading states that were its rivals were at a severe disadvantage.

The Development of Srivijaya

With Chinese recognition given to it, Srivijaya's own capacities brought it to the forefront of Southeast Asian maritime power. Much of what is written about Srivijaya can only be supposition, but it is supposition based on evidence that leaves little doubt as to how this maritime state developed. Strategically placed on the Malacca Straits, Srivijaya came to exert control over all significant trade on the seas in the western section of the Indonesian Archipelago, and between that region of the Archipelago and southern China. Although it does seem correct to think in terms of there having been a Srivijayan capital, this had at least two different locations, and possibly more, over the long centuries of Srivijaya's existence.[9] The capital, additionally, may have been only slightly more important than the other port cities and trading settlements that went to make up this trading empire. For any state or settlement that tried to challenge the Srivijayan monopoly we may suppose that retribution was swift. But equally we may suppose that whatever power existed at the centre of Srivijaya, this was tempered by a readiness to allow the component parts of the empire a very considerable measure of political freedom, provided always that the basic trading arrangements are not infringed.

Srivijaya, like Angkor, was adapted to its environment. For the Khmer state at Angkor hydraulic engineering brought a barely fertile region into a high state of productivity. For the Indonesian-Malay state of Srivijaya the open frontier of the sea made up for the lack of a readily cultivatable hinterland along the swampy southeastern coast of Sumatra and what is today the western coast of peninsular Malaysia. The very sharpness of the contrast between these two states of the classical period is what makes them such good examples of the two broadly differing patterns of historical development that were followed by Southeast Asian states as late as the nineteenth century. It was only in the nineteenth century that major changes came to most of the land-based and largely self-sufficient states of Southeast Asia. As for the role played by Srivijaya as a maritime power between the seventh and fourteenth centuries, this was to pass to others, to Malacca and ultimately, it could be argued, to Singapore in the nineteenth century. But whichever later state held the role of regional entrepot and was the focus of trade in the western maritime areas of Southeast Asia, Srivijaya was the first to show how vital the control of the seas could be. Few of the Portuguese, Dutch or British traders and strategists who fought and manoeuvred to gain an ascendancy in the Southeast Asian maritime world realised that they were the successors of earlier maritime empires and none knew of the Srivijayan state, but in a very real sense they were only the latest to follow a very old pattern.

Yet if Srivijaya was adapted to the environment that existed in its heyday, like Angkor it too was unable to survive once that environment changed radically. A vital change for Srivijaya was the development in the thirteenth century of a Chinese maritime trade with Southeast Asia in which the Chinese themselves now sailed in their own trading junks to sell and buy goods in the region. This development upset the balance that Srivijaya had so long maintained, if sometimes in the face of considerable challenge and difficulty. The expansion of Chinese shipping activity was made more dangerous to Srivijaya's interests by the fact that it came at a time when other Indonesian powers were striving to extend a local suzerainty beyond their immediate power centres. Most dangerously for Srivijaya the Javanese land-based states had come to cherish imperial ambitions and saw Srivijaya's weakened condition as an opportunity to strike a deadly blow.[10] Some time in the late fourteenth century the dominant kingdom in Java was able to eliminate the residual challenge of Srivijaya and to bring to an end that state's long history of maritime dominance.

Vietnam

Vietnam remains a state apart, a very different component of the region. So extensive was Vietnamese cultural and political borrowing from its former colonial master, China, that it is sometimes difficult, certainly at first glance, to see the Southeast Asian elements in Vietnamese history and society. Yet those elements were and are present and throughout Vietnamese history there has been a significant tension between the claims of the non-Chinese elements in Vietnamese life and the claims of the Chinese elements, which were associated particularly with the emperor, his court, and his officials. The place accorded women in Vietnamese non-official society, the distinctively non-Chinese language of Vietnam, despite its multiple borrowings from China, and the Vietnamese peasants' migratory urge are only some of the features of that country's history that seem to link it with Southeast Asia rather than China.

At the official level, however, there can be no denying the force of Chinese ideas. China was a model for Vietnamese official life, an armory from which new weapons could be drawn to combat new problems and challenges as these arose. So much was this the case that an argument could be developed for the greater impact of China on Vietnam than, for example, the impact of India or Cambodia.

By the same token, Vietnam, with its independence achieved in 939 AD, continued over the succeeding centuries to work to maintain that independence, if necessary by fighting for it against China. Once again, understanding of Vietnam's relationship with China has been confusing for some observers since Vietnam was, most clearly, one of China's tributary states. This tributary status, despite the strong cultural links between the two countries, did not mean that Vietnam was ready to accept political interference by China in its internal affairs. Tributary status did mean that Vietnam could not readily act outside its borders in a manner likely to offend its great northern neighbour and suzerain.

If Vietnam was a very special Southeast Asian state, by comparison with those other areas that experienced cultural importation from India, its rise to power and emergence as one of the stronger states of the mainland by the end of the classical period in the fifteenth century further emphasises the major changes that were taking place throughout the region as a whole. For Vietnam's rise to power was at the expense of its southern neighbour, Champa. This Indianised state had, on occasion, been able to challenge the mighty Angkorian empire. As late as the twelfth century the Chams were able to sack a temporarily weakened Angkorian state in a successful water-borne attack on the city after their great war canoes had

travelled up the Mekong and Tonle Sap Rivers. By the beginning of the fourteenth century, in contrast, Champa's former strength had greatly decayed and the Vietnamese were already involved in a process of annexation and long-term attrition that was to lead, eventually, to the obliteration of the Cham kingdom.

As a result of the partial Chinese overlay on Vietnam's court and its officials, the state stood apart from its Southeast Asian neighbours in terms of the precision and formality that attached to the government structure. In theory, and to a considerable extent in practice also, the Vietnamese bureaucracy was open to all who could meet the tests of scholarship. In the Buddhist kingdoms of Southeast Asia (Burma, Thailand, Cambodia, and the lowland principalities of modern Laos) officialdom was, in contrast, a quasi-hereditary affair. Being the son of an official was the vital fact that determined subsequent entry into the ranks of the ruler's administration. In Vietnam merit was taken as the guiding principle, even if it often proved the case that the sons of officials had more opportunity to succeed in their learning and so to enter the official ranks.

Vietnamese officials advised a ruler who was spoken of as the "Son of Heaven," and who was thought to mediate between the physical world and the spiritual world by the correct observance of state and religious ceremonies. Just as the performance of these ceremonies followed a minutely drawn-up set of procedures, so was the rest of Vietnamese official life conceived of as following prescribed patterns. The bureaucracy was a pyramid with the ruler at the apex and with clearly defined links established between that apex and the lowest officials in the provinces who formed the base of this administration. The law was a written code, detailed in form and complete with learned commentaries. Strict rules covered the amount of authority possessed by each grade of official and the qualifications for each grade. And as a further reflection of the character of the state the Vietnamese believed in the necessity of clearly defined borders with their neighbours.

In this, as in so many other ways, Vietnam differed from the other major mainland states of Southeast Asia. For them, the important external cultural influence came from India rather than China. For all of its pervasive importance, however, Indian cultural influence in Burma, Thailand, Cambodia and in the riverine states of Laos was a less clear-cut and obvious affair. Vietnamese officials dressed in the same fashion as Chinese mandarins. With the exception of some court priests such direct borrowing was not a characteristic of the Buddhist courts of mainland Southeast-Asia. In Vietnam, again, official architecture drew directly from China, whereas in the Buddhist states the Indian influence was a more subtle matter, and by the eighteenth century only rarely directly recognisable as a case of cultural borrowing.

The Buddhist Kingdoms of the Mainland

The organization of the Buddhist states contrasted sharply with that found in Vietnam. The pattern of official relationships was in many ways much more complex, in part because it was a pattern lacking the clearly defined lines of authority that were so much part of the Vietnamese system. Where the Vietnamese system sought to control the state in great detail down to the level of the village, the central power in the Buddhist kingdoms followed a very different practice. Control over the more distant regions of the kingdom was readily delegated to provincial governors who were able to exercise almost completely unfettered power, always providing that they did not challenge the king's position as the ultimate arbiter of affairs within the state.

If the pyramid is a useful symbol to depict the disposition of power within Vietnam, a series of concentric circles might be taken to represent the nature of power in the Buddhist kingdoms. The state might be considered as the area contained by the largest of these concentric circles, but it was only at the centre, where the smallest of these concentric circles is located, that the king's power was truly absolute. Beyond that central circle — or beyond the limits of the palace to take the real-life example instead of the graphic concept — it was frequently the case that the king's power diminished in a clear proportion to the distance one moved away from the capital.

As for the border regions, the Buddhist rulers in mainland Southeast Asia, again in contrast to Vietnam, accepted that these were uncertain and

porous. Indeed, given the lack of close links between the centre of the Buddhist kingdoms and the outer regions, as well as the existence of numerous petty centres of power largely independent of their greater neighbours, some writers have argued that to talk of "states" in the traditional Southeast Asian world is inappropriate. Certainly the states of traditional Southeast Asia were very different from the political units described as states in the twentieth century.

The officials who held power, whether at the centre of the state in the king's palace or in the outer regions, were not men who gained their appointments through scholarship. Birth into a quasi-hereditary family, ability, and an opportunity to gain the ruler's notice all played their part in determining advancement. It would be quite wrong to suggest that the rulers of the Buddhist kingdoms did not have clear ideas on what constituted a good official, for the record is clear that they did. But the standards were much more flexible and much more personal than those that applied in Vietnam. In the same fashion the conduct of business within the state was less set in formal pattern, more subject to the personal likes and dislikes of the kings at the highest level, or the officials great and small in the provinces away from the capital.

The king in Thailand was, like his counterpart the emperor in Vietnam, expected to intercede between the world of men and the spiritual world. But the nature of this intercession, and the role assigned to the monarch involved in the act, was very different. In Thailand, and in the other mainland Buddhist states, the king's semi-divine status reflected the fact that the monarch and the throne he occupied were the centre of the kingdom. Monarchy was the lynch pin that held the Buddhist kingdoms together. Despite his title as the "Son of Heaven" the Vietnamese emperor had no equivalent status. The Vietnamese emperors were essential to the existence of the state, but they were not the state. The point may be made clearer when it is noted that the Vietnamese were able to accept a situation in which for more than a hundred years during the seventeenth and eighteenth centuries their emperor was no more than a figurehead, a puppet at the beck and call of one of the great families. However limited a king's power was away from the capital in which he had his palace, and however, such senior officials might have tried to take advantage of a child succeeding to the throne, the idea of a state existing more as a reflection of its officials than of its ruler was not part of the system to be found in the Buddhist kingdoms.

Common to all of the Buddhist rulers of mainland Southeast Asia was a belief — held both by themselves and their subjects — in their semidivine, or near-divine character. The concept of a king possessing magical, divine-like characteristics is a difficult one to grasp, and the more deeply one examines the matter the more complex the issue becomes. For a person seeking to understand Southeast Asia in general terms the following broad points deserve attention. The quasi-divine, magical role played by traditional Buddhist rulers in the states of mainland Southeast Asia involved something more than the concept of "divine right" associated with Christian rulers in Europe. Such European rulers held an office sanctioned by the Christian divinity. But no matter how elevated the status of these kings and queens, they were not semi-divine or nearly god-like themselves. The Buddhist kings of mainland Southeast Asia, on the other hand, were seen as divine, or partially so. Their position as kings was not only sanctioned by the Buddhist faith, and continuing Hindu religious beliefs, they were in themselves removed from the rest of mankind and credited with possessing powers that only the divine or near-divine could hold.

Challengers who succeeded in removing a ruler from the throne immediately tried to claim all of the semidivine powers of their defeated opponent. What is more, with rare exceptions, those who fought or schemed to overthrow a ruling king did so in terms of their own claim to have a more legitimate right to the throne than the actual monarch. The importance of this traditional historical background for more modern periods in Southeast Asia may already be apparent. Given the immensely elevated status that a ruler such as the Thai monarch has continued to be a fundamentally important figure in the modern history of Thailand. Traditional ideas of kingship also help to explain why Prince Norodom Sihanouk of Cambodia was for many years able to reap immense political advantage from the fact that he had been Cambodia's king before abdicating his throne in 1955.

The Later Maritime Kingdoms

Royal figures have also been important in the recent history of the maritime regions of Southeast Asia. If their importance has not been so striking as has been the case for the mainland, the explanation owes something to tradition as well as to the fact that Thailand's monarchy ruled over a country that was never colonised while Sihanouk and his ancestors reigned in a colonial system that allowed at least some of the symbolic importance of the king of Cambodia to be maintained. Unlike the mainland Buddhist monarchies — again excluding Vietnam as a special case — the majority of the rulers of the states in the maritime world were followers of Islam, sultans who acted in the name of their religion as well as their state. As followers of Islam the sultans could not be other than [mere] men.

In Java the rulers of the central Javanese kingdom of Mataram were followers of Islam and, perhaps even more importantly, inheritors of a rich mystical tradition drawing upon Hindu-Buddhist ideas as well as indigenous Javanese religious beliefs and cultural patterns. The rulers of Mataram *were* more than men in a way that many of the sultans of the coastal and riverine states of maritime Southeast Asia were not. These latter rulers were men with special rights and almost limitless privilege, but they were men all the same. The ruler of Mataram ensconced in his *kraton*, or palace, gave formal acknowledgement to Islam but his kingship is more readily understood as having parallels with the Buddhist monarchs of the mainland than in terms of the patterns to be found in many of the other traditional courts of the islands.

Currents of Change

Many important changes took place in the thirteenth, fourteenth, and fifteenth centuries, but no single change is seen as having been sufficient by itself to alter the political map of Southeast Asia from the late thirteenth century onwards. The importance of the Mongol destruction of the state based at Pagan cannot be overstated. But the role of the Mongols in bringing change to Angkor is much less clear. Theravada Buddhism did involve a notably different set of religious values from the combination of Hinduism and Mahayana Buddhism that it partially replaced in Cambodia. Nevertheless, it is far from certain that an official adoption of these values contributed to the decline of the Khmer state at Angkor. Islam was to have great significance as a unifying factor among the coastal populations of the Indonesian islands. The extent to which its arrival in northern Java and northern Sumatra had any quick political "effect" in speeding the decay of the older pattern of state relationships in the Archipelago is more difficult to determine.

Major changes took place in Southeast Asia over a period of more than two centuries as old states were no longer capable of adapting to changed circumstances and as new states proved more attuned to the changed world [but] to search for causes other than in the broadest range of factors that govern the capacity of individuals and kingdoms to survive or to fail is to court disappointment.

The Initial European Presence

The Portuguese, the Spaniards, and the Dutch were the earliest of those from Europe who came to the Southeast Asian region and played a role in its history. In the sixteenth century it appeared that the Portuguese as the first upon the scene would establish a dominant role in the region and gain the major share in the rich trade in spices-the commodity that had drawn Europeans to Southeast Asia in the first place. But Portugal's early successes, including in 1511 the capture of Malacca, the great trading city on the western coast of the Malayan Peninsula, were followed by relatively quick decline as the Dutch became the most important European nation trading in the Malay-Indonesian world. But how important? For the merchants of the ports in the Netherlands, the Dutch who lived, and usually after a very short time died, in Indonesia were important indeed as they developed a commercial system that for a period brought great profit to the Dutch state. But the impact of the Dutch outside their base in Java, and their outposts scattered through the islands was minimal until the middle or even the end of the eighteenth century; for some regions of

Indonesia the impact did not come until the late nineteenth and early twentieth centuries. A similar statement cannot be made in relation to the Spaniards in Philippines.

Early Spanish Influence in the Philippines

The Philippines came into historical focus remarkably late by comparison with other parts of Southeast Asia. We know that trading junks from China and Japan visited the Philippines for centuries before the Spanish established themselves in the northern Philippines during the latter part of the sixteenth century. The records of these voyages tell us frustratingly little about the nature of society in the Philippines and as a result our knowledge of life in the Philippines *before* the Spanish arrived depends largely on the information provided by men who wrote *after* the colonial presence had become an established fact.

In the broadest terms, the Spanish came to an area of Southeast Asia in which authority was for the most part exercised over small communities without any central direction. The exceptions to this general rule were mostly found in the southern islands of the Philippines where the adoption of Islam by traditional leaders had helped them to organise states that used the unifying force of religion to incorporate a number of scattered communities into a single political unit. By the middle of the sixteenth century Islam was slowly gaining ground in the more northerly islands and had reached as far as Manila. But this was a coastal phenomenon and the inland areas remained untouched by the new religion so that the Spaniards encountered a society in which a large village was the essential unit. Authority, as elsewhere in Southeast Asia, rested in the hands of a headman who was through birth and inheritance, or through ability, more prosperous and powerful than his fellow villagers.

The absence of central power in the northern Philippine islands, (the southern islands were never to experience significant Spanish rule away from a few port centers) enabled the Spanish colonial power to implant itself in a way unmatched anywhere else in the region. Unlike anywhere else in Southeast Asia, moreover, the principal agents for the Spanish advance were not soldiers and traders but missionary priests. This state of affairs was unique in the history of Southeast Asia, even though missionary priests played important roles elsewhere. In the Philippines, however, the link between the church and the state was of a different order from that existing during French rule over Vietnam. The church and the state were inseparable in the Philippines, as they were in other parts of the world that fell under Spanish colonial control. This distinctive feature has led some scholars to argue that in order to understand Philippine history and society from the seventeenth century onwards it is necessary to study the Spanish experience in Latin America.

Whether or not one seeks enlightenment from the comparison of the Philippine experience with that of the various countries of Latin America, the impact of Spanish values, particularly Spanish Christian values, on the peasant society of the Philippines was profound. The Philippines became the one country in the Southeast Asian region in which Christianity became more than a minority religion. The presence of Christian missionaries did not, of course, bring immediate change to social patterns in the countryside. Slowly, however, with the combined force of the church and state lending authority to developments, the Spanish colonial impact affected the life of the peasantry, giving new and greater power to the traditional local leaders, yet insisting that power beyond the village or district level could not pass out of the hands of Spaniards.

The ultimate irony of this situation is well known to Filipinos but all too often unknown by others. By the early years of the nineteenth century two hundred years of Spanish rule had brought into being a growing group of native Filipinos whose education fitted them to assume roles in the state and the church that were denied them because they were not Spanish. The resentments this situation caused became the seeds of the Philippine revolutionary movement in the late nineteenth century. Yet there was a further irony again. If the Spanish impact, coming so much earlier and so much more profoundly in the Philippines than elsewhere in Southeast Asia, created a class that resented Spanish political control, it also laid the foundations for a rural economic

situation in which centuries of colonial control developed, strengthened, and gave legitimacy to the high degree of social stratification that remains a feature of Philippine life to the present day.

The 18th Century: A Mosaic of Small States

A political map of eighteenth-century Southeast Asia on which the cartographer tried to indicate the boundaries of the various states by use of different colours would appear as an extraordinary mosaic. It is a difficult task even to count how many colours there would have to be on this map. Instead of the ten states that make up late twentieth-century Southeast Asia a cartographer attempting this task for the eighteenth century could not think in terms of less than forty states — kingdoms, principalities, and sultanates — that required delineation. Many of these states were of minor importance. Both on the mainland of Southeast Asia and in the maritime world one would have to find some way of distinguishing between the states of real importance and those which existed at the pleasure of their suzerains or overlords. But however the calculations are made the political map of eighteenth-century Southeast Asia is notably more complex than a political map of the contemporary world. Moreover, the political map of eighteenth-century Southeast Asia, in contrast to a map of the succeeding century, would have one very distinctive feature. The areas showing a colonial presence would be very small indeed. Apart from the northern Philippine islands and much of Java, the European presence in eighteenth-century Southeast Asia was extremely limited, a few trading posts dotted along the coast-lines of the various regions.

End of an Era

Change of momentous proportions was not far distant for Southeast Asia as a whole as the eighteenth century drew to a close. Many of the changes that came were the result of the Western impact on the region, but other changes had little if any connection with the advance of the colonial

SOUTHEAST ASIA, CIRCA 1750-1800

ASSAM

YUNNAN

CHINA

Pacific Ocean

THREE LAO KINGDOMS

FORMOSA

BURMA

LUANG PRABANG

Macao

LAN NA

Luang Prabang

VIENTIANE

Rangoon

Vientiane

VIETNAM

PHILIPPINES

Bay of Bengal

Champassak

Manila

SIAM

CHAMPASSAK

Bangkok

Philippine Sea

CAMBODIA

South China Sea

Nakhon Si Thammarat

MALAYA

SULU

BRUNEI

MALACCA (MELAKA)

Jambi

SARAWAK

THE MOLUCCAS (MALUKU)

BORNEO

CELEBES (SULAWESI)

Macassar

Portuguese
Vietnamese
Spanish
Sulu
Burmese
Thai
Cambodian
Dutch
Acehnese
Brunei
Jambi
British
JAVA States/Regions

Jakarta

0   250   500   750 km

0   250   500 miles

JAVA

Kupang

I n d i a n   O c e a n

powers. The last three decades of the eighteenth century in Vietnam were marked by political upheaval and by a challenge to established social and economic patterns. The advent of a new dynasty on the Thai throne, the Chakri dynasty, from 1782 onwards, brought a remarkable series of kings to power whose personal energy and ability transformed the state. They did this as much through reinvigorating Thai forms of government as through later selective borrowing from the West.

Changes brought by growing Western influence and changes inspired by outstanding individuals within the ruling groups of the various Southeast Asian states were later to affect the population as a whole. Initially, however, the fact and prospect of change had its greatest effect on the elite. For the peasant the world went on as before, dominated by the cycle of crop planting and harvest, the seasons of the year, and the awesome events of birth and death. Visualising his physical world in the eighteenth century is difficult in the extreme as even the remotest villages of twentieth-century Southeast Asia have been touched and transformed by the modern world. Entering the spiritual world of the peasant during the eighteenth century is even more difficult an exercise. We may sense something of the complexity of this spiritual world, the blend of animistic beliefs with one or other of the great religions or philosophies — Islam, Christianity, Buddhism, Hinduism, Confucianism — that were followed in the states of Southeast Asia. But even the most sympathetic student can only penetrate a certain distance into the religious world of another culture in another age.

Yet for all of the "separateness" of existence between ruler and ruled in the traditional Southeast Asian world it would be wrong not to end with an insistence upon the totality of the world within which these two groups lived. For this too was a feature of the traditional world that was soon to come under challenge as new forces and new ideas penetrated the region.

The courts and kings were separate from the cultivators, fishermen, and petty traders over whom they ruled. But all of these groups inhabited a single, unified world. Just as the serf and the feudal lord of medieval Europe both, in very different ways, sensed themselves to be part of Christendom, so the cultivators or fishermen sensed themselves within the same world as their ruler, whether he was an Islamic sultan, a Buddhist king, a Vietnamese Confucian emperor, or a Catholic Spanish governor. To a considerable extent, the history of Southeast Asia from the beginning of the nineteenth century is a history of the changes brought to this assumption of a settled, single world.[11]

◆   ◆   ◆

AN "AGE OF COMMERCE" IN SOUTHEAST ASIA

— by Anthony Reid

Maritime intercourse continued to link the peoples of Southeast Asia more tightly to one another than to outside influences down to the seventeenth century. The fact that Chinese and Indian influences came to most of the region by maritime trade, not by conquest or colonization, appeared to ensure that Southeast Asia retained its distinctiveness even while borrowing numerous elements from these larger centres. What did *not* happen (with the partial exception of Vietnam) was that any part of the region established closer relations with China or India than with its neighbours in Southeast Asia. The Chinese continued to see Southeast Asia minus the special case of Vietnam as a whole — "the Southern Ocean" (Nanyang). Indians, Persians, Arabs, and Malays named the region "the lands below the winds" because of the seasonal monsoons which carried shipping to it across the Indian Ocean. Both terms stress the fact that it had to be reached by sea, by a journey substantially more difficult than that which Southeast Asians themselves required to reach such central marketing points as Sri Vijaya [Srivijaya], Melaka [Malacca], or Banten. As one observer noted about 1600, speaking primarily of the Archipelago, "these people are constrained to keep up constant intercourse with one another, the one supplying what the other needs."

Until the trade revolution of the seventeenth century, when the Dutch East India Company established an astonishingly regular and intensive shipping network to take a large share of the region's export produce around the Cape of Good Hope, coinciding with an increase in Chinese shipping to the Nanyang, the trading links within the region continued to be more influential than those beyond it.

The period which I have designated "the age of commerce," from the fifteenth to the seventeenth century, was one in which these maritime links were particularly active. The interconnected maritime cities of the region were more dominant in this period than either before or since. The most important central entrepôts had, moreover, for some time been Malay-speaking — first Sri Vijaya and then its successors, Pasai, Melaka, Johor, Patani, Aceh, and Brunei. The Malay language thereby became the main language of trade throughout Southeast Asia. The cosmopolitan trading class of many of Southeast Asia's major trading cities came to be classified as Malays because they spoke that language and professed Islam, even when their forebears may have been Javanese, Mon, Indian, Chinese, or Filipino. It was possible for Magellan's Sumatran slave to be immediately understood when he spoke to the people of the Central Philippines in 1521, and almost two centuries later for Dampier's Englishmen to learn Malay in Mindanao (southern Philippines) and use it again at Poulo Condore, off southern Vietnam. It was during this period that hundreds of Malay words in commercial, technological, and other fields passed into Tagalog;[12] that the major trading centres of Cambodia came to be known by the Malay-derived term *kompong*; and that the Vietnamese adopted such words as cù-lao (from Malay *pulau*, for island). Similarly, Malay words such as *amok, gudang* (storehouse), *perahu* (boat), and *kris* were noted by Europeans in Pegu and even in the Malabar coast of India, as if they were local words. At least those who dealt with matters of trade and commerce in the major ports had to speak Malay as well as their own language.[13]

This period has usually been labelled "early European contact," or "Islamization," or more frequently still by reference to the great states which dominated parts of it — Ayutthaya, Mataram, the Le Dynasty, or Aceh. All these labels tend to obscure the underlying coherence of a period which brought profound and momentous changes to all of Southeast Asia. These would have to include religious change, urban expansion, state formation and strengthening, and involvement in commerce.

Religious Change

Although Islamic enclaves were formed much earlier, the adoption of Islam by the major states involved in the trading route from Ternate and Tidore in the east to Melaka (Malacca) and Sumatra in the west took place essentially in the period 1400-1620. Islam also spread along other major trade routes — from Melaka northeastward to Brunei and Manila, and to Patani and Champa along one of the routes to China. There were no major Muslim gains after 1620, although the full application of Islamic law by states (what we might today call Islamic fundamentalism) reached its peak in the middle of the seventeenth century under sultans Iskandar Thani in Aceh (1636-41), Ageng in Banten (1651-80), and

Hasanuddin in Makassar (1653-69). The latter part of the period also witnessed the conversion to Christianity of most Filipinos, and a proportion of eastern Indonesians and Vietnamese. It appears also to have marked a shift to a more "rational", universalist, and moralist emphasis in the great urban centers of Theravada Buddhism. There was also religious change in Vietnam in the form of the enforcement of neo-Confucian orthodoxy by the state in the fifteenth century. All these changes in one sense fragmented Southeast Asia into different camps, yet in another they led in a similar direction. The first half of the seventeenth century appears to have marked a high point in a progression towards understanding religion as universal faiths emphasizing morality, rationality, and above all written scriptural and legal orthodoxy. Subsequently there was a return to more rural and local forms of religious expression, such as magic, shamanism and ancestor-cults.

The Growth of Cities

Contemporary European estimates of large populations for Southeast Asian cities in the sixteenth and seventeenth centuries should be taken seriously, especially insofar as they are confirmed by evidence of physical size and the dimensions of food imports. It seems probable that Ayutthaya, Pegu, Hanoi, Demak and Melaka all exceeded 50,000 people in the early sixteenth century, while Ayutthaya, Aceh, Banten, Surabaya and Makassar certainly did so in the first half of the seventeenth. Such dimensions were not remarkable by Asian standards, but they were on a par with most of the leading European cities of the day. In relation to the much smaller total population of Southeast Asia than of Europe, India or China, this made the region relatively highly urbanized. In particular it should be noted that the Southeast Asian trading cities were many times more populous than the colonial enclave cities which usurped their economic, but not their political or cultural, functions. Thus it was several centuries before the port cities which fell to European arms or in some cases to hinterland coalitions — Melaka (1511), Brunei (1579), Pegu (1599), Surabaya (1625) and Makassar (1669) — regained their previous populations.

ISLAM IN ASIA

In understanding contemporary Muslims' sense of their history and its impact upon Muslim aspirations today, it is crucial to note that, despite the breakdown of a central caliphal government in the thirteenth century, Islam had continued to expand and flourish politically and culturally. The message and rule of Islam were extended throughout much of Asia and Africa, creating new Muslim community/states that professed a loyalty to Islam and whose government and legal, judicial, and educational systems were influenced to varying degrees by Islam. Thus, from Muhammad's seventh-century Arabia to the dawn of European colonialism in the sixteenth century, Islam was an ascendant and expansive religiopolitical movement in which religion was part and parcel of both private and public life.

The expansion of Islam in Asia produced a variety and diversity of Islamically informed societies. All Muslims shared a common faith, confessing their belief in the one God and in his Book and the teaching of his Prophet. However, Islam encountered peoples of vastly different historical backgrounds, languages, ethnic/tribal identities, loyalties, customs, and cultures. In a very real sense an Arab Islam was transformed into Persian, South Asian, and Southeast Asian Islam through the process of assimilation and synthesis. Despite the common core of belief and practice epitomized by the Five Pillars of Islam, Muslim societies differed in the extent and manner to which religion manifested itself in public life — politics, law, and society.

Islamic ascendancy was reversed dramatically from the sixteenth century onward under the impact of European colonialism. The first trade companies proved to be the vanguard of European imperialism. The presence of British, French, Dutch, Russian, and Portuguese trade companies gave way by the nineteenth century to European economic, political, and (often) military dominance in much of the Muslim world.

By the late nineteenth and twentieth centuries, European legal codes had replaced much of Islamic and local customary laws. The political, economic, and legal penetration of Muslim societies by the West was further extended as modern Western educational reforms were introduced. Traditional political and religious elites saw their power, prestige, and way of life (customs, values) progressively altered by new "modern," Western-oriented classes of professionals and technocrats. By the twentieth century, the West reigned supreme, dominating much of the Islamic world politically and economically. Its impact on social and cultural life was no less threatening.

—John L. Esposito, *Islam in Asia: Religion, Politics, and Society*

State Formation

Around these maritime cities there formed states which owed their power largely to the wealth and military expertise which came with trade. Some of them, such as Laos, Aceh, Banten, Banjarmasin, Makassar, Ternate and in a sense the Spanish Philippines, formed themselves into states for the first time only in the "age of commerce". Others—Siam, Burma, Mataram (Java), Cambodia—assumed something like their modern shape under strong absolutist rulers. A shift towards centralized rule, the mobilization of huge armies, royal monopoly of trade, codification of law, and the replacement of hereditary chiefs by ministeriales, was particularly evident at the end of this period in the first half of the seventeenth century.

Involvement in Commerce

Both internal chronicles and the testimony of visitors made clear that the Southeast Asian courts of the period lived by trade and involved themselves in it. In addition to the ruling circle, there were in each major city a great variety of foreign merchants, some of whom originated outside the region — Chinese, Indian, European, Japanese, Jewish and Armenian — but nevertheless played a role in the life of the cities and often were coopted as court officials. Other commercial communities unquestionably belonged to the region, and of these the Malays (after their diaspora from Melaka in 1511), the Javanese (until around 1620), the Mons of Pegu (until 1599) and the Makassarese and Bugis (after 1600) were the most important. As with commercial minorities everywhere, these groups owed their success partly to their international connections and their mobility, being able to move their operations elsewhere if a particular ruler became too demanding.

This period also marks the apogee of the large Southeast Asian trading ship of 200-500 tons, which contemporary sources always call a "junk." Despite its quintessential Chinese ring in modern ears, the word is Javanese in origin and is the normal word for ship in the Malay maritime codes of the period. The mixture of (northern) Chinese and Southeast Asian features found in the wrecks of the period, and described by European observers, has led to their being dubbed a hybrid "South China Sea junk," in which Chinese living either in South China or Southeast Asia, as well as Malays, Javanese, and Mons, may have sailed, but which were usually built with the more abundant Southeast Asian (especially Burmese) woods. By 1650 these large Southeast Asian ships had disappeared, Southeast Asian traders (except for a few rulers) used small vessels of 20-30 tons, and the term "junk" dropped out of Malay and Javanese usage, to be used by Europeans only for Chinese vessels, which remained large.

A Boom in Trade?

Do these features give the period an underlying coherence? The term "age of commerce" cannot of course explain all that happened in the fifteenth to seventeenth centuries, but it does draw attention to one of the dominant features without which none of the other major changes can be understood. To justify such a term, however, and particularly to identify its boundaries, it is necessary to look at the factors which may have caused the "boom" of the long sixteenth century, already apparent to European historians, to be particularly acutely felt in Southeast Asia. Fortunately the prominence of Southeast Asian products, notably pepper, cloves, nutmeg and mace, in the markets of Europe and East Asia make this possible.

In 1345 Venice concluded a treaty with the Mamluke rulers of Egypt which for the first time established reliable purchases of spices in Alexandria by the annual galley fleets from the Adriatic. Gradually thereafter the Mamlukes consolidated their control of other caravan routes serving Beirut and Damascus. This progress towards peaceful conditions for the caravans taking Asian goods to the Mediterranean from the Red Sea and Persian Gulf ports coincided with a collapse of the Central Asian overland routes. The latter part of the fourteenth century, therefore, marked a sharp upturn in the trade travelling by sea from and through Southeast Asia to the Mediterranean.

While this marks the beginning of a sustained upward movement in Southeast Asian pepper and spice shipments to the West, the trade to China was still vastly more important in bulk terms. Marco Polo had claimed that for every Italian spice galley in Alexandria a hundred docked at the Chinese port of Zaiton (Quanzhou), and China remained the dominant market for Southeast Asia into the sixteenth century. The upswing in demand from China was curiously congruent with that from Europe. At the end of the fourteenth century China began two centuries of expansion in wealth and population. The demand for Southeast Asian products was particularly boosted by the six state trading expeditions of the Ming Emperor Yong La (1403-99). These not only brought home enormous quantities of pepper, spice, sappanwood and other forest products; they also stimulated Southeast Asian production, and left a number of crucial communities of Chinese (often Muslim) traders in the burgeoning entrepots of the region. The leading products of the Nanyang trade, pepper and sappanwood, became for the first time items of mass consumption in China in the fifteenth century, and so abounded in government warehouses that they were used in part-payment of hundreds of thousands of Chinese officials and soldiers.

The fifteenth century, then, appears to have been one of steady growth in the trade to and through Southeast Asia. Despite the Chinese bans on private trade, shipping across the South China Sea continued to grow. This was possible in the first place because Ming official enforcement of the ban was very weak between 1457 and the 1590s, so that merchant junks sailed annually in this period from South Fujian to the Nanyang. Secondly the system of official tribute voyages was at its peak in the fifteenth century, called forth by the expansive initiatives of the first three Ming Emperors. Siam, the most adept Southeast Asian kingdom at exploiting the system, sent 51 tribute missions to China in the period 1371-1420, in response to the 15 missions the early Ming emperors sent to Ayutthaya. After 1420 Peking lost interest, and sent missions only in the two years 1453 and 1482, whereas Siam continued to exploit the trade opportunities offered by sending missions about once in three years. Subsequently tribute missions declined markedly in frequency as other opportunities for trade opened up. Envoys from Melaka, Pasai, Brunei, Ghampa, Cambodia and Java were similarly numerous in the period 1400-1440, though their numbers declined even more rapidly than the Siamese thereafter.

A third means of circumventing the Chinese ban was developed by the island kingdom of Ryukyu, following the end of state trading by the Ming in 1433. Merchants of Fujian settled near Okinawa and conducted their trade under the auspices of the Ryukyu crown, which maintained access to China and Japan by regularly sending deferential but highly lucrative tribute missions to both courts. Ryukyu therefore became a crucial link between Southeast and Northeast Asia during the periods when direct trade was most inhibited. In the thirteen years 1430-1442 at least 17 Ryukyu trade missions were sent to Ayutthaya, eight to Palembang, and six to Java. The pattern was one of decline in the sixteenth century, however, and Ryukyu ceased to be a factor in Southeast Asian trade by the 1550s.

If a particular moment must be singled out for the beginning of Southeast Asia's "age of commerce," the first state trading mission under the eunuch admiral Zheng He (Cheng Ho), in 1405, is the best candidate. These missions were probably responsible for the introduction of Indian pepper plants to northern Sumatra, and the enormous growth in Southeast Asian pepper production for the China market which followed. For the spice trade, and for trading cities such as Pegu, Ayutthaya, Melaka, Pasai, Brunei, Grisek and Demak, the fifteenth century was undoubtedly one of expansion.

The sixteenth and early seventeenth centuries continued the trade expansion of the fifteenth, with Europe and Japan increasingly taking over from China the role of external catalysts for growth. The period immediately following the European discovery of the sea route to Asia in 1498, however, was a very bad one in economic terms for the lands below the winds. The 1490s had seen pepper and Moluccan spice shipments in the Mediterranean at a temporary peak, but these dropped drastically after Vasco da Gama's Portuguese reached India in 1498 — and began to sink or plunder every spice ship they encountered.[14]

NOTES

1. The "official speech" of modern China is derived from the Beijing dialect — called "Mandarin" by Westerners. The present government's goal is to make its use as widespread as the written form, even if it remains a second language for many of the Chinese people.

2. From the word sinitic. Meaning to become more "Chinese-like."

3. See Wm. Theodore de Bary, *East Asian Civilizations: A Dialogue in Five Stages* (Cambridge: Harvard University Press, 1988), pp. 27-35.

4. The name Yangzi (Yangtze) which refers to the river and the surrounding valley is the name best known in the West. The Chinese call it Changjiang or "Long River."

5. Marco Polo's claims about having lived and worked in China were doubted by his contemporaries in Europe and are still questioned by some researchers today.

6. Janet L. Abu-Lughod, *Before European Hegemony: The World System A.D. 1250-1350* (New York: Oxford University Press, 1989), pp. 365, 12.

7. A fifth, and lowest, class may be said to have existed in the relatively tiny number of beggars, executioners, public entertainers, grave diggers, leatherworkers, and butchers. Their descendants, known as *burakumin*, continue to be subject to serious social discrimination in modern Japan.

8. Abridged from: Anthony Reid, *Southeast Asia in the Age of Commerce 1450-1680: The Lands Below the Winds*, vol. 1 (New Haven: Yale University Press, 1988), pp. 3-10.

9. Speculation continues to focus on the area of present-day Palembang (south Sumatra) and may be confirmed in a few years by archeological explorations. Srivijaya is sometimes written Sriwijaya. It was ruled over by the Sailendra dynasty. [—Ed.]

10. The most significant turning point, however, came in 1025 when the South Indian Chola dynasty raided the Malacca regional ports and broke the Srivijayan authority over the all-important Straits of Malacca. [—Ed.]

11. Abridged from: Milton Osborne, *Southeast Asia* (Sydney: George Allen & Unwin, Ltd., 1985), pp. 18-35.

12. Major language of the Philippines.

13. Reid, *Southeast Asia in the Age of Commerce*, pp. 6-7.

14. Abridged from: Anthony Reid, "An 'Age of Commerce' in Southeast Asian History," *Modern Asian Studies*, vol. 24, no. 1, February 1990, pp. 3-7.

Seaborne Barbarians: Incursions by the West

OVERVIEW

With the fall of Constantinople to the Turks in 1453, the European window on Asia was effectively closed. The Europeans of the Mediterranean world felt this loss sorely, for without an alternative trade route to the East, they faced the high costs of a series of commercial intermediaries. Fortunately for them, a "geographical revolution" began at around the same time, led by Prince Henry ("The Navigator") of Portugal whose sponsorship of exploration and research provided Vasco da Gama and his successors with the information, navigational tools, and sailing technology they needed to reach the Indian Ocean by sea via the Cape of Good Hope. Shortly thereafter, their ships were dropping anchor off the ancient trading ports of Southeast Asia in search of valuable spices to carry back to Europe.

The Portuguese were the first to exploit this new capability to reach Asia by sea, but even as they began to plunder local areas of Southeast Asian trade, the Dutch, British, Spanish, and French moved in to challenge them. Most soon made their way to China where, confined to a single port, Guangzhou (Canton) they contended with one another for trade privileges. From the lofty perspective of the Chinese emperor, rivalry among these powers was seen to be mere squabbling among the rabble or "barbarians" of the outside world. China stood in awe of no country, nor did it see any particular need to trade with the

foreigners outside the framework of its ancient "tribute" system.

To make matters worse, Western traders found it difficult to find goods that China would buy. They wanted to exchange goods with China rather than pay silver for its tea and porcelain and they needed access to more ports than Guangzhou. By the late eighteenth century, as Britain came to dominate world commerce, these trade constraints were viewed as an acute problem. The answer, from the British standpoint, was to promote a flourishing trade in opium with China — with devastating consequences for China's society and national wealth. As the trade balance began to turn around in favor of Britain, political tensions with the imperial court in Beijing mounted.

Meanwhile, the commercial role of Southeast Asia shifted from a region of numerous ports for the collection of trade goods to that of a *production* base of important commodities such as rubber, coffee, tin, and rice. To be successful, it was assumed, the production areas required more direct European control over indigenous populations and kingdoms. The vise of colonial rule began to tighten.

It is from this later time, around the middle of the nineteenth century, that the emergence of "modern" Pacific Asia is often marked: the outbreak in 1840 of the first of the so-called Opium Wars between China and Great Britain, other European military victories against Southeast Asian kingdoms, the arrival of America's

Commodore Perry in Japan in 1853, and Western intrusions into Korea.

In fact, the process of change was more gradual and diffuse than such historic thresholds would make it appear. There is no doubt, however, that the Europeans and Americans believed they were bringing to Asia an advanced stage of civilization, later described as "progress," in the belief that the concepts of "modern" and "Western" would always be synonymous.

Advances in art, literature, and technology by vigorous and creative Asian societies over the centuries testify to the "progress" they had already enjoyed, but as the industrial revolution in Europe accelerated, they found themselves at a profound technological disadvantage. The competition from an expansionist West created an urgent need for Pacific Asian societies to adapt and meet the challenge. In the new global economic system each society would have to assert its own integrity and, ultimately, define its own "nationhood" to survive.

EARLY EUROPEAN ADVANCES

The Portuguese Vanguard

By the early sixteenth century, a growing number of Portuguese navigators were following the route around the Cape of Good Hope that had been pioneered by their countryman Vasco da Gama. On reaching the Indian Ocean, they discovered a well-developed Indo-Pacific maritime trading system, stretching from India to the southern coast of China, which, in some respects, was the historical and geographical counterpart of today's intensive Pacific Basin trade (described in chapter 13). As noted in the preceding chapter, Southeast Asia at this time was enjoying the fruits of what historian Anthony Reid has called its "Age of Commerce" (circa 1460-1680). The scope and volume of trade being conducted by Chinese merchants alone astonished the Europeans once the full complexity of the commercial network became

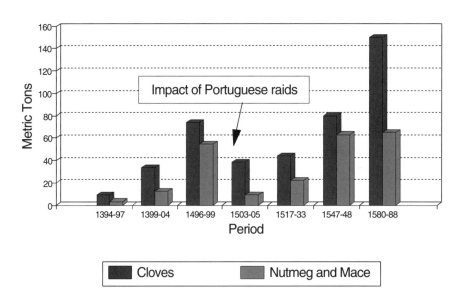

Exports to Europe of Moluccan Spices
Metric Tons Per Year (est.)

Impact of Portuguese raids

Legend: Cloves, Nutmeg and Mace

Graph 2.1

Pacific Century

apparent. The Chinese "junk," the Makassar schooner, and other sailing craft were transporting raw silk, porcelain, ivory, spices, sandalwood, and jewels to ports throughout the South China Sea, Island Southeast Asia, and the Indian Ocean.

Having entered the region in search of the Spice Islands, the Portuguese soon located the key trading city of Malacca on the Malay Peninsula and set about taking it by force. From there they rapidly fanned out during succeeding voyages to make contact with Java, Siam, Indochina and the southern ports of China.

The strategic importance of Malacca derived from its location at the epicenter of trade between the South China Sea and the Indian Ocean. Seasonal shifts of the monsoon (from the Arabic word *mausim*, "season") winds encouraged travel across the Indian Ocean in both directions. A round-trip from Arabia to Southeast Asia could be completed in about six months across what is one of the most pacific of oceans, with many goods eventually reaching European ports.

During the early decades of the sixteenth century, however, there was a sharp drop in this long-distance trade as the Portuguese began to plunder the Muslim shipping routes along the coasts of the Indian Ocean. Traditionally, the Muslim routes had carried goods to the Mediterranean via the Red Sea but now the Portuguese took over the trade and carried it around the Cape of Good Hope.

The Portuguese were unable to hold this advantage for very long, however. An expanding Ottoman Empire, beginning with the conquest of Egypt (1517), strengthened the Muslim traders' capacities to reassert themselves. Meanwhile, key trading ports in Southeast Asia found that by coordinating their resistance they could often match the military prowess of the Portuguese.

This rivalry eventually turned to cooperation as markets grew and the Portuguese saw an advantage in financing rather than fighting their erstwhile Muslim rivals. The growing of pepper for trade spread rapidly into new territories such as

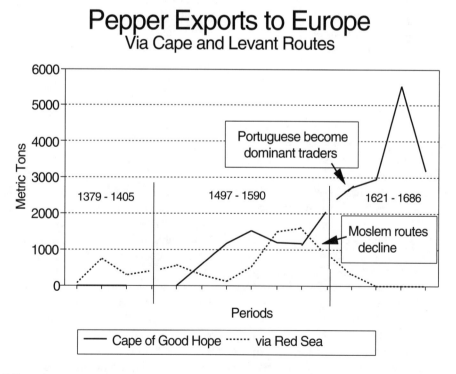

Pepper Exports to Europe
Via Cape and Levant Routes

Portuguese become dominant traders

1379 - 1405   1497 - 1590   1621 - 1686

Moslem routes decline

Periods

—— Cape of Good Hope   ······ via Red Sea

Graph 2.2

The strategic importance of trade in spices from the sixteenth through the eighteenth centuries can hardly be overstated. Since the Middle Ages, the markets of Europe had demanded Asian spices not merely as a luxury taste but as an essential preservative of meat. Arabs were the earliest purveyors of the spices to Europe (primarily mace and nutmeg, but also cinnamon and pepper). By the time the Portuguese arrived in the Indonesian archipelago where the "Spice Islands" were located, spice trading had evolved as a centuries-old tradition throughout East Asia and Central Asia.

The decline of the trade was brought about in part by an "agricultural revolution" in Europe that preceded the Industrial Revolution: New tubers were cultivated that could be used as fodder to keep animals alive throughout the winter. With the need to slaughter surplus animals each fall thus greatly reduced, there was a corresponding drop in the demand for Asia's spices to serve as meat preservatives.

Early Catholic Missions on the Mainland

Portugal's entry into Asia created a new and vital foothold for Christianity in the region. A few small Nestorian and Catholic Christian communities had developed in China during the "openings" of previous centuries between East and West, but by the sixteenth century they had died out. With the Portuguese landfalls in China, a new era opened for Christianity in Asia. Jesuit priests were nonthreatening in comparison with the unbathed, hairy, and seemingly primitive traders whom the Ming Chinese and Japanese alike referred to as "barbarians" (in Japanese, *nambanjin*, or "Southern Barbarians" because they had first appeared from the south). The impact of the Jesuits in China went far beyond religious proselytizing. On their discovery that scholars were held in higher esteem than priests, the learned order began to serve as a conduit to China of new secular information about the world.

Among the first, and certainly the foremost, of the Jesuit missionaries was Matteo Ricci, an Italian, who arrived in Guangzhou in 1582. The missions he established in Nanjing and Beijing thrived to such an extent that by 1650 there were 150,000 converts and by 1700, 300,000. Meanwhile, Dominican and Jesuit missionaries entered present-day Vietnam, laying the foundations for a major French missionary presence in the succeeding century.

Early European Rivalry in Asia

From early in the period of European exploration in Asia, and certainly by the seventeenth century, military conflicts on the European continent were an important factor in foreign trade. Spain, which began the sixteenth century as a rival of Portugal, claimed with it a global monopoly on Christian proselytizing and commerce in any newly discovered territories. This privilege had been bestowed on them by the Vatican which, in light of the earlier discoveries of Columbus, created the Treaty of Tordesillas (1494) in order to control their rivalry. The treaty effectively partitioned the world between them, but its vague terms and the uncertainty in that period of establishing longitudinal position made it difficult to

the west coast of Sumatra which lay beyond immediate Portuguese control. By the 1560s, Muslim spice trading had returned to its former high level, although the advance of new European entrants would eventually overwhelm it once again.

As the Portuguese built their trading empire, establishing a series of coastal fortresses stretching from the Red Sea to China, they gained a reputation for brutal treatment of indigenous populations. Such behavior in China resulted in their expulsion, except for the tiny outpost of Macao south of Guangzhou. For nearly three centuries thereafter, Macao remained a center for western contact with China until nearby Hong Kong took over the role in the mid-nineteenth century.

Figure 2.1   Remains of the Portuguese-built cathedral of Saõ Paulo, Macao.

know the boundary in Asia with certainty. Thus Portugal ventured eastward in search of Asia's spices while the Spanish explored the routes to the west (although the Portuguese had titular claim to part of present-day Brazil).

The result for Spain was the discovery of the New World and Magellan's extraordinary voyage around the tip of South America. Crossing the Pacific in ships smaller than today's harbor tugboats, Magellan encountered the Philippines in 1521. Once the Spanish and Portuguese thrones became united under the rule of Philip II of Spain, the Spanish control over the Pacific Ocean began to tighten further. It was able to establish colonies in the Philippines, appropriating and enlarging the port of Manila in 1570, as well as in the New World. Although the English dealt a major blow to Spanish sea power with the defeat of the Armada in 1588, the Spanish remained largely in control of the trans-Pacific access to Asia into the seventeenth century. Spain's power on the European continent would continue to decline as France's strength grew under the rule of Louis XIV, but for the time being the Pacific seemed to have become a "Spanish lake."

Portugal's power was waning as well. The Dutch, who had emerged as the leading maritime merchants of Europe, sent their traders to Guangzhou in 1604 and 1607 but found themselves rebuffed by the Chinese at the instigation of the Portuguese. In response, the Dutch gathered their forces and attacked the Portuguese at Macao, using the Pescadores Islands southwest of Taiwan as a base. Although also unsuccessful in this effort, they were nevertheless able to maintain intermittent trading contacts with China. Many years later, they were granted permission to build a trading center at Guangzhou (1762). Japan (which only slightly distinguished the Dutch from the Portuguese by calling them *Komojin,* or "Red-Haired People") permitted them to establish a limited presence as well on Deshima Island in the harbor of Nagasaki, even after the Christian persecutions and isolationist policies of the Tokugawa shogun had reached their peak (described in chapter 1). The Japanese took note of the fact that the Dutch were far less interested than either the Spanish or the Portuguese in saving souls. Dutch motives in Asia were almost exclusively commercial.

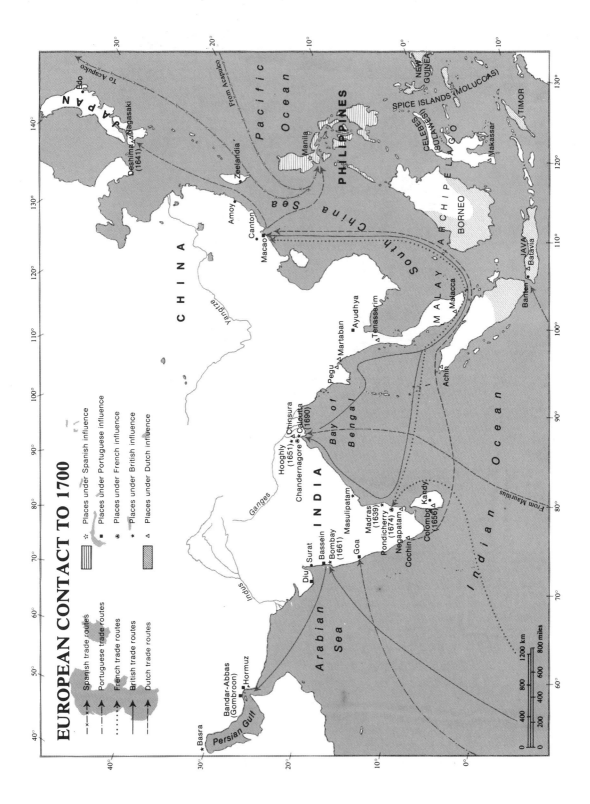

EUROPEAN CONTACT TO 1700

Places under Spanish influence

Places under Portuguese influence

Places under French influence

Places under British influence

Places under Dutch influence

- –×–×– Spanish trade routes
- –·–·– Portuguese trade routes
- ········ French trade routes
- ——— British trade routes
- – – – Dutch trade routes

THE CANTON "FACTORIES"

The old China trade, in the days of sail, depended on the seasonal monsoons. The European ships, coming up the South China Sea, would arrive at Macao with the southwesterly winds of the summer monsoon. They then proceeded up the intricate Pearl River delta, pausing first at Humen (or the "Bogue") to pay a variety of fees. They finally anchored at Huangpu (Whampoa), beyond which the river was too shallow to go. Their cargoes were off-loaded into smaller crafts to be transported the last dozen or so miles to the Thirteen Factories. The return voyage, a few months later, made similar use of the winter monsoon. For those who had set out from Europe, the entire round-trip took slightly more than a year.

— E.J.M. Rhoads, *EAH*

The more immediate Dutch successes came in Southeast Asia, where their East India Company (known historically by its initials in Dutch, VOC) was able to dominate the major commercial centers engaged in the spice trade. Not only did the VOC drive out the Portuguese and hold back the British, the Company went so far as to destroy the spice-producing potentials of certain islands in order to drive up prices. In the course of doing so, the Dutch virtually exterminated entire populations of the Banda Island group. Thus, because it was willing to back its territorial acquisitions with force, the Dutch East India Company became a formidable presence in Asia during the seventeenth and eighteenth centuries, dominating trade across a broad segment of Southeast Asia and the Indian Ocean. In the process, it destroyed the spice-trading livelihoods of the Bugis and Makassar people through blockades and conquests, reducing those formerly prosperous islands to a state of poverty.

With this latter action, the Dutch undermined a component of regional commerce on which they themselves were dependent. Until then, their spice ships had returned from India with fine cloth for sale in local Southeast Asian markets. It was a highly successful business, and during the peak of the export-driven growth and prosperity of maritime Southeast Asia (c. 1620-50), imports of Indian cloth reached a value of about 60 tons of silver equivalent per year. Records of the time show that almost two million pieces of cloth annually arrived

counterpart, the British East India Company, which also had been formed in the late sixteenth century for the purpose of exploiting the spice trade. Dutch belligerence toward the few British representatives who ventured to settle in the Spice Islands reinforced the British East India Company's priority on finding markets in other regions, notably India, where it discovered new and even more profitable commodities to trade. These were destined not only for Europe but for East Asia, primarily China, as Japan remained effectively closed to foreign commerce.

As early as 1685 the Manchu Emperor granted the Company the right to erect a "factory" or trading center at Guangzhou, but it did not begin dispatching ships to that port on a regular basis until around 1715. Thereafter the British began the "Canton trade" which would grow to become a vital part of their commercial empire. Their interest in this trade became more intense following major historical shifts of power and fortune in the mid-eighteenth century. The most important shift came with Robert Clive's pivotal victory against the nawab (provincial authority) of Bengal and his French supporters in 1757 (the Battle of Plassey), which made the British the dominant European power in India. As became clear after the Seven Year's War (1756-63), which pitted Britain and Prussia against France and Austria, the impact of military victories stretched far beyond the European continent. Trading empires in Asia and the Americas required that a nation gain and hold strategic military positions against its rivals. A few years later, Britain suffered defeat in the American revolution, but its economy remained relatively unimpaired. London soon took the place of Amsterdam as the center of world trade and finance. Meanwhile, the British East India Company moved into the power vacuum in India after the Battle of Plassey and became virtually a state within a state. Only gradually was it brought under the direct control of the British government.

from India for purchase by a total Southeast Asian population of barely 25 million. By the 1680s the Dutch were supplying most of this cloth, but once they had eliminated the Southeast Asian trading communities as rivals in the spice trade they terminated the locals' purchasing power as well. Dutch cloth sales plummeted and never recovered their historic levels.

The British East India Company

Like the Dutch, the British had no intention of letting the Spanish and Portuguese dominate trade with Asia. Yet, in its early years, the aggressive expansion of the VOC overshadowed its rival and

Early Regional Financial Flows

Money is the lubricant of trade and in sufficient quantities it becomes a powerful stimulant as well. Prior to the European discovery of the routes to Asia, little of the gold and silver that

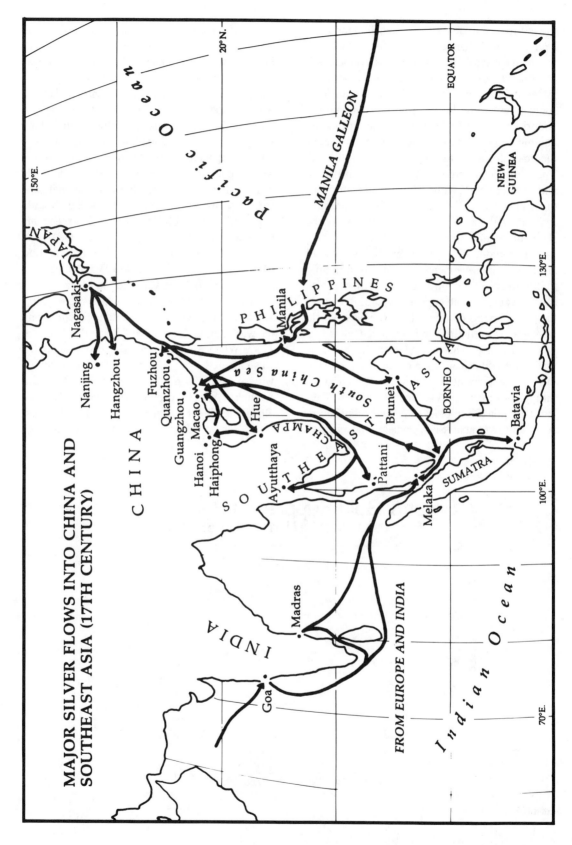

MAJOR SILVER FLOWS INTO CHINA AND
SOUTHEAST ASIA (17TH CENTURY)

Pacific Ocean

150°E.

20°N.

EQUATOR

MANILA GALLEON

NEW
GUINEA

130°E.

JAPAN

Nagasaki

PHILIPPINES

Manila

CHINA

Nanjing

Hangzhou

Fuzhou

Quanzhou

South China Sea

BORNEO

ASIA

Guangzhou

Macao

Hue

Brunei

Batavia

Hanoi

Haiphong

CHAMPA

SOUTHEAST

SUMATRA

100°E.

Ayutthaya

Pattani

Melaka

INDIA

Madras

FROM EUROPE AND INDIA

Indian Ocean

Goa

70°E.

flowed from the West actually reached the East, having been exchanged in India for cloth which was then carried further eastward as a trade good. All this changed dramatically with a boom in silver exports that occurred after 1570 from sources within the Pacific Basin: Japan and the Americas. Spanish America began producing enormous quantities of silver, particularly after the Spanish and Portuguese crowns were united. The silver flowed into Asia through both Pacific and Atlantic routes, with as much as 72 metric tons of silver equivalent being shipped from Europe to India and Pacific Asia each year by the end of the sixteenth century.

Japan produced an even greater amount of silver after improvements were made in mining technology in the mid-seventeenth century. Japan's exports of silver peaked at almost exactly the same time as did those from the New World (see graph) until the shogun banned all silver exports in 1668. This silver fueled the commercialization and urbanization of late Ming society, but before arriving in China it often moved through other parts of Asia, such as Hoi-An (Vietnam), Manila (Philippines), Patani (Malay Peninsula), and Ayuthuya (Siam), where it accelerated

their commercial expansion as well. At the same time, New World silver was being minted as Spanish coins which became so plentiful as to serve as the *de facto* Pacific Asia standard currency.

The initial successes of the Spanish and Dutch were at least partially the result of their access to this Pacific silver trade. Until the shogun's ban, Dutch shipments of Japanese silver had proven vital in financing early Dutch investment in the region, enabling them to consolidate their trade centers. For the Spanish, the twice-annual runs from Acapulco to Manila by the fabled "Manila Galleon," laden with New World silver, became the mainstay of the colony and of the Asian regional monetary system. Carried beyond Manila by Muslim traders, New World silver permeated markets from Mandalay to Macao.

The financial link between Asia and the New World became even more readily apparent during the war between England and Spain that began in 1739. When a galleon crossing from Acapulco was captured by the British, the silver shortage was soon felt in markets across East Asia and Southeast Asia. In response, the Dutch, who were already feeling the competitive commercial pressures from the British, took the unprecedented

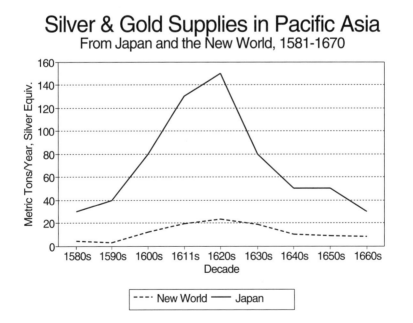

Graph 2.3

measure of sending ships laden with goods across the Pacific from their center in Batavia (Jakarta) to Mexico in a scheme to purchase silver directly from Acapulco. Although rebuffed by the Spanish officials, the Dutch incursions into the Pacific alongside those of the British confirmed a growing awareness that the Pacific could no longer be treated as a "Spanish lake."

The Dutch strove to maintain and expand their trade in the Indonesian Archipelago even though, relative to the British, their fortunes were in decline. This seems largely to have been a consequence of their lack of realistic cost-accounting of the burdens, military and administrative, in maintaining such a remote, far-flung trading regime. It has been argued that the British would have encountered similar difficulties had not the economic boom of the Industrial Revolution buoyed their economy to an extent far beyond that enjoyed by the Dutch whose colonial economy struggled to adjust to the declining market for spices. The British trading regime, based primarily on a growing Europe-India-China trade in cotton and textiles, later on tea and opium, continued to grow and flourish. By the late eighteenth century, British capital and shipping overwhelmed that of any other European nation in the "Far East." For the most part, this trade was with China.

Explorers, Whalers, and the Fur Trade

One of the many remarkable facts about Magellan's voyage is that he managed to sail the entire breadth of the island-strewn Pacific Ocean without sighting a single inhabited spot of land until his landfall at the Marianas in 1521. Nor did the captains of the Manila galleons, in subsequent decades, discover the Hawaiian Islands whose support would have made the arduous eastward voyage across the north Pacific longer but easier. Even the young Spanish explorer Mendaña, outfitted by his uncle, the Viceroy of Peru, sailed right between the two major island groups in the South Pacific, the Marquesas and Tuamotus, without sighting either of them. With a mutinous crew, he struggled across the Pacific to reach the Solomon archipelago in Melanesia, pillaged the region for six months, and returned with charts so inaccurate

that the Solomons remained unlocatable by Europeans for another two hundred years.

Such misadventures make the contrast presented by the British explorer James Cook all the more striking. At a time when knowledge of the Pacific Ocean geography was so deficient that Jonathan Swift would locate Gulliver's Lilliput and Brobdingnag there, Cook's three successive voyages in the latter half of the eighteenth century left little to be discovered in the Oceanic region. He ventured from the far south among the great Antarctic icebergs to the far north where he charted the Aleutian chain of present-day Alaska. In between he discovered and accurately mapped numerous island groups, including the Hawaiian chain where, in one of the few altercations he ever had with indigenous peoples, he was tragically killed.

Lesser but still significant voyages of discovery were made in the Pacific both before and after Cook. The British admiralty sent three notable explorers, John Byron, Samuel Wallis, and Philip Carteret into the Pacific just prior to Cook's first voyage, resulting in the discovery of Tahiti and regions of Melanesia. The French matched the British at the time with a notable voyage (1767-69) through the South Pacific by their explorer, Louis Antoine de Bougainville. Similarly, the Dutch commissioned several explorations of the Australian coastline which they had encountered in their voyages to the Indies (without ever establishing that it was a single continent). So acquisitive was their purpose, however, that they censured their most famous explorer, Abel Tasman, for having encountered no rich treasures or cities in spite of his discoveries of New Zealand and southern Tonga.

With these discoveries by the end of the eighteenth century, Europeans and Americans vastly increased their knowledge of Pacific Basin geography. Still, the Pacific region known as Oceania remained relatively unexploited at first except for such marginal uses as that of Australia as a British penal colony. Then, from around 1780, whaling vessels began to test the potential of the vast ocean regions. Soon, British whalers were entering the Pacific regularly, followed by the Americans. The earliest fleets of both countries searched for sperm whales off the coasts of Chile and Peru, moving on to successive schooling grounds across the Pacific

DEVELOPMENTS IN ISLAND SOUTHEAST ASIA

For the fifteenth through the seventeenth century, the great formative age of Island Southeast Asia, it is possible to deal with the history of the area as a whole — from Aceh and Kedah to Luzon and the Moluccus — in terms of certain great common themes. In that age, trade, stimulated by intense demand for cloves, nutmeg, and pepper, flourished and widened; along the trade routes, Islam spread throughout the islands, and Catholicism came to the northern Philippines; everywhere new port states arose and the Europeans made their entrance in force. These broad movements introduced or deepened certain commonalities of experience throughout much of Southeast Asia — the Malay language as a lingua franca, the widespread fraternity of Islam, the general importance of trade as the economic base of politics, and European naval paramountcy.

By the mid-eighteenth century, if not earlier, these general movements had spent their force. The spread of Malay had halted, not to resume until the twentieth century. Islam was no longer a revolutionary force, and Catholicism, too, in its area in the northern Philippines, was then simply the established religion. Cloves, nutmeg, and pepper were no longer the prizes of world commerce; the economically important products coffee, sugar, tobacco, and tin were, or came to be, concentrated in the three centers of Java, the northern Philippines, and the Straits [of Malacca]. The rest of Island Southeast Asia was economically marginal.

It was also politically marginal. The Spanish had settled down in the northern Philippines, playing no part, aside from perennial disputes with their immediate Muslim neighbors, in the broader politics of the archipelago. The Islamic port states of north-coast Java had been reabsorbed into the agrarian life of Java, and so, in their own way, had the Dutch. Between the mid-eighteenth and late nineteenth century, the Dutch were mainly occupied with exploiting the economic possibilities that political control of Java's large population offered, having neither the capacity nor the inclination for the far-flung naval and commercial dominion they had exercised in the seventeenth century. A third major center was beginning to take shape in just this period, as the English East India Company moved in to establish bases in the Straits Settlements and to exert its influence over the affairs of the Malay Peninsula. But, though the British Navy dominated the seas, and Singapore the commerce, of the archipelago, the British had no desire for territorial rule in those years.

— David Joel Steinberg, ed., *In Search of Southeast Asia*

as each became depleted. A surge of American whaling in the Pacific was stimulated most of all by the War of 1812 which drove the unprotected American whalers temporarily off the Atlantic grounds and around Cape Horn. Once the richness of the Pacific was realized, the Yankee whaling fleets from Nantucket and New Bedford moved in aggressively and by the mid-eighteenth century dominated the scene. The impact of this massive intrusion on indigenous people of the Pacific islands and on unique island ecologies was devastating. Introduced diseases, new competitive species, alcohol, and firearms all took a heavy toll.

Out of the growing trade with China there emerged a second type of commerce that depended on products from these small, semi-isolated islands and the ocean shallows surrounding them. Traders sought desperately for special products that the Chinese would deem worthy of purchase, the manufactured trinkets of the West having made little impression on the emperor and his people. In their search for tradeable goods, the Pacific merchants stumbled on an aromatic Pacific island wood, sandalwood, for which demand became so great in China that every island in the Pacific Basin was soon stripped of it.

> *"If they shall offer you gold or silver in exchange for your articles, you will pretend to hold the same in slight regard, showing them copper, pewter, or lead and giving them an impression as if the minerals last mentioned were by us set greater value on."*
>
> — Dutch East India Company instructions to Abel Tasman

Trepang (the exotic seafloor-dwelling slug used by Chinese in their gourmet foods), pearls, and tortoise shell were objects of intensive exploitation in the island regions as well.

European markets also had an early impact on the exploitation of living Pacific Basin resources, particularly in the northern reaches of the Rim where fur-bearing animals could be hunted and trapped. Russian court circles became extravagant in the prices they would pay for fine furs. Soon the stations of the Russian-American Fur Company stretched from Alaska almost to San Francisco. The ever-competitive Americans steadily pressed the British and Russians traders back during this era, eventually confining both by treaty: the Russians to what is now the southeastern limb of Alaska and the British to points from Vancouver Island northward. In 1867 the Russians retired from Alaska altogether when the region was purchased from them for a mere $7.2 million.

NINETEENTH-CENTURY COMMERCIAL CAPITALISM IN PACIFIC ASIA

The Growth of British Commercial Power

The Industrial Revolution began to gather force at the beginning of the nineteenth century as British manufacturing technology, the most advanced in the world, caused a dramatic rise in the nation's productive capacity. Foreign markets, it was assumed, were the only means by which this new capacity could be absorbed. At the same time, the global labor force began to shift significantly. Asia's population (counting India) constituted two-thirds of the world in 1800. By 1900 it was but 55 percent by current estimates. Europe's population doubled and North America's increased from about 7 million to more than 80 million through mass emigration. (Europe's birth rate at the time was very high; equivalent to many developing countries today.) The growing industrial might of the Atlantic world, then, was underlain by growing and dynamically changing national work forces. Asia was viewed from this perspective merely as a necessary component of European growth. Asian markets offered what appeared to be an outlet for the booming productivity of the new manufacturing era and the intense international competition it spawned.

Among the manufactured goods that rapidly saturated the domestic European markets, textiles presented a special problem. Large investments had been made and thousands of people employed in order to achieve maximum efficiency in production. If new consumers were to be found to justify these large investments, reasoned the British textile barons of Manchester, something needed to be done about the monopoly enjoyed by the East India Company. Particularly with respect to its crown-guaranteed monopoly over trade with India and China, the Company not only prevented the Manchester businessmen from entering the Asian markets, it also imported cheap Indian textiles to compete with them on their own domestic and European turf. A collision between these two powerful interests loomed as the textile producers faced declining markets and rising unemployment.

In the nineteenth century, Great Britain's global economic presence surpassed that of any other nation, its military victories over France having placed it at an increasing advantage in the expansion of its commerce with Europe, the New World, and Asia. By the time the world economy began to accelerate in the latter half of the nineteenth century, the British were sending twice as many ships to China as to all other nations combined. The area officially or actually under British control at the time amounted to a quarter of the surface of the globe. If the so-called informal empire of independent states that were, in effect, satellite economies of Britain were included, perhaps a third of the globe was British in an economic and, in many respects, cultural sense by 1900.

Global trade, in general, expanded significantly. Between 1800 and 1840 the volume of trade worldwide doubled. It increased by another 260 percent between 1850 and 1870 and, as it accelerated, China's place in the global expansion — and the British economy — became all the more significant. The demand for tea, by 1800 a "national drink" in England, was soaring. Britain not only dominated the tea trade, the government earned a tenth of its total revenue from taxing it. The economies of Britain and China were becoming increasingly intertwined.

These trends coincided with the growing phenomenon of "imperialism," a controversial term that has become synonymous with the use of military force to back economic hegemony and territorial aggrandizement. In fact, there is an ongoing debate over the extent to which economic factors actually caused imperialist expansion. The need to project power for its own sake, for example, has also been proposed as a driving force. Various explanations for imperialism are summarized later in this chapter. The focus here will be on the economic and political developments associated with imperialism as it began to transform Pacific Asia.

The British in China: Overtures and Opportunities

From the beginning, the Manchu rulers of China had managed to closely monitor and control their trade with a variety of European trading concerns including a small degree of overland contact with the Russians. As noted above, most of the earliest trade was conducted through the port of Guangzhou where the Chinese demanded that exchanges take place. At first, the advantage was clearly on China's side: The Westerners sought silk and tea but had little to offer in return except gold and silver. In addition, they were required to pay a number of commercial taxes alongside the regular bribery or "squeeze" for local officials. All such exactions were an arbitrary, unpredictable element

from the foreigner's viewpoint but to the Chinese they were entirely legitimate. After all, they had not sought the trade. To them it was all part of the tribute system in which inferior vassal states sought trading privileges with China. As for Western-style commercial treaties, it was unthinkable that any of these vassal states should claim equal and independent status on Chinese soil.

The fact is often overlooked that for nearly three centuries after the first Portuguese maritime contact the Chinese successfully demanded that trade be conducted on their terms. Then, as Manchu power waned and the value of the China trade grew, the Western traders began to contemplate ways to break the restrictions. The rising military power of the British in conjunction with an expanding, liberal trading regime in the Atlantic world reinforced their view that the exactions of the Guangzhou trade should no longer be tolerated.

At first it seemed that policy adjustments by China might evolve smoothly. In 1792 the British sent an embassy led by Lord Macartney to the court in Beijing for the purpose of negotiating the removal of the restraints on their trade. Macartney

Fig 2.2 "China in the Bull Shop." Rival shopkeepers outside [German, French, and Russian]: caption read, "Wonder if he's going to buy anything here. *We* haven't got any orders out of him!"

entered the city at the head of a splendid procession whose banners bore inscriptions in Chinese "Ambassador bearing tribute from the country of England." Perhaps this preemptive obeisance served its purpose, for he was allowed an audience with the emperor without conducting the humiliating "kowtow," or nine full-length prostrations, before the throne. This was the only manifest accomplishment of the Macartney mission, the Qing emperor having expressed no interest either in proposals for new terms or new trade goods.

The British, irritated but undaunted, sent a second mission under the leadership of Lord Amherst, but this time their emissary was treated rudely. Harangued about his unwillingness to perform the kowtow, Amherst was denied even an audience with the emperor. The result was a hardening of positions on both sides with the Chinese more convinced than ever that they had made their point: The barbarians were supplicants who must "tremble and obey" the edicts of the Imperial Court. For their part, the British and the rest of the foreign community (which remained confined to uncomfortable quarters on the outskirts of

Guangzhou) became convinced of the opposite: that the time had come to demand a commercial treaty that would regularize duties and other impositions on free trade.

Since any abrupt demands could easily lead to the expulsion of the traders, it might have taken many years to turn sentiment into action had it not been for three key factors:

- Rapid growth in the opium trade.

- Disputes over national jurisdiction.

- Abolition of the East India Company's trade monopoly in China.

The Problem of Opium

As a trade item, opium was very late in arriving in China. It was used as early as the Tang dynasty for medicinal purposes but, as a drug, its use came about through a juxtaposition of foreign influences. First, China was introduced to the practice of smoking by the Spanish via the Philippines trade in the early seventeenth century. Next, the Dutch demonstrated the mixture of opium with tobacco as a malaria preventative during their occupation of Formosa (Taiwan). The practice then spread across China where it soon became common to smoke opium by itself.

The initial maritime traders in opium were the Portuguese, but other Europeans quickly added it to their China-bound cargoes as it was one of the few trade goods for which they found a strong and growing Chinese demand. Most opium was produced in India where it had long been chewed, not smoked, as a drug. As drug addiction grew in China to alarming levels during the eighteenth century, the Emperor banned its use and the cultivation of its source, the poppy. This only contributed to the demand for foreign opium, however. China's growing consumption of opium in the nineteenth century reached explosive levels, both in terms of its volume and the international political tensions it exacerbated.

As noted earlier, the dominant British role in the opium trade can be traced to Clive's victory in India in the mid-eighteenth century when the British East India Company took control over Bengal, a major production center for opium. Although a significant amount of the drug continued to be produced in China itself, the British promoted the expansion of poppy cultivation in India with the China market very much in mind: The drain of specie caused by the Company's massive purchases of China tea had created a serious imbalance of payments in China's favor. Now the Company was about to reverse the flow.

Wrapped in poppy petals and packed in three-pound balls inside wooden chests, the opium was auctioned to private traders by the Company in Calcutta. The Company itself refused to conduct a direct trade in opium with Guangzhou but took pains to arrange its transport there by specially licensed ships. The hypocrisy of the arrangement was not lost on contemporary observers who noted that every such ship sailed with orders that forbade the transport of opium "lest the Company be implicated" in the trade with the Chinese.

Strong moral opposition to the trade soon emerged among missionaries and physicians who called international attention to the growing problem of opium addiction in China. For their part, the Chinese emperors resisted the importation of the drug officially but only to the extent of prohibiting

REPLY OF THE QING EMPEROR TO BRITAIN'S KING GEORGE III

On you, O king, who live in a remote and inaccessible region, far across the spaces of ocean, but who have shown your submissive loyalty by sending this tribute mission, I have heaped great benefits. Ever since the beginning of history sage emperor and wise rulers have bestowed on China a moral system and code which has been religiously observed by the myriad of my subjects. Your ambassador's request that barbarians shall be given full liberty to spread their religion is utterly unreasonable.

I set no value on objects strange or ingenious and have no use for your country's manufactures, Our Celestial Empire possesses all things. There was no need to import the manufactures of outside barbarians in exchange for our own produce. But as the tea, silk, and porcelain which the Celestial Empire produces are absolute necessities to European nations, and to yourself, we have permitted as a signal mark of favor, that your wants might be supplied at the port of Guangzhou [Canton]. Should your vessels touch the shore [elsewhere] your merchants will assuredly never be permitted to land or to reside there.

Tremblingly obey and show no negligence!

— A decree of the Qianlong Emperor

its purchase by the Guangzhou official (the "hoppo") who had been placed in charge of determining import duties and by conducting police actions of very limited success. Generally, the smuggling of opium was a simple if somewhat inconvenient matter involving the local "Cohong" guild of officially licensed brokers.

There evolved, then, a combination of "push" and "pull" factors in the opium trade: British

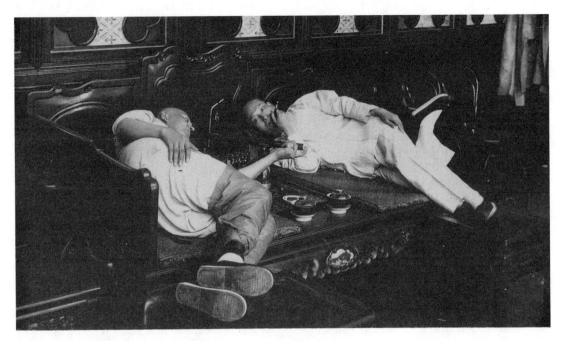

Figure 2.3   An "opium den" in China.

commercial expansion depended on it to balance the cost of purchasing silk and tea while, on the other side, the spread of an internal smuggling system in China corrupted the system from within. Independent British traders, such as the firm of Jardine Matheson, vigorously defended the opium trade on which their personal empire was constructed. William Jardine bolstered his argument by noting that both Houses of Parliament "with all the bench of bishops at their back" had declared it impractical for Britain to give up the drug trade.

"A Drug on the Market":
The Deregulation of Sino-British Trade

The commerce in opium received a further stimulus in 1833 when by an act of Parliament the British East India Company lost its government-approved monopoly of British trade at Guangzhou. At last, the powerful textile lobby had succeeded in toppling its rival. The denial of the trade monopoly, which had been a lucrative source of revenue to the Company, preceded the body's dissolution a few years later (1858) by Queen Victoria.

The immediate effect of the deregulation of the British trade was to cause a flood of new merchants to attempt entry into it, resulting in a vast oversupply of goods being brought to Chinese ports. The trade in opium was no exception, and for a time its price plummeted (the phrase "a drug on the market," i.e., an excessive supply of an item amid saturated demand, comes from this period). Many firms went bankrupt or retired from such commerce.

The more profound effect of the demise of the East India Company was to alter the nature of British representation in China. As long as the Company had maintained control over the China trade, it meant that the British accepted the rules imposed on them by the Qing court and also (from a Chinese perspective) acquiesced to the notion that the Chinese Emperor held a status superior to that of the British crown. This fundamental, if tacit, assumption now had to be confronted, however much the British merchants in Guangzhou might have wished otherwise. No longer were they in the hands of the cooperative Company representative but of Queen Victoria herself.

The arrival in 1834 of the first such representative, Lord Napier, was confrontational from the beginning. Not only did he land outside Guangzhou without first obtaining the customary permission from the Cohong, but as if to compound the insult, he attempted to communicate by means of a "letter" rather than the officially labeled "petition" which reflected the status of a vassal state. On being ordered by the Cohong to return to Macao, Napier refused and retaliated by distributing handbills denouncing the Qing officials. They then cut off his supplies, whereon he ordered his two frigates to open fire on the forts guarding the principle entry to the river and attempted literally to blast his way into Guangzhou. The attack proved ineffective, and after intermediation by more cool-headed parties on both sides, Napier retired to Macao where he died of an illness.

The humiliating failure of Napier's mission left Guangzhou in a precarious state. Although trade continued as before for several years, tensions mounted between the traders and the population. For China, the spread of opium addiction and its consequent drain on the country's silver supply had reached alarming proportions. To the British, it mattered not whether the trade was in opium, cotton, sewing needles, or any other product, for they did not view opium as a nefarious, addictive drug. Laudanum, an opiate, was frequently prescribed for the treatment of "nerves" and for colic in infants. Opium was seen as a legitimate trade item in a widening network of commerce from which, it was said, China could not remain isolated.

The final incendiary touch to the situation came with the appointment of a genuinely incorruptible official, Lin Zexu (Lin Tse-hsü), to oversee the Guangzhou trade in 1839. His draconian measures to stop the drug trade were generally successful, forcing the British to surrender vast stores of their opium stocks. Paradoxically, his actions played into British hands: the office of the Crown in Guangzhou took responsibility for the loss on behalf of the government, thus laying claim to an indemnity from China.

Then, to compound the tensions between both sides, an incident occurred in which some drunken British sailors killed a Chinese man. The Chinese authorities demanded that the sailors be turned over to them for trial, creating a crisis in what had become an increasingly provocative issue in

China's "barbarian relations": the question of national jurisdiction.

Extraterritoriality

A longstanding problem for European ships in Chinese ports of call had always been the matter of who should have authority over the behavior of "rough and ready" sailors on shore. For centuries, the Chinese had been able to maintain their claim to this authority, the most famous case in which they prevailed being that of an Italian sailor named Terranova. In 1821, while serving aboard an American ship anchored in Guangzhou, he was accused in the death of a Chinese woman who apparently had been selling goods next to the ship. After protracted negotiations during which all

---

THE ECONOMICS OF OPIUM

From the opium trade the Honourable [East India] Company have derived for years an immense revenue and through them the British Government and nation have also reaped an incalculable amount of political and financial advantage. The turn of the balance of trade between Great Britain and China in favour of the former has enabled India to increase tenfold her consumption of British manufacture; contributed directly to support the vast fabric of British dominion in the East, to defray the expense of His Majesty's establishment in India, and by the operation of exchanges and remittances in teas, to pour an abundant revenue into the British Exchequer and benefit the nation to an extent of £6 million yearly without impoverishing India. Therefore the Company has done everything it its power to foster the opium trade.

— S. Warren, in a contemporary pamphlet entitled *Opium,* 1839

trade with Americans was halted, Terranova was turned over to the Chinese courts who found him guilty and had him executed.

From the Chinese viewpoint, incidents such as this merely confirmed the generally inferior, possibly even dangerous, state of barbarian culture and society when compared with that of China. They saw the foreign sailors as a generally raucous and violent group that had to be held in check. Besides, all foreigners were by definition subservient to the laws of China, particularly with respect to incidents that occurred on Chinese soil. The Westerners, on the other hand, were appalled by what they saw as the completely arbitrary process of Chinese justice in which courts might try an individual for a crime he or she did not actually commit as long as some vague connection for "responsibility" might be made and an act of retribution taken. The Chinese also frequently practiced torture. Not that this was at all unknown to the Europeans, but when undertaken by "Orientals" against whites it seemed all the more sinister and horrific.

The 1839 case of a Chinese man murdered by British sailors raised these issues anew. This time the British were not inclined to be so compliant as the Americans had been in the Terranova case — nor was their military position so weak. The question was a matter of vital symbolic importance to each side, particularly because it coincided with what were now British claims to a cash indemnity from China for its destruction of their opium. Both countries were willing to back their positions with force. After retreating from Guangzhou to Macao where they held a more militarily defensible position, the British began a series of naval assaults on China.

The First Opium War

That the Chinese seem to have had little appreciation of their relative military weakness at this time is suggested by their initial action in sending a fleet of war junks against two British naval ships at Hong Kong. The British easily destroyed four of the Chinese vessels and went on to blockade Guangzhou in 1840, bombarding it and other coastal cities in 1841. By 1842, the southern capital of Nanjing lay at the mercy of the British fleet (which from the outset had been a relatively tiny force by British standards) and China was forced

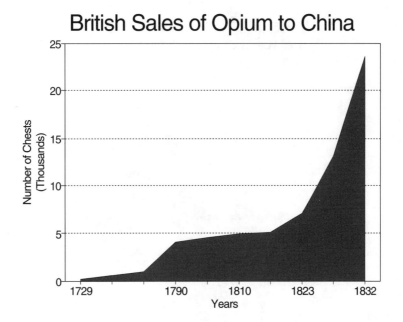

Graph 2.4

to sign what became known as the Treaty of Nanjing. Incorporated a year later into a second treaty (Treaty of the Bogue, 1843) its terms were then used as a precedent by the American diplomat Caleb Cushing to negotiate the Treaty of Wanghia (1844) in the United States which considerably expanded on the rights of extraterritoriality. The French quickly followed suit with their own treaty.

This series of so-called unequal treaties signaled a turning point in China's fortunes. The blow to its prestige was to reverberate and expand throughout the rest of the nineteenth century, exacerbated by a variety of other internal factors, culminating in 1911 in the fall of the Qing dynasty amid revolutionary change (see chapter 4). Most importantly, the new treaty system affirmed the principle of diplomatic equality between China and its treaty partners, shattering the fictive remnants of the ancient tribute system. Only the standards of Western diplomacy could be applied. Foreign trade, no longer confined to Guangzhou, was forcibly expanded to other port cities, such as Amoy, Fuzhou (Foochow), Ningpo, and Shanghai. Tariffs were fixed and subject to revision only on approval of the Western signatories. One of the most important British acquisitions was the Island

of Hong Kong which became a base for rapidly expanding commerce all along the China coast. China's war indemnity to Britain was also heavy, amounting to $21,000,000. Finally, the right of jurisdiction by foreign consuls over their own nationals (extraterritoriality) was established, particularly by the Whanghia Treaty.

From China's viewpoint, it fought the initial war with Great Britain in an effort to stem the opium trade. There can be no doubt of the importance of the economic stakes represented by opium, but it can also be argued that the globalization of commerce in the nineteenth century sooner or later would have encroached on China's perception of its lofty international status. Beyond mere condemnation of the foreigners' actions in that initial confrontation, it is important to understand the forces that moved China and the West toward a collision. These forces had been developing for years prior to the Opium War and involved a broad disjuncture between two great civilizations. Each side believed that it represented the highest manifestation of human social and cultural achievement. China took great pride in the duration and grandeur of its empire, the central core of which was a system of bureaucratic governance and absolute imperial authority based on idealized

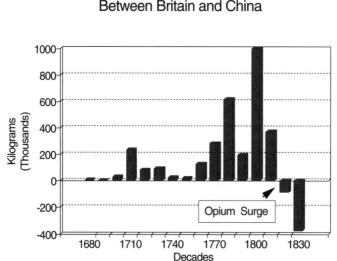

Reversal of the Silver Flow
Between Britain and China

Graph 2.5

Confucian principles. In contrast, the expanding British empire was based on what it saw as natural rules of commerce that must be applied equally among all nations according to the "scientific" principles of economics as defined by such thinkers as Adam Smith. For China, the appropriate signs of progress and advancement were expressed by a highly refined scholarship and philosophical system. For the British, the *sina qua non* of a nation's progress was scientific knowledge, industrial development, and military capability.

Failure of the Early Treaties

What seemed to the foreigners to have been a clear and decisive victory in the 1840-41 "Opium War" was anything but that to the Chinese. As yet, the West had touched only the margin of the country, a fringe of coastal merchants, bannermen, and officials who, even if they had wanted to, could not have conveyed the facts of these developments to the vast populace of the interior. In the Imperial Court, the treaties were viewed as a temporary setback, a matter of current necessity, rather than a historical turning point. The mere fact that the treaties at last required China to deal as a diplomatic equal with the barbarians did not mean that it had altered its assumption of national superiority. Instead, it set out to nullify and weaken in practice that which the treaties had set in motion.

Even without China's maneuvers to weaken their effects, the treaties by themselves were inadequate instruments with which to manage the enormous strains that were building between the foreigners and the Chinese. In particular, the treaties did nothing to ease the tensions in Guangzhou; if anything, they only heightened them.

Meanwhile, Shanghai was becoming the center of foreign commerce. Situated next to the richest silk-producing region in China and populated by merchants who were more accommodative of foreign traders, Shanghai quickly surpassed Guangzhou in trade volume, its exports tripling within eight years after the initial treaties were signed. Shanghai's greater acceptance of Westerners relative to Guangzhou was apparent: foreigners were permitted to establish their own "concessions," that is, residential and working areas within the city. The Shanghai foreign settlement grew rapidly and without disruption, swelled by immigrant Chinese. Even though each foreign concession was subject to the authority of its own government, thousands of Chinese were quick to perceive that the settlements offered a unique refuge from the political turmoil in the provinces. As early as 1854, the Shanghai settlements could count twenty thousand Chinese residents. By contrast, in Guangzhou foreigners continued to be refused entry into the walled city. Several violent clashes followed.

A further source of friction between China and the West emerged in the form of the so-called coolie trade, which responded to a growing demand for labor in Cuba, Peru, and Southeast Asia. Nominally, the Chinese "coolies" were contract laborers but once they were on board the transports the deception of the "contracts" became apparent. The ships became floating hells not unlike the slave ships that crossed the Atlantic from Africa. Both the British and the Americans strove to halt the trade, but its continuance only confirmed China's Imperial Court in its view that the "barbarians" comprised for the most part drug traffickers, criminals, and rapacious merchants. Even the missionaries among them seemed to be obsessed with expanding their influence, seeking to convert the "heathen" masses of China while vying against one another for territory.

In Guangzhou, tensions rose to a point that made open confrontation once again almost inevitable. The ensuing war, the Second Opium War or "Arrow War," takes its name from an incident that finally set the spark to these incendiary circumstances, the Chinese seizure of a ship flying the British flag (see box).

China now faced a growing social and political crisis. Domestic rebellions continued to erupt, (see chapters 1 and 3), population pressures were growing, opium addiction was rampant, and the disruptive influences, both cultural and economic, of foreign commerce continued to penetrate the Chinese interior. The country desperately needed new leadership and a new vision. It required, in addition, a new perspective on the nature of Western societies with which to gauge more realistically its own capacities for competition and adaptation in the new global environment. To its further disadvantage, China at the time had neither a foreign ministry nor official representation in a Western capital except for an ad hoc foreign ministry, the Zongli Yamen. Embassies abroad had been deemed as unnecessary for the Middle Kingdom.

The prospects for a change in this situation seemed to improve in 1866 when Robert Hart, Inspector-General of the Customs Service, went to Europe on leave accompanied by Pin Zhun, a Manchu noble. After visiting the courts of Europe where he was accorded considerable respect as an envoy, Pin Zhun returned to Beijing and delivered an essentially negative report to the court. Relating the outlandish customs of the foreigners, he only confirmed the other nobles in their prejudices that indeed China had nothing to learn from the West. The results of this mission can be contrasted to that of the Japanese who were traveling abroad at the same time, absorbing at every step information to be used in the process of their country's modernization.

This is not to say that the Chinese took no initiatives toward foreign education. A group of Chinese students was sent to the United States in 1872 with the hope by their sponsors, the visionary generals/officials Li Hongzhang (Li Hungchang) and Zeng Guofan (Tseng Kuo-fan), that they would become a vanguard of learning for China in fields such as manufacturing, mining, and shipbuilding. The results were mixed. Some students were reluctant to return home and the overall number sent abroad was limited to a few classes before the project was cancelled. Even so, there emerged a group of Chinese scholars and leaders who formed a "Self-Strengthening Movement" during the late nineteenth century in recognition of the urgent need to make China strong by learning from the West (described in chapter 3).

By 1860 China lay open to new exploitation by merchants and to proselytizing by missionaries. Foreigners, backed by gunboats and the unequal treaties, oversaw the regulation of customs duties. In the view of Westerners at the time, the use of force against China was a result of that country's own backward-looking intransigence. The Chinese view was more fragmented, for although some Chinese enterprises did flourish under the protection of visionary reformers, the country as a whole did not see the necessity for

---

ON HANDLING BARBARIANS

"Barbarian affairs are hard to manage but the basic principles are no more than the four words of Confucius: chung [zhong], hsin [xin], tu [du], and ching [jing] faithfulness, sincerity, earnestness, and respectfulness. . . . Hsin means merely not to tell a lie, but it is very difficult to avoid doing so.

In your association with foreigners your manner and deportment should not be too lofty, and you should have a slightly vague, casual appearance. Let their insults, deceitfulness, and contempt for everything appear to be understood by you and yet seem not understood, for you should look somewhat stupid."

— Zeng Guofan to Li Hongzhang, 1862

CHINA DURING THE QING DYNASTY

States and regions formerly
under Chinese dominance:

Amur, 1689; to Russia, 1858
Dzungaria, 1757; to Russia, 1847
Korea 1627; to Japan, 1895
Taiwan, 1683; to Japan, 1895
Nepal, 1792; fully independent, 1908
Burma, 1769; to Britain, 1886
Tonkin; to France, 1884

| Imperial capital |
| Provincial capital |
| *ZHILI* Province |
| *MANCHURIA* Regions |
| Boundaries of Qing Empire ca.1900 |
| Boundaries of China proper |
| Provincial boundaries |

widespread commercial reform and it deeply resented the enforced "opening." The great success of the Chinese in developing their commercial and intellectual life over the previous centuries made their reformers' calls for radical change all the less compelling.

Cross-Cultural Influences

The clash of cultures, East and West, should not obscure the creative exchanges that also took place between them. Individual Asians will be encountered in later chapters who, while in the vanguard of change, did not slavishly copy Western ideas but used them as tools to define new possibilities from within their own traditions and historical experiences. For their part, Westerners showed an equal capacity to use the encounter with the East to open up new intellectual and artistic vistas that resulted in enduring works of art and literature. The exchange can be traced back for many centuries, but it accelerated after regular maritime contact began. Soon after Portugal's initial forays into the

Figure 2.4   A Chinese court.

East, its builders and architects began to reflect Asian influences. Later on, Chinese art and artifacts became the rage in European court circles, special rooms being set aside for purely Chinese decor. By the late nineteenth century, European artists, such as Van Gogh, would be profoundly influenced by Japanese prints. Debussy would write brilliant music for piano inspired by Indonesian gamelan music, and even architect Frank Lloyd Wright, a visitor to Japan at the beginning of the twentieth century, would redesign American houses in ways that echo, if not fully acknowledge, Japanese architecture.

THE GROWING EUROPEAN PRESENCE IN SOUTHEAST ASIA

The geographic dispersion of European power in Southeast Asia was relatively limited in the seventeenth and eighteenth centuries. Rarely did the newcomers exert a strong influence on the populace beyond the port areas until, as interaction and political pressures increased in the nineteenth century, military conflicts spread their impact into the hinterlands. Even so, the combination of varying geographical circumstances, uneven degrees of contact, and cultural diversity in each instance led to a wide range of responses:

Burma. A dispute over border areas lying between Burma and the British East India Company's territory in northeast India, as well as disputes with British traders, led to a military clash and the temporary British control of Rangoon in 1826. Later, in the early 1850s, events in Rangoon echoed the cultural-economic frictions that had occurred in China a decade before: A local Burmese official tried to discipline the foreigners, leading to a "Second Burma War," and the British acquired the rich agricultural and timber area of Lower Burma. By 1886 they had captured Mandalay and lay claim to the entire kingdom.

HONG KONG: A HISTORY OF EBBS AND FLOWS

The island of Hong Kong was ceded to Britain in 1842 by the Treaty of Nanjing at the end of the Opium War (1839-42), the causes of which have been attributed to conflicts between China and Britain over questions of diplomacy, trade, jurisdiction, and the sale of opium. Yet Britain's decision to resort to arms and to demand the cession of land must also be explained in light of its growing interest and expansion of activities in the East. When Sino-Western trade was confined to Guangzhou under the Cohong system, the idea of securing a place from China had been expressed in Macartney's Embassy (1793), Amherst's Mission (1816), and again in that of Napier (1834). Historical evidence indicates that British merchants were pushing actively in the early 1830s for the acquisition of Hong Kong. Despite the fact that some British had preferred Zhoushan Island and that Lord Palmerston was very dissatisfied with the cession, as Hong Kong was to him "a barren island with hardly a house on it," the island was retained as others realized its strategic and commercial significance, lying right on the path of the chief trade route to China and with a deep and sheltered harbor. The possession was to serve then as a British diplomatic, commercial, and military post in the East.

Kowloon Peninsula, on the northern side of the Victoria Harbor, had been used by the British troops for camping in the 1850s. When China suffered defeat again by the Anglo-French expeditions in 1858, the resulting Convention of Beijing (1860) ceded the peninsula, including Stonecutters Island, to Britain. The extension of the Hong Kong boundaries to include the New Territories on a ninety-nine-year lease was one of the concessions forced on China by the foreign powers following its defeat by Japan in 1895. The demand from Britain in 1898 was based on its claim for the defense of Hong Kong against France, Russia, and Germany in their encroachment for "spheres of influence" in China.

At the time of the British takeover, the island's population numbered about 5,000 farmers and fishermen. After 1841, Chinese laborers, encouraged by prospects of work, began to come to the new settlement and, by 1844, the population reached 19,000. Yet Hong Kong's early growth was unspectacular as compared with Shanghai's development, and conditions were not conducive to attracting emigrants of respectable background. Then the Taiping Rebellion (1851-64) created unsettled conditions on the mainland, resulting in thousands of people of every social class and occupation seeking refuge in the colony. By 1861, the population had risen to about 119,300, of whom 116,335 were Chinese.

Hong Kong's development began with the expansion of population in the 1850s. Its continued growth, however, was the product of a number of factors operating in the second half of the nineteenth century and after. These included the opening of China to Western trade and influence, followed by the opening of Japan (1854) and Korea (1876); the opening of trade routes in the Pacific Ocean and with Europe (Suez Canal, 1869); the development of England as an industrial and commercial power; and its free trade and laissez-faire policy. In addition, the geographical position of Hong Kong, its harbor, and the security provided by the Hong Kong administration were also important reasons for prosperity. Its entrepôt trade at first was mainly with Britain, India, and China, with opium as a major commodity. Later in the century other goods, such as rice, sugar, and textiles, became more important, and the areas of trade were extended to Japan, Korea, Southeast Asia, and the Western Pacific. By 1880 the position of Hong Kong as an entrepôt port was firmly established, handling, on average, about 30 percent of China's external trade. Meanwhile, related commercial enterprises, such as shipping, banking, and insurance, also prospered. After the turn of the century, although Hong Kong was surpassed by Shanghai as the center of British economic interest in China, its intermediary trade with South China, Southeast Asia, Japan, and the Western Pacific continued to increase.

— Ng Lun Ngai-Ha, *EAH*

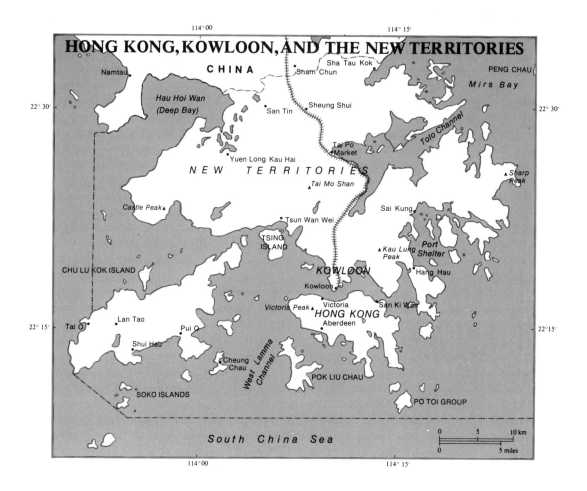

MAP: HONG KONG, KOWLOON, AND THE NEW TERRITORIES

Vietnam. Amid incursions by the French (who held the illusion that Vietnam would be their springboard to the China market) the Nguyen dynasty in Hue struggled to adapt to the growing onslaught of Western ideas and technologies. Emperor Minh Mang, an innovative and progressive-minded leader, even purchased several steamships and tried unsuccessfully to create a working factory in which new ones could be built. Meanwhile, deep schisms appeared in Vietnamese society as the growing number of Catholic converts were seen to defy and undermine traditional customs and beliefs.

In the 1840s, court factions attempted several palace coups and they continued to be a threat after the Tu-duc emperor (1847-1883) was installed. This further weakened the court's ability to conduct institutional reforms that would have enabled it to resist the French incursions more effectively.

Cambodia. From their base in Vietnam, the French were a persistent threat to the weak kingdom of Cambodia, by that time a buffer state between the rival kingdoms of Thailand and Vietnam. Although the ruler, Ang Duong, entertained the possibility of homage to France, it was left to his successor Norodom to finalize the agreement in 1863. In contrast to the way the British extinguished the monarchy in Burma and the French undermined the authority of the Nguyen dynasty in Vietnam, the weak Cambodian king was promoted as the symbolic — but French-controlled — leader of the nation.

Laos. A confusion of petty states and tribal areas in the mid-nineteenth century, the region that is today known as Laos, was the subject of intense competition between the British and French colonialists. The French were eventually to seize the region late in the century under the pretext that Vietnam, which they held entirely, was the traditional suzerain of the Lao states. By 1899 Laos, more a product of imperialist maneuvering than indigenous boundaries, had emerged as a colonial entity that would become an independent state in the postcolonial era.

Thailand. As will be discussed below, Thailand managed to avoid European dominance but was nevertheless profoundly affected by the colonialism that encroached on its borders. In a fortunate combination of geography, internal stability, and skillful political leadership, the kingdom found itself able to buy time, playing the French

THE ARROW WAR

After the Treaty of Nanjing, the people of Guangzhou became increasingly antiforeign and refused to admit the British into the city. The British not only insisted on entering Guangzhou, but also actively sought treaty revision because of their desire to expand trade in China, their demand for resident ministers in Beijing, and their intention to reduce custom duties. Yet the Chinese avoided negotiations [and were led in their opposition] by two xenophobic officials in Guangzhou: Governor-General Xu Guangjin and Governor Ye Mingchen. The new emperor, Xianfeng, was also opposed to Western contact.

Convinced that the treaty system would deteriorate in China if not reaffirmed and extended, Britain finally found a *casus belli* in 1856, when Ye refused to give consul Harry Parks redress for an insult to a British flag lowered by Chinese police from a Chinese-owned vessel registered with the British authorities in Hong Kong the lorcha *Arrow*. The French government, capitalizing on the murder of a missionary, decided on a joint expedition with Britain. The Anglo-French expedition nominally originated in these rather small incidents, in which the rights of the matter were certainly debatable. Nevertheless, the clear-cut underlying issue was whether the Chinese or Western mode of Sino-foreign relations was to prevail.

The Anglo-French forces, led by Lord Elgin and Baron Gros, seized Guangzhou in December 1857 and Tianjin four months later. In June 1858 the Treaties of Tianjin were concluded, containing the following provisions: (1) the establishment of permanent Western legations at Beijing; (2) the opening of ten new ports, including four on the Yangtze River; (3) the permission of foreign travel to all parts of China; (4) the imposition of inland transit dues (*likin*) for foreign imports not to exceed 2.5 percent ad valorem; (5) the payment of an indemnity of six million taels; and (6) the guarantee of freedom of movement throughout China for missionaries.

When the British and French ministers arrived off Tianjin a year later to go to Beijing in order to exchange treaty ratifications, a controversy over the passage to Beijing touched off skirmishes. Elgin and Gros were forced to retreat but returned again in 1860 with stronger forces, occupied Beijing, and burned the Summer Palace. In October they signed the Conventions of Beijing with Prince Gong, the emperor having fled to Manchuria. The new conventions confirmed the treaties of 1858 and included further concessions from China: the indemnity was increased to sixteen million taels; Tianjin was opened to foreign trade; Britain was to acquire the Kowloon Peninsula; and France secured the right for Catholic missionaries to own properties in interior China. Shocked by the Western seizure of Beijing, some Chinese officials initiated the Self-Strengthening Movement through adoption of Western diplomatic practices and military and technological devices.

—Yen-P'ing Hao, *EAH*

CHINA'S ADAPTIVE INSTITUTIONS: THE ZONGLI YAMEN AND THE MARITIME CUSTOMS SERVICE

The **Zongli Yamen** was a subcommittee of the Chinese Grand Council which served as a proto-foreign office at Beijing from 1861 to 1901. China's first major institutional innovation in response to the Western impact, the Zongli Yamen promoted modernization and symbolized China's entrance into the family of nations. To handle diplomatic relations with the West arising from various treaty obligations, the Zongli Yamen (Office for the General Management of Affairs Concerning the Various Countries) was created in March 1861. It was an informal organization, composed of between three and eleven high officials who retained their principal posts elsewhere. It was organized into five bureaus (Russian, British, French, American, and Coastal Defense), with two other offices attached to it: the Maritime Customs Service and the language school called the Tongwenguan.

The Zongli Yamen used international law to protect China's interests in 1864, sponsored the Binchun mission (the first Chinese mission of investigation sent to Europe) in 1866, and secured Anson Burlingame (the retiring American minister to China) as China's first envoy to the Western world in 1868. While the Zongli Yamen marked a forward step, it had weaknesses. All real decisions on foreign policy still had to come from the emperor, and the Yamen was in charge of foreign relations only at Beijing (in the coastal provinces two commissioners for foreign affairs were appointed who reported directly to the emperor).

Although it failed as an effective foreign office, the Yamen, headed by Prince Gong for twenty-seven years (1861-84 and 1894-98), succeeded reasonably well as a promoter of modernization projects, such as modern schools, Western science, industry, and communication. The Zongli Yamen's influence diminished after the 1870s, when Prince Gong lost power with Empress Dowager Cixi and the rise of Li Hongzhang in Tianjin overshadowed the Yamen. It was finally replaced by the newly created Ministry of Foreign Affairs in 1901.

Although regarded by many as imperialistic, the **Maritime Customs Service** of the late nineteenth and early twentieth centuries, nevertheless facilitated foreign trade, gave the imperial court its principal new revenues, introduced the principle of central fiscal control, and fostered China's various modernization efforts.

The foreign inspectorate in the Chinese customs system was created in Shanghai on July 12, 1854 (after the Chinese customs official fled during the Small Sword Society uprising); this practice was later extended to other treaty ports. As head of the Zongli Yamen (Foreign Office), Prince Gong (one of the most progressive and visionary of the Manchu princes) appointed Horatio N. Lay inspector general of customs in 1861; Robert Hart replaced him in 1863. The Service was known in Chinese as the Haiguan, or Maritime Customs, in order to distinguish it from the traditionally established collectorate (Changguan), known to the Westerners as the Native Customs. The traditional Chinese superintendents of maritime customs continued to exercise their functions of banking and remitting duties, but their position gradually lost prominence.

The Imperial Maritime Customs Service, an organization under the authority of the Zongli Yamen, consisted of several offices, such as the inspectorate general's office in Beijing, the statistical and printing office in Shanghai, the office of the nonresident secretary in London, and the offices of the commissioners of customs in various open ports. Under the able leadership of Hart, the Customs became China's first modern civil service, and its staff consisted of some 700 foreign employees (representing twenty-two countries) and 3,500 Chinese by 1895.

(continued on next page)

(continued from previous page)

In addition to applying the customs tariff and collecting a growing revenue for the central government, the Customs provided other useful services: the coastwise lights, charts for navigation, and the services of pilotage and berthing of ships; the modern procedure of customs handling and appraisal of goods; and the publication of essential trade statistics and reports. Its revenue collections were used for many modernization projects: to buy gunboats and equip modern-style troops, to finance the new language schools, to send diplomats and maintain legations abroad, and to create a modern postal service. Because the Customs was staffed by many foreigners and its revenues were used in the twentieth century as security for China's foreign loans and indemnities, however, Chinese patriots condemn it as imperialistic.

Robert Hart (1835-1911), a trusted adviser to the Qing government and a powerful Chinese employee, was a longtime inspector general of the Chinese Maritime Customs Service (1863-1908). He was a prime mover in China's modernization, symbolized the constructive side of the unequal treaty system, and represented Victorian Britain's informed empire in East Asia.

Working hard and supported by Chinese and foreign governments, Hart built up the Customs Service as a modern, administrative arm of the Qing central government that provided financial support to various reform efforts. His concern for the future of the Customs led to his refusal in 1885 to accept the prestigious post of British minister to China. Behind the scenes Hart also was a diplomat who settled the Sino-French War, changed Macao's status, got boundaries delimited with Burma and India, and mitigated the disasters of imperialism.

Hart's tact and capability, coupled with the fact that he was bilingual, endeared him to the court, which took him into confidence as a trusted adviser. In 1865 he submitted a memorandum to the Zongli Yamen (Foreign Office) entitled "Observations by an Outsider," in which he stressed the advantages of mining, railroads, steamships, the telegraph, and Western diplomatic practices. He became deeply involved in the creation of the Naval Yamen in 1885. He promoted the Society for the Diffusion of Christian and General Knowledge (SDK) among the Chinese, translated Western works on international law, started the publication of medical reports, and advocated the inclusion of science and mathematics in the traditional civil service examinations. He returned to England in 1908 and died on September 20, 1911. The Chinese government conferred on him its highest honors, his own country gave him the hereditary rank of baronet in 1893, and he was decorated by thirteen other countries as well.

— Yen-P'ing Hao, *EAH*

and British against one another, until it was able to develop institutions and trade relationships that sustained it as a viable, independent state.

Malaysia. In the mid-nineteenth century, the traditional Malay sultans still ruled in states along the coasts of peninsular Malaya and the northern regions of Borneo and Sumatra. Gradually, they found themselves linked economically to the British who now held Malacca and had established two other settlements: one on the island of Penang and the other an obscure port christened Singapore by its founder, Sir Stamford Raffles, in 1819. Singapore confirmed its creator's reputation as a visionary and pioneer by rapidly becoming a major regional trading center. Together, the three ports, Malacca, Penang, and Singapore, became known as the "Straits Settlements" with Singapore serving as their governmental center. Discoveries of major tin deposits on the peninsula led to a "tin rush" of Chinese miners and an infusion of wealth that radically increased the competition among the sultans, local chiefs, and associations of Chinese miners for the control of

Figure 2.5   The East India Company steamer *Nemesis* is joined by other British ships in destroying Chinese war junks near Canton, January 7, 1841.

territory. The result was a virtual state of anarchy in some areas as rivalries erupted in small wars. Officials in Singapore tried for a time to remain aloof from these disputes, but beginning in 1874 the Colonial Office approved a limited intervention. This proved to be the opening wedge for increasing British control of the region.

Indonesia. The most far-reaching events in the Indonesian archipelago took place on the island of Java where, by the early 1800s, the employees of the Dutch East India Company had reached a working accommodation with the Javanese elite. Put simply, the Dutch backed local Javanese authorities who governed millions of people. This enabled them to exploit indirectly the region's indigenous commerce utilizing an elaborate system of "tribute." For a few years, beginning in 1811, they briefly lost control after the British seized and held Java. Governance in Batavia (Jakarta) was given to Stamford Raffles, but diplomacy and complex power-balancing in

Europe led to its return to the Dutch in 1816. Thereafter, a series of new Netherlands-based administrators entered the scene and attempted to reduce the status of the Javanese elites from powerful vassals to petty administrators whom they could keep under closer control.

The social strains brought on by these changes, involving a shift toward a direct tax and efforts to engage large numbers of Javanese peasants as export crop laborers, erupted in the Java War, a great and destructive rebellion that lasted from 1825 to 1830. After finally suppressing the rebellion, the Dutch sought to rectify the problem by returning to the previous system of "indirect rule" by local Javanese regents. As redefined by the administrator, Johannes van den Bosch, this so-called Culture System actually required far more direct interactions between the Dutch and Javanese than had previously existed. Metropolitan Dutch and Javanese elements began to mix further and the Dutch left their coastal enclaves to enter the life of the hinterland. Even

THE GEOGRAPHY OF COASTAL CONQUESTS

The Malay Coast

Control of coastal areas in Maritime Southeast Asia was often critical to control of much larger territory. By the eighteenth century, European traders dominated the numerous petty kingdoms in small ports and river mouths of the jungle coasts bordering the Straights of Malacca. Rivers penetrated the otherwise inaccessible interiors and provided access to trade with them, but the kingdoms near their mouths were relatively isolated from one another and easy pickings for more powerful forces. European intrusions into the area dispersed and redistributed power among the coastal peoples of Maritime Southeast Asia. Some turned to piracy while others, such as the warlike, seafaring Bugis of Makassar, occupied new territories. In the eighteenth century, they turned the Johore capital of Riau at the end of the Malay Peninsula into a commercial and religious center that was recognized from the Middle East to the China coast as heir to the earlier roles played by Srivijaya and Malacca. Yet in 1784, the Dutch attacked and occupied the Johor port. The British responded by developing the ports of Penang and Singapore as alternatives that drew off Riau's trade.

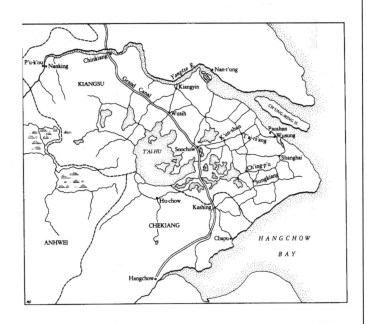

The Yangzi Delta

The strategic value of a river mouth became apparent in the case of the Yangzi, China's most important river. The third longest river in the world (3,900 miles), the Yangzi flows through central China, draining a region in which nearly 300 million people live today. Its network of rivers and canals carry the bulk of China's domestic waterborne traffic.

In the nineteenth century, the Yangzi delta was a much contested prize, and in the 1860s the restored Qing government and the Taiping Rebels vied for its posession. Whoever held the delta controlled the tribute grain collections passing along the Grand Canal, taxes on the commerce of the Shanghai area, and some access to the Maritime Customs revenues.

Western steam-driven gunboats ultimately determined who would control the delta. Once foreigners began to arrive in ships that were no longer dependent on sails, they could maneuver in the confines of the river and penetrate well into the interior. The imposition of a new "unequal treaty," the Treaty of Tianjin (1858), provided access for traders up the Yangzi as far as Hankou. This permitted the British and others to hold the critical region that linked China's northern areas to the rice growing south (see chapter 1). Considerations such as this forced China's government belatedly to give priority to the strategic value of its maritime coast.

PIRACY AND POLITICS IN THE MALAY WORLD

The term "piracy" is essentially a European one and appears in the Malay literature only in the second half of the eighteenth century. The term had the effect of criminalizing activities that the indigenous populations had hitherto considered political or commercial in nature. The indigenous maritime political systems of the Malay world were largely financed by commercial monopolies and by large cosmopolitan entrepôts that drew foreign traders. Raiding, or *merompak*, was a major feature of Malay political activity. It was a principal mechanism of commercial competition, political warfare, and tax collection. It was also the means by which young chiefs proved themselves.

If a warrior chief could unify a large group of sea peoples and set up an entrepôt at some strategic location in a major strait (e.g., Melaka, Johor, Riau, Sulu, etc.), then neighboring states would be subdued and international commerce would be channeled into the entrepôt Exchange, while usually secure, was conducted under the super vision of the ruler. Slave raiding also formed an important part of the system.

After 1800, as English and Dutch colonial empires began to expand in the Malay world, indigenous political and commercial practices were seen to conflict both with liberal principles, such as free trade and antislavery, as well as with imperial aspirations. The foundation of an English base at Singapore in 1819 as a free port effectively destroyed the old Johor sultanate, cutting off the Johor chiefs and their followers from a share in the revenues of the increased trade. The decay of the Malay political system, together with the increased trade, may have actually increased the level of raiding and other maritime violence.

By 1837, the Singapore government began conducting its own raids against Malay villages with "piratical" reputations. Within a few years steamships arrived, and English naval vessels, such as the *Dido* under Sir Henry Keppel and independent adventurers such as James Brooke, began sweeping the Riau Archipelago and the Borneo coast in a campaign that eliminated many of the sea peoples and native traders. The increasing dominance of square-rigged trading vessels owned by Europeans and Chinese also contributed to the elimination of the maritime way of life.

— Carl A. Trocki, *EAH*

so, the Javanese elite (*priyayi*) were less inclined to adapt Dutch ways than the Dutch were to adapt Javanese manners. Both preferred it that way. Not until the beginning of the twentieth century would elements of the *priyayi* begin to venture into what was for them a troubling and dangerous world of Western learning, beginning with the Dutch language.

The Philippines. Catholicism became so widespread in the northern Philippines by the nineteenth century that it was, in effect, a national religion although resistance continued in the southern islands from the Islamic peoples (who were called "Moros" by the Spanish in reference to the Moors who had invaded Spain). Spanish political and economic institutions were not as deeply rooted in the north as was the Catholic faith, yet together these elements reinforced the feeling among the locally born creoles (*Filipinos*, originally applied to Spaniards born in the Philippines; later to all Philippine citizens) and *mestizos* (people of mixed blood) that they and not the newly arrived *peninsulares* (Spaniards born in Iberia) should control affairs in the colony. Tensions increased as the *peninsulares*, pushed out of Latin America by the successful revolutions there, moved across the Pacific to Manila where they were determined that no similar revolutionary trend should be permitted to spawn. Their paranoia fed a rigid, authoritarian behavior that transformed their worst fears into reality.

At approximately the time the Dutch were fighting the Java War, the *peninsulares* had to suppress a regimental revolt comprising disenchanted creole and *mestizo* troops. The resulting trials and executions further stratified Philippine society and led the creole and *mestizo* people toward an identification not with their Iberian heritage, but with their Philippine world, thereby laying the foundation for future Philippine nationalism. The arrivals of new waves of Chinese immigrants further challenged the *mestizos*, particularly those of Chinese ancestry, to forge a new identity with their land. The *mestizo* Chinese had grown wealthy through land acquisitions in concentrated areas such as the island of Negros but over the generations had allowed their Chinese cultural identity to merge with local influences. The resulting search for a new, more secure identity by these and others of mixed heritage led to the acceptance of the term *Filipino* as one that applies to an all-inclusive national group.

The Brooke Dynasty

The commercial role of Southeast Asia thus gradually shifted from that of serving as a group of miscellaneous but linked trading ports where goods could be collected to one of an organized *production* base for important commodities such as rubber, coffee, tin, and rice. To ensure that these areas would be dependably productive and profitable, the Europeans assumed greater control over the indigenous populations and kingdoms. Not only did the encroachment of a new mining and plantation culture evoke local resistance, but ongoing wars among petty kingdoms were disruptive to trade. The Europeans adapted to this challenge by controlling territory under various initiatives and guises, usually by means of force and sometimes under the leadership of private entrepreneurs.

One such person was the English adventurer, James Brooke, whose career in founding the "White Raja" dynasty in Sarawak provides an early example of how the game of competition for resources in Southeast Asia could be played.

Brooke was a child of the imperial age. Born in India, he was wounded in the first of the wars that Britain fought in the nineteenth century to gain control over the kingdom of Burma. In the late 1830s he arrived in Sarawak and soon found himself helping the sultan of Brunei to suppress a local rebellion of Malay chiefs. Rewarded at the age of thirty-eight with control of a Sarawak district, Brooke moved quickly to consolidate his position as a raja. He issued new laws that attracted immigration by Malayo-Muslim and Chinese settlers and guaranteed "law and order" protection to his subjects. His paternalistic reign and that of his successors Charles and Charles Vyner Brooke, saw a period in which Chinese immigration into Malaysia swelled as workers flocked to the British-owned tin mines. The racial divisions created by such immigration were to become a major political obstacle to the formation of the nation of "Malaya" a century later (chapter 8).

The Brookes present a somewhat idiosyncratic example of European dominance in the imperial age because they identified closely with the limited territory and population they controlled. By contrast, their counterparts in the colonial governments saw the much larger territorial claims by their governments as essentially expressions of national will, dominance, and economic necessity. The pace at which the imperial powers sought to control territory accelerated in the later nineteenth century as their mutual suspicions and fears increased. These rivalries, in turn, served to carve out the approximate dimensions of future nation states in the region.

French Incursions in Vietnam

The success of British imperialism in South China inspired the French to pursue similar initiatives in Vietnam. Their immediate pretext was Vietnamese persecution of French missionaries who, as noted earlier, had established an extensive presence in the French-controlled areas of mainland Southeast Asia. In response to the murders of some missionaries, the French navy seized Saigon and the three southeastern provinces around it in 1859-62. The Treaty of Saigon (1862) between

Figure 2.6 A French colonial official rides across a stream on the back of a Vietnamese, symbolizing the relationship between their nations.

Figure 2.7 Chulalongkorn at his coronation. Groomed to assume the throne of Thailand amid the threat of European expansion in Asia, Chulalongkorn traveled widely in his teens and became a careful observer of Western customs and institutions.

France and the Vietnamese court ratified this conquest, in effect creating the French colony known as "Cochinchina."

Further occupation in 1867 of three more southern provinces completed the conquest. Having taken over the Vietnamese territory on behalf of their missionaries, the French began to exploit the area commercially by establishing large rubber plantations.

French colonial policy in Vietnam was at first indecisive, alternating between the social and political "assimilation" of Vietnam into the French system and "association" with traditional Vietnamese institutions, using them to legitimize French rule. The colonial government in Saigon in the early 1860s began by removing higher Vietnamese mandarins from power and replacing them with French officers. This proved impractical, however, because the French did not have enough personnel of their own to keep the system working. In the end, the French retained the most important posts such as the inspectors of indigenous affairs. These were usually professionals who were encouraged if not required to gain a rudimentary knowledge of Vietnamese language, law, and customs.

In the end, the actions of the French in coopting the Vietnamese system undermined the prospects for a peaceful and straightforward transition from colonial rule in the next century. By insisting that Vietnamese institutions be run according to French law and under the supervision of French officials, those Vietnamese leaders who sought to reassert indigenous institutions and a sense of nationhood were forced to turn increasingly toward open resistance. The early manifestations of this resistance and its ideological underpinnings are taken up in chapter 4.

Siamese Interactions with the West

King Mongkut of Siam [present-day Thailand], in contrast to his Vietnamese counterpart, found that he could accommodate Western demands in the interests of preserving his kingdom. He was more fortunate in his geographical location than his neighbor, the Nguyen emperor of Vietnam, in that he was able to manipulate the rivalry between the British (encroaching from

Burma in the north) and the French (pressing on Cambodia from the south). In 1855 he signed a Treaty of Friendship and Commerce with Great Britain and similar treaties soon thereafter with other Western powers. Although Siam eventually had to concede a certain amount of territory in this process, the fundamental integrity of the kingdom was maintained.

Mongkut died in 1868 and was succeeded by his Western-educated fifteen-year-old son, Chulalongkorn (who thereby became King Rama V). Although Chulalongkorn was able to build on his father's legacy and the greater experience he and his brothers had had with the West, an early confrontation with conservatives forced the young king to bide his time. Only as the older generation of ministers died or retired in the mid-1880s was he finally able to seize full power and implement the reforms he considered vital for the kingdom to survive the threats and demands of France and Britain. He began by creating a modern army, overhauling the revenue system, reorganizing the provincial administration and extending the capital's control in outlying regions. His reforms of the educational system and the bureaucracy were to have a far-reaching impact in Thai society.

Chulalongkorn could not prevent the loss of Laos and west Cambodia to France or of Kelantan and other territories to Britain, but within the territory he retained the transportation facilities were vastly improved, particularly by the construction of modern railways. These made the hinterland of Siam much more accessible to international trade and thereby stimulated its economy. With its Western-style law codes and administration, Siam soon gained a reputation for progressive attitudes toward foreigners and so its independence remained essentially unchallenged. Chulalongkorn paid personal visits to European royalty in 1897 and 1907, where he was greeted as an equal by his counterparts.

Impacts of New Technologies

Major technological breakthroughs in the mid-nineteenth century released new energies from industrial Europe toward Asia. Foremost among these achievements was the Suez Canal,

THE NATURE OF "IMPERIALISM"

A number of attempts have been made to explain the nature and impact of imperialism. They range from treating the phenomenon as a movement that developed from economic conditions in the industrializing nations to arguments about the political goals and strategic concerns of the imperialist powers.

The early practitioners of imperialism, whether politicians, journalists, missionaries, explorers, merchants, or military officers, provided various justifications for their activities. Arguments for empire included prospects of economic gain, an enhancement of national power, the scientific value of exploration, and the uplifting task of bringing the benefits of a more advanced civilization and culture to "backward" peoples. Often these arguments adopted the language of a competition for glory and power as each nation sought its "place in the sun," fulfilled a "manifest destiny," assumed a "civilizing mission," or acted as a "chosen people," revealing an underlying drive for supremacy.

After the rationales or apologies for empire had been made, analysts sought the underlying causes of imperialism. Among the earliest explanations were those that viewed imperialism as a historically inevitable part of a capitalist economic system. According to J. A. Hobson, V. I. Lenin, R. Hilferding, and others, accumulations of capital surplus brought a search for markets and profitable investment overseas and permitted imports of raw materials necessary for the industrial system. For Hobson, a liberal, this activity benefited certain industrial interests or investors at the expense of higher salaries and purchasing power for the masses. Lenin, writing after Hobson and during World War I, considered imperialism to be both the highest and the final stage of capitalism. For Lenin, capitalism's contradictions, competitiveness, and drive for monopolistic control had led to a self-destructive, imperialist conflict.

Critics of a predominantly economic explanation of imperialism insist that the costs of empire outweighed any economic gains. They note that overseas investment did not require conquest or direct control, citing in support of this argument the French empire, which offered relatively insignificant markets for either products or investment. Areas of direct dominance in Africa or Asia were often less valuable or profitable than investment in developing areas, a policy favored by Russia or the United States. Moreover, the extraction of raw materials often followed rather than precedednttervention, serving as a benefit but not necessarily as a cause of imperialism.

Arguments for the noneconomic foundations of imperialism initially focused on the extension of great power rivalries into Asia, Africa, and Latin America. The search for national power and prestige led to French expansion as compensation for military defeat in 1871, to a German drive for world power status, to British efforts to contain Russian expansion, to an Anglo-French rivalry and scramble for territory in Africa and Asia, to the competition of all imperial powers for spheres of influence in China. In this analysis, imperialism resulted more from strategic or diplomatic calculations based on an abstract concept of a balance of power than from the manifestation of economic rivalries or pressures. With a nation's strength measured by its ability to project power overseas, heightened nationalist sentiments permitted a mobilization of resources that made imperialism possible.

Other theories have emphasized what may be described as the psychological component of the imperialist impulse. Joseph Schumpeter argued that overseas conquest resulted from the aggressiveness or "atavism" of precapitalist, "feudalistic," and military classes in the industrial states. Others, not necessarily followers of Schumpeter, have concluded that imperialism satisfied and was an expression of a drive for power in which domination was sought for its own sake. This impulse appeared in all imperialist states, whether liberal-democratic, such as Great Britain, France, Italy, or

(continued on next page)

(continued from previous page)

the United States, where the military exercised a minor influence, or authoritarian-imperial, such as Germany, Russia, or Japan, where the role of the military and "precapitalist" classes was more influential.

Although differing in approach, the early theorists of empire agreed that a "new" imperialism emerged after 1870. More recently, scholars have questioned the validity of a distinction between the new imperialism and an earlier time of relative indifference toward imperialism in Europe. For Immanuel Wallerstein and his school, capitalist expansion during the era of commercial empires in the sixteenth and seventeenth centuries marked the beginning of a global economic system, a movement that gained in intensity with the emergence of industrial capitalism at the end of the nineteenth century. For neo-Marxists, the persistence of economic imbalances between "have" and "have-not" nations has meant the continuation of economic, cultural, and political dependencies even after the decolonization of the twentieth century. From a quite different perspective, two British scholars, Ronald Robinson and John A. Gallagher, have insisted that there was little fundamental difference between the "informal" imperialism of the early nineteenth century and the "formal" empires of conquest and domination after 1870. The advocates of empire would have preferred trade without conquest, but turned to the latter when confronted with conditions overseas that required intervention to protect commerce or to keep strategic areas from falling into the hands of hostile authority. Although criticized, the arguments of Gallagher and Robinson have compelled historians to move away from an exclusively Europocentric explanation of imperialism to consider developments in Africa, Asia, and Latin America as part of the process.

Clearly, imperialism has yet to be fully explained by any single, general theory. The result is a series of explanations of varying weights that may be differentially sorted and aggregated to explain individual cases of overseas expansion. Thus imperialism may be described and identified, but its origins, causes, and influence continue to be debated.

—by J. Kim Munholland, *EAH*

completed in 1869, which linked the Mediterranean Sea with the Gulf of Suez and the Red Sea, thereby greatly reducing the sea-route distance between Europe and Asia. Not only could more frequent commerce take place, but the convenience of travel for dependents of colonial officers also increased, resulting in a growing European population in the colonial capitals of Asia.

Steamships at the time had not yet come to dominate global commerce. In 1880 there were still three tons of shipping under sail for every ton under steam-power, but the balance then shifted radically. With the advent of steam-driven commerce, the monsoons no longer governed Indian Ocean traffic. Coaling stations throughout the world became strategic assets. Other advances in science and technology at the close of the century — the telephone, the electric light bulb, the motor car, and the discovery of radio waves — would

not influence developments in Asia for another few decades. Railroads, however, were quickly seen to be essential for major trade-related infrastructure changes and from Malaysia to Manchuria, the lines that were laid invigorated and often created new centers of commerce.

The submarine cable was, in some respects, one of the most revolutionary products to enter Asia. A burst of international cable-laying in the 1860s wove the Asian region, North America, and Europe together so that by 1872 telegrams could be transmitted from London to Adelaide via Tokyo. Communication that was inconceivable just a decade or two earlier was now suddenly available to business representatives and government officials throughout Asia. The idea of global news rapidly caught on as well with the founding of Julius Reuter's telegraph agency in 1851. Within a decade, international news was being

Figure 2.8 The expansion of Western power in Asia was often portrayed as a contest of civilization against barbarism — a mirror image of the Asian viewpoint. Here, the cover of a popular American magazine shows European soldiers with modern arms (a U.S. marine in the foreground) arrayed against Chinese who brandish traditional weapons only.

with the opening of Japan a decade later, was to make the Hawaiian Islands an increasingly important way station on the route to Asia from the Americas. A movement to annex Hawaii began before the Civil War, led by the descendants of missionaries in the islands (who had prospered after they turned to sugar growing). In 1890, these Hawaii sugar magnates staged a coup against the Hawaiian queen Liliuokalani with the intent of having the islands annexed by the United States, but Grover Cleveland, who had just become President, would have none of it. Not until 1898, amid the jingoistic fervor of the Spanish-American War, did the annexation of Hawaii take place.

Prior to the Spanish-American War, the United States' interest in Asia was dominated by commercial concerns and missionary activities. The country lagged far behind the European powers in military preparedness and showed little interest in dominating other countries. In the course of the war that began with Spain in 1898, however, political leaders began to advocate the use of military power to control overseas territory. As a result, the United States acquired the Philippines and soon found itself quelling a bloody nationalist rebellion in the archipelago. America, it seemed, had inherited Spain's role as a foreign oppressor. This was an acutely uncomfortable position for the nation and it soon sought to extract itself from the quagmire (chapter 4).

cabled freely from points around the globe to reach the next morning's breakfast table. Even remote territories became the subject of reporters' "scoops."

As newspapers flourished and literacy in Europe and America increased, the Western armchair traveler gained his impressions of Asia from accounts of adventure travelers and journalists. These reports made Westerners more aware of the "exotic" locations in Asia, but often left them with little information about the societal changes taking place in the region.

American Expansionism

The effect of the Treaty of Wanghia (1844) between China and the United States, combined

The Open-Door Policy

The ambivalent U.S. stance toward such foreign interventions is revealed in its so-called Open Door Policy toward China. The policy arose when the major powers — Britain, France, Germany, and Russia — blocked a militarily ascendant Japan from seizing territory in China and instead grabbed major parcels for themselves, beginning with Germany in Shandong Province in 1897. Russia then carved out a sphere in Manchuria, France in the southern provinces, and Britain in the Yangzi Valley.

From a U.S. standpoint, this was an alarming development, more from the standpoint of its own interests than those of China. Clearly the rules had changed from the previous arrangement whereby the imperial powers had cooperated, propping up

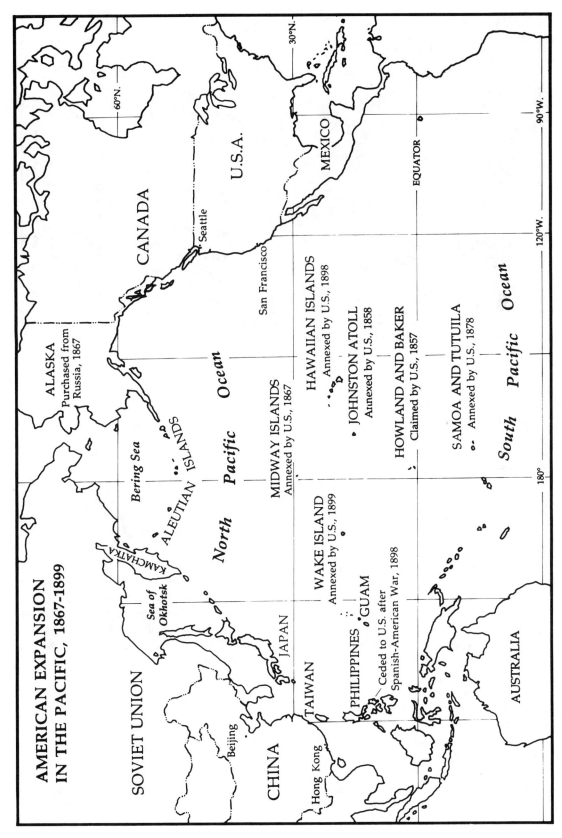

AMERICAN EXPANSION
IN THE PACIFIC, 1867-1899

SOVIET UNION

CANADA

U.S.A.

MEXICO

CHINA

Beijing

Hong Kong

TAIWAN

JAPAN

PHILIPPINES

GUAM

Ceded to U.S. after
Spanish-American War, 1898

WAKE ISLAND
Annexed by U.S., 1899

KAMCHATKA

Sea of
Okhotsk

Bering Sea

ALEUTIAN ISLANDS

ALASKA
Purchased from
Russia, 1867

Seattle

San Francisco

North Pacific Ocean

MIDWAY ISLANDS
Annexed by U.S., 1867

HAWAIIAN ISLANDS
Annexed by U.S., 1898

JOHNSTON ATOLL
Annexed by U.S., 1858

HOWLAND AND BAKER
Claimed by U.S., 1857

SAMOA AND TUTUILA
Annexed by U.S., 1878

South Pacific Ocean

AUSTRALIA

EQUATOR

60°N.

30°N.

90°W.

120°W.

180°

Seaborne Barbarians: Incursions by the West • 115

Figure 2.9   By 1884, hostility to Chinese immigrants had grown so strong in California that murderous raids were conducted on their settlements and restrictive laws enacted to prevent further arrivals.

China's central government, letting it do the administrative work, and avoiding dangerous contests among themselves over territory. A public outcry in the United States over the seizures put further pressure on the McKinley administration whose Secretary of State, John Hay, knew full well there was little the country could do. Its limited capacity to project power abroad was already deployed in the Spanish-American War and soon thereafter its troops were fighting a war in the Philippines.

Rather than attempt a fruitless preemptive action, Hay chose to preserve whatever rights he might claim for the United States by dispatching to the four European powers a series of diplomatic notes, each of which requested that the commerce of all nations be accorded the same rights as those claimed by each nation within its sphere of influence. For example, Germany would not be allowed to preempt the Chinese tariffs on American products and claim them for itself within its sphere.

The Open Door proved to be a highly successful initiative as the four powers could do little but accede to what was arguably a reasonable request. It preserved U.S. commercial interests in China at a low cost and restrained the imperial powers from

exercising their full ambitions within their domains. It was artfully cast as an initiative that supported the government of China, but in fact it implicitly accepted the expansionist territorial grab by the four powers.

From China's perspective, the United States seemed to show special promise as an ally and mediator with the other powers. From the outset of the relationship between the two countries, China assumed that American policy could be manipulated by the lure of trade preferences and railway concessions, a notion that was to cause considerable strain. In fact, U.S. policy did shift in the late nineteenth century in ways that suggested that the "special relationship" might flourish, but the Chinese remained reluctant to become dependent for protection on such a distant and unpredictable foreign power.

Emigration, the Gold Rush, and the Pacific Basin

Yet another impetus toward greater American interaction with Asia, one that would prove far more direct and personal than the diplomatic maneuvers of the Open-Door Policy, was emigration. In the latter half of the nineteenth century, tens of thousands of Asians, mostly Chinese, voluntarily traveled to the United States in search of employment. The 1890 census recorded a total of more than 107,000 arrivals. Most of the Chinese who emigrated to Peru, Hawaii, and Cuba went as contract laborers ("coolies"), but those who traveled to North America more often went as free laborers. The rapid influx of Chinese into California led to an anti-Chinese hysteria in some communities in the 1870s and 1880s, which was fed by images of the "heathen Chinese" brought home by traders and missionaries. The outbreaks of violence against the Chinese settlers (mostly men who hoped to return to China) led them to rely heavily on *huiguan*, district associations for fraternity, mutual aid, and protection.

Many of these Chinese immigrants helped build the transcontinental railroads, particularly the western portions, and by all reliable accounts they formed the most capable of the work crews. It was during this period that America's national infrastructure began to vastly increase the nation's capabilities for future interaction with Asia and the Pacific. By 1883 four different transcontinental routes were in operation across the United States. A fifth was under construction and branch lines proliferated rapidly. As early as 1855 an American-built railroad also began operations across the isthmus of Panama, linking Southampton in England to Sydney, Australia, in a fifty-eight day journey and making Panama a major point of trans-shipment between the Atlantic and Pacific regions.

While railroads were an important avenue of transportation to the Pacific coast, the critical development that drew people there from North America and Asia was the discovery of gold northeast of San Francisco in 1848. The result was an unprecedented migratory stampede that swelled California's immigrant population in the year 1849 from fourteen thousand to about a hundred thousand. During that same time the number of ships docking at San Francisco doubled, hundreds of them to be abandoned by their crews and eventually scuttled or dismantled for timber, so difficult was it to find sailors who could resist the temptation to try their luck in the gold fields. Within another two years, California's population

stood at a quarter million. An explosion of trade followed in the wake of the migrants, with a broad coastal network from Vancouver to Valparaiso carrying a rich variety of foodstuffs. The gold rush expanded and intensified economic activity in key areas of the Pacific Rim (including Australia where gold was also discovered), opening new markets that included growing urban populations with relatively high disposable incomes.

Pacific Asia at the Close of the Nineteenth Century

Urban centers throughout the Pacific Basin had begun to feel the shifts in the global economy by the end of the nineteenth century. The railroad, the steamship, the telegraph (and years later the radio) penetrated the cultures of Asia with more than just Western science, technology, and philosophy. They began to change the pattern, pace, and frequency of interaction within Asia, permitting people to communicate within their societies and across national boundaries as never before. In urban areas streetcars began to appear, filled with people moving to and from their daily work. A sense of connectedness to a larger world was growing, particularly in the burgeoning Pacific Rim cities from Sydney to Shanghai. Regional conflicts throughout the world were now being reported in daily newspapers thanks to the advent of new communications technology. This obvious "connectedness," in turn, stimulated Asian intellectuals to envision the relationship of their countries to the world of nation states and to formulate strategies for new, independent national identities.

Perhaps less clearly appreciated by Asians and Europeans alike was the extent to which the world was about to change, politically and culturally, after the outbreak of World War I in August 1914. As will be stressed in chapter 4, the aftermath of that conflagration became a historical watershed for much of Pacific Asia. Before turning to the rising tide of nationalism and revolution in the twentieth century, however, we must examine what in some respects constitutes *the* Asian revolution of the nineteenth century: the Meiji transformation in Japan.

3

Meiji:
Japan in the Age of Imperialism

INTRODUCTION:
ARRIVAL OF THE BLACK SHIPS

— by Frank Gibney

At 5:00 p.m. on the afternoon of July 8, 1853, the two steam frigates of Commodore Matthew Calbraith Perry's East India squadron and their accompanying two sloops ran out their anchors off the port of Uraga, at the entrance to Tokyo Bay, thus bringing an end to Japan's 250-year seclusion. They also struck a spark to the gathering discontent of several past decades that was to end in the half-controlled explosions of the Meiji Restoration.

Here were the foreign barbarians at Japan's doorstep — with not even a stop at the foreigners' port of Nagasaki — and not a thing could be done to turn them back. Some twenty thousand troops of the Shogun's clan levies clustered in the hills around Tokyo Bay — spears, bows and antiquated muskets and cannon at the ready — but without a prayer of countering Perry's broadsides. At the head of the bay Edo lay defenseless, its packed wooden houses a hostage to naval gunfire and its seaborne food supplies equally so. There was nothing for the Shogun's officers to do but come to some sort of terms with the powerful barbarians.

This was a situation that the Japanese never forgot. Even today, the word *kurobune* — for

Perry's black ships — is used as a catchphrase for unwelcome foreign pressure.

After every effort at threats, temporizations, and delay, the Shogun's officers were ultimately forced to sign a treaty opening Japan to a certain amount of trade with the United States and ultimately other Western powers. Two ports, Shimoda and Hakodate, were set aside for American ships' entry. Although this bare bones' treaty was only a beginning for the Americans, it was enough to start the cycle of recrimination, plot, and counterplot within Japan that destroyed the Shogunate.

Perry's invasion was no casual happening. Just five years after the annexation of California, the still-young United States of America was caught up in the enthusiasm of its westward expansion. Flushed with the easy victory over Mexico and anxious to fulfill the "Manifest Destiny to overspread the continent allotted by Providence," the same Americans who had fought their way across the western prairies were anxious to sail the waters beyond the newly settled Pacific shore. In the China trade since 1787, American seamen now sought to expand their traffic with the Far East. Whaling in particular had become a big industry. The trans-Pacific whalers desperately needed ports for water, coal, and food supplies. Previously, shipwrecked American sailors had had bad experiences when cast up on the shore of Japan. Perry was told, in effect, not to take no for an answer.

"Recent events," his instructions read, "have practically brought the countries of the East in close proximity to our own.... The duty of protecting those Americans who navigate those seas is one that can no longer be deferred." For all his own ceremonial posturing and his sense of an imperialist mission — he had earlier written that the United States, to counter the aggrandizements of Britain and other European powers, might profitably think of annexing the Bonin Islands, Taiwan, and the Ryukyu Islands just south of Japan's main islands — Perry handled his assignment with considerable tact. A man with a profound sense of showmanship, he staged several demonstrations of Western technology for his Japanese hosts, including the presentation of a miniature railroad to the Shogun's men. He was never one to shirk a good ceremonial occasion. His visits on shore, with Marines in full dress and bands playing, were grand enough to impress the protocol-conscious Japanese officials who were sent to deal with him.

Predictably, the Shogun's men dragged their feet on the negotiations. Perry had to return in the spring of 1854, this time with an eight-ship squadron, representing roughly a fourth of the U.S. Navy, before the Treaty of Kanagawa was signed. However, this treaty only initiated the diplomatic process. Thereafter it took America's first resident diplomat in Japan, Townsend Harris, who plied his lonely consul's trade in the treaty port of Shimoda, fully four years of negotiations until a formal treaty was signed. This expanded American privileges and provided, among other things, for the onerous principle of extraterritoriality, i.e., by which American residents in Japan could be tried only in their own courts for any offenses. This was the same "outside law" that the British had already forced on the Chinese; and it rankled. Ultimately enjoyed by the other Western powers trading with Japan, the extraterritorial courts persisted until 1899 — when Japan's own Westernized law was finally accepted by all as valid.

The treaty that emerged in 1858 was a monument to the skill and persistence of the American consul-general. Harris persuaded Shogunate officials that a treaty signed now with the United States, which had no territorial designs on Japan,

Figures 3.1–3.2 Commodore Perry's squadron lives in Japanese memory as "the black ships" because of their belching black smoke and cannon fire, depicted here in a Japanese sketch. Although Japanese pictures portrayed Perry (left) like all "barbarians" as a grimacing, large-nosed creature, he liked his hosts and generally got along well with them.

would forestall the appearance of European warships, which might repeat the hostilities in China. His arguments were given added force by the news that an Anglo-French fleet had attacked and burned the port of Guangzhou in 1857. Shortly afterwards, treaties of a similar nature were signed with Britain, France, Russia, and the Netherlands. Based on Harris's original document, they all secured the opening of additional ports, low customs duties, and the principle of extraterritoriality.

The Shogun's Dilemma

It was an index of Tokugawa weakness that he (the Shogun) had circulated the earlier treaty with Commodore Perry among the *daimyo* (feudal lords) of the leading domains even before reporting it to the court. Their response was mixed. It ranged from cautious acceptance of trade and a gradual opening of the country to defiance and demands that the barbarians be driven from Japan's shores by the Shogun's forces.

The last course seemed hardly possible, particularly to the Shogun's representatives who had actually seen Perry's armament and knew something of the havoc being currently wrought in China's helpless ports by European gunboat diplomacy. The advocates of *sonno joi* ("Revere the emperor and repel the barbarians"), secure in their clan castles, showed no signs of accepting a compromise. This "no compromise" spirit was also evident at the Imperial court in Kyoto. The new resurgence of Imperial loyalty was not lost on younger Court nobles who finally saw a chance to bring the Imperial institution out of the closet, so to speak, and revive the power of the Mikado (the emperor).

In 1858 the Court refused to ratify the treaty. On the contrary, it called on the Shogun to repudiate the treaty and take immediate steps to drive the barbarians from the land. The Court's rejection of the Shogun's treaty was almost without precedent in Japanese history. After later representations by the Shogunate, in the person of Ii Naosuke, the stern and decisive new head of the Shogun's administration, the Court issued a more conciliatory comment and the Shogun made vague promises to keep the barbarians from overrunning Japan. By 1859, however, the treaties

were ratified. The first foreign traders, escorted by European warships and troops, were setting up business in Yokohama. The Shogun's government, already on the verge of bankruptcy, was revealed as fatally indecisive. Ii, who became the supreme Regent of the Shogunate's government, had decided that the opening of the country could not be delayed and put all his authority behind the treaty observance. He set out to discipline both rebellious domain leaders and their allies among the court nobility. He was assassinated in March, 1860, as he was entering Edo Castle. With him died the last hope for decisive leadership in the Shogun's councils. As Katsu Kaishu, one of Japan's early modernizers and a loyal retainer of the Shogun, later commented: "From the day of Perry's arrival, for more than ten years, our country was in a state of indescribable confusion. The government was weak and irresolute, without fixed policy or power of decision."

The "men of spirit" *(shishi)* throughout Japan were shocked by the news of Perry's unopposed arrival, not to mention the treaties that followed it. The *shishi* were a minority of samurai within the clan domains who constituted the "angry young men." Their willingness to use force to have their way was widely recognized. Self-righteous and dogmatic, they were the precursers of the ultranationalist extremists who fomented change in the pre-war Japan of the 1930s.

The actual presence of foreigners off Japan's coast turned theorists into activists quite quickly; in their favorite meeting places, the fencing academies in Edo and the large castle towns where they practiced swordsmanship and other traditional military exercises, the young men argued, talked and postured and took counsel with each other on how they could turn their agitation and concern into some form of action. Many of these "men of spirit" were *ronin*, that is to say, samurai who had left their original *han* (domain) and moved across Japan like high-level drifters, alternately studying and fighting as they went from teacher to teacher. Some of these were still disciples of the traditional Confucian schooling, while others tried to study their Dutch and assimilate some of the new Western learning. There were also young samurai in positions of power. Over the years, daimyo and senior officials of the clans had tended to delegate more and more of their governing to younger men.

Inevitably they came to influence the policies of their respective clans. The Shogun's rule grew weaker — a fact signalized by its palpable inability to handle the problem of foreign penetration — and policy in the various han grew increasingly independent of Edo.

Rise of the "Outsiders"

This was particularly true of Satsuma and Choshu, two of the outer han (*tozama*, those who were initially opposed to Tokugawa rule), which while furthest removed from the direct influence of the Shogunate at Edo, were both large enough and sufficiently independent-minded to serve as focuses of new resistance. Satsuma, the larger of the two, was situated in southeastern Kyushu and had its capital at Kagoshima. The Shimazu daimyo, rulers of Satsuma, had fought against Ieyasu at Sekigahara; and the ancestor of the present daimyo had had to cut his way out of the battle with a few trusted retainers, barely escaping with their lives. Satsuma was a land of farmers and seafarers, as far removed as possible from the new town culture of Edo. Its people were tough, conservative, and very belligerent. The leadership of their domain had taken increasingly independent stands — and had already made contact with the more liberal of the court nobles in Kyoto, as the talk about an Imperial restoration began to increase.

Choshu, the headquarters of the Mori daimyo, was situated in the far southwest of the island of Honshu. Its major port was Shimonoseki. The clan headquarters and stronghold, however, was at Hagi, to this day a quiet harbor on Japan's less populated western coast, whose long rows of eighteenth and nineteenth century houses, once the dwellings of Choshu's samurai nobility, remain remarkably as they were. Choshu, too, had a strong military tradition. Its samurai had kept up their old military virtues and were among the bravest and most competent soldiery that nineteenth century Japan possessed. Choshu was also one of the outer han. Its size had been reduced by the Tokugawa as a punishment for its earlier disaffection. Choshu's long-standing antipathy toward the Tokugawa rule had remained, however.

Yoshida Shoin was born in Choshu to a samurai family. Due to the early deaths of his older relatives, he became the master of Hagi's han school of fencing and military studies while in his early teens. He lived only until the age of thirty. He was beheaded on the orders of the Shogunate in 1859 for plotting to assassinate a high Tokugawa official. He was precocious as a child — having begun to lecture on classical Chinese military tactics to other samurai in Hagi before he was twelve. He also traveled constantly, going almost the length of the country to meet distinguished teachers and new thinkers, both of the traditional variety and people who were exploring Western knowledge, like the redoubtable Sakuma Shozan. He was a perennial activist. Yoshida's first reaction on hearing of the Perry landing was to visit the Commodore and board one of his ships. He and a friend actually made their way to Shimoda and, under the cover of darkness, rowed out to the *U.S.S. Susquehanna* at its anchorage. On being sent to the flagship they asked Commodore Perry if he would take them back with him to the United States to study the sciences there. Perry reluctantly refused and Yoshida and his companion left, only to be imprisoned in cages by the Shogun's officials.

Later Yoshida was allowed to return to Hagi. It was there that he started his famous school, the *Shoka Sonjuku* — literally, "the village school under the pine trees." Viewed from a modern perspective, Yoshida's teachings are rather hard to analyze. On the one hand, he was a traditionalist, full of confidence in the solidarity and virtues of the samurai class. "Even a peasant's will is hard to deny, but a samurai of resolute will," he wrote, "can sway ten thousand men." He was also an ardent imperialist. The highest task to which a Japanese could aspire, he taught, was to become one of the "Emperor's retainers." The society in which Yoshida was reared was still very much a society of the clan domain. Most Japanese of his time were educated to think of themselves as residents of a particular domain — whether Choshu, or Aizu, or Tosa — and not a citizen of a country called Japan. Yoshida was one of the first to break with this idea of loyalty to the domain (han) above all else.

He had seen enough of the world around him to respect the new learning of the West. He was not any blind "destroy the barbarian" zealot. As he once wrote: "the barbarians' artillery and shipbuilding, their knowledge of medicine and the physical sciences can all be of use to us — these should properly be adopted." On the other hand, he was dead set against the way in which the Shogunate had opened the country for Commodore Perry and others. "Japan has been free for about three thousand years," he wrote, "how, one morning, will we be able to bear its control by other men? If we do not give rise to a Napoleon and announce our freedom [he used the English word], it will be most difficult to cure the pain in our heart."

What Yoshida advocated, in short, was a selection of "men of ability and talent" from whatever walk of life or social caste they came from. Samurai feudalist that he was, he nevertheless wanted to scrap the stratified system of hereditary ranks and privileges in favor of mobilizing the resources of the country — and he meant the whole country, not just Japan as divided into several domains — to meet the demands imposed by modernization and, indeed, possible invasion by foreigners.

In today's media-dominated world, Yoshida would be labeled "charismatic;" and in his case the term could doubtless be justified. Ito Hirobumi, Kido Koin, Yamagata Aritomo, Takasugi Shinsaku and others — almost half of the key figures who made the Meiji Restoration and led its government were — Choshu people who had studied at his school. An almost hopeless idealist, he sacrificed all of his personal comforts to what he felt was the cause of truth. He left behind him a clear and undiluted message: Revere the Emperor; work against the Shogun and all

"They were not satisfied with the minutest examination of all these things, surpassingly strange as they must have been to them, but followed the officers and men about, seizing upon every occasion to examine every part of their garments, and showing the strongest desire to obtain one or more of their buttons. Those who were admitted on board the ships were equally inquisitive, peering into every nook and corner accessible to them, measuring this and that, and taking sketches after their manner of whatever they could lay their eyes upon."
—Commodore Matthew C. Perry,
The Japan Expedition, 1852–1854

other officials who were lazy and betrayed their trust; select people of talent for important posts — wherever they come from; be true to one's self and one's ideals. This archetypal angry young man remains a strange and enigmatic figure. Nothing that he wrote reads all that impressively or uniquely in the light of contemporary day. Yet the impression he left on the people around him was almost indelible.

Too Little, Too Late

The final days of the Shogunate represent a bewildering montage of opposing images, ideas and contradictions. Satsuma, Choshu and the other han began to modernize and mobilize their own military forces. In fact, the ultimate Meiji slogan of "Enrich the country, strengthen the army" (in Japanese, *Fukoku Kyohei*) was actually originated in Satsuma by the young Okubo Toshimichi, who was in charge of that clan's modernization plans.

The Shogunate did its best to modernize itself. In 1860 Japan's first mission was sent overseas, primarily to ratify the treaty Townsend Harris had negotiated for the United States, but also to give a selected group of Japanese officials a good view of the world outside. The mission traveled aboard the *U.S.S. Powhattan*, but it was significant that an accompanying ship, the Kanrin Maru, which

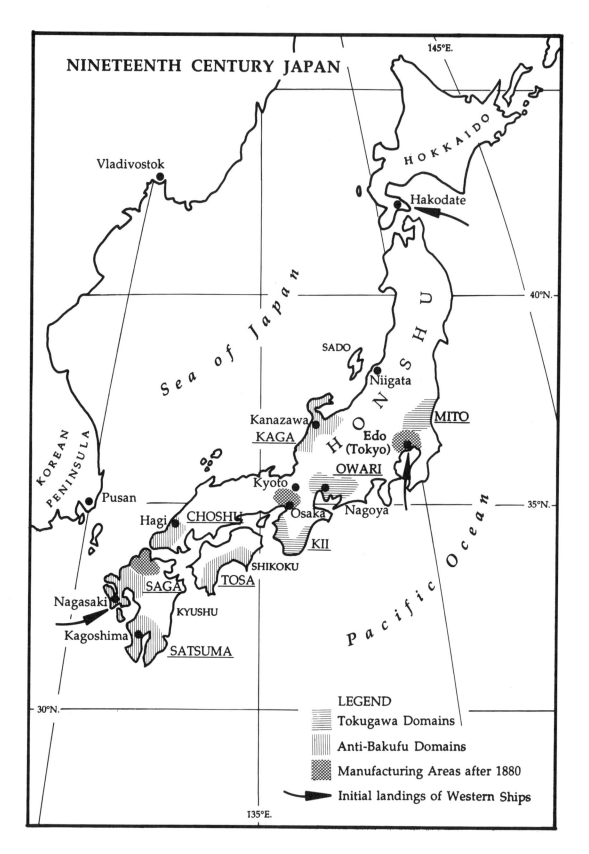

NINETEENTH CENTURY JAPAN

145°E.

HOKKAIDO

Vladivostok

Hakodate

Sea of Japan

40°N.

HONSHU

SADO

Niigata

Kanazawa

KAGA

MITO

Edo
(Tokyo)

OWARI

KOREAN
PENINSULA

Kyoto

Pusan

Osaka

Nagoya

35°N.

Hagi

CHOSHU

KII

SHIKOKU

Pacific Ocean

SAGA

TOSA

Nagasaki

KYUSHU

Kagoshima

SATSUMA

30°N.

LEGEND

Tokugawa Domains

Anti-Bakufu Domains

Manufacturing Areas after 1880

Initial landings of Western Ships

135°E.

carried some members of the delegation, was sailed largely by a Japanese crew under Katsu Kaishu, the Shogunate official who had for some years directed a school for training the first members of Japan's fledgling navy at Nagasaki. It was no small achievement to man an oceangoing ship in a country where just seven years before the highest officials had watched with unbelieving fascination the workings of Commodore Perry's telegraph.

In 1862 the mission was sent to Europe. Other Japanese visitors, unofficial as well as official, began to travel overseas at that time. While those who went to Europe and the United States were impressed, if not shaken, by the industrialization and already complex civilizations of the Western countries, others who traveled in Asia received the complement of this message.

In 1862, on a mission, Takasugi Shinsaku, the Choshu samurai, visited Shanghai as part of a trade mission sent by the Shogunate to look at conditions in China. He was shocked at the apparent corruption of the Qing (Ch'ing) dynasty and its subservience to foreigners. "In viewing earnestly the conditions in Shanghai," he wrote, "I have observed Chinese serving foreigners and Englishmen strutting along the streets of the city. The Chinese are avoided in the streets and their ways have been replaced. In reality, although the territory of Shanghai is part of China, it could be said to belong to the English and the French."

Harsh Lessons

If this message needed reinforcement at home, Satsuma and Choshu both were soon to receive it. In the early 1860's there was a variety of incidents involving foreigners in the new so-called treaty ports, as bands of hostile samurai attacked them. Henry Heusken, Townsend Harris's own interpreter, was cut down on the streets of Edo in 1861. British diplomats were once attacked in their embassy and in 1863 the embassy in Edo was burned down by hostile samurai. The year before, in what became known as the Namamugi incident, a party of English men and women were set on by Satsuma samurai when they misunderstood the signals and did not give place quickly enough for a procession escorting the daimyo. An English-

man named Richardson was killed. In retaliation, a British squadron sailed into the harbor of Kagoshima and, after some losses, set a good bit of the town on fire, and destroyed most of the shore batteries. In June 1863 the Choshu daimyo ordered the shore batteries at Shimonoseki to fire on foreign ships, as June 25 was the date that the Shogun had formally set for the "expulsion" of foreigners from Japan in an earlier memorial to the Emperor. A mixed British, French, and American fleet retaliated, destroyed most of the shore batteries, and caused considerable damage in the town.

These incidents were enough to convince the leadership in both of these han that it was time to come to terms with the West, rather than continue vainly to attack what seemed to be an irresistible force. Thus it was that the most violent antiforeign elements in Japan sharply changed course and set out on a new policy of making friends with the foreigners and learning as much as could be learned from them. Two young Choshu samurai, Ito Hirobumi and Inoue Kaoru, returning posthaste in 1863 from their studies in London, offered themselves as intermediaries in negotiating Choshu's peace with the Europeans.

The Civil War in the United States had distracted Americans from showing the flag much further in Japan. American diplomacy, which had engineered the opening of Japan, was thus rendered relatively inactive for a critical period. The British and French moved quickly to take up the slack. Through the closing years of the Shogunate, the French minister Leon Roches did his best to help modernize the military forces of the Shogunate and shore up its remaining power with loans, trade, and technical advice. The British, on the other hand, decided that the future lay with the Imperialists. Sir Harry Parkes, the British minister, and his assistant, later to be Sir Ernest Satow, started a lively dialogue with the Emperor's party and sympathetic imperialist samurai in the various han which continued through the beginning of the Restoration.

At the Emperor's court Iwakura Tomomi and Sanjo Sanetomi led a faction of the court nobility which, with increasing boldness, asserted imperial independence of the Shogun. They quickly made contact with young reformers from Choshu and other tozama.

Figure 3.3–3.4   One of the more spectacular gifts Perry brought to his Japanese hosts was a scaled-down, working steam engine, shown here in an accurate Japanese sketch. By 1872 the Japanese were operating an imported full-size train between Tokyo and Yokohama with telegraph lines to match. By 1895, they had built their own steam locomotive (below).

Satsuma and Choshu were first opposed to each other, having never been notably friendly in the past. Reform-minded samurai in both these domains, however, had enough in common so that a dialogue of sorts began. Thus, although Satsuma joined with other clans in a military action against Choshu in 1864, by 1865 the tables were completely turned. Although the new regent in Edo, Hitotsubashi Keiki, attempted to call out the different han armies to make war on Choshu, Satsuma and Choshu formed a secret alliance in the same year. This ultimately killed the mission against Choshu and humiliated the Shogunate.

Swordsmen and Patriots

Originally, few of the daimyo and their ruling councils wanted to put an end to the Shogunate as such. However, giving real power to the emperor would represent a radical departure from tradition. Various expedients were proposed for some a sort of "union of throne and Shogunate," but none seemed to work. In Choshu, Satsuma, and the small but influential Tosa han in Shikoku, younger samurai were moving into positions of authority in the han administrations. This made a sharp break with the ruling order of the past.

The transition was not easy, however, and the times were dangerous for public figures of whatever persuasion. Sakamoto Ryoma, for example, the brilliant Tosa samurai who helped forge the Satsuma-Choshu alliance, was cut down by pro-Tokugawa assassins in 1867, on the very eve of the Meiji Restoration.

Patriots of the pre-Meiji period were revolutionaries. They read intensively and talked even more so, but they were far from being theorists. They were activists. These were people who had been raised at the academies of swordsmanship and samurai discipline. An assassination was, to them, a logical extension of a policy, the ultimate way of expressing one's feelings. Some of them could justly be called terrorists, as we now use that term. Almost all of them were idealists — and angry ones.

It would be useful in this connection to quote a classic passage about the Bakumatsu (i.e., end of the shogun's rule, 1853-1868) from H. G. Harootunian's standard work, *Towards Restoration:*

Most principals in the Bakumatsu drama were extremists of one sort or another. It is foolish to suppose that moderation, temporarily extinguished by hotheads brandishing swords at anything that moved, could possibly have provided motivation or energy for a political event such as the Meiji Restoration. The Restoration was propelled above all else by the rage of young men: rage at the coming of the foreigner; rage at the momumental incompetence of the Shogunate, carefully concealed until it was exposed by the opening of the country; rage at the prospects of continuing incompetence and national deterioration; and, finally, rage because they were being denied any opportunity to resolve the problems of the day. If the Restoration was not a revolution in the conventional sense, it was still the result of revolutionary rage which had been nearly dissipated in the struggles of the decade preceding the event; and while later Meiji politicians tried (for obvious reasons) to minimize the revolutionary character of their earlier work, there was no way to conceal an event that had destroyed history and wrenched life from its moorings to give the Japanese a new lease on the future.

The stage was set for a fast-paced, highly complex progression of events that drove the Shogun from power, installed the Emporer Meiji as the supreme authority, and then radically transformed Japan's society and economy.

♦   ♦   ♦

THE MEIJI RESTORATION

—by George Akita

The Meiji Restoration was the pivotal event in modern Japanese history; it is the starting point for any discussion of major developments that followed in the Meiji period (1868-1912) and beyond. The Restoration nearly did not happen. The groups behind the coup d'état that made the Restoration possible entangled themselves in a comedy of errors. On 3 January 1868, however, a coup succeeded, and the leaders declared the restoration of imperial rule (*osei fukko*). The splendiferous reign name, Meiji ("enlightened rule"), only later (October 3, 1868) came to dignify both the coup and the period that followed. The subsequent achievements stand in stark contrast to the thin reed upon which the coup leaders stood that first month of 1868.

For the simile of a pivot to have meaning, we must look backward to the Tokugawa institutions, structures, and developments that shaped the contours of post-Restoration Japan. One of the most critical of these was the vertically structured Tokugawa polity. From Edo, the shogun's government and bureaucracy administered the shogunate's domain and the major cities, and controlled the functions and policies with countrywide implications, such as *sankin kotai* (alternate attendance of lords in the capital), foreign trade, defense, and minting. Then came some 260 domains, governed by the daimyo and their bureaucracies, in effect small "countries" whose autonomy remained intact so long as it did no violence to the shogunate's countrywide responsibilities and concerns. In the domains' villages, towns, and cities were hundreds of self-governing bodies of commoners. If the relationship of shogunate to domain was that the shogunate controlled while the domains administered, that relationship also obtained between the domain government and the self-governing bodies. The number of samurai in the countryside was minuscule. Most lived in castle towns. Here, too, the *chonin* ("city people," that is, the commoners) were given a large measure of autonomy. These tens of thousands of self-contained islands of stability go a long way in explaining Japan's ability to make the transition from the Tokugawa order to the Meiji: the Meiji leaders' efforts were not deflected to coping with the concerns of the great bulk of the Japanese.

The Tokugawa may have been a rigidly status-bound society, but by late in the period it was remarkably free in economic terms. The capitalist economy that is the hallmark of the Meiji period finds its antecedent in the Tokugawa, when one "representative" tenant farmer could turn a tidy profit by raising twenty-five thousand *daikon* (white radishes). Merchants from Osaka, driven by anticipation of financial gain, would annually

flock hundreds of miles to the region described in [the Nobel Prize-winning author] Kawabata Yasunari's *Snow Country* for the chijimi cloth fair. It was, again, the autonomy enjoyed by the commoners that enabled them to thrive in an economy propelled increasingly by market forces and becoming more "national" by the mid-nineteenth century.

A five-hundred-year coal supply was one of only two natural resources significant to modernization available to Japan at the beginning of the Meiji period. The other was its people — industrious, creative, and educated. The Meiji leaders could call upon a body of samurai and commoners whose literacy was comparable to that of advanced, contemporaneous European countries. More important than literacy, perhaps, was the widespread diffusion of the "modern" notion that change for the better was not only possible but desirable. It lessened their burden considerably that the Meiji leaders did not have to drag the majority of the Japanese people unwillingly into the new era.

The new leaders, who in the decades before the Restoration had used words such as "plot" in their letters, now had to build responsibly. All the acts that followed the coup were based on the realistic decision that Japan must not antagonize the Western powers. This first principle in Japanese foreign policy guided the conduct of Japanese leadership to the 1930s. Having made this decision, the leadership then concentrated on domestic reforms, and the Tokugawa polity was the first problem they confronted. A polity divided into some 260 semiautonomous, mutually jealous and suspicious entities was poor material with which to build a modern nation. A unified nation had to be created, and the leaders proceeded slowly and cautiously, a procedure and tempo they followed throughout the Meiji period.

They built on a decision taken in April 1868 by Katsu Kaishu, a bakufu [Tokugawa] official, and Saigo Takamori, from Satsuma, that Edo would be handed over peaceably to the anti-bakufu coalition. The agreement enabled the new leaders to control immediately the administrative center for the former bakufu domain, nearly a quarter of Japan's total area.

Although the bakufu domain was under its control, the government coalition had had to fight its way north. The Boshin War, especially the Echigo (ended September 10, 1868) and Aizu (ended October 8, 1868) campaigns in northwestern Japan, were bloody and closely contested. These campaigns gave the Sat-Cho (Satsuma-Choshu) coalition momentum, since it had won every significant military battle. Each victory enhanced its claim to being kangun, or forces in the imperial service. The Sat-Cho commanders were also gaining experience in leading and coordinating disparate domain forces. The contributions of men and material by other domains meant also that the vertical Tokugawa polity was slowly breaking down. Therefore, when the coalition finally turned to the problem of the Tokugawa polity, the notion that the Sat-Cho leaders were in command was not novel, and it had the support, sometimes lukewarm, of more than a handful of domains.

The Meiji leaders knew what had to be done, but they did not have a master plan. Events were moving too quickly from the fortuitous success of the coup to the country's pacification. They could lean on precedents neither from their own history nor from that of China. The nation-building experiences of the West, so far as they were known, seemed inapplicable to their situation. Their task must have loomed awesomely. This, and the lack of a military force, may account for their caution. The leaders had perforce become prudent and careful in the most revolutionary phase of their lives, for the most circumspect among them, like Ito Hirobumi and Yamagata Aritomo, had participated in terroristic or illegal political actions in the bakumatsu period.

A two-pronged approach was taken, the first part of which involved using the emperor as the focus of transdomainal loyalty and the symbol of the new government's legitimacy. This was the easier part. The Emperor Mutsuhito was a lad of sixteen. He was led before his "subjects," first on a trip to Osaka (1868) and then, accompanied by thousands, to Edo (November 1868-January 1869). These were the first of the one hundred two trips made during his reign, including six grand tours to all parts of the country. Some eighty years later, his grandson Hirohito, too, was to serve the political purposes of rulers by being paraded before his subjects.

The second aspect of this approach involved incremental steps taken judiciously and always through consultation with court nobles, daimyo, and samurai from important domains. The goal was the elimination of the domains. The daimyo had to be dislodged or persuaded to return their territories and their people to the court (the government in Tokyo). The government had neither the power nor the inclination to force the issue, so the first move was made by the four domains that had toppled the bakufu. In March 1869 the samurai leaders of the four domains persuaded their daimyo to return their territories and people to the court (*hanseki hokan*). Some other daimyo followed suit. In July 1869 the government, having taken the precaution of appointing many key daimyo to important government positions, ordered the remaining daimyo to comply. Here again, the transition was eased by appointing all daimyo as governors of their domains. But the daimyo now served as officials of the Tokyo government. It was not until two years later that the government was confident enough to move firmly against the daimyo-governors. Its strength had been bolstered by the formation of the Imperial Guard, composed of ten thousand fighting men from Satsuma, Choshu, and Tosa (April 1871). In August 1871 the daimyo-governors were told that they were no longer governors and that their domains would become prefectures. Samurai, with their own staffs, were appointed in place of the daimyo-governors. The samurai were practiced administrators, having served as such in domain and Tokugawa administrations or in the new government. The use of ex-Tokugawa retainers and supporters reflected the willingness of the new government to use "men of ability" wherever they might be found.

The destruction of the Tokugawa polity and the creation of a centralized, national government was so important that Yamagata Aritomo later called it the "Second Restoration." The confidence that the success of the Second Restoration engendered can be measured by the Iwakura Mission, led by most of the Meiji leaders, which left Japan for more than one and one-half years (1871-73) as an experiment in learning firsthand of the West. It is also measurable by the government's willingness to move apace on socioeconomic renovations affecting two of Japan's most important constituencies, the samurai and the farmers. In their effects on the samurai, these renovations would stanch a drain on the treasury; in their effects on the farmers, they would also help to fill its coffers.

The government first moved against the samurai. It divided the class into two groups: the lower part was made commoners by fiat; the upper part, other than daimyo, remained *shizoku*, or samurai clans. The government assumed responsibility for their stipends, once the domains' function. This may have enhanced the sense of one government over all, but it was an intolerable burden for a government embarking on other costly tasks of modernizing Japan. The leaders moved with care to eliminate this burden. It first offered the shizoku an option to exchange stipends (in rice) for cash and levied a graduated income tax on them (1873). In late 1875 all stipends were converted into cash, but the government still faced annual payments. The following year the government ordered the compulsory commutation of all stipends into interest-bearing bonds (5 to 7 percent) capitalized at between five and fourteen years of income, depending on the size of the stipend. The government was able to immediately reduce its outlay for shizoku support by about 30 percent, and it no longer faced the prospects of continuous payment.

The number of *shizoku* involved, some 311,000, was not trifling. Yet this remarkable socioeconomic revolution, initiated by a part of their number to eliminate the pride of status and hereditary income of all, was accomplished with relatively little bloodshed. If the *shizoku* had had a proprietary interest in the land, as did the gentry in China, the reaction would have been different. Samurai also had become inured to lowering expectations, since they alone among all classes during the Tokugawa had been suffering a consistent drop in income. That many among the lower ranks were already working with their hands during the Tokugawa period softened their demotion to commoner ranks. The tradition of domain loyalty militated against the rise of concerted transdomainal opposition, as did tensions between higher and lower samurai ranks. In addition, there were those like Abe Iwane, who petitioned the governor of Fukushima Prefecture (January 7, 1874) to surrender his 16 *koku* (measure of rice) stipend. His grounds were that keeping it contravened the government's policy of enlightenment (modernization), and was shameful in light of the commoners' struggle to adjust to the new conditions. The governor calculated that among the *shizoku* in the domain 10 to 20 percent shared Abe's enthusiasm. Significantly, the governor recorded nothing of rebelliousness, and this in a stronghold of anti-Sat-Cho sentiment. The enthusiastic minority, driven by idealism, fueled by excitement for the new age, and dispersed throughout the land, may have pulled along many of the uncommitted or doubtful.

The land-tax reform is the third major achievement of the first Meiji decade. By eradicating the cumbersome and inequitable Tokugawa tax system of payment in produce, it laid the basis for a modern capitalist economy that was more efficient in channeling human and material resources for modernization's tasks. To fix the tax base, the government determined the monetary value of 84.44 million parcels of agricultural lands of various kinds and issued 109.33 million certificates of land ownership. This was completed within three and one-half years, from July 1873 to the end of 1876.

The government imposed two conditions on the tax reform to reduce opposition from those who would be most affected. The total tax revenue was to be no larger than that collected under the Tokugawa, and tax burdens were to be uniform throughout Japan. Uniformity meant that tax burdens in some areas rose sharply, but overall the tax burden on most farmers may have decreased slightly; real income rose gradually but surely from 1873 to 1899. A deflationary period in the 1880s, in which the government corrected for the high expenditures of the reform and disorder of the early decade, has drawn much attention, but over the entire Meiji period agricultural output rose nearly 2 percent annually. Efficiency, uniformity, and predictability increased both the effectiveness of market forces and the integration of regional markets.

There were uprisings, some serious, among the cultivators, but nearly all were local and easily pacified. The growth of tenancy and the increasingly desperate plight of tenants compelled to regularly pay taxes in bad times are costs of the reform that are often cited. Recent studies, however, show that tenancy did not rise dramatically and that the lot of the tenant was not generally as bad as has been suggested.

THE SATSUMA REBELLION

The Satsuma Rebellion (or Seinan Senso) pitted Saigo Takamori, its leader, against his former friends and colleagues with whom he had helped established the new Meiji regime. Incensed by the government's retraction of an decision to confront and invade Korea, Saigo had withdrawn to his clan domain in Kagoshima when fighting erupted between his Satsuma bretheren and government officials. Reluctantly, he took command of the rebels, most of whom were disenchanted samurai, eventually committing seppuku (ritual suicide) after losing a final battle at Kumamoto. The rebellion was the culmination of a series of samurai uprisings that began around 1874 in reaction to the liquidation of feudal domains and the loss of special privileges enjoyed by many samurai. It became, in effect, a brief civil war involving a total of 100,000 combatants, of whom over 30,000 died. With Saigo's death, armed resistance to the new government by the samurai ended. The defeat of the samurai rebels by a disciplined conscript army of commoners also demonstrated that not only had the Meiji political and economic reforms bypassed this formerly elite class of warriors but so had Japan's requirements for national defense.

The salient characteristic of Japan's mid-nineteenth century transitional period is the demise of the samurai, in terms of lives lost and pride and status demolished. The danger of samurai uprisings preoccupied the government during its first decade. The middle 1870s saw unrest in the southwest, which had been a center of Meiji support, and where also, perhaps, expectations for the new order had been highest. The government's failure to take military measures to avenge supposed affronts from Korea sparked a demand for representative institutions from part of the governing coalition, inaugurating the movement for "freedom and people's rights" (*jiyu minken undo*) that led to political parties, as well as to samurai insurrections that culminated with the great Satsuma Rebellion of 1877. Yamagata Aritomo's letters to Ito Hirobumi in this decade hardly mention farmers' uprisings; he complained of former samurai's espousal of "people's rights," but he was more concerned by their capacity for armed attack than by their sloganeering. Major enlightenment figures like the educator-publicist Fukuzawa Yukichi (1835-1901), whose treatises circulated in hundred of thousands of copies, deprecated the political agitation of the former samurai.

The three premier leaders of the first decade passed from the scene within a year of one another. Saigo Takamori committed *hara kiri* after the Satsuma Rebellion (1877), Kido Takayoshi died of illness (1877), and Okubo Toshimichi, probably the greatest of Meiji leaders, was assassinated (1878). Their places were taken by Okuma Shigenobu, Ito, and Yamagata. Okuma and his supporters were purged from the government in October 1881 in moves orchestrated by Ito. Such was the nature of political change in Meiji Japan that Okuma would return as prime minister (1898 and 1914) and some of his followers would have illustrious careers in and out of government.

Okuma's ouster left Ito and Yamagata as the two most important political leaders. As they moved front and center, their brush strokes in letters to others changed from the tiny scrawls of the first Meiji decade to large and bold strokes. None of the Satsuma leaders filled the vacuum created by Okubo's untimely death. Only Matsukata Masayoshi made the transition to Choshu leadership, but he was patronized by the Choshu *genro* ("elders") even when he was prime minister (1891 and 1896). Sat-Cho unity, so crucial in the first decade, had given way to Choshu dominance. Consultation did not cease, but by the 1900s Hara Kei's diary notations showed that Matsukata was consulted only occasionally.

Okubo had been the principal actor in laying the foundations of Japan's modern state. The changes were aimed at specific groups: daimyo, samurai, and farmers. The other major reforms were based on the premise that Japan had to tap the resources of all its people. These renovations bear Ito and Yamagata's marks.

Significantly, both came from humble backgrounds. Ito's social status was that of a farmer, and Yamagata's that of a *chugen*, the lowest rank among the samurai.

Reform in education during the Meiji period owed much to the Tokugawa heritage. The Meiji leaders very early carried forward this inheritance by urging the establishment of elementary schools (1869). Within three years, universal compulsory education was decreed. Some farmers violently opposed the loss of their youthful labor to schools, as well as the taxes levied to support the schools, but a national system soon took root. There was little opposition when in 1908 the government added an additional two compulsory years to the original four. By the end of the Meiji, Japan had the world's highest school attendance rate. Widespread literacy had also been achieved.

There was general agreement that education should serve state purposes. The means toward this end, however, were subject to considerable and heated debate. In 1890 authorities concluded the debate through a decree, the Imperial Rescript on Education, which declared "loyalty and filial piety ... [to be] the glory of the fundamental character of Our Empire, and ... the source of Our education." Reading of the document assumed an almost sacral importance in school ceremonies, and its issuance led to a controversy about the compatibility of Christianity, which grew rapidly in the 1880s, with patriotism. Together with the earlier Rescript to Soldiers and Sailors (1882), the statement was designed to provide an ideological and moral foundation for the new Japanese citizen-subject. Nevertheless, both documents were phrased in generalities capable of varied interpretation, and neither service nor educational personnel were as uniform in their response as some writers have suggested. Many teachers, like Red Shirt in Natsume Soseki's Botchan, prided themselves in being at the forefront of Western learning. The textbooks, though uniform throughout Japan from 1903, did not preach a message of narrow nationalism through all their four revisions in the first four decades of the twentieth century. Until the 1930s, there was considerable stress on Japan's international role. The usual

---

ZAIBATSU

Zaibatsu is the term designating Japanese business conglomerates as they existed between the Meiji era and 1945. Mitsui, Mitsubishi, Sumitomo, and Yasuda were the "Big Four," characterized by family ownership, direct control of subsidiaries by holding companies, and a high degree of diversification (covering finance, trading, manufacturing, and mining). Subsidiaries were often required to borrow from the zaibatsu bank and to buy and sell through the combine's trading company.

Although Mitsui and Sumitomo dated back to the Tokugawa era (1600 - 1868), most *zaibatsu* arose after the Meiji Restoration of 1868. Known as "political merchants," Iwasaki Yataro (Mitsubishi) and other entrepreneurs expanded their operations through ties to the Meiji government.

---

portrayal of tight, centralized control over education also breaks down in consideration of the autonomy exercised by the localities, where education accounted for nearly half of town and village budgets in the last five years of the Meiji.

The institution of universal conscription (1873) and the creation of mechanisms for local self-government (1898-99) may be considered in tandem. Yamagata, the guiding force behind them both, had intended them to be so considered. He reasoned that if the nation were to demand military service of its youth, then it should permit their fathers, and later those who had served, the right of self-governance. The Tokugawa heritage of the idea of self-governance has been stressed. There was also Tokugawa precedent for commoners serving militarily alongside samurai. In Tokugawa cities, samurai intendants used commoners for police duties. Both anti-bakufu domains and the bakufu used commoners as regular troops, irregulars, or as vigilantes. Ito and Yamagata had led military

THE GREAT TEACHER: FUKUZAWA

Of all the teachers of Western learning, the most import-ant was Fukuzawa Yukichi (1835–1901). He was one of the great intellectuals in Japan's history — and certainly the most effective in disseminating ideas. Fukuzawa was a con-temporary of the Meiji reformers, the son of a low-ranking samurai family living in Osaka. At the age of nineteen he was sent by his clan to Edo to study Dutch, but soon switched to the study of English upon finding that most foreigners he met in that period could only speak in English or French.

Fukuzawa accompanied the first Japanese official mis-sion overseas on the Kanrin Maru in 1860 and visited Europe thereafter in 1862. In 1868 he founded a small school for teaching Western learning, Keio Gijuku, in Tokyo. It was the ancestor of Keio University, which Fukuzawa himself brought to university status in 1890, following the foundationof the government's Tokyo University in 1877. Some years afterward, in an effort to widen his influence, he established the Jiji Press and became famous in his own right as an editor and publicist.

He was, in the true sense of the word, an educator. His views on the importance of acquiring Western learning impressed several generations of Japanese after him. His first book, Conditions in the West, (Seiyo Jijo), was an effort to describe the institutions and daily life of Western countries, as he himself had observed and read about them in the mid eighteen-sixties. It was unusually popular, its first edition quickly selling 150,000 copies — just behind the best-selling Samuel Smiles. It contained a description of Western institutions like libraries, museums and schools for the blind — all of them unknown in Japan of that day — along with fairly detailed descriptions of education as it was conducted in a variety of countries.

Fukuzawa was at first suspicious that Okubo and the other Meiji Reformers would institute yet another strict authoritarian government, modeled upon that of the Tokugawa. When this was seen not to be the case, he set out to try to influence directly the direction of education in Japan. His next famous work, An Encouragement of Learning, met with the same kind of instant success as had Conditions in the West. Its first lines were memorable: "Heaven never created a man above another, nor a man below another," it is said, "therefore, when people are born, heaven's idea is that all should be equal." They captured the imagination of every achieving Japanese student. Old and young officials alike read greedily almost everything that Fukuzawa wrote and pondered his sweeping criticisms of traditional Japanese learning, his insistence that international learning represented Japan's only salvation.

Fukuzawa was ahead of his time in many respects, notably in his strong feelings about the oppression of Japanese women and the need for their education and opportunities for self-ful-fillment. Although it took a long time for his ideas on this subject to take effect, they were directly responsible for what strides that the Meiji Reformers made in setting up Japanese institutes of higher education for women.

Fukuzawa's later writings assumed an increasing philosophical tone, as he tried to examine precise differences between Western and Eastern versions of civilization and sought methods to harmonize the two. Hardly a revolutionary, he came in later life to adopt an increasingly nationalistic position and sought to distance Japan from the rest of Asia — as a new Western power, so to speak.

—Frank Gibney

SATSUMA PERSONALITIES

Okubo Toshimichi (1830–1878) was born in Satsuma to a samurai family and followed his father into the han bureaucracy while still in his teens. By 1861 he was among the leading policy makers in the han, which was now active in national politics.

His importance and influence in the Meiji government can be charted in the succession of positions he held, ranging from junior councilor in 1868 to state minister in the two most powerful ministries, the Finance Ministry (1871–1873) and the Home Ministry (1873–1874). By this time, holding these positions in tandem with his position as state councillor, he was de facto prime minister, with a hand in fiscal-economic policies and a powerful voice in the "heart and center of the domestic bureaucracy."

Okubo, described as forceful, tough, and of "steely implacable will," was single-mindedly devoted to the creation of the Meiji state, but he was of two minds about the West. On the one hand, he saw the advanced Western nations as a source of learning and it was in this spirit that he led the Iwakura Mission to the United States and Europe. On the other hand, the Western powers were seen as real threats to Japan's independence. They were to be given no pretext to establish a military presence in Japan. He therefore led the decision against military action in Korea (1873), declaring that the "most mature consideration and forethought is essential in order to ... protect the land and its people." This principle guided every major foreign policy decision of the Meiji state.

Matsukata Masayoshi (1835–1924), did not play a significant role in Kagoshima's defense against British bombardment (1863) or fight in battles against the shogunal government. He was, however, favored by Okubo Toshimichi, a native of Satsuma. This circumstance explains his rise in the early Meiji government. From the beginning of his career in 1871 Matsukata was chiefly associated with what became the Finance Ministry. He was finance minister for some fifteen years in all and it was on Meiji Japan's fiscal structure that he left his imprint. His premier achievement was the creation of a stable paper currency backed by silver and then by gold. This policy helped to solve the Meiji government's fundamental fiscal problem, that of earning the people's confidence. Matsukata, however, could not duplicate his success as a fiscal manager in the political arena. Even as prime minister in 1891 he depended on the support of other genro. His lack of political skill and influence contributed to Satsuma's being politically overshadowed by Choshu after Okubo's death.

Kuroda Kiyotaka (1840–1900), was also born in Satsuma. He studied Western gunnery and helped to defend Kagoshima against the British bombardment of 1863. He worked to bring about the Satsuma-Choshu coalition and then distinguished himself in the battles against bakufu forces during the early Meiji period. He went to the United States in 1871 and returned to Japan via Europe. He was appointed prime minister (1888–1889) and held other prominent posts. Kuroda's birthplace, his early career, and the support of Saigo Takamori and Okubo Toshimichi would seem to indicate a stronger role for him and Satsuma in the Meiji government after Okubo's assassination. Although he was duly appointed to high posts, he was never able to win a place for Satsuma as Choshu's equal. The reason may have been his instability stemming from alcoholism. His appointments, despite his disability, indicate that the Meiji leaders were sensitive to the requirement of maintaining a balance between Satsuma and Choshu in the government.

—George Akita, *EAH*

Ito Hirobumi (1841–1909) was the only person of peasant stock among the Meiji leaders. During Ito's youth, however, his father was adopted into a samurai family of modest rank. Ito was swept up by the convulsive events that led to the Meiji Restoration, and participated in the attack on the British legation and the assassination in 1862 of Hanawa Jiro, a National Studies (Kokugaku) scholar. After an unauthorized trip to England in 1863, however, he rejected his radical antiforeign views and became a proponent of Western learning.

Ito's talents were recognized by the leaders of the Meiji government, Kido Takayoshi and Okubo Toshimichi. He became governor of Hyogo Prefecture before he was thirty years old (1868–1869) and then went to the United States to study fiscal and currency questions (1870). In 1872 he collaborated with Okuma Shigenobu to build Japan's first railroad. He succeeded Okubo as home minister when the latter was assassinated in 1878, and three years later, in a masterful, bloodless purge, ousted Okuma from the government and succeeded him as finance minister. Since he was also state councillor, he became, as had Okubo before him, de facto "prime minister." It is a measure of the quality of Meiji leadership and of the political stability they had created that Ito went abroad for a year and a half (1882–1883) to study under leading European constitutional scholars immediately after the purge.

The two decades following Ito's return may be described as the "Ito years," in which he enjoyed a series of political successes and was the principal architect of the new European-style governmental structure. In 1884 the Imperial House Law and the peerage were established, followed in 1885 by the creation of the cabinet system. He became Japan's first prime minister (1885–1888) and again held that post on three separate occasions (1892–1896, 1898, 1900–1901). Ito was the first president of the Privy Council that was founded in 1888 to discuss the Meiji Constitution he had helped to draft. The promulgation of the constitution in 1889 was followed by the establishment in 1890 of the two-house Diet, in which Ito was the first president of the House of Peers. More significantly, Japan was the first Asian state to hold a national election for members of a legislative body.

His domestic achievements were matched by foreign affairs successes. He was prime minister when, with Mutsu Munemitsu, he accomplished what had eluded other Meiji leaders, an agreement with Great Britain (1894) to do away with extraterritoriality in 1899. During the same tenure Japan fought and won its first major war, against China (1894–1895).

Ito displayed to an exceptional degree the qualities characteristic of Meiji leaders: pragmatism, flexibility, moderation, and a preference for compromise and workable, realistic solutions. These traits were evident in two of his final major achievements. He formed the Seiyukai (1900), a political party composed of members of a former antigovernment party and bureaucrats, a political mix still evident today. He was Japan's first resident-general of the Protectorate of Korea (1905–1909). He favored an even-handed, moderate policy of reform that would respect Korean sensibilities even while Japan's national interests were served. He was assassinated by a Korean in Harbin on 26 October 1909.

—George Akita, *EAH*

Yamagata Aritomo (1838–1922) was born into a samurai family of the lowest rank in Choshu. He was the single most influential military figure in modern Japan, and his descendants still refer to him as gensui ("field marshal"). He became adept at spearmanship and in 1863 was a commander of the Choshu Kiheitai, a military force composed of samurai and commoners. He was wounded in the defense of Shimonoseki against Western warships (1864). He then led forces in pacifying northern Japan for the new Meiji government.

Yamagata was one of the earliest in the government to go abroad, traveling to Europe and the United States from 1869 to 1870 to study Western military systems. He was an architect of the National Conscription Law, enacted in 1873. That year, he was appointed army minister. In 1874 he became state councillor in recognition of his growing importance. He helped crush a series of minor revolts against the Meiji government in the 1870s and headed the imperial forces that put down Saigo Takamori's Satsuma Rebellion (1877). The following year, he was appointed chief of the Army General Staff.

Like other Meiji leaders, however, Yamagata was not a one-dimensional figure. He served as home minister (1883–1889), and during his tenure he reformed the police system and helped to establish the local government system that helped pave the way for parliamentary government. In late 1888 he took his second trip abroad, again to Europe and the United States, to study local government. When he returned in 1889, he was appointed prime minister and held that office when the first Diet session was convoked. He resigned in 1891 but became justice minister (1892–1893) and president of the Privy Council (1893), a post he held for a total of more than seventeen years, but not consecutively). In 1894, after the outbreak of the Sino-Japanese War, he led the First Army in Korea, only to have illness force his return.

Yamagata was also a diplomat, concluding the Yamagata-Lobanov Agreement (1896) and supporting Katsura Taro in bringing about the Anglo-Japanese Alliance (1902). In the meantime, he had his second tenure as prime minister (1898–1900). He was chief of the Army General Staff during the Russo-Japanese War (1904–1905), but his main activities after this were in behind-the-scenes political maneuverings. After Ito Hirobumi's assassination (1909), he became the principal organizer of cabinets.

Yamagata was the complete statesman. He was a master garden architect and accomplished in composing poetry, chanting nō librettos, and performing the tea ceremony. He was a learner who read avidly and listened attentively, especially to those recently returned from abroad. His accomplishments ranged from military to civil and foreign affairs. He preferred compromise to confrontation and prided himself that he had never dissolved the Diet as prime minister, a point he emphasized by contrasting it with the several dissolutions ordered by his archrival Ito. He was extraordinarily cautious in dealing with the Western powers, recognizing Japan's weakness in the face of any combination of the powers.

—George Akita, *EAH*

units of commoners in the bakumatsu period. The conscription system nonetheless was revolutionary in making commoner participation in the nation's armed forces regular and universal. Initially the innovation was not popular. Samurai were outraged at the destruction of a monopoly they had enjoyed for centuries. Farmers preferred shouldering hoes to guns. Elements from both groups rebelled. All were put down.

The conscription system should not be perceived as the beginning of a militaristic, expansionist Japan. Rather it should be seen in relation to the Meiji leaders' decision that war with the West was unthinkable. The army was to provide for domestic stability and security. The leading Western powers to whom Japanese leaders looked for inspiration all had citizen armies. The army was a vehicle for social mobility as well, and this further helped to promote social stability. The basic training provided to lowly recruits and the technological education provided officers created new opportunities for many.

The generalization that the Meiji transformation was tightly controlled from the center does not withstand an accounting of Meiji economic development. In the first twelve years, it is true, industrialization was encouraged through government owned and managed pilot plants.

On November 5, 1880, however, as part of Matsukata's deflationary policy, most government-owned plants were offered for sale. The outstanding feature of Meiji economic development, which built on Tokugawa antecedents of growing domestic manufacture, interregional trade, and population mobility, is that it followed Adam Smith's "natural pattern" of progress from agriculture and handicrafts to light and then heavy industry. Moreover, the stimulus for Japan's modern economic growth was the capitalistic domestic market. Foreign and colonial markets, at their maximum (1927-36), accounted for but a 20 percent share of Japan's gross national product. Significantly, the Japanese were becoming an economic challenge to the West. Western cotton spinning machines were not fully introduced into Japan until the late 1870s. But by 1897 exports of cotton yarn surpassed imports, despite protective tariffs imposed by the West. By the first decade of the twentieth century Japanese cotton goods had driven American merchandise from the Korean

"Western culture has drawn its inspiration from within, naturally, but the present future of Japan feeds itself from without and thus depends on the strength of others, not fulfilling itself ... this leads me to feel great pessimism about Japan's future."

—novelist Natsume Soseki, 1911

and Manchurian markets. By the 1920s they had captured the Asian market from China to India.

The capstone of the Meiji transformation was the establishment of constitutional government. Yamagata saw it as such and called it the "Third Restoration." Perhaps this was the most revolutionary innovation. Others can be seen as built on Tokugawa institutions and trends, but the concepts of legally enshrined individual rights and limitations on governmental powers were alien. Further, the idea of parties and factions went against the grain; majority rule sanctioned by law was a thoroughly novel conception, and public oratory and competition for votes would have been unthinkable in Tokugawa Japan. So the Meiji leaders proceeded slowly. The landmarks are clear: the consultative assemblies of governors in Tokyo (1875); the creation of prefectural assemblies (1878); the imperial promise (1881) to promulgate the constitution in 1889; the creation of the peerage and cabinet systems (1885); the establishment of the local government system; and the gradual elevation of the emperor to a position "above the clouds," to prepare him for his role as a constitutional monarch (the last grand imperial circuit was in 1885).

The Meiji constitution, the establishment of the Diet (1890), and their unceasing travels to the West show the Meiji leaders' recognition that Western strength was based as much on political institutions as on technology and arms. This may have been a crucial reason for the success of their reforms.

The sharing of political power on a national scale, minimal at first, was achieved without revolution by the masses, and this was a source of considerable pride. There was widespread interest

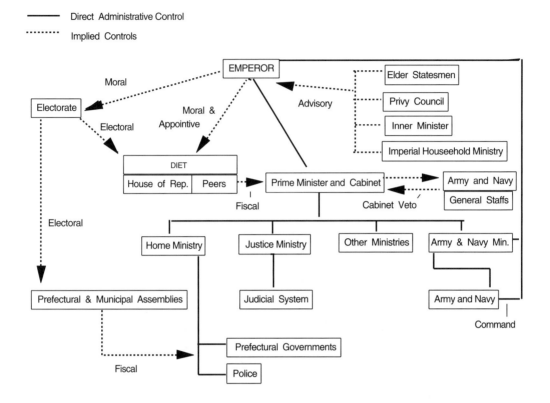

Graph 3.1   The Meiji Government

THE MEIJI CONSTITUTION

Ito had decided that the best form of government — and one most congenial to Japan of that time — was the limited form of constitutional monarchy in vogue in Bismarck's Germany. Accordingly, several German advisors were hired to come to Japan to assist in the drafting of the constitution.

The Meiji Constitution, which emerged in 1889, in many ways represented a forward step. It guaranteed male suffrage (although this was based on property rights). It provided for basic individual freedoms. It set up a bicameral legislature with broad powers, including that of the budget. Yet it failed to develop a strong sense and guarantee of popular rule by leaving a great many rights and prerogatives to the Emperor and those who represented him.

The Constitution was particularly weak in its control of the military, who were placed directly under the command of the Emperor. The custom, also, that the War Minister or the Navy Minister had to be a serving General or Admiral on the active list, gave the military an automatic veto power over the selection of any cabinet. Over the years this became a fatal pattern.

—Frank Gibney

The Changing Pattern of Japanese Trade
1878 - 1922

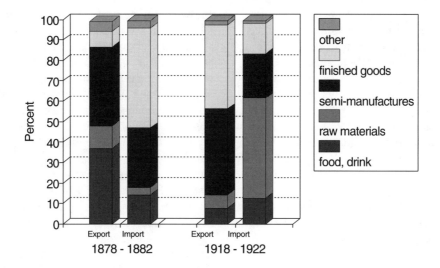

Graph 3.2

The Growth of Japanese Trade
Five-Year Periods Beginning 1878

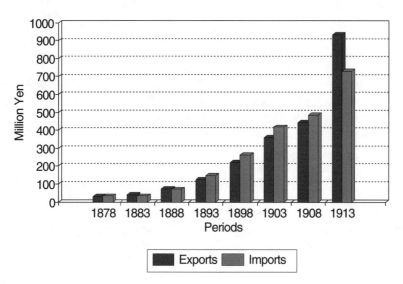

Graph 3.3

in and demand for constituent assemblies, however, and the government was determined to control the timetable for their creation. There were legal restrictions on the political opposition, and opposition leaders were jailed and fined, but the path to constitutional government was not strewn with the bodies of the opposition. Once the constitution was established, the Meiji leaders never reverted to the status quo ante — this in the face of the growing strength of the political opposition, which increased with every passing election, until a working two-party system was in place (by 1924). This is an achievement still unmatched by any non-Western country.

In a memorandum submitted in 1880, Yamagata could not conceal his pride in the government's domestic achievements: "It is true that the Meiji Restoration's achievements are outstanding ... [but these gains] are nothing compared to the question of Japan's relationship with other countries, which in turn is tied to Japan's rise and fall." This is a clear statement on the Meiji leaders' priorities. They were prudent in their dealings with the Western powers and were willing to go to great lengths to accommodate themselves to these powers. Japan was involved in three major wars during the lifetime of the Meiji leaders: the Sino-Japanese War of 1894 to 1895, which brought Japan international equality and an alliance with England (1902); the Russo-Japanese War of 1904 to 1905, which consolidated the path to empire; and World War I, which offered Japan the opportunity to consolidate its position in China. The genro [the Sat-Cho oligarchy], however, were hesitant in 1914, and this contrasted with the confidence of the younger leaders, including civilians such as Foreign Minister Kato Komei, who directed negotiation of the Twenty-one Demands (presented to China in 1915 in order to extend Japanese rights on the mainland). Hara Kei commented in the Taisho period (1912-1926) that as long as Yamagata lived, Japan would never fight America, however much younger army officers talked about it. When Yamagata died (1922), Tokutomi Soho wrote that if Yamagata could have written his own epitaph, it would read: "After me, the deluge." Both men were right.[1]

♦   ♦   ♦

REGIONAL DYNAMICS: THE NEW JAPAN AND ITS ASIAN NEIGHBORS

The Meiji Restoration is rightly called the first, and even now, the most successful self-modernization of a non-Western country. It is justly regarded as the most striking instance of an assertive and creative Asian interaction with the hitherto overpowering encroachment of Western ideas, Western economics, and Western imperialism on the East. For many throughout Asia, Japan became the new standard-bearer of an Asian resurgence against the West. In a sense this proved correct, from the grandiose plans of Japanese pan-Asian thinkers through the successful war on Russia down to the attack on Pearl Harbor in 1941.

Yet behind this lay a great historical irony. Japan's first military triumphs came at the expense of China and Korea, the countries that had influenced Japan so much. The war organization built up by Yamagata's General Staff, constructed carefully on European models, first went into action against fellow Asians. Even the Russo-Japanese War, while dramatized as a struggle of East against West, was at root a dispute over which colonial predator would dominate Manchuria and Korea. Japan's victory resulted in the crude military annexation of its closest Asian neighbor, Korea, and dominance over China, a society it had long admired.

To compound the irony, Japan's attempt at hegemony over China and Korea succeeded, at least temporarily, precisely because their efforts at modernization and internal revolution had failed, while Japan's had produced sudden and spectacular success. In the process, the Japanese grew contemptuous of neighbors they had once treated with respect. After hostilities began in 1894 the Chinese forces were revealed as weak and ineffective against both the Japanese Army and Navy. Japan's historic awe for China's power and culture had been diminishing and now it turned to ridicule as Tokyo's popular press and wood-block print artists caricatured the ineptness of the "Chinks" (*Chanchan* was a Japanese term of derision used). Behind the popular contempt and the nationalistic disparagement of China, one suspects, lay a kind of disappointment at having

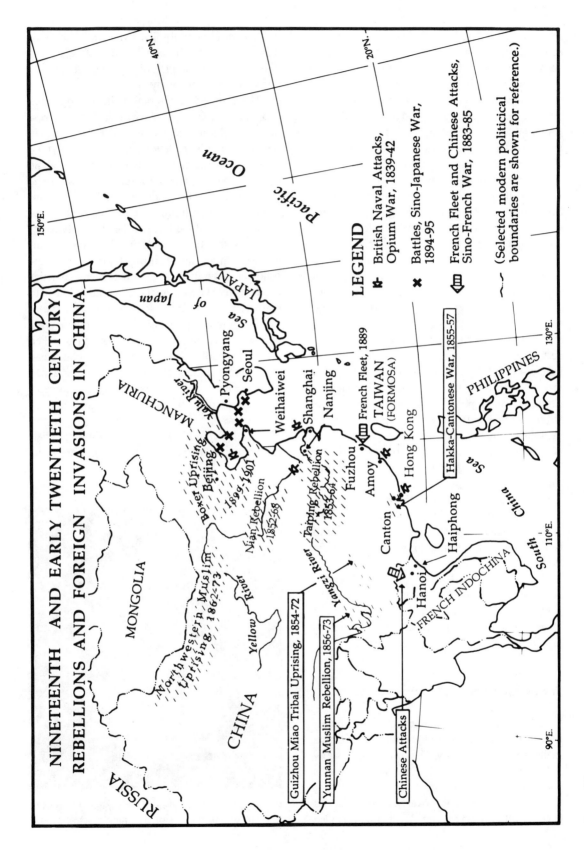

NINETEENTH AND EARLY TWENTIETH CENTURY
REBELLIONS AND FOREIGN INVASIONS IN CHINA

RUSSIA

MONGOLIA

MANCHURIA

CHINA

Yellow River

Northwestern Muslim
Uprising, 1862-73

Nian Rebellion
1852-68

Boxer Uprising
Beijing
1899-1901

Yangzi River

Taiping Rebellion
1853-64

Nanjing

Shanghai

Weihaiwei

Seoul

Pyongyang

Yalu River

Sea of Japan

JAPAN

Pacific Ocean

150°E.

40°N.

20°N.

130°E.

110°E.

90°E.

Fuzhou

Amoy

Canton

Hong Kong

TAIWAN
(FORMOSA)

French Fleet, 1889

Hakka-Cantonese War, 1855-57

PHILIPPINES

South China Sea

FRENCH INDOCHINA

Hanoi

Haiphong

Guizhou Miao Tribal Uprising, 1854-72

Yunnan Muslim Rebellion, 1856-73

Chinese Attacks

LEGEND

- British Naval Attacks,
  Opium War, 1839-42

✕ Battles, Sino-Japanese War,
  1894-95

⬇ French Fleet and Chinese Attacks,
  Sino-French War, 1883-85

--- (Selected modern political
  boundaries are shown for reference.)

respected China and the Chinese for so many centuries. In a sense, nineteenth century China became a victim of its past reputation.

Why was China unable to transform itself in the manner of Meiji Japan? What differences of culture, society, geography, and economy slowed China's advance toward modernization? This was the blunt question posed by Prime Minister Ito to China's great statesman Li Hongzhang (Li Hungchang) in Shimonoseki where Li had come in 1895 to sue for peace at the conclusion of the Sino-Japanese War. "Ten years ago I talked with you about reform," said Ito. "Why is it that up to now not a single thing has been changed or reformed?"

Li replied, "Affairs in my country have been so confined by tradition that I could not accomplish what I desired. I am ashamed of having excessive wishes and lacking the power to fulfill them." His answer is especially revealing in that he took personal responsibility for his country's failure. Li, as the governor of the maritime province of Jiangsu (Kiangsu) and commissioner for China's northern ports (it was he who created the North Pacific Fleet), served as a representative of the Qing court. As such, he became a key figure in matters dealing with the seaborne "barbarians." There being no Great Wall to guard the coast of China, officials such as Li were expected to handle foreign affairs issues with the Western powers in the course of their provincial duties. Li, moreover, was charged by the imperial government to be the chief overall negotiator for China with the Western powers.

Li's strategy was both to control the Western invasion and use it for China's modernization. The story of his career is instructive insofar as it reveals the achievements, as well as the shortcomings, of the late Qing dynasty establishment.

Li Hongzhang and the Taiping Rebellion

Li rose to power in the midst of serious rebellions and social unrest throughout much of China in the nineteenth century. The origins of this disorder lay not with the attack of the West on China's ports, but with the growing internal instability of Chinese society. Famine, poverty, corruption, and banditry all were on the rise. The population also was increasing rapidly. The extent and variety of the crises facing the country, both foreign and domestic, were completely unprecedented in the history of the Manchu dynasty.

The most serious internal challenge originated in Guangxi (Kwangsi) Province. There a frustrated scholar and mystic named Hong Xiuquan (Hung Hsiu-ch'uan), having been exposed to missionaries in Guangzhou, had a vision in which he declared that he had seen Jesus Christ (whom he considered to be his "elder brother"). Hong concocted a new religion out of this vision and declared himself the King of the Heavenly Kingdom of Great Peace, in Chinese, Taiping (T'ai-p'ing). Under the Taiping banner, he drew followers from the underworld of secret societies and cults that had sprung up as a kind of law unto themselves in much of south China. Many elements of pre-Meiji Japan's discontent were present in the Taiping movement, which attacked Confucian traditions as well as the Manchu rulers. The Taiping leaders, at least originally, preached an amalgam of militant Christianity and communal egalitarianism, but their impact was ultimately destructive.

Lasting from 1850 to 1864, the Taiping Rebellion was one of the last premodern wars to be

Figure 3.5 Li Hongzhang, who initially hoped to use the Western invasion to China's advantage.

Figure 3.6   Although the Confucian schools and examination system remained in place throughout the 19th century in China, mission schools offered training in mathematics, science and languages.

fought anywhere. Its immense cost in lives and fortunes severely crippled China at a critical point in its growing relationship with the West. Only with the installation in 1860 of a new boy emperor, followed a year later by a power struggle that threw out the worst (but not all) of the reactionary, xenophobic elements in the court, was Beijing able to mount an effective counterattack. It was barely in time. A key leader in crushing the Taipings was a Confucian scholar named Zeng Guofan (Tseng Kuo-fan) who became a successful commander of the Manchu armies with the help of Western mercenaries, such as F.T. Ward of Salem, Massachusetts and the fabled British General C.G. "Chinese" Gordon.

One of Zeng's understudies was Li Hongzhang who was given command of the Anhwei Army. After several important victories over the Taiping he was made governor general of Tianjin (Tientsin) and went on to forge alliances with key Westerners such as the powerful British (and pro-Chinese) Inspector General of Customs, Robert Hart. A varied string of crises in foreign affairs made Li indispensable to the court in Beijing, and he gradually became the de facto foreign minister of China at a time when no office of that name existed.

Li understood as well as any Japanese leader the urgent need for his nation to adapt Western learning if it was to survive. In fact, the rapid advances of the Japanese concerned him deeply. Western science was not unknown in China. Another alert bureaucrat, Wei Yuan, had written the detailed account of Western accomplishments studied by the pre-Meiji reformers in Japan. In fact, much of the Western technology and invention known to Japanese mid-nineteenth century reformers had come to them through China. Li tried to encourage the literary bureaucracy in Beijing to give greater emphasis to science and mathematics and the court approved their addition to the official curriculum in 1867. The subjects even became a part of the examinations a decade later, but their inclusion continued to meet with strong resistance within the traditional literary bureaucracy.

Figure 3.7 China's "power behind the screen," the Empress Dowager Cixi is often seen as a symbol of antireform sentiment in China, but her views were conditioned more by a need for political control than by resistance to change.

Unable to find central support for bureaucratic restructuring, Li undertook reforms and innovations within his own considerable authority. He was one of the more visible leaders of a diffuse, reform-minded body of bureaucrats that came to be known as the Self-Strengthening Movement, although they were never "organized" as such and had widely varying interpretations of what reform should mean in China. Li placed his proteges in managerial positions in new industries and joint ventures of his own creation such as textiles, telegraph, and mining companies. He also sought desperately to build and man a new navy with which to counter the rising regional influence of Japan. The speed and thoroughness with which he was able to prepare China for future military confrontations was seriously hindered by a semi-ossified bureaucracy.

Progress was also slowed by the self-aggrandizing Empress Dowager Cixi (Tz'u-hsi),

a formidable and cunning presence who held power "behind the screen" for the final four decades of the Manchu reign. (She herself dealt perhaps the single worst blow to the Chinese navy when she misappropriated most of the funds intended for its modernization to enlarge the Summer Palace in Beijing.) The traditional view of Cixi, shaped by the fact that she presided over a crumbling empire, has been of an inflexible, narrow reactionary. In fact, her views of her country and her role in it were similar to those of some of China's most successful emperors. For her, as for her predecessors (and successors in the twentieth century), the overriding necessity was to maintain political control at the center. This, rather than a principled resistance to change governed her actions. The Emperor Meiji may seem to stand in contrast to her by having presided over rapid change in Japan, but although he was influential, he was controlled by a ruling clique.

The far more powerful Cixi was in no mood to permit outsiders such access to imperial decision-making.

To maintain herself in power and to ensure that political control would not devolve to the provinces, the Dowager Empress allowed the reactionaries in her court to block all reform efforts on a national scale, including those proposed by Li. When, in 1898 during a brief period known as the One Hundred Days, a small group of reformers managed to gain the impressionable young emperor's authority to issue dozens of "radical" decrees, Cixi used her influence to overthrow the new advisors. The leaders of the reform group, two brilliant scholars named Liang Qichao (Liang Ch'i-ch'ao) and Kang Youwei (K'ang Yu-wei), escaped execution only by fleeing to Japan. There they taught and inspired many of the emigre Chinese revolutionaries who were eventually to help bring the Manchu dynasty to an end.

Li Hongzhang was not one of these, however. When his initiatives were blocked by Cixi or the court aristocracy, he bided his time; whenever he was pilloried for negotiating peace terms with foreigners (such as concessions to the French in 1884 to settle their claims in Annam, part of Vietnam), he endured the insults. Singlehandedly, he had tried to set up several modern factories and an arsenal in China. Whenever one of these business ventures collapsed, he would try again in another sector. He was, in short, the quintessential servant of China and the imperial court; a power seeker who also had the interests of the state firmly in mind.

Meanwhile, under the influence of foreign legations and special trading arrangements, China's so-called treaty ports began to behave more and more like independent city states. In spite of Cixi's efforts to prevent it, the centralized authority in Beijing grew weaker even as its dependence on trade taxes increased.

By the end of the century, the Qing dynasty was to find itself engaged in a disastrous military confrontation with the new regime in Japan (described below), resulting in Li Hongzhang's negotiation of the humiliating Treaty of Shimonoseki.

Li and others like him in China fought, nevertheless, a skillful diplomatic retreat by using the endemic rivalry and mistrust among the Western powers to encourage a balance of forces. In this turbulent period, the overlapping interests of nations were far too complex to permit any leader to plan with confidence. To understand what followed, we must return to developments in the land that remained the pivotal element in East Asian political relationships: Korea.

Korea: The Fulcrum of Power in East Asia

As a result of its relative weakness early in the Meiji period, Japan's diplomatic inititatives were limited; yet the Meiji government managed to find such opportunities early on. When some ship-wrecked fishermen from the Ryukyu Islands to the south were killed by aborigines on Taiwan, Japan turned their misfortune into a diplomatic incident. Assuming the role of the Ryukyus' protector, Japan responded by sending a punitive expedition against Taiwan in 1874.

Alert leadership in Beijing would have protested but the Chinese were preoccupied with rebellions in Central Asia and agreed to pay Japan an indemnity by way of settlement. In the logic of the imperialist world at the time, Japan thus established a recognizable sovereignty over the Ryukyus. Apart from adding some useful and symbolic real estate to Japan, the expedition to Taiwan accomplished one other function, however unintended: The ships that had been purchased for transporting the troops were turned over to Iwasaki Yataro's fledgling Mitsubishi company, which ultimately developed the global merchant fleet of N.Y.K. (for Nihon Yusen Kaisha).

The priority for the Meiji leaders was not the Ryukyus, however, but Korea. They desperately wanted to find a way to "open" Korea much as Commodore Perry had "opened" their own country. The reasons for this geographical focus were partly strategic, because of Korea's proximity to Japan; partly ideological, i.e., to transform the "corrupt" regime of their neighbor; and partly economic, to secure additional food supplies and a market for Japan's nascent industries.

Ironically, the United States gave them an opportunity to do so in 1871 when it sent a punitive expedition to Korea. The so-called U.S. Asiatic Fleet, consisting of five warships based in China under Admiral John Rogers, received orders to attack Korea after the Koreans had sunk and burned an American merchant vessel, the *Sherman*, as it sailed up the Taedong River to the city of Pyongyang. All those aboard the ship had been killed. In the retaliatory move, American marines succeeded in capturing a key fort on Korea's Kanghwa Island, but Rogers lacked the strength to press his temporary advantage and so withdrew.

In this incident the Meiji government saw an opportunity to undertake one of its first official diplomatic initiatives: It offered to serve as an intermediary in the dispute over the sinking of the *Sherman*. Tokyo's real aim was to establish a working diplomatic relationship with Korea, but to the Taewon'gun,[2] Korea's conservative regent, the Japanese emissaries looked like all the other "barbarians" in Western dress. He refused either to meet them or recognize their diplomatic credentials.

Korea began to impose an ever-increasing isolation on itself. Like Japan's earlier "men of spirit," some of Korea's *yangban* (gentry) watched with growing horror the depredations of the West in China — not to mention the spreading influence of French Catholicism within their own borders. The retreat from Kanghwa by the U.S. marines convinced the Taewon'gun that his isolationist policy was working. This, combined with the desecration by foreigners of his father's grave three years earlier, reinforced his resolve to declare the country off-limits to all foreigners except for Korea's ancient benefactor, China. Korea thus became viewed by Westerners as "The Hermit Kingdom." For a time it receded from their view, each power pursuing other preoccupations: Britain in India, France in Annam (Vietnam), and Russia in Siberia and the Kurile Islands. The United States, meanwhile, struggled to rebuild from the damage of the Civil War.

Pleased with his apparent success, the Taewon'gun confidently erected monuments across the land proclaiming his own version of Japan's "*sonno joi*" antiforeign policy. Korea, he said, must "fight back when invaded by the Western barbarians." The nation would not be "sold out" in peace negotiations. A reformer in his own mind, he sought to return Korea to its Confucian foundations while maintaining its ancient fealty to China. His emissaries thus continued their pilgrimages to the Chinese court to request its help and advice, seemingly ignorant of China's own growing predicament.

The Old Order Passes

The official isolationism of the Korean court was powerfully reinforced by the preachments of a new creed, called *Tonghak*, or Eastern Learning. Founded by a wandering aristocrat named Ch'oe Che-u in 1860, it seemed a bulwark against the encroachments of *Sohak*, or "Western Learning," as Roman Catholicism at the time was called. Paradoxically, Tonghak echoed in some ways the secular strategies being advocated elsewhere in East Asia at this time, each of which sought to utilize Western intellectual traditions. In Japan, one of the early students of "Dutch learning," Sakuma Shozan, had coined the phrase "Eastern ethics and Western science" as an expression of his strategy to capture the techology of the Europeans without losing Japanese cultural identity. Similarly, the Qing official Wei Yuan had urged his countrymen to "learn the superior science of the barbarians so that we can control them."

In Korea, Ch'oe proclaimed a vision that combined elements of indigenous and foreign faiths, including Christianity. Although Tonghak advocated loyalty to the king, it contained a profoundly populist, anti-establishment appeal and rapidly gained converts among impoverished people throughout the country. Like the Taipings in China, the Tonghaks envisioned a new regime that would be built on the ashes of the old order. Ch'oe's initial strategy for achieving a paradise on earth, in which all people would live in harmony and equality, called for an evolutionary — not revolutionary — process. Nonetheless, Ch'oe was suspected by the court of fostering rebellion and was tortured and executed. His successors led a large scale uprising, the first of its kind in Korea, that ended in defeat in 1894 but not before it had precipitated a war between China and Japan over who would "help" Korea put down the rebellion. Japan emerged victorious in this contest and consolidated its grip over Korea. Thus, in the end, the Tonghaks achieved part of their goal: The old order fell into its death throes partly as a result of their rebellion. But instead of paradise on earth

Korea gained a regime dominated by a foreign power — Japan. To understand this chain of events, it is necessary to consider the assymetry of power and uneven pace of change between Korea and Japan.

Korea's agony in the late nineteenth century was that of a country whose leadership was slow to adjust to social changes and external pressures. The rulers during its Yi (Chosun) dynasty were even more reactionary than the Manchu die-hards in Cixi's Qing court. There were several reasons for this, not the least being that Korea's aristocracy, or *yangban*, had begun to disintegrate under the pressures of factionalism and poverty. The *yangban* themselves had hardly been exemplars of what might be called civic duty in the Confucian sense. Obsessed with court politics, they spent too little time managing their estates and imposed increasingly burdensome taxes on the peasantry. But as more and more of them sank into poverty and effectively lost their status, the credibility of Confucianism itself came under heavy pressure. Meanwhile, those still in power became so rapacious in their taxes and land seizures that open peasant revolts began to break out in several provinces.

The seeds of Ch'oe Chu-e's Tonghak religion thus fell on fertile soil all across Korea. As its adherents grew in number, the authorities in Seoul tried to suppress it. They were distracted by what seemed, after all, a far greater threat: the increasing efforts by foreign powers to "open" Korea to international trade and most especially by the persistence of the Japanese. The first humiliating treatment of the Meiji envoys by the Taewon'gun came close to provoking Japan into launching a punitive campaign against Korea in 1873. Although Saigo Takamori's plan to invade Korea at this time was scuttled by his colleagues, Okubo and Kido, two years later the Japanese were able to make their point to Korea by using Commodore Perry's technique of displaying superior naval power. By 1876 the Koreans were sufficiently intimidated by Japan to sign with it the Treaty of Kanghwa, which opened two ports to Japanese trade. The other colonial powers, stirred by Japan's success, moved rapidly to make their own treaties with Korea. They were encouraged and assisted in their efforts by Li Hongzhang, who saw the need to introduce counterbalancing forces against Japan in a country that he and the authorities in Beijing still deemed to be China's fiefdom.

Korea was unprepared for the suddenness of these developments and the blows fell heavily on its economy. The treaties it had been forced to sign were modeled on the unequal treaties imposed on China and, initially, on Japan. These permitted foreigners to buy land and establish businesses independent of Korean law. Foreign capital, mostly Japanese, moved rapidly into circulation in Korea. Not only did this accelerate the debasement of the local currency (one European traveler complained of having to load an entire donkey train with copper coins in order to have sufficient funds for a trip in the provinces), but Korean wealth began to be siphoned off at an alarming rate. The fundamental measure of this wealth was rice which the Japanese bought up in enormous quantities, raising the price beyond what ordinary Koreans could afford.

A small court elite quickly saw that Korea must engage in a race to modernize or fall increasingly under the domination of Japan or other colonial powers. Yet the larger community of Confucian scholars in Korea objected. They demanded not an opening to Western ideas but the reverse, including strict controls over the import of books. In spite of a few desultory steps toward governmental reform by Korea's King Kojong, the views of the conservative majority held sway in Seoul and further precious time was lost.

By now the court had come under the domination of a faction headed by the king's wife, Queen Min. Her father-in-law, the Taewon'gun, was shunted aside, eventually to be kidnapped by the Chinese and hauled off to Beijing after he tried to regain power through a coup. Observing this turn of events, Japan sent troops to try to effect greater control of the situation in Seoul, but they were blocked by overwhelming Chinese forces. Li Hongzhang had stationed a permanent garrison in Seoul under the command of one of his most aggressive generals, Yuan Shikai (Yuan Shih-k'ai), who would emerge years later as a strongman in China's revolution.

Korea had now become the focal point of Sino-Japanese conflict. For a time, Japan had hopes of outmaneuvering China by fomenting an internal uprising in Seoul and establishing a reform-minded, pro-Japanese government led by

Kim Ok-kyun, a reform-minded scholar who had studied under Fukuzawa Yukichi in Japan. On the night of December 4, 1884, during a festive dinner party, Kim and his followers seized control of the royal palace and called in the local garrison of two hundred Japanese troops to protect them. They quickly announced a new political program and for a day or so appeared to have staged a successful coup. General Yuan, however, counterattacked with his 1,500-man Chinese garrison, overwhelming the rebels and their Japanese defenders.

The failure of this coup, which has become known as the Kapsin coup (after the year-name), marked a tactical turning point in Japan's relations with Korea. Abandoning all hope of "reform" in Korea and thereby of controlling it from within, Japan reverted to bold, strong-arm tactics. The government in Tokyo cooly denied all responsibility for the revolt and the Koreans had no choice but to accept the demands of the Japanese for reparations. Beijing agreed to a mutual withdrawal of Japanese and Chinese forces from Seoul.

Undeclared War

Japan was now well-positioned to take advantage of any new crisis. The withdrawal of Chinese forces had occurred just as the Japanese general Yamagata's armies were completing a massive buildup. Meanwhile, Japan's aggressive shipping companies were beginng to dominate the carrying trade for Koreans. Large-scale Japanese fishing enterprises overwhelmed thousands of

Figure 3.8 Factional politics, endemic to the Korean court, pitted the family of King Kojong, led by his conservative father the Taewon'gun, against the family of his wife, Queen Min.

Figure 3.9 Stabbed to death in her own quarters by a Japanese assassination squad, Queen Min represented the last strong center of indigenous political power in Korea in the nineteenth century.

Korean fishermen, and the mounting export of Korean rice along with other daily necessities impoverished and weakened the Korean economy. The response by the court in Seoul, now dominated by Queen Min's faction, was merely to impose even greater taxes to compensate for its lower revenues.

Popular protests rose. By 1894, the government tried to placate the rebels, but it was too late to avoid major bloodshed. The Tonghaks demanded an end to rice exports to Japan and a complete restructuring of power and privilege in Korea. Unable to comply even if he had wanted to, King Kojong turned to China for help in quelling the uprising.

By previous agreement, China and Japan were required to inform one another if they intended to move troops into Korea. China thus notified Japan that in response to the king's request it was about to send troops and a fleet to Korea to quell the Tonghaks. Japan reacted immediately by landing its own invasion force at Inchon. On July 25, 1894, without a declaration of war, Japanese warships intercepted and destroyed the Chinese fleet off Asan Bay in the Yellow Sea.

Most European military experts had predicted that China would be the victor if war broke out between China and Japan. The action of war quickly demonstrated how far the balance had turned in Japan's favor. After a series of swift victories, the Japanese drove the Chinese forces northward out of Korea. The strategic naval base of Port Arthur (Lushun) on the Liaodong (Liaotung) Peninsula was captured, as well as the island of Taiwan.

At this point, China desperately sought peace terms. Its fleets had been destroyed and its provincial forces had fallen back in the face of a better equipped and better trained Japanese army. With the Japanese public calling not for peace but for ever greater victories, China's early conciliatory initiatives were spurned and Japan's bargaining position became even stronger. By the time Li Hongzhang was finally permitted to sit down with Ito at the peace table in Shimonoseki in 1895, he had little left with which to bargain.

The resulting treaty imposed a staggering penalty on China. Not only was China required to pay Japan a crushing indemnity of 360 million yen, but it had to recognize Korea's "independence" (giving uncontested suzerainty over Korea to Japan), cede to Japan the Liaodong Peninsula, the Pescadores Islands, and the island of Taiwan, and open several more ports to Japanese trade.

Perhaps Li Hongzhang, the inveterate balancer of forces, knew all along that the European powers would never permit Japan to achieve such a dominant position. At any rate, his hopes were fulfilled within a week of the signing of the treaty when France, Germany, and Russia demanded that Japan give back Port Arthur and the Liaodong Peninsula. Shocked and outraged by this "Triple Intervention," the Japanese public supported an all-out military buildup to prevent any such future humiliation. By 1897 military spending had increased to 55 percent of the national budget!

Two years later China leased Port Arthur to Russia. The czar's government then fortified it heavily and turned it into a major base for Russia's Pacific fleet. Meanwhile, Germany appropriated similar interests on China's Shandong peninsula, as did France in Henan along with a ninety-nine year lease in Guangzhou Bay to the south. Britain obtained a lease on Weihaiwei in 1898 and set up its sphere of influence in the Yangzi Valley.

The United States did not participate in this division of the spoils (which was accomplished by intimidation and force), holding instead to Secretary of State John Hay's "Open-Door Policy" that called for equal commercial access to China by all nations, and, later, the maintenance of China's territorial integrity. But this did nothing to prevent the incursions by the imperial powers, nor could the United States have prevented them if it wished, for it was too weak militarily at the time. What forces it possessed were committed toward developing a base in the Philippines which, from the standpoint of Japanese and European observers, represented a new imperialist path for the United States.

In spite of the "loss" of the Liaodong Peninsula, Japan's victory in the Sino-Japanese War made it a force to be reckoned with. Russia, for one, became alarmed at the growth of Japanese power in Korea, which bordered its sphere of influence in Manchuria and threatened its nearby port of Vladivostok. In 1896, amid the pomp and circumstance of the coronation of Czar Nicholas II, Li Hongzhang signed the Li-Lobanov Treaty in which Russia agreed to protect China against any

Japanese attacks. In exchange, Russia received rights to build a railroad across Manchuria linking Harbin with Port Arthur.

In Korea, the Japanese remained thwarted by Queen Min's faction at the royal court (which now had the support of the Russians). They quietly plotted her assassination with the help of the Taewon'gun. In the early morning of October 8, 1895, a band of assassins stormed the palace, found the Queen and stabbed her to death. An immediate cry of outrage rose from the diplomatic community, two of whose members had witnessed the crime. In a daring countermove, the Russian minister in Seoul, Alexander de Speyer, formed an armed escort which took King Kojong from his palace and placed him under the protection of the Russian legation.

After this, Russia began to establish ever-closer ties with the Korean government, training its army and financial experts while guaranteeing the security of the king. By 1898 all commands in the new Korean army were being issued in Russian. Yet no nation, including Russia, approached Japan in its ability to aggressively dominate Korea's overseas trade, three-fourths of which was with Japan by the turn of the century. Japanese railroads, Japanese timber industries, Japanese telegraph services, and many other business interests controlled by Japan dominated life in Korea.

The Boxer Rebellion

At this point, a domestic antiforeign uprising emerged to play a pivotal role in the politics of Asia, one that grew out of the rage of the common people over their displacement and exploitation at the hands of foreigners and the incapacities of their traditional government to prevent it. Called the "Boxers" from a mistranslation of the Chinese name, *Yihetuan*, (United in Righteousness and Harmony), the movement soon established a covert alliance with the Manchu court which saw it as a force to drive out the Westerners. By 1900 the so-called rebels had laid siege to the foreign legations in Beijing and Tianjin after killing thousands of Christian converts and 250 foreigners, mainly missionaries, throughout China.

Inside the legation walls in Beijing, the foreign diplomats, businessmen, and their families ate their racing ponies one by one as they awaited relief from a force made up of soldiers from virtually every nation represented in China. Japan contributed the largest number of troops to this effort, but soldiers also participated from Russia, Great Britain, France, and the United States. Eventually, they succeeded in freeing all the foreign legations and went on to thoroughly loot the city of Beijing. The Empress Dowager and the young emperor fled to Xi'an to permit things to cool down.

In his last diplomatic negotiation, and perhaps his most ignominious, Li Hongzhang papered over the fact that the Empress Dowager had supported the Boxers. The protocol he signed with the imperialist powers in 1901 kept the treaty system intact and arranged for yet more concessions, heaping another monstrous indemnity on China's already crushing burden of foreign payments. He died a few weeks later.

Russo-Japanese Tensions

Russia used the Boxer crisis to considerable advantage. While sending a few troops to the Beijing relief expeditions, the czar's government argued that the railroad from Port Arthur must be protected from falling into rebel hands. Large Russian forces were moved into Manchuria, where they became a virtual army of occupation.

With Russia now her chief rival for hegemony in Asia, Japan sought to find a counterweight. The obvious choice was Great Britain, the czar's ubiquitous competitor in the "Great Game" of empire. Japan persuaded Britain to renegotiate their "unequal" commercial treaty (a pattern soon to be followed by other nations), and eventually the British agreed to a formal Anglo-Japanese Alliance (1902), the first between an Asian nation and a European power. The stage for the Russo-Japanese War was now set.

Russia, besides widening its ties to the Korean court, gave even greater priority to its interests in Manchuria, where both China and Japan had requested Russian troop withdrawals. Tensions rose over Russia's continued Manchurian deployment.

A few leaders on both sides sought to avoid war. Prince Ito, convinced that Japan could not

MEIJI JAPAN AND THE FAILURE OF THE KABO REFORM, 1894-1896

Japan's victory in its war with China in 1894 opened up a new opportunity for it to promote a reform-minded, pro-Japanese government in Korea. Working with Korean reformers, the Japanese persuaded the Taewon'gon to lead the new government, thereby appealing to the Tonghak insurgents who remained a formidable protonationalist force in Korea. The result was a short-lived but important movement known as the Kabo ("1894") Reform. Lasting from July 1894 to February 1896, the movement was led by many key figures in the Korean "enlightenment" politics of the 1880s (the period of the abortive "Kapsin Coup"). These were people who had studied or lived in Japan and the United States and were committed to nationalism, egalitarianism, and modern capitalism.

Meiji Japan was a model for this idealistic reform movement during which 210 reform bills were adopted by a special Deliberative Council and a dozen royal edicts, setting forth the goals of the reform, were promulgated by King Kojong. The Reform had the following objectives:

1. *Full Korean independence as a nation.* Unequal treaties with China were abrogated and Chinese privileges in Korea abolished. A new Ministry of Foreign Affairs was created and plans were made for establishing foreign legations. Education reforms emphasized schooling that would instill a sense of Korean national identity and the use of the national *hangul* script was encouraged.

2. *A cabinet-centered constitutional monarchy.* Seven new ministries were established under a Japanese-style Cabinet. Local administration was revamped to provide greater control from the center under the supervision of the home minister.

3. *Increased national wealth.* Fiscal authority was concentrated in the new Ministry of Finance and a modern taxation system was introduced. Modern banking and monetary sytems were established. Legal restrictions on private entrepreneurs were eased and plans were made for state support of new industries and national infrastructure.

4. *Strengthened military security.* A new military command system was created. Plans were laid for a Military Academy and officers training school. Modern police units and administration were introduced in all major cities.

5. *A new system of education.* The traditional government examination system was abolished and in its place an integrated system of modern elementary schools, high schools, and colleges was introduced. Some two hundred students were sent to Japan for education at government expense.

6. *A modern judicial system.* Executive powers were separated from judicial powers. A modern court system was introduced and criminal rights, as well as the rights of the families of criminals, were improved.

7. *Sweeping social reforms.* Class distinctions between the *yangban* elite and commoners were abolished along with slavery. Early marriage was prohibited (no sooner than twenty for men; sixteen for women). The western calendar was adopted. Most controversially, an order was issued — and briefly enforced — that Korean men cut off their traditional topknot.

The Kabo Reforms, which occurred during a period of political turbulence and intense foreign rivalry in Korea, encountered stiff resistance from the Koreans themselves. This was partially due to Confucian conservatism, but anti-Japanese passions were enflamed during the reform period when the Japanese murdered Queen Min. King Kojong subsequently fled to the protection of the Russian legation and the reform movement collapsed. Two pro-Japanese cabinet members were murdered; the others fled to Japan. Yet the memory of the Kabo Reform movement did not die. Early in the next century many of its goals were to be revived by a new generation of Koreans this time in defiance of their colonial masters, the Japanese.

Japan had the advantage of fighting close to its main sources of supply. With control of the seas, the Japanese quickly landed troops above Port Arthur. There, General Nogi Maresuke threw wave after wave of troops against entrenched machine gun positions in a lesson that seemingly went unnoticed by generals on the European continent a decade later. From Tokyo, Yamagata, now Chief of the General Staff, urged Nogi to press on against the naval base — "the most important element in the victory or defeat of our army."

After spectacular losses, Nogi's forces prevailed. Later on, Mukden fell in a collision of armies numbering 300,000 on each side. In the meantime, Russia's Baltic fleet was making its way painfully around the world after having its use of the Suez Canal denied by Japan's new ally — Great Britain. Immediately on its arrival in the Tsushima Straits, which separate Japan from Korea, Admiral Zinovi Rozhdestvensky found

Figure 3.10 The foreign population of China was oblivious to the discontent that was rising against it. Thousands of missionaries and their Christian converts were slain by the "Boxer" rebels shown here.

defeat Russia, argued for a conciliatory posture in the face of mounting public jingoism; Foreign Minister Katsura Taro complained of being reviled by the press "as a traitor and a coward" because he sought to avoid the conflict. But Russia's policy, under its new Far Eastern Viceroy, Admiral Eugene Alexiev, remained both belligerent and ill-informed as to Japan's growing military capabilities. By 1904 Japan's leaders had lost all patience and they launched a surprise naval attack on Port Arthur, sinking virtually the entire Russian squadron at anchor. Two days afterward, Tokyo issued an official declaration of war.

Once again part of the Asian mainland became a battlefield for great armies. But this time it was well-equipped, modern "imperialist" forces that fought one another, amid unprecedented carnage and suffering, over a barren winter landscape which each deemed to be an incalculable prize.

Figure 3.11 As a multinational force fought its way to their relief, the heroics of the defenders of the foreign legations in Beijing became the grist of tabloids throughout the Western world.

Admiral Togo's warships lying in wait. The Russian fleet was utterly demolished.

Most of the great powers, alarmed by Russia's expansionist policies, had leaned toward a preference for a Japanese victory. Once it had been achieved, however, they became wary of the rising power in the East. Kaiser Wilhelm II's use of the phrase, *die Gelbe Gefahr* — "the Yellow Peril" — reflected the racism inherent in this concern. For his part, however, President Theodore Roosevelt was almost openly "pro-Japanese" and quite pleased with the war's outcome. Committed throughout to Hay's "Open Door Policy" of keeping the war out of China, he felt it was time to suggest a peaceful solution. "We may be of genuine service," he had written to Hay in 1904, "if Japan wins out, in preventing interference to rob her of the fruits of victory." In the summer of 1905 the then-Secretary of War, William Howard Taft, met with Japan's foreign minister in Tokyo and signed the Taft-Katsura agreement in which both nations agreed to respect each other's "paramount interest" in Korea and the Philippines, respectively. Roosevelt then urged Japan and Russia to accept him as a mediator for a peace treaty.

Japan's leaders realized full well that their nation, not yet a mature industrial power, would be unable to sustain such a costly war effort for very long. For their part, despite the czar's intransigence in the matter, Russian leaders saw little hope of readily reversing their staggering losses. Accordingly, both nations accepted Roosevelt's offer to negotiate a peace, and a treaty was finally concluded in Portsmouth, New Hampshire, in the fall of 1905.

News of the succession of victories in Manchuria had been received throughout Japan in an ecstasy of nationalistic pride. The people thought they would be heir to vast new territories, a fabulous indemnity at the czar's expense, and new respect from the Western world. Some even imagined a Japanese empire extending from the Pacific through Russia's Far East to Lake Baikal. Instead, the Portsmouth Treaty gave Japan no indemnity at all. Japan did obtain substantial Russian holdings in Manchuria, as well as the southern half of Sakhalin Island, but this was far below the public expectation.

When word of the settlement reached Japan, it was met with stunned disbelief. A succession of

Figure 3.12 Japanese troops during the Russo-Japanese War. The carnage of the land war anticipated the slaughter that was to come a decade later in the trench warfare of World War I.

riots erupted over the "betrayal" of Japan in the negotiations. Little did the protesters understand that with their nation's victory in this war they had arrived at one of the critical turning points in contemporary Asian history, one that began to alter fundamentally the way other Asians viewed their own capacity to challenge the incursions of the West. Japan exemplified the ability of an Asian nation to adapt the so-called Western Learning to its own needs and turn it against its originators. The goal set by the Meiji founders half a century earlier to "enrich and strengthen" Japan seemed now to be fulfilled by this extraordinary victory over a European power — and it offered hope that other Asian nations might emulate Japan's performance.

Meiji Japan and the Roots of Revolution in Asia

Tokyo in the early years of the twentieth century became a haven for Asian revolutionaries. Foremost among them were refugees from China who had fled after failing at their own attempt at reform, called the Hundred Days Reform. They placed high hopes in the reforming influence of Japan, particularly following the Sino-Japanese

War. These included the original radical reformers of the One Hundred Days campaign, Kang Youwei, but also a new, more internationally oriented figure named Sun Yat-sen.

Sun had returned to Japan from London in 1897 something of an international celebrity because of a highly publicized incident in which the Chinese legation in London had tried to kidnap him. He quickly gained a number of Japanese backers who, under the banner of "Pan-Asianism," sought to bring about Japanese-style reforms in China. Hundreds of Chinese students who had been sent for their education in Japan flocked to Sun. They were quickly radicalized by his ideas and inspired by the lectures and writings of his learned rival Liang Qichao. From his base in Tokyo, Sun attempted to stage several uprisings in China, all to no avail. He was eventually banished from Japan after the Qing court brought extreme pressure to bear on Tokyo, but he kept up his contacts with Japan's pan-Asianists, an odd mixture of nationalist and radical thinkers.

On coming to power, finally, in the Chinese Revolution of 1911, he had considerable Japanese support.

Japan's defeat of Russia in 1905 inspired revolutionary leaders in Southeast Asia as well — and they were supported and encouraged by the Japanese in the new "Pan-Asia" societies. The Philippine patriot, Jose Rizal, moved to Japan in the late 1880s and lived there for more than a year. Two of Vietnam's most influential early nationalists, Phan Boi Chau and Phan Chu Trinh, moved to Japan specifically for the purpose of learning how the Meiji leaders had succeeded in their efforts to counter the European thrust. By this time France had consolidated its hold over all of Indochina and only a few pockets of resistance were left. Phan Boi Chau was strongly influenced by the Japanese example in his writings and he saw in the restoration of the Meiji emperor the potential for a modern "restored monarchy" in Vietnam. At one point he even brought Vietnam's Prince Cuong De to Tokyo to plan the restoration before

Figure 3.13 Many Japanese saw themselves as the leaders of change and "liberation" in Asia, but they ruthlessly exploited Korea as a colony and military foothold on the mainland.

changing his views in the direction of a democratic republic. Chau frequently exchanged ideas with Sun Yat-sen and helped found in Tokyo an organization of Asian nationalists from countries as diverse as China, Korea, India, and the Philippines. This "East Asia United League," supported by radical Japanese Pan-Asianists, became a vehicle for mobilizing a broader base of support for insurgencies in Asian countries in the early twentieth century. By contrast, Phan Boi Chau's compatriot, Phan Chu Trinh, soon became suspicious of Japanese intentions in supporting Pan-Asian nationalism. He left Tokyo and returned to Vietnam to agitate against colonial abuses and begin his own reform programs. Within a few years he was arrested and imprisoned by the French authorities.

One group of Asia's radical nationalists was conspicuously not encouraged in Tokyo. These were the Koreans, the heirs of the Kapsin revolutionaries of 1884. The reformer Kim Ok-kyun had been assassinated in 1894 by a pro-Chinese Korean government agent, ironically provoking an outcry in Japan that had helped mobilize public support for the Sino-Japanese War. Kim's successors in Tokyo in the early 1900s found little support among the Japanese for their ideas about national reform and independence. Korea was made a Japanese protectorate in 1905 and Japan had no intention of relaxing its grip.

In 1907 King Kojong made a last desperate bid for outside help. He sent envoys to the World Peace Conference being held at the Hague, where they appealed to the international delegates for help. Embarrassed and angered by this display of independence, Ito — now Korea's Governor General — forced the abdication of King Kojong and installed Kojong's son as king. The Korean army responded by attacking local Japanese units in Seoul before fleeing to the countryside. With peasant support, Korean nationalist guerillas continued to inflict heavy casualties on the Japanese. This grass-roots revolt was finally suppressed in 1908, but not before some twelve thousand Korean guerilla fighters had been killed.

Ito justified the brutal repression of the Koreans as being the more "moderate" of the solutions advocated in Tokyo at the time. He had, in fact, consistently advocated a policy of compromise in an effort to win the Korean's support. Sadly, he was given little time to try more moderate policies. In 1909 he was assassinated by a Korean patriot, An Chung-gun, at the Harbin railway station as he prepared to meet with the Russian finance minister. His death provoked an even more brutal repression of Korean dissidents, culminating in 1910 with the formal annexation of Korea by Japan.

With this action, the hope of other Asian reformers for an enlightened Japanese pan-Asianism was effectively stilled. When even a liberal like Fukuzawa Yukichi could call Japan's war on China "a battle for the sake of world culture" there seemed little hope that Japan would genuinely identify with the aspirations of other Asians. Even the enlightened crusader for popular rights Okuma Shigenobu noted unctuously: "The harmonization of Eastern and Western civilizations has always been and will depend on the intellectual power of the well-informed class of the Japanese nation."

◆   ◆   ◆

MEIJI JAPAN: AN ASSESSMENT
— by Mikiso Hane

Despite all the difficulties and problems that beset the people, the Meiji era can nevertheless be considered to have been a magnificent half-century for Japan, perhaps the most remarkable such period in all her history. She emerged, with a modern army and navy, from a secluded feudal nation into one of the world's major powers. Japan had industrialized sufficiently during this period to lay the groundwork for the next phase of her growth, in which she was to rank economically among the major industrial nations. She had adopted Western political and legal institutions and was consequently accorded equal treatment by the Western powers, who relinquished the special privileges they had acquired from her in the mid-nineteenth century. Party government had not yet come into its own, but it was definitely on the horizon. Constitutional government, though imperfect, had unquestionably become an established institution; and if rule-of-law had not yet become a reality, at least rule-by-law had come about.

Some critics have labeled the Meiji government "totalitarian," but there was certainly nothing like the kind of authoritarianism that had prevailed half a century earlier. There were still, of course, aristocrats and commoners, and the gap between the rich and the poor did continue to grow. However, there was legal equality and, theoretically, an open society with some degree of social mobility had come into existence. Universal education had been introduced [1872]; in 1900, tuition fees were eliminated; and in 1907 compulsory education was extended to six years. Despite the two-year extension, school attendance was over 98 percent in 1908.

The extent to which Japan was modernized by the end of the Meiji era is a matter of controversy. Okakura Kakuzo remarked at the turn of the century, "Accustomed to accept the new without sacrificing the old, our adoption of Western methods has not so greatly affected the national life as is generally supposed. One who looks beneath the surface of things can see, in spite of her modern garb, that the heart of Old Japan is still beating strongly." A later Western observer saw vestiges of old Japan in "the ideal of feudal loyalty, the patriarchal system, the attitude toward women, the exaltation of the martial virtues."

Vestiges of traditional Japan were still strongly embedded in the social practices and the attitudes of the people. In the rural areas, in particular, the traditional ways and values still governed all phases of the people's lives. Western individualism certainly had not permeated the society, and it would appear that even later, in the Taisho era, when "democracy" was in ascendancy, the rugged individualism so characteristic of Western societies never really triumphed. This was also true in the highly competitive business world where the contending parties typically organized themselves around groups. Family-centered business empires like the Mitsui, Mitsubishi (Iwasaki), Sumitomo, and Yasuda constituted cliques of financial and business interests. Lafcadio Hearn, writing at the turn of the century, observed that the Japanese continued "to think and to act by groups, even by groups of industrial companies." Hearn goes on to point out that,

In theory the individual is free; in practice he is scarcely more free than were his forefathers. Old penalties for breach of custom have been abrogated; yet communal opinion is able to compel the ancient obedience. No man is yet complete master of his activities, his time, or his means. The individual of every class above the lowest must continue to be at once coercer and coerced. Like an atom within a solid body, he can vibrate; but the orbit of his vibration is fixed.

The ruling class deliberately fostered and strengthened the familial characteristics of Japanese life in the new institutions that were emerging. We have already noted this in the concept of the state and the emperor. In the industrial realm, factory owners were depicted as being fathers of the workers, and as such they were expected to manifest a paternalistic interest in their welfare by, for example, sponsoring mutual aid societies and training the girl workers in the domestic arts of sewing and flower arrangement. In return the workers, as children, were expected to be obedient and loyal to their employers, their fathers. Even the large business combines, the *zaibatsu*, were basically family-centered organizations. In the army also an effort was made, after the Russo-Japanese War, to equate the relationship between the company commander and the soldier with that of father and son. Paternalistic "benevolence" and "humaneness" failed, however, to humanize the army, which on the contrary became one of the most mercilessly disciplinarian and inhumane institutions in the world.

Bearing these qualifications in mind, we can still say that Japan at the end of the Meiji era was well on the way to becoming a modern, industrial power. The question is frequently raised about why Japan managed to modernize in fifty years or so while China, which was exposed to the West much earlier, fell so far behind. No doubt, a complex webbing of intertwining reasons accounts for this, but first some of the obvious differences in the situations facing the two countries should be noted. For one thing, Japan was a much smaller, more compact nation in which there was a stable, fairly centralized political system in existence even during the Tokugawa period. In China, the pull toward regionalism got stronger as the central government weakened, whereas in Japan, even though the regional forces managed to overthrow the central government, they replaced the bakufu with a much stronger central government instead of establishing diverse regional ones. Throughout the country, as a result, it could effectively enforce its policy of "enriching and strengthening" the nation.

Another obvious difference in the situations facing the two countries is that the Western powers interfered much less in the internal affairs of Japan than they did in China, which was ultimately reduced to the status of a semicolonial nation. Still another noteworthy difference has to do with the fact that Japan was ruled by a military class that by its very nature was much more practical than the Confucian scholar-officials of China. The challenge posed to Japan, and to China for that matter, was primarily military. The Japanese warriors immediately recognized the need to adopt Western arms and military techniques if they were to modernize and thus cope effectively with the foreign threat. They further realized that any program of modernization would depend heavily upon the adoption of Western science, technology, and industrialization. They were even willing to adopt Western political and social systems if these were deemed necessary for national survival.

In striking contrast to this rather pragmatic approach on the part of the Japanese military class, the Chinese ruling class was immersed in a sense of cultural superiority and enthnocentrism. This is quite understandable when you consider that China had been the center of the Asian world — which to the Chinese was the entire world — for thousands of years. China had a civilization that could be traced back three thousand years or more, and her institutions, values, and ways had served the needs of the society for more than two thousand years. As far as the Chinese were concerned, the golden age was in the past and if disorder or troubles came about, they occurred because the people had departed from the traditional values and ways. As a result, whenever the country was faced with difficulties, and this includes the crisis in the nineteenth century, the ruling class endeavored to reform the institutions and tighten the moral standards to approximate as nearly as possible those of the golden age of the past. It did not seek to resolve the problems by introducing innovations or by adopting alien institutions and values.

Japan, on the other hand, had been historically receptive to outside influences. As we observed earlier, for several hundred years after the fifth century she readily adopted and adapted Chinese civilization on a large scale. Subsequently from time to time she continued to subject herself willingly to influences from Korea and China. In the sixteenth century she even welcomed the advent of Christian missionaries. The ultimate rejection of Christianity was not due to cultural intolerance; it was strictly the result of political considerations. This long inbred tendency to learn and borrow from other cultures led the Japanese, when they were exposed to Western civilization in the nineteenth century, to reject the counsel of the seclusionists and turn enthusiastically to the importation of things Western. There was no psychological barrier to hinder seriously an all-out effort at modernization. Economic developments in the later stages of the Tokugawa era were sufficiently favorable for a fairly rapid transformation to take place from a feudal economy to a modern economic system.

Another key factor that contributed to the relatively rapid modernization of Japan was the attitude or character of the people. The masses had been trained to be obedient and work hard during the centuries of feudal rule. Lafcadio Hearn made this observation about their tradition of obedience: "The probable truth is that the strength of the government up to the present time has been chiefly due to the conservation of ancient methods, and to the survival of the ancient spirit of reverential submission." Hearn goes on to comment about the great sacrifices willingly made by the people and their unswerving obedience "as regards the imperial order to acquire Western knowledge, to learn Western languages, to imitate Western ways."

Undeniably the Japanese have always been a well-disciplined, industrious, and energetic people; and unlike people living in extremely impoverished countries, hard work enabled them to survive. These qualities should not, however, be considered as having given the Japanese an edge over the Chinese because the latter were also extremely diligent and industrious. Nevertheless, it is true that the Chinese were probably less regimented than the Japanese because they were not ruled by a sword-bearing military class that was ready to cut down any commoner who stepped out of line. The virtues of hard work, thrift, self-discipline, obedience, and selfless service had been instilled in the Japanese people by the edge of the sword.

It is also possible that the Japanese in the nineteenth century possessed a much more dynamic outlook than their contemporaries in China. Like the Chinese, the Japanese were influenced by Confucianism but, in addition, they were molded by Shinto and the outlook of the warrior. Also, Zen Buddhism flourished to a greater extent in Japan than in China. Shinto had the effect of accentuating national pride, the sense of being unique, and the desire to excel. The samurai outlook fostered activism, stressed spiritual discipline, physical superiority, and military excellence. Zen Buddhism, which influenced the samurai more than the other classes, made the ruling class vigorous, decisive, and highly disciplined.

Another noteworthy factor is that Japan was endowed with a large number of exceptionally able leaders during the critical years of Meiji. These men had the foresight and willpower to chart the course of Japan and channel the energy of the people into enterprises that contributed to "enriching and strengthening" the nation. The Meiji Restoration was brought about by four outstanding leaders, Saigo, Okubo, Kido, and the court noble Iwakura. They were succeeded as architects of the new Japan by statesmen like Ito, Yamagata, Inoue, Matsukata, and Okuma. At the center was an enlightened monarch who knew precisely who could be trusted and relied upon. At the nongovernmental level there were outstanding educators and philosophes, like Fukuzawa, who helped to create the necessary climate of opinion for the advancement toward "civilization and enlightenment."

In the business realm a significant number of enterprising leaders emerged from the samurai class to build the new industrial society. Iwasaki Yataro would be an especially prominent example, and as one economist notes, "the role of the samurai families in founding Japan's business class can hardly be exaggerated." There were even some business leaders who emerged from an agrarian background, like Shibusawa, although his would be an exceptional case. The traditional merchant houses, of course, provided their share of leaders even though they tended to adhere more closely to merchandizing and banking. They did not actually turn to industrial activities until new blood was injected into them from the former samurai class. In this respect, also, Fukuzawa played an extraordinary role in that his academy produced a large number of exceptionally able businessmen who became key executives in the major companies and thus played crucial roles in the industrialization of Japan.

Another factor to be noted is the relatively high rate of literacy that prevailed in Tokugawa Japan. This meant that not only was the samurai class literate but also the leaders among the villagers and some common peasants were able to read and thus could be exposed to ideas from the West through books, tracts, and journals dealing with "civilization and enlightenment," as well as scientific and technological matters. The Meiji leaders were consequently able to count upon a fairly large body of informed and intellectually sophisticated leaders at the middle and even lower levels of the society to assist in the task of propelling the nation toward modernization.

At the end of the Meiji era it would have been difficult to assess whether or not modernization would be beneficial to the nation and the people as a whole. In fact the answer is still not available today, but Japan like other modern, industrial nations is now faced with the task of reevaluating the entire process of modernization and the consequent changes that science, technology, rationalism, and individualism have brought about. For the Japanese of the Meiji era, modernization was already a mixed blessing. The cost was borne primarily by the masses in terms of the following: the greater burdens imposed upon the peasantry; the dehumanizing practices that accompanied industrialism in the exploitation of factory and mine workers; and the brutalizing effects of modern militarism.

The Meiji leaders envisioned as the object of modernization, not so much the well-being of the people, as *fukoku kyohei*, the enrichment and strengthening of the nation. In terms of the goals they had established, they were well on the way to achieving their objectives. In the process, however, the masses were treated merely as means to an end, as laborers and cannon fodder. Voices were, nevertheless, beginning to be heard speaking up for the rights and welfare of the masses. The reign of Emperor Taisho was to be characterized by the ascendancy of democratic forces.[3]

◆　　　◆　　　◆

CONCLUSION

— by Frank Gibney

The death of the Emperor Meiji on July 30, 1912, and the mourning that accompanied it were a study in contrast. In September, while Japan and the world marked the Emperor's demise with the pomp and circumstance attending the passing of European crowned heads of state and Japan's modern soldiers draped their flags in mourning, the leading military figure of the realm, General Nogi, committed suicide in the samurai ritual fashion, along with his wife — the final gesture of a warrior following his lord and the wife following hers in death. All their countrymen were most impressed.

Many have since quoted the comment of the novelist Natsume Soseki from his novel, Kokoro: "at the height of the summer, Emperor Meiji passed away. I felt as though the spirit of the Meiji Era had begun with the Emperor and had ended with him. I was overcome with the feeling that I and the others who had been brought up in that era were now left behind to live as anachronisms."

Anachronism was a key word. If there was any common denominator shared by most Japanese of that day, it was a sense of colliding time frames, as Japan came out of one era and, in a sense, another world to meet the movers and shakers of a Western-dominated century — and to become one of them. For the Meiji people, contradictions were the very stuff of life. Their era was launched with slogans that called simultaneously for "expelling" all foreigners and the "opening" of the country to the West — an acceptable contradiction once it became clear that without opening their country to the technology of the foreigners,

they would be powerless to expel them. Similarly, the movement for "civilization and enlightenment" (*bunmei kaika*) expressed the widely held view that an internationalist culture was a good thing for the country to adopt. At the same time, the political guardians of Japan were dedicating all their energies to fulfilling the goal of *fukoku kyohei* — "enrich the country and strengthen the army." Here was not an internationalist goal, but something more like the marching song for a potential garrison state — yet it was also a strategy by which Japan could join the ranks of the imperialist nations.

Contradictions emerged as well in the new sense of democracy that the Meiji reforms created. On the one hand they brought forward tendencies that equalized Japan's previously stratified society, yet they were accompanied by the idea of a restored Emperor and an Emperor system founded on the ancient myths of Japan's island history. What a mixed bag it was. With the growth of free speech came the emergence of state censorship. With the spread of a party system based on an increasingly widening number of voters came also a strengthened view of the bureaucracy as some kind of guardian of the state.

The timing of Japan's Meiji transformation was critical. The global era in which it happened featured great strides in technology, not to mention the consolidation of the modern nation states in Europe. Capitalism was in fashion and state-assisted capitalism by no means unknown. It was natural that the Japanese would fit in this era. The forces that drove Meiji — the urge for achievement, self-expression, and increased industry — were exactly the forces that were vibrating through the European world at that time. To the Japanese, their energies released after two and one half centuries of relative seclusion, this was an era in which to be reborn. "Our history begins today," as the early Meiji students had said to a foreign visitor.

At the same time, across the Pacific, the United States was embarking on its own journey of growth, discovery, and aggrandizement. The American enthusiasm for expansion, then kindled, was to last, with few interruptions, for more than a century. Hawaii and the Philippines were both annexed by 1900. By the time of the Emperor Meiji's death in 1912, the power balance in the Pacific had begun to shift. The British still guarded the life lines to the Australian and Asian regions of the Empire, and other European warships continued to drop anchor in the waters off Shanghai, but the emergent guarantors of Pacific power were to be Japan and America as Europe drifted toward its first great war of the century.

Theodore Roosevelt, who consistently supported Japan in its modernization, had seen "nothing ruinous to civilization in the advent of the Japanese to power among the great nations." He also cast a prophetic eye on the future when he wrote, at the time of the Russo-Japanese War, "I am perfectly well aware that if they win out, it may possibly mean a struggle between them and us in the future, but I hope not and believe not."

In the end, Japan succeeded in modernization — as distinct from "westernization" — and made the transition with an intensification of many basic cultural values rather than a loss of them. The Meiji era was a watershed in Japanese history. It re-cast Japan in a new mold, albeit one in which much of the old remained. Whatever aspect of modern Japan we study — politics, business, literature, scholarship — the modern roots go straight to Meiji.

Beyond this, Meiji prefigured the whole era of Pacific modernization. Indeed, it strongly informed and invigorated the ideas of transformation that were taking firm root in other parts of Pacific Asia. After Meiji, neither Japan, its neighbors, nor the world was ever quite the same.

NOTES

1. George Akita, "Meiji Period," in *Encyclopedia of Asian History,* eds., Ainslie T. Embree, Robin J. Lewis, Richard W. Bulliet, Edward L. Farmer, Marius B. Jansen, David S. Lelyveld, and David K. Wyatt, vol. 2 (New York: Charles Scribner's Sons, 1988).

2. Taewon'gun was the title meaning "Prince of the Great Court" that was bestowed on Yi Ha-ung, the living father of King Yi Myong-bok and the effective ruler of Korea from 1864 to 1873. The Taewon'gun's son, who was posthumously entitled King Kojong, ascended the throne in 1864 at the age of 12.

3. Mikiso Hane, *Modern Japan: A Historical Survey* (Boulder: Westview Press, 1986), pp. 185-90.

4

The Rise of Nationalism and Communism

OVERVIEW

World War I is appropriately viewed as a great rift in world history, the scale and ferocity of its destructiveness to so many nations at once having been unlike anything previously experienced. Europe and America soon came to look back with nostalgia at the *Belle Epoche*, the age that preceded the Great War, but their nostalgia was not shared by Asians for whom the pre-war period often recalls harsh colonial rule. If there was a watershed in this period for much of Asia, it is to be found in the year immediately after the war: 1919.

It was during this turbulent period that Asians focused their attention on the Versailles Treaty, the agreement that would set the terms for a new world order to emerge from the shattered fields of Europe. Western leaders and intellectuals at the end of the century's second decade who saw themselves as the shapers of the world's future were startled to find that Asians had their own visions of the future — visions that were forged not in the trauma of war but in the experience of colonial repression and economic exploitation. By 1919 there had emerged a younger and bolder strata of Asian leaders who sought to combine political power, their own cultures, and new ideologies and philosophies to build modern, independent nations. Japan, which saw itself in the vanguard of Asian nationalism, was eventually swept along by a new generation of militant "reformers" who were obsessed with the need to cleanse their

nation of corrupting Western influences — and to lead other Asians in doing the same.

In the two decades that followed the first World War, China in particular was caught up in increasingly violent social and political change. Yet the great majority of those who advocated change were peaceful, moderate reformers, particularly in the first decades of the century. The turmoil that grew, eventually to engulf them and the entire Pacific Basin by mid-century, was not merely a struggle for power by and among elites; it derived from a confluence of forces that were building up both internally and in response to foreign influences. The Pacific War was not an inevitable culmination of these influences; at various stages the region found itself "ratcheted" towards ever greater crises that national leaders and the League of Nations failed to resolve.

The circumstances varied enormously. By the 1930s, the Philippines, in a complex interplay of opposition and cooperation with the United States, seemed to be moving along well toward formal decolonization, but all the other major colonial areas such as Indonesia, Vietnam, and Korea struggled against their masters. Not until the hammer of the Pacific War broke the hold of the European powers, opening fresh opportunities for change and strengthening indigenous capacities for nation-building, could the resistance movements really press their advantage.

Each of these emerging nations depended critically on the abilities of political leaders. The strongest leaders were those who invoked

> *"All subject peoples are filled with hope by the prospect that an era of right and justice is opening to them ... in the struggle of civilization against barbarism."*
>
> —Letter from Ho Chi Minh to President Woodrow Wilson, 1919

traditional values and thereby inspired large numbers of followers. Their allies — and sometimes their skeptics — were the writers, artists, and scholars who could also express the frustrations and aspirations of the people.

A number of Western teachers, missionaries, and philanthropists sought to encourage these aspirations for a new, decolonized Asia. The American evangelical missionary Sherwood Eddy, for example, was deeply sympathetic to the Korean independence movement. Following his return from a tour of Asia he wrote a glowing account of the region's promise which he published in a 1913 book entitled, *The New Era in Asia.* Hopes were indeed buoyant all across Asia during the preparations for the Versailles Conference. The negotiations would not only settle the claims of the war in Europe but also assert the inalienable rights — especially political self-determination — of peoples throughout the world. President Woodrow Wilson was the standard-bearer for this cause. The enormous stakes were widely understood by intellectuals and students, particularly in China, Korea, and Vietnam.

At first, Asian leaders believed that surely Asian views on peoples' rights of self-determination would be heard in the aftermath of the "war to end all wars." It was an optimism twice misplaced by leaders such as Vietnam's Ho Chi Minh. Ho first made his appeal to an indifferent audience at the 1919 Versailles Peace Conference and again at the outbreak of World War II. The resistance he organized in Vietnam against Japan believed that the forces of democracy and human rights would prevail; that once the Japanese were driven out of Vietnam the French would be prevented by their American and European allies from returning.

Dynamics of Nationalist Movements

Nationalist sentiments can be traced back into the nineteenth century to individual reformers and peasant resistance movements, but a distinction needs to be made between the resistance movements of the nineteenth century and the revolutions of the twentieth century. The nineteenth century goal was to repel foreign intruders. The twentieth century goals were both to repel colonials and forge *new nations.* Peasant revolts of the earlier period were reactive to the changes imposed on their cultures. The twentieth century nationalist movements sought much more: the complete renovation of their governments and societies.

The term "nationalist" is barely a century old. It was first applied to the right wing ideologues in France and Italy who sought to expand their countries' territories. Early nationalist movements in Asia did not merely repeat those in Europe, but they were tempted by the same simple solutions of fascist ideology and organization. China's nationalist leader, Chiang Kai-shek mobilized a secret army of "blue-shirt" toughs in the manner of Hitler's brown shirts and, years later, Indonesian President Sukarno quoted the Italian whom he so much admired, Benito Mussolini, urging his countrymen to spend a year "living in danger" to confront neighboring Malaysia. This does not suggest that nationalism in Asia was led by a group of "fascists," but the increasingly tense and turbulent political conditions enabled some leaders to draw upon feelings of xenophobia, rage and humiliation. Governments, in turn, responded with greater paranoia and repression. Yet the majority of people in most countries were initially willing to follow moderate reformers before the momentum of events turned them toward armed struggle.

In the colonial settings, nationalist aspirations escalated into destructive political confrontations because the authorities left no room for compromise. Equally important, they were unable to appreciate how much they themselves were contributing to the momentum of political change. This was especially the case in societies where the colonial powers inadvertently nurtured Asian nationalism by combining political repression with opportunities for Western (or Japanese) education. The most talented and capable indigenous leaders were offered the benefits of colonial education but denied professional opportunities to use it. Strains grew rapidly between traditional values and new ones, between efforts to adapt modern Western material techniques and the need to maintain a distinctly non-Western cultural identity, and between the impulse to assimilate the intruder and the urge to expel him completely. The the earliest collisions with colonial authority began in the Philippines.

THE PHILIPPINES

Early Nationalism

The Philippines found itself severely strained by the collapse of Spanish rule in Latin America early in the 19th century. The vital lifeline of the galleon trade came to an abrupt halt and with it the vast flow of silver from the New World. Manila thereafter found itself directly dependent on Spain while it became peripheral to Spanish interests.

The loss of the empire in Latin America was a trauma for the Iberian-born[1] Spaniards (*peninsulares*) who were forced to move to the Philippines. The prospect that the same upheaval might occur in their Pacific colony made them oppose any changes that seemed to undermine the authority of the Spanish crown. When increasing numbers of the *peninsulares* arrived from the fallen New World empire, a schism grew between them and the native-born Philippine bureaucrats who were mostly *creoles* (Spaniards born in the colonies) and *mestizos* (persons of mixed blood).

The burgeoning trade in the nineteenth-century Pacific Basin opened up new economic opportunities in the islands and further undermined Spanish control. As the agricultural export economy began to boom, based not on plantations but on independent small holdings, foreign banking and trading concerns (Chinese, American, and British) sprang up to stimulate it further. The Spanish governors that came and went with increasing frequency did not comprehend change throughout the archipelago and clung to an outmoded vision of their Old World status. Their obtuseness focused a nascent nationalist resentment against them.

"In a colony, liberal and rebellious are synonymous terms."

—Sinibaldo de Mas, 1843, arguing for the closure of colleges in Manila

Early Filipino reformers lacked a central monarchy around which they could rally a nationalist movement. Their initial goals, which had been encouraged by their education in Jesuit colleges in Manila, were rather modest: They sought basic educational and economic rights and hoped to be assimilated into Philippine-Spanish society. As their numbers grew, they became identified as a special group, the *ilustrados*, at the pinnacle of the indigenous Filipino society. Their stature enabled them to lead the way toward a new identity for the entire Philippine community.

A watershed event occurred in 1872 with the execution of three Catholic clergymen. Two of the men had offended a new governor by advocating liberal reforms; the third merely had the misfortune of working with them in the Manila cathedral. Their deaths and a small insurrection to which they were falsely linked led many Filipino intellectuals to go abroad to escape further repression. Ironically, they settled in Spain where their key vehicle of resistance became a newspaper, *La Solidaridad*.

In 1892, one of the most eloquent of their number, the novelist Jose Rizal, returned to the Philippines and organized a nonradical group concerned with educational and economic advancement. Within a few years, Rizal was arrested on false charges amid a new Spanish reign of terror. He was executed in 1896. Although not himself a political leader, Rizal was the inspiration for what became the Philippine Revolution (1896–1898) led by Emilio Aguinaldo (1869–1964). Spawned by a separatist society known as the Katipunan, the revolution ended in a military stalemate. Aguinaldo, along with his staff, accepted exile to Hong Kong only to return a few months later at the outbreak of the Spanish-American War aboard an American ship with the intention of founding the first Philippine Republic. His return launched

Figure 4.1   The execution of Jose Rizal, 1896.

a new era in Philippine history during which not only the ideal but also the working definition of nationhood matured.

♦   ♦   ♦

PHILIPPINE NATIONALISM TO WORLD WAR II

— by David Joel Steinberg

Emilio Aguinaldo's place in history was salvaged by the accident of American intervention in the Cuban revolution. The Spanish-American War that resulted suddenly altered the balance of power as Commodore George Dewey, under orders to destroy the enemy's navy in the Pacific, sailed into Manila Bay and obliterated the Spanish squadron [May 1, 1898]. Though his continued presence there was ostensibly in order to await, and destroy, the Spanish relief column, Americans had already begun to realize that they had gained a Far Eastern base for expansion. The Spanish, equally aware of changed circumstances, attempted to recover Filipino loyalty by offering various concessions, including a consultative assembly to be composed of *ilustrados*. Their efforts failed both because of the residue of *ilustrado* hostility and because of the American navy's return of Aguinaldo from Singapore via Hong Kong.

His repatriation reestablished the revolution, but with a significant difference: Aguinaldo got widespread support from the *ilustrados* by surrendering his power to them. Although he continued to surround himself with relatives and Cavite supporters, he felt out of his depth and abdicated political decisions to the *ilustrados*, especially to his new adviser, Apolinario Mabini. *Ilustrados* outside the Tagalog areas were induced to join the movement out of allegiance to and confidence in their Tagalog compatriots. The radical, as opposed to the nationalist, goals of the Katipunan were abandoned as private property was guaranteed and as the suffrage was limited to those "distinguished for high character, social position, and honorable conduct." Aguinaldo's initially clumsy announcement of a "dictatorial government" was rapidly altered to the declaration of a "Philippine Republic" by Mabini, who also persuaded Aguinaldo to declare national independence on June 12, 1898.

The new government quickly took control of the countryside from the Spanish, establishing its capital at the provincial city of Malolos. Under Mabini's direction, it moved to fill the void created by the collapse of Spanish power. Throughout Mabini's writings, including his *True Decalogue* and *Constitutional Program*, runs the theme that the country required a simultaneous external and internal revolution. He was romantic, authoritarian, and nationalistic. He saw unity and discipline as essential to any social regeneration, hence he favored a strong executive and a weak, consultative legislature. The great majority of the *ilustrados*, however, were suspicious of Aguinaldo's power and favored a strong legislature as a means of insuring their control. Felipe Calderón, for example, afraid that the "military element, which was ignorant in almost its entirety, would predominate;" wanted to see the military neutralized "by the oligarchy of intelligence, seeing that congress would be composed of the most intelligent elements of the nation."

During the six months in which the Filipinos were establishing a government, the Americans were debating whether or not to demand final possession of the Philippines in future peace negotiations with Spain. Captain Alfred Thayer Mahan's theories [see below], Social Darwinism, the lure of the China market, and missionary zeal encouraged the Republicans in Washington to advocate retention of what had been won. While Kipling urged America to take up the white man's burden, Mr. Dooley, less reverently, noted that it was less than two months since most Americans had learned whether the Philippines were islands or canned goods. After testing the mood of the country, President William McKinley announced that he had no choice but "to educate the Filipinos, and uplift and civilize and Christianize them, and by God's grace do the very best we could by them." Maintaining that "the march of events rules and overrules" his actions, he strengthened Dewey's flotilla until the Americans had more than 10,000 troops around Manila Bay. The Spanish in Manila, preferring to surrender to the Americans rather than to Aguinaldo's Filipino troops, conducted a sham battle which ended on August 13 with capitulation to Dewey. The Philippine forces that had been blockading the city were prevented from entering, and the tenuous

alliance between Americans and Filipinos collapsed as their joint enemy, Spain, surrendered.

McKinley's selection of delegates to the Paris Peace Conference with Spain, his refusal to see Aguinaldo's representative, and the actions of his field commanders made it clear to those in Malolos that a strong colonial power was about to replace a weak one. Unexpectedly, however, the Filipinos found support in rising anti-imperialist sentiment in America. The debate in Congress and in the country created strange alliances. Combining idealism with racism, the anti-imperialists polarized much of American society in a way that took the Republican leadership by surprise. McKinley, suddenly on the defensive and not sure of getting the necessary two-thirds vote for ratification of the peace treaty in the United States Senate, ordered his commander in the Philippines to promise the Filipinos a regime of "benevolent assimilation." To the Filipinos, however, that merely made clear McKinley's annexationist intentions. On February 4, 1899, under circumstances that have long been disputed, fighting broke out; the Americans made no real effort to reestablish a truce. Two days later, after narrowly defeating a number of anti-imperial and Democratic amendments, the United States Senate decided to retain possession of the Philippines by ratifying the peace treaty with Spain. The imperialist margin of victory was one vote.

Translating that decision into reality proved both costly and embarrassing. The alliance between *ilustrados* and Aguinaldo mobilized a much larger segment of the nation than had participated in the 1896 revolution. While the Americans could win set battles against Filipino troops, they were frustrated by the guerrilla techniques of a war of national liberation. As the Americans bogged down literally and figuratively on the battlefield, the Republican administration became concerned for its own political fortunes, aware that the Democrats planned to use anti-imperialism as a central campaign issue in the coming presidential election.

The Americans broke the back of Filipino resistance by splitting the tenuous alliance between the *ilustrados* and the provincial followers of Aguinaldo. Jacob Schurman, head of the newly arrived Presidential Commission, promised that America would satisfy the views and aspirations of educated Filipinos in creating a new government. The message was clearly understood. While it is far too simple to claim that all *ilustrados* became Americanistas, it is true that the American offer weakened the consensus forged by Aguinaldo's capitulation to the *ilustrados*. The Americans called for negotiations; Mabini, as *de facto* foreign and prime minister, took a hard bargaining position. When his negotiator proved too sympathetic to the Americans, he was arrested. The *ilustrados* from their dominant position in the legislature, forced Aguinaldo to dismiss Mabini and to replace him with their candidate, Pedro Paterno, who advocated compromise. The generals around Aguinaldo, most importantly Antonio Luna, called Paterno a traitor. As American military power increased, and as the government of the Philippine Republic was hounded from place to place, *ilustrados* began to slip away quickly and return to Manila. General Luna, an implacable foe of appeasement and one of the few *ilustrados* in the military, emerged as the alternative leader of the republican movement. He constituted a threat Aguinaldo could not tolerate; in circumstances that are still not clear, Luna was shot by Aguinaldo's followers. Mabini openly accused Aguinaldo of ordering Luna's death. Whatever the truth of the matter, his death ended the revolution. Aguinaldo, though not captured for some time, became a harried fugitive, isolated from power.

The tension between the *ilustrados* and Aguinaldo was not simply a class struggle. It was, among other things, a contest between two world views — the urban, cosmopolitan, and educated versus the rural, unsophisticated, and innocent. Aguinaldo lost control because he lacked the range of experience needed; the *ilustrados* talked circles around him, and yet they seemed to him city slickers, men who had become so westernized that they had lost touch with the people and with the traditional verities. The *ilustrados*, for their part, saw Aguinaldo as a bumpkin, a peasant. They recognized his hold on the imaginations of the common folk but, from their urbanized and internationalized perspective, thought it foolish to continue struggling against the Americans when the opportunities were so great not only for themselves but for what they saw as the best interests of the country. In effect, the Americans

made a deal with the *ilustrados*. At the price of collaboration and allegiance, they were offered the chance to fill the vacuum created by the Spanish withdrawal. The Americans ended all friar power, agreed to limit the franchise, guaranteed private property, and acknowledged the social and economic realities of Philippine life. The Americans needed the *ilustrados* to end the war, break the resistance, and demonstrate America's altruism. The *ilustrados* turned to the Americans to achieve hegemony politically, dominance socially, and security economically. Both groups had much to gain; neither was to be disappointed.

The Filipino-American War and the anti-imperialist debate combined to alter rapidly American objectives in the archipelago. Whatever the dreams of the early expansionists, the Republicans had by 1900 arrived at a policy of self-liquidating imperialism. The Americans saw their mission as providing tutelage and protection so that, in due time, the Philippines could become self-governing and independent. Whether out of guilt or by shrewdness, America rationalized its imperialist adventure by conferring upon it the benefits of American-style democracy. "The destiny of the Philippine Islands," wrote Schurman, was "not to be a State or territory . . . but a daughter republic of ours — a new birth of liberty on the other side of the Pacific," which would stand as a monument of progress and "a beacon of hope to all the oppressed and benighted millions" of Asia. Implicit in William Howard Taft's condescending phrase "little brown brother" was the eventual maturation of the ward. The Americans, arguing that the colonial government had to conform to the Filipinos' customs, habits, and even prejudices, supported a strong, centralized government, dominated by educated and conservative Filipinos, to whom would be permitted increasing power as the nation developed.

By 1900, therefore, the basic pattern of Philippine national development had been established. For the next twelve years, Taft — first as governor-general, later as secretary of war, and finally as president — shaped that policy. He not only moved to minimize "the bitterness and distrust" by getting "Filipinos of education, intelligence, and property" to cooperate, but he also encouraged the *ilustrados* to alter the character of

Figures 4.2–4.3   A Minneapolis newspaper exulted that America had "snared" the Philippines (above), but enthusiasm in the United States waned after casualties mounted on both sides in the bloody war that followed (below).

Philippine society from "the medieval-religious type" to one in which "the modern lawyer-politician" dominated." Establishing civil government on July 4, 1901, Taft modeled Philippine governmental structures on American examples. Noting with satisfaction that the Filipino people, especially those he felt were of the better class, were happy with the Philippine Act of 1902, Taft went on to hold municipal and local elections and, subsequently, provincial and national ones. He encouraged *ilustrados* to hold office on the premise that no American should be appointed to any office in the Philippines for which a reasonably qualified Filipino could be found. As early as September 1901, three ranking *ilustrados* had been appointed to the seven-man ruling commission.

The seeming success of American policies in the Philippines obscured their fundamental contradiction. In order to end nationalist resistance to American rule and to extricate itself from an ideologically embarrassing situation, the Republican leadership had promised to shape colonial policy to comply with *ilustrados* aspirations and prejudices. By 1908, Taft realized that America had paid a high price to gain *ilustrados* collaboration. While theoretically committed to "popular self-government" and to the extension to the masses of sufficient education "to know . . . civil rights and maintain them against a more powerful class and safely to exercise the political franchise," Taft was alarmed that American policy might actually be "merely to await the organization of a Philippine oligarchy or aristocracy competent to administer government and then turn the Islands over to it." In offering the *ilustrados* power, the Americans also accepted a particular social system and pattern of land tenure. Education, it was hoped, would in time redress the balance of economic and political power. Taft noted that the "work of instruction in individual rights will require many years before the country is rid of the feudal relation of dependence which so many of the common people now feel toward their wealthy or educated leaders." Consequently, though independence might be the goal of American policy, it could scarcely come rapidly if early pragmatic expedients were to be reconciled with idealistic commitments.

During the first few years, the Americans prohibited any open advocacy of independence, but by 1907, during the National Assembly elections, politicians campaigned as Immediatistas and Urgentistas. The two groups fused into the Union Nacionalista and won fifty-nine out of eighty seats. The new Nacionalista Party, moreover, quickly turned to a group of young leaders, relegating the older *ilustrados* to positions of ceremonial impotence. Sergio Osmeña, at the age of twenty-nine, was elected Speaker of the new Assembly over Paterno, who was seen as "too Spanish." A new generation of younger men — led by Osmeña and Manuel Quezon — gained control of the nationalist movement and dominated it for the next forty years.

The key issue in both the United States and the Philippines was the timing of independence. The Nacionalistas, aware of the political value of the call for immediate independence, advocated it publicly. The opposition, eventually led by Juan Sumulong, came out for a more gradual approach. Like Taft, Sumulong believed that premature independence would establish an oligarchy rather than a democracy. His voice went unheeded, however, as nationalist rhetoric made independence the all-embracing goal. The issue became even more pressing after Woodrow Wilson's victory in the American presidential election of 1912, since the Democratic Party had consistently advocated rapid independence. Under the influence of former Democratic colleagues with a record of anti-imperialism, Wilson appointed F.B. Harrison governor-general with instructions to increase the tempo of decolonization. Harrison established a Filipino majority on the commission and increased the Filipino representation in the bureaucracy from 71 percent to 96 percent. In Washington in 1916, the Democrats passed the Jones Act, which promised independence as soon as a "stable government" could be established. The Clarke Amendment, which specified the time limit as four years, was passed in the Senate and only narrowly defeated by the Republicans in the House. Since independence seemed imminent, especially after Wilson's advocacy at Versailles in 1919 of worldwide self-determination, Harrison abdicated his supervisory functions and permitted the Filipinos to modify American institutions to satisfy indigenous desires.

Harrison actively supported the independence mission that went to the United States in

1919. Quezon and Osmeña, despite their political rhetoric, were far less eager for immediate independence than Harrison, since what they privately wanted was the benefits of self-rule without the liabilities of ultimate authority. Quezon secretly was willing to accept a twenty-five-year Commonwealth. Such an arrangement would have left problems of defense, currency, and free trade to the Americans while placing political, social, and economic power securely in the hands of the Manila elite. Quezon was spared the embarrassment of publicly admitting his plan, however, by the accident of the American election returns. Just as the fate of the archipelago had been shaped by the 1900 election, so too was its independence delayed by the Republican victory in 1920. The Warren G. Harding administration, unhappy about the lax quality of the Harrison era and about a series of economic scandals, dispatched Leonard Wood and William C. Forbes to investigate. Their mission concluded that "it would be a betrayal of the Philippine people ... and a discreditable neglect" of national duty to withdraw "without giving the Filipinos the best chance possible to have an orderly and permanently stable government." Recommending that the office of governor-general be strengthened, the Wood-Forbes mission postponed the independence that had seemed so near.

Quezon and the Nacionalistas dominated Philippine nationalism up to World War II. Opposition critics like Sumulong were relegated to a peripheral position. The one major challenge to Quezon's position came in 1930-33, when a concatenation of factors, including Democratic victories in the American Congress and for Franklin Roosevelt, the rise of Japanese militarism, growing opposition to retention of the Philippines by American labor and farming groups, and racial hostility toward Filipino immigrants, combined to make the American Congress again receptive to Philippine independence. The Hare-Hawes-Cutting Bill, advocating independence after a further ten-year Commonwealth period, was passed by the American Congress after Osmeña and Manuel Roxas had lobbied in Washington for it. It was vetoed by President Herbert Hoover, passed despite his veto, and then blocked in the Philippines by Quezon, who was afraid that Osmeña might regain his earlier position as the architect of independence. During the bitter pro- versus anti-independence fight in the Philippines, the Nacionalista Party again split. Quezon, the master politician, used his patronage and leverage to block the Hare-Hawes-Cutting Bill and then negotiated (as he had known he could) a slightly more favorable bill from the newly elected President Roosevelt. The measure was known as the Tydings-McDuffie Act. Osmeña, much to Sumulong's disgust, again decided not to establish himself as an opposition leader and ran as Quezon's vice-presidential candidate in the elections for the new Commonwealth government.

In summary, the forty years from 1901 to 1941 contrast sharply with the last decades of the nineteenth century. Whereas in the earlier period the political structure of society was undergoing profound reorganization, later it remained relatively stable. On the other hand, the twentieth century saw striking increases in the numbers of people involved in urbanization, in education, in the franchise, and in modernization. In the late nineteenth century, the *ilustrados* represented a minute percentage of the nation; by 1941, the actual number and the relative proportions of the educated had dramatically increased. Geographic, linguistic, and ethnic distinctions became less important as local patterns were replaced by national ones. People of every economic class and social category came to identify with Philippine nationalism — the flag, the anthem, and the abstraction. Thus, while the dichotomies of tenant and landlord, urban and rural, rich and poor, elite and peasant increased rather than decreased, all strata found a common locus of loyalty in the Commonwealth. Nationalism could supply cohesion, even though it left unanswered substantive questions of direction and identity. The success of Philippine nationalism led one Filipino to write that they were "an Oriental people standing at the portals of Asia, in deep sympathy with its kindred neighbors yet with hands outstretched to the cultures of Spain and America." In the prewar period, Filipinos took great pride that their nation could offer a model for other Southeast Asians to emulate. The optimism of the period was to be tempered by the problems of independence.[2]

◆   ◆   ◆

INDONESIA

The Rise of Indonesian Nationalism

Several outstanding figures led the movement for independence in Indonesia; the most prominent were Sukarno (1901-1970) and Mohammad Hatta (1902-1980). These leaders found inspiration in the anti-Dutch resistance movements of the previous century such as the Java War (1825-1830). To this still-powerful sentiment they added a new impetus brought about by decades of Western contact — in particular, their exposure to Western education and political concepts. The newly-educated people rose to prominence as spokesmen for an emergent national consciousness. We will examine the roles of these two leaders, Sukarno and Hatta, but it is useful also to note that their Western education was shared by thousands of others, as described in the following section.

◆　　◆　　◆

SOCIAL CHANGE AND NATIONALISM

— by John R.W. Smail

On January 12, 1900, as the new century was dawning, a young Javanese woman called Raden Adjeng Kartini wrote, in Dutch, in a letter to a friend, "Oh, it is splendid just to live in this age; the transition of the old into the new!" The exclamation point was Kartini's, but the vision was true for her time; a new age was opening in the Netherlands Indies. In the early years of the century, the many societies of the archipelago, including her Javanese one, were coalescing in a new and more comprehensive Indies society. The export economy was booming, new investment capital was pouring in, muddy-streeted towns were becoming modern cities. The government, fortified by a freshly proclaimed colonial ethos, the "Ethical Policy," was beginning to penetrate the life of the village with a host of new development programs. A new sense of change and purpose was in the air.

Kartini was aware of all this. But for her the new age was first of all in her own mind; she had needed new eyes to see the society now taking shape so rapidly around her. Her life story, as it is recorded in her published correspondence [*Letters of a Javanese Princess* (1964)], was a voyage of self-discovery. Its special quality came not from her earliest childhood in the *priyayi* (Javanese elite) establishment of her father, the regent of Japara, but from her education in the local European primary school. There she learned Dutch, thus gaining access to all that modern European thinking had to offer. It made her voyage difficult and often painful, for she remained deeply attached to her Javanese heritage. But it enabled her to see the new Indies around her and at least to begin the task of defining a place for herself in it.

What happened to Kartini happened in many different ways to many others in the early-twentieth-century Indies; not only to Javanese, Sundanese, Makassarese, and Minangkabau but also to Eurasians, Chinese, and the Dutch themselves. The outer political history of the period was the story of how, at the height of Dutch colonial rule, the initiative passed to its subjects, who, developing a nationalist movement, challenged that rule and prepared for its demise. The inner political history of those years consisted of a series of self-transformations by all who came to play roles in that outer history. In the older Java and in the islands beyond it, numerous different societies, indigenous and immigrant, lived side by side, either having little to do with each other or, where they did interact, accommodating fairly easily to each others' cultures. After 1900, the tightening frame of modern Indies society pressed them more closely together, dissolving the old accommodations and challenging the established culture of each separate group. All came under strong pressure to redefine their cultural identities and find places for themselves in the emerging social order. Before politics, therefore, came education, both in the narrow sense of schooling and in the more fundamental sense of self-discovery.

Education in Dutch-language secular schools was most significant for the depth, and especially the breadth of the transformations it engendered among the peoples of the Indies, yet the beginnings were slow. In the nineteenth century, the government developed a small but good system for its European nationals, but before 1900 only a handful of high-ranking "natives," such as Kartini, were allowed to attend European primary schools. The number increased in the years of the Ethical Policy, reaching 4,000 in 1905 and 6,000 in 1920. Those privileged students, still largely from the traditional elite classes in the different Indies societies, also predominated among the very small numbers of indigenous people who went on through the new European secondary schools and colleges (Engineering School, 1920; Law School, 1924; Medical School, 1927) or to study in Holland.

Meanwhile — alongside this European school system always intended primarily for the Dutch themselves — a separate government system of Native schools was growing. Most of the Native schools of the nineteenth century, as well as the very large system of village schools developed after 1907, used local languages as the medium of instruction and hence had much less cultural impact. But the "Dokter Djawa" School, which came in time to graduate fairly completely trained "native doctors," used Dutch as the language of instruction after 1875. For that reason, its few hundred students played a disproportionately large role in the political and cultural movements of the first two decades of the twentieth century. It was after 1900, however, that the government Dutch-language Native system really developed. Between 1907 and 1914, the existing Native primary-level schools evolved into Dutch Native Schools (DNS), which provided primary education for "natives" entirely in the Dutch language. During the following decade, a latticework of new schools was built above the DNS to provide higher education for a few "natives" and transfer routes to advanced training in the parallel European system. But it was the government Dutch Native Schools, with 20,000 students in 1915 and 45,000 in 1940, that were decisive — perhaps the most important single institution in twentieth-century Indies history.

Dutch-language secular education had many consequences. Most obviously it opened a new route for upward social mobility into urban positions as civil servants, teachers, white-collar workers in private business, journalists, lawyers, and doctors. It also provided a new criterion of social status, which had a double effect. On the one hand, Dutch education placed all those who had it above those who did not. Graduates from the European system ranked above those from the Native system, and so on upward to the handful who had advanced degrees from the Netherlands. It was a new, easily calculated hierarchy of standing, which put those lower down in an often painful position and left the peasant an outcast.

On the other hand, this criterion necessarily challenged the old status hierarchy, which was based, within each indigenous society, mainly on birth. A lower *priyayi* official who had an education as good as, or better than, that of the hereditary regent he served under found it difficult or unpleasant to use the humble "high" Javanese when speaking to him, as required by traditional status ranking. Virtually all of the modern movements of the early twentieth century, therefore, had a strong anti-"feudal" aspect. By the same token, the new criterion increasingly called into question the high status the Dutch inherited with their skin. The engineer Sukarno was fully as well educated as the lawyer governor-general who exiled him in 1933, but he could not possibly have attained that office.

Dutch education, finally, gave easy access to the self-proving truths of modern science, to new and conflicting political visions, to whole schools of literature not necessarily better but certainly different and stimulating. More deeply, the very fact of thinking in a foreign language, as several tens of thousands came to do, imposed a new geometry on what they thought.

The experience of these changes defined, in both social and cultural terms, a new group that rose in the early-twentieth-century Indies, the secular urban intelligentsia of indigenous origin. But that educational experience did not of itself provide them with a new identity. They were no longer traditional Bugis, Minangkabau, or Javanese — though they continued to think in those languages too, with all that implied. Nor, evidently, in a racist Indies, were they Dutch or Eurasians or *peranakan* Chinese[3] — though they shared a language and much else with them. Their predicament gave rise to a whole series of efforts in the early decades of the century to create new identities. This quest was not in origin a political one, but the politics of the time were very largely determined by it.[4]

◆   ◆   ◆

POLITICAL LEADERSHIP

Like many others in Asia, Indonesians can trace a watershed point in their history to the year 1919, but unlike the rest of the region where hopes ran high that new principles of human rights would be established by the Versailles Treaty, Indonesian hopes were building around a charismatic leader named Tjokroaminoto and his mass movement, the Sarekat Islam (Islamic Union) which promised to alter the relationship with the Dutch. These expectations were dashed in that same year when a few violent local protests were harshly repressed by the Dutch authorities. The Sarekat Islam rapidly splintered with one faction creating itself in 1920 as the Indies Communist Party (known by its Indonesian initials as the PKI) while another allied itself with the world-wide pan-Islamic movement of the time.

Meanwhile, many of the elite who would eventually help lead the new nation of Indonesia continued to go abroad to study, Hatta among them. He spent ten years in school in Rotterdam where he converted the local Indies' students society into a potent political organization. He saw clearly that education would be the key to creating a sufficiently broad indigenous leadership for an independent Indonesia. Prior to his return to Batavia (Jakarta) in 1932, he helped found the National Education Club with the aim of establishing nationalist cadres for resistance to the Dutch. For his activities in the Indies he was exiled to outer islands and could not return to Java until the outbreak of World War II.

Sukarno did not go to Holland but studied architecture and engineering in Bandung before co-founding and becoming the first chairman of the Indonesian Nationalist Party (PNI) in 1927. The party was aimed specifically at fostering a national identity and boasted that it did not depend on communist directives from Moscow or Islamic guidance from Istanbul. With the formation of PNI and Sukarno's charismatic leadership, the idea of Indonesian nationhood suddenly captured the popular imagination. Dozens of organizations were created or changed their names to include the word "Indonesia" and, in general, the notion of a national entity exclusive of the Dutch but inclusive of the territory to which they laid claim

SUKARNO

Sukarno was a complex figure, combining elements of Javanese tradition and modernity in his leadership. To some he was a catastrophic president, wasting resources on grandiose policies. To others he remained the father of the nation. Politically resourceful, he was skilled in balancing rival factions, but with his mercurial style and his external appearance of confidence went signs of an inner vulnerability. At times he would act decisively, as in forming PNI in 1927, handling the Japanese in 1942-45, and introducing Guided Democracy in 1957-59. At other times he appeared hesitant and uncertain. He posed as a revolutionary but recognized the fragility of the republic, and it could be argued that his revolutionary rhetoric disguised a desire to preserve the social status quo. Perhaps his greatest achievement was his projection of a vision of a unified Indonesian nation in an archipelago of great ethnic, religious, and geographical diversity.

—John D. Legge, *EAH*

became an accepted concept. A tectonic-like societal pressure had been building which suddenly released itself in a creative outpouring of new or rejuvenated associations, each seeing itself as part of a larger whole. The Indonesian national anthem and a national language were created at this time, the latter a transmutation of the underlying common Malay tongue.

The Dutch closely monitored the key political groups and did not hesitate to use repressive tactics against them. Sukarno, in particular, was seen as a threat because of his ability to draw massive crowds. In 1929 he was arrested, tried and convicted for "creating a public disturbance." Released from prison in 1931 and re-arrested in 1933, he was exiled to the remote outer islands where, like Hatta, he remained until the Japanese forces swept down to overwhelm the Dutch in 1942. These developments are taken up in chapter 5.

CHINA

China: 1919 and the May Fourth Movement

For China, the year 1919 stands alongside the year of the Chinese Revolution itself (1911) as a pivotal time in its modern history. In particular, the month of May 1919 continues to resonate in Chinese political life as an inspiration toward political reform — to an extent that made the prospect of its celebration by students in 1989 a cause for dread among China's aging leaders. They, who had once led protests themselves, recognized the potential of youth-led mass movements to unseat those at the center of power.

On May 4, 1919, several thousand students from Beijing's thirteen universities gathered in protest at the Gate of Heavenly Peace (Tian'anmen), having learned that the Versailles Peace Conference had confirmed Japan's claim to the German-held territory on China's Shandong province. To the shock of the Chinese diplomats at the Conference, it was revealed that the matter had been decided long before: in 1917 Japan had signed a secret covenant with Britain, France and Italy to guarantee its claims after the war was over. The Chinese students were furious and their demonstration soon became violent. They found the Japanese ambassador and beat him severely, then went on a rampage that had to be quelled by the police. Amid the arrests and reprisals that followed, an unprecedented wave of protest swept across China with strikes and demonstrations by students, laborers and merchants.

This was the beginning of what is today called the "May Fourth Movement." In some respects it marks the political birth of "modern" China in this century but more usefully it can be seen as the galvanizing of a new generation of urban Chinese intellectuals to oppose foreign imperialism. The May Fourth Movement occurred within a broader process of cultural change known as the "New Culture Movement" which embraced a wide range of new ideas and artistic forms. More profoundly, it expressed a broad societal disillusionment over what by then was clearly a failed revolution, for amid much confusion and turmoil, the Qing Dynasty had finally fallen. It its place had emerged a ruthless general-turned-president

followed by an era of equally ruthless warlords who presided over their separate territories. Many had expected the revolution to occur, but few had predicted such an ignominious outcome. In fact, during the first decade of the new century there were reasons to be optimistic.

The Late Qing Reforms

Several years before the death of the Qing Empress Dowager Cixi in 1908, efforts at key reforms had at long last begun amid broader stirrings of pro-active rather than reactive, anti-foreign nationalism. The final humiliation suffered during the Boxer Rebellion, when the Empress Dowager was forced to retreat from Beijing before a vengeful army of the imperial powers, broke any final resistance to the notion that China needed to find ways to change and adapt more rapidly. One of the first and most difficult reforms occurred in the field of education, then still dominated by the Confucian classics and official examinations. A new system, modeled strongly on that used by the Japanese, was inaugurated in January, 1904 but with the old examination system left in place. The old system continued to attract the "traditionalist" students who were office-seekers while the most able of the "modern-minded" youth flocked to schools established by foreign missionaries. In order to attract the best students, the government had little choice except to abolish the examination system altogether, which it did in 1905.

Other reforms focused on the need to revamp the central administration. In previous centuries, in an essentially agrarian society, a decentralized system of governance had worked well. Ultimate power — but little day-to-day control — was located in Beijing. By the beginning of the twentieth century a more centralized means of control was sorely needed; one that could provide a responsive, fast-acting, legal and fiscal system. Yet the provinces had become even more economically and politically independent of control from Beijing, partly because of inept leadership there. The burgeoning wealth of the treaty port communities contributed to this widening political gap between the center and the provinces. Thus, the creation of new ministries in Beijing (such as a

Foreign Ministry and Finance Ministry) in the first decade of the twentieth century was met with resistance by provincial officials. The Manchu princes in Beijing further complicated matters by seizing key positions that permitted them to undermine or delay needed reforms.

Cixi is usually portrayed as a reactionary and a primary obstacle to reform in China while she lived, but the record also suggests that she saw the need for reform. Like the emperors who had come before and the new Chinese leaders that would follow, she was obsessed with maintaining centralized control in Beijing. What troubled her was the demand for power-sharing by outsiders and provincial elites. Her obsession tended to undercut the very changes that she sought to promote. The reforms being carried out just before her death challenged the authority of local elites and aggravated all the more the clash between the center and the periphery.

The Chinese people were also beginning to recognize a new sense of nationhood. In 1905 they organized a boycott of American goods in a protest against increasingly blatant, racially-biased U.S. immigration rules. The boycott demonstrated a new assertiveness by the Chinese people in their perceptions of the world and their rightful place in it. Unlike the xenophobic Boxer Rebellion, the boycott responded to the desire by the Chinese to maintain the right of travel and access to the outside world and particularly their right to seek their fortunes abroad. Overseas Chinese communities in locations throughout the Pacific Basin responded with support. From the Philippines to Singapore, from Bangkok to Vancouver, Chinese participated in the boycott. Modern undersea cable communications enabled these disparate port-centered communities to coordinate their activities and positions. Even so, the leadership, coordination, and agreement over the specific goals of the boycott began to break down and it faltered within a year of its implementation. President Theodore Roosevelt remained unmoved and even Woodrow Wilson, in his 1912 Presidential campaign, was to denounce "oriental coolieism" as "a most serious industrial menace."

As if to place a final curse on her country just before she died, the Empress Dowager apparently ordered the murder of the only viable adult successor to her power, the 37-year-old Guangxu emperor. With his death, the possibility for a stable, reformist government became remote. Instead, the three-year-old Puyi was named emperor (the subject of a popular motion picture, *The Last Emperor*) with a weak regent guiding the government. The enfeebled regime assembled a cabinet to oversee its ministries, then stacked it with Manchus, further infuriating the reformist groups. The country was ripe for a complete change of government.

The Revolution of 1911

The historic change, when it finally came about, occurred amid intrusion and manipulation by Japan. Some Japanese even assert that they caused the 1911 revolution. The Chinese say they did not. In any case, there is no question that the Japanese encouraged the overthrow of the Manchu court and sponsored successive coup attempts, all of which failed, in the years leading up to the revolution. These activities were launched from Tokyo by revolutionary Chinese groups under the sponsorship of right-wing Japanese organizations who saw themselves as the leaders of a new Pan-Asian alliance against Western imperialism. The first step in creating such an alliance, they reasoned, would be to sweep away the old order in China (Korea having already been annexed by Japan). Thus, there emerged a natural partnership between the Japanese Pan-Asianists and the Chinese reformers.

Those Chinese who enjoyed the protection and sponsorship of Japan fell into two general groups: One was led by the esteemed scholar in exile, Kang Youwei and his protege, Liang Qichao. Kang advocated a new government in Beijing that would be based upon moderate reforms led by the then still-living Emperor Guangxu. Once that possibility had been eliminated by the deaths of the emperor and the Empress Dowager, Kang's formulations (which included the establishment of Confucianism as a state religion) seemed less relevant. Liang then began to speak with a more independent voice, still fundamentally at odds with his rival, the leader of the radical faction, Sun Yat-sen (Sun Zhongshan).

Sun had been collecting funds from abroad since 1895 when he attempted to foment an

Figure 4.4   Many of the Chinese who were able to study a new curriculum in the classroom became the reformers and revolutionaries of their generation.

uprising in the Guangzhou region. His activities, coordinated with secret societies within China, resulted in several additional, badly botched efforts to overthrow the government. When the moment of the revolution finally came, led by a secret society not directly under Sun's control, he was in the United States raising funds.

Internal tensions in China had grown to an explosive potential by 1911. New conspiracies were being uncovered every day by the imperial authorities, particularly in the upper Yangzi region where resentment was boiling over efforts by the Beijing administration to arrange a loan from foreign banking groups to convert existing railways into national ownership, thus removing them from local provincial control (a key point of contention in the "center versus periphery" competition).

A bomb explosion in a factory in Hankou led to several arrests and executions as yet another plot by a secret society was uncovered. In this case, however, many army members were found to have been behind the bombing. Once discovered, they had little to lose and decided to launch a full scale revolt. Surprisingly, the Manchu governor-general

fled instead of quashing the rebellion, giving the rebels time to consolidate their power and for anti-Manchu popular support to spread and gain confidence. Soon all the southern, central, and northwestern provinces had declared their independence under the leadership of local army officers. There was little fighting in what became known to the Chinese as the Xinhai Revolution.

Upon hearing the news of the revolution, Sun was tempted to rush back to China but he realized the new government badly needed foreign capital. He travelled on to London to obtain a major loan, hoping by the same stroke to make the British in China a counterbalance to the growing Japanese influence there. Once back in China, he was sworn in to be provisional president of the new government, but in a very short time the new administration faced chaos. It was one thing to rally people to the cause of ending the Manchu reign and quite another to give them a clear blueprint for the future. Into the breach, amid threats of growing factionalism, civil war and foreign intervention, stepped the formidable general, Yuan Shikai, the only man with the experience and authority to keep the country stable. Sun readily resigned in

TWO CHINESE REVOLUTIONARIES

Sun Yat-Sen (Sun Yixian, also known as Sun Zhongshan; [1866-1925] was the leader of the 1911 Chinese republican revolution and the Guomindang, (Kuomintang, or Nationalist Party). Sun has been called "the father of the republic."

Sun came from a farming family in Guangdong Province. When he was fourteen years old he joined an older brother in Hawaii, where he attended school. Subsequently he became a Christian, and received a degree from the Hong Kong College of Medicine in 1892. Exposure to foreign practices, the influence of Christian principles, and anger over the Manchu Qing dynasty's failure to defend China during the Sino-French War (1884-1885) pushed Sun toward revolutionary ideas. His first political acts came during the Sino-Japanese War (1894-1895), when he organized the Revive China Society (Xingzhonghui) in Honolulu and plotted a rising in Canton (Guangzhou) with revolutionary friends and secret society leaders. Discovery of this plot forced Sun to flee to Japan, and thereafter the Qing government considered him a dangerous enemy.

Sun became internationally famous in 1896 because of the publicity surrounding an unsuccessful Qing attempt to kidnap him in London in order to bring him back to China for trial and presumably execution. Subsequently, he spent several years in Japan. Although his early contacts had been mainly with secret societies and Overseas Chinese, he now made the acquaintance of liberal, pan-Asianist, Japanese adventurers. More important, he met Chinese students, who were coming to Japan in increasing numbers after 1902. Radical students formed the basis for the Revolutionary Alliance (Tongmenghui) established in Tokyo during 1905. Sun was director, and the party adopted his "Three Principles of the People" (nationalism, democracy, and the people's livelihood — a gradualist conception of socialism) as its platform.

Sun was involved in establishing party branches in Southeast Asia and in preparing for uprisings in South China between 1907 and 1908. When these failed, his leadership was challenged within the party. Moreover, the Qing persuaded other Asian governments to expel him. Most of the following years were spent raising funds and recruiting in the United States and Europe, and Sun did not return to China until more than two months after the 1911 Revolution had begun. He was elected president of the provisional republican government, but he soon resigned in favor of Yuan Shikai to break the stalemate between revolutionary and imperial armies and to facilitate the Manchu abdication.

With Yuan's encouragement, Sun then concentrated on plans for railway development, although he was nominal director of the new parliamentary party, the Guomindang. However, he angrily returned to politics after the assassination of the Guomindang's parliamentary leader and took part in the unsuccessful "Second Revolution" in 1913. Thereafter, Sun consistently sought to overthrow Yuan until the latter's death in 1916, and then worked to defeat militarist contenders to control the national government in Beijing.

Sun failed to reorganize revolutionaries effectively into a conspiratorial Revolutionary Party (Gemingdang), personally loyal to him, and also did not succeed in rallying opposition to northern militarists in the name of restoring the 1912 constitution. The governments he formed with unreliable militarist allies in Canton were short lived. When forced to retire to Shanghai, he wrote articles later published as *Principles of National Reconstruction (Jianguo fanglue)* and began work on *The Three Principles of the People (Sanmin zhuyi)*. Repeated frustrations pushed him toward new tactics: in 1919 he revived the Guomindang, and in 1921 decided to establish a rival national government at Canton. Sun, as president, launched a "northern expedition" to unify China, but southern army commanders refused to move far from home and ousted Sun as president.

(continued next page)

After this failure Sun adopted an entirely new approach of alliance with the newly formed Chinese Communist Party and cooperation with the Soviet Union. With the help of Soviet advisers, the Guomindang was reorganized into a disciplined, centralized, pyramidal structure, and the Whampoa Military Academy was established to train a loyal, revolutionary officers corps. The First National Congress in January 1924 elected Sun party leader for life, and Sun's Three Principles were expanded to stress anti-imperialism and party unity, and the "Three Policies" of alliances with the Soviet Union, the ChineseCommunist Party, and the workers and peasants were added to party doctrine. Unable to begin another northern expedition immediately, Sun went to Beijing for negotiations with northern warlords. There he died of cancer, leaving behind a political testament enjoining his followers to complete the revolution that he had begun.

The movement toward revolution in China was far too broad to have had only one leader. Within the narrower circles of the professional revolutionaries, Sun was more hampered than his colleagues by the enmity of the Qing government before 1911. Unable to operate freely in Asia, he was pushed toward the peripheral position of international spokesman and fund raiser. He was, however, also able to transcend, to some extent, the divisions among revolutionaries, and his dedication, optimism, and personal magnetism inspired strong loyalty.

—Mary Backus Rankin, *EAH*

Liang Qichao (1873-1927) was one of China's most skilled publicists of reform ideas in the crucial era between the 1890s and 1920s. He belonged to a transitional generation that had been educated in the traditional educational system but that refused to follow the conventional career opportunities. Instead, he opted for the medium of the recently developed Chinese press, where he played a leading role in expanding the political and intellectual horizons of China.

With China's defeat in 1895 by the Japanese, Liang began to edit reform periodicals and to publish essays dealing especially with educational reform. During this period he also established societies for studying China's problems and promoted the ideas of Kang Youwei. Although Liang did not play a prominent role in the reform movement of 1898, he had developed a reputation as a leading thinker behind the reform proposals and was forced to flee to Japan with the coup d'etat of September 1898. While in Japan he continued to publish ideas that helped promote the political revolution of 1911 and 1912. Among these ideas were the promotion of new institutions, including a constitution and a parliament, as well as such concepts as individualism and a public-spirited citizenship.

Liang returned to China in October 1912 and formed a political party that supported constitutional reform and competed with Sun Yat-sen's revolutionary party. Liang supported liberal democratic government and opposed Yuan Shikai's monarchial attempt in 1916 and an imperial restoration effort in 1917. But his principal impact remained as a publicist popularizing new ideas on literature, law, finance, politics, and current events, providing in part the basis for the intellectual revolution of the May Fourth era. By the 1920s Liang lost his enthusiasm for the West and returned to his Confucian roots, emphasizing Confucianism's altruism as a response to the wholesale westernization being promoted in China. The new generation had produced new leaders who overtook Liang, however, although all acknowledged their indebtedness to his essays and periodicals.

—Adrian A. Bennett, *EAH*

favor of Yuan, who then proceeded, over the following two years, to bitterly disappoint Sun and the other revolutionaries while he vigorously, if ruthlessly, held together a centralized government. Yuan used bribery, assassination, and brute military force to maintain his power at the expense of the liberal reformers. He eventually attempted to re-establish a monarchy with none other than himself on the throne.

The Asian Powers and China on the Eve of World War I

In 1914, when the initial fighting of the First World War finally broke out in Europe, Japan declared its entry on the side of Great Britain. In spite of its mutual defence treaty with Japan, Britain was reluctant to see the Japanese join the war. The British correctly assumed that Japan would use the state of war with Germany for a pretext to expand its dominance in Asia. The Chinese government was similarly concerned that the division among the European powers, all of which had summoned their forces home in preparation for war, would give Japan a free hand in Asia — particularly in China. They petitioned the United States to exclude China from the area of hostilities, an action that Japan took to be unfriendly, but China's fear was well-grounded: Japan quickly demanded of Germany that it deliver up the entire leased territory of Jiazhou and the port of Qingdao which the Germans had grabbed in 1898. (This was sweet revenge; the Germans prevented Japan from seizing those lands as spoils of the Sino-Japanese War.) In addition, a vast region of the North Pacific — the island chains of Micronesia — fell under German and now Japanese domination. Ominously, these lay directly across the route of access by the United States to its newly acquired colony in the Philippines.

Confirming Chinese fears, Japan followed its takeover of the German-held territories with an ultimatum to Yuan Shikai in 1915 known as the "Twenty-One Demands." The demands ranged from extensions of leases and concessions already held by Japan to new rights for Japanese farmers and businessmen residing in China. The Twenty-One Demands verged on turning China into a Japanese protectorate. After the most extreme of them were dropped Yuan capitulated, sparking deep outrage in China and a boycott of Japanese goods. Isolated politically, Yuan died in 1916.

With his death, China entered a period of political fragmentation commonly named the "warlord era." For the next ten years, powerful generals at the head of independent armies held provincial and regional authority. Their pillaging and over-taxation of the countryside completely undid the benefits of a successful campaign that had been conducted against opium just before the 1911 revolution. Meanwhile, Japan became increasingly bellicose toward China and it quickly replaced the Western powers as China's most serious imperialist threat.

The Guomindang and the Chinese Communist Party

Against this turbulent background there emerged two powerful factions in Chinese politics, both intensely nationalistic, whose leaders were fundamentally opposed to one another. Both groups have survived to the present day, still opposed to one another: the Guomindang on Taiwan and the Chinese Communist Party on the mainland. Both have erected elaborate memorials to Sun Yat-sen whom each still claims to be its founding father. In the beginning, they were united under Sun's leadership within the party he helped found in 1912, the Guomindang (Kuomintang, KMT, or Nationalist Party). Through Sun's charismatic leadership and his fundraising skills, he managed to hold together the disparate groups, aided by a brilliant political organizer, Song Jiaoren.

When the KMT captured 45 percent of the two houses of the new China parliament in 1913, the party's ascent to nationwide power seemed certain. Yuan Shikai dashed any such hopes by assassinating Song and confronting the KMT with brute military force. Sun fled to Japan where, disillusioned, he reorganized his party into a secret military organization, effectively ending the old KMT and causing splinter groups to form. By the time Yuan died and Sun was able to return to China, the country had been effectively carved up by the warlords. Sun proclaimed his new KMT

> *"There must be preparation, there must be method, there must be sacrifice."*
>
> —Zhou Enlai, August 1919

to be the legitimate government of China, based in Guangzhou, but he was forced by China's contending power brokers to retreat to the Shanghai foreign concessions.

The failure of the Western democracies to aid Sun and his party in the face of these threats left him bitterly discouraged with parliamentary solutions to China's problems. He was attracted to the new Bolshevik government in Russia which, after the Russian Revolution of 1917, loudly proclaimed its opposition to imperialist expansion by the West. In 1920, Sun met with agents of the Comintern, the name given to the Third Communist International, established in Moscow in 1919 to coordinate communist parties around the world. After the founding of the Chinese Communist Pary (CCP) in 1921, Sun agreed to allow their formal participation in the reconstructed KMT. Almost immediately, members of the CCP and the Comintern agents began to exercise an influence in the KMT out of all proportion to their numbers. The Comintern agents, such as Gregor Voitinsky and Adolph A. Joffe, operating on direct orders from Moscow, initially helped Sun reorganize the KMT into a centralized, disciplined party modeled on Lenin's Bolshevik Party. In 1923, the new permanent representative of the Comintern, Michael Borodin, arrived with $1 million in aid and he became a powerful figure in the newly invigorated party. At its first party congress in 1923, the KMT laid out a revolutionary manifesto in which it vowed to engage in a "determined struggle against imperialism and militarism, against the classes opposed to the interests of the peasants and laborers.... Such is the meaning of the Three Principles." With this, the party transformed Sun's 1905 platform, "Three Principles of the People" (nationalism, democracy, and the people's livelihood), into a call for mass mobilization of peasants and workers. A new KMT foreign policy emerged that

reflected the change in attitude. No longer did it seek aid from the West; instead it demanded an end to the unequal treaties.

The next task was to create a KMT army. With Soviet funding, arms, and advisers, Sun established a military academy at Whampoa near Guangzhou under the leadership of a young military specialist trained in Tokyo and Moscow, Chiang Kai-shek (Jiang Jieshi). A key CCP member, Zhou Enlai, was placed on his political staff. For a military expedition against the northern warlords (the so-called Northern Expedition) the KMT started to rally laborers and workers to its cause, but once again, the most notably influential and effective members in this endeavor were the members of the Chinese Communist Party.

The Appeal of Marxism-Leninism in Asia

It is no coincidence that at a time when slogans such as "science and democracy" were being used by Chinese intellectuals in the 1920s, the "science" of social revolution in the ideas of Karl Marx held a special appeal. In China and throughout Asia, Marxism was a powerful tool for explaining what had gone wrong in the world and how it could all be made right again. This was especially true of Lenin's interpretation of Marx. "Leninism" provided a *doctrine* of imperialism which explained the basis of Western colonial behavior in economic terms, a firm *prediction* that such behavior was ultimately doomed, and a *methodology* for fighting back by means of a specialized, disciplined organization. No other intellectual framework at the time offered such a potent combination, backed by the formidable organizational talents of Comintern agents.

After Asian claims to self-determination had been spurned at Versailles in 1919, a key concept pushed by Lenin gained strength: Nationalism and anti-imperialism were profoundly linked as motivators of revolutions. Intellectuals in Asia who sought to mobilize people on a large scale were especially drawn to this element of Marxism-Leninism.

Lenin considerably strengthened the prestige of the Soviets by offering to give up nearly all the old claims and privileges of the czars to territory in China. The most valuable possession, however, was the Chinese Eastern Railway in North Manchuria that connected the Trans-Siberian Railway with Vladivostok. This Lenin retained. In 1929, control of the railway provoked a major dispute between the two countries.

Moscow did not immediately become a "Vatican" for Asian revolutionaries. Party training and education in Moscow was a highly-regarded form of practical experience, but the traditional pull of the European capitals continued to exert its influence, sometimes with the aid of colonial sponsorship. Vietnamese and Chinese journeyed to Paris, Indonesians to Amsterdam, Filipinos to Madrid and Barcelona where in each case they formed expatriate and anti-imperialist associations inspired by European socialist labor movements. These were the seedbeds from which sprang many leaders of nationalist movements in Asia. Vietnam's Ho Chih Minh even helped found the French Communist Party.

The value that Asians placed on European models and education varied considerably. The Vietnamese became profoundly disillusioned with the French who refused to apply to them the ideals of "liberty, equality, and fraternity." Nor was Marxism-Leninism by itself the basis for nationalism in Asia and elsewhere. The fundamental issue was the right of a people who shared a common heritage and territory to define its own community and governance. Ho Chi Minh said, "It was patriotism and not Communism that originally inspired me."

Moscow did exert its own special pull by virtue of its centrality and prestige within the international communist movement. Particularly among the succeeding generation of leaders and intellectuals who supported communism in East Asia, Moscow education and training was a great asset and remained an enduring influence in their thinking and their careers. Even Ho, prior to his wanderings across the face of Asia in the 1920s and 30s, was summoned to Moscow for training by the Comintern. From there, he was sent to Guangzhou where he served as an interpreter for the Comintern within Sun Yat-sen's KMT. His primary mission, however, was to recruit radical Vietnamese patriots living in exile for membership in a new organization, the Vietnam Revolutionary Youth League, which became a major force in Vietnam's growing nationalist movement.

The arguments of Karl Marx (1818-1883) had little intrinsic appeal to the intellectuals of Asia. His audience had been the industrial proletariat of Europe to whom he offered the vision of irrepressible, "objective" historical forces that would propel them from their current economic status toward liberation. What could this offer the agrarian peasant societies in Asia? A strict interpretation of Marx suggested they had little to hope for except to wait for capitalism to grow and mature in their midst. Then and only then would come their turn at revolution.

This quickly created a dilemma among fledgling communist groups. Their meetings, rather than being effective strategy sessions, often deteriorated into arguments over abstract ideological issues. After attending the "First Congress" of the Chinese Communist Party in Shanghai in 1921, a Comintern agent reported that it would never be effective. Lenin, however, was quick to seize the potential of the discontent in Asia and predicted that the peasant-based colonies represented the "weakest link of imperialism." National liberation movements in outlying rural areas, he said, would trigger a proletarian revolution in the metropolitan regions. Lenin assigned a place for everyone: peasants would make the revolution; intellectuals would organize and guide it. To those who suggested that this strategy was just a pipe dream, he could point to the reality of the Bolshevik Revolution. The dramatic political success of the Russian Bolsheviks deeply impressed Asians. There was a widespread belief — not at all taken lightly by governments and industrialists in that period — that the masses could indeed "rise up" in a worldwide revolutionary transformation.

The Appeal of Marxism-Leninism in China

What led China to choose the path of communism? Some suggest that the primary influence was the inspiration provided by the Bolshevik Revolution and Lenin's compelling theories. Others trace the foundations of Chinese communism to a rapid radicalization of its nationalist leaders in the period around 1919. Still others make a compelling argument that it was the direct intervention of the Comintern itself that turned the tide. This latter view is supported by the fact that the

Figures 4.5–4.7 **FUTURE LEADERS OF THE CHINESE COMMUNIST PARTY.** During their youth, the divergent paths of these three future leaders of the Chinese Communist Party would profoundly affect their ambitions for China's relationship to the world. Both Zhou Enlai (top) and Deng Xiaoping (bottom) traveled abroad and studied in France where these pictures were taken. Mao Zedong (middle), on the other hand, remained in China where he developed his own utopian vision of an on-going Chinese revolution.

"May Fourth" movement tested diverse ideologies, the foremost of which was *anarchism*, not communism.

Anarchists believed that the abolition of authority structures, both state and family, would leave people free to return to their "natural state of goodness" wherein they would, without coercion, form small social units. It was not unusual at that time in China to espouse anarchism or some other socialist ideal. Most Chinese were politically tolerant and shunned the idea of class struggle that would later become the hallmark of communist belief. Without a committed, well-organized team of Comintern agents, communism might have been much slower in gaining a foothold.[5]

The grim, "radicalizing" environment of China in the early decades of the century aided the Comintern agents. A growing urban-based labor movement was increasingly outspoken in its anger over working class conditions and widespread urban poverty. It required no leap of the imagination to believe that China's misery was "rooted in the global forces of capitalism." When the Comintern first began to send its agents to China in 1920, most Chinese intellectuals still knew very little about Marx and Lenin. Anarchist experiments in communes were clearly failing. Communism offered a persuasive, concrete alternative to anarchism: the class struggle and the creation of a "dictatorship of the proletariat." With the help of their Comintern advisers, the early Chinese communist activists began to mobilize.

Early Vicissitudes of Communism in China

Even though Lenin's new formulation of revolutionary change appealed to the future leaders of the Chinese Communist Party (CCP), they soon split over the question of how to interpret it. The first leader of the CCP, Chen Duxiu, argued that cities should be the focus of the revolution and rural areas would follow their lead. His faith in by-the-book Marxist doctrine was complete, including the notion that "objective laws" of history would ultimately determine China's economic development and revolutionary fate. By contrast, Li Dazhao called for a more hands-on

> ### STRIKE-BREAKING
> ### IN CHINA: 1923
>
> [On February 7] the leader of the [railroad] union's Wuhan branch, Lin Xiangqian ... was arrested [at the command of the local Chinese warlord] and told to order his union members back to work. When he refused, the workers were assembled on the platform, and he was beheaded in front of them. His head was hung on a station telephone pole. Despite a scattering of sympathy strikes from other unions, the railwaymen went back to work on February 9. This was a new kind of war.
>
> —Jonathan Spence,
> *The Search for Modern China*

approach to change. The peasants in the countryside were China's real hope, he said, and should take priority in the Party's national mobilization. The latter view would eventually predominate within the CCP under the label of "Maoism," but first the Party itself was to suffer grievously at the hands of its initial ally, the KMT.

Sun Yat-sen died in 1925, leaving behind a disunited KMT whose leadership was deeply distrustful of the CCP. To make matters worse, his death came at a time of a new crisis in Sino-Japanese relations. Strikes that had been organized against Japanese factories in Shanghai culminated in violence on May 30, 1925 when foreign police fired on demonstrators and killed several of them. A storm of fires and protest erupted in cities across China over what became known as the May Thirtieth Incident. These demonstrations were broadly antiforeign and their intensity served notice to the foreign community throughout China that its continued presence in the country could no longer be taken for granted. Suddenly, both the KMT and CCP found students flocking to their cause. The communists recruited a wide base of workers and labor organizations. Within a few months, however, the growing KMT-CCP schism erupted in mutual accusations over the assassination of a prominent communist.

THE PEASANT MOVEMENT IN SOUTH CHINA

The movement with the greatest impact on the future was that among the peasants. It started in 1922 in Haifeng and Lufeng, two scenically spectacular counties in eastern Guangdong not far from Hong Kong. It was here, over the next six years, that most of the characteristic forms of the Chinese revolution were to crystallize.

Like much of the far south, Haifeng and Lufeng were an area of large lineages. These owned perhaps half the arable land as collective property. They also had their own armed forces, and government control over them was never strong. There was an exceptionally high rate of tenancy (around 70 per cent), though about two-fifths of the tenants had rights of permanent tenure. The people were of a remarkable ferocity, many of them being members of the Red or Black Flags, semi-secret organizations of nineteenth century origin that periodically engaged each other in savage fighting. It was a common ritual practice to eat parts of slaughtered enemies.

Recent developments had opened a political space for a peasant movement. An increase in economic differences between the richer and poorer members of same lineage, and the exploitation of the humbler members by the lineage managers, had weakened peasant faith in the bonds of kinship and led them to join bodies like the Flags. The traditional local leaders were losing the trust of those below them, especially as they conducted their own affairs more and more on the basis of pursuing their own wealth and power, rather than of social obligation. A symptom of this trend was a new form of rural armed force, the gentry militia, recruited for the defense of the privileges of the local notables. Security of permanent tenure was crumbling, and traditional taxes were augmented with new levies to pay both for the increased number of troops and for new projects, such as modern education, from which the peasants benefited little.

But peasant resentment was never class resentment. (That was a notion imported from outside by the intellectuals.) It was outrage at the absence of equity and fairness within the accepted framework of social relationships. The motive of their actions was to restore equity, achieve social respectability and assure economic security. Their method was equally traditional: to find a protector — whether lineage or secret society leader, warlord or Communist cadre — a man of destiny in whom they could believe, and who would give them what they wanted. There was thus at all times a divergence of interests between the peasants, struggling against economic exploitation, and the professional revolutionaries, who strove to exploit them politically, so as to seize power on the basis of their discontent, and then transform society.

— Caroline Blunden and Mark Elvin, *Cultural Atlas of China*

In March, 1926, Chiang Kai-shek suddenly made a power play by declaring martial law in Guangdong Province and arresting several CCP leaders. Meanwhile, Stalin issued cables to Borodin and other agents commanding them to undertake impossible missions of mass mobilization. At his order, the communists mounted an insurrection in Guangzhou during which they and city workers briefly held the city before being slaughtered in the streets by the anti-communist troops of local warlords.

The factions temporarily papered over their differences. Each needed the other for support to ensure the success of the Northern Expedition. After capturing Nanjing and Shanghai, however, Chiang moved against the CCP in April, 1927. Allied with the notorious underworld godfather, Du Yushang (Tu Yueh-Sheng, or "Big-eared Tu") who headed the powerful "Green Gang" in Shanghai, Chiang launched without warning a carefully coordinated armed attack against labor groups and the CCP throughout the city, slaughtering several thousand people. Among the few who escaped was Chiang's colleague from the Whampoa Military Academy, Zhou Enlai.

With this stroke, Chiang and the Green Gang took over the Chinese Revolution. The foreign community in Shanghai rejoiced and Henry Luce, publisher of *Time* magazine exulted that Chiang had "impeached" the communists. In fact, Chiang presided over a disintegrating situation: He had accomplished his Northern Expedition mainly through deal-making with untrustworthy warlords, the CCP was still alive and re-organizing within a rural base in Jiangxi province, and the Japanese soon moved to consolidate their hold in China by seizing control of northern Manchuria in 1931. Japan created the puppet state of Manchukuo there in 1932, an even more ominous development. Yet rather than give priority to driving out the Japanese, Chiang became increasingly obsessed with eliminating the resurgent Communist Party.

By then the communist leadership included Zhou Enlai, general Zhu De, and a rising commissar named Mao Zedong, a new voice in the CCP. Opposed to the directives from Moscow that called for an urban revolution in China, Mao

Figure 4.8　Chiang Kai-shek addressing his troops in China.

Figure 4.9　Communists gunned down in the streets of Guangzhou, 1926.

instead followed the views of Li Dazhao which said that the party should adapt its policies to local conditions and patiently cultivate a rural revolutionary base.

Chiang, meanwhile, surrounded the Communist army in Jiangxi province. In 1934, when the military noose began to tighten, Mao's ideological strategies became secondary to sheer survival. In a desperate attempt to avoid annihilation, the Communists broke out of the circle and headed west to begin an epic journey in contemporary Chinese history called the Long March. Of the 100,000 troops that began the March, barely 5,000 survived the 370 days and 6,000 miles of fighting across eighteen mountain ranges and twenty-four rivers. The Communists leaders argued bitterly among themselves and suffered terrible defeats. Yet they remained convinced, after arriving in the relative security of remote Shaanxi province, that they were destined to rule China. The basis of their success was their ability to manipulate major currents of discontent in the countryside.

In the meantime, Chiang placated the Japanese to an extent that alarmed nationalistic soldiers and students. When the Japanese army took over northern Manchuria, Chiang's own army forcibly detained him in Xi'an and compelled him to

negotiate an alliance with the CCP. Chiang capitulated to his troops' wishes just in time: the Sino-Japanese War erupted in 1937 when the first shots were fired at the Marco Polo Bridge outside Beijing (see below). For his part, Mao found that the crisis with Japan enabled him to further consolidate his position as supreme leader of the CCP while using Zhou's diplomatic skills to handle day-to-day relations with Chiang and the Nationalists. Wherever possible, the communists held the countryside and built a peasant-based infrastructure for the future contest with Chiang.

Cultural and Economic Changes

A period of cultural experimentation and change in China that lasted from roughly 1916 to 1926 is often called the "New Culture Movement." Its political centerpiece was the May Fourth Movement of 1919, which served to carry the new cultural ideas to a wider population. Writers and artists played vital roles in the New Culture Movement as described in the following overviews.

◆   ◆   ◆

THE NEW CULTURE MOVEMENT

— by Guy R. Alitto

The New Culture Movement was first associated with Chen Duxiu (1879-1942) and his magazine *New Youth*, which he founded in 1915 in Shanghai. In its pages, Chen issued a clarion call to young China to destroy all of old China, its institutions, habits, ethics, and thought as well as all its authorities and patriarchies. His call for cultural revolution was not in itself completely unprecedented, but in the decade previous to 1916 tens of thousands of foreign-trained intellectuals had returned to China's cities, where a totally new class, the modern student of Western-style schools, had sprung up. Within a year *New Youth* had become the most influential periodical in the nation and Chen had become the leader of a sizable group of kindred spirits all over China.

Chen advocated a wholesale adoption of rationalistic Western culture and civilization, which he epitomized by the terms *science* and *democracy*. Quite unmoved by appeals to Chinese cultural identity and national pride, he and his coterie obstreperously flaunted the foreignness of their cultural revolution by using the transliterations of English words (*saiensi, demokelaxi*) instead of the Chinese terms. In the New Culture Movement there is something of the implacable rationalism of the French Enlightenment. Its war cry "Overthrow Confucius and sons" was in the same spirit as Voltaire's "Ecrasez l'infâme."[6] This intellectual outburst dealt a shattering blow to Confucianism and ushered in a new iconoclastic attitude toward all of the Chinese past.

The intellectuals related their frustrated nationalism and their Western-oriented anti-traditional cultural iconoclasm on two levels. First, they identified the political establishment, which they held responsible for China's appalling failure as a modern nation, with Chinese tradition and Confucianism. Second, they assumed, as had previous generations, that in order to achieve the wealth and power of the Western nations, China had to borrow culturally from them. In the seven decades previous to 1919 China had gradually increased the scope and depth of these borrowing to include more and more of Western culture. In the 1860s and 1870s it had begun with military hardware and related technologies. In the 1870s and 1880s this was expanded to include economic institutions and organizations. In the twenty years following that, China imported Western science and scholarship, as well as education and government, and began to send its young abroad for study. Finally, in 1912, even the monarchy was abandoned for a Western-style democratic republic, together with its political processes and organizations. Yet throughout the entire period, China seemed to become poorer, weaker, and increasingly abused internationally. The conclusion that the young intellectuals drew was that the only thing Western left to borrow — and the only thing Chinese left to jettison — was culture itself, the whole way of life and its underlying spirit.

A crucially important figure in the May Fourth Movement was the chancellor of Beijing University, Cai Yuanpei (1876-1940), whose tenure (1916-1926) both coincided with and made possible the May Fourth Movement. Cai's devotion to absolute academic freedom, his liberal attitude toward experimentation, and his encouragement of the talented young made the university the center of the movement as well as the intellectual hub of the nation. In 1917 Cai appointed Chen Duxiu the university's dean of arts and letters, which brought him together with a host of like-minded men returned from study abroad. Cai was equally devoted to diversity, appointing men from a wide spectrum of intellectual and political viewpoints. Another of his appointments, university librarian Li Dazhao (1889-1927), more conservative culturally than most, was yet a co-founder of the Chinese Communist Party. Significantly for later history it was Li, not Chen, who was Mao Zedong's mentor during his brief sojourn at Beijing University in 1918-1919.

Individualism, Iconoclasm, and other Isms

One of the dominant concepts of the May Fourth Movement was the liberation of the individual, a value that ran directly counter to the very keystone institution of Chinese society, the family. The new urban educated youth began to ignore, and sometimes aggressively violate, the ancient principles of family organization. Sons and daughters ignored marriages arranged by their parents and openly defied traditional customs and codes. Fu Sinian (1896-1950), the student marshal of the May Fourth demonstration and later a famous scholar, titled a 1919 article on the Chinese family system "The Source of All Evil." Thus, the basic unit of Chinese society and the entire hierarchic network of social relations and obligations that had shaped it for millennia were under unprecedented and systematic attack.

The sacred authorities of the past became fair game to the new intellectuals. Confucius and the ancient sages went from being demigods to villains. Inspired by Western critical scholarship, a new generation of historians, such as Gu Jiegang (1895-1980) and Qian Xuantong (1887-1939), set out to prove that the sage-king founding fathers of China were myths and that the Confucian classics were mere assemblages of later interpolations.

Wu Zhihui (1864-1953), a major intellectual of the period, advocated putting all the ancient writings "into the toilet for thirty years."

The modern press burgeoned during the May Fourth era as foreign-trained intelligentsia and their students founded hundreds of new magazines devoted to introducing Western thought and culture. These publications also provided a forum in which, for the first time in China, national, social, and intellectual problems were discussed. The general tone and inspiration of most can be surmised by their names: *New Tide, New Woman, New Society, New China, New Man, New Learning, Youth and Society, Young China, Young World*, and so on. Older, established publishers began to follow their lead, and replaced their editors with younger, aggressively modern-minded men. Their editors and contributors infused hundreds of Western-derived "isms" into the Chinese scene, all of which were widely discussed and debated: feminism, Ibsenism, utilitarianism, anarchism, naturalism, relativism, Bergsonism, and so on. The issues and controversies in their pages were, in a way, a telescoped recapitulation of those of the nineteenth- and early twentieth-century West. Translations from Western languages became a major industry. In the decade after 1915, tens of thousands of translations of Western writings — everything from Nietzsche and Freud to William James and Charles Seignobos — were published. Much of Western fiction also was rendered into Chinese, so that by the 1920s Shakespeare, Tolstoy, and Dumas were as well known as traditional Chinese literary greats.

Hu Shi and the Colloquial Literature Movement

One of those cultural innovations associated with May Fourth that had the most immediate and profound effect was the general abandonment of China's classical written language (*wenyan*), which had not been a spoken tongue for thousands of years if ever) for a language closer to modern colloquial Chinese (*baihua*). The New Culture figure most closely associated with this idea was Beijing University professor Hu Shi (1891-1962), a student of John Dewey and enthusiastic disciple of American pragmatism and liberalism. While still a student in New York, Hu published articles calling for all serious literature to be written in *baihua* to produce a "living literature" instead of the dead, sterile, stylized writing of the past. Chen Duxiu immediately and vociferously supported him and began publishing *New Youth* in *baihua*. Despite strenuous opposition from some of China's older literary authorities, it was an idea whose time had come. In 1920 the Ministry of Education decreed that *baihua* would be the language taught in public schools. By the 1930s, almost all writing was in some form of baihua. Thus, the previous three thousand years of Chinese writings of all sorts was rendered largely inaccessible to later generations. By the same time, Chinese writers almost universally had adopted the Western literary forms of novel, short story, play, and poetry, and the native Chinese forms began to disappear.

The earliest and most famous *baihua* writer was Lu Xun (pen name of Zhou Shuren; 1881-1936), also a professor at Beijing University for a time. His bitterly satirical stories of rural life struck Chinese traditional culture and society blows more telling, perhaps, than all the polemics of Chen, Hu, and their colleagues. His novelette *The True Story of Ah Q* (1921) is the only modern Chinese piece of fiction to have won universal international acclaim. After 1949 the Communist authorities enshrined him as the creator of the *baihua* literary revolution and the foremost cultural revolutionary of the May Fourth period. The 1920s saw a profusion of literary coteries, all of which based themselves upon various European literary theories. As in Chinese thought in general, the 1920s saw a steady leftward drift in the literary scene, and by the early 1930s Marxist theories of "revolutionary" literature dominated.

Split in the Movement

By the 1920s the intelligentsia, which had just a few years before thought of the "West" as a monolithic entity comprehensively symbolized by "science and democracy," now began to perceive its inner tensions and complex alternatives. Out of this came a permanent split within the ranks of the May Fourth intelligentsia. In the summer of 1919

Li Dazhao organized the Society for the Study of Marxism in Beijing. Simultaneously in Shanghai, Chen Duxiu organized the nucleus of a Chinese Communist Party, which in July of the next year held its first congress. The May Fourth Movement was after this composed of two broad groups, a left wing oriented toward political action and social revolution, and a liberal wing that maintained a scholarly aloofness toward politics and devoted itself to gradual cultural reform.

The impact of the May Fourth Movement, however profound, was limited to a relatively small group of urban intellectuals. All these tides from the West left the vastness of rural China unaffected. Only decades later did nativized forms of these influences begin to transform the rural Chinese and their traditional way of life.[7]

♦   ♦   ♦

LU XUN

— by Jonathan Spence

Lu Xun had unquestionably emerged as the most brilliant writer of the movement, and his words were guaranteed an attentive audience. After so many years of apparently failed endeavor — as a medical student and a translator in Japan, as a minor bureaucrat and antiquarian in his native Zhejiang province and in Beijing — he found his full voice in 1917, when he was thirty-five years old. Most of his greatest stories were published between that same year and 1921, including the famous "True Story of Ah Q," which portrayed the 1911 revolution as a muddled and inconclusive event, one controlled by charlatans and issuing in the deaths of the ignorant and the gullible. Lu Xun saw it as his task to direct the searching beam of his critical gaze onto the cultural backwardness and moral cowardice of the Chinese. He was harsh in his criticisms and often pessimistic in tone, even though his stories are full of compassion. He had come to understand his mission as a writer, he told a friend, through this image: He was a man standing outside a great iron box in which the people of China had fallen asleep. If he did nothing, they would all suffocate; if he banged and

banged on the outside of the box, he would awaken the sleepers within, who might then be able to free themselves. Even if they could not escape, they would at least be conscious of their fate. The central idea here was not far from Mao Zedong's in his essays on Miss Zhao.[8] But whereas Lu Xun believed that through his work the Chinese at least would die thinking, Mao had insisted that they die fighting.

Lu Xun hated the Confucian legacy and attacked it with bitter satire. He constantly reiterated the "Ah Q" theme, that the so-called "revolution of 1911" had changed nothing of significance in the Chinese character but had just brought a new set of scoundrels into office. He felt that revolutionary political activism might one day bring about constructive social change, but he feared that the admixture of progressive thought with superstition and apathy made that possibility problematic. He regretted bitterly the difficulties in China of speaking across class lines, and of keeping any hope alive in such a fragmented world. In the beautiful ending to one of his finest stories, "My Old Home," published in 1921, he mused aloud that "hope cannot be said to exist, nor can it be said not to exist. It is just like roads across the earth. For actually the earth had no roads to begin with, but when many people pass one way, a road is made."

This was as much a central statement of May Fourth movement thinking as Hu Shi's, although more ambiguous and perhaps more pessimistic. But Lu Xun, like the other prominent figures in the movement who were aged thirty or older, largely confined his actions to the domain of words. When Chen Duxiu began passing out forbidden words with his hands and was arrested for it, this marked a new activism, a second stage. Younger students with a bolder vision of the future seized on this activist strain and claimed the need to expand it into a third stage. For them, it was gratifying that their predecessors had believed they could "overturn the earth with their pens." But for these younger radicals the true meaning of May Fourth lay in the recognition that the time had come "to struggle against the forces of darkness with our bare fists."[9]

♦   ♦   ♦

A GOLDEN AGE OF CHINESE CAPITALISM

Between approximately 1911 and 1937, a successful Chinese business class arose amid (indeed, in spite of) the fierce contests for political control in China. The initial stimulus was the first World War because the European nations, focusing their energies on that conflict, reduced their economic involvements in China. Chinese entrepreneurs soon replaced the European imports and services for which there continued to be a growing demand in China. Chinese banks sprang up: savings banks, postal banks, and credit cooperatives all serving an expanding economy. By 1920 a National Bankers' Association formed to enforce standards and help maintain currency stability. Chinese exporters and processors of raw materials prospered from the global increase in prices created by the Great War. Even Chinese currency appreciated due to the rise of silver prices on the world market.[10]

The focus of this activity was Shanghai, a massive, cosmopolitan city where Chinese and foreign businesses alike could prosper. Shanghai fostered the growth of independent guilds and chambers of commerce which, under a different chain of future events, might have provided the basis for more democratically-oriented politics. Here lived and flourished members of the great Chinese business families, some of which got their start outside of China in overseas Chinese communities. These were among the truly indigenous "Pacific Basin" enterprises of the early twentieth century: The Jian family began a

---

THE WOMEN'S MOVEMENT IN CHINA

The women's movement drew on a variety of late traditional antecedents. Unconventional philosophers like Li Zhi, novelists like Cao Xueqin, poets like Yuan Mei (who encouraged and published women writers) and satirists like Li Ruzhen (author of *Flowers in the Mirror* showing women playing the roles of men) had all pointed to the waste of talent caused by the underestimation and mistreatment of women. Taiping women soldiers and the "Red Lanterns," the young female counterparts of the Boxers who were so active in Tianjin in 1900, offered models of military and political activism. The pioneer of female emancipation in China, Qiu Jin, who was born in 1875, was influenced by these antecedents, and by the old stories of female knights errant, most of them fictional. She rode horseback, used a sword, drank heavily and wrote verses, but also engaged in revolutionary activities, practiced making bombs, taught girls military drill and started the *Chinese Women's Journal.*

The Suffrage Alliance of 1912 had stormed the Nanjing parliament in an unsuccessful attempt to secure equal political and social rights for women, but it was only in the early 1920s that the movement acquired a mass basis. It was split between a social revolutionary wing and a more strictly feminist wing. Xiang Jingyu, the foremost woman Communist of the decade, complained that most educated women only wanted westernized families, participation in business and personal liberty. She kept her harshest strictures for the "romantics," girls who believed in free love and individual happiness.

There was a conflict between feminist mobilization and revolutionary mobilization that was never resolved. In the countryside, peasants, who had often paid large sums for their wives, were alienated from the revolutionary peasant movement when the women's associations began to grant divorces. But, if the women were not given divorces, they would not back the peasant movement. There was also an inter-generational conflict. Mothers-in-law, who in fact exercised the day-to-day control over their sons' wives, rarely welcomed the loss of the services of their daughters-in-law.

— Caroline Blunden and Mark Elvin, *Cultural Atlas of China*

shipping empire out of Guangzhou in the nineteenth century, moved into massive cigarette exports to Southeast Asia and developed the ocean-spanning empire of the Nanyang Brothers Tobacco Company which grew to challenge the mighty British American Tobacco Corporation. Similarly, the prosperous Kwok family started its entrepreneurial life in Sydney, Australia and maintained close ties to the branches of the family as far away as the Philippines and Fiji. In China and Hong Kong their import-export company, Wing On, became a household name.

The beginning of the end for this flourishing of modern Chinese enterprise came in 1927 with Chiang Kai-shek's triumph over the Communists in Shanghai. Chiang immediately set about sapping the strength of the wealthy Chinese business class, particularly in Shanghai, and co-opting businessmen into his corrupt bureaucracy. Among these businessmen were members by marriage or birth in the Kong family of Shanxi province whose fortunes had swelled when they became banking and distribution agents for the British Asiatic Petroleum Company and other foreign firms. When they became financial ministers and affiliated bankers to Chiang's Guomindang, they succumbed to demands for inflationary policies and an eventual looting by the KMT of the national treasury.

From Chiang's perspective, however, there was little choice: He could not impose a general income tax because it had been tried and found nearly impossible to collect. Foreign businesses were too powerful to be taxed heavily. Land taxes went to provincial authorities who were beyond his control. Only the Chinese entrepreneurs were subject to serious taxation. The levies fell so heavily on them, however, that even major companies like the Jian family's Nanyang Tobacco Company were driven into virtual bankruptcy. By mid-century, what Chiang had begun the Chinese Communist Party would finish off.

Foreign firms remained a dominant economic force in China in the 1920s and 1930s. World bankers and industrialists viewed China as a market of almost boundless potential. Thus, even while Chinese-owned businesses expanded and flourished, the foreign share in total investments in China remained strong — at around 77 percent in shipping, for example.

The majority of both foreign-owned and Chinese enterprises were indifferent and often brutal to their Chinese laborers. Hours were long, medical insurance non-existent, and factory housing conditions horrific. Child labor became ever more prevalent: An infamous example was young girls using their bare hands to pluck silk cocoons out of vats of scalding water.

Meanwhile, the foreign community of Shanghai prospered. The skyline of the Bund, a row of tall buildings housing the great banks and hotels along Shanghai's famous waterfront promenade, is little changed today and remains an icon of the late imperial age in China. Shanghai was more than just a commercial center; it was a playground for the self-indulgent rich, "the Paris of Asia," and a symbol of decadent imperialism.

The city held a special attraction for wealthy Chinese because it was a center for new movements in Chinese culture. There was remarkably little social intercourse between the foreign and Chinese communities of Shanghai, but by the 1930s the city had become the center of a burgeoning Chinese movie industry. Here, a struggling but mediocre Chinese actress named Jiang Qing got her start, rising later to become the formidable and culturally imperious Madame Mao Zedong.

VIETNAM

Roots of Early Nationalism

Vietnamese nationalism, slow to flourish, developed a fierceness and tenacity that responded directly to the ruthlessness of the French colonizers. Paradoxically, young Vietnamese who converted to Catholicism and whom the French deemed capable of proselytizing for the faith were granted French education, but the danger always existed that these students would pursue lines of reasoning not intended by the priests.[11] Some of them did advocate social and administrative changes for Vietnam that were opposed not only by the French authorities but also by traditional, Confucianism Vietnamese.

Nguyen Truong To[12] (1827-1871), who stood out among the earliest reformers, was a bureaucrat and monarchical loyalist who had received a

Figure 4.10 This Vietnamese cartoon from early in the century shows peasants routing the French. The caption reads, "Wipe out the gang of imperialists, mandarins, capitalists, and big landlords!"

classical Chinese education. To was supported at an early age by the French missionary priest, Gauthier, who taught him French and took him back to Italy and France in the 1850s. There he visited factories and was received by Pope Pius IX, who made him a present of a hundred Western books. Upon returning to Vietnam, To sent a stream of memorandums to the emperor Tu-duc for an institutional revolution to be led by the emperor. His blueprint for reforms included a specialization in law, science and agriculture by civil servants, all of whom would be tested on their specialties. The Tu-duc court was incapable of carrying out reforms that attacked so many vested interests and To died in 1871, acutely depressed over his inability to prevent his country from drifting toward disaster.

The Emergence of Organized Resistance

To's efforts, although unsuccessful, were appreciated in later years, but the next generation of Vietnamese was sharply divided between those who tried to accommodate the foreigners and those who wanted to expel them. Pham Quynh, a conservative, used his journalistic talent to call for cooperation with the French and preservation of the monarchy. Because of his moderate views, Pham received official support for his cultural journal *Nam Phong*. It promoted a distinctive Vietnamese literature and the adoption of *quoc ngu*, the romanized form of the Vietnamese written language. By contrast, more radical nationalists such as Phan Boi Chau refused to join the imperial bureaucracy and formed the Vietnam Renovation Society (Duy Tan Hoi) in 1904 for the purpose of overthrowing the French. Yet Chau too called for a constitutional monarchy under Prince Coung De of the ruling Nguyen dynasty.

Like other Asian nationalists of the period, Phan Boi Chau was inspired by the 1905 Japanese victory over Russia. Among Vietnamese reformers and intellectuals, Meiji Japan was *the* model in Asia for an action program to which Vietnam should aspire. Phan Boi Chau led this enthusiasm and established headquarters in Tokyo in the hope of receiving Japanese aid. He soon made the acquaintance of "pan-Asianist" patron Okuma Toshimichi and became a disciple of the Chinese dissident in exile, Liang Qichao. He smuggled copies of his history of Vietnam's loss of independence back to secret branches of his Renovation Society scattered throughout Vietnam. Soon, over two hundred Vietnamese students had moved to Japan to find inspiration and education in its universities, part of the so-called Dong Du (Eastern Travel) Movement. The French became so alarmed by the trend that they pressured the Japanese to expel all the students and eventually Phan Boi Chau himself after it became clear that he lay behind several schemes to stir up revolution in Vietnam.

The Meiji influence continued to be felt in Vietnam even after the Dong Du students returned. In 1907, the founding in Hanoi of the famous Dong Kinh Free School (also known as the Tonkin Free School) was the outstanding expression of the Meiji inspiration. Modeled on the Keio School (today's Keio University) in Tokyo, the Dong Kinh School opened its doors to any and all students, their tuitions paid by elite Vietnamese families. Within weeks nearly a thousand students registered for classes that ranged from "Economics" to "Literature." Echoing the Meiji reformers' penchant for cutting hair as a sign of modernity, the school students recited a jingle, "Cast away your stupidities, throw away your foolishness. Today we'll have a haircut, tomorrow we'll have a shave." The French were quick to see the dangers to themselves in this indigenous, independent education. They soon closed the school and imprisoned several of its teachers and leaders. Only in 1918 did the French create a "University of Hanoi," but its curriculum and activities remained under their strict supervision.

Phan Boi Chau turned to China where he persuaded the South China division of Sun Yat-sen's new Guomindang (KMT) Party to support a Vietnamese party modeled after it. Thereafter, the Chinese model of revolutionary change held sway among Vietnamese revolutionaries, replacing the technocratic approaches of the Meiji influence. A hunted man in south China, Chau was finally caught by French agents during a visit to Shanghai and returned to Vietnam where he lived under house arrest until his death in 1940. The more moderate reformers fared no better. The French manipulation of the old-guard Confucianists as a bulwark against change left little

to work with for any progressive-minded Vietnamese intellectual.

One other Vietnamese reformer did gain fame for his advocacy of a more Western-style, republican government. Although little-remembered today outside of Vietnam, the protests and arguments of Phan Chu Trinh in the early 1920s against the very concept of a monarchy had a profound effect on Vietnamese popular thinking. When he died in 1926, his funeral in Saigon elicited mass demonstrations all over the country He thus ushered in a new phase of Vietnamese nationalism, one that no longer accepted patronizing hand-outs from the French to a few privileged elite and which increasingly questioned whether Confucian traditions were sufficient to guide Vietnam toward an independent future.

World War I provided another powerful stimulus for change in Vietnam: the French transported nearly 100,000 Vietnamese to Europe to be workers during the conflict. These people returned to Vietnam with impressions of both the failure of European civilization and the freedoms accorded the citizens of an independent state. It is not known how many of them actually emerged years later to support the Vietnamese Nationalist Party, founded in 1927 in Hanoi, but their orientation by then was not toward Japan or Europe but China. Chiang Kai-shek's unification of major regions of China in his "Northern Expedition" helped to inspire members of the new Vietnamese Nationalist Party. Modeled on KMT principles, the organization attempted to launch an armed resistance but most of its members were soon arrested or killed by the French police.

Ho Chi Minh and the Indochina Communist Party

Early in the century, the young Ho Chih Minh scorned the furtive efforts to restore an independent monarchy, conceding that they were useless against the overwhelming technology and organization of the French. Ho gained considerable experience of the world aboard ships at sea, during life in London (where he was first exposed to Marxism), and later in Paris. He was astute enough to see the opportunity to go "over the head" of France in 1919 with an appeal to the

> *"In Europe, socialism is so extremely popular and so greatly developed, yet people over here are indifferent to it like sleepers who do not know anything. ...If you have understood how to live, then you must protect each other — in the old days even our forefathers understood it. Only through that did the expression arise: 'Nobody breaks chopsticks which are in a bundle,' and 'many hands make a big repercussion.' "*
>
> —Phan Chu Trinh, 1925

global community. At the Versailles Peace Conference, Ho presented a petition demanding independence for Vietnam according to the principle of self-determination. Although the appeal was rejected, it brought Ho to the attention of the emergent communist elite in France and the Soviet Union. By the mid-1920s, Ho was in China organizing expatriate Vietnamese radicals. For the next ten years he moved around Asia in the service of the Comintern, pursued by French agents.

More than any other figure outside Japan (where a far different agenda for Asia was in the making) Ho Chi Minh tried to develop a broadly regional response to the West that would end, once and for all, its domination over Asia. In the 1920s and 1930s, Ho was alternately in Guangzhou, Rangoon, Bangkok, Singapore, or Hong Kong (and in Moscow) working tirelessly to develop the international network which, he envisioned, would rise up and expel the colonialist powers.

Ho's vision of Vietnam's role in this revolution and in Southeast Asia generally was reflected in his Indochina Communist Party, whose branches in Laos and Cambodia he made subservient to his control from Vietnam. Ironically, in founding the Indochina party, Ho accepted the patronage of the French Communist Party even though its commitment to the dissolution of the French Indochinese empire could hardly have been strong. This left him open to attacks by his arch-rivals, the Trotskyists, who had a strong following in the south; Ho's Indochina Party was strong in the north of the country. Further defeats came at the hands of

the French themselves who successfully crushed Ho's "soviets" in the north-central provinces.

In May, 1941, after Japan had launched the Pacific War and had established effective control over the French in Vietnam, Ho held a meeting of the Central Committee of the Indochinese Communist Party just inside the country along its border with China. There, he announced the formation of the League for the Independence of Vietnam — the Viet Minh. Its purpose was not merely to resist the Japanese occupation but also to build up a guerrilla force that could oppose any efforts by the French to return at the close of the war. With his usual prescience and skill, Ho maneuvered within the wave of calamity that was spreading across Asia, setting his sites on its aftermath in Vietnam when, in the initial struggle for independence, he would be the communists' undisputed leader.

KOREA

1919 and the March First Movement

Koreans, too, responded *en masse* to the Versailles Treaty, but with one important distinction: they were pro-active instead of reactive to the unfolding of events in Europe. Rather than wait for the results of the Versailles negotiations to be completed in the initial months of 1919, a small group of Korean patriots seized upon the March 3 commemoration day of King Kojong to stage a protest. They timed their action two days in advance of the commemoration in order to take advantage of the crowds massing in Seoul for the occasion, but even they underestimated the pent-up forces of Korean nationalism that were about to be unleashed.

On the afternoon of March 1, thirty-three of them gathered in a restaurant called the T'aehwagwan where one read aloud a Declaration — not a petition — of Independence. It stated, simply and forcefully, that Koreans were a free, united people with 5,000 years of history in their making and that their statement reflected "the moving principle of the present age . . that cannot be stamped out, or stifled, or gagged, or suppressed by any means." All of them were arrested on the spot by Japanese police.

The intent of this declaration was to launch an entirely peaceful city-wide and nation-wide demonstration that expressed the people's resolve to be an independent nation, free of Japanese rule. By pre-arrangement, students gathered in a nearby park to read the declaration. Then, crying "Long live Korean independence," they set out through the streets of Seoul to lead demonstrations that quickly spread to cities throughout the peninsula, then further north to the Korean communities in the Manchurian region held by Russia.

Stunned by the massiveness and boldness of the protests, the Japanese responded with brutal violence. They mobilized army and navy units and police who opened fire on countless peaceful demonstrations. By their own count, the Japanese killed over 7,500 Koreans and wounded another 16,000 but the numbers were probably far greater. Schools, churches and houses were burned.

From this nation-wide slaughter there emerged a more organized Korean resistance movement directed mainly by those who fled the country after the March First Movement. To understand this new period of Korean nationalism and its key players, it will be necessary, first, to return to the beginning of the decade and the legacy of the nineteenth century reform movements.

The Independence Club

During a pivotal moment in the history of late nineteenth century Korea, a small group of reformers led by Kim Ok-Kyun turned to Japan for support when they attempted to overthrow the old regime and advocated a bold new set of reforms (the short-lived Kapsin Coup of 1884). Japan's motives in the Kapsin Coup and subsequent incidents were anything but philanthropic, however. Their ultimate goal was to wrest control over Korea from China. By 1910, when Japan formally annexed Korea, all hope had died that the Japanese would one day allow Korea to develop into an independent nation in a manner similar to that being contemplated by the United States for the Philippines.

Even so, from the 1890s forward, an educated group of Koreans began to lay the groundwork for an independent society they felt certain would one day emerge in Korea. The word, "independence,"

became a standard for the movement they sought to encourage, their most famous institution being "The Independence Club" and their newspaper, the *Independent*. Published by the American-educated Dr. Philip Jaisohn, it served during its brief lifetime as both their voice and inspiration. Jaisohn had been a friend and supporter of Kim Ok-Kyun. In 1896, upon being invited to return to Korea as an advisor to the Privy Council, he seized the opportunity to do even more, becoming a leader of the independence movement, the "Independence Club."

The movement had three principle goals. First, it tried to safeguard the nation's independence and, wherever possible, to roll back foreign aggression. Independence Club members urged Korean leaders to adopt a neutral foreign policy that favored none of the rival powers in Asia. Second, the Club promoted "self-strengthening" that harkened back to the Kabo Reform period of 1894-96 (chapter 3). Third, it wished to establish democratic rights for the Korean people.

◆   ◆   ◆

PHILIP JAISOHN AND THE INDEPENDENCE CLUB

— by Vipan Chandra

Philip Jaisohn soon took upon himself the mission of not only strengthening the national consciousness of Koreans but also educating them about the achievements and merits of what he called the Christian civilization of the West. Partly for this reason, he persuaded the government to help him set up a Korean-language newspaper. Weaning Koreans away from China meant to him the exclusive use of the purely native script *han'gul*, the study and glorification of Korea's own national heroes, the celebration of Korea's indigenous achievements, and an awareness of the contrasts between the weak and backward-looking civilization of China and the forward-looking and prosperous civilization of the Christian West. A newspaper published jointly in *han'gul* and English was begun on 7 April 1896 and remained wedded to these themes in its editorials. It was

Figure 4.11   Korean Resistance fighters executed by Japanese in the early 1900s.

appropriately called the *Independent (Tongnip sinmun)*.

In July 1896 Jaisohn moved to enlist the throne and high government officials as well as members of the public in the launching of three commemorative projects that he believed would be symbolic reminders of the independence that both China and Japan had recognized and pledged to respect through the Sino-Japanese Treaty of 1895. These three projects were the Independence Gate, the Independence Hall, and the Independence Park. The first was to be built at the site of a gate where envoys from China had been traditionally received by the Korean government according to the rules of the suzerain-vassal relationship between the two countries. The second was to be constructed where a guest house for Chinese dignitaries had stood. Both old structures seemed symbols of Korea's humiliation and needed to be supplanted. An association was formed for this purpose, and it soon came to be known as the Independence Club. Among those prominent in it were Yun Ch'i-ho, an American educated young Christian official

named Yi Sang-jae, Han Hyu-sol, An Kyong-su, and Namgung Ok, all of whom may best be described as reformist Confucians. The park project was abandoned later owing to lack of funds, but the other two were completed in 1897.

Independence Hall became the site of many public discussions and debates, conducted by the club according to Roberts' Rules of Order, on all manner of questions dealing with the related themes of national independence and social, political, and economic advancement. The Hall thus joined the newspaper in the crusade for public enlightenment. Although the club had its own official monthly organ called *The Great Korean Independence Club Report (Tae Choson tongnip hyophoe)*, the *Independent* remained its more eloquent, though unofficial, mouthpiece.

The club seemed to have struck a responsive chord across the nation. Thousands read its ideas through the *Independent*. Hundreds attended its frequent debates in the Independence Hall. Seeing this popularity, Jaisohn gradually expanded the forum of his editorials to include such sensitive political questions as popular sovereignty, the inalienable rights of the people, the duties and responsibilities of government officials, the need to guard Korea from the pernicious effects of collusion between corrupt Korean officials and self-seeking foreign powers (especially Russia), the necessity of popular participation in government through a national assembly, and the like. The club also began to form branches across the country. Jaisohn's idiom was suffused with arguments influenced by Locke, Rousseau, and Bentham that made both the monarch and the conservative officials nervous. Consequently, he was pressured to return to the United States, which he did in mid-May 1898. Yun Ch'i-ho then took over the leadership of both the club and the newspaper.

Yun and his associates, many of whom were young men fired with Jaisohn's idealism, not only kept the club's activism alive but also gave it a militant edge. Syngman Rhee (Yi Sung-man), the future first president of the Republic of Korea, was especially noteworthy among them. Against Yun's advice, the younger members of the club often moved its activism onto the streets, forging an informal alliance with many smaller popular groups representing a cross section of the society and holding frequent mass meetings and demonstrations. In late 1898 this activism led to a confrontation between the club and the government over the question of whether or not the Privy Council ought to be transformed into a modern legislative assembly. The club's proposal showed an eagerness to see the Privy Council function as a kind of one-chamber parliament to which the council of ministers would be accountable for the performance of its functions. The club's arguments for this proposal were drawn from Western democratic theory as well as the populism expressed in the writings of the ancient Confucian philosopher Mencius. At first King Kojong (r. 1864-1907) accepted the proposal. To many conservatives and to the monarch, however, the proposal soon looked like a subversive attempt aimed at eventually turning Korea into a republic. Alarmed at this possibility and irritated by the club's activism, the conservatives persuaded the king to ban the club in early November 1898.

The Independence Club left a lasting imprint on Korea's political development. It made Korean nationalism a deeply felt force in the psychology of the people. Many Koreans continue to draw their inspiration from the club. For the first time, many people thought of themselves as citizens with inherent rights rather than as subjects with nothing but duties toward the state. This too remained part of the club's long-term bequest to the nation.[13]

♦   ♦   ♦

THE NEW KOREAN ENLIGHTENMENT

Although the Independence Club ended in 1898, its demise was really just the beginning of a new wave of independent intellectual and cultural activity in Korea. A growing number of the most promising young intellectuals graduated from the Confucian academies only to cut off their *sangtu* (topknots) in a symbolic break with the traditional past. The period is sometimes referred to as the Korean Enlightenment because it harkened back to the time of "enlightenment thought" in Korea in the 1880s and represented a bursting forth of fresh perspectives and ideas in the national consciousness. A key development was the Korean translation by a senior intellectual, Chuang Chi-yon (1864-1921), of the reform ideas of Liang Qichao, thereby exposing many younger people for the first time to Western theories of democracy and social development. One of these younger leaders, Sin Ch'ae-ho, turned to journalism and history to express a growing sense of outrage over the acquiescence of Koreans to Japanese demands. Sin blamed the centuries-old relationship with China (that is, Korea's ritual subservience to China in an expression of the East Asia power balance) for having created a national consciousness that tolerated a state of subordination. Further, he argued, Chinese preeminence in the relationship had created an attitude of cultural "dependency" in Korea that needed to be broken through the discovery of new symbols and goals. Yet, for a time, it may have been the Chinese who lagged behind the Koreans, so rapidly did the latter develop new associations and periodicals written in modern vernacular.

Japanese Colonial Policy in Korea

Japan's goal in Korea was to bring the populace to voluntarily accept its leadership and control. The first step in this process was to control Korea's educational system. Koreans had launched thousands of new private schools between the time of King Kojong's 1895 edict on education (deemed for all citizens to be "truly of fundamental importance in preserving our nation") and the Japanese annexation of Korea in 1910. The Residency-General closed many of these schools and took over the curriculum of those that remained. In the end, they were converted into vocational training schools that prepared Koreans for work in the Japanese system and helped instill in them Japanese values. By the 1930s this policy even required all classes to be conducted in Japanese. Koreans, like all other subject peoples in the emergent Japanese empire, were forced to bow each morning to the Japanese emperor. Most traumatic of all was the Japanese demand that they abandon their Korean names for new Japanese names. This action, carried out in a society that had for millenia revered the names of its family lineages, was enacted on February 11, 1940, Japan's National Foundation Day.

The spread of Japanese language and cultural values through the educational system created a profound dilemma for the Korean resistance movement. To prevent a steady erosion of Korean identity and self-confidence, the movement strove through literary efforts to preserve Korean culture. Ironically, the most able Korean students moved to Japan for an advanced education where they were exposed to radical elements within the Japanese university system.

Korea's land provided another major arena for Japanese control. Japanese acquisitions of forest and upland as well as river basin regions eventually amounted to 40% of the entire country. The overall impact of Japan's measurement and codification of the land rewarded the wealthy Korean landholders. At a time when population pressures were growing, the Japanese land survey strengthened the power of Korean landlords by formalizing their legal rights of ownership. Meanwhile, tenants incurred ruinous debts to pay rising rents.

The Japanese colonial policy vastly strengthened Korea's transportation and communication infrastructure, but Koreans were pressed into labor gangs to build the railroads and telegraph lines that spread rapidly across their country. At the end of the colonial period, Korea could boast one of the most advanced transportation and communication systems in Pacific Asia.

To finance the Japanese-run government, the Koreans were forced to borrow from Japan, incurring a crushing debt. Korea's banks were controlled by Japan with the result that few Korean business enterprises could afford to expand because they lacked significant access to capital. Even a mass movement to repay the debt was suppressed in 1907 by Japan's Residency-General (the controlling political power in Seoul) who accused it of being "anti-Japanese."

Resistance Movements

Although they could not foresee the extreme measures that would be imposed on them in the decades ahead, Korean reformers and revolutionaries at the beginning of the century had sufficient cause for alarm. Prior to the annexation, they were able to express their views through a limited number of publications, in particular the newspaper *Korea Daily News* whose owner, the English journalist Ernest Bethell, remained free from censorship by virtue of the British-Japanese alliance. Eventually, even this and the expatriate newspapers within reach of Japan were closed or "reformed." Other means of expression were not so easy to control, however. A rich literary movement produced a new genre of realistic novels such as Yi Kwang-su's *The Heartless (Mujong)* in 1917. Popular songs called *ch'angga*, sung to Western-style melodies, became all the rage because their message-within-a-message was one of national pride and dignity.

Secret societies sprang up devoted to the modernization of Korea. The country's annexation by Japan in 1910 strengthened such movements and led some Koreans (such as Sin Ch'ae-ho) to choose a life of exile and protest. After the traumatic events of 1919, a fully-formed Korean Provisional Government-in-exile emerged, based in Shanghai. Its first President, a distant relative of the Korean royal family, Yi Sung-man, became better-known to the West as Syngman Rhee. It was

Export & Consumption of Korean Rice
1912 - 1936

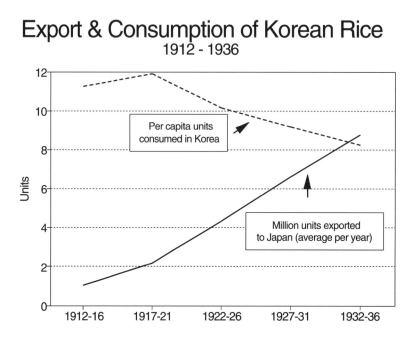

Graph 4.1   The Japanese ate increasing amounts of Korean rice while the Koreans ate less. Units are in a traditional Korean measure, *sok*.

not the connection to royalty that brought him to the leadership position, however, but his stature as a former member of Independence Club, a survivor of imprisonment and torture, and a holder of a PhD from Harvard. A Christian, Rhee was briefly a YMCA evangelist in Korea before being driven out by the Japanese in 1913. From a base in Hawaii, he continued to campaign for Korean independence, but his combative style in factional disputes within the international resistance movement led the Provisional Government to impeach him - an act he refused to recognize. In 1940 he moved to Washington to gain recognition for his Provisional Government by the United States, where he began to acquire an enthusiastic following of American supporters.

Increasing Industrialization

The Japanese colonial grip on Korea steadily tightened, but the excesses of the colonial government in suppressing the 1919 March First Movement were followed by a relatively more sophisticated approach under the direction of a new Governor-General, Admiral Saito Makoto. His so-called Cultural Policy relaxed controls over the life of the colony but at the same time expanded the size and capability of the police force for internal security.

Korea became a vital component of Japan's foreign economic network. In the 1930s, over half of Korea's entire rice production was exported to Japan with the result that per capita consumption of rice in Japan was twice that of Korea. At first, the Japanese-Korean relationship was classic colonialism: Korea had to export raw materials to Japan, its almost exclusive trading partner, while Japan exported manufactured goods to Korea. Beginning in the 1920s, however, Japanese capital began to move across the Sea of Japan in the form of investments in new plant and equipment on the Korean peninsula. This process accelerated dramatically after the 1931 Mukden Incident (see below) when it became clear that Japan would need massive munitions and other manufacturing capacities on the Asian mainland in order to realize its ambitions of Pan-Asian dominance. The effect of the new Japanese investments was to vastly improve Korea's manufacturing capabilities until,

Koreans Employed in Industry
Within Korea, 1932 to 1943

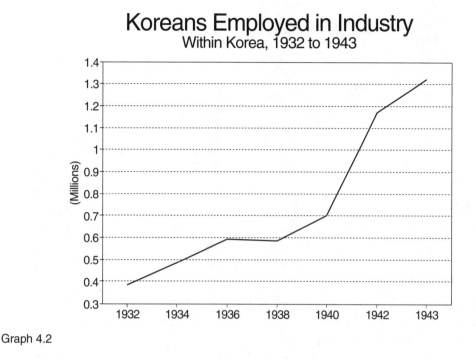

Graph 4.2

by 1939, nearly half the total exports from Korea to Japan were manufactures.

From the turn of the century, Koreans had begun to invest in their own service and manufacturing industries as a means of laying the groundwork for independence, but their size was insignificant in comparison with Japanese enterprises. Indigenous Korean manufacturing capabilities in the 1920s were far from moribund, however. One of the best-known — and very popular with Koreans — was Kim Song-su's Seoul Textile Company. Launched in that fateful year of 1919, the company symbolized Korea's determination to build an indigenous capacity for the new industrial age. Using Korean capital and Korean labor, the company found a ready market for its heavy cloth in the rural population. Kim Song-su's two other major contributions during this era were the founding of the nationalist-oriented newspaper *Donga Ilbo*, still one of Seoul's major dailies, and the support of Posung College, later to become Korea University.

Governor-General Saito's conciliatory policy following the 1919 demonstrations permitted the Korean publication of two national newspapers and a variety of magazines. These did much to revive Korean nationalism and intellectual discourse in the 1920s at a level of moderation that was tolerable to the Japanese. National movements began, such as the Korean Production Movement which attempted to support entirely Korean-produced goods and services. Although it was a significant rallying point in the 1920s, Japanese economic advantages and growing ambivalence by Korean businesses, particularly those subsidized by Japan, undermined the movement in the 1930s.

Japanese colonial control became harsh once again in the 1930s, leaving Korean intellectuals frustrated and internally divided over an appropriate response. Korea was becoming industrialized, with a steady movement of the population into manufacturing jobs at the lowest positions of production and supervision. Japanese consumer products and popular culture continued to pour into Korea, and the pressures against a distinct Korean identity continued to mount. In 1934 Japanese became the only language of instruction in schools, and the following year Korean officials and students were required to participate in Shinto

Figure 4.12   Kim Il Sung of North Korea (left) and General Zhu De of China (in the 1950s).

ceremonies. The appointment of a new Governor-General in 1936, Minami Jiro, who had been a Minister of War and one of the most aggressive generals in Japan's occupation of Manchuria, signaled the advent of a new authoritarianism and close supervision within Japanese-imposed mass organizations.

Under these pressures, lasting for several years, Koreans saw no alternative but to compromise in order to survive in their professions. This amplified the level of fear, suspicion and resentment among themselves. It was a legacy that would haunt individuals and communities for years after the Japanese had gone.[14]

With the outbreak of the Pacific War in 1941, Japan's manpower needs increased dramatically. To fill the demand for workers in factories and mines in Manchuria, Korea and Japan, millions of Koreans were uprooted from their families and sent off to work far away. In 1944, at the war's peak, fully 16 percent of the Korean population — 4 million people — had been deported outside

Korea to Japanese labor camps. Those in remote areas such Sakhalin Island would be stranded and isolated after the war, confined by the new borders of the cold war.

Korean Communists

Shanghai became the center for the Korean resistance movement after 1919. It was the seat of the Provisional Government under Syngman Rhee and the early headquarters for the Korea Communist Party (Koryo Kongsandang). Beginning as the Korean Socialist Party in the Soviet Far East city of Khabarovsk in 1918, the Party soon changed its location to Vladivostok. Then, under the leadership of Yi Yong-hwi and with the "Communist" part of its name newly substituted for "Socialist," the Party moved on to Shanghai in 1920. From the outset it received substantial financial support from Moscow. Other expatriate left-wing movements sprang up as well, including an anarchist group of Korean students in Tokyo who actually attempted to assassinate the emperor, but the Communists were the ones with staying power. They benefitted from Moscow's financial backing and also from the organizational expertise of Comintern agents.

The highly efficient Japanese police force in Korea arrested the initial wave of Party members when they first attempted to secretly build networks inside Korea. In 1927, in a remarkable show of unity with other Korean resistance groups, the Party joined more moderate nationalists in forming a common front, the Sin'ganhoe, to formally oppose Japanese rule. For a brief time the Sin'ganhoe was allowed by the Japanese to be a legal organization in Korea but by 1929 most of its leaders were in jail. The organization disbanded and the Communists went back underground.

Once again fragmented, Korean resistance forces operated in Manchuria (the Communists among them were absorbed into the Chinese Communist Party) from where they launched raids against Japanese troops in Korea. These Korean guerrilla groups also joined the Chinese forces in fighting the Japanese inside China. After Japan triumphed in Manchuria, the Korean Communist troops scattered, some northward to the safety of Soviet-held territory where they were trained by the Russians for use in the event of a Soviet campaign in the Far East.

During this period, a unit commander in the Korean Communist forces, Kim Il Sung, made a favorable impression on his Russian hosts. Although poorly educated and xenophobic (Kim was in some respects the spiritual heir of the authoritarian Taewon'gun who governed the "Hermit Kingdom" from nineteenth century Pyongyang) he nevertheless was identified by the Soviets to be an able and intelligent leader. In the same way that Syngman Rhee had begun to work assiduously in the United States to build a base of political support, Kim Il Sung developed his relations with the Soviets. At the end of World War II he returned to Korea accompanied by the Soviet Army. Poles apart in their ideological, diplomatic, and religious orientations, the two leaders were to become symbols of intransigent divisions within the Korean peninsula itself. Their dispute, greatly amplified by the great power rivals that backed them, is taken up in chapters 8 and 9.

JAPAN

Response to the Versailles Conference

Like much of the rest of Asia, Japan was bitterly disappointed over the results of the Versailles Conference, but for different reasons. Although the great powers had agreed to Japan's demands that it receive rights held by Germany in the Pacific Islands of Micronesia and allowed it to acquire German rights to holdings in Shandong province, the Conference had denied Japan's important and legitimate request that the Versailles signatories recognize the concept of racial equality. It may be that the request was a negotiating ploy and that Japan's leaders knew it would be rejected. Nevertheless, this open rebuke of Japan's standing in the world community stung its leaders and its people, contributing to the distrust of Western moves in the following decades.

Japan had hardly participated in World War I except to take over the German territorial holdings. It also seized the opportunity to replace Soviet control in the upper region of Northeast Asia when, for differing reasons, forces of the World War I allies invaded the Soviet Maritime Province in 1918. The United States reluctantly joined this ill-starred intervention, which was bitterly opposed by the local populace, having agreed with the Europeans that allied prisoners of war should be rescued from the region. The Americans balked, however, at using that pretext to intervene in the continuing Russian civil war. The U.S. contingent, like the British and French, numbered only a few thousand. The Japanese sent 72,000 men and refused to withdraw them even after a peace agreement had been achieved. Only under pressure from the Soviets did they withdraw from the Maritime Province in 1922.

On balance, World War I was highly profitable for Japan. While Europe remained mired in the exhausting and destructive struggle, Japan continued to rapidly build its economy. Its entrepreneurs benefitted from the boom in global economic demand as did their counterparts in China. Diplomatically, however, the conclusion of the Versailles Treaty reinforced Japan's belief that the nation's interests would be taken into account only if it could project military power.

The Washington Conference

In 1920 the three major maritime forces of the world were Great Britain, the United States, and Japan. Each country intended to match or exceed the naval power of its two rivals and a massive naval arms race was about to begin. The rationale for this obsession with naval power had been established in the previous century by an American naval officer, Alfred Thayer Mahan. His thesis, described in his famous work *The Influence of Sea Power on History*, held that a nation's control of the seas made it the master of nearly any international situation, a view that by 1920 was standard orthodoxy in major world capitals. It was also obvious, however, that if more than one country committed itself to achieving Mahan's goal, an upward spiral of warship building would ensue. By virtue of agreements arrived at in the multinational Washington Conference of 1921-22, the major powers managed to establish the basis for a military equilibrium in the Pacific and, temporarily at least, avoided an excessive build-up.

An equally important outcome of the Washington Conference was its decision to dissolve the British-Japanese alliance that had prevailed for the previous two decades. In its place the conferees created a new multilateral arrangement involving France, Great Britain, Japan, and the United States. Both the United States and Canada had pressed for an end to the Japanese-British alliance, believing that Japan's interests in the Pacific would increasingly run counter to their own. The British placed a higher priority on relations with the Americans and looked for a diplomatic means of ending the alliance with Japan. In the end, the Washington Conference satisfied everyone except Japan: it lost a premier and exclusive ally, it accepted an inferior war fleet size to that of the British and Americans (a ratio of 5-5-3), and its diplomats were troubled by the generally belligerent American stance toward them in the course of the negotiations.

The overall effect of the agreement diffused the concentration of power and responsibilities in the Pacific Basin and it seemed to dilute the capacity of any single player to influence events. American diplomats were pleased. Having earlier been forced by Congress to back away from joining the League of Nations, they believed nonetheless in collective responsibility and naively assumed that the results of the Conference would secure peace in the Pacific. They did not sufficiently appreciate that the Conference provided for no system of control. No sanctions or mediation were established that would come into play in the event that the various parties' interests began to collide.

Such collisions soon began to occur over China. Although China attended the Washington Conference and was the object of effusive, flattering speeches regarding its sovereignty, neither Japan nor the Western powers were willing to relinquish their special privileges there. All of them had economic interests in mind, but in addition the West felt a need to remain strongly present in order to restrain Japanese influence in Beijing. That Japan sought wider influence on the mainland was clear enough, but this seemed only a minor problem to the West in the early 1920s when Japan gave the appearance of a country moving briskly in the direction of a liberal democracy. For this reason, Japan-United States relations in the 1920s were generally calm, although eruptions occurred. A particular sore point was a bill, passed by Congress, that excluded Asian immigration altogether.

Economic Turmoil: Aftermath of the War Boom

On the domestic front, Japan faced the daunting challenge of making its post-Meiji government work. Although World War I had brought an economic boom in Japan, it also precipitated a serious crisis for the government. In response to spiraling demands for rice in urban areas and speculation over its price, the cost of this basic staple in the Japanese diet began to skyrocket. During a ten-day period in mid-1918, for example, rice prices surged 50 percent. Protests grew into violent clashes with police. From August through September in 1918, the so-called "rice riots" spread to nearly all parts of Japan. The government was able to quell the disturbances only through the use of armed forces in combination with measures to import cheaper rice from Taiwan and Korea.

With the end of World War I and the re-entry of the European powers into international economic competition, Japan confronted the same challenges of rapid industrial change that faced other countries. Its rapid growth years were over, at least temporarily. Massive layoffs followed an industrial slowdown, resulting in large-scale labor disputes. Fearing that anarchist and communist movements would spread within militant labor groups, the authorities set severe penalties for participation in organizations that they deemed "contrary to the national polity" or that opposed the ownership of private property.

Hostility and paranoia toward leftist political groups, and the potential for xenophobia in Japan, were revealed in the mass hysteria that erupted after the great Kanto earthquake of 1923. The immense quake caused fires to break out all over the city of Tokyo, turning it into a virtual inferno. Landslides and tidal waves added to the loss of life, which totaled more than 100,000, with half a million injured. Rumors spread, which were repeated by newspapers and believed by the army and police, that the many Koreans living in Japan had started the fires and were looting and raping in mobs. Japanese police and vigilante groups killed hundreds of Koreans and Chinese in response. The fantasy was spun further by members of the government who accused socialists and communists of inciting the Koreans to riot. This allowed them to arrest, and in isolated cases kill, leftist political leaders, further radicalizing those who escaped the net.

The Growing Influence of the Military

From 1918 to 1930 democratic party government prevailed in Japan, but the political parties were financed and strongly influenced by the great family combines, the *zaibatsu* (Mitsui alone held 15 percent of the national wealth in its 120 corporations). Corruption in the form of bribes for party officials was common. Government leadership lacked continuity during this period — six ministers were assassinated while others were discredited. Criticism from the military grew as the officers, most of whom came from rural Japan, deplored the poverty in the countryside and the government's emphasis on industrial development. They were deeply angered by the corruption of the politicians and Japan's "weak" foreign policy.

As a result, the senior civilian politicians and military leaders who ruled Japan were increasingly at odds with one another, particularly in matters of foreign policy. Even so, on a number of occasions the civilian politicians supported the demands of the military. For example, the major political party known as Minseito delivered its leadership over to General Tanaka Giichi who, after becoming prime minister in 1927, twice sent Japanese troops into China. On both occasions, the intent was to stop Chiang Kai-shek's "Northern Expedition" from succeeding in its effort to unify China. Many Japanese felt that they could not afford to let Chiang's strength grow to a point where he might challenge their economic hold on the Shandong peninsula. Clashes between Chinese and Japanese troops on the peninsula during a period known as the "Shandong Intervention" (1927-1929) were especially bloody in the principal city of Ji'nan and led to the further tightening of the Japanese military grip over Shandong.

From this point on it became increasingly difficult to sustain civilian control over the army, particularly so-called "Kwantung Army."[15] Originally a garrison in the Kwantung (Guandong) Leased Territory on the strategic Liaodong Peninsula, the Kwantung Army grew in the 1930s to become a massive twelve division army of occupation by 1940. From 1919 its officers reported to no civilian authority but only to the war minister and general staff in Tokyo. Officers in the Kwangtung Army engineered the assassination of a Chinese warlord and, in 1931, created an excuse to invade all of Manchuria.

The incident that provoked the invasion, the so-called Mukden Incident (or "Manchurian Incident"), involved a bombing by the Japanese of their own railroad tracks near Mukden (Shenyang) for which they then blamed the Chinese. This permitted the Kwantung Army, whose ostensible purpose was to protect the South Manchuria Railway, to claim self-defense and advance beyond its zone. By 1932 all Manchuria lay under Japanese military control. In defiance of League of Nations condemnations, the Japanese installed China's long-deposed emperor Puyi to be the head of their new puppet state of "Manchukuo" and designated the Kwantung Army commander to be their "ambassador."

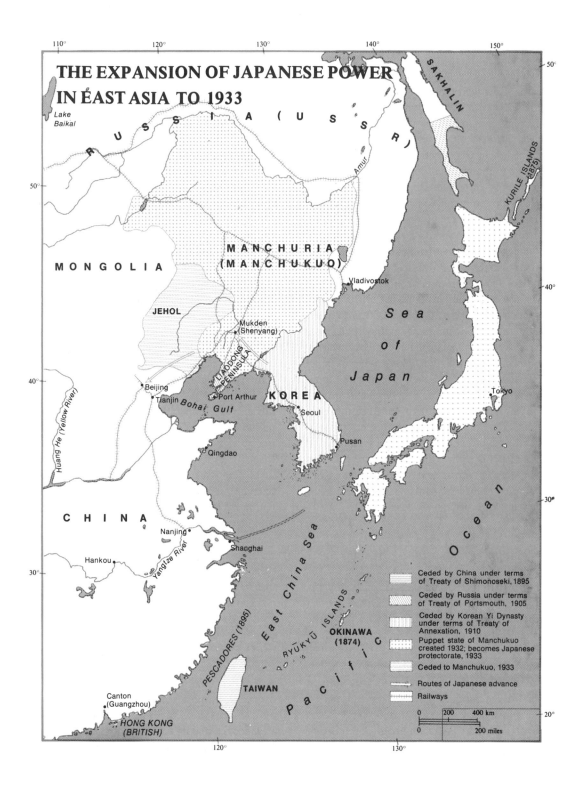

THE EXPANSION OF JAPANESE POWER
IN EAST ASIA TO 1933

Lake
Baikal

R U S S I A   (U S S R)

SAKHALIN

Amur

KURILE ISLANDS (1875)

MONGOLIA

MANCHURIA
(MANCHUKUO)

JEHOL

Vladivostok

Mukden
(Shenyang)

LIAODONG
PENINSULA

Beijing

Tianjin

Bohai Gulf

Port Arthur

KOREA

Seoul

Sea
of
Japan

Tokyo

Huang He (Yellow River)

Qingdao

Pusan

CHINA

Nanjing

Hankou

Yangtze River

Shanghai

East China Sea

Pacific   Ocean

PESCADORES (1895)

RYŪKYŪ ISLANDS

OKINAWA
(1874)

TAIWAN

Canton
(Guangzhou)

HONG KONG
(BRITISH)

Ceded by China under terms
of Treaty of Shimonoseki, 1895

Ceded by Russia under terms
of Treaty of Portsmouth, 1905

Ceded by Korean Yi Dynasty
under terms of Treaty of
Annexation, 1910

Puppet state of Manchukuo
created 1932; becomes Japanese
protectorate, 1933

Ceded to Manchukuo, 1933

Routes of Japanese advance

Railways

0	200	400 km

0	200 miles

The use of an incident to spark a conflict is often employed as a justification for an invasion, one whose ostensible purpose is to restore safety, order, or other "legitimate" interests of the invader. Countries may create or take advantage of a provocation in this manner only to find themselves bogged down and unable to withdraw from the arena of conflict. Japan was to be no exception to this pattern when it embarked, in 1931, on a course of ever-deepening military involvement in China against fierce Chinese resistance.

The dangers were apparent to Japan's civilian leaders. In early 1932 one of Japan's more experienced and moderate statesmen, Inukai Tsuyoshi, became prime minister and quickly moved to curb army actions in Manchuria in accordance with the wishes of the Showa Emperor[16] (Hirohito, who had succeeded the Emperor Taisho upon the latter's death in December 1926). Enraged by Inukai's plans to restrain the army, a small group of young military officers burst into his home and shot him to death on May 15, 1932. Remarkably, the assassins were only lightly punished; one of them was released after serving five years of a fifteen year term. Previous assassination plots against civilians had received similarly light treatment, for by then the civilian politicians had become frightened and avoided further showdowns with the military. The previous year, another Prime Minister, Hamaguchi Osachi, died of wounds from an assassin's bullet. Also assassinated were an ex-Finance Minister, Inoue Junnosuke, and the chairman of the Mitsui interests, Takuma Dan.

The Inukai assassination, in particular, marks the effective end of republican government in Japan, just as the Mukden Incident the year before marks, in retrospect, the veering of Japan toward a path of aggression and self-destruction. From the time of Inukai's death until after World War II the system of government by civilian parties ceased to function. Instead, a succession of Prime Ministers emerged primarily from the ranks of the army and navy. At the same time, the military's demands grew ever more difficult to resist. Japan's admirals demanded parity in warships with the U.S. and Britain. The "allies" refused, and so Japan withdrew from the London naval conference, abrogating all previous agreements controlling the size of battle fleets. A naval arms

"Talk is useless!"

—Assassin's reply to Prime Minister Inukai Tsuyoshi when he shot him on May 15, 1932

race, earlier forestalled by the Washington Conference, now began in earnest. Meanwhile, the Japanese army sought to widen its control in China.

Democracy and the Role of the Emperor

A dwindling minority of Japanese intellectuals tried to divert the nation from this militant, confrontational course with the rest of the world. A free and open national debate was sorely needed. Yet Japan's experiment with democracy had only begun and those with dissenting views against the conservative government were often treated not as a loyal opposition but as outright enemies. The first truly general election in Japan occurred only in February 1928 — previous elections were limited to the aristocracy and people of substantial income (women still could not vote in 1928). Even then, the powerful Minister of Home Affairs, Suzuki Kisaburo, warned the populace in a national broadcast the day before the election that a vote against the ruling party was tantamount to a vote against the authority of the emperor.

The emperor came to define in the minds of Japanese politicians, intellectuals, and the general public the very essence of the nation, its purpose, and the role of each individual in it. A struggle ensued for the "hearts and minds" of the Japanese people over the question of who the emperor really was and what he represented. Was he not only a direct descendent in the world's oldest royal lineage but also, because that descent began with the Sun goddess, imbued with divine and mystical qualities? Did he really embody "Japan" as the supreme head of a single national family, the Japanese people? Or was he instead simply the chief executive and most senior authority, albeit deeply revered, of what had become the legal state of Japan? Devout believers in the first definition

婦選獲得同盟宣傳デー

三月廿日

Figure 4.13   Prior to World War II, Japanese women were not allowed to vote in political elections, but this did not prevent some among them from publicly demonstrating for such rights.

could be molded to do nearly anything in the name of the sovereign, but if the public became convinced of the latter meaning they would have to assume greater responsibility for their own actions as individuals and as a nation.

The National Mood

Japanese tend to look for symbolic events that encapsulate a national mood or consciousness during certain periods. In 1927 the suicide of the brilliant novelist, Akutagawa Ryunosuke, author of "Rashomon" and more than 100 other stories, stunned the nation and became such a symbol. In a "Note to Old Friends" which he left behind, one passage seemed to stand out and became the most-quoted phrase of the time, *bonyari shita fuan*: "indefinable anxiety."

Was it some "indefinable anxiety" that underlay a chain of suicides throughout the year 1933 when a total of 804 men and 140 women jumped, day after day, into the Mihara volcano? Did "indefinable anxiety" compel the escapist behavior of the "mobo" and "moga" (modern boy and modern girl) who patronized dance halls, musical revues and movies (where the producers' buzzwords were "ero," "guro," and "nansensu" — eroticism, grotesqueness, and nonsense)? Was "indefinable anxiety" responsible for the sudden rise of cult religions? One new religion, the *Omotokyo* (Great Fundamentals) grew to some 8 million adherents among the impoverished peasantry and townspeople. Alarmed especially by the "imperial" behavior of the movement's messianic leader, the government banned it and all other cults.

Perhaps it is not possible for a simple phrase to explain such broad cultural trends, particularly since Japanese pundits took the phrase out of context from Akutagawa's carefully worded insight into his deteriorating mental state, but there can be little doubt that these were anxious times in Japan. Policy-makers fretted over an exploding population, envisioning an archipelago teeming with unemployed millions. The Great Depression had descended worldwide, exports were plummeting, and in Japan unemployment had reached alarming levels. Japanese watched obsessively the trends in American hemlines because their most vital export industry — silk — rose and fell according to the length of American hosiery. Their vulnerability to the whims of foreign fashion were a more concrete source of anxiety than the one implied by Akutagawa.

The upheaval in values combined with such national vulnerability to foreign forces fostered xenophobia and political extremism. In the ranks of the military, extremists were both well-organized and determined. They aimed to purify Japan of deteriorating economic and social conditions, most of which they blamed on foreign influences: a breakdown of family values, lack of public discipline and sacrifice for the nation, and a takeover of the nation's wealth by a few greedy and ambitious men. They believed intensely in Japan's capacity to lead Asia into a new era and were willing to sacrifice their lives, if necessary, to bring this about. A special, divinely-endowed nation such as Japan, they argued, must defend its purity against foreign corruption and at the same time establish foreign bases that would place it in greater control of its destiny.

National Debate and the Trial of Minobe

During the brief Taisho Period (1912-1926) that followed the Meiji Period, the processes and institutions of parliamentary democracy gained ground. The emperor was in poor physical and mental condition and therefore unable to govern, and the ruling clique (*genro*) could no longer dictate the course of policy. It found itself repeatedly turning to political parties for support. By 1918 a prime minister, Hara Kei, could draw upon a power base in a political party rather than relying on the *genro*.

These steps toward democratization were accompanied by a broadly moderate political outlook in the population as a whole, but the political system had not matured sufficiently to manage

"And one clouded stream that never ran dry was that choked with the scum of humanism, the poison spewed out by the factory at its headwaters. There it was, its lights burning brilliantly as it worked even through the night — the factory of Western European ideals. The pollution from this factory degraded the exalted fervor to kill, it withered the green of the sakaki's leaves."

—Mishima Yukio, *Runaway Horses*

(Appearing after the war, Mishima's characters often gave voice to pre-war anger with "polluting" influences from the West.)

inflammatory debates and a rising tide of intolerance by extremists. The foremost debate was over the nature and role of the emperor. According to the theory put forward by law professor Minobe Tatsukichi, the emperor should be seen an "organ" of the state, someone whose function is similar to that of a chairman in the legal structure of a private corporation. This was far too "ordinary" a position as far as many conservative nationalists were concerned. They felt that to suggest the emperor was nothing more than a chairman of the board amounted to a sacrilegious act. Instead, they insisted the emperor was a being of mystical qualities whose stature placed him above the state and identified him with the very spirit of the nation.

Minobe presented both a personal target and a means by which his ideas could be defeated. The arch-conservatives excoriated him in the House of Peers and, when he attempted to defend himself on the platform in the House, denounced his testimony as unpatriotic. Minobe was ruined. His books were banned and he lost his teaching post. The specter of his downfall haunted other independent intellectuals and marked the beginning of the end of freedom of thought in Japan. From then on, political theories were strictly supervised. The emperor's "great august will" determined one's moral behavior and under his "guidance" the family system became the framework within which

> *"There was nothing more frightening than not being a Japanese, not being the child of the emperor. It was more frightening than dying. The reason that I'm not afraid of death is that even if I die his Imperial Highness will live. As long as his Imperial Highness continues to live, there's no possibility that I will ever vanish into nothingness.... As long as I am a Japanese I have nothing to fear, as long as I am the emperor's child I have nothing to fear."*
>
> —Oe Kenzaburo,
> *The Youth Who Came Late*

the whole society operated. Here, then, was an ideal situation for extremists to increase their influence over national policy: a supreme and mystical authority, removed from the people, whose pronouncements were strongly subject to manipulation.

Kita Ikki and Japan's Angry Young Men

From the beginning of the century, Japan was able to parlay its limited strength into spectacular successes, such as the 1905 victory over Russia. The general sense of progress and achievement that resulted from this prevented conservative extremists from gaining widespread popular support. Confined to social enclaves such as the Amur River (or "Black Dragon") Society, these nationalists sponsored private intelligence gathering and forays by Chinese revolutionaries onto the mainland. Conditions had yet to ripen before their radical members in the military would be able to capitalize on the disillusionment, anxiety and frustration that built up in Japan after World War I.

The Versailles Conference's backhanded treatment of the racial equality clause and a general unwillingness by the Western powers to affirm Japan's "appropriate place" in the uppermost ranks of world nations, particularly in Asia, were sources of resentment. All this lent support to the rightist claim that Japan's mission should be

to lead a revitalization of Asia, throwing out the Western powers in the process.

In 1919, one of those who supported this view, the 36 year-old Kita Ikki, decided to return to Japan from China where, as an observer for the Amur River Society, he had been deeply embroiled in post-1911 KMT politics. The murder of his friend, KMT master strategist Song Jiaoren, had deeply embittered him against the Japanese government. In his book entitled *A Private History of the Chinese Revolution*, he blamed the government for Song's death because it had not backed the KMT.

Aboard the steamer carrying him back to Tokyo, Kita carried the manuscript of his latest and most inflammatory work, *Outline Plan for the Reorganization of Japan*. The *Plan* called for the nationalization of existing wealth in Japan, the creation of a welfare state apparatus, and the liberation of Asia from Western imperialists under the banner of a "revolutionary Japanese empire." Unpublished until 1923, the book was heavily censored by the authorities but clandestine uncensored copies circulated among his adherents.

Kita became popular with a number of young army officers. They were especially attracted to some of the most incendiary aspects of his plan which called for the replacement of the ruling elite by a coup d'état, the suspension of the Constitution, and the imposition of martial law. His ideas combined democracy, imperialism, and fascism in a self-contradictory brew that nevertheless intoxicated a growing number of the enthusiasts in the military. On the snowy morning of February 26, 1936 a group of them came within a hair's breadth of overthrowing the Japanese government. With *obi* belts tied over their uniforms to hold their swords in traditional samurai style, the officers fanned out across the city of Tokyo at the head of truckloads of rebel troops. They stopped at newspaper buildings to drop off propaganda leaflets and visited centers of power with assassination squads, killing or seriously wounding senior officials.

Uprisings and assassinations had occurred before in the post-Meiji era, but nothing like this. The scale of the revolt was unprecedented. Upon hearing the reports early that morning, the Showa Emperor responded not with support of the rebels (who had announced that they were acting on his behalf) but by ordering their arrest. By thus

Figure 4.14 Amid rumors that war is about to erupt between China and Japan in 1937, Japanese soldiers conduct traffic in the Chinese seaport of Qingdao, then under their control (note the Japanese flag, right), while residents rush to prepare for the conflict.

designating the "patriots" as mutineers, the emperor sealed their fate. The forces of the Imperial Guards division and the First Division mobilized. Naval vessels in Tokyo Harbor put their marines ashore while troops from nearby prefectures began moving toward Tokyo. Sandbags and barbed wire sprang up in the center of the city. Civil war seemed imminent.

Only the moral weight of the imperial condemnation prevented bloodshed. Returning from the Imperial Palace, the martial zone commander issued a message to the rebel troops informing them of the command issued in the emperor's name and called upon them to surrender. He promised them a pardon if they did so immediately. An NHK[17] radio announcer echoed the appeal to the soldiers, "Return to your barracks now. It is not yet too late. Your parents and brothers are weeping to see you become the nation's traitors." In response, most of the non-commissioned insurgents returned to their units. The revolt crumbled. The radio announcer's phrase, "it is not yet too late," was to be repeated often in subsequent years by those Japanese who tried to turn the military from its disastrous ambitions.

Although he had been informed of the plot, Kita Ikki had no direct role in it. Still, he was arrested along with the main conspirators, tried in a military court, and executed in 1937. Enshrined thereafter as a martyr, Kita's image resurfaced in future decades in conservative, Japanese political literature. Nor did his death and that of the other key insurrectionists slow the momentum toward a military takeover of the government: many officers remained in the ranks who had been sympathetic to the goals of the rebels.

The Sino-Japanese War

One night in 1937, Chinese and Japanese troops exchanged shots near the Marco Polo Bridge outside Beijing. The incident precipitated an escalating series of clashes that launched the Sino-Japanese War. Japan moved new troops into China and captured Shanghai after a fierce struggle. On December 1, the Imperial Headquarters in Tokyo ordered an attack on Nanjing (Nanking). The attack lives in Chinese memory as one of the most infamous events of twentieth century warfare — the "Nanjing Massacre." Estimates by the Chinese suggest that more than 100,000 soldiers and civilians in Nanjing were slaughtered indiscriminantly by Japanese troops who entered the city after encountering virtually no resistance. The troops were bitter over their severe losses in the earlier fighting and held racist attitudes towards the Chinese. Both factors contributed to the complete breakdown of discipline. They became a pillaging, raping, murderous mob. The massive loss of life was repeated elsewhere in China and by late 1938 Japan controlled, from north to south, a vast swath along China's coast.

The realistic accounts of the arrogance, cruelty, and greed which distinguished the Japanese Army operations in China were shocking enough, but in the United States they were reinforced by a onesided view of what was happening inside Japan. Frank Gibney and others have pointed out that moderate opinion in Japan was actually quite strong. Many dedicated people wanted peace — bureaucrats, editors, diplomats, socialists, and not a few professional navy men. The balance between a militarist and a reasonably democratic Japan was delicate, even as late as the mid-thirties. It was tipped, in the end, by the willingness of Japanese big business (*zaibatsu*) to profit from the army's aggression. There was also national pride in the success of the Japanese armies in an area where Western armies had already done their share of land grabbing.

One of the few balanced views of Japan presented by the American press during that time was an impressive special issue, "The Rising Sun of Japan," which *Fortune* magazine published in 1937. Not only did *Fortune* see Japan's China adventuring in some historical perspective, but the editors pointed out the effects of the corollary Japanese economic advance into world markets, expedited by the artificially devalued yen. Their judgment was accurate and in some ways, prophetic:

> "The Japanese were no longer merely dressing up like a great power and talking like a great power — they were actually doing what the great powers had long reserved the special and peculiar right to do. They were appropriating pieces of Asia. And that wasn't

"I'll ask you something. Suppose ... suppose His Imperial majesty had occasion to be displeased with either your spirit or your behavior. What would you do then!"...

"Like the men of the League, I would cut open my stomach...."

"Indeed! Well then, if he was pleased, what would you do!"

Isao replied without the least hesitation. "In that case too, I would cut open my stomach at once."

—Mishima Yukio, *Runaway Horses*

all. Indeed it wasn't the half. Trade statistics began to come in. The Japanese, not content with pricking the diplomatic pride of the powers, were picking their purses as well. And not only picking their purses but picking them at a time of world depression when world markets were shrinking overnight. . . . Japanese exports of textiles, up 117 per cent from 1924, had somehow, in 1930, passed the diminished British total and now led the world. In Malaya, British cotton sales were off by half in three years while Japanese sales had mysteriously almost doubled. The same thing was true in Ceylon. In India the Japanese were underselling not only the British mills but the Indian. All through Africa the story repeated itself. Six Johannesburg factories closed in 1933 as the result of unforeseen and ruinous Japanese competition. Japanese textile exports to Kenya and Uganda rose to six times the British....

The Dutch found themselves yielding leadership to the Japanese in their own Javanese markets and were eventually driven to imposing quotas and restrictions which infuriated the natives and seriously diminished Dutch prestige. The Germans were violently concerned about Japanese competition not only in their South American markets but in Germany itself. America was in the same stew, with imports of Japanese goods into such countries as Ecuador 750 per cent *higher in 1934 than in 1933, and with the Argentine textile market almost lost to Japanese competitors....*

There was no sinister explanation. The great competitive superiority of the Japanese is not a superiority in natural resources of which they have few, nor in resources of capital, which are limited, nor in mechanical genius, which is still rare, but in a homogeneous, highly integrated, and beautifully adapted social organization permitting a unification of national effort not possible in any other country.... She acquired the industrial revolution by mail order and fitted it to her preregimented population like a ready-made house dress to a perfect thirty-six....

At present the Japanese masses are educated in the hands and the eye and the ear but not in the mind. Their hands are educated to work in one world: their minds are left to live in another. The methods of propaganda, of censorship, of "moral education" of police terror, now in use and now effective, may retain their power for some time unless a serious war occurs."[18]

By the time this assessment was made, 1937, Kita Ikki's earlier dream of a China united under Sun Yat-sen and supported by Japan had long since been buried. In its place Kita's spiritual heirs in the military had substituted disdain for China and a determination to overtake its historic role as the dominant Asian power. This might have been Kita's choice as well, for he was too zealous a nationalist to support China once its interests clashed with those of Japan and his aspirations for military rule in Japan began to be realized once total war broke out between the two countries. The military permitted titular civilian leadership, but placed Japan on an emergency footing with government decision-making largely under its control — a dictatorship not by one individual but by a cohort of officers.

Amid further international condemnation of their actions in China, Japanese leaders assessed their strategic position with growing alarm: bogged down in China, they faced a hostile Soviet Union to their north and unfriendly British and American forces to the south. In 1940 they signed a military pact with the Axis powers, Germany and Italy, who by then had launched World War II in Europe. Already, Japan felt surrounded and increasingly vulnerable in Asia. General Tojo, Minister of War, later said, "rather than await extinction it was better to face death by breaking through the encircling ring to find a way for existence."

NOTES

1. Born and raised in Spain.

2. David Joel Steinberg, ed., *In Search of Southeast Asia: A Modern History* (Honolulu: University of Hawaii Press, 1987), pp. 273-81.

3. A distinctive culture of Javan Chinese.

4. Steinberg, ed., *In Search of Southeast Asia*, pp. 292-93, 302-04.

5. See Dirlik Arif, *The Origins of Chinese Communism* (New York: Oxford University Press, 1989).

6. Literally, "crush the infamous thing [superstition]."

7. Guy R. Alitto, "May Fourth Movement," in *Encyclopedia of Asian History,* eds., Ainslie T. Embree, Robin J. Lewis, Richard W. Bulliet, Edward L. Farmer, Marius B. Jansen, David S. Lelyveld, and David K. Wyatt, vol. 2 (New York: Charles Scribner's Sons, 1988), pp. 515-17.

8. A bride who in 1919 had committed suicide in protest against her arranged marriage.

9. Jonathan Spence, *The Search for Modern China* (New York: W.W. Norton & Co., 1990), pp. 318-19.

10. See Marie-Claire Bergère, *The Golden Age of the Chinese Bourgeoisie, 1911-1937,* trans. Janet Lloyd (Cambridge: Cambridge University Press, 1990).

11. Education for the Vietnamese people as a whole remained extremely limited. At any one time there were only a few hundred university-level Vietnamese students being educated by the French.

12. Vietnamese family names come first in the three-word sequence; personal names come last. In keeping with customary Vietnamese practice, we cite Vietnamese by their given names, not their family names. Thus, Nguyen Truong To is referred to as To. Some rare exceptions to this rule occur, as in the case of Ho Chi Minh, who is always referred to as Ho.

13. Vipan Chandra, "The Independence Club," in *Encyclopedia of Asian History*, eds., Ainslie T. Embree, et. al. (New York: Charles Scribner's Sons, 1988).

14. Dilemmas for Koreans in the entire interwar period are analyzed in Michael B. Robinson, "Nationalism and Social Revolution, 1919-1931," and "Forced Assimilation, Mobilization and War," in *Korea Old and New: A History*, Carter J. Eckert, et. al. (Seoul: Ilchokak Publishers, 1990), pp. 276-326.

15. In Pinyin, this would be the "Guangdong Army," but so many records still refer to it in the Wade-Giles version that the usage is retained here.

16. *Showa* is the title of Emperor Hirohito's reign. In accordance with Japanese custom, deceased emperors will be referred to here by their reign names. For example, Hirohito's grandfather, Mutsuhito, is best known by his reign name: Meiji.

17. NHK is the quasi-national broadcasting system analogous to Britain's BBC. NHK stands for *Nihon Hoso Kyokai* (Japan Broadcasting Corporation).

18. The observations and the quote from *Fortune* are taken from: Frank Gibney, *Japan: The Fragile Superpower*, 2d ed. (New York: New American Library, 1985), pp. 44-45.

5

Maelstrom: The Pacific War and Its Aftermath

OVERVIEW

Japan and the Pacific in 1940

By late 1940, World War II in Europe was already well into its second year and a power vacuum was growing in Pacific Asia. France and the Netherlands, the subjugators of Southeast Asia, were now themselves the victims of aggression by Germany. It seemed only a matter of time before Britain too would capitulate and its colonies along with the others would be "ripe for the picking" by Japan.

Earlier that year in Japan, a new power clique of ministers had agreed to strengthen the country's ties with the then-victorious Axis powers, sign a nonaggression pact with the Soviet Union, and build a "New Order in Asia" that would incorporate the European colonies into a Japanese empire. Many of the Japanese foreign service officers who were sympathetic to Great Britain and the United States, and thus might have blocked such initiatives, had been removed from key posts. After negotiating a military pact with Germany and Italy that was aimed specifically at the United States, Foreign Minister Matsuoka Yosuke visited Moscow in 1941. There, Stalin agreed to a nonaggression pact with Japan and assured Matsuoka that "We are both Asiatics" and "Japan can now move south."

The idea of a "New Order in Asia" emerged into the full light of domestic Japanese politics and

was renamed the "Greater East Asia Co-prosperity Sphere." The concept of such a sphere encountered no serious public debate or opposition, for by then democracy in Japan was dead. On October 12, 1940, at the instigation of Prime Minister Konoe, all politicians voluntarily merged into a single party, the "Society for Assisting the Imperial Rule." Journalists and politicians tailored their statements to satisfy military leaders, leaving the Japanese public with an increasingly distorted picture of the world in which the United States and Britain were depicted as decadent and weak. Thus did Japan move toward expansionism and war not by following a charismatic, fanatical leader such as Hitler (although some in the West argued that the Emperor served a similar purpose), but through the spontaneous cooperation of the political parties themselves.

War and Occupation

This chapter first examines the growing confrontation between Japan and the United States in the 1930s that culminated in Japan's surprise attack on the American fleet at Pearl Harbor. The war of attrition that followed, conducted on a scale never before seen, ended with the still-controversial decision to use the atom bomb against Japan. The signing of the surrender documents on the deck of the *USS Missouri* in Tokyo Bay on September 2, 1945, with General Douglas MacArthur presiding, formally began the period known as the allied Occupation of Japan (in reality, an American Occupation). It was to last until April 28, 1952 when the San Francisco Peace Treaty, containing provisions for the defense of Japan by the United States and the renunciation by Japan of its conquered territories, went into effect.

The scene of destruction that greeted the occupiers of Japan in the summer and fall of 1945 is difficult to imagine today against the backdrop of its modern metropolises. Not only had the United States dropped atomic bombs on Hiroshima and Nagasaki in August, 1945, but Tokyo had been systematically fire-bombed, resulting in destruction which in some ways exceeded that caused by each of the atomic blasts. Not surprisingly, some of the American occupiers felt it would take many decades to rebuild Japan. Its merchant fleet and factories lay in ruins alongside the smoking embers of the cities. The Japanese people were demoralized and struggled just to find food and shelter.

No one could have foreseen the extraordinary recovery that was to take place over the next four decades. Senior officials of the American occupation forces confidently predicted that it would take Japan until the end of the century to bring its economic output up to world standards. Yet, as had been the case in the late nineteenth century Meiji period, Japan would once again surpass all expectations.

As unlikely as Japan's rapid recovery may have been to observers in Tokyo in 1945, its origins can be found in the unique juxtaposition of the prewar experience and postwar circumstances that faced both the victors and the vanquished during the critical years of the American Occupation.

General Douglas MacArthur was appointed Supreme Commander for the Allied Powers (SCAP) and took complete authority over the Emperor and the Japanese government, although the actual administration of the country's day-to-day internal affairs was turned over to Japanese rather than American bureaucrats. It could hardly have been otherwise: The United States did not have sufficient personnel skilled in both the Japanese language and administration to take over the government. Thus, the survival and skillful maneuvering by the Japanese government, even in the face of a complete national defeat and occupation, was the key to the speed of the initial stages of recovery.

The Birth of Nations in Southeast Asia

The final part of this chapter addresses the aftershocks of the Japanese incursions into Southeast Asia where with their initial victories they both liberated and subjugated the former European colonies. The initial defeat of the European overlords by the Japanese left an indelible impression in the minds of the formerly subjugated populations of Southeast Asia. With the war's end, leaders in Indonesia and Vietnam were quick to seize the advantage to declare the creation of new, independent nations. Indonesia soon emerged victorious from its struggle, but long and bitter fighting still lay ahead for Vietnam. Meanwhile, the United States reached agreement with the Philippines concerning its independence, amid social turmoil in the devastated archipelago. We conclude with a survey of the postwar assertions of Asian national identities and rising cold war tensions.

◆　　　◆　　　◆

JAPAN AND THE UNITED STATES AT WAR

— by John Curtis Perry

Why did the United States and Japan go to war? For the Japanese it was part of the unresolved struggle with the Chinese, an East Asian land war which had been going on sporadically since 1931 and the seizure of Manchuria. For the United States, war in the Pacific was, of course, part of the global World War II waged also against the Germans and Italians.

The United States and Japan had slipped into a position of increasing incompatibility during the 1930s. The mood of compromise and harmony struck by the Washington Conference and lingering throughout the 1920s now evaporated; relations across the Pacific took on a sharp and competitive edge. In Japan, strong civilian leadership vanished; and the military, principally the Army, wrenched power from other competing elites. Yet the nation did not lie in the hands of a ruthless, conspiratorial, and irrational Nazi-like gang, although many Americans saw it that way.

For one thing, no such certainty or unity of purpose existed within Japanese leadership. The now freshly stated goal was national security, to be achieved through a self-sufficient economy. Was this so new or so irrational? Was it so different from that of the Meiji era? Was it so inconsonant with the world of the 1930s?

The Japanese argued that they were simply seeking those advantages enjoyed by the other powers. Japan, one of its statesmen remarked, "had to have a special position in China in order to have the same degree of economic freedom as Great Britain and the United States of America with their vast internal markets," the British with their empire, the Americans with their huge continental spaces.

China, a presumed solution to the constriction of Japan, remained a problem to the Japanese. As we know, the Japanese were riding a tiger there. All they could wrest from the obdurate Chinese was territory. No popular support welled up from those whom the Japanese "liberated," and the Japanese failed to grasp the intensity of Chinese revolutionary nationalism.

Americans, bound by sentiment to China, preached the principle of self-determination. Were China to be incorporated in a Japanese led Pan-Asianist sphere, America's economic and cultural role there would be severely compromised, perhaps even ended. One of the premises of Pan-Asianism, in China as in Japan, was, after all, the elimination of the remnants of Western imperialism and the inroads of Western culture and values. As Secretary of State Cordell Hull put it, the United States was at the "Oriental crossroads of decision," in that there seemed no way both to accommodate Japan in China and to preserve an independent American presence and role in East Asia.

Even so, the evidence suggests that the China problem alone would not have provoked war between the United States and Japan. Too many Americans felt China was not worth it; too many Americans opposed war at all, in any form; too many Americans sensed that Chinese nationalists were themselves so anti-foreign that American interests in China would be endangered whoever should win. And people like Ambassador Joseph Grew in Tokyo thought that the Japanese would in the end wind down their involvement in China

Figure 5.1 Depicting the League of Nations as an "Unarmed Cop," this cartoon reflected the dismay of the American public over Japan's brutal treatment of the Chinese.

for reasons of their own, having to do with the expense and unpopularity of the war at home in Japan. Diplomat John V. A. MacMurray, in a prescient memorandum of 1935, perceived that China was the geopolitical meeting point of several contending forces, which held each other in balance to a certain degree. The elimination of one of these forces, Japan, would therefore open the way for another, such as the U.S.S.R.

What eventually stirred the leaders and shapers of American diplomacy was not the fate of China, but rather the "European Connection" — the relationship they perceived between war in Asia and war in Europe. Both Secretary Hull and the President considered the war in China their line of defense against the spread of war to Europe. This was because they believed that peace depended upon the credibility of the international community's commitment to collective security,

Figure 5.2   Japan's invasion of Vietnam drew increasing public attention
and anger in the United States as depicted in this 1941 cartoon.

and the strength of its consensus that aggression was immoral and inadmissible in international relations.

Failure to respond effectively to aggression in Asia would encourage outbreaks of violence elsewhere, Hull and Roosevelt judged. They were encouraged in making this connection by the seemingly interlocking character of events on three continents — in close succession there came the Italo-Ethiopian war (1935), the Spanish civil war (1936), and the reopening of war in China (1937) — and by growing evidence of what appeared to be parallels between European fascism and what was emerging in Japan. Comparisons among Germany, Italy, and Japan were strengthened by the soundings for a German-Japanese alliance (1938) and the actual conclusion of the Tripartite Pact (September 1940). Although that alliance was to be of little real importance to the Japanese, to Americans it was compelling evidence that the Nazis and the Japanese were but birds of a feather.

After the outbreak of the European war in 1939, and particularly after the fall of France in 1940, there was a growing tendency in Washington to regard what was going on as "one war, in two theaters," to use the phrase of the State Department's Stanley K. Hornbeck; or, as Roosevelt himself put it, "a single world conflict," requiring in the United States "a global strategy of self-defense."

The linkage of American security interests in Asia and Europe was a somewhat paradoxical development. On the one hand, it greatly strengthened American resistance to Japan. With only one exception namely, the decision in July 1939 to give notice of the ending of the American commercial treaty with Japan in order to open the way for economic sanctions — all the critical stages of escalation in United States containment of Japan occurred after the outbreak of the European war and were directly related to European considerations.

Thus the fall of France, in June 1940, was followed within a month by the American decision to place exports of aviation fuel and high-grade scrap iron and steel under license, and within three months by Ambassador Grew's

Figure 5.3   When Japan invaded the southern half of Indochina in July, 1941, the United States, Britain, and Holland retaliated with an embargo on all shipments of oil and raw materials to Japan. As this U.S. cartoon suggests, it was assumed that the Japanese would yield, but instead they seized the oil of the Dutch East Indies and attacked Pearl Harbor.

famous "green light" message from Tokyo giving his assent to the use of economic sanctions against Japan. That same month, in September 1940, Japan invaded northern French Indochina with the helpless acquiescence of French colonial officials there; and the United States responded by placing an embargo upon the export of scrap metals to Japan. So also, in July 1941, after the German invasion of the Soviet Union had freed Japan from the threat of Soviet land power in northern China, Japan overran the remaining parts of French Indochina, and the United States responded with its trump card, the freezing of Japanese assets, which automatically ended the export of all American oil to Japan.

Finally, to take another example, it was the urging of Winston Churchill at his Atlantic Conference meeting with Franklin Roosevelt that the United States do something to protect British Malaya and the Netherlands East Indies — with their tin, rubber, bauxite, and oil — that prompted Roosevelt to issue his very thinly veiled warning to the Japanese ambassador in August 1941 that any new military expansion that threatened American interests would bring active intervention.

On the other hand, and this is the paradoxical element, the same linkage that served to strengthen the American position against Japan served also to define it as peripheral: a function of America's much greater and more vital interest in the survival of the anti-fascist allies in Europe. China, and East Asia more generally, became the occasion and the immediate issue of a steadily deepening confrontation of the United States with Japan; but it was not the ultimate American concern.

If events in Europe had not raised the specter of a twofold world, divided between fascist aggressors and peace-loving democracies, and if the Japanese had not exacerbated the resulting tensions by striking southward to seize the oil and mineral resources of the European empires in Southeast Asia, it is most unlikely that the United States would have frozen Japanese assets and imposed an oil embargo. And had there been no oil embargo hanging over the Japanese Navy, it is not at all clear that Japan would have resigned itself to a war that many of its own officials knew in their inmost hearts was likely to end in defeat.

Out of this paradox grows one of the great ironies of Japanese-American relations during the late 1930s: namely, that while there was some fatalism, especially in the navies, about the inevitability of eventual war between the two potential hegemonic powers of the Pacific, prior to 1941 neither side really expected that a war would result from their current confrontation over China. In Japan, it seemed axiomatic to Premier Konoe and the Pan-Asianists that America, which had always confined itself to rhetoric in East Asia, would do so again and would eventually accept the logic and the profits of the Japanese redivision of the Asian world into a new set of spheres. This is one reason why they pressed ahead so hard and so recklessly.

In America, on the other hand, one of the strong arguments for the use of economic sanctions had always been that they would prevent war by breaking the momentum of Japanese expansion and making clear the risks involved — which is why the United States applied sanctions on the assumption that they might gain peace. It was the perception of global issues in the East Asian context that escalated the American response beyond anything Japan had thought probable, and placed the Japanese in the untenable position of having either to fight or to back down because of dwindling oil reserves. The matter was urgent; without oil the Navy could not put to sea. On September 6, the Konoe[1] cabinet decided tentatively for war and set the wheels in motion.

Many Japanese conceded that the American war-making potential was quantitatively far greater than that of Japan; America was larger, richer, and more industrially developed. In fact, in 1941, Japan had only one-tenth the productive capacity of the United States. This meant, for example, that the United States could build two million trucks during the war, the Japanese only

155,000. In addition, Japan suffered from the disadvantage of having a large part of its military strength and air power already committed to the China theater.

What the Japanese counted on to offset this was the supposedly qualitative superiority of their war-making capacity, particularly the discipline and almost mystical spirit of many of the officers and men, and the priority that would predictably be given by Americans to the European theater of the war. If a flabby America, badly wounded at the beginning, fought with less than half its strength in the Pacific, then a smaller but highly disciplined and purposeful enemy might bleed it badly enough to destroy its spirit. And in that case, there was hope for a limited Japanese victory: a settlement of a rather eighteenth-century character involving a loss of wealth, prestige, and overseas territories, but leaving the home governments and territories intact. Thus Japan blundered into a twentieth-century total war, expecting a limited war like those of the past.

Like Hitler grappling with the British "nation of shopkeepers" whose spirit he proposed to break, the Japanese underestimated American will — underestimated, in fact, the degree to which their own surprise attack at Pearl Harbor was a factor in strengthening rather than weakening American will, but in other respects their hopes were not entirely forlorn. Indeed, historian Samuel Eliot Morison goes so far as to say that their strategy "nearly worked."

The United States was committed from the outset to a Europe first strategy. Even before America's own entry into the war, President Roosevelt had become convinced that the survival of Britain as a great power was essential to the security and well-being of the United States; and in the so-called ABC Conferences between members of the American and British military staffs, during the first three months of 1941, he allowed American strategists to define Germany as the enemy of highest priority, should America ever enter the war, and to base their contingency planning upon that premise. Until 1945, American war plans did indeed call for the bulk of American power to go to the European theater.

An American decision made early in the war seemed to give further credence to the notion that the United States was fighting a limited war against Japan. This was the giving of highest priority in the allocation of resources to the development and deployment of strategic air power for massive strikes in 1943 against the industrial heartland of Germany. This carried several implied advantages for the Japanese. Obviously, it meant that most American airplanes would be flying thousands of miles away from Japanese troops and ships. More subtly, it meant that the United States had committed its primary emphasis to a weapon — the strategic bomber — that could not then, or in the foreseeable future, be used against Japanese cities and factories, because the distances from America's existing bases were too great. The maximum range for heavy bombers then was 1,500 miles.

THE SIGNIFICANCE OF PEARL HARBOR

The catalyst for the American entry into World War II was Japan's surprise attack on the U.S. Pacific fleet at Pearl Harbor on December 7, 1941. Prior to the attack, the American people had been deeply divided over the necessity of U.S. entry into the foreign conflicts, including the one in Europe. Many prominent Americans traveled to rallies around the country in a campaign to oppose any direct entry by America into World War II.

Meanwhile, Japan sought to negotiate with the United States to gain a free hand in China and break the embargo that America had imposed on its oil supplies. As negotiations deadlocked, the Japanese leaders reasoned that a swift, decisive and devastating blow would force the America to negotiate a settlement from a position of weakness. It was a major tactical (and cultural) blunder. The outraged American people were immediately united in a determined effort not only to fight the Japanese, but to accept nothing from them but unconditional surrender.

Concomitantly, the emphasis upon air power led to a drastic reduction in the projected size of the American Army. In September 1941, the War Department had estimated that 215 divisions would be necessary to defeat the Axis powers. In fact, only eighty-nine American divisions were formed during the war. The decision for a small Army simply ruled out of the question any thought of committing major American ground forces in China or continental Southeast Asia. It left most of Japan's landholdings outside America's sphere of effective action. And this, in turn, is one reason why American planners became convinced by 1945 that they would need the assistance of the Soviet Army in Manchuria at the end of the war: namely, that there just were not enough American troops available to invade and occupy both the Japanese home islands and Manchuria at the same time. If Japanese armies on the continent decided to fight on after those in the homeland were crushed, it would be useful to have Russian military power to help subdue them.

The United States assumed that the Chinese were incapable of defeating the Japanese Army in their country and would have to receive massive assistance from some outside source. The American strategy in China during the war was to promote Chinese unity and supply China with as many of its military needs as America could without disrupting major Allied efforts in Europe and in the Pacific islands and to do this in the hope of draining off Japanese strength by making the Chinese land mass a great sponge for Japan: what Russia had been for Napoleon and was being for Hitler.

The steady erosion of American confidence in the military and domestic policies of the Kuomintang [Guomindang, the Chinese Nationalist Party discussed in Chapter 4] discouraged realistic hopes that China could do much more than soak up an uncertain amount of Japanese military resources. And after Chiang Kai-shek intrigued successfully for the removal of General Joseph Stilwell,[2] and ruled out the possibility of a Chinese offensive directed by American officers, Washington substantially gave up on China and let that front stagnate. So there was no real expectation that the Chinese by themselves could take on the remaining Japanese armies in Manchuria in 1945, even in their then debilitated state.

THE COORDINATED ATTACK

Pearl Harbor was by no means an isolated strike in the Japanese stragegy for Pacific conquest. Almost simulataneously with the attack on the American base at Hawaii, Japanese forces struck against the U.S. installations in the Philippines and swept down upon Southeast Asia. In spite of a valiant American-Filipino defense in the Philippines, General Douglas MacArthur was forced to leave for Australia, abandoning his forces on the Bataan peninsula. British forces in Singapore were even less prepared. Although they had long expected a Japanese attack, they had taken few measures to strengthen their defenses, so confident were they of their superior military capabilities. Combined Japanese land and naval forces soon overwhelmed the British in Hong Kong and Singapore. From the latter base, the Japanese invaded Indonesia, forcing the Dutch to surrender in only nine days.

The final focus of the Japanese attacks was Burma where the capital of Rangoon served as a supply base via the "Burma Road" to Chiang Kai-shek's troops in China. Again, the British forces were unprepared. Even after a sustaining severe losses from an aerial bombardment, they refused Chinese offers of help in the defense of Rangoon until it was too late. By April, 1942, the Burma Road was closed and the Sino-British force withdrew to China. As in Indonesia, the Japanese occupation of Burma was facilitated by Burmese nationalists whose support as fellow Asians the Japanese had been cultivating for at least a decade prior to their invasion. The British colonialists had no such good will to draw upon.

What the Japanese had not counted on was the pattern of events that led the United States to undertake a limited offensive in the Pacific only half a year after Pearl Harbor, beginning in the summer of 1942. The attack on Pearl Harbor had destroyed the American battleship fleet but missed the aircraft carriers, which were cruising at the time. This was an extraordinary piece of luck, because naval aviation was improving to such a degree that in the ensuing war carrier-borne airplanes, rather than battleships, decided the control of the seas.

As it happened, American naval aviation was considerably more refined than its Japanese counterpart.[3] In May 1942, at the battle of the Coral Sea, American carriers broke the Japanese offensive in southern New Guinea and frustrated the Japanese fleet in its attempt to isolate Australia. It was, incidentally, the first battle in history in which no ship on either side sighted the enemy. At the battle of Midway, June 1942, American carriers won control of the central Pacific by sinking four large Japanese carriers and turning back the Japanese battleship fleet.

These early victories in the theater of the war in which many Americans were most interested,

coming at a time when large-scale European operations had not yet even begun, persuaded American strategists to depart from their overall plan and authorize a limited offensive in the Pacific. Interservice rivalries led to the undertaking of a two-pronged offensive. The Navy thrust across the central Pacific through the Marshalls, the Carolines, and the Marianas, slicing through that Japanese spider web. The second prong was an Army thrust up from New Caledonia in the South Pacific, by way of the Solomons and New Guinea, to the Philippines, capitalizing on the use of Australia as a staging area. Although it was hard going, the Japanese resisting with stubborn determination, there were limited successes from both these drives. Admiral Chester Nimitz's commanders won Tarawa, and General Douglas MacArthur's troops dislodged the Japanese from the eastern tip of New Guinea, where the dark, dripping, lush jungle made fighting particularly difficult. MacArthur had been adamant that liberation of the Philippines be high on the list of Allied priorities.

Accordingly, the Pacific theater took on a momentum that had not originally been foreseen, either in Tokyo or in Washington. By the end of 1942, not only the Navy but the Army as well had

Figure 5.4 Admiral Chester Nimitz's sweep across the Pacific began in the Gilbert Islands where an assault on the flat, barren atoll of Tarawa against suicidal counterattacks from its defenders cost so many Marine lives that it raised a controversy in America over the correctness of the Pacific strategy.

Figure 5.5 In the Pacific War, as in past wars, Japanese officers frequently entered a battle with drawn swords.

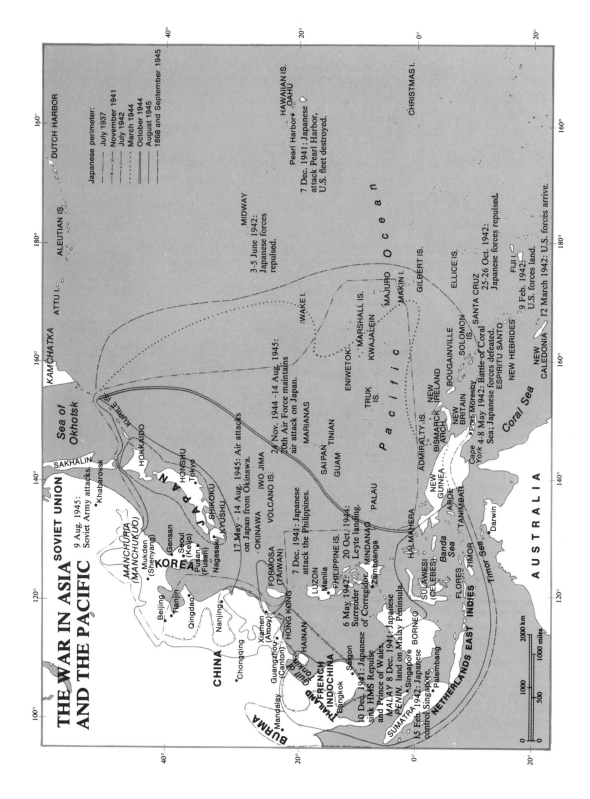

THE WAR IN ASIA AND THE PACIFIC

Japanese perimeter:

—·—·—	July 1937
—x—x—	November 1941
········	July 1942
·········	March 1944
————	October 1944
————	August 1945
————	1868 and September 1945

SOVIET UNION

9 Aug. 1945: Soviet Army attacks.

DUTCH HARBOR

ALEUTIAN IS.

ATTU I.

KAMCHATKA

Sea of Okhotsk

SAKHALIN

•Khabarovsk

KURILE IS.

HOKKAIDO

HONSHU
•Tokyo

SHIKOKU

KYUSHU

Nagasaki•

JAPAN

17 May - 14 Aug. 1945: Air attacks on Japan from Okinawa.

OKINAWA

VOLCANO IS.

IWO JIMA

24 Nov. 1944 - 14 Aug. 1945: 20th Air Force maintains air attack on Japan.

MIDWAY

3-5 June 1942: Japanese forces repulsed.

HAWAIIAN IS.
•OAHU

Pearl Harbor

7 Dec. 1941: Japanese attack Pearl Harbor, U.S. fleet destroyed.

CHRISTMAS I.

P a c i f i c   O c e a n

WAKE I.

MARIANAS

SAIPAN
GUAM
TINIAN

PALAU

ENIWETOK•

MARSHALL IS.

KWAJALEIN

TRUK IS.

MAJURO I.

MAKIN I.

GILBERT IS.

ELLICE IS.

SANTA CRUZ

25-26 Oct. 1942: Japanese forces repulsed.

FIJI I.

9 Feb. 1942: U.S. forces land.

12 March 1942: U.S. forces arrive.

NEW CALEDONIA

NEW HEBRIDES

ESPIRITU SANTO

SOLOMON IS.

BOUGAINVILLE

NEW IRELAND

NEW BRITAIN

BISMARCK ARCH.

ADMIRALTY IS.

NEW GUINEA

Port Moresby•

Cape York

4-8 May 1942: Battle of Coral Sea; Japanese forces defeated.

Coral Sea

HALMAHERA

SULAWESI (CELEBES)

Banda Sea

AROE

TANIMBAR

Timor Sea

TIMOR

FLORES

•Darwin

A U S T R A L I A

NETHERLANDS EAST INDIES

BORNEO

Palembang•

SUMATRA

Singapore•

15 Feb. 1942: Japanese control Singapore.

MALAY PENIN.

8 Dec. 1941: Japanese land on Malay Peninsula.

10 Dec. 1941: Japanese sink HMS Repulse and Prince of Wales.

Saigon•

FRENCH INDOCHINA

Gulf of Tonkin

HAINAN

HONG KONG

Bangkok•

THAILAND

Mandalay•

BURMA

CHINA

•Chongqing

Guangzhou (Canton)•

Xiamen (Amoy)•

Nanjing•

Qingdao•

Tianjin•

Beijing•

MANCHURIA (MANCHUKUO)

Mukden (Shenyang)•

KOREA

Gensan•

Seoul (Keijo)•

Pusan (Fusan)•

FORMOSA (TAIWAN)

LUZON

Manila•

PHILIPPINE IS.

MINDANAO

Zamboanga•

6 May 1942: Surrender of Corregidor.

7 Dec. 1941: Japanese attack the Philippines.

20 Oct. 1944: Leyte landing.

0	500	1000	2000 km
0		1000 miles	

Figure 5.6 The image of Japan in the United States reached its nadir in wartime propaganda. Drawn two weeks after the Japanese attack on Pearl Harbor, this *Chicago Tribune* cartoon invoked once again the racist term, "Yellow Peril."

more forces deployed in the Pacific against Japan than in the European theaters against Germany and Italy. And the next year, in 1943, when British opposition forced the postponement of major landings in France until 1944, American strategists decided to have both Nimitz and MacArthur undertake major Pacific offensives. By November 1944, when the Air Force began strategic bombing of the Japanese mainland from newly liberated Guam, the Navy had already cut off the home islands from access to the resources of Southeast Asia and the American submarine service was wreaking havoc with Japanese merchant shipping.

The War in Asia and the Pacific

In the early phase of the war, within five months after Pearl Harbor, the Japanese had over-run a huge area; the entire northern Pacific west of the international date line lay in their hands, and more than 100 million people had fallen under their dominion. India on the west and Australia to the south trembled. Were they to be next?

If one adds occupied China and Korea to Japan's new conquests, they now embraced nearly one-quarter the population of the globe. Japan's success severed old ties between much of East and Southeast Asia and the Western world. It gave powerful impetus to local nationalisms, Japan's armies thus playing a role similar to that of the soldiers of Napoleon in Europe 150 years before as dissolvers of old allegiances. For the Westerner in Asia, things would never be the same again.

Capricious, arbitrary, and often harsh, Japan's military leaders built a war-won empire of only negative importance. The victors failed to bind the far-flung territories into effective support for the

Figure 5.7   Aerial view of central Tokyo, August 1945. The Allied fire bombing of Tokyo killed more people than the two atomic attacks on Hiroshima and Nagasaki. The raid of March 10, 1945 left 85,000 dead in its wake.

demands of the Japanese war machine. Petroleum and all the other resources so desperately required did not flow to the north as had been anticipated. That all of Southeast Asia was brought under one rule for the first time in history would have no lasting significance. Japan failed even temporarily to win the allegiance of the peoples of Southeast Asia, and whatever cooperation developed between Southeast Asians and Japanese was purely from expedience. The marriage was unequal, short-lived, and strictly one of convenience. And it generated a legacy of hatred which, long after the war was over, would plague the Japanese trying to build economic linkages with that part of the world.

Bombing supplemented blockade and gave the coup de grace to Japan's emaciated economy. The machinery virtually ground to a stop; the people were brought to the brink of starvation. Bomb tonnage dropped on Japan was far smaller than what the Germans received from the Allies, but the vulnerability of Japan's cities — most of their buildings were wooden — made the impact very great. Incendiary raids were particularly destructive, and they were cheap for the attacker:

1.4 American bombers were lost for every square mile of Japanese city destroyed. In the great raid of March 10, 1945, fifty square miles of Tokyo burned, in a greater disaster than the cataclysmic earthquake of 1923.

For most Japanese, the atomic bombs, when they fell in August, were simply one more agony in a lengthy catalogue of disaster, their genetic effects not clearly understood. After the war, Americans in large numbers read with sickening horror John Hersey's vivid report, Hiroshima, and came to realize what the new age of nuclear warfare meant to humankind. And in the years since, Americans and Japanese both have pondered the dropping of the two bombs — their necessity at the time, and the moral implications of their use.

The bombs speeded the concluding of the war but until the very end, responsible officers in the Imperial Japanese Army were still talking of a last-ditch stand, defending the precious homeland with sharpened bamboo spears wielded by every man, woman, and child. Those Japanese who wanted peace steadily gathered adherents, but the need to achieve a consensus among the governing elites made the process agonizingly slow.

The guns were stilled on August 14. And what had the great conflict accomplished? Millions of lives had been lost or maimed, countless treasure expended, immeasurable suffering endured. For Americans, the human costs were far less than for the Japanese. The destruction of Japan solved only the problem of Japanese militarism. Inexorably, Americans were sucked into the resulting power vacuum in northeastern Asia — and with incalculable results.

JAPAN'S AMERICAN INTERLUDE

In Germany, Americans found that invasion and desperate large-scale fighting at the end of the war brought not only the ravaging of much of the material culture but also the collapse and disappearance of most of the apparatus of government. In Japan, Americans arrived to find the civil government completely intact and smoothly functioning. American authority could be relatively easily superimposed on top of Japanese structure. The American decision to insert themselves in this fashion, like that of squeezing out the Allies from administrative control, was made before the occupation began.

The question of the future of the Emperor remained unclear until the drafting of the new constitution early in 1947 in which he was declared to be simply a symbol of the state. At war's end public opinion in the United States had strongly favored doing away with the imperial institution, but the Emperor's name was absent from the list of war criminals drawn up by the occupation authorities in the spring of 1946, and to the Japanese, American policy implied that the Emperor could be retained. This proved a powerful incentive to them to cooperate with the Americans.

The American decision to use the Emperor, along with the rest of the Japanese civil government, happened to be entirely consonant with customary Japanese patterns of governance. The only change was that the orders now came from an alien source, from outsiders. For in Japan real power was traditionally concealed behind a facade of those — like the Emperor — nominally exercising power. So when SCAP issued orders or informally made suggestions, the Japanese

Figure 5.8   The contrast between the shorter, formally-attired Hirohito and the informally dressed MacArthur emphasized to the Japanese the overpowering self-confidence of the American occupiers. The photograph, widely reproduced, has since seemed to have forecast the awkwardness — and the necessity — of the post-war relationship between Japan and the United States.

carried them out and found the process reasonably comfortable.

MacArthur's mandate was sufficiently vague as to allow considerable opportunity for creativity. Like the Meiji reformers three-quarters of a century earlier, MacArthur and his men were pragmatists when it came to specific programs. The Meiji leaders were concerned primarily with building military strength; the MacArthur group were concerned primarily with wiping out such strength. The Americans began, acutely aware of past failures in other military occupations. The general himself had been in the Rhineland after Germany's defeat in 1918. That had not been a success, a fact he well knew.

Uncertainty as to how long the occupation should last and conflicting views of what Japan ought to be in the future were among the dynamic elements keeping the situation in a state of flux, and preventing those in charge from developing and executing an overall detailed plan. Among the

"AT THE COST OF A FEW EXPLOSIONS"
Japan's Surrender and the Decision to Use the Atomic Bomb

On August 6, 1945, a B-29 flying at 36,000 feet dropped a single atomic bomb on the city of Hiroshima. In the holocaust that followed, 100,000 people died instantly while many thousands more were condemned to a slow, agonizing death from burns, shock, and radiation poisoning. Three days later, a second bomb fell on Nagasaki, killing 35,000 more.

President Truman's public statements subsequent to these events suggested an unshaken certainty over the rightness of his decision to use the bomb. In fact, it was one that he loathed having to make and it reflected the extent to which he and the U.S. leadership had been deeply affected by the events of the war. Years of U.S. wartime propaganda had reduced the image of the Japanese to that of vicious, subhuman fanatics. Kamikaze attacks against U.S. ships, the atrocities against U.S prisoners of war, and the fanatical resistance on the islands of Iwo Jima and Okinawa hardened Truman and others in their beliefs. "When you deal with a beast you have to treat him as a beast," wrote Truman in justifying the use of the bomb.

It should be remembered also that as yet there had been no 'experience' of the bomb's horrors. To Churchill, for example, it seemed like a deliverance when he learned that the bomb was available for use:

> "We seemed suddenly to have become possessed of a merciful abridgement of the slaughter in the Far East. To bring the war to an end, to avoid indefinite butchery, to give peace to the world, to lay a healing hand upon its people by a manifestation of overwhelming power at the cost of a few explosions, seemed, after all our toils and perils, a miracle of deliverance."

The decision had been further rationalized by Japan's apparent rejection of the Allies' statement at their Potsdam Conference that nothing less than unconditional surrender would be required. Perhaps, also, the use of the bomb was hastened by the prospect of the Soviet Union's entry into the Pacific War. Having initially rejected Allied entreaties that he throw his Siberian forces against Japan, Stalin had finally agreed to do so during the Yalta Conference in exchange for what turned out to be a steep price: the restoration of Soviet special rights in Manchuria, its probable control over the Korean peninsula, the return of the southern half of Sakhalin Island, and the annexation of the Kurile Islands. Whether or not the use of the atomic bomb was also seen by the United States as a pointed demonstration to the Soviets of its new-found power, there can be little doubt that the Americans and many Japanese felt an even greater sense of urgency in bringing the war to closure as Soviet troops surged across Manchuria toward Korea in August, 1945.

Would Japan soon have surrendered without the use of the atomic bomb? Was a second atomic attack really necessary? These questions continue to be debated without clear resolution. It seems likely that the cost in Japanese lives would have been even greater had there been an assault using conventional forces (the fire-bombing of Tokyo was at least as fatal in its impact as the nuclear detonation at Hiroshima) but the question of when (and if) the Emperor would have acted in the absence of a nuclear attack is a matter of speculation. In any case, in the shocking aftermath of Hiroshima and Nagasaki, Japan seemed to feel that it had undergone an ultimate atonement and victimization for the war while the onus for using the bomb remained on the United States. This stigma was to linger not only because the bomb had been used against civilian populations, but against Asian civilians, a theme that Chinese leader Zhou Enlai would skillfully play upon a few years later.

disparate individuals working at GHQ were former businessmen, Wall Street lawyers, ex-New Deal bureaucrats, Midwestern agricultural experts, teachers, and career Army officers. One has the feeling that each had his own private vision of what Japan ought to be.

Furthermore, the changing world political climate had a powerful impact on the evolving occupation: growing hostility toward the U.S.S.R., with whom the American relationship had always been ambiguous; and, with the triumph of the Chinese Communist revolution in 1949, the collapse of American hopes there. These tensions obviously caused Americans to reflect on the inadvisability of a continuing hostility toward Japan. Perhaps Japan could replace China as America's Far Eastern ally. In 1948, Thomas E. Dewey nearly became the first Republican President since Herbert Hoover. The climate of opinion in the United States had grown more conservative. This too had its impact on the evolution of American thinking about Japan. Critics of the occupation — Americans and Japanese, then and later — charged that the American authorities, aided in unspoken alliance with Japanese conservatives, backed away from significant democratic reform. In fact no political reforms were changed, or even social ones, though there was a decided scaling down of economic reforms.

Japanese responses to the occupation were not, of course, simply passive. Prime Minister Yoshida Shigeru, longtime professional diplomat, who, with his cigars, his wing collars, and his Rolls-Royce, liked to play the part of the English aristocrat (nothing pleased him more than to be likened to Winston Churchill), proved a wily manipulator of the Americans — who did not perceive the degree to which the Japanese guided their conquerors. Americans, although keenly aware of Japan's economic borrowing, were largely ignorant of the long Japanese tradition of conscious cultural borrowing, of adaptation, of preserving the essence of their own ways while taking on the appearance and manner of another.

The first order of business for the occupiers was to disarm the Japanese, to destroy their ability to make war. Getting the soldiers and sailors out of uniform was accomplished entirely by the Japanese themselves, rapidly and efficiently. With

Figure 5.9 Entitled "The Real Japanese Diet," a pun on the word 'Diet' which is Japan's parliament, this racist cartoon underscored American certainty during the Occupation that Japan could be transformed from within if it could be forced to consume the unpalatable bowl of "MacArthur's Orders."

equal speed and competence, the Japanese moved six million of their people, on everything from aircraft carriers to sailing ships — soldiers, officials, teachers, technicians, clerks, engineers, wives and children — back home from the far-flung former empire. These individuals had to begin life all over again in a homeland which some of them had never seen before.

Much of the imperial Navy had been sunk or severely damaged in the fighting. What ships survived, their ferrying duties successfully completed, were now either distributed as spoils to the Allies or scrapped. Although the imperial Army on the home island, unbloodied by conflict, had been largely intact, by December 1945 it too had ceased to exist.

Vast quantities of war materiel remained from both services, and much of it — like guns, tanks, airplanes, and ammunition — had to be ferreted out and destroyed. This time-consuming and dangerous task was accomplished under American supervision but largely by Japanese hands.

All of this was perfectly straightforward; the Japanese were cooperative. The unexpected ease with which the breaking up of the great war

Figure 5.10   Yoshida Shigeru, then Prime Minister of Japan, signing the Treaty of Peace of San Francisco, September 8, 1951. The Treaty took effect the following year.

machine was accomplished swelled American expectations of what could be done in Japan and how fast they could do it. More complicated than destroying the means to make war was the question of how the victors should cope with Japan's will to make war. Disposing of the instruments was insufficient; the Japanese had to be convinced of the foolishness of using war as a means of solving national problems.

This meant altering Japan's political culture. Democracy, the Americans thought, would be the best form of government for the Japanese, the kind most likely to insure peace. It was "good for us, therefore it should be good for them too," the theory being that social justice and civil liberties ought to lead to rational political behavior. The idea is certainly plausible but is not one about which there was much speculating. It was taken as a given, and plans sprang from the assumption.

Although the reformers could build upon Japan's experience of the 1920s with a British type of political system, the Japanese required new institutions to root the sources of authority firmly in the people. All the people should choose the Diet, a parliament to which a cabinet and prime minister would be responsible, with a place made in political life for those hitherto politically inert, inarticulate, or voteless: labor, women, and

youth. The old leadership, blamed for bringing about the war as well as for inhibiting popular government, had to be excised and cast aside. The Japanese anticipated that Americans might concern themselves with a wide array of Japanese affairs. One military government officer, stationed out in the provinces, was startled to be asked by a middle-aged Japanese woman, "Does military government have a plan whereby the Japanese people can get sexual satisfaction?"

Americans judged that Japan required sweeping changes, and they were ready to see them carried out in legal codes and local government, through the police, in land-holding patterns, and in the organization of big business. Many believed the large combines, *zaibatsu*, to have been powerful anti-democratic forces which had promoted war.

Since a continuing successful democracy could not be established by fiat, particularly one issued by a foreign occupying army, reform had to begin with the Japanese educational system so that the youth of the nation would grow up to demand democracy, to support it, to fight for it. Teachers, curricula, ways of teaching and learning, all required change. Americans laid out the pattern of what they wanted done with Japan's schools; the Japanese carried it out. Nearly a million teachers and education officials were, for a starter, screened for suitability to the new spirit of democracy.

The Japanese were constantly exhorted to follow the American model, but few Americans seem to have thought very much about whether that model was appropriate to Japan. New teachers and new courses eliminated the ultranationalism and militarism to which the Americans so vigorously objected. Coeducation became prevalent. The initial enthusiasm of Japanese boys for having girls in their classes was somewhat dampened by the realization that the girls were not going to clean the classrooms for them. New methods of teaching were attractive to many Japanese, particularly the students. A large number of schools and colleges were suddenly elevated to university status and school years reorganized so that the Japanese could have junior high schools like the Americans. All this put severe demands on the limited amount of money postwar Japan had to spend on education and that budget was already

REMEMBERING THE OCCUPATION

Many Japanese still think of the occupation as an excuse, a straw man to beat, for their own lack of decision, as with the businessmen who blame the occupation's labor policies for an unruly union movement, but are disinclined to fight the issue out themselves. For others, however, it remains part of a dream (good or bad), a piece of an inspiration, an irritating but stimulating experience. It was the only time in Japan's history that a foreign guest ever arrived, went past the entry hall, and stayed for dinner.

Similarly, it is doubtful that the names of MacArthur's occupation personnel will go down in Japan's annals. They had their moment. But for those who lived through that time, Japanese and American, the memory of the experience remains amusing and sad, prideful and embarrassing. In a sense, the experience was too strong, too heady. It fostered in both peoples an attitude and a relation to each other which was not, in the long run, healthy, but which took a long time to die. History will probably record that, on balance, those years reflect credit on both players in the game.

—Frank Gibney,
Japan: The Fragile Superpower

strained to the utmost by the need to repair and to replace the damage of war: burned-out school buildings, smashed laboratory equipment, and lost books. Yet in this specific field of reform, as in others, the Americans conspicuously failed to engage the sympathies of the Japanese intellectual community. These people — scholars and critics, writers and journalists — were much more drawn to Marxism. They became the hottest and most persistent critics of American policies and the American presence in Japan.

Land reform was one of the two most important specific changes carried out at the prodding of the occupiers. Here was an area in which the reformers could be virtually as radical as they liked, for the sturdy Jeffersonian farmer tilling his own soil was an image pleasing to almost all Americans. Unlike the breakup of big business in Japan, land reform did not strike uncomfortable parallels with what might want doing in the United States. But the Americans were not merely agrarian reformers, they were more revolutionary than that.

The occupation authorities recalled that the Meiji constitution had served the needs of both parliamentary democracy and military oligarchy. Freedom requires highly specific guarantees; and although a constitution may be less important for what it says than how people choose to interpret

it, the law is nonetheless of great importance for spelling out human rights.

Therefore, the Americans instigated a new constitution, the second of their two most important reform measures for Japan. This constitution of 1947 provides, among other civil rights for citizens, specific legal equality for Japanese women, something that Americans had yet to secure more than 30 years later. Douglas MacArthur thus goes down in Japanese history as, among other things, a radical feminist.

Article Nine, the most controversial and most radical clause of the constitution, renounces war and pledges that Japan will not maintain armed forces. The clause has inhibited armament; it has not prevented it. For both the American and Japanese governments have chosen to interpret the law as allowing the Japanese to maintain armed forces for self-defense. The constitution remains unchanged.

Japan emerged from the occupation with a working democratic system and a high degree of social stability; the nation was poised for the brilliant economic success which would flower in the 1960s. No one, even the Japanese, anticipated such a triumph. Americans perceived Japan as a weak client state long after reality was quite different. Only from a purely military point of view did Japan remain weak. The misperception was serious, because it inhibited Americans from responding to Japan's economic power. The occupation mentality lingered; Americans were not ready to learn anything from the Japanese. The burst of study and learning about Japan in America inspired by the demands of war was not sustained; and the Japanese continued to exhibit more interest in and to learn more about the United States than Americans about Japan.

Looking back at the occupation, for the United States the experience was a high point of national self-confidence. "We knew what was best for the Japanese," said one of the occupiers. Many would have agreed with him, including a lot of Japanese. The paradox is that despite profound American ethnocentrism and despite profound American ignorance of Japan, the occupation went well. Japan has a much greater aversion to armaments and their use than any other power; Japan remains friendly to the United States. Sir George Sansom, the great British scholar-diplomat, musing about the occupation, said, "Although I could criticize, I could write a long book showing all the mistakes the American government made, I think the thing was a great success."[4]

NATIONALISM AFTER W.W. II

With its defeat and occupation, Japan may have been on the periphery of events in the Pacific Basin, but the legacy of its conquests in Southeast Asia was immediate and profound. The fact that it had evicted the colonial powers from Asia left an indelible impression on the former colonial populations. Once they had witnessed both the quick defeat and ruthless subjugation of their former European overlords, the prospect of any return to the previous status quo became unthinkable. In the following excerpts from a survey of Southeast Asia after the war, we explore how the nationalist momentum that had been building before the war advanced rapidly in the post-war era in Indonesia, the Philippines, and Vietnam.

◆   ◆   ◆

INDONESIA

—by John R. W. Smail

At the outbreak of war in 1941, the Netherlands Indies was in a nearly perfect state of what the Dutch called *rust en orde*, calm and order. The rapid changes of the previous decades, while creating deep social tensions, had not shaken colonial stability. Dutch rule, occasionally disturbed earlier in the century, was secure and nowhere effectively challenged from within. Indies society — a mosaic of numerous folk societies and small ethnically defined urban communities — was intact in its complex order. The small, mainly Dutch-educated elite of "Indonesians" was itself just another such urban community embedded — alongside similar Dutch, Eurasian, and Chinese ones — within the frame of the plural Indies structure.

The Japanese occupation ended the old order, overturning the politically and economically dominant elites, herding the Dutch into concentration camps, and harassing Chinese and Eurasians in various ways. By hasty improvisation, the Japanese drastically simplified the Indies' plural legal structure and, more important, the plural education system, which it replaced with a unitary system using Indonesian as the medium of instruction. The export industries collapsed, unbacked occupation currency caused a huge inflation, and rationing led to black markets and widespread corruption. Hundreds of thousands of peasants were marched off as slave labor to die in various parts of Southeast Asia.

In one sense Japanese rule simply exchanged one externally based colonial power for another. The Japanese maintained the basic Dutch administrative system, continuing to rule through established elites. But their political style was fundamentally different: Where the Dutch were conservative and aimed to keep their subjects quiet, the Japanese were totalitarian and sought to stir them up. They mounted a relentless, provocative propaganda campaign designed to enlist the energies of their new subjects in their own

Figure 5.11   Streetcar in Jakarta during the Indonesian revolution.

desperate war effort. On Java, where the occupation had its strongest impact, the Japanese set out to enlist the Muslim and secular nationalist elites in their cause. In particular, a succession of widely publicized Japanese-controlled mass organizations gave the nationalist intelligentsia opportunities inconceivable in Dutch times to build connections and gain access to a broad public. Established prewar leaders, such as Sukarno and Mohammed Hatta, publicly supported Japan in order to spread the nationalist idea of Indonesia. The Japanese actively indoctrinated young people in schools and a host of special organizations. Finally, the Japanese built up a well-trained military force of 65,000, officered up to the battalion level by Indonesians — a development quite without colonial precedent.

Japanese colonial rule ended in August 1945, as abruptly as it had begun and before most of the Indies had been reconquered by the Allies. Competing forces moved quickly to fill the vacuum of power thus created. The first to act were the older-generation nationalists who had built up a

momentum of leadership during the Japanese occupation. In Jakarta on August 17, two days after the Japanese surrender, Sukarno and Hatta proclaimed the independence of Indonesia. In the next two weeks, a small committee quickly sketched the outlines of the new Indonesian state: a constitution, a cabinet, Sukarno as president, and Hatta as vice-president. The colonial response came soon enough; on September 29, the first British army units began landing at Jakarta. Representing the victorious Allies, they supported Dutch administrators whose task was to restore Dutch colonial rule.

The ensuing collision opened a long and bitter struggle, which lasted until the achievement of Indonesian political independence in December 1949. Specifically, in September 1945 it precipitated a mass movement, a violent upheaval that swept over most of Java and Sumatra where three quarters of all Indonesians lived, and pinned British troops and Dutch officials to their coastal footholds. It was this social upheaval, and not simply the political struggle for independence,

Figure 5.12 Indonesia fielded a highly motivated guerrilla movement against the Dutch which included women.

that made the Indonesian revolution the central event and experience in modern Indonesian history.

The mass movement rose first because of the sudden disappearance of effective government. The Japanese administration had collapsed overnight; the British had few troops available and were only marginally interested; the Dutch had the motive and precedent for rule but, until 1947, few troops; the Republic, finally, was at first only an idea, with almost no machinery for enforcing its will. In any society, absence of government stirs deep fears and generates powerful impulses aimed at recovering the lost commonwealth. In Indonesia, in September 1945, those emotions were fixed most immediately and massively on the symbol of the Indonesian Republic, and the mass movement, which arose with startling suddenness, was founded on an impassioned Indonesian nationalism.

It was above all men and women in their teens and early twenties who responded in this way, and hence the outpouring is called the *pemuda* movement. (*Pemuda* literally means youth, but in the revolution it took on a deeper connotation of activism, militance, and patriotism.) The movement swept over *pemuda* of all classes and ethnic groups, uniting them in a common commitment to the cause of independence and a powerful sense of liberation and idealism. *Priyayi pemuda*, (aristocrats in the movement) dropped their titles and abbreviated their aristocratic names; men vowed not to cut their hair until freedom had been achieved; young women left home to work in the Indonesian Red Cross; a cult of heroes sprang up. These primarily political energies, moreover, spilled over into other domains, producing a flowering of specifically Indonesian painting, fiction, and poetry inconceivable a few years earlier.

The other side of idealism is fanaticism. The political significance of the *pemuda* movement lay in the violence it mobilized and sanctioned. It began in mid-September with ever-larger parades and demonstrations; shifted to attacks on Japanese posts, offices, and garrisons; progressed to fighting the British; and reached one climax in the battle of Surabaya in early November, in which the larger part of a British division would have been destroyed had Sukarno not intervened. The movement's domestic political impact, however, was more significant. In the extreme disorder it created throughout Java and Sumatra, all established claims to political and social leadership were subject to a drastic test. Those unable to justify themselves, to adapt to revolutionary conditions, or to defend themselves were abused, driven out, or killed. Minority groups — Dutch, Chinese, Eurasians, and Ambonese — suffered particularly heavily from looting and atrocities. A wave of local "social revolutions" spread over the area between Aceh and Surakarta, challenging the traditional local elites on which Dutch, Japanese, and now Republican rule rested, destroying some and driving most into cautious retreat.

The enormous but unchanneled power of the *pemuda* movement decisively influenced political developments at the national level. It brought what was from one viewpoint a struggle between two small elite groups, the Dutch and the Dutch-educated Indonesian nationalists, out into the arena of mass politics. In particular, it greatly complicated the affairs of the small group of older nationalists who had founded the Republic. These men had declared independence and created the Republic, but they lacked a mass organization like the Viet Minh because they had been isolated from the masses both by Dutch and Japanese design and by their own precocious cultural and political development. Nor did they have much taste or aptitude for military organization. During the first months of the revolution, they made no effort to establish a national army, which left the field wide open for *pemuda*. As a group, the founders and leaders of the Republic were urban politicians — committee men and orators. Characteristically, they organized themselves in terms of political parties, which grew in great profusion in late 1945 and after. Few if any of their parties gained mass followings during the revolution; like their predecessors, the prewar parties, they were mainly vehicles of intra-elite politics.

Until mid-1947, the Dutch were quite as willing as the Republicans to negotiate. Holland was exhausted by the German occupation. The Dutch had been lucky, with the help of the British and the Republic itself, to be able to hold out against the *pemuda* in their enclaves in the major cities of Java and Sumatra. The negotiations themselves dragged on until November 1946, when they produced a compromise satisfactory to neither party. Meanwhile, the Dutch had reoccupied the more sparsely populated islands outside Java and Sumatra with little resistance. In December 1946 they established the state of East Indonesia — comprising the Celebes, Bali, and the rest of the eastern archipelago — as the first in a series of regional member states in a projected federal system, which they could expect to control from the center.

By July 1947, the Dutch had assembled enough divisions to launch a "Police Action" in which they easily seized West and East Java and the plantation and oil areas of East and South Sumatra. Though the United Nations began to intervene at that point, the Dutch were able, in January 1948, to compel the government of the Republic to acquiesce in those conquests. In the occupied areas, they quickly established new federal member states based politically on more conservative social groups-hereditary elites, former cooperating nationalists, Chinese, Eurasians, and others-which had been badly shaken by the *pemuda* movement. The next step was logical: in December 1948, the Dutch launched their second "Police Action," quickly occupying most of the remaining Republican territory and capturing Sukarno and Hatta.

The success of the campaign proved fatal for the Dutch. The Indonesian army, released from the restraints of *diplomasi* [a program for attaining independence by negotiations], turned to guerrilla war; the United Nations swung sharply against Dutch policy; and the leaders of many of the Dutch-made federal states — nationalists too — took a more independent line. The Netherlands had to give way; the Republican leaders, as ever, were ready to negotiate. The Hague Agreement of November 2 brought a settlement: political independence for Indonesia; temporary retention of Western New Guinea by the Netherlands; and guarantees for Dutch investments in Indonesia. On December 27, 1949, the Dutch flag was hauled down for the last time.

In the course of the revolutionary upheaval most inhabitants of what the early nationalists had christened "Indonesia" came to think of themselves as Indonesians — a supra-ethnic national identity not to be found elsewhere in Southeast Asia except the Philippines. During the same years the Indonesian language — also supra-ethnic — acquired a new emotional significance, while the unitary Indonesian language school system was permanently built in. It would be difficult to overrate the importance of these developments in the long run for the future of the sprawling multiethnic nation of Indonesia.[5]

THE PHILIPPINES

— by David Joel Steinberg

The war broke the hermetically sealed isolation created by the colonialism and gave Filipinos a sense of their place in Asia. The wartime use of the Tagalog language and the glorification of indigenous institutions generated a new pride. In 1935, Pio Duran, an apologist for Japan, had been considered a pariah for advocating the idea that the Philippines was "inextricably linked" to Asia, yet after the war his message became a key component in the thinking of establishment leaders like Claro Recto, Ferdinand Marcos, and Carlos P. Romulo.

The war also heightened social, political, and economic tensions between tenants and landlords, patrons and clients, exiles and captives, city dwellers and rural *tao* (peasants), guerrillas and collaborators. Thus the Hukbalahap (People's Anti-Japanese Army), while a guerrilla resistance movement in central Luzon, was equally a peasant effort to redress grievances with landlords. Not all guerrillas were radicals, not all conservatives were collaborators, not all peasants were Huks, and not all landlords were absentee landlords. But the disruptions of war and of occupation gave the Huks a special opportunity. Those under indictment for collaboration claimed to be vindicated by Roxas's victory. While presidential amnesty for political collaboration was declared early in 1948, the issue has lingered for decades.

The war years also led to disillusionment with the United States. Dissatisfaction began as early as 1942, when Quezon had bitterly complained to Charles Willoughby that "America writhes in anguish at the fate of a distant cousin, Europe, while a daughter, the Philippines, is being raped in the back room." Most Filipinos felt that the United States owed them generous postwar support, not merely because they had been allies but especially because they had fulfilled handsomely the obligations of *utang na loob* that cemented the "special relationship." Instead, the Filipinos were crushed to discover that the United States seemed

Figure 5.13 This American poster appealed to the Filipinos to join the resistance against the Japanese. While many of the Filipino elite cooperated with the Japanese, the majority sided with the United States. After the war they expected the Americans to respond generously.

preoccupied and insensitive. The relative meagerness of post-war economic aid, especially in comparison with the far more substantial support given Germany and Japan, and the crude way in which the United States tied its aid to postwar concessions, soured many Filipinos. They expected American gratitude; instead, the United States proved to be niggardly, calculating, and neocolonial.

The United States had retained the giant military installations at Subic Bay and at Clark Air Field on 99-year leases. These bases and the American claim to have made the Philippines a "showcase for democracy" were threatened by the Hukbalahap rebellion. As communism triumphed in China and Vietnam, America became increasingly afraid that it could triumph in the Philippines as well. Cold War ideology, therefore, helped to shape the areas of continuing involvement. Military and geopolitical concerns came to dominate Washington's priorities, angering Filipino nationalists like Senator Claro M. Recto. Such concerns led the Americans to endorse the political oligarchy and to address socioeconomic issues with military solutions.

Corruption, low morale, inflation, and economic exhaustion prevented the Manila government from defeating the Huks. Roxas, prior to his death in office in 1948, and his successor, Elpidio Quirino, simply lacked the strength or appeal to break the agrarian uprising led by a charismatic peasant, Luis Taruc, even though the United States was supplying increasing military and economic aid. The 1949 presidential election, in which Quirino defeated the wartime president, Jose Laurel, through bribery, fraud, and violence, weakened democracy. In 1950, the country went through an economic, moral, political, and military crisis. In October of that year, the Central Bank had to borrow to meet government payrolls.

The emergence of Ramon Magsaysay altered the history of the Philippines. Born in a bamboo hut, the son of a teacher who became a blacksmith, he was no scion of an elite family. Magsaysay, a guerrilla leader during the war, became Quirino's secretary of defense. He made three great contributions in his years as secretary. First, he infused a corrupt and demoralized army with a new sense of purpose and esprit de corps. Second, Magsaysay's intelligence network enabled him to arrest en masse the Communist Party Politburo and to seize documents that listed sympathizers. Third, and most important, he got the army to guarantee that the 1951 congressional elections would be honest. By protecting the ballot box he restored a degree of confidence in the electoral process. He won an easy victory in the presidential election of 1953. Gathering a brain trust of bright young men, he broke the Hukbalahap uprising by a combination of heavy military pressure against those who refused to surrender, amnesty for those who did, and a series of resettlement schemes to ease tenancy in the Huk areas. By the time of his death in a plane crash in 1957, he had done much to restore vitality and cohesiveness to the nation.[6]

◆   ◆   ◆

VIETNAM

— By Alexander Woodside

The Japanese occupation of Vietnam from 1941 to 1945 transformed the unpromising revolutionary prospects there as completely as did Japanese occupying armies elsewhere in Southeast Asia. In addition to undermining the reputation of French military power in Vietnamese eyes, the Japanese invasion gave the Vietnamese Communists an opportunity to blend their esoteric dogmas with the more easily understood nationalist cause of resistance to both the French and the Japanese.

Until January 1945, the Japanese armed forces had no more than 35,000 men in Indochina. They were content to let the colonial government, responsible to the neutral Vichy regime in France, preserve order. The disappearance of the Vichy regime by the fall of 1944, and the American invasion of the Philippines, changed Japanese calculations. In early 1945, Japan increased its forces in Indochina, achieving absolute military superiority. And on March 9, 1945, the Japanese struck. They overthrew French colonialism and eliminated the French army as any sort of threat in "French Indochina" in less than twenty-four hours. The Emperor Bao Dai signed a proclamation, under Japanese guidance, which reclaimed Vietnam's rights of independence but said that Vietnam now considered itself to be an "element" in Japan's Greater East Asian system.

But the Viet Minh were the ultimate beneficiaries of the Japanese coup. Viet Minh leaders had been planning an uprising in Indochina, in order to seize power in a colony strangely divided between the French and the Japanese, for almost a year. They had created a "liberation army" in the Cao Bang hill country in December 1944. It comprised some thirty-four people on the day it was formed and was commanded by Vo Nguyen Giap, a brilliant former Hanoi schoolteacher. By the spring of 1945, the small but growing Viet Minh forces had carved out a "liberated zone" which ran right across the north's mountainous borderlands and had also infiltrated the Red River delta. American officers who were attached to the U.S. Office of Strategic Services in China wanted Ho Chi Minh's cooperation in rescuing American pilots shot down over northern Vietnam. To get it, they aided the Viet Minh army and trained its technicians. There is an extant letter from Ho to two such Americans, dated May 9, 1945, which says in English, "I will be very much obliged to you of taking care of our boys. I wish they can learn radio and other things necessary in our common fight against the Japs … Yours sincerely Hoo."

Apart from the prestige they gained in being associated with the increasingly victorious Americans, the Vietnamese Communists were also able to take advantage of a terrifying famine which ravaged northern Vietnam from the end of 1944. Hundreds of thousands of Vietnamese starved to death; Tonkinese rivers were full of corpses. Survivors were reduced to eating the roots of plants. Giap's new army entered northern villages, seized the fatally prominent granaries which were storing rice for landlords or for the Japanese army, and distributed their rice to hungry peasants. The Viet Minh combined the slogans "National independence" and "Destroy the paddy granaries and resolve the famine," under the conscious inspiration of the 1917 Bolshevik slogan, "Peace, bread, and land." The famine thus enabled them to overcome conservative village notables who had previously opposed them. Village chiefs were invited or compelled to destroy their own seals of office. "People's committees" replaced them.

After Japan surrendered to the Allies in August 1945, Viet Minh forces seized major cities and towns, sometimes by mobilizing scythe-carrying peasants to invade them. The Communists were determined to gain superficial control of as much of Vietnam as they could before the French could return to resume their rule. Bao Dai's government at Hue, although it enjoyed support from civil servants and other members of the urban intelligentsia, had no military power of its own. Bao Dai later wrote that he "felt isolated in a dead capital city" in 1945. Being impressed both by Viet Minh arms and by Viet Minh connections with the Western powers, he therefore abdicated his throne when the Viet Minh demanded this, handing over the dynastic seal to Ho Chi Minh's representatives in a remarkable public ceremony. Fortified by the emperor's acceptance of his legitimacy, Ho announced the birth of a Communist-run Democratic Republic of Vietnam (DRV) in Hanoi on September 2, 1945, with himself as president. As

he did so he quoted from the U.S. Declaration of Independence and referred also to the French Revolution's Declaration of the Rights of Man of 1791. This entire performance reflected Ho's belief (not shared by some of his politburo colleagues) that the Vietnamese revolution would be destroyed if it could not muster the support of many diverse constituencies inside and outside Vietnam. Buoyed by the genuine outpouring of popular patriotism that the events of 1945 had encouraged, but aware as well that Chiang Kaishek's Chinese government would crush the DRV if it thought Ho's new government was vulnerable, Ho and the Viet Minh carried out an "August Revolution," which appealed to the "extremely festive" soldiers and peasants and shopkeepers in Hanoi (as one American military eyewitness described them). But they stopped far short of communism. The colonial tax system was abolished. Mass education was introduced. The course of this moderate revolution was, however, also darkly punctuated by a series of political murders, as Communist assassins killed a number of distinguished non-Communist intellectuals.

Ho Chi Minh's great political skills were tested to the utmost to save his revolution in 1946. In the fall of 1945, a Chinese army of 180,000 men occupied northern Vietnam as if it were a conquered country, bringing with them worthless wartime Chinese currency and a disorderly crowd of porters, wives, and children. Their pretext was that they were exercising Nationalist China's mandate, as one of the major allied powers, to receive Japan's surrender. But they also undoubtedly hoped to replace Ho's government with anti-Communist politicians more favored by Chiang Kaishek. Instead of attacking the Chinese invaders, Ho cunningly welcomed them as "friends." To enlarge his Vietnamese support, and also to confuse the Chinese, he announced (November 1945) the outright dissolution, on paper, of the Indochina Communist Party itself as a "sacrifice" to the need for a "national union" government in which non-Communists would feel at home. The party then went underground and publicly reappeared in 1951.

Most daringly of all, Ho invited the French armed forces to return to northern Vietnam, so that he could use them as a counterweight to the Chinese occupation. (The French had already reentered southern Vietnam, aided by the British.) By an arrangement of March 1946, France recognized the DRV as a free state and negotiated the withdrawal of the Chinese army from the north. In return, Ho's government accepted membership in a proposed French Union (an ambiguous commonwealth version of the old French empire) and allowed the French army to reoccupy northern Vietnam for five years. Viet Minh orators, significantly, compared this 1946 deal with France to the Treaty of Brest-Litovsk of 1918, when Bolshevik Russia had accepted a shameful treaty with a decaying German empire in order to consolidate its political system. But the French now dreamed of using Cochinchina as the fulcrum of a French-controlled Indochinese Federation that would permit the preservation of their Southeast Asian empire, except northern Vietnam. In the summer of 1946, Ho made his last effort to flatter the French into peaceful decolonization. As president of the DRV, he paid a state visit to France in which he explained patiently that Cochinchina was as much a part of Vietnam as Brittany was a part of France and that Vietnamese independence would serve the "greater honor" of France. His effort failed. War between the Viet Minh and the French broke out at the end of 1946 and lasted until 1954.

The French colonial regime thus won the opportunity to perish in a revolutionary war which it never really understood. The military thinking of the Vietnamese Communists, as explained trenchantly by Vo Nguyen Giap, included such principles as the value of continuous attack over stationary defense (because attacking deepened the political consciousness of the people and more passive defensive postures did not); the importance of learning how to use small resources, cleverly deployed, to defeat larger resources not so wisely managed; the value of surprise; the flexible use of different types of forces, ranging from a main army equipped with the most modern weapons available to local self-defense forces armed with hoes and pickaxes; and, most crucial of all, the total involvement of the population, old and young, male and female, in fighting the enemy. To get such popular involvement, the Viet Minh launched a drive against illiteracy. Everyone was to be taught how to read, from prostitutes to fishermen to monks and nuns to highland minorities. The education itself was an odd mixture of information and indoctrination. Viet Minh "Library for the Masses" primers dealt with such diverse topics as the evils of fascism, the importance of having a national assembly, the nature of railway locomotives, and the futile superstitiousness of praying for rain. The French soon found themselves submerged in a strange guerrilla war in which peasant children could be spies and toothless old women could be laying mines.

By 1949, Mao Zedong's Communists had seized power in China, vanquishing Chiang Kai-shek. The Viet Minh gained a strong if possessive ally. In 1953, the increasingly desperate French tried to lure the Viet Minh into fighting a classic set-piece battle, of the sort the Western military mind could understand and Western artillery and air power could dominate, in the Dien Bien Phu valley near northern Vietnam's border with Laos. Giap's peasant army, supplied by coolies who transported to Dien Bien Phu — by animal carts and bicycles — everything from heavy artillery to rice, unexpectedly surrounded the French garrison there by the spring of 1954 and forced them to surrender. Dien Bien Phu was the worst defeat any Western colonial power ever suffered on the battlefield at the hands of an Asian people it had once ruled. Yet the Viet Minh still failed to reunify Vietnam on their own terms.

At an international peace conference at Geneva, convened soon after the collapse of Dien Bien Phu, the Vietnamese Communist government was pressed by its allies, the Soviet Union and China, to accept less than it thought was its due. The Geneva Agreement of 1954 required a final French withdrawal from Indochina. But the agreement arranged a partitioned Vietnam in which the Communist regime, based in Hanoi and confined to north of the seventeenth parallel, had to coexist for at least two years with an anti-Communist southern Vietnamese state based in Saigon. At the time the Geneva Agreement satisfied the Chinese desire to exclude American military interference in Indochina and the post-Stalin Soviet formula that Asian revolutionary movements should develop peacefully. It anticipated nationwide reunification elections in Vietnam in 1956. The new South Vietnam and its American patron refused to sign the Geneva Agreement and resisted these elections, which were not held.[7]

Figure 5.14   The Nonaligned Movement, begun at the Bandung Conference in Indonesia in 1955, continued to thrive under the leadership of (from left) Egyptian President Gamal Abdel Nasser, Pakistan's Ayub Khan, Indonesia's Sukarno, and China's Zhou Enlai, all of whom are gathered here for a tenth anniversary meeting in Cairo in 1965.

♦   ♦   ♦

THE BANDUNG CONFERENCE IN THE POSTWAR SETTING

"The population of Asia will never forget that the first atom bomb exploded on Asian soil."

With these words in April 1955, China's premier, Zhou Enlai, galvanized an audience in Bandung, Indonesia, comprising most of the rising stars of the Asian and African developing world. Present were Indonesia's Sukarno, Egypt's Nasser, India's Nehru, and Burma's U Nu, along with delegations from twenty-four other nations.

The Bandung Conference and Zhou's speech signaled a new level of coalition-building in the developing world during the early postwar era. It also signified a diplomatic threshold for several nations in Southeast Asia. Their new vision initially rejected close alignments with either the United States or the Soviet Union amid the growing cold war tensions between the two superpowers. The political heritage of the Pacific War was still fresh in the minds of Asia's leaders for whom "liberation" by the Japanese had not only ended the colonial era but exacerbated internal divisions among their own populations. This memory, and the Great Power maneuvering and confrontation

that had followed the Pacific War, demonstrated to the participants at Bandung their continued vulnerability. Developments in the Soviet-American rivalry were now seen as translatable into the Asian arena with unsettling implications for their own fragile systems.

Global economic interdependence had already been demonstrated by the devastation of the Great Depression in the 1930s. Now, World War II and its aftermath propelled nations toward a new network of political interdependencies as well. In response, the leaders of new African and Asian nations sought to build a "Nonaligned Movement" that could assert itself politically while standing apart from the growing cold war confrontation. In the years that followed, true neutrality proved to be an impossible goal for many of these nations, and within the movement the diplomatic influence of Soviet client states, such as Cuba, increased. For a number of Asian countries such as Indonesia, however, the memory of Bandung was to carry a special resonance that would sustain their commitment to speak on behalf of the developing world.

The battle lines of the cold war confrontation were readily apparent to the participants at Bandung in 1955. A defeated Chiang Kai-shek had fled in 1949 with his Guomindang troops to the island of Taiwan where he lobbied for U.S. support while Mao Zedong proclaimed the formation of a new communist regime on the Chinese mainland. Korea stood divided between a communist-aligned north and an American-allied south, following a devastating civil war in 1950-53 that pitted American forces directly against both the North Koreans and the People's Liberation Army of China (see chapter 9). In Vietnam, where fears of Chinese and Soviet influence over Ho Chi Minh had convinced Washington to support the returning French colonials against him, a crushing French defeat in 1954 led the Americans to shore up anticommunist resistance in yet another divided Asian nation.

Zhou Enlai was the master of this situation during the Bandung Conference. Not only did he imply that Asian leaders might usefully invoke their "Asian" identity to shore up their regional relationships, he skillfully drew some of the previously neutral countries toward his side by sounding conciliatory toward the United States over the problem of the newly-signed U.S. security treaty with Taiwan (1954). China's Asia-Pacific strategy during this critical period has yet to be understood on the basis of open archival research and discussion within the PRC itself, but it is clear that China's growing sense of independence from the Soviet Union and its desire to reassert its traditional political centrality in the region partially underlay Zhou's strategy at Bandung. During the previous year in Geneva he had demonstrated to an international audience his cosmopolitan sophistication as he lunched with Charlie Chaplin and his diplomatic skill as he joined other foreign ministers in trying to forge an agreement for stability in mainland Southeast Asia following the French withdrawal. He even used the Geneva Conference as an opportunity to block Vietnam's ambitions to dominate the kingdoms of Laos and Cambodia by agreeing that they should be treated as separate and independent nations in the postcolonial period, and in both Geneva and Bandung he enunciated principles of "peaceful coexistence" while at the same time condemning the American plan for an anticommunist Southeast Asia Treaty Organization (SEATO).

Zhou recognized that a moderate stance by China toward its Asian neighbors would aid its future diplomatic strategies in the region and the world. Not only countries such as India and Burma, which as ideological neutrals had aided China in diplomatic discussions over the Korean peninsula and the former French colonies, but also Southeast Asian nations such as Indonesia were important potential allies.

Yet concerns ran deep in Southeast Asia over the role of the overseas Chinese whose economic success in enclave communities had long been a source of both envy and fear. Would these Chinese become the instruments for China's meddling in the internal affairs of other Asian countries? Chinese immigrants — even those who were several generations removed from their mainland roots — were seen by Southeast Asians as people who made little distinction between their ethnicity and their nationality. It was a distinction that China itself had refused to make, having often treated the overseas Chinese as citizens of China. But Zhou sought to allay these fears even prior to Bandung by declaring that the overseas Chinese should "respect the laws of the government and the social customs of the countries in which they live."

China's soft line soon hardened as Mao, celebrating the fortieth anniversary of the Bolshevik Revolution on a visit to Moscow in 1957, declared that "the east wind prevails over the west wind." By 1959 China's internal power struggles amid Mao's haste to enact a utopian society forced Zhou to throw his support to Mao. China began more openly to champion struggles of national liberation in the Third World, a development that deeply troubled countries such as Indonesia, with its large and active communist party, and Malaya, where amid a communist insurgency the British were still working out a constitutional transfer of power.

Japan remained on the periphery of these developments except to serve as a key if passive component in the U.S. strategy to contain communism in Asia. Its reversal of fortune seemed complete as, at Bandung, remnants of its former empire consulted with one another and asserted their views on Pacific relations. Japan struggled to recover under American tutelage while newly-visible Asian leaders emerged who refused to bow to a Eurocentric world order: Ho Chi Minh had defeated the French at Dien Bien Phu, Sukarno had thrown out the Dutch, the Malays were negotiating their independence with the British, and China's *de facto* ambassador to the third world,

Zhou Enlai, bestrode the Asian stage as an inspirational figure.

However isolated politically it may have been from these developments, Japan was gathering itself for a new assertion of influence in the Pacific, one that would draw on its greatest strengths as a nation — its human talent and economic organization. It is to this process of recovery, its extraordinary achievements, and its international implications that we turn next.

NOTES

1. Prince Fumimaro Konoe, Japanese Prime Minister from 1937-39 and 1940-41.

2. Stilwell, who had long experience with China prior to the war, frequently clashed with Chiang Kai-shek over the latter's unwillingness to engage the Japanese.

3. At the very outset of the war, the Japanese air carrier groups were more skilled in overall battle coordination than their American counterparts. Japanese pilots, on average, had more flying experience and the new Mitsubishi-made fighter (the "Zero") was recognized by both sides to be superior to any fighter in the U.S. arsenal in 1941. Yet within two years the United States surpassed Japan in the training, experience, quality of equipment and numbers of its forces in the Pacific theater. [—Ed.]

4. James C. Thomson, Jr., Peter W. Stanley, and John Curtis Perry, *Sentimental Imperialists* (New York, NY: Harper & Row, 1981), pp. 190-98, 201-02, 211-16.

5. David Joel Steinberg, ed., *In Search of Southeast Asia: A Modern History* (Honolulu: University of Hawaii Press, 1987), pp. 418-22.

6. Ibid., pp. 431-34.

7. Ibid., pp. 356-61.

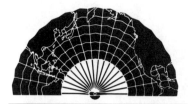

6

Miracle by Design:
The Postwar Resurgence of Japan

OVERVIEW

World War II may have devastated Japan physically but its surviving population retained its most
important asset: a collective knowledge and experience of how to build and operate an industrial
economy. With so much destroyed, Japan was able
to start afresh by building on its prewar economic
experience as well as on the guidance and assistance of the United States. This chapter describes
how the nation reconstructed itself and rose to
become a great economic power in less than forty
years after the end of the war. In the process of this
change, new businesses and institutions arose that
were guided not by the old guard scions of industry
but by younger men eager to rebuild their country
and to steer it away from the disastrous militarism
of the 1930s and early 1940s. The new institutions
evolved as amalgams of Occupation reforms and
older Japanese traditions. Just as the Meiji Restoration integrated Western technology into Japanese
culture, so the postwar reformers reinvigorated the
Japanese economy but they changed it less than
they thought.

As Japan's economic recovery removed it from
the role of a dependent, developing nation to that
of a manufacturing and financial powerhouse, its
relations with its foreign trade partners changed,
resulting often in acrimonious trade disputes.
Japan was accused of using an initially under-

valued currency and protectionist barriers to pursue a "beggar thy neighbor" trade policy. At the
same time, the Japan-U.S. economic relationship
became highly interdependent. America could not
do without Japan as a lender of capital. Japan could
not prosper without the openness of the American
market. The nations had become, in the words of
one Japanese business executive, like two mutually antagonistic prisoners chained together and
forced to cooperate. By the late 1980s, Japan had
become a global export powerhouse, creating new
trade frictions with Europe and the United States.
But its maturation as an industrial trading economy
exposed it to global economic forces that have
slowed its once-rapid growth, leaving it stagnant
and floundering without effective leadership.

THE EARLY POSTWAR PERIOD

The diverse group of Americans who were
assembled to administer the Occupation of Japan
knew relatively little about their host country and
they did not feel compelled to learn a great deal
about it. They saw themselves not only as victors in
possession of the superior skills, ideology, and technology that had won the war but also as mentors to
a malleable Japanese society and they assumed that
the status of Japan as a dependent "pupil" of the
United States would continue indefinitely. The

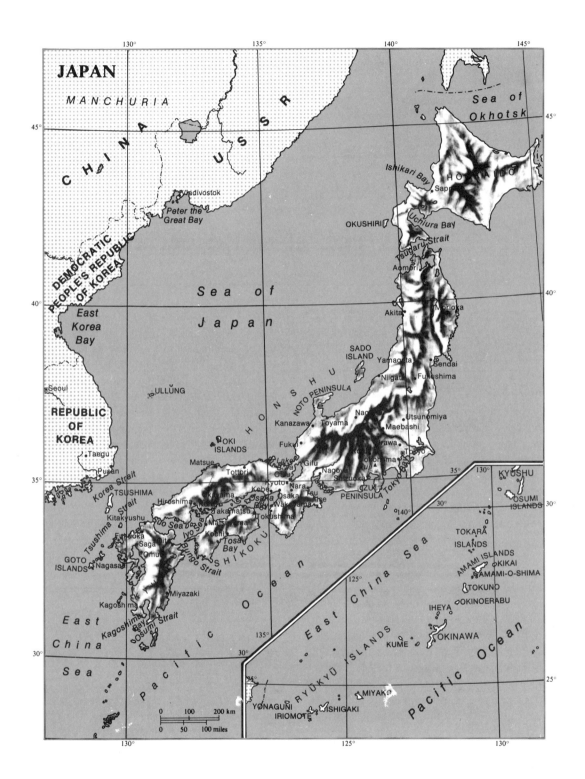

JAPAN

MANCHURIA

CHINA

U.S.S.R.

DEMOCRATIC
PEOPLE'S REPUBLIC
OF KOREA

East
Korea
Bay

Sea of
Okhotsk

HOKKAIDO

Ishikari Bay

Sapp

OKUSHIRI

Uchiura Bay
Tsugaru
Strait

Aomori

Akita

Morioka

Vladivostok

Peter the
Great Bay

Sea of

Japan

Seoul

ULLŬNG

REPUBLIC
OF
KOREA

Taegu

Pusan

Korea Strait

TSUSHIMA

Tsushima Strait

Kitakyushu

Fu oka

Saga

Omu

GOTO
ISLANDS

Nagasa

Kagoshi a

Kagoshima
Bay

Osumi Strait

East
China

Sea

SADO
ISLAND

Yamagata

Niigata

Sendai

Fukushima

NOTO PENINSULA

H O N S H U

Kanazawa

Toyama

Nag

Maebashi

Utsunomiya

rawa

OKI
ISLANDS

Matsue

Tottori

Lake
Biwa

Gifu

Otsu

Nagoya

Toky

Kyoto

Nara

zu

kayama

Kobe

Osaka

Wak yama

Bay

Ise

PENINSULA

Hiroshima

Kure

akamatsu

Tokushima

ZU

Matsu ama

Iyo Sea

Kouhi

Tosa

Bay

Bungo Strait

SHIKOKU

Miyazaki

Pacific

Ocean

KYUSHU

OSUMI
ISLANDS

TOKARA
ISLANDS

AMAMI ISLANDS

KIKAI

AMAMI-O-SHIMA

TOKUNO

OKINOERABU

IHEYA

OKINAWA

KUME

East China Sea

RYŪKYŪ ISLANDS

YONAGUNI

IRIOMOTE

ISHIGAKI

MIYAKO

Pacific Ocean

0   100   200 km
0   50   100 miles

Japanese themselves tended at first to reinforce this prejudice even as they followed American prescriptions for economic recovery.

Land and Industrial Reforms

General Douglas MacArthur's first steps as supreme commander of the Occupation forces were to ensure that all production of military material had ended and to close down, with the exception of the Bank of Japan, all state financial institutions and corporations. Factories were stripped of their equipment to provide reparations to the countries Japan had attacked, and the managers of major corporations were purged. The government was barred from making payments to companies for their losses under wartime contracts, with the result that various industrial concerns and banks plummeted into bankruptcy and were forced to restructure.

The holding companies of the *zaibatsu*[1] were abolished and their shares placed on the open market, forcing the components of each combine to operate as independent companies. All cartel activities were prohibited under the Anti-monopoly Law. Ultimately, a number of giant corporations were broken up under the Decentralization Law. Still, the old *zaibatsu* were simply reorganized around their banks which turned out to be an even more effective arrangement. In the end, only 18 corporations were dismantled in this way, but the dramatic pace of the reforms sent shock waves rippling through industrial circles.

One of the most far-reaching changes wrought by the Occupation was the forced sale of land holdings to the tenants who had once occupied and farmed them. Before the war, the land system still had many characteristics of a semi-feudal state. Now the owner farmer was to become the mainstay of Japanese agriculture. Land reform and the encouragement of labor unions, imposed by SCAP, would otherwise never have developed spontaneously in Japan. The Occupation was, in some respects, an "imported revolution."

A major challenge that faced the Occupation in the early years was a growing conflict between labor and business. The political left, long held down by the pre-war government, now gained great influence over the workers movement. A momentary alliance of conservatives, militants, socialists and communists rose up to better their economic lot. Leftist militants wanted far more than high wages, however. They wanted worker control of the factories, and actual political power.

In May 1947, a union coalition called for a general strike. The response to the call was overwhelming: Five million people pledged to stay away from their jobs. Just hours before the strike was to begin, MacArthur stepped in and forbade the strike, declaring that the country had only a four-day supply of rice and fuel. Any massive work stoppage would be devastating to the nation.

The Dodge Mission to Japan

By 1948 cold war tensions had begun to mount in East Asia. The United States began to revise its policy toward Japan with the aim of strengthening and accelerating its economic recovery. Soon, Japan's war reparation payments were discontinued and basic industries such as coal and steel were given priority by economic planners. Inflation, due to poorly controlled credit and currency allocations, plagued the recovery for several years until Washington sent Detroit banker Joseph Dodge to Japan. Dodge's mission was to halt inflation, remove government controls over trade, and generally bring the Japanese economy back to full strength so that American aid would no longer be needed. The measures he prescribed seemed draconian at first: a strictly balanced budget, an end to subsidies of all kinds, an end to lending by the Reconstruction Finance Bank, and a fixed exchange rate for the yen. This was bitter medicine indeed. Japan plunged into recession and labor unrest increased.

Japan's "Korean War Boom"

Just as it appeared that Dodge's cure might be worse than the disease, the recession was swept away by an economic boom caused by the outbreak of the Korean War in June 1950. Suddenly, industries ranging from textiles to coals and paper went into full production with a ready market in the U.S. military. The Japanese-produced goods were paid for in dollars, bringing in desperately needed foreign currency, with the result that annual foreign currency income leapt to $800 million per year through 1953, enabling Japan to import goods worth nearly $2 billion annually. Japanese companies did not lose time exploiting this precious opportunity. They modernized and expanded production, soaking up the excess labor in the cities and countryside and thereby stabilizing the economy well beyond the end of the Korean War.

In the Meiji era, Japan's leaders had believed that a rich nation required a strong army. In the post-war recovery, they believed exactly the opposite: the nation's path to richness lay in a weak or nonexistent army. As a result, Japan resisted the cold war overtures of the United States to rearm against communism. However much the pacifist stance may have involved a calculation of economic benefits, there can be no doubt that the tragic consequences of the war had left the Japanese population with an abhorrence of militarization.

Labor-Management Relations: The Nissan Strike

As noted above, the initial efforts by the Occupation officials to support the growth of labor unions backfired quickly when, in 1947, a coalition of unions called for a nationwide strike and MacArthur had to step in to forbid it. The Occupation officials made it clear that unions should be allowed to be free and vocal — but not disruptive. There began a not so subtle campaign against radicals even as the number of strikes led by communist organizers increased. A critical point was reached with the Nissan Strike of 1953, a confrontation whose aftermath was to change forever the face of the Japanese workplace.

On one side of the conflict was Nissan's militant union. Its members were fighting for higher wages, control of the factory floor, and an industrywide union. There was virtually no strike fund, which, for many Nissan workers, meant little food and tremendous hardship. For a time the workers were sustained by the passionate rhetoric of their leader, Masuda Tetsuo. Masuda was a brilliant, charismatic speaker who had been politicized by his war experience. He returned home committed to the self-determination of workers, independent of companies, communists, or any

other groups. He refused to make any compromise in the union's position.

Nissan was prepared for a long strike. Its management had obtained a massive loan from the Industrial Bank of Japan to tide them over, and had also extracted a promise from its major competitors, Toyota and Isuzu, not to compete for Nissan's market share while production was down. There is an old Japanese saying: The nail that sticks up will be hammered down. It was clear that to Nissan and its industrial and financial allies, Masuda was the nail.

After six months Nissan had won. It broke its militant union and replaced it with another more to management's liking. Masuda's refusal to compromise cost him the support of conservatives and workers too poor or tired to continue the struggle. The loss broke Masuda's spirit: He was fired by Nissan and wandered at loose ends until his death eleven years later.

The outcome of the strike fundamentally changed the character of Japan's large, export-oriented businesses. From that day on, there would be company unions, but no industrywide unions. The livelihood of the workers would be tied to the company's success. They had surrendered a large part of their independence in a trade with management, and the trade was this: There would be no more disastrous strikes, no more stoppages. The workers would also take a drop in wages and lose control of the shop floor. In exchange, there would be no layoffs. None of this was written down. It was an industrywide arrangement whereby power in the factory was restored to management but, for this, management had paid a price. To keep the peace, Japanese companies would go to such lengths to keep workers employed that American observers later characterized the system as "lifetime employment." It was a deal, however, that applied only to those in the public sector and in the large export-oriented firms — comprising about a third of Japan's industry. Employees in the smaller supplier firms did not benefit and often became the shock absorbers for the system, in terms of layoffs and paycuts. Women were also underpaid.

The concept of "lifetime employment" forced employers to view their workers differently. Instead of treating labor as a cost of production — to be hired and fired as the company's fortunes

Productivity Growth
(GDP per Man Hour)

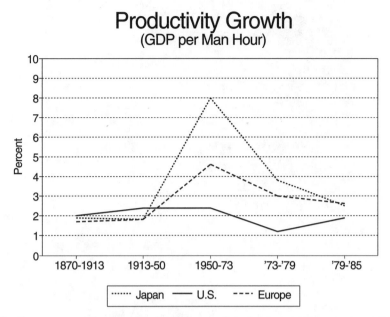

Graph 6.1   Postwar recovery boosted productivity growth in Japan and Europe above the United States.

rose and fell — Japanese executives were pushed into treating their workers as human capital — a valuable resource to be developed. Knowing they had to hire employees from cradle to grave, managers spoke in terms of hiring the "whole" individual, not just a particular skill, and they invested heavily in training programs and solicited the worker's participation and ideas on how to improve the company by means of "quality circles." Production workers would rotate jobs throughout the factory allowing the company to be flexible in responding to market changes and to increase productivity more effectively. Labor productivity soared — it more than doubled in the years between 1960 and 1980. In key areas such as steel, automobiles, and electrical machinery, Japan's productivity eventually surpassed that of the United States.

Post-Occupation Industrial Policies

The first and most important step toward the goal of increasing national wealth lay in industrialization. The Occupation came to an end in 1952 as decreed by the San Francisco Peace Treaty, and the Japanese government quickly took steps to foster industrial reconstruction. Government-funded banks, in particular the Japan Development Bank, played a critical role in supplying government funds to strategic industries by means of long-term, low-interest loans.

The initial strategy called for a departure from the prewar emphasis on light industries. Instead, the government gave priority to the heavy industries: electric power, coal, shipping, and steel. Other industries also were encouraged to expand their capacity through a series of special tax exemptions and reductions for steps taken to accumulate new machinery and sophisticated technology. Meanwhile, business leaders sought changes in the antimonopoly law that had been imposed by the American occupiers. In effect, the law was modified to permit the formation of cartels, ostensibly to protect major industries, such as textiles, from the most severe effects of a recession. Companies were also permitted to hold interlocking shares. Both of these changes were to provide a major impetus to the growing power and influence of Japan's industrial conglomerates.

To be able to purchase the equipment it needed from abroad, Japan had to be able to use foreign currency — something which, in spite of the Korean war boom, was always in short supply.

The Postwar Resurgence of Japan • 245

Figure 6.1   Central city of modern Tokyo; the Ginza District.

Scarce dollars had to be rationed, in effect, and the government carefully controlled the kinds of imports that companies were permitted to purchase. This encouraged the production of needed goods at home by "infant" industries while foreign industries were essentially shut out. The government was especially generous in permitting the acquisition of foreign technologies. This even took the form of legislation to foster specific industries, such as machinery and electronics.

By skillfully acquiring new technologies from abroad and taking advantage of steadily opening world markets, Japan was able to generally maintain its strong growth from the 1950s on.

Acquiring New Technology

In the 1950s, new technologies that Japan needed to acquire for its industrial development were being developed primarily in the United States. These included synthetic fibers,

electronics, petrochemicals, and other products that would promote vigorous growth. Even prewar technologies had to be imported at that time in order to reconstruct the economy and provide for domestic production of such items as automobiles and home appliances.

Massive investment plans were implemented, some of which seemed extravagant at the time. Kawasaki Steel, for example, constructed a massive integrated steelworks in Chiba Prefecture which, it was first thought, would result in an oversupply. In fact, the rapid expansion of the Japanese economy absorbed all the steel that Kawasaki could produce. Similarly, Matsushita Electric foresaw strong demand for home appliances and began to specialize in that field. Shipbuilders utilized new techniques, such as electric welding and construction in block units, so that by the mid-1950s they were the world's largest producers.

Wartime producers of guns and equipment turned their skills to the manufacture of sewing machines, cameras, and binoculars. Civil engineering firms acquired the earthmoving equipment that had been introduced for the construction of new power plants. Agriculture became more productive with new rice-growing methods. All of these developments reflected a Japanese capacity to draw on their existing expertise and knowledge (which clearly had reached a high level by the time of World War II), as well as aggressive corporate strategies, cooperative labor relations, and the most promising technologies for industrial development.

Investment tended to breed more investment in a kind of chain reaction. Capacity leaped in the steel, cement, and electric power industries. Large industrial complexes sprang up along the Pacific seaboard in places like Kawasaki, Yokkaichi, and Mizushima, each of which was centered on steel mills or petrochemical plants and had the facilities to offload, process, and ship raw materials at the lowest possible cost.[2]

THE FAST GROWTH DECADES

The early stages of rapid growth in the 1950s included periods of brief recession when the government was forced to tighten the money supply to correct a dangerous imbalance of payments, but each time the economy rebounded quickly and the boom resumed.

As Japan entered the 1960s it had regained a significant degree of its ability to compete in international markets. A more self-confident government, headed by Prime Minister Ikeda Hayato, unveiled an "income doubling" plan which envisioned, on the basis of an average growth rate of 7.2 percent, a doubling of the Gross National Product (GNP) every ten years. This high growth rate meant that workers would be in an almost continually strong demand and led to a rapid depopulation of rural areas as labor moved to the Pacific belt of booming industrial cities.

The resulting growth curve was not a smooth one. Recessions in 1962 and 1965 finally led the government to pump money into the economy through deficit spending, thereby departing from Joseph Dodge's previously unviolated rule that the budget must be balanced. Nor were the social

costs minor ones. Urban crowding and alarming rates of industrial pollution of the country's air and water led to increasing public disillusionment. Like other parts of the world, college campuses in the late 1960s in Japan were scenes of frequent demonstrations. Yet the national growth rate continued largely unimpeded and in fact exceeded the expectations of the government: in the latter half of the 1960s the Gross National Product was growing at an average rate of 11.6 percent.

Changing International Conditions

Japan was able to build its economy rapidly during this period due to another legacy from Joseph Dodge: the pegging of the exchange rate to exactly 360 yen to the dollar. This gave Japanese exporters a strong cost advantage in countries such as the United States. In the early years, the weak yen had not been a serious threat to U.S. industries which were going through their own boom period. But by the early 1970s it was clear that the rapidly strengthening economies in Europe and Japan no longer justified an artificially strong dollar relative to their currencies. For a period in 1971, President Richard Nixon slapped a 10 percent surcharge on imports and called on Europe and Japan to revalue their currencies. The yen began to grow stronger (meaning that a lower number of yen was required to purchase one U.S. dollar) and by early 1973 the era of floating rather than fixed exchange rates had begun.

Japan had considerable difficulty at first with the adjustment to this new environment. In an effort to compensate for slowing exports, the government pumped new money into the economy through spending programs and lower interest rates. The result was a serious bout of inflation. A new prime minister, Tanaka Kakuei, took office in 1972 with a bold plan to "remodel the Japanese archipelago" with massive projects, such as highways and Shinkansen "bullet trains," that were to tie the mid-size cities of the nation together. This, combined with the proposal for ambitious new welfare programs, contributed greatly to the inflation scare.

Yet a more frightening blow was about to fall. In October 1973 war broke out in the Middle East and the Organization of Petroleum Exporting Countries (OPEC) decided for the first time to use oil as an economic weapon: it sharply reduced the supply of available oil, then announced a fourfold increase in the price. Of all the industrialized nations, Japan was by far the most dependent on oil to sustain its economy. Fully three-fourths of its national energy requirements were being satisfied by oil imports. Inflation soared well into the double-digit range as a speculative panic took hold in the country. The government resorted to draconian cuts in its budget and imposed high interest rates to curb the trend. Eventually it succeeded in keeping the economy under control, but the high-growth era had effectively ended for Japan. Thereafter, an era of stable, slower growth began with new industry leaders encouraged by the Ministry of Trade and Industry (MITI): autos, electronics, machine tools, and machinery.

A second oil crisis following the Iranian revolution and Iran-Iraq War in the late 1970s did not fall so heavily on Japan, thanks to a quick response once again by its government to control inflation. The key to recovery in both oil crises was not domestic demand, however, but the boom in Japanese exports — cars, electronics, and other products — which grew far more rapidly than imports. By 1977 Japan's burgeoning trade surplus had become a global issue.

Growing Trade Frictions

As global attention began to focus on Japan's consistently high trade surplus, the role of a consistently weak yen — which made Japanese exports inexpensive abroad, thereby undercutting domestic producers in the United States and Europe — came under renewed sharp criticism by U.S. policymakers. Yet the policies of the Reagan administration and the Federal Reserve in the early 1980s made a strong dollar and weak yen almost inevitable: High interest rates in the United States and deep budget deficits led to a voracious demand for U.S. Treasury bonds. With abundant savings to invest by now, Japanese money poured in to help finance the U.S. deficit — worsening all the more the Japan-U.S. trade gap.

Initially, the battlegrounds between Japanese and U.S. policymakers were chosen sector by sector. In 1978, for example, the United States introduced "trigger prices" which set a floor price for Japanese steel in the United States This was a protectionist measure designed to prevent "dumping" of steel by Japan into the U.S. market at a price that was below the cost of producing and shipping it. The U.S. steel industry, having been forced to grant world-record wages to strongly unionized steel workers, neglected to upgrade and modernize its plant and equipment. As a result, the increasingly inefficient industry sought government protection from the new producers in Europe and Asia. Despite the fact that American consumers of automobiles and other products were major beneficiaries of the high quality, low cost foreign steel, successive congresses and administrations responded positively to the steel lobby.

The Japanese trade battleground moved on to other sectors, with Europe joining the fray. France, to cite an extreme example, declared that the flood of Japanese video-cassette recorders would have to be processed entirely through a single small customs house. More generally, a chorus of complaints arose from the world trading community about the formal and informal barriers to imports that had been erected by Japan since the war. Under growing pressure, Japan agreed in 1985 to a massive currency realignment (the "Plaza Accord") among the Group of Five major industrial nations. The yen rose rapidly and previously competitive industries in Japan, such as automobiles and electronics, saw a major decline in their profits. They began to move production offshore to lower-cost areas in Asia. Still, Japan's trade surplus with the United States was slow to fall (and remained high with other Asian nations as well), and bilateral frictions continued to mount even as formal barriers to trade in Japan continued to drop.

At one point in the mid-1980s the United States went so far as to negotiate a cartel-like agreement with the Japanese to force the price of semiconductor chips upward. The reason for such action lay in the fact that massive investments were by then required to remain competitive in the semiconductor business. This worked increasingly to the advantage of a capital-rich country like Japan. A massive flow of low-cost Japanese chips to the United States — some of which were probably being "dumped" to capture large market shares and drive U.S. producers out of business — led to the desperate measure of

Hours (actual) Worked in Manufacturing
Production Workers: 1978 - 1988

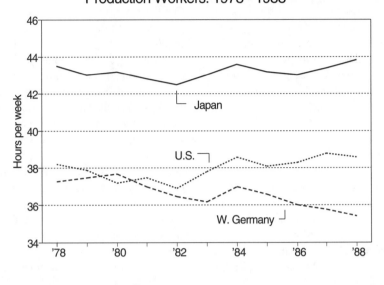

Graph 6.2

trying both to regulate the floor price of the chips in the United States and to mandate a minimum share for the United States in the Japanese domestic semiconductor market. Although the U.S. market share in Japan did increase in the years that followed, the most dramatic and immediate effect was to provide windfall profits to Japanese producers who found their chips suddenly selling at a mandated higher price just as demand for them exploded. Korean companies benefited even more. Their huge gamble as new entrants into the chip production industry was repaid handsomely and they used the profits to finance their expansion in the business. Initially, the U.S. chip producers barely managed to hold their own while the larger American industry groups — the users of computer chips — suffered a competitive disadvantage from the even higher costs of production.

As an early experiment in "managed trade," the chip pact had mixed results, hurting some and helping others while increasing total U.S. market share in Japan. By the late 1980s, however, the United States decided to take a different tactic with Japan. Rather than debate specific barriers in each sector in drawn-out, bitter confrontations,

the Bush administration forced a reluctant Japanese bureaucracy to sit down to talks about "structural impediments" to trade that were said to exist within the Japanese economy. Amid criticism from both sides of the Pacific that the goals were unrealistic and amounted to an effort to change Japanese culture, an initial agreement was penned in 1990 which, on the surface, indicated that Japan and the United States had agreed to broad reforms in both economies.

For its part, Japan agreed to enact reforms that would (1) direct capital surpluses toward massive public investments in Japan to improve the quality of life and at the same time stimulate demand for foreign goods and services; (2) change land policy to moderate the distortions caused by high land prices; (3) revise large-scale retail store laws to permit easier entry by foreign retailers; (4) eliminate the monopolistic, anticompetitive behavior of the large Japanese business conglomerates (*keiretsu*); and (5) make more "transparent" (i.e., clarify the actual procedures of) the various laws regulating the entry of foreign firms into the Japanese market.

As its part of the agreement, the United States pledged to lower its budget deficit, raise its rate of national saving, and improve the quality of public education to make its firms more competitive. This unusual agreement reflected both the level of frustration that had arisen on each side as well as the profound interdependence of the two economies. Over the ensuing years, each side made only limited progress in addressing its part of the bargain, but the list of corrective measures remains a common reference for what ails the two economies and encumbers their relationship.

Japan's Standard of Living

It is important to keep in perspective, alongside an accounting of Japan's dramatic postwar recovery, that there were areas in which things did not develop exactly according to plan. The failure was most notable in the area of living standards. The famous "income doubling" plan was to have not only doubled the GNP every two years, it was to have dramatically raised the nation's standard of living, including public services and housing. Clearly, the Japanese people enjoy a higher standard of living today than do the people of many other nations, but the standards that might be assumed on the basis of the nation's per capita GNP are, alongside similar figures for North America and Western Europe, woefully inadequate.

The majority of Japanese today cannot hope to own their own homes, land and housing prices having soared far beyond their reach. The purchasing power of their daily earnings is considerably weaker than that enjoyed in the West where the costs of common goods and services are sometimes as much as a third lower than in Japan. The transportation infrastructure in Japan has lagged behind national growth so badly that urban commutes of four hours per day on crowded trains are not uncommon. At the same time, American-style urban pathologies are rare: Homicides and drug addiction in Japan are far below the Western norms.

Japan's Self-Perception

These contrasts and paradoxes can be explained in part by the cultural norms that permit a highly regimented growth at the expense of each family's personal material enjoyment and by an economic system that holds as its highest objective the strengthening of major industries. Such are the circumstances from which some observers, both Japanese and non-Japanese, have inferred that Japan cannot be compared to any other nation socially, culturally or economically. In fact, the effort to understand what is and is not "different" about Japan has come to dominate an international debate about what it means to be Japanese and what is special about Japanese economic behavior.

It is impossible to characterize a national personality in any rigorous fashion. Of particular concern to scholars has been the need to avoid subjective evaluations that might reinforce racial and cultural prejudices. For these reasons, many prefer to leave discussions of Japanese social and cultural behavior to the Japanese themselves. So how do the Japanese describe themselves? As an insular, inward-looking nation, not given to bold leadership moves in the international community and deeply concerned about their vulnerability, as a resource-poor island nation, to external forces.

In fact, some of these aspects of Japan's self-identity did begin to shift slightly during the 1980s under the influence of its own successes and pressures from its international trading partners, but Japan's concept of its role in the Pacific and global communities, a concept that was defined by the early postwar prime minister Yoshida Shigeru, has remained static for most of the postwar period. The "Yoshida Doctrine," as it is sometimes called, advocates a pacifistic, nonmilitary role for Japan and forms the core of its contemporary diplomatic identity.

Japan's Diplomatic Identity

Japanese Prime Minister Yoshida Shigeru, who played a key role in shaping the post-war economy, was fond of saying that "history provides examples of winning by diplomacy after losing in war." Yoshida proceeded to do just that, using the disputes between the two giant victors of World War II, America and the Soviet Union, to position Japan as a potential bulwark of democracy against communism. This required skillful

Figures 6.2-6.3 Japan's self defense forces, while significant in size by the standards of most nations, are restricted in their structure and activity. They are often called upon for rescue duties in times of natural disaster, as in the case of a landslide, right. Below: destroyers of the Maritime Self-Defense Force.

persuasion at the outbreak of the Korean War in resisting U.S. Secretary of State John Foster Dulles' efforts to establish a large Japanese military (which would have undone the MacArthur-imposed constitution). Acceding only to U.S. military bases in Japan and a limited degree of rearmament, Yoshida's successful resistance to a new military buildup left Japan free to benefit from the vast procurement bonanza that accompanied the Korean conflict.

The basic ingredients of post-Occupation Japan's security policy began to take shape: First, political-economic cooperation with the United States would undergird Japan's economic growth. Second, a small national defense expenditure would leave industry free to commit itself to productive industrial development. Third, Japan's own security would be guaranteed by the U.S. "nuclear umbrella" in exchange for allowing the Americans to situate bases in Japan.

Yoshida's defense policies were further modified in the 1960s and 1970s to emphasize the defensive rather than offensive military capability of Japan's armed forces. Japan constructed its policy well aware not only of American ambivalence toward its potential rearmament, but also the apprehension throughout the rest of Asia that Japan's military capabilities might once again be put to aggressive use.

THE 1980s:
RETHINKING FOREIGN POLICY

Although the Yoshida Doctrine remains the centerpiece of Japanese foreign policy, a small but growing constituency of new leaders has slowly begun to reconsider some of its basic tenets. The harbinger of this shift was the appearance of a prime minister whose more charismatic and aggressive style in the mid-1980s belied the weak political faction from which he had emerged.

Nakasone Yasuhiro took office in 1982 at a time of rising trade tensions with the United States. As a young legislator during the American Occupation, he had petitioned General MacArthur for a revision of the constitution and the creation of an independent Japanese defense force, views that remained essentially unaltered as he assumed the position of prime minister. Nakasone's ideas were not those of the mainstream politicians, and the fact that such a political maverick could achieve the leadership post reflected a compromise among deadlocked factions of the dominant Liberal Democratic Party (LDP) rather than a broad shift of popular sentiment. Yet his distinctive style of leadership struck a responsive chord domestically and also appealed to foreign leaders.

Stirrings of New Nationalism

No longer content to remain quietly on the sidelines in meetings of world leaders, such as the Economic Summit, Nakasone occasionally sought center stage. He spoke boldly both at home and abroad of the need for a new vision of Japan's international role and a restructuring of its major institutions to permit easier integration with the world community. Symbolic of the new self-respect and assertiveness for Japan, which Nakasone sought to promote, was his decision to be the first postwar prime minister to visit the Yasukuni Shrine during the commemoration of the end of World War II. Because Yasukuni is the place where so many soldiers of World War II — including those found guilty of war crimes — are memorialized, this action appeared to many to be an attempt at reviving the dangerous nationalism that had plunged the Pacific into war, but Nakasone's stated purpose was to put aside confidently the national sense of shame and turn toward a new respect for national traditions, commitment, and sacrifice. Nevertheless, angry student demonstrations erupted in other parts of Asia in response to the Yasukuni visit, particularly in China and Korea where formal diplomatic protests also were heard, for it seemed to outsiders to indicate Japan's willful amnesia over its atrocities in those countries.

Both Nakasone's vision of Japan's appropriate role in the Pacific and the Asian response to it in this instance reflect an ongoing tension in the relationship, one dominated by a searing memory of Japan's militarism that reaches back, in some cases at least, to the previous century and perhaps further. Now that Japan has begun to again dominate the Pacific region through trade and investment (and in ways that its prewar nationalists could only dream of, as described in chapter 13), the nations it once held by conquest worry all the more about its long-term behavior. Thus, the resurgence of an armed, militantly aggressive Japan is unthinkable to its Asian neighbors, and any sign that might indicate such a change is met with diplomatic anxiety and public anger in many parts of Pacific Asia.

It is also an anxiety felt by the Japanese themselves. In 1960, left-wing political parties held demonstrations throughout Japan in an unsuccessful effort to prevent the conservative government from signing a security treaty with the United States that would lock Japan into the American strategy for containing communism in Asia. The result, in combination with the Occupation-imposed "peace provision" in the constitution, has deprived the Japanese of taking ultimate charge of their own national security. Ironically, that responsibility is precisely what the political Left now seeks to avoid. Even though its rhetoric is generally anti-American in tone, the Left is forced to cling to an American-made constitution that prevents Japan from taking military actions abroad. Most Japanese share the Left's pacifist sentiments. They are uncomfortable in situations that require Japan to take positions on military action in international affairs. Such was clearly the case in 1990-91 when Japan, like its former Axis partner Germany, demurred from sending its own troops to help oust Saddam Hussein from Kuwait even though in principle the country supported the allied effort and pledged US $13 billion to help fund it.

The Japanese are proud of their pacifist stance in situations of world conflict, but Japan's conservatives continue to chafe under conditions that Nakasone described as the "unfinished business" of the postwar era: the unrevised, American-imposed constitution, the ill-defined role of the emperor, the lack of patriotism in public education, and the enduring stigma of Japan's behavior in World War II.

Frustrations of an Economic Superpower

In contrast to the concern with which Japan's neighbors react to any reconsideration of its military role, a shift in Japan's thinking about its economic behavior has been strongly encouraged by non-Japanese. Many nations, the United States in particular, have accused Japan of economic nationalism that could undermine the rules of the global trading system as a result of the massive current account surpluses it has built up. From the Japanese perspective, however, the notion that an immense current account surplus should be viewed as a national crisis is entirely open to debate, particularly because part of the surplus has been used to lend sorely needed capital to the rest of the world. In any case, the surplus is diminishing. More fundamental, however, are criticisms aimed at changing the very structure of the Japanese economy, as was the case in the "structural impediments" argument.

The issue of whether Japan's economic structure can and should change has provoked one of the most intense political and intellectual struggles of Japan's postwar domestic politics. On one side are those who wish primarily to preserve the nation's economic gains, the political *status quo*, and their ideas of what it means to be Japanese. On the other are leaders who seek to reorient the nation's economy and its institutions so that Japan will be more accepted by the world community and able to play a stronger leadership role in it. Still others, while advocating change, are pessimistic that Japan is capable of playing any type of aggressive international role.

Why should this latter view be suggested of a nation that has become the world's second-largest economy and its largest aid donor? A variety of factors have been proposed, a few of which are listed below:

- Japan's historic dependence on trade has made it naturally cautious in diplomacy.

- Since the Meiji period, Japan has felt at the mercy of other world powers.

- The wartime trauma has give rise to pacifism and a preference for noninvolvement in foreign political matters.

- The country lacks a strong executive office from which decisions are made.

- Decisions in Japan are made by consensus, leading to a slow, "reactive" behavior in foreign relations.

- Private factions and coalitions constrain government policymaking.

- A passive, reactive policy is intentional and works to Japan's benefit.

These explanations have been much debated in and outside Japan. It is perhaps significant that a broad debate usually precedes any major shift of policy in Japan and it may be that such a shift is underway. The initial stirrings could first be seen during the tenure of Prime Minister Nakasone, but the debate was forestalled by an illusory economic boom in the late 1980s. The intensity of the debate only mounted once again when, in the early 1990s, Japan endured the greatest economic debacle of the post-war era, one for which blame could clearly be assigned to government policies and institutions.

JAPAN'S SAVING SYSTEM:
AN EXAMPLE OF GOVERNMENTAL INTERVENTION

There are several ways in which the government has influenced the structure of Japan's special institutions. Many of these institutions it created directly in the course of its "industrial rationalization" campaigns of the 1930s or in the prosecution of the Pacific War. When the government did not create them directly, it nevertheless recognized their usefulness for its own purposes and moved to reinforce them. The savings system is an example. It is possible, as many commentators have urged, that the savings of private Japanese households — the highest rate of saving as a share of GNP ever recorded by any market economy in peacetime — is due to the natural frugality of the Japanese. But there are strong external pressures that encourage the Japanese to save: a comparatively poor social security system; a wage system that includes large lump-sum bonus payments twice a year; a retirement system that cuts a worker's income substantially before he reaches the age of sixty; a shortage of new housing and housing land, as well as a premium on university education for one's children, both of which require large outlays; an underdeveloped consumer credit system; a government-run postal savings system with guaranteed competitive interest rates; the lack of a well-developed capital market or other alternatives to personal saving; and a substantial exemption from income taxes for interest earned on saving accounts. The government is quite aware of these incentives to save and of the fact that money placed in the postal savings system goes directly into Ministry of Finance accounts, where it can be reinvested in accordance with government plans. Innate frugality may indeed play a role in this system, but the government has worked hard at engineering that frugality.

—Chalmers Johnson, *MITI and the Japanese Miracle*

PUZZLES IN THE
JAPANESE "MIRACLE"

Japan has often seemed like the odd man out within the global trading system, partly because its capitalist economic system operates differently from that of most other nations. We will discover (Chapter 7) that other Asian countries have pursued variations on the Japanese model, but the focus of the debate has been on Japan and the role its government has played in its economic successes and failures. As Chalmers Johnson has observed, competing explanations of the Japanese "miracle" can be divided into four categories:

1. **No miracle occurred** (i.e., governmental intervention was irrelevant to the success of the economy alongside the natural interaction of capital, labor, markets, and so forth). This, he suggests, begs the question because it merely assumes that, as a matter of principle, governmental intervention can make no difference in an economy.

2. **National character, basic values, and consensus** (i.e., Japan has a natural advantage as a homogeneous society whose members have a unique, culturally derived capacity to cooperate with one another). Here, Johnson asks two important questions that remain essentially unanswered by the "national character" school. First, why should the Japanese be cooperating especially well in this day and age? During much of their modern history, they have experienced violent factionalism and internal upheaval. Second, might not the government have played a key role in fostering today's strong, societal cooperation?

3. **Unique structural features** (i.e., Japan enjoys good labor-management relations, a unique savings and banking system, general trading corporations, and so forth). This argument holds that Japanese private industry has three special advantages - what the Japanese refer to as their "three sacred treasures" — a lifetime employment system that ensures labor stability, a more efficient seniority-based wage system, and

The One Percent Ceiling
Japan's Defense Budget, FY 1980 - 1990

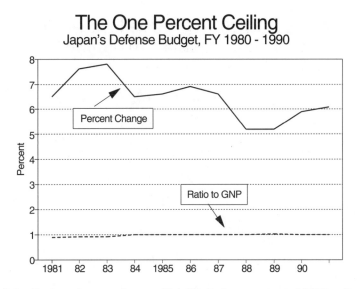

Graph 6.3   Postwar Japan set an unofficial limit of one percent of GNP on its defense spending, far lower than many industrial economies. Measured by NATO standards, the expenditure in 1989 would have been approximately 1.6 percent of GNP.

passive, company-dominated labor unions. Johnson does not disagree with the idea that these features provide special advantages to Japanese companies; he even goes further to suggest that several other unique Japanese institutions and practices also lend substantial advantages to the major Japanese companies under the umbrella of a kind of corporate welfare. However, these institutions have developed with significant encouragement from the government.

4. **"Free Rider"** (i.e., Japan exploits the alliance with the United States through its low defense expenditures, cheap access to key technologies developed in the United States, and easy access to a huge U.S. market). Although postwar Japan has set an unofficial limit to its defense expenditures of 1 percent of the GNP, the "cheap defense" argument is undermined by the rapid growth of South Korea and Taiwan — both with very high defense expenditures. With internal civilian investment in these economies occurring at a very high level, defense burdens were negligible.

As for the role of export markets, Johnson does not deny their considerable benefit to Japan, but notes that by the late 1960s Japan's exports were only 9.6 percent of the GNP compared, for

example, with Canada's 19.8 percent. From 1953 to 1972 Japan had a consistently lower dependence on imports and exports than the major European nations. Particularly in the late 1980s, Japan's strong growth was driven primarily by domestic rather than export forces. Technology transfers, like export markets, have been an important ingredient in Japan's economic resurgence, but Johnson argues that it misses the point to suggest that Japan's acquisition at low cost of important technologies from the West, especially from the United States, was only a "free ride." It was, he says, the heart of the matter.

The importation of technology was one of the central components of postwar Japanese industrial policy, and to raise the subject is to turn the discussion to MITI [Ministry of Trade and Industry] and the Japanese government's role. Before the capital liberalization of the late 1960s and 1970s, no technology entered the country without MITI's approval; no joint venture was ever agreed to without MITI's scrutiny and frequent alteration of the terms; no patent rights were ever bought without MITI's pressuring the seller to lower the royalties or to make other changes advantageous

Japan's Imports from the United States
Manufactures as Share of all US Imports

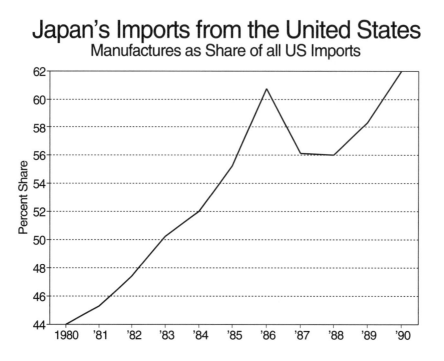

Graphs 6.4-6.5   The good news/bad news use of statistics in connection with trade disputes between Japan and the United States is illustrated here by the top graph indicating that Japan's imports of American manufactures have risen as a percent of all its imports from the United States. The lower graph, however, reveals that when Japan's manufactured imports from the entire world are counted, the United States' position actually eroded in relative terms during the 1980s.

Japan's Manufactured Imports
1980 - 1990

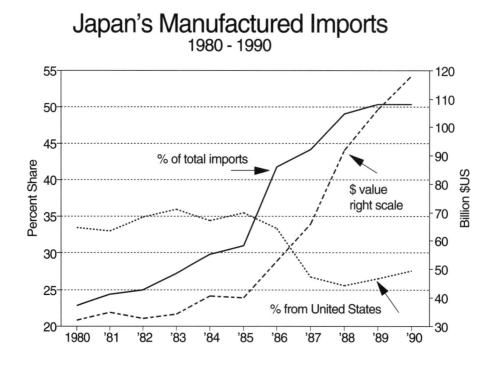

to Japanese industry as a whole; and no program for the importation of foreign technology was ever approved until MITI and its various advisory committees had agreed that the time was right and that the industry involved was scheduled for "nurturing" (ikusei).

From the enactment of the Foreign Capital Law in 1950 (it remained on the books for the next thirty years), the government was in charge of technology transfers. What it did and how it did it was not a matter of a "free ride" but of an extremely complex process of public-private interaction that has come to be known as "industrial policy." MITI is the primary Japanese government agency charged with the formulation and execution of industrial policy.[3]

The major distinction between the Japanese and U.S. economies, from Johnson's viewpoint, is that the former is "plan rational" while the latter is "market rational." That is, the formulation and execution of a plan underlies the Japanese national economic strategy, whereas in the United States the economy is expected to respond only to basic market forces with limited regulation by the government. In Japan, an elite bureaucracy drafts most of the significant legislation, controls the budget, and generally sets the major policy directions for broad segments of the national economy. These bureaucrats retire at age fifty to fifty-five and move from their senior government posts into equally senior posts in private companies. This type of close cooperation between the corporate and governmental bureaucracies ultimately creates a system that Johnson calls the "capitalist developmental state."

Although it is a product of historical evolution and undoctrinaire experimentation rather than a single person's creative genius, the capitalist developmental state is probably Japan's most important invention. It combines private ownership of property with state goal setting. The state operates not by displacing the market, as under socialism, but by becoming a player in the market-creating incentives, supplying capital and information, lowering risks for approved activities, providing pro-

tection from foreign competitors, encouraging competition in strategic industries, and facilitating changes of industrial structure in order to keep as many high-value-added jobs in Japan as possible. The Japanese system was (and is) somewhat comparable to what in the United States is called "the military industrial complex." It is based in part on an intentional blurring of the public and the private. Achievements of privately owned and managed enterprises are regarded as national achievements, but any profit that results is treated as private property.

During the Allied Occupation following World War II, American reformers set out to dismantle this system. As we know today, they actually succeeded only in modernizing and rationalizing it. Many of the Occupation's reforms were long overdue in Japanese society, and many Japanese leaders not only welcomed them but helped the Occupation to achieve them. These included such policies as land reform, extending the vote to women, eliminating the military from political life, and insisting that the emperor was only a symbol of the state, as he had normally been in the centuries before Meiji. But in one area, reform of industry, the Americans proved to be fundamentally misinformed about Japanese economic realities, blinded by their own ideology, and vacillating in terms of their goals for the economy.[4]

Strong governmental planning initially protected fledgling industries and steered companies into serving long-range national goals. The new government institutions were reinforced by a powerful culture of austerity — a determination on the part of all Japanese to sacrifice and work hard to rebuild the devastated country. Under ordinary circumstances, this type of "plan rational" economy worked well, generally outperforming the American system. Yet it relies on a broad consensus within the Japanese economy, something that broke down when, in 1971, President Richard Nixon imposed without warning an embargo on soybean shipments to Japan and, also without consultation, dramatically shifted U.S. policy toward China. The national confusion that followed these so-called "Nixon shocks" and, two years later, the 1973 oil-price shock demonstrated the weakness in the Japanese system.

Japan's businesses, on the other hand, have demonstrated special strengths. First, they have benefited from a host of new executives who came on stream after World War II, eager to learn and willing to sacrifice short term profits for long-range goals. Second, a reformed version of the *zaibatsu* evolved which integrated the functions of finance, marketing and distribution. It subsidized growing companies with the profits of established firms. Third, high savings rates and low interest rates made the cost of capital to these companies relatively lower than for many of their competitors abroad. Lastly, a new system of labor relations evolved which, as previously noted, coaxed astounding productivity increases out of Japan's work force.

The last element was extremely important, for the Japanese economic miracle was, and continues to be, built on the sacrifice of the individual. In some industries, such as car manufacturing, Japanese workers may now be the best paid in the world, but they also work the longest hours. Nor are white collar executives exempt from this sacrifice. Competition among the major Japanese firms for the domestic market share is so intense that it is not unusual for management to demand vast overtime from engineers and managers if it is felt that the company is falling behind. This ability to elicit sacrifice from the work force toward the achievement of ever higher goals gives Japan's industry a critical edge over the competition from other countries.

Challenges to the Japanese Stereotype

Some analysts argue that the role of the Japanese government has been exaggerated or at least is no longer as relevant as it once may have been. In fact, it is widely acknowledged that today MITI does not exert the influence it once held over businesses. There is, in addition, growing recognition that Japan's system is more chaotic than it first appears and is often indecisive and incoherent when it comes to national strategy and policy development. This view sees Japan as no longer operating according to some well-conceived "master plan." Rather, it is like any other country

in that it is subject to domestic pressures to raise its standards of living and to remove the contrast between the purchasing power of Japanese citizens at home versus that of those abroad. In response to both domestic and U.S. pressures, Japan has begun to apply a greater part of its massive current account surpluses to upgrading the nation's housing and infrastructure. In the process of doing so, less of its capital will be available for foreigners to borrow for their own development.

This perspective also suggests that as Japan is buffeted by international economic pressures, various parts of its society will respond differently, leading to social fragmentation and therefore a more pluralistic and complex nation. The essential trends can be summarized as follows:

- New institutions, such as industrial organizations, are defying or inhibiting controls by governmental agencies.

- International alliances among transnational corporations are further diluting governmental control as well as the individual's notion of Japanese "uniqueness."

- Political factions are increasing their power at the expense of government bureaucracies whose influence, therefore, is declining.

- A more affluent middle class is emerging that is not so willing as was the wartime generation to permit the government to define its interests.

- A weak chief executive and weak political structures inhibit clear-cut decision-making.

The Persistence of Global Trade Frictions

The changing conditions of the Japanese economy and polity, cited above, further complicate the resolution of trade disputes with its foreign trade partners. The central theme of the disputes has been the persistent and massive trade deficit of these countries with Japan, although by the 1990s it was declining from record heights established in the 1980s. In their more reflective moments, officials on all sides have acknowledged that the annual trade deficits, often as not,

Share of Patents Granted by the European Patent Office

Country	1982	1985	1988	1991
United States	27.0	27.4	26.2	25.0
Germany	23.1	21.9	21.4	20.0
Japan	**12.9**	**15.3**	**18.0**	**22.3**
France	9.6	8.6	8.5	8.6
United Kingdom	8.5	7.7	7.2	5.2
Newly Industrialized Economies	0.1	0.1	0.2	0.4

Table 6.1   Japan's growing technological prowess in the 1980s is reflected in the rapid increase in the relative number of patents it received globally.

distort the economic issues facing each country. The assumption has grown in the minds of many in the West, however, that for a bilateral trading relationship to reflect "fairness" it should be approximately in balance. Such a notion contradicts the theory of comparative advantage which expects a nation to run surpluses with some countries and deficits with others. Imbalances are especially predictable in the case of Japan, a country with virtually no raw materials to export but one possessing a great capacity to pay for its imported agricultural and industrial needs through the export of manufactured goods and services. Its deficit with some countries is made up for by a surplus with others.

Neither Japan or the United States dominates the other's trade. Japan is the second-largest market for the United States and America is Japan's largest trading partner, but the total global transactions of each are much greater than the focus on the trade imbalance implies.

The Role of Capital

Arguments surrounding trade relationships with Japan tend to ignore the role of capital in determining trade balances. A trade surplus implies that a country produces more than it consumes. In effect, it collects IOUs from deficit countries. Deficits are not always bad if they involve the "borrowing" of resources from other countries to enhance long-term productivity (as occurred in the United States in the late nineteenth and early

twentieth centuries), but they are detrimental to a nation's interests when they are used merely to finance a budget deficit (as occurred in the United States in the 1980s).

When a country increases its demand for capital (say, as a result of its budget deficit), it raises its own trade deficit at the same time. The process can be understood as follows: An increase in borrowing from abroad forces the country to compete with other borrowers for capital, something that is normally done by raising interest rates. Higher rates make the country's currency more attractive globally and so its value rises with the demand. But a more expensive currency means that the country's goods abroad are also more expensive relative to their foreign competition. The result: export sales fall off while imports of comparatively cheaper goods rise. In other words, the trade deficit rises. Trade barriers, whether in Japan or elsewhere, play a relatively minor role in this process.

The Keiretsu

A frequently-cited trade complaint against Japan, one that figured prominently in the Structural Impediments negotiations, concerns the structure and operations of its large conglomerates, the *keiretsu*, literally, "affiliated chain." These are Japanese corporate alliances that typically include a bank, a trading company, and several manufacturers. Famous names, such as Mitsui, Mitsubishi, and Sumitomo, are actually

A Keiretsu Case

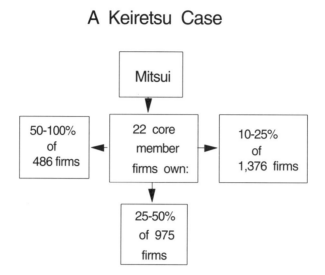

Graph 6.6 The interlocking *keiretsu* system in Japan stands in fundamental contrast with the way capitalism is organized in the United States and it presents a formidable front to its competitors at home and abroad. Here, the Mitsui *keiretsu* is shown as it appeared in 1974. By 1989, 71% of publicly held companies in Japan were held by other companies.

groups of companies, each of which owns parts of the others. Their senior officers meet frequently and tend to prefer doing business with one another rather than outsiders. The difference from the prewar *zaibatsu* groups is that *keiretsu* lack a central holding company and do not involve interlocking directorates. Core member firms do own one another's equity, but not in large enough amounts to exert bilateral control. The result is an arrangement that is said to operate outside the rules of ordinary free market competition. Since most of the *keiretsu* shares are "stable" (not traded) and are held by other large companies, they are not subject to the wishes of their small shareholders — or foreign shareholders. Most importantly, it is said that they change the rules of free competition in high technology industries. By cooperating internally to create leverage and dominance in buying, trading, and selling products, they are able to overwhelm any "go it alone" small firm.

The Japanese counter that the *keiretsu* system enables their managers to focus on long term goals, protects them from hostile takeovers, and fosters stable ties between suppliers and custom-

ers, thus making their system more efficient. Yet recent studies suggest that such efficiencies only arise in the case of special industries such as automobiles. Even so, the *keiretsu* remain a formidable organizational innovation that some firms in the West have begun to emulate rather than attack.

The Japanese assert that concerns about the *keiretsu* are a distraction from the essential point: that the fundamental causes of the U.S. trade deficit have been its massive budget deficits, lagging productivity growth, and the low savings rates in the private sector. Unless there is improvement in these areas, there is little hope of closing the U.S.-Japan trade gap. Tariff and nontariff barriers have only marginal effects on current account balances. To the extent that they have some impact, the Japanese point out that compared with other OECD[5] members, Japan is one of the more "open" countries in terms of tariff levels. They cite the thousand Kentucky Fried Chicken outlets or the six hundred McDonald's outlets as evidence of their receptiveness to foreign businesses. As further evidence of this openness, look also at Japanese television, they say, where advertisers use

Import Content of Manufactured Goods
Developed Countries in the 20th Century

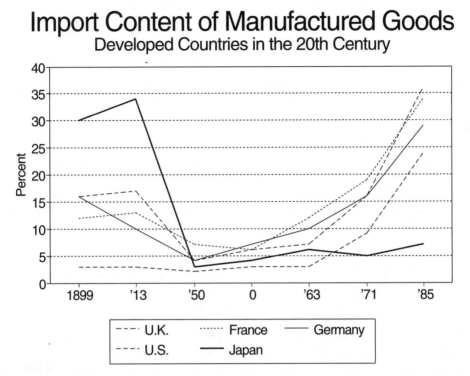

Graph 6.7   In comparison with other developed nations, Japan remained strongly resistant to using imports in its manufacturing production through the mid-1980s.

non-Japanese celebrities to enhance the image of their products.

The Japanese also call attention to the fact that in the 1980s Britain, France, and Italy had a combined GNP and population larger than Japan's and yet together they absorbed fewer American imports than did Japan. At the same time, the size of Japan's trade surplus as a ratio to the Gross National Product has diminished steadily, from 4.5 percent in 1985 to less than 1.5 percent 1990. The share of manufactured items in total imports rose from the 30 percent level in 1985 to more than 50 percent after 1989.

The Political System

If shifts in the structure of the Japanese economy are taking place, so are changes in its political system. The country has developed innovative institutions, both private and public, that have contributed to its success, but credit must also be given to a political system dominated by a single party, the Liberal Democratic Party (LDP). Formed as a coalition of political factions, the LDP has governed Japan without interruption since 1955. Its success in doing so has been attributed to several factors:

- Factionalized and ineffectual opposition parties.

- Dominance over an effective, elite government bureaucracy with close ties to business.

- A record of economic success that discourages opposition.

Today, the system is under increasing stress as it searches to identify a new generation of leaders while remaining under the control of an older oligarchy. Chalmers Johnson points out in the following passage that the system will have difficulty adapting to the new circumstances facing the nation.

◆   ◆   ◆

JAPANESE DEMOCRACY
AND POLITICAL STABILITY

— by Chalmers Johnson

Generally speaking, the postwar system worked well so long as the only people participating in it were Japanese and the economy was growing at a double-digit rate. But whenever the bureaucrats were divided among themselves or the unintended consequences of their own policies started to mobilize the people, as was the case with pollution, the machinery slowed down. It fell apart completely whenever the Japanese were forced to deal with international problems or when they had to conform to standards not of their own making — as, for example, in ratifying the Japanese-American Security Treaty in 1960, in normalizing relations with South Korea in 1965, in normalizing relations with China in 1972 and 1978, and in attempting to deliver on Japan's innumerable promises to the rest of the world to open its domestic markets to international trade. Each of these issues produced major internal political instability, sometimes resulting in the resignation of the prime minister, or else there was only a pretense of a policy for external consumption while internal patterns continued unchanged.

Given its structural contradictions, Japan currently lacks the capacity for true political leadership. Its most experienced leaders acknowledge that public opinion, as distinct from the influence of special-interest groups, has almost no effect on the political system except in a crisis and that the equivalent of public opinion in other systems is pressure from abroad (*gaiatsu*).

During the 1950s and 1960s the LDP reigned over the political process, spending most of its time raising money for its own reelection and fighting off charges of corruption; the bureaucrats initiated all major policies; and the electorally significant interest groups whose votes the LDP needed, primarily farmers in thinly populated but never reapportioned districts, were paid off.

Big business is not a separate interest group in Japan; it is the prime beneficiary and virtual *raison d'être* of the Japanese system, as the theory of the capitalist developmental state stipulates. For that reason it is meaningless to speak of the role of big business in Japanese politics; the two are indistinguishable. The Japanese system of political economy as it was formulated in the 1950s, and particularly after the Security Treaty crisis of 1960, intentionally favored manufacturing over all other activities, exporters over importers, producers over consumers, and industrial needs over environmental needs. The intent of the system was to rebuild Japan economically and free it from dependence on U.S. foreign aid and offshore procurements. Over time vested interests developed around these priorities, including vested interests in the continuing reign of the LDP and the groups the party relied on to ensure its reelection. Tension began to build within the system during the late 1960s as the need to alter the priorities of the high-growth system (by, for example, ending protectionism and servicing domestic demand) increasingly clashed with the old arrangements to keep the LDP in power.

During the 1970s the relationship between the LDP and the bureaucracy also began to change. Long-serving LDP politicians began to rival and challenge the bureaucrats in terms of policy expertise. Some politicians became known as *zoku giin*, (literally, "tribal Diet members" but actually meaning sectoral policy specialists and deal makers). This had the effect of politicizing policymaking much more than it had been in the past, since politicians were more susceptible to the favors of special-interest groups than the bureaucrats. The end of high-speed growth and the appearance of large government deficits also meant that the bureaucracy could no longer dominate the system by giving everybody something. Interministerial conflicts over jurisdiction grew as the issues facing Japanese society changed but the ministries did not; the politicians were often called on to resolve these disputes. New interest groups tended to cultivate politicians because rival older interest groups had already developed symbiotic relationships with the ministries (for example, securities trading companies favored politicians because banks were already close to the Ministry of Finance). And smart bureaucrats, thinking of their own soon-to-come *amakudari* ("descent from heaven") into the private sector, avoided highly controversial subjects, such as defense or school textbooks, that might embroil them in political conflict.

Big Business, Politicians, and Bureaucrats
Japanese Networks in the Privatization of NTT

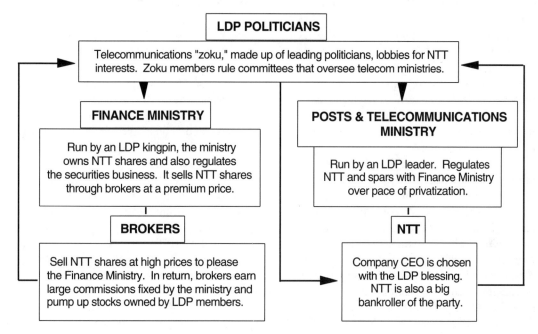

LDP POLITICIANS

Telecommunications "zoku," made up of leading politicians, lobbies for NTT interests. Zoku members rule committees that oversee telecom ministries.

FINANCE MINISTRY

Run by an LDP kingpin, the ministry owns NTT shares and also regulates the securities business. It sells NTT shares through brokers at a premium price.

POSTS & TELECOMMUNICATIONS MINISTRY

Run by an LDP leader. Regulates NTT and spars with Finance Ministry over pace of privatization.

BROKERS

Sell NTT shares at high prices to please the Finance Ministry. In return, brokers earn large commissions fixed by the ministry and pump up stocks owned by LDP members.

NTT

Company CEO is chosen with the LDP blessing. NTT is also a big bankroller of the party.

Graph 6.8   When Japan's giant telecommunications company, NTT, was partially privatized in the 1980s, the networks stemming from the *zoku* in the Diet played a critical role. The big losers in this complex game were the Japanese consumers: Many bought NTT shares at US$ 14,230 apiece, only to see them eventually plummet by 58%. Total loss: $42 billion. In 1991, a new scandal broke out over the revelation that major Japanese securities firms were secretly paying back their "big" customers for major losses. The LDP strongly resisted, but finally relented, at efforts to summons the officials for testimony before the Diet.

The result was the appearance of what Karel van Wolferen has called the "truncated pyramid," meaning a Japanese system in which no one was ultimately in charge. The economy ran on unchecked, and no one could cause it to change course: prime ministers went to Washington or to summit meetings and made promises, but with their only authority coming from their fellow faction leaders in the LDP, they lacked the power to force the bureaucracy to act; the bureaucrats spent more and more time servicing *zoku giin* as a way of fighting their own turf battles; and the old vested interests dug in their heels against the promises made to foreigners and consumers.

As the last months of Showa [the reign of the Emperor Hirohito who died January 7, 1989] unfolded, the anomalies of the Japanese political

process began to pile up. Japan emerged as the world's richest nation in terms of per capita income, even though its per capita consumption changed hardly at all (indicating that it was not the Japanese "people" who were getting rich). The figures for 1988 were $23,765 as Japan's per capita Gross National Product, compared with $19,050 for the United States, even though per capita consumption in Japan was only 63 percent of the U.S. level.

All of this was capped, on December 9, 1988, by the resignation of Miyazawa Kiichi, the minister of finance, because his secretary admitted making $181,130 on an insider stock trading deal [involving the well-known Recruit Company]. Prime Minister Takeshita himself temporarily assumed the post of minister of finance because there were no other senior members of the party who had not been equally involved in the stock scam, even though associates of the prime minister had also received stock from the Recruit Company before it was officially listed on the stock exchange and for sale to the general public. Typical of experienced *mikoshi* [persons in positions of authority], the LDP faction leaders received their bribes — actually advance payments for future favors — in the form of payments to their secretaries, whereas the senior bureaucrats and businessmen involved, new to the game, accepted theirs in their own names.

Before it was all over, Takeshita resigned as prime minister when the LDP's popularity in the public opinion polls fell to under 2 percent. Uno Sosuke replaced him but promptly made the situation worse by seeming to insult Japanese women through his extramarital liaisons. The prosecutors eventually indicted some thirteen people on charges of bribery, but only two were politicians, even though some sixteen politicians admitted publicly that they had received payoffs from the Recruit Company. The long-suffering Japanese public finally had had enough. In the upper-house election of July 23, 1989, they failed

for the first time to give the LDP its customary majority.

The election turned on many issues other than the Recruit scandal. Probably the most important was the phenomenon known as "rich Japan, poor Japanese," meaning that the upward revaluation of the yen against the value of the U.S. dollar by some 60 percent since 1985 had made the Japanese the world's richest people on paper but not in their lives. They still commuted to work for an average hour and a half each way in incredibly overcrowded trains, lived in minuscule apartments that they could never afford to buy, and spent more than a third of their household income on food. To add insult to injury, the Ministry of Finance forced the LDP to enact a poorly constructed and inequitably administered sales tax at precisely the same moment the Recruit scandal revealed that LDP members and other insiders were being paid millions of yen by people trying to buy access to the government.

The fundamental problem of Japanese politics since the Meiji era has been to contain the social tensions generated by extremely high-speed economic growth. Writers in English-speaking countries commonly believe that

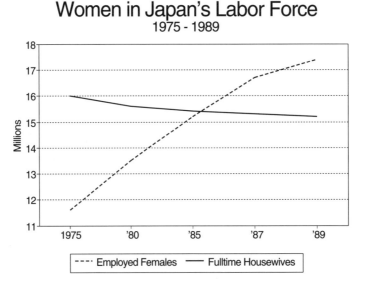

Women in Japan's Labor Force
1975 - 1989

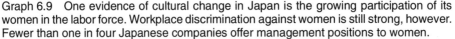

Graph 6.9   One evidence of cultural change in Japan is the growing participation of its women in the labor force. Workplace discrimination against women is still strong, however. Fewer than one in four Japanese companies offer management positions to women.

economic growth, particularly if it is achieved under capitalist auspices, facilitates political stability and even democratization. The opposite is actually the case.

As we have seen, Japan's industrialization occurred from above for political reasons in accordance with the goals of small, self-appointed elites. In the Meiji era these elites were the oligarchs who had engineered the Restoration; in the 1930s these elites were militarists and their bureaucratic and industrial collaborators who came to power essentially through coup d'état; and in the 1950s and 1960s these elites were economic bureaucrats of the central government who were attempting to rebuild Japan and restore self-respect to its people. The economic interventions of these elites have produced three clear cycles in which bureaucratism displaced underlying trends of democratization. Hidaka Rokuro periodizes them as follows:

Cycle One: (a) Meiji Restoration, 1869 to circa 1890, a period of "enlightenment" with movements toward liberty, people's rights, and democracy; (b) 1890 to circa 1912, a period of nationalism and imperialism, in which democracy waned.

Cycle Two: (a) 1912 to 1931, a period in which attempts were made to bring the absolutist system under democratic constraints, known as the era of Taisho Democracy; (b) 1931 to 1945, a period of militarism, ultranationalism, and the suppression of all democratic tendencies.

Cycle Three: (a) 1945 to 1960, a period of intense democratization in the wake of Japan's defeat and the reforms of the Allied Occupation; (b) 1960 to 1989, a period of high-speed economic growth based in part on single-party government and the avoidance of political problems.

Concerning the main postwar cycle, Hidaka argues:

In the prewar period, the state unified the Japanese people by fostering loyalty to the Emperor. Today, the state coopts the people by elaborately redistributing profits to meet the people's expectations. The high-growth economy made the ability to redistribute profits possible. The postwar period can be divided into two phases: the phase of postwar democracy and the phase of high-economic growth.

The high-growth economy of Japan, which began in the 1960s, created a new state completely different in quality from the Japanese state during or immediately after the war.

It is possible that the social forces mobilized and set in motion by the political crisis of 1989 will lead to renewed and sustained democratic development in Japan. The strongest reason for optimism is that some of the people who voted against the LDP were motivated by personal frustrations. Too often in the past Japan's attempts at democracy were based on foreign examples or pressures and lacked indigenous roots. In order to thrive, democracy in Japan must be something that the Japanese people themselves create.[6]

◆   ◆   ◆

THE MODERN JAPANESE ECONOMY

Resurgence in the late 1980s: The "Bubble" Economy

As described previously, Japan's high-growth era came to an end with the first oil crisis. After 1973, annual GDP growth rarely climbed above 5 percent, reflecting not only the aftermath of that crisis but also a larger, more mature economy that appeared to be headed towards convergence with other industrial nations. From 1973 to 1986, growth was only slightly greater than that of the United States.

This situation changed dramatically in the late 1980s as stronger growth rates resumed. Between 1986 and 1991, Japan maintained an average GDP growth rate of 4.9 per cent against only 2.1 percent in the United States. Japanese firms enjoyed very low-cost access to capital (by means of highly regulated financial markets and high domestic savings) and their stocks were buoyed by inflating land prices. From this strong domestic base, Japan's corporations expanded aggressively with marketing and acquisitions in other countries. As Japanese electronics firms began to purchase major Hollywood film studios and prominent American landmarks such as Rockefeller Center

Japan's GDP Growth, 1970-1995

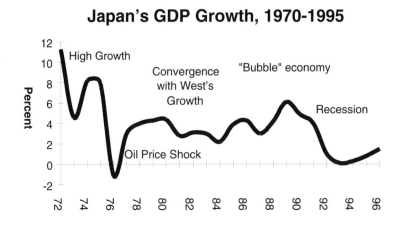

Graph 6.10   After 1973, the growth of Japan's maturing economy seemed headed for "convergence" with that of other industrial nations, but in the late 1980s it accelerated — then fell into a recession-like doldrums.

in New York, it seemed that the postwar Japanese economic expansion had no limits.

The Bubble Bursts

The foundation of the 1980s economic surge was in fact quite fragile. By the late 1980s, the already-expensive cost of real estate in Japan had reached levels that seemed to defy logic. The paper value of all Japanese property was several times greater than all the land in the United States, a nation 25 times its size. The most dangerous development in the upward land price spiral came in April, 1990 when the Ministry of Finance gave housing loan companies, called *jusen,* an exemption from restrictions on real estate-related loans. The *jusen* soon began to engage in reckless lending in the belief, common to such companies, that land prices would not decline in the near term. By the time the price downturn did arrive, the *jusen* had racked up trillions of yen in debts, most of which went bad, creating one of the worst political and economic crises in Japan's post war history. Most major banks were affected as well. At the depth of this financial crisis, Japan's banks were estimated to be carrying $367 billion in bad loans, over a quarter of which may have been linked to firms owned by gangsters (*yakuza*). This economic downturn, which reached unprecedented

duration and severity, fell upon Japan beginning in April, 1991. Inflation-adjusted GDP growth fell to an average of only 0.6 per cent per year between 1991 and 1995. The recession deepened not only as a result of a steady fall in real estate prices but also because plant and equipment spending rates dropped as well. This category of purchases had risen so dramatically during the bubble period that it had contributed a full percentage point to GDP growth. Like the accelerating land prices, such growth fed the demand for yet more plant and equipment. Once the cycle was interrupted, a vast overcapacity drove the process into reverse and exerted an equally strong negative pull on GDP growth.

In an effort to turn around the economic slowdown, the Japanese government tried to stimulate the economy through large public works spending and tax cuts. This had a positive, if limited, effect but it did not revive public confidence. At last, Japan began to confront the fictions that had made its economy seem invulnerable. In particular the system of bureaucratic governance, once lauded for its ability to manage the economy, was exposed to public criticism. The authorities in the once-vaunted Ministry of Finance, in particular, were seen to be inept in their early efforts to remedy the economic slowdown.

Critics of the system pointed out that Japan's huge success in the 1980s had been largely a consequence of an artificial environment. A temporarily depreciated yen, the value of which had dropped 20 per cent between 1978 and 1982, had given the already-competitive Japanese firms a huge price advantage in global markets, enabling them to pour profits into new technologies. This advantage was reversed in the 1990s. The yen strengthened so much that Japan's exports were overpriced in most markets. This meant that exports would play no significant role in the Japanese recovery. The belief that Japan could always "export its way out of a recession" proved false.

The recession also led to a painful reevaluation of the management of Japanese firms. What had once seemed farsighted, strategic foreign investments by these firms was viewed in a new light as the dollar value of those assets fell. By some estimates, exchange rate shifts led to losses of nearly $400 billion in only a few years. Perceptions of Japanese technological prowess were similarly revised. A US government review of 27 "critical" technologies, such as biotechnology and computers, found that Japan did not lead in any of them.

Political Upheavals

In August 1993, after 38 years of controlling the post of Prime Minister, the LDP lost its ruling position in a general election. Disenchantment with the LDP had become so pervasive that a new prime minister, Morihiro Hosokawa, was able to form a successful political coalition on the basis of a pledge to reform Japanese politics. A period of extensive political turmoil ensued. Within a year, the top leadership position changed again as 71 year-old Tomiichi Muruyama, head of the left-leaning Social Democratic Party of Japan, became prime minister as part of a politically opportune coalition with the LDP and another party. Amid a sluggish economy, a surging yen, and a variety of controversial political issues, Muruyama's weak and indecisive leadership was doomed to failure. An assertive, rising star in the LDP, Ryutaro Hashimoto, seized the reins of leadership in 1996 as part of the same coalition, but more turbulence ensued as his powerful rival, Ichiro Ozawa, head of the then-largest opposition party in Japan, Shinshinto, launched an intensive political attack. The focus: a controversial plan to use government

money to help bail out the troubled housing load companies, the *jusen*.

The rise to power of personalities like Hashimoto and Ozawa occurred amid a major alteration of Japan's system of electing the lower house of its parliament, the Diet. In January, 1994, the Diet enacted new rules to more effectively create a "one person - one vote" system. The rules were expected to put an end to personality-centered campaigns which were heavily associated with graft. The plan combines 300 single-seat districts with 200 seats awarded according to a party's proportional share of the vote total.

The impact of the new electoral system will take some years to determine. Although it may eventually cause some power realignments among parties, critics of the reform have observed that the old ways of local and intraparty maneuvering still prevail. This may be partly due to the fact that Japanese political races after the cold war lack the clarity of ideological cleavages that have remained in some other countries. Indeed, the Japanese voter is often confused or, worse, apathetic at the sameness of the political parties and leadership choices.

The 1993 political upset appeared on the surface to be a firm reprimand from the voters to the established LDP politicians. In fact, nearly every incumbent was re-elected, even those who had been tainted by bribery scandals. The illusion of fundamental change was heightened when a significant number of LDP politicians broke away and founded a new party with the aim of reforming the political system. But in fact, the LDP retained its dominant role in Japanese politics. Its only major concession to change was to share power with minority parties in coalition governments.

The slow pace of political reform in Japan stems from a formidable opposition: Japan's bureaucrats. In particular, the Ministry of Finance (MOF), whose officials comprise a united, broadly-based front, exerts significant influence over the politicians. Whether they are active in government or retired into strategic positions in industry (*amakudari*), the officials and former officials of the MOF use a wide range of instruments to discipline those who oppose their views. A typical tactic is selective enforcement of tax violations. For example, when Japan's auto market was initially opened to foreigners, Japanese auto dealers who bought foreign cars were exhaustively audited and found guilty of normally unenforced tax rules.

In spite of its formidable reputation, the MOF came under heavy criticism for mishandling the Japanese financial crisis in the mid 1990s. As a result, Hashimoto was able to launch a credible effort at long term financial reform in Japan which, if successful, would moderately curb the ministry's influence.

Japan Reconsidered

The influence of Japanese bureaucrats has become the subject of intensive comment and analysis, both within and outside Japan. Once largely overlooked as a basis for understanding Japanese development, scholars like Chalmers Johnson drew attention to the role that powerful government institutions have played in Japan throughout the century.

The prolonged Japanese recession of the early 1990s stimulated a fresh round of debate about the role of such institutions in the Japanese economy. The so-called "revisionist" school, represented by writers such as Johnson, Eamonn Fingleton, and Karel van Wolferin[7] pointed to the origins of Japan's financial debacle, especially its mismanagement by the Ministry of Finance, as a confirmation of their view that Japan's economy functions under the tight control of bureaucrats. Others argued that the collapse of the bubble economy merely confirmed that Japan is subject to the same laws of economics as any other country, i.e., by pushing exports and resisting imports it weakened its competitive advantage at home. Both conclusions are valid. A Japanese observer, Mikuni Akio, summarized the problem:

There were two motives behind [Japan's economic] system. The first was to expand Japan's productive capacity as quickly as possible. The second was to keep control of Japan's productive assets out of the hands of foreigners. The strains in this system first started appearing in the late 1960s, when Japan began running chronic trade surpluses. The result has been constant upward pressure on exchange rates. The increasing value of the yen should have served as a signal to Japan's policy elite that it needed to shift the driving force of the economy from exports to domestic demand. But Japan, alas, has lacked the political infrastructure capable of carrying out such a wide-ranging shift.[8]

If the revisionist view has gained widespread credibility, its proponents differ in their interpretation of Japanese intentions. Leon Hollerman, for example, believes that collusive bureaucratic oligarchy has been implementing a well-constructed master plan by which it will turn Japan into the "headquarters economy" for the world.[9] Contradicting him, van Wolferin can see no sign of or capacity for a master plan. Instead, he describes a powerful but directionless Japanese bureaucracy that operates according to its own conservative institutional codes without reference to any specific national objective except to increase indefinitely Japan's productive capacity and, not incidentally, the relative power of the bureaucracy. The US wartime occupation removed the only powers that might have checked this process, he argues, leaving the ministries to regulate an economic system without regard to consumer welfare or even profitability. The result is a Japan that retains vast productive overcapacity in its domestic economy but has a low yen-purchasing power in the rest of the world (because trade imbalances have strengthened the yen) — and it has no political institutions or leadership with which to change this dangerous course.

The Future of the Japanese Economy

The late 1980s boom and the 1990s recession, viewed against the longer postwar history of Japan, represent extremes that are unlikely to recur, but the economic downturn did reveal fundamental structural weaknesses in Japan's economy that had been masked by years of high growth and cheap capital. It is now recognized that even if Japan returns to a steady growth path which may accelerate from time to time, these problems will not be resolved easily.

The nation's gross financial liabilities continued to mount during the recession period as the Ministry of Finance was forced to use economic

Comparative Rates of Return on Capital, 1955-90

	Japan	United States	United Kingdom	Germany
1960	28.3	14.4	23.3	23.8
1970	18.0	12.4	15.1	14.0
1980	7.8	8.7	10.5	8.9
1990	3.9	5.9	7.9	5.3

Table 6.2   In the 1960s, when Japan and Western Europe were still building up their capital stock, returns on investment were double the rates found in the United States. By the 1990s, however, Japan's rate had dropped nearly a third below that of the US.

stimulus packages that were debt financed. By one measure, the gross financial liabilities of the government as a share of GDP have come to be among the world's highest (83 per cent in 1995). This share of GDP is not so alarming after government assets are deducted from the gross amount (11 per cent in 1995), but the ultimate effect remains unclear, and the national debt burden on future generations is a growing concern in Japan.

The economic boom years also hurt Japanese corporations by instilling in their managers a false sense of security and confidence. They were encouraged in this view by foreign companies, particularly in the United States, which began to copy elements of Japanese management as part of an overall restructuring. Most importantly, a process of painful "downsizing" and related efficiency measures stimulated many firms in the U.S. and some in Europe to make dramatic gains in productivity. As these companies laid off employees and shut down their less productive factories, Japanese firms continued to hire new employees and add capacity. The result was a cost structure in a number of Japan's industries that was badly bloated by international standards.

Today, Japan faces a serious problem of lagging productivity growth. That is, the cost of producing a particular good or service in Japan has become so high by world standards that it affects Japan's ability to compete with foreign firms. After years of strong productivity growth (Graph 6.1) Japan nearly caught up by this measure with the rest of the industrial world, but early productivity gains have now slowed. The cause is widely believed to be a consequence of Japanese bureaucratic regulation and the government's sanctioning of noncompetitive behavior among firms. This means, in turn, that the economic welfare of the

average Japanese will continue to lag behind the industrial development of the nation.

Lagging productivity growth is ascribed, in part, to policy environments that discourage competition and innovation. For years, the Japanese government defended its restrictions on competition as being necessary to protect consumer health and welfare. But there were also undeclared reasons, such as protecting powerful political lobbies. Agricultural producers and small retailers were particularly favored. Equally debilitating to the long term health of economy was the government's resistance to foreign direct investment which limited firms' exposures to new production and management techniques.

Today average Japanese productivity levels remain well below those of the United States and Germany, although in some manufacturing sectors such as motor vehicles, steel, consumer electronics, and machine tools, Japan is preeminent. In the increasingly critical area of services, however, Japan lags badly. A McKinsey study in 1992 found a 56 percent gap between the United States and Japan in retailing and a 23 percent gap in telecommunications.[10] The productivity of these and other services is important because up to half of the sales value of manufactured goods comes from service inputs.

Productivity is also strongly affected by basic scientific research and development. Japanese research has tended to be more applied than in the United States and Europe ("applied" research is conducted with a specific product or process in mind rather than for the more abstract knowledge gains involved). Yet there is growing evidence that fundamental research may contribute up to three times the productivity gains of applied research.[11] Japan's domestic investment boom of the late 1980s included massive increases in R&D, but the returns on these "practical" areas of research in Japan have been disappointing. For example, Japan contributes disproportionally less than would expected to global scientific knowledge. In 1993, 34 percent of the world's scientific literature was produced by American authors, 8.8 percent by Japanese authors.[12]

CONCLUSION: ADAPTING TO A GLOBAL ECONOMY

Japan: Groping for Growth

The deeply held Japanese faith in government bureaucratic management of industry was shaken by the nation's economic troubles in the 1990s. What had seemed to the world to be an economic juggernaut was revealed more accurately as a uniquely deformed economy. Alongside a powerful export machine that pumped out autos, elec-tronics, semiconductors, and machinery stood a host of feeble, protected industries in retailing, banking, farming, textiles and other areas. In retrospect, it was seen that the post-war "miracle" in Japan had been based on unsustainable trade surpluses. Eventually, global economic forces imposed severe penalties on the protected Japanese economy as its surpluses exerted upward pressure on the value of its currency, making it ever more difficult for Japanese companies to sell abroad from their protected home base.

As Japan confronts the possibility of another period of historic change, significant perhaps as the Meiji era or the Occupation, it must alter an established, rigid economic structure of its own making. The decisions of the early post-war era have created the habits of the present one and they will resist fundamental alteration. Whether new institutions and a deregulated economy will emerge through forceful leadership remains to be seen. What appears certain is that, should the 21st century bear witness to a second Japanese miracle, it will be by a different "design" — or no design at all.

NOTES

1. Business conglomerates controlled by wealthy families. The four leading *zaibatsu* were Mitsui, Mitsubishi, Sumitomo, and Yasuda.

2. See Takafusa Nakamura, "An Economic History of the Showa Era," *Economic Eye*, vol. 10, no. 2, Summer 1989, pp. 4-16.

3. Chalmers Johnson, *MITI and the Japanese Miracle*. (Stanford: Stanford University Press, 1982), pp. 16-17.

4. Chalmers Johnson, "The People Who Invented the Mechanical Nightingale," *Daedalus*, Summer 1990, pp. 74-75.

5. Organization for Economic Cooperation and Development, an intergovernmental body of industrialized nations headquartered in Paris.

6. Johnson, "The People Who Invented the Mechanical Nightingale," pp. 79-88.

7. McKinsey Global Institute, *Service Sector Productivity* (Washington, D.C.: October 1992), Exhibit 2E-11.

8. Mikuni Akio, "A New Era for Japanese Finance," in *The Asian Wall Street Journal*, July 2/3, 1993.

9. Chalmers Johnson, *Japan, Who Governs? The Rise of the Developmental State*. W.W. Norton, 1995, 384pp.; Eamonn Fingleton, *Blindside: Why Japan is Still on Track to Overtake the U.S. by the Year 2000*, Houghton Mifflin, 406pp.; Karel van Wolferin, *The Enigma of Japanese Power*, Knopf, 1989.

10. Leon Hollerman, "The Headquarters Nation," in *The National Interest*, (Fall, 1991).

11. Frank Lichtenberg, *R&D Investment and International Productivty Differences* (Working Paper No. 4161). Cambridge, Massachusetts: National Bureau of Economic Research, 1992.

12. National Science Board, *Science and Engineering Indicators, 1996* (Washington DC: 1996) Appendix Table 5-32.

7

The New Asian Capitalists

OVERVIEW

When the USSR and East European communist governments collapsed in 1989-1991, self-congratulatory comments could be heard throughout the West about the "victory of capitalism." It seemed only a matter of time before the struggling command economies in Asia (e.g., China, North Korea, Vietnam) would succumb to similar forces of change. For reasons connected with their successful revolutionary histories, however, Asian communist states are likely to come to terms with capitalism differently and more slowly than those in Europe. Government planning continues to play a major role in these communist societies.

The capitalist governments of Asia, too, have intervened heavily in the management of their economies — far more so than most of their counterparts in the West. Classic economic theory suggests that a high degree of governmental interference in making excessive "choices" for the private sector is doomed to failure, and there have been such failures in Asian capitalist states. Yet as Japan's early record of growth illustrates, forceful intervention can also have positive results (leading some observers to suggest jokingly that, for a time at least, it was "the only communist system that worked"). The success of government intervention in Asia has become the subject of much debate inasmuch as it challenges traditional free market assumptions. It is a complex issue and the results of government intervention must be measured over

many years. In the previous chapter, we examined Japan's success in the post-war era and the extent to which early strategies of success may have undermined later dynamism and growth. Here, we undertake a similar review of the successes, crises, and failures of other capitalist states in Pacific Asia.

All capitalist systems generally share the characteristics of private ownership of property and the means of production and they encourage private initiative to respond to market (supply and demand) forces, but there is considerable variation world-wide among them in the nature and degree of state intervention. A major difference with the "command economies" has been that the capitalist economies allow true price mechanisms to operate: markets are the primary determinants of product values.

Japan dominates Pacific Asian capitalism, both in size and example. Its largest businesses, which form interlocking networks in the *keiretsu* system, tend to make their strategic priority the control or domination of markets — often with the support of the Japanese government. The alternative "free trade" emphasis reverses the order of priority: Markets should be allowed to develop without being manipulated by governments and companies are expected to fend for themselves. In fact, the two approaches have mutually influenced one another over the years. On the one hand, Asian governments have sheltered or controlled their key business sectors, with Korea going even further than Japan in controlling the behavior of its businesses.

More recently, however, a counter-trend has begun in which many governments are privatizing state-owned or controlled entities and cautiously deregulating their business environments. This has been prompted not only by the need for investment capital but by the demonstrable need to maintain globally competitive industries.

In the early postwar era, Pacific Asian economies were major beneficiaries of the lower tariff barriers that resulted from global trade liberalization under the aegis of a new institution, the Geneva-based General Agreement on Tariffs and Trade (GATT). Amid a steady expansion of world trade, they turned toward export-driven economic strategies and saw their national revenues soar. The scope and scale of their dramatic post-war economic growth owed much in particular to the vastness and relative openness of the American market.

Besides Japan, the high-growth economies of East Asia (South Korea, Taiwan, Hong Kong and Singapore) have led the regional growth trend, but other countries have begun to move up rapidly. Historically, their economies shared several characteristics. First, their governments participated in strategic planning and cooperated with the private sector to promote specific national industries. Second, all shared a commitment to export-oriented growth. This implied an acceptance, in the manufacturing sector, of the principle that both quality and fair price are to be measured by international standards and that wages will be tied to productivity. Third, all shared high levels of savings and investment. Most have exceeded a savings and investment rate of 20 percent or more of GNP which is widely held to be a level at which development becomes self-sustaining.

This chapter will examine the economic expansion of these economies, using South Korea to illustrate the range of factors and choices confronting a "late developer." In examining Korea, and in the final section, we ask what role, if any, Confucian traditions may play in promoting economic development.

Complexities of the Economic Boom

The strategies and circumstances of the growth policies pursued by Pacific Asia's capitalist economies have varied considerably from one country to the next in terms of timing, sequence, and prioritization. They are summarized in the accompanying table by William Overholt.[1] All such strategies have not been pursued in each country, nor has there been an ironclad formula for economic success in the region generally. Amid the turmoil that followed the Pacific War, economic setbacks and political crises were the norm in the early stages. The Philippines stumbled badly in the course of its economic development and in spite of rapid growth rates, poverty is still a massive problem in several other Asian economies. Moreover, economic development has given rise to a host of new social and environmental problems which will be taken up in later chapters. For now, however, we will concentrate on the success stories.

◆   ◆   ◆

DEVELOPING ECONOMIES OF THE ASIA-PACIFIC REGION

— East-West Center

Since 1960 the market economies of Pacific Asia, with few exceptions, have been growing at average annual rates of 6 percent or more. Growth rates in China and some Southeast Asian countries have been only slightly lower over the same period. This level of economic performance is far higher than that of any other world region. If present and foreseeable trends continue, by the end of the century the western Pacific rim countries will have an aggregate economy comparable in size to those of Western Europe or North America.

Japan is the premier developed economy in the Asia Pacific region. In 1960 it accounted for approximately 20 percent of the region's income and 3 percent of that of the world. In 1975 these figures stood at approximately 50 percent and 9 percent, respectively. In the intervening years Japan graduated from the status of a developing country to that of a developed country. A century-long process of catching up with the advanced developed nations had come to a close. Once Japan was at the forefront, the country's growth rate dropped, from approximately 10 percent annually in the 1950s and 1960s to about 5 percent or less after the oil shock of 1974. It will continue

PACIFIC ASIAN STRATEGIES FOR ECONOMIC DEVELOPMENT

- Stimulate a sense of nationhood, if necessary by antagonism toward the developed powers.

- Clean up institutions:
  - Purge corrupt timeservers, and incompetents.
  - Install Western-trained technocrats.

- Crack down on crime, political strikes, and disorder.

- Repress pressure groups that cause patronage, corruption, and inflation.

- Come to terms with the advanced industrial countries in order to share their capital, markets, and technology.

- Keep military budgets small, development budgets high.

- Shift to export-led growth.

- Reform income distribution:
  - Land reform.
  - Labor-intensive industry (cheap labor, textiles, agriculture, and consumer electronics).
  - Huge investment in education.

- Coopt the Left with egalitarian reforms, the Right with growth: Give the masses a stake in society.

- Create large, modern firms to enhance trade.

- Acquire technology, capital, and trading from multinational corporations and international banks.
  - Use technocrats and nationalistic leadership to maximize benefits for the country.

- Move up a ladder that starts with labor-intensive sectors:
  - Agriculture and raw materials.
  - Textiles, shoes.
  - Light industry, especially consumer electronics.
  - Heavy industry.
  - High technology.

- Use authoritarian means, if necessary, to accomplish the above.

—William Overholt

Real Per Capita Growth
Developing Nations, 1980s & Forecast

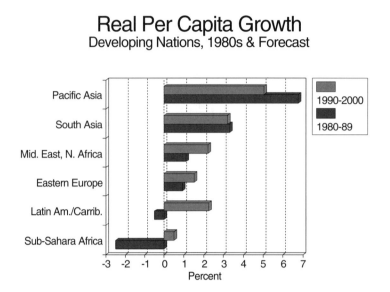

Graph 7.1

to grow at rates below those of its East Asian and Southeast Asian neighbors. Nevertheless, by the year 2000 Japan will still account for over 40 percent of the value of goods and services produced in Asia and the Pacific.

With the possible exceptions of Hong Kong and Singapore, no other Asian and Pacific developing economies can be expected to follow Japan into the ranks of the fully developed economies before the end of the century. Nevertheless, since the mid-1970s the new cutting edge of economic growth in the region has moved west and south to: (1) South Korea, Taiwan, Hong Kong and Singapore; (2) the resource-rich countries in Southeast Asia (Malaysia, Thailand, Indonesia and, since 1992, the Philippines); and (3) the People's Republic of China.

Neither theoreticians or practitioners of development have been able to agree on a definitive set of answers to the question of how economic growth occurs. Clearly, however, there must be substantial investment in public and private infrastructure, and this requires a high rate of savings and effective means of channeling savings into productive investment. The labor force must be better educated and trained. Technology must be upgraded and foreign exchange receipts increased to buy needed raw materials and technology from

abroad. The government must provide a stable political climate and a relatively predictable policy environment to encourage economic activities.

No countries have met these challenges more successfully than Japan and the newly industrialized economies (NIEs) of East Asian and Southeast Asia — Hong Kong, Singapore, South Korea, and Taiwan. Why have these economies been so spectacularly successful? There may be disagreement on the weight that should be placed on different factors, but there is consensus on some main elements in the East Asian and Southeast Asian economic success stories.

First, the international orientation of the economies of Japan and the NIEs allowed them to exploit opportunities in a generally favorable world economic environment and to overcome limitations in the domestic market. Exports have been encouraged through favorable tax and credit treatment, the monitoring of export opportunities, and realistic foreign exchange rates.

Second, the East Asian economies had a substantial start on economic modernization during the prewar period. This is obviously true of Japan, which by the 1930s had an industrial base sufficient to fight a major war. Much of this was destroyed in the war, but considerable progress had already been made in developing a modern

Structural Change: Korea and Taiwan
Percentage Labor Force in Sectors

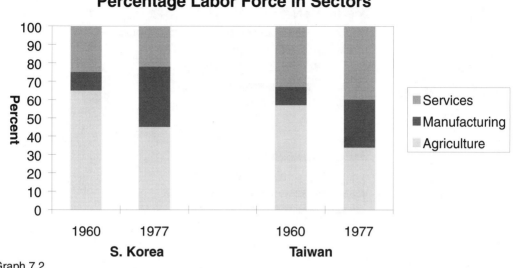

Graph 7.2

industrial infrastructure, acquiring managerial and technical expertise, and training the labor force. In South Korea and Taiwan the colonial experience, for all its repugnant aspects, did result in the development of rural infrastructure including roads, irrigation works, electrification, and farm organizations, all of which bolstered agricultural production and laid the groundwork for decentralized industrialization. Hong Kong and Singapore, as colonial entrepôt centers, also had benefited from the early development of commercial and educational infrastructure.

A third factor has been political consensus on economic development as an overriding national objective, which except in the case of Hong Kong justified a strong governmental role in charting and guiding economic growth. In Japan, catching up with the West had long been a national goal both before and after the war, and it was only in the late 1960s, when this task was essentially completed, that other values such as environmental protection and leisure time became more important. In South Korea and Taiwan economic growth was seen as an aid in achieving political goals of strengthening and legitimizing the government. The Singapore government also placed great emphasis on the need for economic modernization as a key in Singapore's struggle for national "survival."

It has frequently been noted that the developmental orientation of Japan and the NIEs was facilitated by a combination of sociopolitical characteristics unusual in developing economies: (1) the absence of wealthy landowning classes, which are often biased against industrialization and may siphon off surpluses derived from increased agricultural productivity; (2) relatively weak labor movements; and (3) strong economic bureaucracies with considerable independence in shaping policies. Except in Hong Kong, the government's role was particularly prominent in the early stages of industrial development. Close government-business relations, protection of infant industries (that is, start-up industries that are not yet able to stand up to large, international competitors), vigorous promotion of exports, government guidance in directing credits and foreign exchange to favored industries, and the establishment of public sector enterprises are characteristic of most East Asian economies.

Fourth, there has been a high degree of political stability: all of the independent East Asian and Southeast Asian high-growth economies have been ruled by centrist or conservative political forces that have favored close alignment with Western countries. There has been strong authoritarian control in some cases. This stability has meant predictability and consistency in government policy, which

Growth in the NIEs

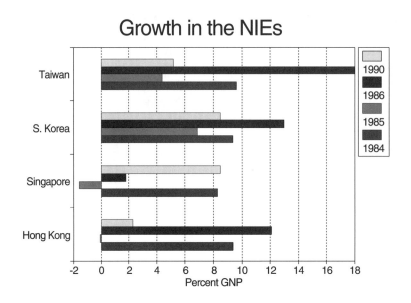

☐	1990
■	1986
▨	1985
■	1984

Graph 7.3 Economic slumps in the mid-1980s illustrate the difficulties of upgrading small economies like Singapore and Hong Kong.

encourages private savings and long-term investment. Profits have remained to be invested at home. Uncertainty about the political order, as in South Korea after the assassination of Park Chung Hee or in Hong Kong just prior to the Sino-British agreement of 1984 on the colony's future, have been associated with economic recessions.

Perhaps the most elusive factor is the cultural one. Japan and the newly industrialized economies are said to share Confucian values, which emphasize hard work, savings, discipline, secularism, entrepreneurship, and educational attainment. Such values do not automatically lead to economic development in the absence of other necessary conditions and policies, but they may encourage an orientation that is conducive to the formulation of policies at the public level and modes of behavior in the private sector that promote economic growth. The "Confucian factor" is taken up later in this chapter.

The Newly Industrialized Economies (NIEs)

The economies of South Korea and Taiwan have undergone profound structural change in the past three decades. These economies are today so

thoroughly identified with exports of industrial goods that it is difficult to recall that as recently as 1960 both could be described as natural resource-based economies. In 1960 the agricultural sector provided 37 percent of South Korea's domestically derived production (gross domestic product, or GDP) and 33 percent of Taiwan's. Primary products, mostly farm goods, accounted for 86 percent of South Korea's exports and 73 percent of Taiwan's. By 1983, however, agriculture's share of GDP had dropped to 14 percent in South Korea and 9 percent in Taiwan. Industry's share in South Korea had increased in 1960 from 20 percent to 40 percent of GDP, and in Taiwan from 25 percent to 44 percent. Industrial goods now account for more than 90 percent of the exports of both economies. No other developing countries have experienced such a remarkable shift of economic structure over such a short period of time.

This economic transformation owed its initial impetus to increased agricultural productivity, which provided surplus labor for the manufacturing sector and generated savings that were turned into productive investments. In the early 1960s both South Korea and Taiwan had adopted import-substitution, industrial developmental strategies, encouraging the growth of domestic

TAIWAN

Japan's first overseas possession, Taiwan was intensively developed and rigorously administered by the Japanese colonial bureaucracy. Japanese colonial policies were in large part shaped by the needs and interests of the home islands rather than those of the Taiwanese, who were permitted little voice in the management of the Colony. This colonial relationship was reflected in the Japanese policy slogan "Agricultural Taiwan-Industrial Japan." Nevertheless, Japanese colonialism yielded substantial benefits to the Taiwanese. Under Kodama Gentaro, the fourth governor-general, and his energetic and talented civil administrator, Goto Shimpei, a series of administrative and economic reforms were carried out in the early 1900s, marking the initial stage of the remarkable modernization and economic growth that the island enjoyed under Japanese rule over the next forty years.

Through the 1920s Taiwan played an important role in satisfying Japan's growing demands for agricultural products and raw materials. In the 1930s, as Japan began to prepare for war, Taiwan was intensively developed as an industrial base. Early in the Pacific War the island was a staging area for Japanese offensives into Southeast Asia, but by 1944 Taiwan came under heavy American aerial attack. On 25 October 1945 Japan surrendered Taiwan to the government of China in accordance with the Cairo Declaration of 1943. Misrule and oppression by rapacious Chinese troops resulted in the bloody Taiwanese uprising of 1947 and the brief formation of an autonomous republic. This was quickly suppressed by Chinese troops.

In 1949, as the Chinese Communists took power on the mainland, the Nationalist regime of Chiang Kai-shek and the remnants of his army escaped to Taiwan. Initially, the US government refused to provide military protection, but two days after the outbreak of the Korean War on 27 June 1950, President Truman ordered the Seventh Fleet to protect Taiwan from Communist attack. This presidential directive prevented the Communists from uniting Taiwan with the mainland. As a result, the governments in both Beijing and Taipei (Taibei) continue to claim to be the legitimate authority for all of China.

Retreating from the Communist victory on the mainland in 1949, Chiang Kai-shek established the seat of government of the Republic of China (ROC) in Taipei. As president, he was responsible for perpetuating the policy of mainland recovery and rejecting all compromises with the People's Republic of China (PRC). In maintaining his claim to represent all of China, Chiang reorganized the government to place more control in the hands of the mainlanders. This policy created tensions between the mainlander refugees (about two million) and the Taiwanese (about nine million). Security controls were increased and martial law was employed against both Communist and Taiwanese "rebels." Since Chiang concentrated on military and political preparations for retaking the Chinese mainland, he delegated the economic policies to a pragmatic group of technocrats. As military reconquest became an improbable dream and Chiang aged, he withdrew into an austere and ascetic life. He died on 5 April 1975 at the age of eighty-seven. His body is temporarily interred near Taipei, awaiting a final resting place in China.

Following Chiang Kai-shek's death, power was turned over to his son Chiang Ching-kuo. He [did] not abandon his father's ultimate goal of mainland recovery, but actively concentrated on economic reforms, reindustrialization, and modernization. Under Chiang Ching-kuo, Taiwan became more than just a province of China supporting a hostile competitor to Beijing. Reelected in 1984 to another six-year term, Chiang Ching-kuo chose the Taiwanese-born technocrat Lee Deng-hui to be vice president. The "taiwanization" of the political regime is a major issue for the leaders of the Republic of China.

Economically, the island has shown spectacular growth. Success has been made possible by the strong Japanese legacy, substantial U.S. aid, an energetic land reform program, state intervention, and a growing class of technocrats.

— Richard C. Kagan, *EAH*

SINGAPORE

Singapore and Penang were the staging areas for British economic penetration of the Malay Peninsula. Chinese miners and planters, moving in from the Straits Settlements, pioneered the economic development of the peninsula. In the 1870s, when conflicts between different groups of miners arose, the British government intervened and extended its political hegemony over the Malay states of the peninsula.

By the beginning of the twentieth century, Singapore had been displaced by Kuala Lumpur as the administrative center of the British colonies in the federated and unfederated Malay states. But as the terminus for the Malay railroad system and as the banking and commercial center of the region, Singapore retained its primary role as the economic capital of the British empire in the Malay world.

The ease with which Singapore was taken by the Japanese in 1942 demonstrated the uselessness of trying to maintain such a colony if the state did not already control the surrounding air and sea routes. Following the war, the British began the process of decolonization. With its overwhelming Chinese population, Singapore was seen as incompatible with the political aspirations of the Malays. Thus, the Federation of Malaya remained administratively separate from Singapore, and each began to develop its own political structure. The 1950s were marked by outbreaks of communal violence between Malays and Chinese as well as by British moves to destroy communist or socialist movements in both Singapore and the Federation of Malaya.

As Singapore moved toward independence in the 1950s, a number of political parties emerged, among them the Socialist Front (Barisan Sosalis) and the People's Action Party (PAP). The latter was led by Lee Kuan Yew, a London-trained lawyer who by the early 1960s had emerged as the clear victor in the power struggle to dominate the new state. Following a one-year attempt to rejoin Singapore to the rest of former British Malaya in the Federation of Malaysia, Lee led Singapore to full independence in 1965. The PAP and Lee then dominated Singapore into the 1980s. During these years the island republic made the transition from entrepôt to an export-oriented manufacturing center and attained an impressive degree of economic progress.

—Carl A. Trocki, *EAH*

---

manufacturing through import protection or subsidies. However, these policies gave way at a rather early stage to policies designed to encourage outward-oriented, export-based industries founded on the comparative advantages in labor. This did not mean that previous import-substitution programs were dismantled, but that policies discriminating against exports were eliminated or altered. Exporters were given subsidized credits and were exempted from duties on imported capital goods and raw materials. Exchange controls and multiple exchange rates were abolished, and many quantitative restrictions on imports were lifted.

The export-oriented industrial strategies of the NIEs helped them overcome the limitations of their relatively small domestic markets, but also placed them among the world's most highly trade-dependent economies. Lacking the basic raw materials for industry, the NIEs carved out a special place in the world economy as manufacturing centers, making full use of their comparative advantage in relatively abundant and disciplined labor. Later, as population growth began to fall and surplus labor from the agricultural sector diminished, labor-intensive manufacturing industries began to lose their advantage to more capital and technology-intensive industries.

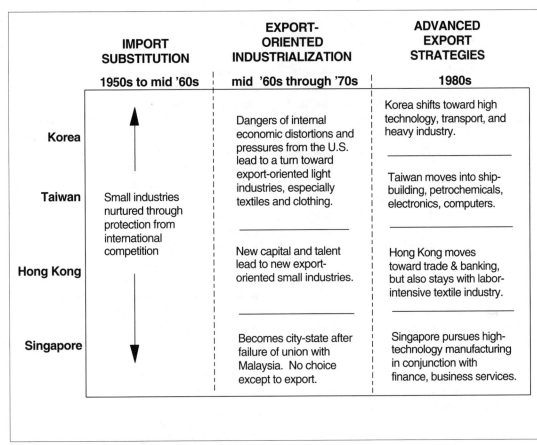

	IMPORT SUBSTITUTION	EXPORT- ORIENTED INDUSTRIALIZATION	ADVANCED EXPORT STRATEGIES
	1950s to mid '60s	mid '60s through '70s	1980s
Korea		Dangers of internal economic distortions and pressures from the U.S. lead to a turn toward export-oriented light industries, especially textiles and clothing.	Korea shifts toward high technology, transport, and heavy industry.
Taiwan	Small industries nurtured through protection from international competition		Taiwan moves into ship-building, petrochemicals, electronics, computers.
Hong Kong		New capital and talent lead to new export-oriented small industries.	Hong Kong moves toward trade & banking, but also stays with labor-intensive textile industry.
Singapore		Becomes city-state after failure of union with Malaysia. No choice except to export.	Singapore pursues high-technology manufacturing in conjunction with finance, business services.

Graph 7.4   Changing economic strategies of the NIEs.

The critical economic challenges the two economies now face derive from their heavy dependence on external trade and from the uncertainties inherent in their current transition away from labor-intensive industries. Because the growth sectors in their economies are so dominated by exports of manufactured goods and so dependent on raw materials and fuels from abroad, the NIEs have become highly vulnerable to international economic conditions. Access to supplies at favorable prices was threatened by the two oil shocks in the 1970s, but despite short-term economic difficulties both economies were able to compensate by increasing exports. A more difficult adjustment was required by the recession in the early 1980s, which affected demand in export markets. By the mid-1980s, as exports boomed again, both economies had weathered this crisis, but the boom increased their dependence on the U. S. market.

Uncertainty about exports has augmented longer term problems associated with upgrading industries. The economic authorities in both countries believe the development of more capital and technology-intensive industries is needed to compensate for the decline of the NIEs' labor advantages. In Taiwan, however, business caution about the viability of new industries and concern about the greater initial investments required to develop new product lines in competition with producers in Japan and other developed countries have discouraged investment.

South Korea probably faces more serious adjustments. Its home industries have received more protection and subsidies than those of Taiwan. Moreover, South Korea more explicitly sought to follow the Japanese path, emphasizing heavy industries such as steel, shipbuilding, and automobile manufacturing, which entail heavy investments. The small business and agricultural sectors have been relatively less developed, and the large-scale industries accounting for more than a quarter of South Korean income are controlled by a small and rich new business elite. Unlike Taiwan, South Korea had a low rate of domestic savings at the beginning of its industrialization process. Although domestic savings had increased from 1 percent of GDP in 1960 to 26 percent by 1983, investment has exceeded savings, requiring substantial borrowing from abroad. Some economic projects, including harbor improvements and hydroelectric and nuclear power projects, have been delayed to avoid incurring new debts.

The two smaller NIEs, Hong Kong and Singapore, are city-states whose per capita incomes (US$ 21,650 and US$ 23,360 respectively, in 1994 using the World Bank Atlas method) have increased so quickly that they are the only economies in the developing world to have effectively closed the absolute gap between their income levels and those of the industrialized nations of the north. Both cities play a prominent role as regional centers for financial and other services. Their developmental strategies, however, have differed considerably. Hong Kong has been a free trade economy whose colonial government has believed in a minimum of government regulation of the economy. Singapore experimented briefly with an import-substitution strategy of industrialization in the mid-1960s but subsequently abandoned it in favor of export growth. Its government has been much more actively involved in economic development, establishing state corporations and playing a crucial role in setting wage rates. Whereas investment in Hong Kong has been led by domestic capital, Singapore's industrialization has relied more heavily on foreign investment.

Both economies have experienced economic difficulties in recent years, a result of the general recession in the early 1980s and other special factors. In Hong Kong uncertainty over the outcome of Sino-British negotiations on the colony's future affected investor confidence and has led to some capital flight. Singapore benefited to some extent from Hong Kong's difficulties in the early 1980s, but by 1985 the Singaporean economy was seriously troubled. Its petrochemical and petroleum-refining industries were depressed by a worldwide glut in supplies. Singapore's role as a refining center, the world's third largest, was undercut by new competitive facilities in the oil-producing countries of the Middle East, Indonesia, and Malaysia until the Gulf War in early 1991 led to a boom in Singapore refining. Electronics, another growth industry in Singapore, consisted mainly of subsidiaries of Western companies and was depressed in the mid-1980s as the U.S. industry began undergoing a major restructuring. Shipbuilding and repairing has been adversely affected by excess capacity.

Although Singapore's mid-1980s economic slump was short-lived, it illustrates the difficulties of upgrading a small economy. In the late 1970s the Singapore government encouraged large across-the-board wage increases to give priority to more capital and technology-intensive activities; this policy is now thought by some to have priced Singaporean labor too high.

The Resource-rich Economies of Southeast Asia

The members of ASEAN (the Association of Southeast Asian Nations) comprise Brunei, Burma, Indonesia, Laos, Malaysia, the Philippines, Singapore, Thailand, and Vietnam. The smallest, Brunei, is an oil-rich sultanate with a per capita income that had already reached approximately US$ 20,000 annually by the mid-1980s. Another, Singapore, has been described as a rapidly growing, newly industrialized economy. The remaining four ASEAN countries (known as ASEAN-4) — Indonesia, Malaysia, the Philippines, and Thailand — are middle-income countries (using the World Bank classification) with 1994 per capita annual average incomes ranging from US$ 880 for Indonesia to US$ 3,520 for Malaysia. All are comparatively rich in terms of primary products. Agricultural and mineral products, such as petroleum (for Indonesia and Malaysia), tin, rubber, palm oil, coconut products, rice, sugar, and tapioca have been the mainstays of their economies.

The ASEAN-4 economies have had high rates of growth and have undergone structural transformation, although the degree of change has been less rapid than for the NIEs. Thailand has had the best overall growth performance, with average

Average Annual GDP Growth of ASEAN
In Constant Prices, 1950-85

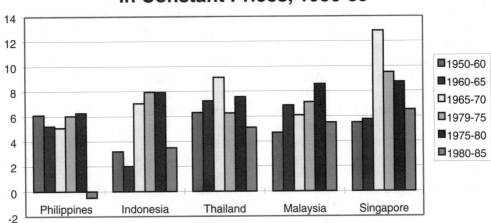

Graph 7.5

annual real per capita income increasing by 4.2 percent between 1965 and 1989. Malaysia at 4.0 percent and Indonesia at 4.4 percent have also done well, Indonesia having leapt ahead after a slow start before 1966. The Philippines has the poorest record among these countries, with per capita income increasing by an average annual 1.6 percent between 1965 and 1989. This would be a respectable performance in any other region, but it is less satisfactory in comparison to its neighbors and was tarnished by a serious economic in the 1980s.

The share of national income contributed by agriculture has declined over the past quarter century in all of the ASEAN-4 economies and now is in the 20 percent to 25 percent range, although half or more of the labor force is working in agriculture. During the same period agricultural production has expanded more rapidly than population growth in all four countries, although only one (Thailand) is self-sufficient in food. The growth of Malaysia's food production, about 50 percent per capita during the 1970s, reflects the introduction of high-yielding plants, a doubling in the application of fertilizers, and high government priority on programs to help the rural sector, whose predominantly Malay popu-

lation has considerable political power. Thailand has succeeded in diversifying its agricultural sector from rice into higher-value crops, such as tapioca maize, pineapples, and sugar, and into fish farming. Increased food production in Thailand, however, has depended heavily on the expansion of arable land — now reaching its limits — and the yields for some staples have been lower than in other Southeast Asian countries. Thailand has begun to shift to an agricultural strategy emphasizing increased productivity on available land.

Indonesia's achievement of rice self-sufficiency in the 1980s has been one of the most impressive agricultural performances in the Asia-Pacific region. During the 1970s and 1980s, rice output increased by nearly 5 percent annually, and yields now exceed the Southeast Asian and South Asian average. This is a consequence of the availability of fast-maturing seeds, incentives for increased fertilizer use, and multiple cropping made possible by expanded irrigation. The Philippines also concentrated on achieving self-sufficiency in rice, reaching this goal in the 1970s. However, its agricultural sector suffered setbacks along with the rest of its economy until the mid-1990s, necessitating periodic rice imports.

Economic growth in rural areas is essential, both to provide employment opportunities for a still rapidly expanding labor force and to increase demand for the expanding manufacturing sector. The manufacturing sector has become more important in exports, already accounting for 62 percent of the value of the Philippines' exports by 1989 (compared with 6 percent in 1965), 54 percent of Thailand's (from 3 percent in 1965), 44 percent of Malaysia's (from 6 percent in 1965), and 32 percent of Indonesia's (from 4 percent in 1965). The Philippines was the first ASEAN country to develop import-substitution industries in the 1950s and 1960s, protecting them through high tariffs, exchange controls, and an overvalued exchange rate. Although deregulation began in the 1960s and a period of relatively rapid growth occurred in the 1970s, the lagging rural economy acted as a drag, failing to create sufficient income or savings to sustain overall growth. As the limits of the domestic market were reached, industrial expansion lost momentum. Recognizing this at the beginning of the 1980s, the Philippine government sought to promote manufactured exports, but the industrial sector remained biased toward production of capital-intensive and final-stage consumer goods, a legacy of the earlier period. The protectionism surrounding these inefficient domestic-based industries is being reduced.

In the early 1980s, the Philippine economy was buffeted by declining terms of trade for primary product exports, such as copper, sugar, and coconut products, and by high inflation and a heavy external debt. A massive capital outflow and the near collapse of the banking system following the assassination of Benigno Aquino in August 1983 (described in chapter 8) propelled the country into a full-scale economic crisis. In 1984 a financial rescue package was negotiated with the International Monetary Fund requiring a number of politically difficult reforms. The Philippines permitted the peso to fall, adopted an austerity budget, reduced trade restrictions, and disbanded some monopoly arrangements in the agricultural sector but then failed to implement these reforms effectively. Unlike that in the NIEs, the economic bureaucracy in the Philippines has been weak. Broader development goals frequently have been subordinated to the self-interest of those with political influence, but reforms enacted after 1992 have reduced the protection afforded local industries and have stimulated new foreign investment.

In contrast to the Philippines, Indonesia's economy was buoyed in the 1970s by the rising price of petroleum, by far its principal export. The post-1966 Suharto government brought political stability and macroeconomic reforms, such as the freeing of foreign exchange markets and the imposition of budgetary discipline. The industrial sector grew at an average annual rate of 11 percent between 1970 and 1982, although this was more a product of the oil boom than of the planning process. Support was provided through import restrictions and the heavy subsidization of public enterprises and large-scale, capital-intensive projects, such as the Asahan aluminum project in Sumatra and the Cilegon cold-rolling steel mill. Heavy bureaucratic controls, a legacy dating from Dutch colonialism, remained characteristic of the Indonesian economy.

This approach did little to improve the competitiveness of Indonesian manufacturing, which remains oriented toward the protected domestic market. Indonesia's capital-intensive industries have limited ability to provide employment for the growing labor force or to generate related economic activities. Petroleum exports had contradictory economic effects, providing the foreign exchange needed for development projects but also helping to maintain a high value for the rupia, thus undermining the competitiveness of Indonesia's other exports and its manufactured goods in their home markets.

When oil revenues began to decline sharply in the 1980s Indonesia devalued its currency, canceled some large-scale projects, cut subsidies for consumer goods, such as domestic fuel and rice, and initiated reforms of its banking and financial institutions, its tax system, and the management of its customs, tariffs, and harbors. Efforts to diversify exports have had some success; textile and plywood exports have grown rapidly. The abundance of natural resources and low-cost labor are definite assets. How these physical and human resources are used will determine the pace and direction of growth. In the aftermath of the oil bonanza Indonesia has demonstrated considerable ability to carry through new policy directions in a less favorable economic environment.

THE NEW NIEs

Japan is fond of employing the metaphor of a flock of geese flying in a "V" formation to describe the way it would like to see East Asia's economy develop. Japan is out there in the lead, followed at a respectful distance by the NIEs — South Korea, Taiwan, Hong Kong and Singapore. The poorer members of ASEAN (Indonesia, Thailand, Malaysia and the Philippines) take up the rear. The metaphor appeals to the Japanese sense of harmony, but these particular geese are a bit more unruly than the image suggests. Some of the laggards are catching up on the leaders.

. . . The growth of GDP in Malaysia and Thailand is expected to exceed that of the NIEs. Even the economy of lumbering Indonesia will probably expand [at about] the same rate as those of Singapore and South Korea. As a result, the "V" formation is flattening slightly and there are at least three good reasons to think that its shape is changing permanently.

The first is that the economies of Malaysia and Thailand have "taken off" in the sense that industrialization is accelerating at a rate comparable with the speed at which South Korea and Taiwan built up their manufacturing bases in the early 1970s. In Thailand, manufacturing output has grown at an annual rate of more than 16 percent a year since 1988 and at an even faster pace in Malaysia.

The second factor is demographic: the population of the proto-NIEs is younger than that of the "old" NIEs. Their labor forces are growing faster as a result. Malaysia's pool of labor is expected to expand by 2.9 percent a year in the 1990s, five times faster than Singapore's. The NIEs, therefore, have to produce more goods and services per worker than countries like Thailand simply to grow at the same rate.

Third, foreign investment has been pouring into Malaysia, Thailand and Indonesia over the past five years or so. It has provided a much bigger impetus to growth in these three countries than in Taiwan and South Korea, but not as much as in Singapore, 80 percent of whose manufacturing investment comes from abroad.

The NIEs themselves are slowing down for similar reasons to those that caused the rate of Japanese economic expansion to halve after the first oil shock of 1973. One reason is that services are growing as a proportion of their economies and annual productivity gains have therefore halved.

Can Malaysia, Thailand and Indonesia keep it up? Many people say "no," because their inadequate infrastructure is expected eventually to strangle economic growth. In actual fact, however, this kind of bottleneck tends to cap the rate of expansion rather than to cut it drastically.

As for the three factors mentioned earlier, the first, industrialization, tends to take on a momentum of its own. Once economies become less dependent on the production of raw materials, opportunities for trade and specialization tend to grow exponentially. Demographics — the second factor — looks set to support rapid economic growth well into the next century.

Foreign investment seems more problematical. On the face of it, the capital flow from Japan and the NIEs depends on the vagaries of exchange rates. But it will probably continue to infuse Malaysia, Thailand and Indonesia for the foreseeable future. The savings surplus is dwindling rapidly in Japan and Taiwan, and has disappeared in South Korea, but capital from all three of these countries will continue to look for cheaper homes in the rest of Asia.

If this admittedly rosy prospect is correct, East Asian economic integration is about to enter a new phase. The first was the supply of raw materials to Japan by the poor countries of the region. The second phase, now nearing its end, is the supply of components to Japan. The next stage is the export of finished goods, not just from the NIEs, but from countries like Thailand and Malaysia, too. The geese are still flying Japan's way.

— Nigel Holloway, *Far Eastern Economic Review*

Malaysia's Changing Export Structure
by Commodity Classification

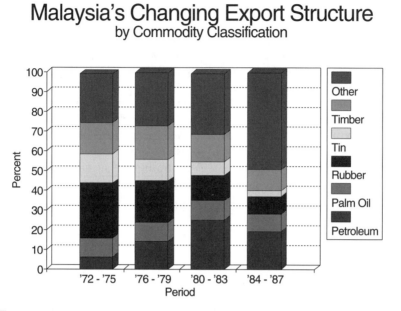

Graph 7.6   The changing structure of Malaysia's export economy indicates its transition toward a stronger industrial base that promises to place the nation, along with Thailand, in the category of a NIE within a few years.

In both Thailand and Malaysia there has been relatively steady industrial growth. Manufacturing was initially related to processing primary products, such as vegetable oils, finished wood products, and rubber products. More recently, new, mostly light industries, such as electronics and textiles, have appeared, which use few local materials but exploit the two countries' competitive advantages in labor. In Malaysia, in particular, there has been a heavy emphasis on manufacturing for export from free-trade zones. The business communities of both countries have continued to be dominated more by traders than by industrialists. Partly for this reason import protection has been relatively mild, with some exceptions.

Today, the Malaysian and Thai governments stress larger-scale industrial projects, such as Malaysia's ambitious scheme to become an automobile manufacturer and Thailand's plan to develop an industrial center along its eastern seaboard (adjacent to new gas fields) as an alternative to Bangkok. The hope is that these new ventures will complement rather than displace light indus-

tries and the incentive policies that enabled them to flourish. These ventures are locally controversial, some opponents arguing that too rapid a leap into more capital-intensive production — relying on imported materials, equipment, technology, and management — may run counter to comparative advantage and soon come up against the kinds of constraints and needs for adjustments experienced by South Korea (described later in this chapter).

The ASEAN-4 countries have had remarkable success on many other fronts related to economic development. They have reduced population growth, improved their educational systems, and strengthened the quality of other public services. Some measures of social welfare, including access to safe water, availability of medical care, and increased food supply, have shown remarkable improvement. On the other hand, the benefits of economic growth have not been shared as equitably as in the East Asian countries. Measurements of income distribution from the late 1980s cited by the World Bank show that the poorest 20 percent of the population received only 4.6 percent of

DOES RAPID ECONOMIC GROWTH IN ASIA THREATEN THE PROSPERITY OF DEVELOPED COUNTRIES?

There has been ambivalence in the Western advanced countries about the rapid growth and industrialization of the Asia-Pacific region. Some fear the continuing strong Asian economic and export performance threatens the prosperity of their own countries. This fear frequently underlies the protectionist sentiments growing in some Western economies. There are good reasons to be wary of protectionist thinking, however.

- The Asia-Pacific region has become a center of dynamic economic development; therefore, countries that adopted protectionist policies would partly isolate themselves from the benefits of increased economic efficiency, reduced prices, and expanded consumer choice that become available with freer trade.

- As economic growth continues in the Asia-Pacific region, its economies become increasingly important markets for the exports of other countries. Because of the growth of incomes in the region, for example, the share of U.S. exports purchased by Asian developing countries has increased significantly. The share and amount of U.S. products purchased by Japan has also been growing.

- Opportunities for high return on direct investments expand with dynamic growth in Asia-Pacific economies. These investments provide incomes and may help expand markets for investors while providing recipient countries with the capital and technology needed for continued growth.

- Economic growth in Asia and the Pacific has improved the political and security environment there to the benefit of the entire world. Countries in the region contribute positively to maintaining the security of their region, reducing the burden on outside powers. As they have developed economically, foreign aid provided to these countries on political, security, and humanitarian grounds has decreased.

Imports from Asia-Pacific countries have hurt specific industries in the United States and Western Europe and are beginning to affect some industries in Japan, but they are helpful and not harmful to the national prosperity of these countries when they are based on comparative advantage as determined by market forces. Most economic studies show that more jobs are gained than lost as a result of freer trade and that protectionism results in reduced economic momentum and income growth.

household income in Malaysia, 6.5 percent in the Philippines, 6.1 percent in Thailand, and 8.7 percent in Indonesia. Rapid aggregate growth may increase the absolute incomes of the poor, but less directly and not as much as those in middle- and higher-income categories, thus increasing internal income gaps. This, however, is a problem the region's policymakers recognize and are trying to address.

The ASEAN-4, with the exception of Malaysia, have potentially large internal markets. Savings are slightly higher than the average for countries at a similar socioeconomic level and investment rates are even higher. Except for the Philippines, most have financed this gap prudently by borrowing cautiously in international markets. In general, their governments have consciously sought to improve their economic performances.

Income Inequality and the Growth of GDP in Developing Economies

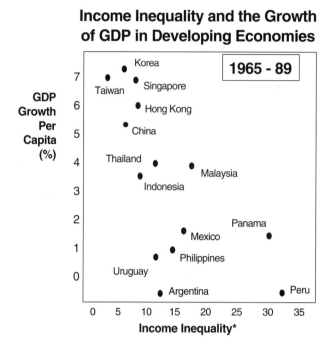

* Income inequality is the ratio of the income shares of the richest 20 percent and poorest 20 percent of the population. Data on income distribution are from surveys conducted mainly in the 1960s and early 1970s.

Graph 7.7

The somewhat slower aggregate growth performances among the ASEAN-4, compared with the NIEs, can be partly attributed to their larger agricultural sectors in which expansion is slower. It may also reflect their more pluralistic societies. Growth objectives often have come into conflict with other more pressing political needs, and there has been less opportunity for the development of a strong economic bureaucracy that is autonomous from domestic political forces opposed to growth. Given these constraints they have had remarkable growth and, except for the Philippines where economic technocrats are trying to encourage fundamental reforms in a difficult domestic and international environment, a continuing high growth rate can be anticipated in this region.

Equity and Redistribution

Economic policies in developing nations have strongly influenced the equality of income distribution within their populations. There are significant differences between the levels of income inequality in Pacific Asia and those in Latin America, as illustrated in the above graph. During the period in question, Latin American countries imposed discriminatory taxes on their farmers and protected their industries far more than did most of the Asian countries. Also, the fast developers in Asia invested heavily in widespread public education, regardless of sex or ethnicity. As a result, women in countries such as Malaysia and Indonesia entered the wage labor force in greater numbers; a factor in improved income distributions. Successful land reform, which raises the incomes of the poor and contributes to social stability, was carried out successfully in Asian economies such as China, Japan, Korea, and Taiwan but not in Latin America or the Philippines.

The conventional wisdom has been that early stages of economic development require a high level of income inequality so that the wealthy elite will boost the nation's capital stock and fast growth will occur. The contrasting growth patterns of Asian and Latin American countries have contributed to a reevaluation of that assumption.[2]

Low-Income Economies of Southeast Asia

More than a hundred million people live in the low-income Southeast Asian economies of Burma (Myanmar), Vietnam, Kampuchea (Cambodia), and Laos. Burma, with more than forty million people, has been pursuing its own brand of socialism since 1962 and has one of the lowest standards of living in the world (less than US$ 250 per capita in 1994). After years of stagnation, in the late 1970s and early 1980s there was a period of growth in Burma exceeding 6 percent annually, fueled by increased rice production and exports. However, exports remained at a third of their highest prewar level. Foreign debt has increased rapidly, reaching more than US$ 4 billion by 1989; debt service payments equivalent to 30 percent of export value have encouraged Burma to diversify exports and increasingly to look abroad for foreign assistance. Until the late 1980s, no foreign investment existed in Burma and the government did not solicit investment despite its foreign capital needs. (Subsequently, companies in Thailand bought major timber-cutting concessions in Burma's rich tropical forests.) The private sector, theoretically nationalized in 1962, still accounts for more than half of production but current economic plans continue to call for a substantial increase in the state sector of the economy and a reduction in the private sector. Other indicators of socioeconomic development, such as longevity, access to clean water, and availability of medical care, are at far lower levels than in the ASEAN countries.

Vietnam also has had a serious foreign debt problem with little success in attracting foreign investment until it altered its investment laws in the 1990s. Early hopes that this country would concentrate on economic reconstruction following reunification were dashed by its 1978 invasion of Kampuchea (chapter 11) and by the mid-1980s more than 40 percent of Vietnam's budget was devoted to defense. Among Vietnam's many prob-

lems are fertilizer shortages, lack of petroleum for nonmilitary use, a poor transportation network, and inadequate power supplies. The most important economic priority is to continue to boost agricultural production. Like China, Vietnam has introduced a system allowing lands of the cooperatives to be tilled by individual families or small groups under a contract quota system.

Laos and war-torn Kampuchea have limited current economic prospects; maintaining an adequate food supply is the major economic problem for both, and they depend heavily on foreign assistance. Nevertheless, Kampuchea has long-term potential based on its endowment of rich agricultural lands.[3]

◆　　　◆　　　◆

KOREA'S ECONOMIC DEVELOPMENT IN HISTORICAL PERSPECTIVE, 1945-1990

— by Carter J. Eckert

The development of the South Korean economy is one of the great stories of the post-World War II era. It is a tale whose drama is heightened by breathtaking contrasts: a per capita GNP of about US$ 100 in 1963 versus a figure of nearly US$ 5,000 as the year 1990 began; a war-ravaged Seoul of gutted buildings, rubble, beggars, and orphans in 1953 versus the proud, bustling city of the 1988 Summer Olympics with its skyscrapers, subways, plush restaurants, boutiques, first-class hotels, and prosperous middle class; a country abjectly dependent on foreign aid in the 1950s versus a 1980s economic powerhouse - a factory to the world for everything from clothes, shoes, and electronic goods to steel, ships, and now even automobiles and semiconductors. Given these remarkable facts, it is not surprising that many popular writers and even a few scholars have taken to calling South Korea's economic transformation "the miracle on the Han."

The term "miracle," however, actually fails to do justice to the complexity of the story by implying that South Korea's growth was somehow contrary to reason or extraneous to history. Nothing, of course, could be further from the truth. Growth was stimulated and conditioned by a number of international, social, political, and cultural factors-all deeply grounded in Korean history. Indeed, even though the most visible and striking aspects of South Korean development occurred after 1961, the post-1961 period of rapid growth can be fully understood only in the context of a long historical process that began in the late nineteenth century. The process and impact of economic growth, moreover, have also posed some fundamental problems and challenges for South Korean society, culture, politics, and international relations that the "miracle" sobriquet tends to obscure.

INTERNATIONAL FACTORS

Historical Background

While the credit and responsibility for South Korean development ultimately rests with the Koreans themselves, the influence of foreign powers in shaping the country's economy has been extraordinary. Korea's crucial geopolitical position at the cross-roads of northeast Asia has brought the peninsula into intimate and sustained contact with two of the most dynamic and expansive economies of the twentieth century, Japan and the United States. From the Korean viewpoint especially, the contact has not always been a happy one, and many scholars in South Korea, let alone in the north, have argued that foreign interference before and after 1945 has worked to distort a natural development of the economy that was already underway in the late nineteenth century. Such a view is deeply tinted with nationalist feeling and laden with presuppositions about the nature of economic development, but it correctly emphasizes the extent to which economic growth on the peninsula has been conditioned by external forces.

What can hardly be denied, however, is that Korea's special historical relationships with the major core countries of the international capitalist system have played a key role in fostering economic growth, even if a number of Koreans have found certain aspects of that growth objectionable. What, then, were these special relationships?

And how have they affected the development of the South Korean economy?

Before the late nineteenth century, Korea's international orientation was toward China, and the interaction between the two countries was less economic than diplomatic and cultural. After the Hideyoshi Invasions of the late sixteenth century, Koreans regarded Japan with a wary eye, and even though diplomatic relations were restored with the Tokugawa shogunate in 1609, Japanese were never permitted to go beyond Pusan, and the shogun was obliged to communicate with the Korean court either through sporadic Korean embassies to Edo or through the medium of Tsushima, a Tokugawa island domain that also maintained a semi-tributary relationship with Korea. From the Korean perspective, Japan was a peripheral, even culturally inferior, member of the Sinitic world order, and although the shogun was formally accorded a status equal to the Korean king by Korean diplomats, Koreans in general never demonstrated the kind of interest in and respect for Japan that they historically showed for China.

All this changed with the Western invasion of East Asia in the 1800s. The dynamo of Western power and imperialism was its great capitalist industrial base, and East Asian history since the 1840s has to a large extent been an attempt to come to terms with this new global economic force. Japan's early success in this regard gave it military and economic superiority in the region and compelled the surrounding countries, including Korea, to emulate Japan's achievement or face the threat of Japanese hegemony. By the turn of the century, there were signs that both Korea's government and private sectors were finally

This section is taken with permission from *Korea Old and New: A History* by Carter J. Eckert, Ki-baik Lee, Young Ick Lew, Michael Robinson, and Edward W. Wagner (Seoul, Korea: Ilchokak Publishers, 1990). It is strongly recommended for those interested in further exploring Korean history.

Figure 7.1   In the vicinity of Seoul in the late nineteenth century.

beginning to reform the economy and society along Western (and Meiji Japanese) lines, but it is impossible to say where such reform would have led had it been allowed to continue. In the end, it proved to be too little and too late to stem the Japanese advance, and Korea became a Japanese colony in 1910.

Impact of Japan's Colonialism

It was thus Japanese colonialism that ultimately laid the foundations for a modern transformation of the economy. To be sure, colonial development was geared to Japanese, rather than Korean, goals and needs. But the changes effected were nevertheless historic. To appreciate how far reaching they were, one need only compare photographs of Seoul in the late Choson period with similar photographs taken in the mid-1930s. The former show a city that seems distant and alien to the modern eye — less a city, in fact, than an overgrown village of thatched-roof cottages that the famous nineteenth-century explorer Isabella Bird Bishop likened to an "expanse of overripe mushrooms." By contrast, pictures of Seoul in the 1930s show a city that is distinctly modern and familiar.

The altered face of Seoul was part and parcel of a general physical transformation of the country that occurred as colonial industry expanded with Japan's penetration of the Asian continent, especially in the 1930s and 1940s. Railways, roads, rice mills, textile factories, hydroelectric plants, smelters, oil refineries, shipyards, and even new cities were built to service the empire. The growth of manufacturing, in fact, averaged about 10 percent per year, and by 1940 about half of all factory production was in heavy industry, located mainly in the north. By any standards such industrial growth was impressive; in the context of colonial rule, it was exceptional, a clear reflection of Korea's vital strategic role as Japan's military-economic link to the Asian mainland. Much of this industrial base was later lost to South Korea through the peninsula's partition and civil war, but some important elements, including the railway system and the textile industry (centered in the south), remained as a framework for reconstruction in the 1950s and for rapid export-led growth in the 1960s.

The physical changes wrought by colonialism, however, were probably less important for later South Korean development than the accompanying social changes. A small population of Japanese dominated the modern, urban sector of the colonial economy, but by 1945 millions of Koreans had been induced or forced into new modes of life and thought by the industrialization process. Between 1910 and 1941, the number of Koreans living in cities of 20,000 people or more increased over threefold, from about 6 percent to 20 percent of the total population. Perhaps four million Koreans (about 16 percent of the population) were in Japan and Manchuria by 1945, and many of these people, especially the two million or more in Japan, were also living in cities.

Most of the new Korean urban populace consisted of factory wage workers who only a short time before had been tilling the land literally in the footsteps of their fathers and forefathers. As a political safety valve, however, the Japanese had also opened the door for a small number of Koreans to develop into a urban elite of businessmen, bureaucrats, white-collar workers, technicians, lawyers, doctors, and other modern professionals. Together the workers and the urban elite provided the social core and framework for a new capitalist society that continued to develop with American support and aid in the south after 1945.

Japan's Post-War Influence

Liberation ended Korea's colonial tie with Japan, and regular diplomatic relations between Seoul and Tokyo were not resumed until 1965, in part because of an implacable anti-Japanese stance by President Syngman Rhee. Private personal and professional relationships formed by Koreans and Japanese during the colonial period were by no means entirely severed, however, and for South Korea's elite, largely educated in the Japanese language, Japanese newspapers, magazines, and books continued to be a source of the latest information on everything from fashion to economic trends and industrial technology. Japan itself, moreover, remained a model of national and economic development for such people, especially as it began to reemerge as an important international economic force in the late 1950s and early 1960s. In that sense at least, the ROK-Japan Normalization Treaty, when it finally came in 1965, was less a break with the past than a resumption of an historic relationship under new conditions and on different terms. Indeed, although such a treaty had long been urged by the United States, South Koreans themselves took the initiative when the opportunity presented itself. Soon after Rhee was overthrown in 1960, South Korean official and private contacts with Japanese counterparts mushroomed, with Japanese-speaking Korean bureaucrats and businessmen of colonial vintage leading the way and working through a network of ex-colonial officials in Japan. And President Park Chung Hee, who was himself an elite product of the colonial military system, fluent in Japanese and deeply influenced both intellectually and emotionally by his training during Japan's period of Asian military industrial supremacy, seems to have needed little or no persuasion to continue this process after seizing power in 1961.

The normalization treaty of 1965 signaled the beginning of the second period of major Japanese influence on the Korean peninsula since the late nineteenth century, and opponents of the treaty in fact compared it to the forced Korea-Japan Kanghwa Treaty of 1876 that had first opened Korea's ports to international trade. In one sense the comparison was misleading, since it was the South Koreans who were initiating normalization in the early 1960s, though the Japanese themselves certainly welcomed such a treaty for both political and economic reasons. On the other hand, normalization once again opened the door to widespread Japanese activity in Korea, and the results in terms of economic ties between the two

Manufacturing Productivity

Index (1970 = 100)

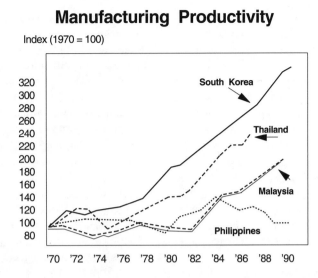

Graph 7.8   Korea's manufacturing productivity, boosted in part by heavy Japanese investment, has outpaced even the faster growing ASEAN nations.

countries were immediate and dramatic. ROK-Japan trade had been growing since the 1950s despite the lack of formal diplomatic relations, but until 1965 the preponderance of South Korea's trade had been with the United States. Within little more than a year after the signing of the normalization agreement, however, Japan surpassed the United States as South Korea's most important trading partner and continued to hold this position throughout the period of rapid growth in the 1960s and 1970s. Since 1971, moreover, Japan's investment in South Korea has been considerably greater than that of any other country, accounting for about 54 percent of all foreign investment since 1962 (compared to about 26 percent for the United States).

The benefits of normalization for South Korean economic growth were enormous. At a time when American aid was being reduced and the Park government was desperately seeking alternative sources of capital to finance its new development plans, the treaty provided South Korea with US$ 300 million in grants, US$ 200 million in public loans, and US$ 300 million in commercial credits (raised to US$ 500 million in 1967) over a ten-year period. In 1982 the Chun Doo Hwan regime negotiated a second loan agreement for US$ 4 billion with the Nakasone government that reaffirmed the Japanese economic

commitment to South Korea and eventually helped pay for the 1988 Summer Olympics in Seoul. Since 1965 Japanese private capital and technology have also flowed into South Korea in large quantities, propelling economic development. The recent triumph of the Hyundai subcompact car in the United States is a case in point: Mitsubishi owns about 10 percent of the Korean company and provides the car's engine and other key components.

The close economic interaction between South Korea and Japan has clearly been facilitated by geography. Seoul and Tokyo are only two hours apart by air and in the same time zone, and the economic advantages for both countries in terms of shipping costs and delivery times are obvious. Geographic proximity has also made the peninsula a continuing object of Japanese political and strategic concern and given Japan an incentive for contributing to the growth of a cooperative capitalist economy in South Korea.

Cultural similarity stemming from both countries' historical involvement with Chinese civilization and from the more recent heritage of colonialism has also played an important role in creating a special economic relationship. Language, for example, has been more of a bond than a problem. Since Korean and Japanese grammar and syntax are very similar in many respects and both written languages make use of borrowed Chinese characters, Koreans and Japanese can master each other's languages with relative ease; with its comparatively simple sound system, Japanese is in fact particularly easy for Koreans to learn, and more and more younger South Koreans have been studying Japanese in schools, universities, and private institutes as economic relations between the two countries have progressed. The generation that has dominated South Korea over the last twenty-five years, moreover, was educated for the most part in the Japanese language, and key government and business figures in both countries have consequently been able to deal with one another comfortably and confidently in the Japanese language.

In addition to a relative absence of language problems, the Japanese have found in South Korea a government-business structure and culture that is strikingly like their own — even down to the informal parties of wine, women, and song that invariably follow serious business discussions in both countries. They have also found a people who, though generally more direct and out-spoken, possess a similarly keen sense of hierarchy and status. Indeed, there is surely no other foreign country in the world perhaps not even Taiwan where the Japanese have felt more at home doing business than in South Korea.[4]

Today as Seoul is sprouting flashy new suburbs like Apkujong-dong that increasingly resemble Shinjuku and other districts of Tokyo, plans are being laid by American and South Korean authorities to move the American military command out of the central part of Seoul which it has occupied since 1945 and to return the command's 700-acre compound of offices, barracks, schools, landscaped homes, and myriad recreational facilities (including clubs, movie theaters, swimming pools, a full-scale library, a baseball diamond, and an 18-hole golf course) to South Korea. Somehow this conjunction of events seems appropriate and symbolic: in the long-term judgment of history, America's total economic impact on Korea will probably shrink in comparison with Japan's. Nevertheless, for a period of about thirty years between 1945 and the mid-1970s, the U.S. played a critical role in the South Korean economy. Most of this complex story has yet to be written, but the following points seem clear.

The first and perhaps most important point — so obvious as to be forgotten — is that the United States since 1945 has been the decisive factor in the creation and maintenance of a political environment on the Korean Peninsula in which South Korea's particular capitalist development has taken place. Such a political framework was first established in 1945-48 by the United States Army Military Government in Korea (USAMGIK). What needs to be emphasized is that without American backing in 1945, Korea's nascent capitalist class, tainted by colonial collaboration, would in all likelihood have been severely purged or swept away in the politics of liberation, and the capitalist system itself would, at the very least, have been greatly modified.

In 1950, the United States again intervened in Korea to push back a North Korean invasion and saved the existing capitalist system a second time. Since then the U.S. has signed a mutual defense treaty with South Korea (1953) and maintained tens of thousands of American troops and even tactical nuclear weapons on the peninsula, while pouring vast sums of money into the development of South Korea's own military forces. The construction of this massively fortified political citadel has been an important prerequisite for continued capitalist development of the peninsula, especially in the first two decades after liberation.

In addition to insuring a political environment conducive to capitalist development, the U.S. has directly or indirectly sought to foster economic growth in South Korea. To be sure, interest in Korea has from the beginning been political and strategic rather than economic: support for South Korea since 1945 has been part of a global containment (and occasional rollback) of international communism centered on the Soviet Union. Nevertheless, American policymakers have also tended to see the development of a strong capitalist economy in Korea (and elsewhere) as an integral part of their anticommunist strategy and have consequently provided South Korea with large amounts of the two things it has needed most: capital and technology.

Between 1946 and 1976 the U.S. supplied a total of US\$ 12.6 billion in economic and military assistance to South Korea — more dollars per capita of aid than to any other foreign country except South Vietnam and Israel. Although the growth rate achieved in the 1950s as a result of such assistance was only about 4 percent, American aid was clearly the crucial factor in South Korea's post-colonial economic survival between 1945-50 and in the country's postwar reconstruction after 1953. Indeed, between 1953 and 1962 American aid financed about 70 percent of South Korea's imports and accounted for nearly 80 percent of total fixed capital formation, mainly in the areas of transportation, manufacturing, and electric power. One of the most notable aid accomplishments was the resuscitation of the South Korean textile industry. Building on its colonial base, the textile industry experienced its most rapid expansion in history between 1953 and 1957, with growth rates averaging about 24 percent per year; by 1957 the industry had achieved complete import substitution in cotton, woolen, rayon, and knitted textiles and was beginning to explore possible export markets. Also worth noting is that nearly all of the American aid to South Korea before 1964 was provided on a grant basis, thus making it possible for the country to begin its export-led growth in the 1960s without a backlog of debt. Since then South Korea has gradually freed itself from a reliance on American economic grants, but it has continued to depend on U.S. support for concessional and commercial loans from the World Bank, the International Development Bank, the International Finance Corporation, and other international public and private lending institutions. American military aid, moreover, which totaled about US$ 6.8 billion in the thirty years after liberation (not including the military equipment supplied during the Korean War), has also been an important factor in economic growth by freeing domestic resources for development.

The influx of American capital into South Korea has been accompanied by a corresponding flow of American technology and technical expertise. Aid has helped finance technology transfers from American firms and the creation of official research and development organizations like the Korea Development Institute and the Korea Institute of Science and Technology (KIST), while the U.S. itself has since 1945 been the primary training ground for South Korean economic and industrial technocrats, many of whom have been supported by aid funds.

American economic experts and technicians associated with the U.S. AID Mission in South Korea have also played a key role in shaping the South Korean economy through their allocation of aid funds for specific projects and their participation in the formation and implementation of South Korean government development plans. While the full dimensions of this particular American contribution are only now being investigated by scholars, it is clear that the direct and personal involvement of Americans in the South Korean economy has been extraordinary. Indeed, in the early 1960s the U.S. AID Mission in South Korea was one of the largest in the world, and AID officials had full access to South Korean government information and personnel. American experts spoke of "tutoring" President Park in economics and did not hesitate to use AID funds as leverage to force the South Korean government into compliance with their economic suggestions.

The special U.S.-ROK relationship also gave South Korea privileged access to U.S. markets. Until recently the U.S. more or less accepted South Korean protectionist policies as a necessary part of the growth process and accorded many South Korean exports duty-free status under the General System of Preferences (GSP), a program instituted in 1976 to promote trade with developing countries. Although the U.S. has gradually been withdrawing such favors as ROK development has proceeded, the economic gains to South Korea over the years have been considerable. In 1987, when the U.S. drastically reduced the scope of the GSP, South Korea accounted for about 14 percent of all GSP preferences. Today South Korea sends about 40 percent of its exports to the U.S., and in 1987 it enjoyed a US$ 10 billion trade surplus with its former aid donor.

South Korea also reaped important economic benefits from its role as America's chief ally in the Vietnam War. In 1964-65 the Lyndon Johnson administration launched a major diplomatic effort to secure troop commitments for the war from European and Asian countries, both to create the impression of international solidarity with the United States on the war issue and also, secondarily, to reduce the burden on U.S. combat forces. Only Australia, New Zealand, the Philippines, Thailand, and South Korea responded positively, and South Korea eventually emerged as the most important contributor by far, dispatching a total of about 300,000 troops to Vietnam between 1965 and 1973.

In return, the South Koreans demanded and received a remarkable package of military and economic payments and perquisites formalized in the so-called Brown Memorandum of 1966 (Winthrop Brown was the U.S. ambassador to the ROK at the time). In addition to agreeing to equip, train, supply, and pay all the ROK forces used in Vietnam, the U.S. further agreed to modernize the ROK forces in South Korea itself and to suspend the program, instituted by the U.S. in the early 1960s, to shift the burden of American military aid to the ROK defense budget. The U.S. also promised additional AID loans to the ROK and pledged itself to procure from South Korea insofar as possible and practicable supplies, services, and equipment for the various military forces in Vietnam, as well as a "substantial amount of goods" required by the AID Mission in South Vietnam for its work in rural construction, pacification, relief, logistics, and other areas. South Korean contractors, moreover, were to be given "expanded opportunities" to participate in American construction projects in South Vietnam and to provide other services, including the employment of skilled Korean civilians.

Vietnam quickly developed into an economic bonanza for South Korea. Although rapid export-led economic development was already underway in the country by 1965, the Vietnam War boom, like the ROK-Japan Normalization Treaty, gave the economy an important lift during the critical take-off period — similar, in that sense, to what the Korean War did for Japan in the 1950s. In 1966 the war accounted for 40 percent of South Korea's crucial foreign-exchange receipts, and by 1970, the last year for which we have published data, the total U.S. payments to South Korea under the Brown Memorandum were estimated by the U.S. Department of Defense to be nearly US$ 1 billion.

The economic effects of South Korea's Vietnam's venture, moreover, went far beyond the simple acquisition of foreign exchange. Many South Korean business firms, including two of the largest business conglomerates or chaebol, Hanjin and Hyundai, got their first big economic boost from the war. Cho Chung-hun, Hanjin's founder, set up a land and marine transport company in South Vietnam and eventually assumed responsibility, with the blessing of the U.S. Army, for the whole operation of the port of Qui Nhon. In 1967 Cho also established an air and sea transport firm in South Korea, mainly to carry South Korean products and workers to South Vietnam; two years later he took over an ailing Korean Air Lines from the government and used the Vietnam trade to help turn the company around and elevate Hanjin into the ranks of the major chaebol by the mid-1970s.

The Hyundai story was no less spectacular. Hyundai and other South Korean construction companies became major contractors for the U.S. Army in South Vietnam and later made use of their Vietnam contacts and experience to expand into the international construction business, most notably in the Middle East. Between 1974 and 1979 South Korea's top ten chaebol took home nearly US$ 22 billion in Middle East construction sales, of which Hyundai's share alone was over US$ 6 billion.

INTERNAL SOCIAL AND POLITICAL FACTORS

Early Impediments to Development

External influence, however important, is not sufficient to explain South Korea's economic growth; internal factors have also been crucial. In many countries the existence of a powerful landed elite opposed to agrarian taxation and reform has been a serious historical impediment to industrialization, and we can appreciate the significance of this point by looking at the Philippines and numerous Central and South American countries even today. On the other hand, the fact that Japan's traditional elite was a stipended urban bureaucracy without binding economic ties to the land has often been cited as one of the main underlying reasons behind Meiji Japan's rapid transformation into an industrial society. Another problem for many countries has been the lack, for a variety of reasons, of a dynamic class of entrepreneurs and/or of a class of dependable, efficient industrial workers; without such critical social elements to support and sustain the growth process in a developing country, the injection of foreign capital and technology into the economy is likely to be wasted effort.

In the late nineteenth century Korea had one of the most entrenched landed aristocracies in the world, and the refusal of this class as a whole to countenance any serious change in the economic and political status quo was a major factor in the country's ultimate inability to meet the challenges of imperialism and ward off colonial domination. Colonialism removed this class from political power but strengthened and sustained it economically, so that in 1945, in spite of the existence of a new urban industrial sector built up largely by imported Japanese capital, the countryside was still dominated by the old landed elite. Nevertheless, by 1945 a progressive segment of this class had already begun to transfer some of its landed wealth into commerce and industry, and subsequent land reforms in South Korea under the American military government, North Korean occupation during the war, and the Syngman Rhee regime finally eliminated the landlords as a class and opened the door to full-scale industrialization of the South Korean economy.

Many post-reform landlords were, in fact, highly successful in making the transition to industrial society: a Harvard study conducted in 1976, for example, concluded that the vast majority of the country's business leaders have come from the landbased traditional elite. The process of transition, however, was not simply one of shifting assets from the land to urban enterprise. South Korean landlords were given government bonds denominated in rice as compensation for reform, but the bonds eventually lost about 90 percent of their value in the marketplace, largely because of the government's failure to redeem on schedule; they thus never provided a financial basis for landlord reinvestment in industry. Nevertheless, many landlords, anticipating reform, had already concluded satisfactory private sales with relatives and tenants by the time the reform was actually implemented , and even those landlords who were wiped out by the reform continued to retain the high level of education and the personal connections that have always been important factors for success in Korean society. In any case, by the mid-1950s not only was landlordism no longer an obstacle to economic growth, but former landlords themselves and their children were already well on their way to becoming businessmen or white-collar professionals of one kind or another.

Entrepreneurial Growth

Korean entrepreneurs have, in fact, been an important and constant part of the country's modern history, skillfully availing themselves of every major economic opportunity since the late nineteenth century. With the opening of Korea's ports in 1876, Korean landlords and commercial agents called *kaekchu* or *yogak* made fortunes in the new international trade in export rice and imported manufactures, thus initiating a process of capitalist accumulation and growth on the peninsula that continues in South Korea today. By the turn of the century, a number of these newly enriched Koreans were beginning to establish modern banks and commercial enterprises, but it was really the colonial period (especially after 1919) that saw the emergence of a nascent industrial capitalist class, which developed in cooperation with Japanese colonial economic interests. This story is perhaps best epitomized by the rise of the Kim family of Koch'ang County in North Cholla province from small enterprising landlords in the late nineteenth century to commercial and industrial magnates by 1945, but there were other similar, if less dramatic, cases of colonial entrepreneurship whose importance we can now more fully appreciate. No less than three of South Korea's top four *chaebol*, for example, were founded by men who began their business careers during the colonial period: Yi Pyong-ch'ol (Samsung), Ku In-hoe (Lucky), and Chong Chu-yong (Hyundai).

Since 1945, and especially since 1961, the process of capitalist growth has greatly accelerated in South Korea. Although there has been considerable entrepreneurial continuity throughout the post-1945 period and even extending back into the colonial period, each new economic opportunity since 1945 has also tended to spawn additional entrepreneurs, and some in each case have generally been able to carve out a lasting place in the economy. Broadly speaking, the main opportunities have come in connection with the following circumstances or events: the gradual sale of former Japanese properties by the South

Figure 7.2　Like a traditional Korean acrobat, depicted here in a performance in 1894, South Korea finds itself conducting a balancing act between the demand for foreign goods by its new "consumer society" and policies that discourage purchases of such goods.

Korean government at exceptionally favorable prices during the 1950s; the demand for goods and services (at inflated wartime prices) during the Korean War; the political economy of aid dependency and import substitution during the Rhee years, when fortunes could be made through the acquisition of foreign exchange, exclusive import licenses, public contracts, aid funds and materials, and cheap bank loans — all government-controlled; the new policies of export promotion after 1961, which gave exporters in targeted industries special licensing, tax, and financial privileges; the aforementioned economic environment created by South Korea's participation in the Vietnam War, and the subsequent construction boom in the Middle East, where South Korea captured almost 7 percent of the market and became the sixth largest international contractor in the region. By the mid-1980s, the combined sales of South Korea's top five chaebol (excluding intra-firm transactions) accounted for nearly 66 percent of GNP, and two of them, Samsung and Hyundai,

were, according to Fortune magazine, among the fifty largest business firms in the world.

The Korean Labor Force

Equally if not more important than such entrepreneurship in the development process has been the contribution of South Korea's workers. The growth of elementary and secondary schools during the colonial period and the participation of millions of Koreans in the pre-1945 industrialization of Korea, Japan, and Manchuria left the peninsula with an impressive pool of literate and experienced workers by 1945. Since then this pool has been continually enlarged in conjunction with the proliferation of new schools and the reconstruction and expansion of the manufacturing industry. Very few countries have been as blessed as South Korea with such a well-educated and adept working class in their early stages of development. Indeed, for so-called late- or late-late-developing countries like South Korea, where success in the international market depends to no small degree on the ability of the country's workers to adapt quickly to changing foreign technologies, the existence of such a work force is a special desideratum.

South Korea's workers have not only been quick and skillful; until recently they have also been cheap. A number of factors have made this possible: the country's low standard of living in the early stages of the growth process; the workers' low pay relative to business profits; poor working conditions (especially at the smaller factories); the longest average work week in the world (about fifty-four hours); workers' forbearance in the face of such hardships, especially in the 1960s and early 1970s; and until recently the refusal of the South Korean government to permit workers freely to organize and take collective action in their own interests. For the past twenty-five years low labor costs have consistently been South Korea's chief, if not only, comparative advantage in the international export market; one of the main reasons, for example, that South Korean companies were able to compete so successfully in the Middle East construction market in the 1970s was their ability to offer package deals that included the utilization of thousands of experienced and inexpensive South Korean workers.

The Role of Government

By the early 1960s South Korea already had many of the essential ingredients for rapid economic growth: international political support, access to foreign capital and technology, a small core class of entrepreneurs, and a reserve of actual and potential workers, quick to learn and cost-competitive in the international market. As the economist Alexander Gerschenkron has pointed out, however, late development assumes an active economic role for the state, and until 1961 South Korea did not have a state structure committed to and capable of galvanizing all its valuable international and social resources toward economic growth.

The problem of creating such a state had plagued Korea since the late nineteenth century. The late Choson state had lacked both the necessary vision and the autonomy from civil society to take the lead in the industrialization process, and it was the Japanese who finally provided Korea with the kind of strong, autonomous, and developmental state that could initiate and carry out industrialization. The American military passed this state structure on virtually intact to the newly inaugurated ROK in 1948, but Syngman Rhee converted it into a political tool to perpetuate his own power, thus fostering a pattern of nonproductive interaction among the ruler, bureaucracy, and social elite that was reminiscent of the late Choson dynasty. The ill-starred Second Republic that followed Rhee made economic growth a priority and began to revive a development plan that the Rhee government had originally drafted and then neglected, but the new government was overthrown before the plan could be implemented. Even if the Second Republic had continued, however, there is considerable doubt whether the new ruling Democratic Party of Chang Myon, with its intimate ties to existing socioeconomic interests, would have been able to carry out the kind of economic transformation effected by the military under Park Chung Hee.

The Park government represented a return to the relatively autonomous and economically oriented state of the colonial period. The relative autonomy was a function of the Park group's position outside the South Korean socioeconomic, and even military, elite. Like the political leaders of Meiji Japan and the Kuomintang on Taiwan after 1949, Park and his followers were comparatively free of entangling personal and economic connections with the civil society and thus under far fewer constraints than their immediate predecessors with regard to making economic changes. This point, of course, should not be exaggerated — hence the term "relative autonomy." Park never carried out what can be described as a genuine social revolution, and from the beginning he was to some extent dependent on the goodwill and cooperation of various key sectors of the society especially the business elite whom he disliked and distrusted (at least at first), but who were important in his plans for economic development. The South Korean state, moreover, has never enjoyed the same degree of autonomy vis-à-vis the international political and economic order that it has with respect to domestic forces. Nevertheless, the point to be noted here is that compared to the Chang Myon, or even the Rhee, government, the Park regime was notably unhampered by ties to the existing South Korean establishment.

Such freedom allowed Park and his officials to devise a series of five-year economic development plans beginning in 1962 that were based largely on perceived economic efficiency, with initially little input and no serious interference from the civil society. Economic planning and monitoring were centered in a new Economic Planning Board (EPB), established in 1961, which was composed primarily of professional economists and other so-called technocrats, and headed by a Deputy Prime Minister who was himself a prominent technocrat. Probably the most important economic policy change of the Park government was its shift in the early 1960s from an import-substituting to an export-led economy, a move that both the Rhee and the Chang Myon government, with all their vested social, economic, and bureaucratic interests in import-substitution would have found difficult if not impossible to carry out. Since then, the state has continued to act as the general manager of the economy, supervising a major transition in the 1970s from an emphasis on labor intensive light industries like textiles to capital/technology intensive heavy industries like shipbuilding, petrochemicals, heavy machinery, electronics, and automobiles.

Official development plans were implemented in all the relevant sectors of society through a combination of state controls and incentives. As in the colonial period, labor and business were treated very differently. When workers, for example, began to demand better conditions and more freedom in the late 1900s and early 1970s, the labor laws were structured into an elaborate system of restraint on union activity, and the workers themselves were ruthlessly put down by the police and other security forces; only recently has the government modified its harsh treatment of workers to some extent. Businessmen too have ultimately been subject to the state's monopoly of violence, but in general Park and his successors have chosen to cultivate a cooperative relationship with business, leaders, gradually bringing them into the economic decision-making process through both formal and informal channels, lavishing public praise and honors on them for achieving or exceeding development goals, and selectively allowing them to become rich.

At the same time, however, the state has been able to make businessmen adhere to its official development programs through the manipulation of a number of key economic controls, three of which have been particularly effective. One has been the state's allocation of business licenses, which precisely define and limit the scope of a firm's activity; all businessmen have been required to obtain such licenses from the appropriate government ministry or department in order to establish, modify, or expand a company. A second lever of control has been the government's domination of the financial system; through its ownership or supervision or all the country's banks and its power to set interest rates, the government has been able to direct capital into industries targeted for development and to make or break even large conglomerates. Even commercial loans induced from foreign countries have generally required approval and guarantee by the government. Finally, a third government control over business has existed in the Office of National Tax Administration (ONTA), which has been used by the government to insure that business expenditures and profits flow into approved areas, and to penalize or even ruin businessmen who have seriously violated the official guidelines and regulations or somehow offended the government authorities.

THE ROLE OF CULTURE AND TIMING

National Identity

The correlation of economic development with such things as access to international capital and technology, entrepreneurship, industrial labor, and a strong, developmental state seems direct and unequivocal. The role of culture and timing in this process, though probably no less significant, is far more difficult to pinpoint and delineate. Nevertheless, it is important to try, and the following general observations may be regarded as a tentative step in that direction.

Nationalism has often been cited as a cultural factor in economic growth, especially in late-developing countries, where it can function as an ideology of popular mobilization and legitimacy during the hardships and social disruption of rapid economic growth. Certainly nationalism has played such a role in the historical development of Japan, and to some extent in Taiwan after 1949; and although it does not seem to have been an important factor in the growth of Hong Kong or Singapore, perhaps this is because both are really city-states rather than nations. On the other hand, the absence of a strong national identity and pride or, conversely, the presence of deep subnational loyalties to a particular tribe, religion, or region has proven to be a serious obstacle to economic growth in many parts of the world.

In Korea there has been no such obstacle. One of Korea's most striking characteristics is that it has been a unified country, from the triumph of the Silla state in the seventh century CE to the artificial political division of the peninsula in 1945. Between 668 and 1910, moreover, there were only three Korean dynasties, and the third alone lasted over 500 years. Linguistic, ethnic, and religious divisions among the population have had little impact on the country's history, and only in the last decade or so has regionalism become an important socioeconomic and political issue as a result of South Korea's geographically skewed pattern of economic growth. In spite of numerous invasions and occupations, the Koreans have remained remarkably homogeneous, so much so in fact that they use the same term, *Han minjok*, to mean both "Korean nation" and "Korean race," and, indeed, do not clearly differentiate between the two ideas. (The Japanese also fail to make this distinction, but the Chinese in the PRC, at least since 1949, use the term "Chinese nation" or *Chung-hua min-tsu* to embrace a variety of ethnic minorities.)

Korea was not only unified for well over a millennium before 1945; until the twentieth century it was an active and leading participant in East Asia's Sinitic world civilization. If Japan's cultural achievements came largely from a departure from Chinese culture, Korea's came from a process of creation within the Chinese tradition, and its accomplishments often rivaled, and sometimes even surpassed, those of China itself. In the realm of Neo-Confucian culture alone, Korea's contributions were "stellar," to borrow the adjective used by Columbia scholar Wm. Theodore de Bary, and were creatively adapted to Korean conditions and needs. Indeed, Choson Korea's aristocratic elite were both self-consciously cosmopolitan and Korean at the same time, and they were capable, during China's Qing dynasty, for example, of looking down on China for abandoning cultural standards they themselves continued to uphold.

Although extra-familial loyalties in traditional Korea were focused on the ruling dynasty rather than on the abstract idea of Korea as a nation state, the country's essential homogeneity and historically based sense of cultural attainment helped pave the way for modern Korean nationalism, which gradually developed in reaction to foreign imperialism and occupation in the late nineteenth and twentieth centuries. Colonialism, in particular, intensified nascent nationalist feeling by providing a clear external enemy and by leaving many Koreans with a passionate post-colonial resolve to match or outdo the economic achievements of their former colonial overlords. The very fact, moreover, that the colonizer had been Japan, a culturally similar-indeed, from the Korean perspective, inferior country, rather than a totally alien Western nation, gave Koreans confidence in their ability to duplicate Japan's economic success. All these feelings — the continued strong sense of national unity and destiny and the catalytic bitterness and anger (*han* in Korean) of the colonial experience — have been consciously and effectively harnessed in the service of economic growth by South Korea's developmental state.

Confucian Tradition

The postwar economic rise of East Asia (especially Japan, Korea, Taiwan, Hong Kong, and Singapore) has spurred a new interest in Confucianism, and there are presently a number of academic projects underway in the United States to explore the role of Confucianism and Confucian institutions in the process of rapid economic growth. Everyone involved seems to agree that Confucianism has indeed played such a role, but defining it — indeed, defining Confucianism itself — has proved to be more difficult than many people had originally anticipated. Nevertheless, such projects have already gone a long way toward raising some of the fundamental questions that need to be confronted in dealing with this complicated topic, and substantive studies are likely to be published in the next few years. Such Western interest in Confucianism is of course highly ironic, since for decades scholars had followed the lead of Max Weber in considering Confucianism the main cultural impediment to economic development in East Asia; even research on the cultural origins of development in Japan, the only East Asian country at the time that seemed to demonstrate a capacity for economic growth, was focused primarily on Japan's indigenous cultural roots, especially those that were most reminiscent of the complex of values associated with Weber's so-called Protestant ethic.

In the case of Korea, perhaps the best way to approach this issue is through a few caveats, some of which may apply to one or more of the other East Asian countries as well. First, despite the recent focus on Confucianism, it is important to keep in mind that it is only one of several great religious or philosophical traditions in Korea. Two others which predate Confucianism and continue to exist in South Korea today are Buddhism and shamanism, but so far no one has seriously investigated their role, if any, in the country's economic growth. Nor has anyone sufficiently considered the impact of Christianity in this regard (Christianity has been growing in Korea since the late Choson period and now embraces about 25-30 percent of South Korea's population). As the anthropologist Vincent Brandt has suggested, moreover, the communitarian values that are generally associated with Confucianism and regarded as an ethical resource in late development (in contrast to the spirit of individualism associated with the original industrial revolution in the West) are only half of the Korean story; Brandt has pointed to an equally deep and persistent countervailing tendency in Korean culture toward individual self-assertion, and it may well be that this combination of opposing values and the tension between them, rather than communitarianism alone, provide a better explanation of Korea's particular type of development, with its aggressive entrepreneurship and, simultaneously, its close government-business relations.

A second point to remember is that many of the so-called typical Confucian values now seen as factors in South Korea's economic growth — filial piety and family loyalty, a perception and acceptance of the state as an active, moral agent in the development of society, a respect for status and hierarchy, an emphasis on self-cultivation and education, and the concern with social harmony mentioned above — were already present in varying degrees in Korean culture long before Neo-Confucianism became the country's ruling ideology in the Choson dynasty. What the Choson state's adoption of Neo-Confucianism seems to have done is to have given these values a more richly constructed philosophical framework and to have diffused them throughout the society at much deeper levels than ever before.

A third point to be considered in assessing the impact of Confucianism on South Korean growth involves coming to terms with the phenomenon that finally led Weber to conclude that Confucianism was a hindrance to economic development: the failure of a country like China or Korea to achieve an economic breakthrough at a time when Confucian influence in the society was at its peak. One might argue, of course, that strong negative factors, such as the existence of a powerful land-based aristocracy, overrode the positive force of Confucianism, but history does not really support such a view; Korea's aristocratic elite, for example, were well-educated Neo-Confucians and opposed economic and social reform on solid Neo-Confucian grounds.

A much more convincing explanation of this problem has been put forward by Harvard historian Tu Wei-ming. Tu avoids positing any kind of direct causal relationship between Confucianism and economic growth and even acknowledges the likely debilitating effect of a conscious, studious commitment to Neo-Confucian ethics on the development process. He suggests, however, that once the orientation of a society has shifted toward modernization, many of the values mentioned above, now internalized and no longer conscious, can provide a cultural basis for the requisite economic transformation. Following Tu, one may therefore conclude that the effect of Confucianism on East Asian economic growth has been a case of "unintended consequences," similar in that sense to the effect of Calvinism on early

Western capitalists. A good example of such an "unintended consequence" in South Korea has been the country's development of an exceptionally well-educated population, capable of rapid assimilation and adaptation of foreign technology and economic expertise. Instead of reading Mencius and Chu Hsi, ambitious South Koreans now read Paul Samuelson and Martin Feldstein, but the respect for education and commitment to self-improvement through study remain much the same as in the Choson dynasty.

The Role of Timing

Timing, even more than culture, is one of those elusive variables of development that tend to defeat economic model-making and give the whole process of growth a stubbornly fortuitous cast. The reason, of course, is because timing, by definition, involves a conjunction or concatenation of events or situations that are usually unpredictable and unique. One good example of such timing was South Korea's economic opportunity in Vietnam, which came precisely at a time when the country was in dire need of new sources of foreign exchange. Another was the construction boom in the Middle East, which came just as the Vietnam War was winding down, and after South Korean firms had already acquired a decade of experience in the international construction industry in Southeast Asia as a result of the Vietnam War.

There have been other such examples, but two in particular deserve mention because their impact has been even more continuous and profound than the benefits from Vietnam and the Middle East. One concerns the international market as a whole. Until recently South Korea has been able to keep its own markets relatively closed to the world while having wide, and often preferential, access to the international market, both as a source of capital and technology and as a destination for South Korean exports. The importance of such access can hardly be overestimated for a country whose rapid growth since 1961 has been fueled almost entirely by exports. For some time now, however, the international market has been growing increasingly tighter for Korea, a function of the economic decline of the

United States and the rise of a number of other low-wage economic competitors (Thailand, Malaysia, and China), and there seems to be a perceptible drift toward protectionism and the development of regional economic blocs centered in East Asia, North America, and Western Europe. In retrospect, it seems that South Korea has been doubly fortunate, first in that its period of reconstruction in the 1950s came at a time when the United States was still willing and able to channel large amounts of concessional aid to developing nations, and second, in that its subsequent period of export-led growth occurred when the international market was still relatively open and outside pressures to open its own domestic market were slight to nonexistent.

South Korea's important cooperative economic relationship with Japan since 1965 has also been deeply affected by factors of timing. First, the relationship was initiated, structured, and developed by what was, in effect, Korea's last colonial generation, i.e., Koreans who had reached maturity (age 20 and above) while the country was still under colonial rule. Many of these Koreans already had personal connections dating from the colonial period with Japanese who were, or had subsequently become, influential elements in Japan's political and business elite. All spoke Japanese fluently (in some cases even better than Korean) and were well accustomed to, even genuinely comfortable in, Japanese social and cultural settings.

Second, the South Korea-Japan economic relationship has also grown because of the complementary nature of the two countries' economies, a function largely of the different historical timing of each country's industrialization. Since the colonial period Japan has been the moving force in the development of what some scholars have suggested is a transnational northeast Asian political economy. Both in the colonial period and again after 1965, Korea has in fact developed more in conjunction than in competition with the Japanese economy, often serving, like Taiwan, as a base for declining Japanese industries as Japan has moved upward through each product cycle and through progressively more advanced stages of industrialization. One sees this phenomenon perhaps most clearly in textiles, the oldest industry in both countries, but it has also been present in steel, shipbuilding, automobiles, and other industries as well.

Problems and Prospects

South Korea's transformation into an urban industrial society has raised the country's general standard of living far beyond the dreams of even the most visionary of the Choson dynasty's state-craft writers and justly commanded the attention and respect of the world. The legacy of this great change, however, has been mixed. A look back over the past one hundred years or so, for example, shows a history of industrialization that has been intimately connected with invasion and foreign occupation, war and other forms of organized violence, political repression, and the immiserization of millions of people.

The problems and issues raised by the country's economic growth have also been numerous and profound, and many are in fact a natural outgrowth of the various factors, discussed above, which have contributed most to the growth process. Reliance on foreign capital has given South Korea's business firms exceptionally high debt-equity ratios (some in the range of 8-1) and the country as a whole one of the largest foreign debts in the developing world, equal in 1986 to about 50 percent of South Korea's total GNP. A similar dependence on foreign technology (as late as 1980 only about six-tenths of 1 percent of GNP was spent for research and development) has also left the country with a weak indigenous technological base at a time when international economic competition is making the acquisition of new foreign technology increasing difficult, even at the high prices South Korea is now willing and able to pay. As noted above, South Korea's strategy of export-led growth is also beginning to run into protectionist barriers, especially in the crucial U.S. market.

South Korea's strong developmental state, which has jealously planned and guided the economy since 1961, has now become as much of a problem as a boon to continued growth. The increasing complexity of both the domestic and the international economy suggests a pressing need to transfer more of the economic decision-making power to the private sector. Even so, apart

from the knotty problem of infringement on vested political interests that such a shift would pose, there is some question as to the ability of the private sector in certain key areas like commercial banking, so long under the control or protection of the government, to adjust quickly or easily to such a change.

Distribution of Wealth

The main social problem of South Korean development involves the question of economic justice in the distribution of wealth. In promoting export-led growth, the state has cultivated a junior partnership with the country's entrepreneurs and simultaneously kept workers' wages down to maintain comparative advantage in the international market. Although since 1961 both entrepreneurs and workers have benefited from the general rise in living standards and absolute poverty has been notably reduced, the entrepreneurs have reaped a disproportionate share of the new national wealth, especially in view of the workers' crucial contribution to the rapid growth of the economy. In the first decade of rapid growth, for example, annual business profits averaged about 20 percent, but real wages rose only about 9 percent. Since 1970, moreover, there has been a perceptible trend toward income inequality, a significant increase in relative poverty (income less than one-third of the national median income), and a striking concentration of national wealth in the hands of the business elite; between 1974 and 1984, for example, the estimated combined GNP share of value-added for South Korea's top five chaebol alone grew from 3.6 percent to 12.1 percent. None of these statistics would make any difference, of course, if South Korean workers were satisfied with what most U.S. and South Korean economists have praised as a relatively equitable distribution of wealth compared with other developing countries. But recent political events suggest that the workers are in fact far from satisfied, and South Korea's residual Confucian culture has always been much less tolerant of such income disparity than Western capitalism.

The contradictory linking of nationalist ideology and external dependency in the growth process has also posed cultural and political challenges for South Korea. The cultural challenge has been to retain and develop a uniquely Korean identity while absorbing a constant and intense barrage of foreign cultural influences. Given the enormity of this task, it is hardly surprising that South Koreans in the last twenty-five years have tended to shift uncomfortably between two extremes: indiscriminate cultural imitation on the one hand, and militant cultural chauvinism on the other. Recently the pendulum has moved toward the latter, and traditional culture (both high and low), disdained as late as the 1960s by many South Koreans as unprogressive or simply embarrassing in a Western-oriented world, has been enjoying a renaissance of interest and respect. Folk culture in particular has become a new source of pride and inspiration, especially to nationalist (*minjok*) or populist (*minjun*) artists who have consciously identified the core of the nation with the history of the common people (or masses). Nevertheless, the question of how to be both modern and Korean at the same time remains a deeply felt problem in the society and is often reflected in South Korean newspaper and magazine articles, as well as television programs, that attempt to define — if only to celebrate — those things which are indisputably Korean.

The contradiction between nationalism and foreign dependency has also made potential political instability a structural problem for the state, the capitalist class, and perhaps even for South Korean capitalism itself. To understand why, one first has to remember that the whole process of capital accumulation in South Korea has taken place largely through the establishment of transnational state and class relationships, and that although actual foreign ownership of South Korean assets has been strictly controlled and limited by the state since 1948, such external linkages have kept both the state and the private sector in a relatively vulnerable economic position with respect to the outside world, and especially vis-à-vis the United States and Japan. South Korea's market liberalization in the past decade has been a case in point: although domestic as well as international forces have moved the country toward liberalization, there is no question that South Korea's heavy dependence on the U.S. as an export market has also limited its

ability to withstand U.S. pressures to liberalize certain sectors of the economy, especially agriculture and services.

The economic relationship with Japan in the past two decades has been far more dependent and uneven than with the U.S. Indeed, according to Chang Key-young (Chang Ki-yong), former Deputy Prime Minister and head of the EPB in the period of transition to rapid export-led growth, the Park government consciously sought to promote an "organic division of labor" between Japan and South Korea that would marry Japanese capital and technology to cheap and unorganized South Korean labor. Park was, of course, successful in this endeavor, and the result has been a highly unbalanced relationship: South Korea's own economic growth has now become structurally linked to Japan's, both through the product cycle, mentioned above, and through an exceptional South Korean reliance on imported Japanese intermediate goods (between 60 percent and 100 percent of the total required, depending on the product). Ironically, U.S. pressures on South Korea to liberalize the economy have actually increased Japan's economic leverage in South Korea because of American inability to compete effectively with Japanese products.

The existence of such inherently unequal economic relationships with external powers is a politically volatile issue in South Korea because of the peninsula's history of foreign invasion and domination since the late nineteenth century and because successive South Korean governments since 1961 have not only fanned nationalism in South Korean society as a mobilizing ideology, but also consistently used nationalist themes, including economic self-reliance, as a justification for official policies. Many South Koreans have been disturbed and dismayed by the country's external economic dependency and by the apparent contradiction between official words and deeds, but the sharpest criticism has come from a small but growing radical left.

In the past decade or so, the radical left has carved out an important niche in nearly all of South Korea's major intellectual circles and has gradually been redefining Korean nationalism within the discourse of Western/Japanese neo-Marxism and dependency theory. The result has been a scathing attack on the government and the

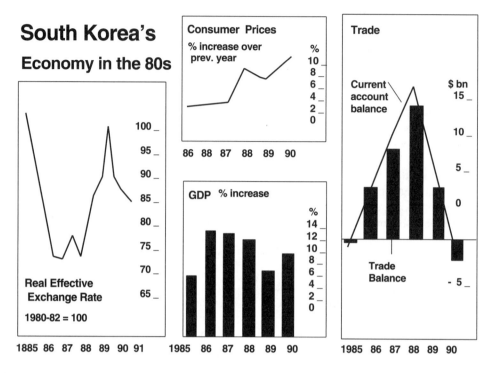

South Korea's
Economy in the 80s

Real Effective Exchange Rate
1980-82 = 100

1885 86 87 88 89 90 91

Consumer Prices
% increase over prev. year

86 88 87 88 89 90

GDP % increase

1985 86 87 88 89 90

Trade

Current account balance

Trade Balance

1985 86 87 88 89 90

Graph 7.9

South Korean Pay Pressures
Union Membership and Wage Levels

Democratization movement builds

'81 '82 '83 '84 '85 '86 '87 '88 '89

—— Manufact. Wages   ▉ Union Membership

Graph 7.10

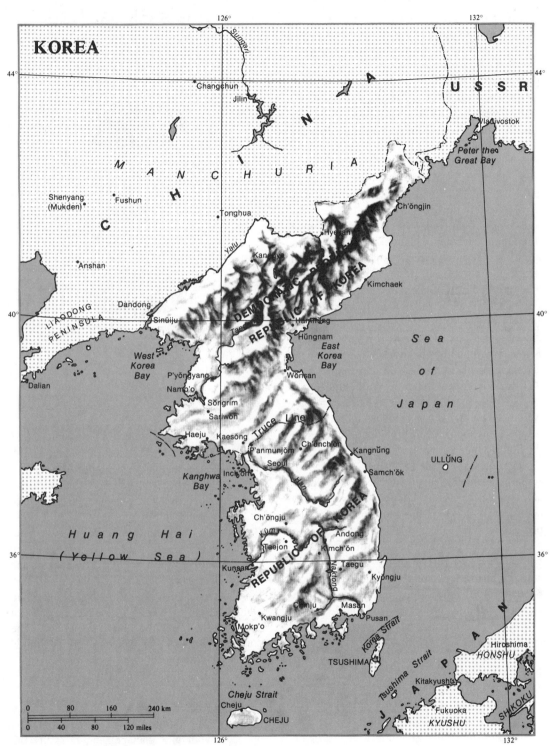

KOREA

44°   44°

Changchun
Jilin

Sungari

C H I N A   U.S.S.R.

M A N C H U R I A   Vladivostok

Peter the
Great Bay

Shenyang   Fushun
(Mukden)   Tonghua   Ch'ŏngjin

C   Hyesan

Anshan   Kanggye   Kimchaek

Yalu
Dandong   DEMOCRATIC PEOPLE'S
40°   40°
LIAODONG   Sinŭiju   Taedong   Hamhŭng
PENINSULA   REPUBLIC OF KOREA

Hŭngnam
Dalian   West   East   S e a
Korea   Korea
Bay   P'yŏngyang   Bay   o f
Namp'o   Wŏnsan
Sŏngrim   J a p a n
Sariwŏn
Truce Line
Haeju   Kaesŏng   ULLŬNG
Ch'unch'ŏn
P'anmunjŏm   Kangnŭng
Seoul
Kanghwa   Inch'ŏn   Samch'ŏk
Bay
Han
Ch'ŏngju
H u a n g   H a i   Andong
Kŭm   REPUBLIC OF KOREA
36°   (Y e l l o w   S e a)   Taejon   Kimch'ŏn   36°
Kunsan   Taegu
Naktong   Kyŏngju
J   A   P   A   N
Chinju   Masan
Kwangju   Pusan
Mokp'o   Korea Strait   Hiroshima
HONSHU
TSUSHIMA   Tsushima Strait   Kitakyushu
SHIKOKU
Cheju Strait   Fukuoka
Cheju   KYUSHU
CHEJU

0   80   160   240 km
0   40   80   120 miles

1:6,000,000

126°   132°

capitalist class for foreign toadyism, and even treason, and a scholarly investigation into what is perceived to be the anti-nationalist historical origins of Korean capitalism itself. Curiously, most of this criticism has been focused on South Korea's economic relationship with the United States rather than with Japan, even though the latter is much deeper, more unequal, and, in the long run, probably more important. Such myopia is understandable, however, in view of America's overarching political and military role in South Korea since 1945 and its direct and critical involvement in the economy through at least the mid-1960s. With some 40,000 troops stationed throughout the country, the U.S. has also been a highly visible and, especially since the Kwangju Incident, controversial, presence in South Korea, whereas the Japanese economic influence has so far been more subtle and hidden. If, as expected, Japan's economic penetration of South Korea grows in the next decade as a result of South Korea's current liberalization and Japan's new and increasingly important role as a financial, as well as an industrial, superpower, the imbalance in the ROK-Japan economic relationship may well become more conspicuous, more widely debated, and more politically uncomfortable for the South Korean government.

Through most of the 1980s the South Korean economy seemed strangely immune to these deep and complex problems. Economic development continued to advance at a rapid pace (over 12 percent between 1986 and 1988), thanks in large part to a decline in international oil prices and interest rates, the revival of the U.S. economy, and the increased competitiveness of South Korean exports following an appreciation of the Japanese yen. A current account surplus, first registered in 1986, allowed the government to reduce its foreign debt from a peak of about US$ 47 billion in 1986 to about US$ 35 billion in 1980, and there was even widespread talk among government officials of South Korea's becoming a net creditor as early as 1992.

By the end of the decade, however, it was clear that some of the structural weaknesses of the economy were beginning to take their toll. Political reform in 1987 opened the door to a long suppressed social conflict between capital and labor that interrupted production, raised wages

Korea's Global Trade

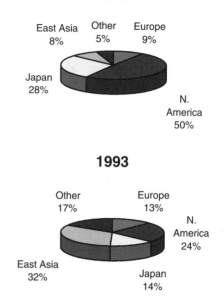

Graph 7.11.

(in some cases by as much as 30 percent in a single year), and unnerved a business community accustomed to unequivocal support from above and no interference from below. At the same time, economic liberalization, especially in the form of a steady appreciation of the won after 1987 (including a 15.8 percent increase in 1988), exacerbated an already difficult situation by reducing the competitiveness of South Korean exports and raising the cost of imports. By the mid-1990s, South Korea's current account had slipped into annual deficits of over $5 billion, yet the national growth rate remained above 7 percent. The country's trade deficit worsened as its limited number of export categories were insufficient to offset massive imports of machinery and equipment.

Such problems do not beget quick or easy answers. The continuing bitter confrontation between labor and management, probably the most serious obstacle to growth the country presently faces, is a product of nearly thirty years of institutionalized oppression and distrust, and it will take much time and effort on both sides before a new institutional arrangement is devised that strikes a satisfactory balance between a commitment to productivity and a concern for the rights and needs of the working class. But the prospects are by no means bleak. Barring a major economic or military crisis, a return to the authoritarian past is not likely to be tolerated by the general public. And if the current economic problems are allowed to run their course in an atmosphere of free speech and association, they may well turn out to be no more than a necessary transition to a period of new growth, less dramatic, perhaps, than in earlier decades, but ultimately more equitable and stable.[5]

EDITOR'S POSTSCRIPT

Amid nationwide strikes and protests in early 1997, Korea confronted the incompleteness of its economic and democratic transformation. An effort by the ruling majority party to enact a law that swept away key job protections for workers and permitted draconian measures by internal security forces in search of suspected terrorists outraged the labor unions. Their members took to the streets in protest and brought several key chaebol to a standstill. While participation in the strike was widespread, it was not uniform across industries, reflecting a growing perception among many well-paid Koreans that by crippling their employers, they might endanger their own survival in a competitive global economy.

◆   ◆   ◆

CONFUCIANISM AND ECONOMIC GROWTH

Introduction

It has long been accepted that cultural orientation plays a role in the economic behavior of individuals and even nations. Economists and economic planners, however, generally have tended to regard culture as a repository of traditions that inhibit modernization and economic development. The rapid growth of the Japanese,

South Korean, and Taiwanese economies in East Asia has forced a reassessment of this attitude and drawn new attention to positive ways in which culture might contribute to economic development.

Why do these East Asian economies have such high savings rates? Why have their societies been able to adapt so readily to industrialization, seemingly with a minimum of social disruption? What accounts for the apparently harmonious relations between government and industry or between management and labor? Why is income relatively equitably distributed in these countries, and why, when it is not, does the inequality attract so much attention?

To some observers the Confucian tradition common to the high-growth Asian economies seems to be important in answering some of these questions. As an ethical system Confucianism is concerned with correct relations between superiors and inferiors and stresses mutual obligations,

Figure 7.3   Confucius

such as correct example on the part of the former and loyalty on the part of the latter. Individualism is subordinated to harmony within a group; the family was traditionally the paramount social group. In government, Confucianism supports enlightened authoritarian rule by a centralized bureaucracy, not popular democracy. In traditional Confucian societies, government was supposed to be the preserve of an educated bureaucracy, chosen through examination rather than inheritance or political connections.

These values appear to undergird the strong role of government bureaucracies, company loyalty, and cohesive social relations found in many high-growth East Asian economies. Confucianism also values frugality, discipline, and hard work. Some observers of East Asian growth have raised questions about its role, however. Why have Confucian societies only comparatively recently experienced high growth rates? Why, as recently as the 1950s, did Western scholarship regard Confucianism as an explanation for poor economic performance in Korea and China? Why have some Confucian societies, including Vietnam and at times mainland China, failed to grow rapidly, while other societies without Confucian traditions have done well?

Obviously there is not just one explanation for economic growth. Most economists would continue to look first to noncultural factors, such as the presence or absence of economic incentives. However, the East Asian economic success stories raise intriguing questions about the complex connections between culture and economic development. These are receiving more systematic attention from social scientists in both the East and West as indicated in the following section.[6]

THE CONFUCIAN FACES
OF CAPITALISM

— by Gilbert Rozman

Capitalism East and West

At first glance, capitalism in many parts of Asia seems to operate the same as in the West. Businessmen take risks with their own companies, large and small; managers fill the adminis-

trative ranks, and government officials move the levers of state financial and regulatory control. In fact, the two regions are conspicuously different, particularly in those parts of Asia with Confucian traditions. The contrasts occur not so much in the types or categories of people in the system, however, as in the longstanding ideals by which they operate.

It is important to avoid stereotypes in explaining these differences, for as will be emphasized, there are exceptions to every rule in business. Nevertheless, the ways businesses are developed, managed, and regulated are not the same in the East as they are in the West. The contrasts occur mainly in terms of three categories: (1) the individual's view of his or her freedom of action in the creation and conduct of business; (2) the structure of obligations in which such action takes place; and (3) the appropriate role of government in fostering and controlling business development.

Ideals in the West, especially in the United States, combine the rugged individualism of the venture capitalist with the contractual bureaucratic management of the Master's in Business Administration. Both have risen to prominence under the relatively laissez-faire supervision of government regulators. Particularly in the 1980s, the magnetic lure of junk bonds, the intense competition for a place in a small number of elite business schools, and the surge of deregulation (with its dramatic if not always intended results in sectors ranging from airlines to savings and loans) demonstrated Americans' strong preference for free-wheeling, individual-centered business activity.

By contrast, business practice in Asia often reflects a far greater reliance on the group as manifested by three ideals: (1) the long-range entrepreneurship of the small family firm in accordance with longstanding traditions (the shop is often combined with the home); (2) hierarchical solidarity within the large enterprise (traditionally it was the merchant house, becoming the industrial or financial conglomerate in recent times) with its grand show of building its own community of workers; and (3) ready government intervention by today's incarnation of the Confucian bureaucrat who still competes through examinations for the top slots in the civil service.

Small businessmen using family labor, managerial personnel committed to their larger firms, and bureaucrats, maintaining a tight hold on the reins of the economy, all work together within a market setting, guided by a distinctive regional ethos in support of the advancement of capitalism. With the understanding that these are capitalists who draw heavily on not only their own but Western traditions and adapt constantly to global economic forces, let us refer to them here as "Confucian capitalists," for they are distinctive as the architects and builders of prosperity in many parts of Asia today.

Whenever a cultural term is applied to an economic phenomenon, certain caveats and explanations are in order. First, to suggest that capitalism in Asia has a distinctive, "Confucian" aspect is not to reduce Asian economic development to a set of cultural artifacts or "national character" traits. Rather, it allows us to relate Asian policy choices and institutions to certain cultural antecedents that make the reasons for such choices easier to understand. In other words, the Confucian perspective provides us with a frame of reference within which we can see broadly shared regional attitudes and practices that have influenced the development of capitalist institutions in Asia. This does not mean that some of these characteristics may not occur outside of the Asian region, in Germany for example, but it does suggest that their occurrence in Asia fits a pattern and has a historical basis. Thus, the suggestion that capitalism in certain successful regions of Asia may have a distinctively "Confucian" dimension — within which there are several variations — complements rather than contradicts explanations that are of a more structural or policy-focused nature.

Second, there is of course in each region of the world variation from country to country and over time. Although here we try to paint regional differences between East and West in broad brush strokes, there are also important intraregional variations to keep in mind. These include not only different national traditions but contrasting experiences over the past century in colonization, in the time at which industrialization was introduced, and in policy approaches in the creation of new institutions.

Third, Confucianism itself has changed over the centuries and has emerged as several different traditions that reflect its distinctive historical development in each country. Within the common framework of the Confucian tradition shared for more than a thousand years by the peoples of China, Korea, and Japan, there were significant variations.

Briefly stated, China especially encouraged family entrepreneurship separate from the state. Intermediate organizations were weakly developed, and an enormous gap opened between the public and private spheres. Confucianism became closely identified with "familyism," under the distant emperor and the central bureaucracy. Korea achieved a pattern of state sponsorship in cooperation with large family-run firms. Stability rested on a strong bureaucracy working closely together with a sizable aristocracy. In contrast to these patterns, Japan in its premodern history favored intermediate-level firms ready for intense competition. Japan's decentralized tradition of samurai solidarity and loyal service spread also to the country's merchant organizations, cooperating with local administrations but also vying with each other. Imperial authority was relegated to the background in Japan while filial piety of a son to his father was balanced with other types of loyalty. Korea and Japan had imported Confucianism, relying more on formal education to encourage its spread.

Colonization during the modern period created yet another set of influences in Asia, these having to do with the introduction of different capitalist practices and institutions. The British, for example, were reserved and distant in their business development in Singapore and Hong Kong. The Japanese, by contrast, intervened intensely in Taiwan and Korea. Particularly in Korea they established the model (which the Korean adopted with a vengeance after World War II) of strong bonds between the state and a small number of dependent industrialists.

In the history of Asian economic development, the timing of a nation's entry into industrialization has been critical. Japan was among the most fortunate in this respect. It launched a vigorous modernization process late in the nineteenth century when it was clear that a strong state apparatus would be necessary for survival in the competition with Western imperialism. With a few exceptions, the smaller capitalist countries began their independent modernization only in the 1950s or 1960s when America offered support for free trade and assistance to countries on the frontline of communist expansion. Lastly, China shifted suddenly in the 1980s to a new course of sustained growth utilizing capitalist forces and an "open door" to investment by foreign firms, including other East Asian firms, flush with cash. Each of these initiatives took place in a different international environment. As we search for regional commonalities, we need to keep such sources of variation in mind.

The Importance of Confucian Teachings

It used to be thought that capitalists would be able to succeed in Asia in spite of the Confucian heritage, not because of it. After all, the formal Confucian tradition frowned on merchants, placing them at the bottom of a four-class hierarchy, far below China's scholar-bureaucrats, who themselves were traditionally trained as generalists unprepared for the technical orientation required of modern officials. Japan's samurai, it was said, were taught to scorn commerce and to cling to their hereditary ranks. Orthodox Confucianism cast suspicion on easy money from "unproductive" commercial activities and on lavish consumption by those unworthy of their wealth. The "slow start" toward modernization in China and Korea seemed to confirm all this for observers who concluded that there would emerge only Western-style capitalists, not Confucian ones.

A different viewpoint about the importance of Confucian teaching is now surging in popularity. First, the living body of Confucian teachings, despite its ritualistic language often dating from 2,500 years ago, was not really so inimical to commerce nor so narrowly focused on the past that it stunted economic growth. Increasingly over the past millennium the state and the elite guardians of the tradition appreciated the need to work closely together with the merchants in an already quite commercialized economy. Indeed, China was long in the forefront of world development, for example in the earliest proliferation of rural periodic markets from roughly the seventh century CE and in the rise of many vast cities. (As late as 1800 at least half of the world's ten largest cities

with a population of more than 500,000 were found in China.) Until Western commerce realized a qualitative leap forward after the beginnings of global trade in the sixteenth century, China may have remained economically in the lead. Korea and especially Japan (where the urban population quadrupled from the late sixteenth to the early eighteenth centuries) also developed advanced economies by premodern standards.

East Asian leaders governing from large administrative centers closely integrated into national marketing networks grew more realistic about the importance of merchants. Large provincial merchant associations founded branches in cities across China without government objection. Japan's more than 250 feudal lords both borrowed heavily from merchants and granted them special rights in the hope of expanding exports for their domains. In these circumstances it should come as no surprise that Confucian teachings inspired merchant house codes intended to foster such qualities as loyalty and diligence.

The increasingly knowledge-based management of premodern East Asian societies was to prove beneficial for their modern development. In spite of this, Westerners (and early Asian reformers) at first dismissed Confucian learning as a handicap. They saw it as merely a process of training in textual memorization or interpretation. In fact, a great deal more than memorization arose from the learning environment created by Confucian traditions, extending even beyond the broad dissemination of basic knowledge and literacy. Rather than closing people's minds, Confucian traditions were as capable of opening them, teaching many individuals to "learn how to learn." That is, it gave them the tools to observe, interpret, and take on new knowledge. It also taught them to internalize ethical principles, such as diligence, self-sacrifice, and delayed gratification. The result was often a very high level of Confucian discourse about society and even government, despite strict censorship against criticisms of the ruling dynasty or the principles by which it was legitimized.

Literacy rates in China climbed sharply, with an estimated 40 percent of males having been exposed by the nineteenth century to a basic knowledge of the necessary characters for simple reading. If nothing else, education in Confucian teachings inspired the most highly trained to serve their community and country, while preparing the bulk of the peasantry (ranked high — above artisans and merchants — on the ideal class hierarchy) to view learning as the path to improving their lot in life.

While it is a fact that the countries of East Asia did not generate their own industrial revolution, Confucianism played a role in the transformation once it occurred. These countries were latecomers to modernization and the challenges they faced were those of borrowers and adapters rather than technology path-breakers. At the same time, they sought to create domestic conditions that would permit them to develop their own, home-grown business capacities. In doing so, they learned to rely more on activist state bureaucrats and/or existing family organizations for help rather than on the strength and spirit of individualistic ambitions. Even in cases where a dominant individual with a flair for business emerged to build a company, the process by which he did so upheld the ideals of a hierarchical, family-modeled institution.

The new thinking about Confucianism, then, is that it was at least as capable of creating conditions that favored industrialization as impeding it. Yet there can be little doubt that temporary barriers arose across much of the region that interfered not only with the modernization process but also with any contribution that Confucian traditions might make to it. Even amid the late Qing reforms, for example, there were Manchu rulers and Chinese bureaucrats who clung to the old structure of power in China and interfered with change. In the warlord and early Republican eras that followed, modern family-based enterprises began to flourish, only to be taxed heavily and often required to make irregular payments. Japan further undermined business development when it plunged the region into harsh occupation and war. Finally, China's and Korea's Communists sought to destroy the Confucian past rather than to make use of it. Thus, in the absence of constructive political leadership and stability, the countries of the region could not easily draw on their traditions and apply them in ways appropriate to modernization — but the traditions themselves remained applicable to the modern era. As the economic gap between these countries and the industrialized world continued to widen, it became all the more apparent to them that they must switch to a new but parallel track, one that brought the support of state organization and leadership to the forefront in the pursuit of capitalist goals yet did not necessarily break with tradition. Japan, of course, was instrumental in demonstrating how a successful model of this nature could be devised.

What, then, were the specific Confucian traditions that helped stimulate the process by which these late-arriving nations rose so rapidly in the global economic order? The key elements were the ideals and practices that exalted the long-term wellbeing of the family:

- The stern but benevolent father.

- The loyal child who, despite his or her filial piety, can never fully repay a deep debt to the parents.

- The ancestors to whom proper worship and acknowledgement must be given and who underscore the importance of perpetuating the family under favorable conditions.

- The highly formalized yet still diffuse roles specific to each family relationship (e.g., that between older and younger brother, between husband and wife, and so on).

As the core of the society, the family became the model for other organizations. All types of East Asian capitalists have developed under the influence of these family-based attitudes.

Confucius was, of course, not a capitalist himself. He was a teacher, one who tutored young men in virtuous thought. He was also a frustrated statesman, traveling from state to state, eager to serve a ruler by applying his high-sounding ideals for a harmonious state. Beginning with his disciples, Confucius wanted to train a generation of men who aspired to become sages. By convincing a ruler, he hoped to create a model state in which peace would result from correct social conduct rather than from coercive controls or strict laws. Because he was primarily concerned with improving social relations, Confucius established a precedent for focusing on education, ritual, and organizational restructuring. Officials, landowners, and townspeople all found merit in his teachings. They were urged to seek self-improvement through intense study, purification of their minds, and cultivation of a worldview centered on service to family and lord.

The "Confucianization" of China advanced gradually, spurred by varied forces including social mobility and popular religion associated with ancestor worship. The Confucianization of Korea and Japan, on the other hand, occurred later and more rapidly, penetrating deeply into family life only as recently as the last premodern era (Korea's Yi dynasty from the fourteenth century and Japan's Tokugawa period from the seventeenth). Many Confucian practices initially centered on the imperial house or the elite. Eventually, all groups found ways to adapt the tradition to their own circumstances. For the majority of the people a kind of "mass Confucianism" guided at least family-related behavior. For many businesses, especially in Japan, there also emerged "merchant house Confucianism," flexibly applying principles such as ancestor worship and family solidarity to the organization of the firm.

The Small Family Business

The central concepts of Confucianism are best understood not as a religion to be accepted on faith nor as a philosophy to be scrutinized for logical consistency, but as a practical guide to living. One reason the concepts spread so widely in Asia is because they worked so well. As the body of Confucian rituals grew, it supported and enriched the family and community. To honor the family one was urged to devote oneself to both its prestige and its prosperity.

"This-worldly" in its orientation, Confucianism teaches individuals of both high and low birth to strive for success in their lifetime and in the long-term interests of their direct descendants. One need not reconcile oneself to one's current lot in life, it says. Human nature is inherently good and perfectible. Education is for everyone. Moral cultivation can be expected to pay rich dividends. Unlike serf or closed-class societies in which hope for advancement may be tightly circumscribed, the Chinese tradition gained credibility by a generally open market for land and open channels for social mobility. In this environment, families could anticipate that hard work, savings, study, and attention to market opportunities would improve their standing in society. Such circumstances fostered a competitive and even, within understandable premodern limitations, an entrepreneurial spirit. Yet the entrepreneurial strategy was substantially different from that found in the West and, again, it was the family that conditioned the strategy.

East Asian families were reared in the operation of family farms. They usually owned their own land. Often they would farm additional land as tenants under contract or they might lease part of their holdings to others. They grew accustomed to marketing as part of their production and appreciated the vagaries of a commercial economy. Part-time commercialized handicrafts or peddling alerted them to the option of nonagricultural careers as well.

In ordinary circumstances the path to success was not through leaving the family to find one's fortune, but through relying on family assistance. Resources in densely populated East Asian countries were scarce. Connections were essential if one was to gain placement as an apprentice, establish a branch shop, or obtain the support of a guild formed by persons from a common local place of origin. Thus did the family, through its multi-generational links to the community and the outside world of business, serve the interests of an aspiring entrepreneur. Entrepreneurial skills did not normally originate in risky commercial undertakings, however. They were an outgrowth of a wide range of business orientations extending from the familiar surroundings of the family farm through associations into which families carefully deposited their offspring.

Hugh T. Patrick and Thomas P. Rohlen refer to small enterprises, especially small-scale family enterprises, as "the economic, political, and social heart and backbone of Japan." They comprise at least two-thirds of Japan's economic pyramid, adding a dynamic element "in entrepreneurship, job creation, output, and political clout." Located in or near the family home, they draw on the labor of many unpaid and paid family members.[7] Even in recent decades of prominence for large firms, the small-scale sector continues to grow and to play an important role in continuing economic dynamism.

Similarly in Taiwan we find that small employers rely not only on family labor but also on the entrepreneurial aspirations of workers eager to earn start-up capital for their own future firms. Family-centered entrepreneurship in Chinese settings — in the 1980s at last spreading to southeast China as the barriers erected by the communist government were being removed — is more pronounced than elsewhere. Using women, the elderly, and even children as laborers, the household business has been quick to respond to changing conditions. Able to utilize family savings or credit from relatives as well as space otherwise available for family living, this type of firm can draw on additional land and capital as well as labor. It enables vast numbers of the population to become involved in modernization before the process is very advanced and continues to give flexibility to the economy even when the country has become quite wealthy.

The Chinese family has shaped modern industry just as industry has redefined the nature of the family. Yet in this symbiosis neither has been changed to the extent observers once predicted. Those who expected industrialization to cause families to break apart, following a Western pattern of devolving from "extended" to "nuclear" families and perhaps fragmenting even further, have been foiled by family entrepreneurship. On the other hand, Chinese traditionalists who wishfully anticipated the continued importance of the extended family and the ideal Confucian relationships in the household find that there have been enormous changes in family size, structure, and customs. The small-scale family firm is the prime setting for this mixture of tradition and change in capitalist industrialism.

Throughout the region the dynamism of small-scale family businesses reflects the depth of entrepreneurial ambition. Land reform, implemented in several countries in the first postwar decade, and subsequent restrictions on the accumulation of land have served to channel talent into nonagricultural businesses. In Japan the presence of subcontracting links to larger enterprises and the strong support for small firms provided by government loans and protective legislation have produced a highly integrated industrial structure in which products emerge through dispersed but closely coordinated businesses. In Taiwan such integration has not been as great, as family firms do not easily change into other types of entities even when they grow quite large.

Entrepreneurial capitalism is consistent with the regional tradition of idealizing the small family-run business as a place where the work ethic and human affection are in balance. It is moral to work hard for one's family. If it becomes clear that a child's access is barred to a calling of higher prestige, often because of undistinguished high school performance, the family is likely to play a major role in placement. Many families have the skills and experience to use the additional labor themselves rather than placing it elsewhere.

Management

East Asian managerial practices take personal values seriously. They strive to create a corporate culture different from the formalistic, contractual ideals of what Max Weber described as rational bureaucracy. While drawing heavily on nineteenth-century European factory organization, Japan led the way in inserting its own traditional elements. Already in the Tokugawa era, merchant houses had developed around a family core through the addition of relatives, apprentices, who might in some cases become adopted sons, and youths from the same local area as the family. Even when the organization became quite large, the family metaphor was applied. The diffuse and even unlimited commitment of a dutiful child was owed in return for the protective, if stern, care of the patriarch.

Merchant house codes started from the premise that the structure and values of the family organization would also help the business achieve a profit and create a moral environment. Consistent with the family model, rewards depended less on the individual's specific achievements than on how long and well he served the enterprise. This often meant that with age came more rewards. Just as family success was attributable to each member's fulfillment of his or her roles in a virtuous and harmonious manner, so the firm's prospects were also linked to harmony and diligent role performance. The merchant house fostered an ideology of ancestor worship for its founder and his successors. The history of the firm emphasized pride in distinctive traditions over many generations and in the moral quality of ancestral teachings. Each employed a regular cycle of rituals and ceremonies to smooth the way for harmonious human relations.

The East Asian approach to management draws on popular beliefs that credit business achievements to the spiritual qualities of organizations. Employees are often hired through personal recommendations that praise their personality qualities and suggest that they are consistent with company needs. Particularly in Japan, orientation sessions are both long and demanding, concentrating on character building and linking work to higher social goals. The company teaches values at an abstract level and proceeds to reenforce them through many group-oriented practices.

As capitalism matures, the risk-oriented founders of entire industries gradually give way to the more cautious managers of well-established enterprises. The organization man or the salaryman becomes the mainstay of the economy. This transition has proven relatively easy in the East Asian region. In the words of Roderick MacFarquhar, "If Western individualism was appropriate for the pioneering period of industrialization, perhaps post-Confucian 'collectivism' is better suited to the age of mass industrialization."[8]

The educational demands made on the employee who is rising through the ranks of an established bureaucracy are different from those required by self-made men who found their own niches back when modern organizations were appearing for the first time. Today, formal educational criteria are followed closely in filling the managerial ranks of the larger firms and, as a result, managerial capitalism has emerged in tandem with "examination hell"[9] as the source of a modern meritocracy.

The Confucian tradition valued education without distinctions on the basis of social standing at birth. It espoused the perfectibility of man through years of study. As Hung-chao Tai remarks, today East Asian "parents, teachers, and students treat education almost like a national religion, and government and society devote considerable resources to a frantic expansion of schools and classes."[10] It is no wonder that this region's expansion of enrollment at both the secondary and higher educational levels has proceeded extremely rapidly in the postwar era.

Japan has deeply influenced the development of managerial capitalism in the region. Hong Kong, with its great reliance on small-scale family businesses, and the People's Republic of China, with its socialist industrial sector, have, for different reasons, been slow to share in this form of capitalism until very recently. Korea and Taiwan, however, have evolved along the path taken by Japan. Perhaps influenced also by their more public adherence to Confucian traditions, including the "ladder of success" through examinations, they achieved their early industrialization under Japanese occupation. It is important to look back at Tokugawa history for the roots of managerial capitalism.

Through the seventeenth and eighteenth centuries Japanese merchants developed their own culture within a governmental system that would not tolerate any substantial economic reform but which nevertheless eagerly solicited their services and depended on their large commercial network. The samurai became the model for all other classes, leading to the acceptance of parallel social ethics. The proud and powerful Osaka merchants, working in what was called the "kitchen of Japan," were known for "their high regard of business traditions, guild rules, and their sense of self-reliance." "They worshipped profits . . . in a spirit of ancestral obedience and loyalty."[11] Osaka was not alone; the values of central merchants were widely disseminated through the more than two hundred castle towns.

In Japan more than China the education of merchants acquired a distinctive character by the early nineteenth century. Schools for townsmen emphasized the public value of mercantile virtues. In the process of this education, merchant values became elevated and Confucianized rather than denigrated. This became the background for the Meiji era blend of moral training and utilitarian skills.

Varied forms of employment existed in Japan prior to 1868 and new forms emerged under Western influence. Some enterprises used large numbers of unskilled men. Others drew young, unmarried girls into textile factories. Only in the first decades of this century did the forces of late development and tradition come together to establish what Ronald Dore calls the "enterprise family system." By then, employers had become preoccupied with reducing turnover and retaining skilled personnel. The bureaucracy worried about social tensions inconsistent with what it assumed should be promoted by a legitimate, benevolent, Confucian-based government. Workers began prodding for organizational change and turned to strikes and union solidarity out of a sense of injustice. All these forces contributed to the growing notion of a "macro-family."[12]

Dore's suggestion that the full-fledged realization of the Japanese system of management emerged so soon has been disputed by historians who see it as a creation of the ideologically charged atmosphere during the war years or even of the desperation to cling to scarce jobs in the immediate postwar period. Some detect in the Confucian language of "familyism" not the unfolding of traditions, but rationalizations. That is, institution-builders are said to have reinvented Confucianism, invoking it to win worker loyalties at low cost.

There can be little doubt that businesses have sought to exploit the advantages that the tradition implies for themselves. Political leaders have been even more aggressive in touting the virtues of Confucian teachings when it suits their purposes. The stern prime minister of Singapore, Lee Kuan Yew, lectured his people repeatedly on the Confucian virtues. In 1990 the Chinese communist authorities decided to give especially strong attention to the annual rites at Confucius' birthplace, Qufu. In both cases, as well as others that could be cited in Japan, Korea, and elsewhere, Confucianism is not only invoked, it is reinvented to suit the purposes of the moment.

Particularly in their search for skilled employees to be groomed for managerial roles, East Asian enterprises are likely to take a familistic approach. They do not simply pick recruits from want ads or impersonal recruitment procedures. Instead, new employees are carefully chosen based on prior credentials, such as family background, educational success, and examination scores. The factors to be weighed most heavily are not specific skills but moral character and general aptitude. Recommendations from persons with a stake in seeing the applicant succeed

play an important role. Just as traditionally a great deal of attention was given to choosing a bride or an adopted son to become a new member of the ongoing family, the choice of a fast-track employee has rarely been left to chance. Hiring is aimed at producing a loyal, permanent employee.

Still, times are changing for the large corporation just as they are for families. The system that gives most of its preferences and benefits to older, more experienced employees has come under increasing pressure. Young employees who are increasingly restless and leisure-oriented now question the need to maintain such strong commitment to a business. Women have begun to join the hired labor force in large numbers and now use equal employment opportunity legislation to gain equal treatment, undermining the preferential system. Previously, they were a silent minority in the firm and lacked the home-based supports enjoyed by the devoted company man backed by a no less devoted housewife and "education mama." Firms increasingly feel the dual pressures of a greying population, with small replacement cohorts entering the work force, and rising pension and health care costs as a result of the broadening of social welfare benefits. In light of this, large wage differentials based on seniority and early retirement are much more difficult to achieve.

Nevertheless, even as changes in the employment system occur, some features persist. Managers try to use personal, face-to-face moral suasion to control and motivate workers. Senior management is still reluctant to rely on formal, contractual relations that might be interpreted too literally by their business partners and, if need be, by lawyers. Traditionally, East Asians use mediators rather than lawyers, their go-betweens playing a more diffuse role and vouching for the moral character and goodwill of the other side.

Even as the requirements of capitalism shift in our age of globalization and high technology, a growing school of observers argues that the model of the firm-as-community with its meritocratic selection based on educational levels and its attention to the social significance of work, establishes a pattern that is better suited to the current stage of modernization than those found in the West.

C is for Chinese Culture
C is for Confucius
C is for Court Cases
C is for Charity

C IS FOR CARTOONS!

SINGAPORE'S CLASSROOM

Figure 7.4 Typical of how some political leaders in Asia have used Confucianism as a rationale for their policies, Singapore Prime Minister Lee Kuan Yew frequently lectured his people on behavior according to Confucian principles. Here, he is depicted in such a role related to a court case involving an opposition politician.

Bureaucratic Capitalists

Just as there are contrasting patterns in the motivations and rules that guide business behavior between Asia and the West, so are there differences in their approaches to governmental service. In both cases, individuals can be motivated by ideals of service to the team, but in the West these tend to be reinforced by incentives and rewards that are of a personal nature, individuals being honored for their own service-oriented achievements more often than the group itself. Similarly, the limits which the "team" can impose on the individual, either as a member of the bureaucracy or as an outsider subject to its regulation, are far apart in the two cases.

Generally, the rhetoric of service to others is far more pervasive in the Confucian-based societies of Asia than in the West. Through an appeal to their sense of responsibility, workers are more likely to be encouraged to work harder. Senior government officials occupy the top of this pinnacle of public responsibility, insisting that they are serving the interests of the national community. Their credibility is heightened not only because of

the common rhetoric of service to others — those managing firms take credit for serving the community of workers and those in small shops often claim to be laboring on behalf of their family — but also through the high prestige accorded to public service.

China, Japan, and Korea developed large state bureaucracies and endowed them with an aura of indispensability. Long before the nineteenth century the officials selected for appointment were often men of remarkable learning. Modern capitalist officials are, in some sense, the heirs to this tradition of service by those chosen as the best and the brightest.

Observers of Chinese and Japanese public administration often remark about the "tenacity of culture." In the case of China, the traditional structures that once exercised political responsibility were treated as elevated above but coexisting with the society itself. At the top was an "elitist high Confucian culture that glorified the established authority of the better educated and rationalized their claims of superiority on the basis of possessing specialized wisdom."[13] Combined with a genuine meritocracy, this tradition at the top facilitated the creation of what Chalmers Johnson calls a developmental state. Alternatively, the same bureaucratic tradition combined with a dogmatic ideology and a fear of professional elites could produce a government that responded only to the interests of a small number of power holders as came to be the case in late twentieth-century China.

East Asian administrative elites are the products of the highest-ranked universities and of demanding civil-service examinations. They enjoy high prestige, and they often "rule," especially with regard to developmental needs, while politicians only "reign." While they often have to contend with the encroachments of elected politicians, public confidence in their essential contributions toward both stability and development helps to preserve their high standing.

In the postwar era one East Asian country after another has experienced a crush of eager applicants for higher education in top universities that open the way to access to the honored positions of government service. Belief in the fairness of this competition and the universalism of the standards used, as in the centuries of imperial China's examination system, sustains a national consensus on the justice and competence of public administration. At times this equanimity is shattered by scandals, but the blame usually is placed on the politicians rather than on the career civil servants. Postwar democratizing tendencies from the West have helped reduce bureaucratic arrogance. The resulting blend of meritocracy and democracy has served the needs of capitalism well.

In the cold war era, analysts transfixed by the dichotomy of capitalism and socialism were apt to treat the former as a unitary phenomenon. Variations in the forms of capitalism were downplayed and said to be the result of "stages of development" or remnants of a fast-disappearing past rather than an on-going regional adaptation that would be tested by future competition. With the dismantling of socialist economies, we are more likely to perceive diversity in the capitalist world. In fact, we need new theories of capitalism, including attention to how the ideals held by capitalists vary in the two principal regions of modernization.

For their part, the East Asian capitalists are adapting to the demands of international, technology-based competition with great success and it matters not to them what models we construct of their behavior. Like their ancestors, they have adopted the ideals that work best for them. Whether one wishes to see their practices as capitalism with a Confucian face, or perhaps even as Confucianism with a capitalist face, their versions of capitalism will continue to challenge the West in the decades ahead.

◆   ◆   ◆

THE "OVERSEAS" ETHNIC CHINESE

The ethnic Chinese, in their totality, comprise one of the most important economic forces for Asian Pacific growth. Over the centuries, Chinese emigrants have departed the mainland individually and in groups to seek their fortunes in the farthest corners of the Pacific Basin. Their economic success stories have contributed to an historical stereotype of impoverished Chinese who struggled in a strange land, achieved wealth, and either built a prosperous home or returned to China, or did both. The real picture is somewhat more complex.

It is tempting to contrast the image of poor Chinese immigrants in Southeast Asia who arrived a century ago from the mainland to work in the mines, ports, and railroad yards of European and American colonies with today's wealthy and powerful Chinese business tycoons. The latter are commonly believed to be the descendants of the impoverished immigrants. In many cases, however, today's wealthier families among overseas Chinese came from medium-income families of the mainland whose access to family capital, knowledge of commercial practices, and use of personal networks helped them advance rapidly ahead of the less-advantaged immigrants.

The extraordinary success of the Chinese immigrant communities throughout Southeast Asia has been a target of considerable debate and concern by the indigenous populations. Two characteristics, their business acumen and the discrimination practiced against them, have earned the ethnic Chinese the label "the Jews of Asia," comparing them with the Jewish communities of old

Overseas Chinese
Percent Ethnic Chinese in:

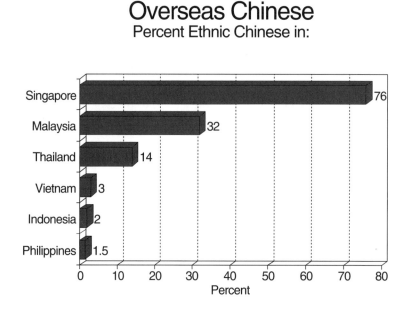

Singapore	76
Malaysia	32
Thailand	14
Vietnam	3
Indonesia	2
Philippines	1.5

Percent

Graph 7.11

Europe. In several countries, the ethnic Chinese own or control a major portion of the national economy. Most of the corporate economy of Thailand and Malaysia is controlled by ethnic Chinese, and they are estimated to own half the private assets in Indonesia where they comprise just 2 percent of the population.

Why should an immigrant group be so successful in commerce while the local indigenous populations fail to keep pace with them? Political and intellectual leaders in Southeast Asia, such as Jose Rizal of the Philippines, Mochtar Lubis of Indonesia, and Mahathir Mohamad of Malaysia, have all openly pondered the question of why local populations are not as "good at business" as the Chinese.

A search for plausible answers has focused on the Chinese Confucian traditions. Indeed, cultural explanations, Confucian or otherwise, are widely accepted in the region with a shrug of the shoulders, evidenced in such common expressions as "Chinese like to take, Malays like to give," and "Chinese like to sell, Thais like to buy." It is true that professions built around trade are not held in

high esteem in many indigenous communities of Southeast Asia, but explanations for the Chinese success extend beyond aphorisms to embrace social and economic factors. Although we have yet much to learn about the reasons for Chinese success, the following conditions have helped them to advance:

Historical Factors

The most powerful Chinese families in Southeast Asia are descendants of mainland families who were already engaged in trade at an intermediate level. They moved into large niches of opportunity created by the colonial powers. The demand for labor was especially great where new mines and plantations were opening up. Wealthier Chinese quickly learned to serve as "middle men," who exploited the labor of poorer local Chinese immigrants.

This same historical position of relative strength continues to benefit the ethnic Chinese today. There is an enormous advantage to already being established in business, with insider networks and access to capital, in an area of expanding opportunity.

Social Environmental Factors

Catastrophe sometimes forced whole communities of Chinese to emigrate. In normal times, those who moved into Southeast Asia were from a more adventurous, risk-taking subset of the population, who did not plan to settle permanently outside China. They expected to make a fortune through short-term, high-return investments after which they would return home. This meant that the astute and well-funded of the Chinese arrivals tried to become "middle-men" from the outset and attempted to achieve monopoly positions in specific economic niches of the colonial economy.

The colonial powers used the Chinese to exploit labor but denied them any hope of entry into positions of status in society or government. Such discrimination forced the Chinese to excel within the confines of commerce. In addition, the fact that their children could not attend local Western schools meant that they had to send them abroad - often to schools that surpassed the quality of the local institutions. Their success was also aided by a steady expansion of personal networks, locally and abroad, that provided them with special favors, advantages, and access to capital. At first, such networks were made up of other ethnic Chinese, but when the wealth and power of these individuals increased so did the penetration of their networks into the substrata of both the colonial and indigenous societies. The networks were an essential element for survival in communities that discriminated openly against them.

The Chinese Family

It has always been an advantage in building family ties among overseas Chinese that an individual in Hong Kong can feel comfortable arranging a marriage with a Chinese in Vancouver. Cultural homogeneity provides stability and security within and among Chinese communities, particularly those who are islands in a sea of racial discrimination. *Yet the ethnic Chinese communities in Asia are not a homogenous group overall.* Local circumstances force Chinese families to adapt and change, as Rozman suggested previously. This adaptability has enabled them to adjust their own culture to local nuances and to modify "who they are." Some of the new generation of Chinese in Southeast Asia feel a diminishing emotional tie to the mainland, yet they have not lost their "Chineseness."

Historically, the solidarity of the Chinese family unit has been a critical factor in commercial survival. Other Asian populations are "familistic" and utilize extended networks, but ethnic Chinese have learned to use their networks to assemble a wider range of business-related inputs: from access to additional capital to exemptions from onerous regulations. They are, in other words, adept at "putting it all together." Their flexibility and adaptability means that today they are as likely to build large businesses with the help of professional outsiders as family insiders.

Contemporary Adaptations

The above factors raise the question of how the Chinese will survive in the new commercial age of Pacific Asia. Conditions that once provided them with significant advantages have now begun to change dramatically. When governments owned large business enterprises and regulated them closely, the Chinese were able to utilize their special contacts to maintain the "inside" track against potential competitors. In today's environment of deregulation and privatization in Asia, the Chinese entrepreneur must compete in an increasingly open field for information and capital.

Yet the ethnic Chinese continue to demonstrate an extraordinary adaptability to the changing circumstances of international commerce. The success of Chinese firms in Thailand indicates that not only are ethnic Chinese able to draw on the capital, technology, and expertise of large foreign firms to grow into very large firms themselves, they are beginning in some cases to beat their foreign partners at their own game. Thai firms, such as the Saha Union Corporation, illustrate that the ethnic Chinese can thrive as owners and managers of large conglomerates in Southeast Asia,

SUCCESS AND EXCESS: THE CASE OF THAILAND

With the collapse of Thailand's currency in the summer of 1997, Paul Krugman seemed to be vindicated in his much-criticized thesis about the "myth" of the Asian economic miracle. Luxury cars were repossessed all over Bangkok as the over-heated Thai economy suddenly lurched and nearly came to halt. A humiliated Thai government had to request a rescue package from the International Monetary Fund (IMF) and closed 42 ailing financial firms. Meanwhile, a brief period of panic currency selling affected other Asian developing countries and several stock markets dived. Many observers suggested that an era come to an end.

In some respects, it had. The euphoric period of almost unrestrained growth in Thailand had ended, but contrary to Krugman's belief, in most developing Asian economies the fundamentals remained sound. Even so, Thailand served as a warning to those that might similarly be veering toward an easy-credit, low-reinvestment strategy governed by insider deals and corrupt government.

Thailand is a case study in the dangers of economic success. Fast growth and a flood of foreign investment combined with an under-supervised financial sector left too much capital in the hands of private financiers who were poorly-equipped to recycle it. Their lending spree resulted in a mountain of highly questionable loans. Most important, a dwindling proportion of the money was being re-invested in Thailand's physical plant, equipment, and education, the mainstays of a competitive economy. As low-cost manufacturing competitors rose rapidly in nearby China, Indonesia, and Vietnam, Thailand saw its export position shrink. The final element in the crisis was a succession of corrupt, inefficient and indecisive governments that overruled the economic discipline of previous generations. Inevitably, a period of slower growth and painful readjustment ensued.

Annual GDP Rate (%)

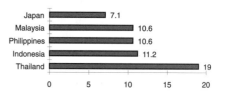

Interest Expense for Nonfinancial Companies as % of GDP, 1995

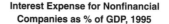

Japan	7.1
Malaysia	10.6
Philippines	10.6
Indonesia	11.2
Thailand	19

Return on Equity (%) *

*Listed Thai companies, excluding banks finance, property, telecommunications

Ratios of Secondary School Enrollment of Males

Taiwan	94 %
S. Korea	92
Hong Kong	73
Philippines	71
Singapore	70
India	60
China	59
Thailand	34

In 1993

with more than a single "model" for their success. Both a family patriarchal system and the dispersed authority of professional managers have proven to be effective modes of organization for a new generation of ethnic Chinese businesses.

CONCLUSION:
DEBATING THE "MIRACLE"

Alternative Views of Success

The economic vitality of Pacific Asia has become the envy of the developing world, but its nature and causes are subjects of ongoing debate. The phenomenon of "late development," in which countries become industrialized and integrated into the world economy, occurs when economic reforms coincide with historic opportunities for change. As noted in the preceding section, the Confucian tradition in Pacific Asia has also contributed to this process. It exploits an overall familistic solidarity that extends to a social contract shared by the entire nation. Analysts continue to disagree over which elements — history, policy, or culture — have been most influential in each economy and we still have much to learn about these interactions.

The debate took a new turn in the 1990s with the assertion that dramatic growth in Asia is qualitatively no different from that achieved by the Soviet Union in its early years. As reasoned by economist Paul Krugman, Asia is similar to the USSR in having managed to achieve high growth for a period only by virtue of massive inputs of capital and labor. Eventually, the USSR stagnated as it encountered diminishing returns from such inputs. The same will be the case for East Asia, Krugman argued in a famous article in *Foreign Affairs*[14] which predicted that continued high growth in the region will eventually confront the reality of low productivity, resulting in an economic slowdown.

Asian growth has indeed been stimulated by massive capital and labor inputs so that the problem of productivity growth is a genuine concern. But breaking economic growth into its components involves difficult and uncertain methodologies. Krugman based his conclusions on the

GDP Growth

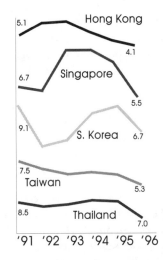

Graph 7.12   The slowing growth rates of several Asian economies in the early 1990s demonstrated that their respective monetary authorities could engineer "soft landings" for the overheating economies, but it also engendered fears of future stagnation.

so-called "factor productivity" growth data for Singapore, Hong Kong, Korea, and Taiwan which many analysts have questioned. If, for example, low productivity leads to low growth in real incomes, real wages in manufacturing in Singapore and other economies would not have increased by anywhere from 40 to nearly 90 percent during the 1980s. Such gains would have been difficult to achieve under Krugman's assumptions of low productivity.

Krugman further argues that diminishing returns from domestic capital have caused the East Asian economies to begin exporting their capital to other parts of the region. This, in fact, is a measure of success, not a lack of profitable investments at home. In each of the Asian "tigers," labor-intensive industries have moved off shore while profitable ones stayed and increased their wages. Lastly, East Asian economies are unlike the command economy of the former Soviet Union. They have responded to market forces and produced quality products that have broad international acceptability.

Still, Krugman's skepticism about the Asian success story provides a useful caution for Asia's planners. There has been, as he suggests, a rapid growth of capital stock and labor inputs, even if that was to be expected at the early stages of Asia-Pacific development. The challenge for these economies will be to advance their productivity further as competition and wages continue to mount. This continuing pressure underlies much of the economic foment in Pacific Asia. Having decided to open their markets and compete on a global scale, the Asian economies now have little choice but to pursue further liberalization. The results will be felt throughout the world.

NOTES

1. William Overholt, "The Moderation of Politics," in *The Pacific Basin: New Challenges for the United States*, ed., James W. Morley (New York: Academy of Political Science, 1986), p. 39.

2. World Bank, *World Development Report, 1991: The Challenge of Development* (New York: Oxford University Press, 1991), pp. 137-39.

3. Excerpted and updated from East-West Center, *Asia-Pacific Report: Trends, Issues, Challenges* (Honolulu: East-West Center, 1986), pp. 17-26.

4. A powerful undercurrent of resentment and distrust by Koreans against Japanese continues to occasionally disturb the bilateral political relationship, however. [—Ed.]

5. Carter J. Eckert, "Korea's Economic Development in Historical Perspective, 1945-1990," in *Korea Old and New: A History*, Carter J. Eckert, et. al. (Seoul: Ilchokak Publishers, 1990), pp. 388-418.

6. Introduction adapted from: East-West Center, *Asia-Pacific Report: Trends, Issues, Challenges* (Honolulu: East-West Center, 1986), p. 21.

7. Hugh T. Patrick and Thomas P. Rohlen, "Small-scale Family Enterprises," in *The Political Economy of Japan: The Domestic Transformation*, eds., Kozo Yamamura and Yasukichi Yasuba, vol. 1 (Stanford: Stanford University Press, 1988), p. 331.

8. Roderick MacFarquhar, "The Post-Confucian Challenge," *The Economist*, 9 February 1980, p. 67.

9. The highly stressful process of written examinations which determine the quality and rank of schools and, ultimately, jobs that will be available to the graduate.

10. Hung-chao Tai, ed., *Confucianism and Economic Development: An Oriental Alternative?* (Washington: The Washington Institute Press, 1989), p. 25.

11. Johannes Hirschmeier and Tsunehiko Yui, *The Development of Japanese Business 1600-1973* (Cambridge: Harvard University Press, 1975), pp. 32, 41.

12. Ronald Dore, *Taking Japan Seriously: A Confucian Perspective on Leading Economic Issues* (Stanford: Stanford University Press, 1988), p. *vii*.

13. Lucian W. Pye, *The Mandarin and the Cadre: China's Political Cultures* (Ann Arbor: University of Michigan, Center for Chinese Studies, 1988), p. 39.

14. Paul Krugman, "The Myth of Asia's Miracle," *Foreign Affairs*, November/December, Vol 73. No. 6. 1994.

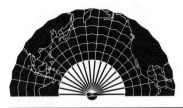

8

Power, Authority, and the Advent of Democracy

OVERVIEW

By the time a wave of peaceful democratic transitions and political liberalization movements had swept Eastern Europe and part of Latin America in 1989, several nations in Pacific Asia were already deeply immersed in their own democratic transformations. The most dramatic of these occurred in 1986-88 in the Philippines and Korea, but throughout the region in the late 1980s the stirring of democratic forces was being felt. Rising middle class wealth was an important stimulus for these movements, even if in some cases it merely strengthened democratic impulses that had begun much earlier. This chapter will focus on the exercise of power, authority and the transition toward democracy in several capitalist states that are undergoing such transitions, leaving the echoes of democratization within the communist states of Vietnam and China to be dealt with in later chapters.

The rise of Asian nationalism and independence movements both before and after World War II stirred debates over what form new governments should take, but such concerns were often overwhelmed by the struggle for political control. Once independence movements had managed to prevail, factional rivalries and instability complicated early efforts to establish independent judicial structures and representative forms of government. The search for workable, stable forms of democracy resulted in compromises, modifications, and setbacks that in Western eyes might be seen as the "failure" of democratic reform.

In fact, democracy was not the highest priority for most developing Asia-Pacific governments in the early postwar period. The fundamental concern was with economic and political stability backed by a sufficient base of power and authority. As a result, the outward forms of democracy, such as legislative bodies, did not necessarily reflect truly representative government. Leaders often bolstered their mandates to rule by promising social stability and rapid rates of economic growth even if their governments might not be deemed "democratic" or sensitive to human rights. By the late 1980s, however, a resurgence of democratic impulses revealed that authoritarian control could no longer be rationalized merely on the basis of economic growth and stability. Those in power had to confront the reality of a rising, affluent and influential professional class whose access to news, ideas, and information from "outside" had made them less tolerant of authoritarian control. As will be seen, even the emergence of this new constituency has not always led to significant political change, but leadership transitions of one sort or another have begun or are about to occur across the entire map of Pacific Asia. All will be influenced by ongoing political, economic, demographic and cultural changes in the region.

"If we were to run elections among China's one billion people now, chaos ... would certainly ensue.... Democracy is our goal, but the state must maintain stability."

—Deng Xiaoping to George Bush,
February 1989

POWER AND AUTHORITY IN PACIFIC ASIA

Ideals of Behavior

Asia-Pacific societies share with the West the sense that unmanaged political power is dangerous, but unlike Westerners they do not conceive of their political development as derivative from some early, more primitive state. Rather, they see themselves as having had to maintain always a precarious balance between stability and chaos. Nor do they view political power and authority as being inherently dangerous, except when authorities have discredited themselves through incompetence or ruthlessness. This general acceptance of authority derives from deeply rooted notions of what is appropriate and obligatory behavior on the part of those who legitimately exercise power, the broader patterns of which can be compared and contrasted between East and Southeast Asia.

In Southeast Asia, power arrangements were traditionally mirrored in a social hierarchy interlaced with a broad network of personal obligations. By maintaining their stations within this hierarchy, people believed they were contributing to the cosmic order and the preservation of stability. The pinnacle of their order was a semidivine ruler, as noted in chapter 1. Kingly powers were to be used to maintain this harmony, not so much by intricate social management as by mediation with powerful cosmic forces.

Authority in East Asia, particularly China, had a similarly divine connection as typified by the "Mandate of Heaven," also described in chapter 1, with which every successful and legitimate ruler was said to be endowed. Governance soon came to be viewed in secular terms as Confucianism grew dominant and authority was imbued with concepts of ethics and order. Society looked upon the supreme ruler as the ideal of proper conduct. His exemplary behavior and moral authority were expected to bring benefits to everyone, and beneath him each individual accepted his or her place in a carefully ordered hierarchy.

There are certain disadvantages to a Confucianist system that grants so much responsibility to so few people, as in the case of China where governmental authority was granted to a supreme leader, his ministers, and an elite group of bureaucrats. This relatively small body was expected to serve a great number of people impartially. At the same time, the elites' Confucian tradition required them to give total loyalty to their family and clan, creating a fundamental and insoluble contradiction — one that has underlain charges of corruption and nepotism against power-holders from China's distant past down to the present day.

Managing Competition and Criticism

In both East and Southeast Asia, leaders were traditionally revered to a degree that made it dangerous to criticize their rule, however constructively. Voices of dissent could be taken as a challenge to the entire system of order. Even the most prestigious Confucian scholar in China, for example, risked imperial retribution if his criticism was seen as undermining the authority of the court. If this stifling of criticism might seem "authoritarian" to Westerners, it was also a "paternalistic" relationship between patrons and clients that helped maintain the social order. The problem, particularly in the East Asian Confucian system, was the absence of any means by which legitimate adversaries could contest publicly and peacefully for power. Those who held the throne considered themselves to be the representatives of the entire society, not merely a constituency within it. Competition for power took place through intrigue and personal attacks, the tactics most compatible with a stable hierarchical system.

If these general attitudes toward power and authority are shared broadly between societies with Confucian traditions, there are also important differences between them. As noted by Lucian Pye, one of the most striking contrasts occurs between China and Japan:

> *"In contrast to the Japanese approach to power, which evolved out of feudal pluralism and was based on primary relationships, the Chinese started with the ideal that all power should emanate from above, from the center, from a single supreme ruler. In contrast to the near anonymity of the low-postured Japanese leaders, the Chinese have consistently made their top leaders into larger-than-life figures. Sun Yat-sen, Chiang Kai-shek, Mao Zedong, and Deng Xiaoping are names that dominate the history of modern China, while only the aficionados of Japanese history can recount the names of those involved in carrying out the Meiji Restoration or can list the prime ministers who made the Japanese economy the third greatest in the world . . The Chinese conviction that all power should reside in the central authority . . has been one of the most powerful factors in shaping Chinese history."*[1]

A further contrast between Chinese and Japanese power relationships can be seen in the extent to which Japan finds it much easier to accommodate competitive forces within its society than does China. Whereas Japan has long accepted the struggle for supremacy among factions, as occurred regularly among feudal lords, China sought to repress such aggression as inimical to social harmony. In Japan, the network of loyalties and obligations extended beyond the family to include whatever superior governmental authority the family acknowledged. Thus, a changeable hierarchy of competing families emerged that also accepted the authority of a central Japanese leadership. By contrast, the Chinese hierarchy developed not among families but within an officialdom whose members were expected to harmonize their relationships in support of a supreme ruler and an idealized vision of an orderly state. Japan's dramatic leap toward interaction with the West in the nineteenth century involved broad factional competition and dynamic societal changes that China's leaders would have found unacceptably chaotic and dangerous.

> *"The gentleness tempered with severity used in governing the household is indeed like that which is required in governing the state."*
> —Yen Zhi Tui, sixth century
> Chinese scholar

To summarize, a key challenge for developing nations in modern Pacific Asia has been to permit competition for power and legitimate authority among constituencies without undermining the basic social order. We will examine how this problem has been confronted, first in Southeast Asia where it is complicated by colonial legacies and ethnic divisions; then in East Asia where rapid economic growth and national political boundaries have influenced the course of democracy in Korea and Taiwan.

TRIALS OF DEMOCRACY IN SOUTHEAST ASIA

Thailand: Steps Toward Parliamentary Democracy, 1932-1945

Thailand's escape from colonial occupation, as noted in chapter 2, came at a price: King Mongkut and his son, Chulalongkorn, had to accept serious encroachments on the territory of what was then called Siam by both France and Great Britain. Yet by playing the imperial ambitions and strategies of the two rivals against one another, they bought precious time in which to educate and effectively modernize a fledgling bureaucracy that would soon manage the emergence of modern Thailand.

Although Thailand entered the twentieth century with an enlightened monarchy bent on forging a modern state, the search for a more representative form of government, such as a constitutional monarchy, was not on the king's agenda. Chulalongkorn and his successors resisted the increasing pressure from some members of the royal family and a growing number of Thai intellectuals to modernize politically as well as economically. In 1912 an unsuccessful military coup attempted to install a republican form of government. It was to be the first of many coup attempts in the decades to come.

Resistance by the throne to democratic reform was rooted in doubts about the suitability of democracy for Thai society. Calls for parliamentary democracy troubled the kings and the senior princes who responded that the society lacked a middle class or educated electorate. In their view, a parliament would have power without real accountability to a knowledgeable and aware populace. They were especially concerned that a parliament might quickly become dominated by Thailand's ethnic Chinese communities.

Yet modernization required an enlarged bureaucracy. By the late 1920s the size and power of the Thai bureaucracy itself created a constituency for constitutional government that could no longer be contained. Leading the call for change were elements of the Western-educated military who in June 1932 staged a bloodless coup and installed a constitutional regime. Although the immediate period that followed (1933-38) could hardly be called more democratic than the one it replaced (power was still highly concentrated in the hands of the reformers), it succeeded in moving forward with a liberal program of mass education and public health under the constitutional monarchy of the boy-king Ananda, led by prime minister Phraya Phahon. The military officers who had formed the People's Party for purposes of staging the coup rapidly increased their power and influence at the expense of their civilian counterparts, mainly because they were a more cohesive, organized political force.

During this period, until the end of World War II, Thailand's only formally recognized political institution was its unicameral legislature which was half appointed, half elected. The People's Party was dominant and absorbed a broad spectrum of the political elite, but it was not formalized as a legal entity. Its potential role in educating and mobilizing the populace was left to the bureaucracy whose membership overlapped considerably with that of the legislature. As a result, the legislative and bureaucratic processes became closely intertwined and political parties as such emerged only a decade after the end of the war.

With the fall of Phraya Phahon's government in 1938, Thai politics entered a strongly national-istic and authoritarian period under Prime Minister Luang Phibun Songkhram, a former army colonel who cooperated closely with the occupying Japanese during World War II. Phibun's government collapsed with the defeat of the Japanese and was replaced by his rival Pridi, who had helped stage the 1932 coup and later led underground support for the Allied powers during the war. Pridi was not able, however, to break the grip of the military over Thailand's government.

Thailand's Military-Civilian Balance of Power

The Japanese surrender gave Thailand's legislative body, the National Assembly, a significant role in government for the first time. A civilian coalition attempted to minimize the role of the military in politics but the result was highly unsatisfactory: Political bickering and economic hardships led to eight cabinets and five different prime ministers in the span of two years. Finally, in November 1947 the military staged a coup. By early 1948 the old constitution had been abandoned and a general was the new premier. Yet even this new government proved unsatisfactory to the military because the constitution still limited their direct involvement in politics. By late 1951 the same generals who organized the 1947 coup staged the so-called silent coup of 1951 that enabled them to retain greater control. The resulting "semidemocratic" government has been subject to innumerable coups ever since, most of them bloodless, as competing factions led by the military continue to rise and fall.

What would seem on the surface to have been a chaotic postwar political development in Thailand was actually a process through which political forces remained in a dynamic balance. An elected parliament was permitted to function even though the real center of power was the executive branch, controlled by elite military and bureaucratic groups. A further stabilizing influence has been the king who remains by far the most revered leadership figure in Thailand. By the early 1990s King Bhumibol had survived more than a score of prime ministers and thirty cabinets by staying above politics except in matters of extreme national crisis when the mere hint of his

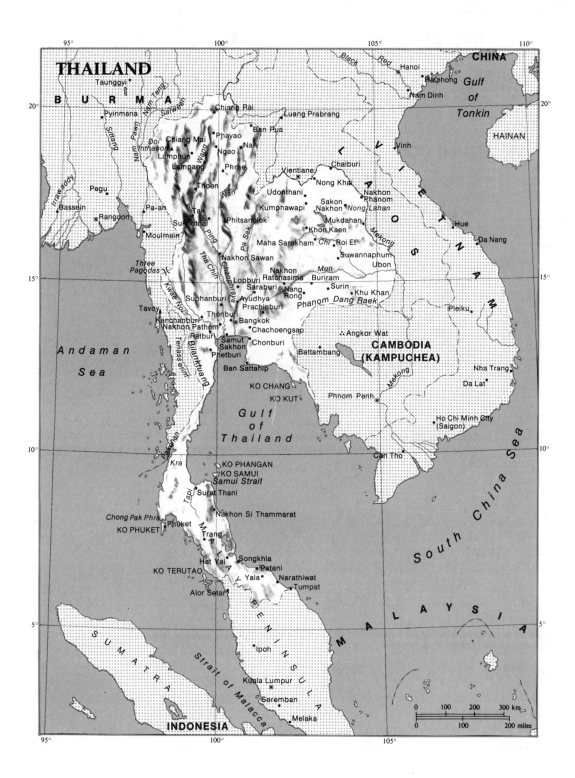

Figure 8.1   Thailand's generals have long been the governmental power brokers. This picture, taken in 1984, shows then-Supreme Commander Arthit Kamlangek in the center. On retiring from the military, Arthit became deputy prime minister in the democratically elected administration of former general Chatichai Choonhavan. After the 1991 bloodless coup, both Arthit and Chatichai were briefly imprisoned, then sent abroad "on vacation."

disapproval restrained military leaders from ill-advised attempts at coups. As a focus of loyalty and national cohesion, his support for a political regime is deemed essential to its survival.

However unique the position of the king may be, the ideal of behavior he represents is also expected of the ordinary political authorities in Thailand. Officials, it is said, should be compassionate, accommodative, and supportive of their subordinates without intimidating them. The responsibilities of a benevolent superior to his subordinates serve as a counterweight to any exploitation that might otherwise develop in the relationship. This has contributed to the stability of Thai political changes since power is not seen merely as a repressive force but as an expression of superior stature and an ability to serve a dependent public.

The use of military coups to effect political transitions seemed to diminish in Thailand by the early 1980s as yet another general-turned-civilian,

Prem Tinsulanonda, took the position of premier. Prem's rule was to be challenged several times, including another unsuccessful coup attempt in 1985, but he remained acceptable to a broad enough coalition of Thai parties to last until 1988 when the first truly democratic election of a new premier in many years, former general Chatichai Choonhavan, took place. At the same time, business leaders and members of the parliament appeared to be increasing their ability to play a forceful role in Thai politics.

On February 23, 1991, however, the image of a receding military role in Thailand's parliamentary democracy was shattered by yet another coup under the leadership of the military Supreme Commander General Sunthorn Kongsompong and his deputy General Suchina Kraprayoon. The United States, acting on principle, quickly terminated all development assistance programs to Thailand as a sanction against the coup even though most of the Thai people,

BURMA'S AGONY

The Burmese strongman, Ne Win, seized power in a military coup in 1962 and, until an outbreak of popular protest in 1988, he held the country in the vise grip of a loyal army and secret police. Ne Win officially retired in 1989 but remained in charge behind the scenes. The military government slaughtered many unarmed antigovernment protesters in Rangoon during the 1988 demonstrations. A year of confrontation followed between civilians and the army in which additional thousands were killed. In retaliation, the authorities used a technique similar to that employed by Cambodia's infamous Khmer Rouge: they depopulated and razed entire neighborhoods of Rangoon known to have supported the democracy protests, moving the inhabitants to shanty towns rife with disease.

In 1990, having become confident that the opposition had been rendered ineffective by the previous year of repression, the authorities decided to permit a showcase popular election. To their shock, a sufficient number of candidates within a broad opposition coalition were elected to lay the groundwork for a representative national assembly.

Yet no action to create such an assembly was permitted and by 1991 most of the opposition leaders had been rounded up and jailed, the most prominent among them being Aung San Suu Kyi, winner of the 1991 Nobel Peace Prize and daughter of the revered "founding father" of modern Burma, Aung San.

Burma stands out in Asia for the thoroughness with which its authoritarian government acts to control opposition voices. Today the country is effectively held by an indigenous army of occupation recruited from impoverished rural areas. More than half the gross national product is devoted to "defense."

while apprehensive, had welcomed the military action. King Bhumibol had been consulted and effectively condoned the coup. What had happened since Chatichai's election to precipitate yet another democratic crisis?

Although he was a product of Thailand's military apparatus, Chatichai had taken measures to place the military more firmly under his authority. His moves were deeply threatening to powerful military rivals who were determined not to relinquish their considerable control over the bureaucracy, nor were they supportive of Chatichai's aggressive efforts to privatize public utilities in which they had financial interests. The fact that his administration also stood widely accused of rampant corruption made it much easier to justify his overthrow. The generals soon named an interim prime minister, the respected businessman Anand Panyarachun, but they also moved to stack the membership of a new National Assembly whose new members they appointed. Nevertheless, the military cast themselves in the role of

reformers and crusaders as they announced a crackdown on the pervasive influence (including in the National Assembly) of gangland figures. They also indicated that they would change the constitution so as to remove the linkage between the legislative and administrative branches, a notorious cause of graft.

Some Thai observers accuse the 1991 coup of having upset the delicately balanced interests of the military, the elected Assembly, the monarchy, the middle class, and the business community. For them it represented a "regression" to the earlier system of government-by-coup. Others suggest that the stabilizing role of the military and its disgust with rampant corruption in Thai politics signaled a shift, however modest, toward a more regular and "clean" political system. They believe that it was Chatichai, not the military, who upset the balance of interests. In any event, the coup signaled a continued dominant role for the military in Thailand, one that future civilian governments will ignore at their peril.

MALAYSIA: THE TRIAL OF PARLIAMENTARY DEMOCRACY, 1957-1969

The Ethnic Setting

The stark division of Malaysia into two parts by the South China Sea is matched by its deep division ethnically, one that has given the term "communal politics" a special meaning in that country. Malays constitute slightly less than half the population. The second largest group, the ethnic Chinese, comprise roughly thirty-five percent and dominate the nation's commercial and professional spheres. They reside mostly in the urban areas of Borneo and the west coast of the peninsula. The Malays are Sunni Muslims whereas the Chinese and the other major indigenous group, the Indians, follow their own religious traditions. Occupation, race, and religion are thus all closely correlated in Malaysia. As a group, the Chinese are much better off economically than the Malays.

This diversity and the pressures it places on the Malay population lie at the center of Malaysian politics. To be a Malay is to be a Muslim, yet unlike the political environments found in the Middle East, the pressures on Malaysia's Muslims are divided between accommodation of diversity and the shunning of it. On the one hand, Malays recognize that they lack a majority status in their country and are reliant on strategies of compromise to achieve political dominance. On the other hand, the identification of Islam with "Malayness" and the fact that Islam is interpreted as an entire way of life has made it difficult for them to accept the intrusion of the modern secular world or the customs of other ethnic groups in their midst. Further complicating the picture are the Malay traditions on which the Islamic faith has been superimposed. A set of non-Islamic folk beliefs rooted in Malay traditions imparts a distinctive quality to Islam in Malaysia and provides a clear example of how Islam was modified by the many cultures in Asia wherein it spread and flourished.

Political Evolution

As elsewhere in the region, Japanese occupation during World War II had a profound effect on the economics and politics of colonial "Malaya." Those who held out against the Japanese in a steady

Malaysia's Ethnic Mix

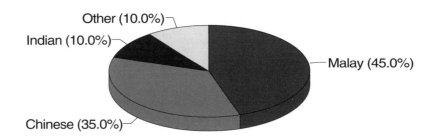

Graph 8.1

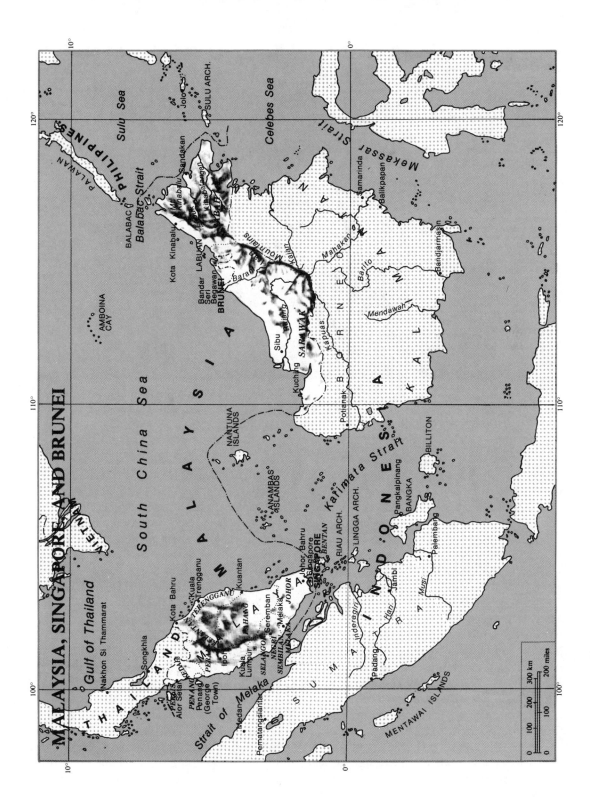

Figure 8.2   One of the most famous scenes in Malaysia's modern history. Prime Minister Tunku Abdul Rahman cries "Merdeka!" ("Freedom!") after reading the Proclamation of Independence on August 31, 1957.

guerrilla warfare were primarily ethnic Chinese Communists whereas the Malays were far less resistant to the invaders. This contrast only served to heighten tensions between the groups after the British returned to Malaya in 1945. In attempting to initiate some local self-government, the British sought to encourage the notion of "citizenship" as applying to all residents including the non-Malays. To move the independence process along, the Malay elite accepted that citizenship rights should be extended to non-Malays prior to independence, but that "special rights" would, at the same time, accrue to those who were indigenous Malays. This informal and profoundly ambiguous "bargain" was intended to display a united front to the British and convince the latter that stable government could be formed in their absence.

At first the British attempted to reorganize "Malaya" politically as a unified state which excluded Singapore (still to remain a separate colony) and abrogated the rights of the sultans of the separate states. This proposal alarmed the Malays who saw it as a serious diminution of their power in the future independent nation. They

organized massive protests and soon formed what was to become the dominant political party of the nation: the United Malays National Organization (UMNO). In the face of such resistance, the British abandoned their original proposal and replaced it with one calling for a Federation of Malaya, still excluding Singapore and the British territories of Borneo, but resembling the old order of state structure and nonelective councils dominated by Malays.

In the years that immediately followed, two other important political organizations were formed, the Malayan Chinese Association (MCA) and the Malayan Indian Congress (MIC), both of which were created as ethnic parties. By 1952, the MCA and MIC had teamed up with UMNO in countrywide legislative council elections to form an intercommunal Alliance Party. This was the supposedly united front which the British accepted as the precondition to independence, even though the British clearly would have preferred parties that combined different ethnic groups rather than a political "alliance" of parties divided along ethnic lines. Constitutional talks ensued which resulted in independence for Malaysia on August 31, 1957.

This delicately balanced, multiethnic coalition was led by Tunku Abdul Rahman, a man whose special appeal was that he had not only led the struggle for independence, but also appeared to be above communal chauvinism. The British administration, too, needed a figure with the Tunku's attributes, someone who believed in British notions of popular government, including parliamentary democracy. Yet even the Tunku could not successfully balance ethnic demands without paying a political price. In the end, many Malays saw him as having "sold" the country to the non-Malays, while non-Malay leaders close to the Tunku could no longer keep their own followers in line in the face of greater demands for opportunities and access to the system.

The Alliance, as it came to be known, remained dominated by the Malay majority but it suffered a serious loss in the 1969 elections. In fact, the opposition, while fragmented, gained a total of 52.5 percent of the votes to the Alliance's 47.5 percent.

To the Malay elite who led the Alliance it seemed that Malay political supremacy, the core of national stability, was seriously in doubt. Amid the victory celebrations of non-Malays and rumors that one or more state governments would be led by non-Malay chief ministers, counterdemonstrations by UMNO supporters led to four days of communal rioting that left nearly two hundred people dead.

The "May 13" rioting of 1969 remains the great political watershed of Malaysian postwar history. Although the rioting was soon contained, the nation was deeply shocked by it. A state of emergency was declared immediately and a "National Operations Council," controlled by the Malays, temporarily replaced the parliament.

Responsibility for diagnosing and solving the problem was given to a high-level National Consultative Council whose recommendations, when implemented in 1971, led to the restoration of parliamentary democracy. The Council concluded that the Malay (or *bumiputera*) population had lost faith in the "bargain" struck on its behalf in the years prior to formal independence. That bargain was understood to have guaranteed Malay access to a greater share of the nation's wealth and the protection of the distinctive Malay cultural heritage. These assurances needed to be reinforced, it

was agreed, through measures that included guarantees for educational access, Malay language instruction, and special redistributions of wealth and ownership rights in commerce and industry. After 1989 the Alliance was reformed into the Barison Nasional (National Front, or BN) comprising at times as many as ten different parties including a larger number of Chinese groups.

By 1971 a broad coalition of Malays and non-Malays had reached an agreement that destabilizing issues, particularly those related to the political dominance of Malays, could no longer be questioned or raised in any way in the course of public debate. Paradoxically, then, as Malaysia returned to parliamentary government in 1971 it did so with the understanding that democracy Malaysian-style would hereafter be contained within strict guidelines of political discourse.

The new, multiethnic "grand coalition" of political parties that followed the 1969 riots placed the Malay leaders on a much firmer footing. Concern over the potential instability that would result from a renewal of interethnic violence reinforced the institutional changes that were imposed during the brief period of nondemocratic emergency rule. An increased strength of the communist insurgency in the 1970s, combined with the prospect that Vietnam might attempt to militarily dominate Southeast Asia (described in chapter 11), also impelled the diverse interest groups of Malaysia toward compromise and accommodation.

Mahathir and the "Limiting of a Limited Democracy"

Running directly counter to these stabilizing forces was the increasingly authoritarian voice of Dato' Seri Dr. Mahathir Mohamad, the prime minister who took over in 1981. Mahathir's policies placed new strains on the Malaysian system of internal cooperation.[2] Unlike his predecessors, he had not been educated in Britain and his experience was that of a young professional rising amid the opportunities and frustrations of a multiethnic, developing country. The result was a new "style" in Malaysian politics and a new voice that seemed to echo the views of early Asian revolutionaries who rejected the models provided by the West.

DILEMMAS OF INEQUALITY:
MALAYSIA'S NEW ECONOMIC POLICY, 1970–1990

The 1969 race riots in Malaysia changed profoundly the way the Malaysian government managed its economy. Prior to 1969, the government had taken a relatively hands-off approach to economic development, assuming that standard market-oriented approaches would provide the necessary "trickle down" effect to the poorer *bumiputera* (indigenous Malay) population. The Malays in control of the government interpreted the riots in economic terms and decided that such a passive approach would only lead to new frictions. This conclusion led to the creation of a "New Economic Policy" (NEP). The goal of the NEP was to eradicate poverty among all races in Malaysia as well as any connection between race and occupation. In effect, the aim was to redistribute wealth over a twenty-year period. Malay ownership of corporate assets was to rise to 30 percent while non-Malays would own 40 percent. Foreign ownership, it was agreed, would shrink dramatically over the same period.

The results of the NEP were mixed. Thousands of jobs did open up to Malays in the higher productivity manufacturing and service sectors, but major regions comprising mostly rural Malays continued to stagnate. In general, job creation for Malays did not keep pace with their accelerating entry into the labor force.

The Chinese were nevertheless opposed to the NEP because it clearly discriminated against them. Malays were given preference in government contracts, Chinese business expansion was regulated, Chinese businesses were forced to hire Malay managers, and they had to sell shares at discounts to Malays. At the same time, the Chinese could see no prospect that they would gain political equality with the Malays if the NEP succeeded.

For the first ten years of the NEP, the greater part of corporate asset redistribution was affected by purchases of strategic stakes in firms by government investment companies. In the 1980s, under Mahathir's influence, the focus shifted towards privatization. Stakes in state companies were sold to the public, especially Malay investors. This, too, met with limited success until government measures in the late 1980s succeeded in bolstering the capital and skills of Malay businesses. This privatization effort continues today.

In the end, the NEP (which was more or less abandoned in 1991) had a dampening effect on the most vital and dynamic part of the Malay economy: the ethnic Chinese businesses. In this respect, it was counterproductive even though it may have succeeded in its larger goal, which was to ensure national political stability. Malay elites were not blind to this cost, but they faced a difficult choice. Unless they could hold out the prospect of economic improvement to poorer Malays, creating a vision of the future that placed them on an equal footing with the Chinese, the divided nation might again have been plunged into civil strife.

Malaysia presents an example of the complex choices facing leaders in a developing country where there are stark income inequalities. Economic models will not tell them how to make the choices that face them: between free market capitalism and interethnic equality; between free-for-all democracy and political stability.

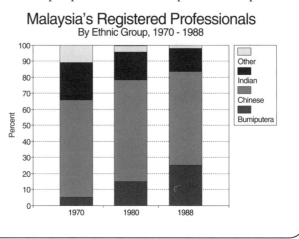

Malaysia's Registered Professionals
By Ethnic Group, 1970 - 1988

ONE-PARTY RULE IN SINGAPORE

In 1984, when Singapore Prime Minster Lee Kuan Yew's Political Action Party (PAP) won the general elections with seventy-seven out of seventy-nine parliamentary seats, what should have been hailed as a landslide in other countries was viewed as a defeat for PAP: For the first time since independence it had failed to score a clean sweep.

Voting is compulsory in Singapore. So is voting for PAP some would say, since constituencies voting for the opposition automatically lose the extensive services of community organizations controlled by PAP. One of the regime's reactions to the 1984 shock was to intimidate further those who participated in opposition politics. In 1987, for example, twenty-two young Singapore professionals were rounded up and detained without trial for months on the grounds that they were engaged in a Marxist conspiracy. Most were later released after many weeks of harsh interrogation. Similarly, the regime launched an all-out attack against key independent news sources, such as the prestigious regional weekly magazine *Far Eastern Economic Review*, expelling its correspondent and virtually banning its distribution.

On the other hand, the regime's response to the 1984 elections was to inquire urgently into how PAP had failed its constituency and what needed to be done to bring that constituency back. The "strongman" rule in Singapore, which formally ended in 1990 when Lee passed the premiership to his chosen successor, Goh Chok Tong, belies the glib generalization that power corrupts. Lee's leadership, exemplary in the Confucian sense, was never tainted by accusations of corruption or self-seeking. He sought, in a paternalistic way, to determine the interests of his society, to protect it from perceived dangers, and to guide it in adapting to global economic change.

Instead, Dr. Mahathir called for his countrymen to "Look East," that is, to learn the work ethics and strategies of Japan and Korea. His aim was to combine private and public sector enterprise in ways that would accelerate the country toward industrial modernization.

At first, Mahathir's approach seemed to indicate a "liberal" political trend when he released detainees under the Internal Security Act (ISA). This tolerance of dissent soon evaporated, however, as he began to claim a mandate to rule derived from the majority support he garnered at the polls rather than from any parliamentary processes. A more confrontational style of politics appeared that opened divisions within his own party and within the Malay community at large. By 1986, in an unprecedented development, Mahathir's chief deputy and heir apparent, Dato' Musa Hitam, resigned. The party was effectively split into two factions.

In subsequent elections, Mahathir still managed narrowly to defeat the opposition in elections, but his position was weakened by the internal dissension. Racial polarization in the country grew worse. Mahathir reacted by cracking down on the freedom of expression. Beginning in October 1987, he had some 106 persons rounded up and imprisoned under the ISA, and he closed three local daily newspapers. Mahathir said that the arrests were necessary to prevent racial conflagration and the disruption of public order, but they also enabled him to silence some of his most dangerous critics.

The Nature of Democracy in Malaysia

Democracy since the crisis of 1969 has been sustained in Malaysia at the cost of significant curbs on political freedoms, particularly those of the press. These limitations have been justified by the view that too much political discourse in an ethnically divided society like Malaysia is more likely to inflame passions and result in political violence than it is to resolve them. One observer has called the result the "limiting of a limited democracy."

On the other hand, politics in Malaysia since the 1969 crisis have been stable. Although fully democratic conditions have not been allowed, there has been a sense of broad political participation. General elections continue to be held, the leadership succession continues under constitutional authority, and a significant political opposition is allowed to operate. In short, it is a resilient political system which in spite of occasional convulsions and crises has served the needs of a divided, tense, multiethnic society. Ethnic and religious factors explain why the rules of the game remain so "tight" and why the predominance of a secure Malay majority remains essential to the stability of the nation.

INDONESIA: FROM "DEMOCRACY" TO "GUIDED DEMOCRACY," 1950-1966

Background

In considering the political development of Indonesia, it is important to keep in mind that it is a vast archipelagic nation of more than a thousand inhabited islands. The island of Java contains more than half the population of Indonesia and exerts a powerful influence over the course of Indonesia's economic and political development.

Despite a huge Muslim population of more than 130 million, Indonesia is not an Islamic state. Unlike Malaysia, where the constitution declares Islam to be a state religion (but which remains vague as to whether Malaysia is an "Islamic state"), Indonesia prides itself in officially embracing all religions. At the same time, Islam occupies such a special place in Indonesian society that there is a separate state system of Islamic education and Islamic courts. Moreover, the ethnic Chinese in Indonesia have been under even greater pressure than in Malaysia during the post-independence period. Indonesia (like Thailand) requires the Chinese to speak the national language (special Chinese language schools are permitted in Malaysia) and to adopt indigenous names. Restrictions on Chinese in Indonesia became especially severe after President Suharto came into power, with chambers of commerce,

guilds, and Chinese-language books all forbidden. The regulations eased slightly after diplomatic relations with China were restored in 1990.

The independent, federated United States of Indonesia emerged in 1949 after being shaped by two fundamental forces: Dutch colonial rule and the Japanese occupation which was followed by a protracted military struggle with the returning colonial forces (chapter 5). In this sense, Indonesia is the product of artificial boundaries that were super-imposed on an ethnically diverse island world. Initially, this forced a federalist structure on the new nation, with considerable autonomy given to the outlying, non-Javanese regions. But the revolution's leaders, whose intent had been to establish a republic with a centralized authority located on the island of Java, deeply resented this fact. With the final departure of the Dutch, they moved quickly to establish a republican, parliamentary structure with Sukarno as figurehead president.

There followed several years of rapid turnovers of cabinets and shifting alliances among political factions. The Indonesian Communist Party (Partai Komunis Indonesia, PKI) expanded rapidly during this period and made a startlingly strong showing in the popular vote in the 1955 elections. Meanwhile, tensions were growing between the export-producing "Outer Islands" and the import-consuming, densely populated center of Java. By 1956 regional army commanders in the outer islands of Sumatra, Kalimantan, and Sulawesi (Celebes) had, with the backing of the local populace, formed resistance movements to the Javanese authorities. These leaders saw even Sukarno as a threat as he began to denounce Western-style, liberal democracy as inappropriate to Indonesian customs. In 1958 the resistance flared briefly into armed revolt on Sumatra. Islands such as Aceh and South Sulawese were hotbeds of Islamic insurgencies, angered by the refusal of Indonesia's leaders to incorporate Islam into the new constitution.

Although the Sumatran insurgency and other uprisings were quelled, they left the nation in a state of political paralysis. With the backing of Nasution, the leading general of the revolution, Sukarno discharged the constituent assembly and launched a new system of governance known as "Guided Democracy," the influence of which

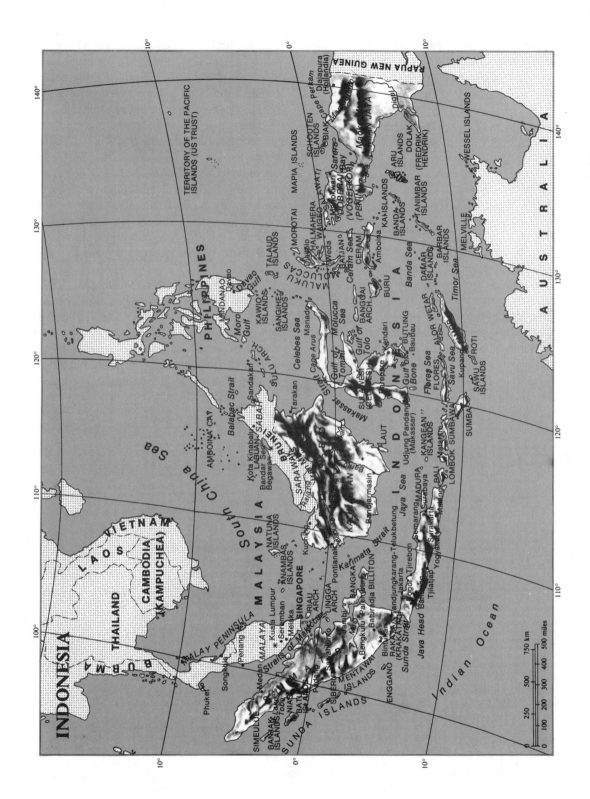

continues to be felt in Indonesian politics. These developments and their consequences are described below in excerpts by two leading analysts.

♦   ♦   ♦

SUKARNO AND GUIDED DEMOCRACY

— by Ulf Sundhaussen

Sukarno was influenced by traditional Javanese thought, as well as Marxism, Western European social democracy, and Islam, without being totally committed to any of them. Rather, he attempted to synthesize them and thereby become acceptable to all major streams of thought as the great unifier of this diverse society. Yet, at the beginning of his Guided Democracy, he practically disenfranchised most ethnic minorities as

well as the intellectual community. During the following years he argued for a continuing revolution and the unity of nationalist, religious, and communist parties for this common cause, only to see his dream collapse in a huge bloodbath.

Future generations are unlikely to see him as the "great unifier" he purported to be, but may hail him as the founder of a viable form of Indonesian democracy. His criticism of liberal democracy had started in 1949, culminating in a number of speeches he made at the end of 1956 and the beginning of 1957, when he stressed that he was a Democrat; however, "I do not desire democratic liberalism. On the contrary I want a guided democracy."

Sukarno opposed Western parliamentary practices and majority decisions — "50 percent plus one are always right" — as essentially enhancing rather than solving conflict, putting minorities forever in the position of permanent losers. Rather, he felt Indonesia should return to the age-old form of democracy practiced in the villages, where deliberations were held until consensus emerged, in the

Indonesia's Ethnic Groups

Ethnic Group	%	Location	Major Religion
Javanese	45	Java	Orthodox santri, abangan
Madurese	7	Madura/Java	Orthodox santri
Sundanese	14	Sumatra	Modernizing santri
Coastal Malay	7	Sumatra	Modernizing santri
Minangkabau	4	Sumatra	Modernizing santri
Batak	2	Sumatra	Christian., Mod. santri
Acehnese	2	Sumatra	Modernizing santri
Buginese	4	Sulawesi	Modernizing santri
Minehasa	2	Sulawesi	Christianity
Balinese	2	Bali	Hindu
Dayak	1	Kalimantan	Animism, Islam, Christianity
Ambonese	1	Moluccas	Christianity, Islam
Papuan	1	New Guinea	Christianity, Animism
Chinese	3		Confucianism, Buddhism, Other

Table 8.1   Many Indonesian Muslims are the so-called *abangan* who adhere to the "Javanese religion," an amalgam of animism, elements of Buddhism and Hinduism, with Islam only the last layer. The *abangan* have resisted Islamization of society with as much determination as Christian, Hindu, and Buddhist minorities. Even the "good" Muslims, the *santri*, are divided into an orthodox and a modernizing yet devout wing, competing with each other through different parties and organizations. (Ulf Sundhaussen)

spirit of mutual cooperation. This, in his view, was true democracy, brought about under the guidance of a trusted elder who could summarize and aggregate all expressed sentiments and pronounce the decisions of the assembled.

Musyawarhara ["deliberation"] became the apparent practice in the legislative assemblies of his Guided Democracy. Yet this kind of democracy must be pronounced a failure not so much because it had proven unworkable, but because these assemblies were unrepresentative, with no elections ever held during Guided Democracy, and large groups excluded from the process of decision-making, which increasingly came to rest solely in the hands of the president. The army's attitudes toward democracy have been no less ambivalent. Although alienated by the early socialist cabinets and the conduct of parliament between 1952 and 1950, army leaders have in the main supported or at least tolerated the system of parliamentary democracy as long as parliamentarians were able and willing to put together government coalitions. Only when parliament ceased to function did they seek to involve themselves in the processes of decision-making, not as usurpers of all power but as one of the forces determining the fate of the nation.

Of particular importance are the views of Nasution, who has had by far the greatest impact on the evolving ideological platform of the army. As a Batak from North Sumatra he was well aware of the ethnic problems of the country, and while he abetted the smashing of the federalist order he has also continued to call for adequate preservation of the rights of the Outer Islands. He committed himself implicitly, and often enough explicitly as well, to maintaining some form of democracy.

At the beginning of Guided Democracy civil servants, as well as cabinet ministers, had to choose between party membership and their jobs, and their promotions and assignments became dependent on their allegiance to the president and his policies. The military, under its concept of the "dual function" — both as an agency in charge of external defense and internal security, and as one of the sociopolitical forces of the land — had started to penetrate all state branches and services from 1958 on. But with the ascendancy of the New Order many, if not most, of the top jobs in the civil service came to be occupied by military officers.

These different penetration patterns have prohibited the bureaucracy from becoming an autonomous, truly professional service. Equally damaging has been the fact that Sukarno allowed civil service salaries to decline to such an extent that state employees could not possibly feed their families on their official income and were thus forced into succumbing to the temptation of corruption. It is only because of the widespread suffering of the masses as well, and the existing feudal values with their inbuilt respect for authority, that the bureaucratic arm of the state did not suffer irreparable damage.

Almost the same maladies affected the armed forces. From 1945 on, party politicians have tried to use the military for their own particular purposes in total disregard of the need to keep officers out of politics if the military was to abstain from intervention. The relationship between the officer corps and the politicians was so tense that one of the earliest goals of the army was to remain free from party ideologies, and to serve the nation rather than the ever-changing "government of the day." The army headquarters had loyally served the democratic order and ceaselessly attempted to inject into civil-military relations a rational and professional system of prerogatives until parliamentary rule was abandoned by the politicians in early 1957.

The army has not increased its political power by coups against legitimate governments, but rather has stepped in whenever vacuums needed to be filled, especially in 1957 and 1960. It has come to see itself as the savior of the nation from rapacious and incompetent politicians, as well as rightist and leftist extremists endangering the unity of the country, a role that has become enshrined in military doctrine.

During Guided Democracy, and increasingly so under the army supported New Order [see below], the life of autonomous social, occupational, and cultural organizations, trade unions, and business associations has been gradually strangled. Only in the last ten years or so have new forces striven to attain a degree of autonomy like, for instance, KADIN (the Chamber of Trade and Commerce). But with the state still the major investor and main proprietor of banks, mines, industries, and trading houses, even potentially independent-minded businessmen can rarely afford to lose government contracts by exhibiting too much autonomy. While private fortunes are being made, though, they are often made by Chinese businessmen who depend on the government and the army for their personal safety, the myriads of licenses and concessions required to do business in Indonesia, and the truly lucrative connections. The trade union movement remains firmly under state control.

The most important democratic thrust in Indonesia was that toward what can be described as "confederate" democracy, involving primarily not individuals, but whole minority groups intent on seeking a degree of autonomy within the larger framework of the state, with a system of democratic dialogue as the means to achieve and maintain that autonomy. Almost all significant ethnic minorities, as well as the Catholics and Protestants, were strongly in support of such democratic order, and the major parties representing their interests were all staunch defenders of parliamentary democracy. When their political rights appeared to be threatened they were prepared to oppose the essentially Javanese and increasingly authoritarian government, sometimes even to the extent of taking up arms in defense of their perception of democracy.[3]

◆   ◆   ◆

DESCENT INTO CHAOS

— by John R. W. Smail

Indonesian political power rested in a competitive alliance between the army, with most of the machinery in its hands, and Sukarno with his vintage charisma along with the loyal support of the PKI. This oddly constructed political tripod remained surprisingly stable during the descent into chaos. Exports shrank as army officers made away with the assets of former Dutch plantations, Java no longer reliably supplied the staple foods its growing population required, inflation rose faster and faster. The government launched two major "confrontations," the first (1960-62) against Holland for recovery of West New Guinea, which it successfully achieved in 1962, the second (begun

in 1963) against the newly formed state of Malaysia. For these campaigns, among other reasons, Sukarno's government imported a great deal of Soviet military equipment. In due course it proceeded also to expropriate British and Indian assets, in addition to the earlier Dutch ones. Sukarno himself propagated a stream of new slogans which became part of an official ideology in which all civil servants and students were indoctrinated. In 1964 the PKI, more and more openly sponsored by Sukarno in alliance against the army, shocked the rural leadership of Java with a vigorous land reform and rent reduction campaign.

As Guided Democracy moved into 1965 the mounting inflation turned into a classic hyperinflation. The army worried about what Sukarno might do next for the PKI and stood by its guns. The PKI, unable to do anything but mount another strident campaign, agitated for a people's militia, which might arm some of its supporters, and clung ever tighter to Sukarno. As for Sukarno, his extraordinary talent seemed spent.

The crisis burst before dawn on October 1, 1965, when a group of middle-rank officers assassinated six senior generals and proclaimed their own assumption of power under Sukarno's aegis. In Indonesia the coup is officially attributed to the PKI; foreign scholars diverge widely in their interpretations. At any rate it was the aftermath of the coup — suppressed within a few days by forces shrewdly deployed by General Suharto — that was decisive.

With both Sukarno and the PKI shaken by apparent complicity in the coup, and the martyrdom of the six generals for a rallying cry, the army set out to destroy the PKI forever. In late October, after an ominous three-week silence, the massacres began, in Central Java, then East Java, then Bali. Army units themselves seem to have killed comparatively few people; they provided assurance of support and sometimes firearms, but it was mostly neighbors and youth bands who did the killing. Hundreds of thousands were massacred, systematically and — most awfully — without resistance. (Estimates of the number of victims range, shakily, from fewer than a hundred thousand to a million. The main killings outside Java and Bali were in North Sumatra. In Aceh and West Borneo large numbers of Chinese were also massacred.)[4]

Amid these horrors, on March 11, 1966, Sukarno was tactfully compelled to transfer effective authority to Suharto, and Indonesia passed from what later come to be called the "Old Order" into the "New Order." On the one hand Suharto moved swiftly on economics and foreign policy. At home, aware that he could do nothing with hyperinflation raging, he built a strong connection with a group of U.S.-trained Indonesian economists, his "technocrats" of the sixties, seventies, and eighties. Abroad, he promptly canceled Sukarno's two major foreign policy initiatives of the moment, military "confrontation" with Malaysia and intimate association with China. These steps opened the way to closer connections with the West and Japan and therefore to the possibility of help for Indonesia's ravaged economy. As the capitalist bloc warmed to these overtures, Suharto and his technocrats promptly took steps to return Dutch and other nations' expropriated assets and to promulgate an attractive law on foreign investment. There followed a steady and generous flow of aid from abroad.

On other matters, especially domestic politics, Suharto moved slowly and with great care. He understood the enormous appeal of Sukarno's political language and persona and was careful to copy much of the former and back away from direct confrontation with the latter during the arcane constitutional maneuvers of 1966 to 1968. It was not until March 1968 that Suharto was elected president and not until June that he was able to appoint his own cabinet.[5]

♦   ♦   ♦

BRAVE NEW ORDER

General Suharto's initial moves on succeeding Sukarno were to consolidate a base of political support in Java through political appointments and purging the military of leftist officers. An Operations Command for the Restoration of Security and Order (KOPKAMTIB) was established as a means of maintaining a close watch on domestic political developments and any potential breaches of national security. The vague state ideology begun by Sukarno called the *Pancasila* (Five Pillars), consisting of Belief in One God, National-

ism, International Cooperation, Democracy, and Social Justice, was retained. Over a period of years the government *de facto* political party, GOLKAR, forced various opposition groups, one Muslim and the other secular, to unite under two artificial parties. Both have been riven by factionalism that has prevented them from mounting a serious challenge to the regime.

Sukarno's close control of the press was similarly retained by Suharto, except that where Sukarno had banned right-wing publications Suharto banned those of the Left. Some limited amount of independence was granted to a daily newspaper and a weekly magazine, but press closures in the 1990s reflected an increasingly defensive posture by the regime in the face the visible corruption of Suharto's immediate family.

Another Sukarno legacy has been retained in the parliament: While GOLKAR clearly dominates the electoral process and the parliament, non-GOLKAR groups are permitted a voice through the Guided Democracy practice of *musyawarah* ("deliberation") and *mufakat* ("consensus"). This results in a potentially significant if somewhat invisible role for the opposition: If it refuses to give its consent to a bill during a process of discussion in committees, the legislation is likely to be shelved before it reaches the plenum. Nevertheless, the parliament remains a weak instrument in they eyes of most observers.

The demise of what was once briefly a parliamentary democracy in Indonesia has troubled scholars of democratic change because it seems to imply that there has not been popular support for full democratic reform. Javanese political culture, a dominant force in the Indonesian government, might be viewed in this sense as unsupportive of democratic values. In the Javanese cosmology, power is a neutral force bestowed on the sultan. Anyone acquiring it independently does so at the expense of the sultan, including opposition groups whose acquisition of power undermines the political "potency" of the state. On the other hand, some authorities including those in the army have proved capable of self-critical review in response to frank criticism. Army abusers of human rights in East Timor, following Indonesia's forceful takeover of the former Portuguese colony in 1975 (Chapter 11), were eventually disciplined, for example.

PROPAGANDA AND THE POWER OF THE PUPPETS

Every Sunday morning at 11:15 four popular clowns appear on Indonesian TV for fifteen minutes. They are Semar, a hideous pot-bellied dwarf; Petruk, a scrawny, long-nosed creature; Gareng, a deformed midget with sores; and Bagong, a bald and stupid froglike character. They sing, they cackle, they shriek. They are also related to gods; furthermore, they are immortal. Javanese viewers find them hilarious. But non-Javanese may find the program a little too didactic — for the clowns sing, cackle, and shriek about such matters as paying taxes on time, birth control, and agricultural development.

Javanese do not mind being lectured. It even appears they positively like being told how to behave, as long as the lecture has an aesthetic appeal. In fact, ethics and aesthetics in Java are often indistinguishable. To be Javanese literally means to be civilized, and to be civilized means to behave beautifully. The highest expression of Javanese manners is also the finest repository of Javanese aesthetics, namely *wayang*, and specifically *wayang kulit*, the shadow puppet theater. To Javanese *wayang* is something spiritual, ethical, and aesthetic, and it is to this theater that the four popular clowns belong, the ugly exceptions in a world of grace and beauty.

It is typical of the way Indonesia is governed these days that the clowns, whose traditional function is to be critical of their masters, are now used for government propaganda. Even the Dutch tolerated being made fun of by *wayang* clown characters played by actors. The Japanese, however, during their occupation of Indonesia, did not and several actors were executed. The present Indonesian Government does not go quite that far, but direct criticism is out. A few years ago a traditional Sundanese clown called Kabayan was banned from TV for being too satirical. Now, he, too, is used to disseminate government messages.

—Ian Buruma, *Far Eastern Economic Review* (August 9, 1984)

Islam is another factor that has been cited as a potential barrier to the development of democracy in Indonesia. In view of occasional outbreaks of violent Islamic extremism, concern has been expressed that Indonesia could one day be subject to an Islamic revolution of sorts. Such an outcome is unlikely, however, in view of the way in which Islam has developed in Indonesia. As in Malaysia, its influence has been moderated by Indonesian Malay traditions. Differences exist within the Indonesian Islamic movements as to their appropriate role in politics. Indonesian Muslims seem unlikely to rally under the universal banner of Islam, being subdivided historically into a variety of distinct regional identities.

Democracy remains an elusive goal for a determined minority in Indonesia. By the mid-1990s, in anticipation of parliamentary elections in 1997 and the Presidential election in 1998, that minority began to advocate more democratic processes. One of the most prominent voices was that of Megawati Sukarnoputri, daughter of former President Sukarno. As the head of the Indonesian Democratic Party, or PDI, one of the approved political parties in Indonesia, her outspoken statements at potential attractiveness to a discontented public clearly unnerved Suharto. In 1996, the regime engineered her dismissal, sparking the most visible political demonstrations to be seen in Jakarta since Sukarno's demise. The arrest of numerous Megawati supporters confirmed the extent to which independent, organized opposition still arouses suspicion and anxiety in the Indonesian government. At the same time, new and more independent voices are being heard from a newly formed Indonesia human rights commission and retired ministers who are willing to criticize the government. Although constrained by Suharto's limited of tolerance of dissent, the vanguard of a more openly critical generation continues to test the boundaries of authoritarian control.

THE PHILIPPINES: FROM INDEPENDENCE TO MARTIAL LAW, 1946-1972

Among the several Asian nations struggling to define for themselves the appropriate role of democratic institutions, perhaps none has weathered as long a succession of crises, almost as an ongoing phenomenon, as the Philippines. The historical and cultural forces affecting Philippine democracy have been especially volatile and contradictory, for beneath a broad Philippine commitment to democratic ideals lies an authoritarian heritage grounded in church, home, and community.

Amid the vast destruction left by the Japanese occupation, the Philippines at the end of World War II was poised to embark on a new era based on a strong sense of national identity that was increasingly an Asian identity as well, but its political fortunes have seen radical swings since then. The Philippines became the first colonialized nation in Asia to achieve democracy and seemed destined for a bright future under the leadership of Ramon Magsaysay. His death in a plane crash in 1953 was a critical blow to the country, until at last another promising politician appeared on the scene whose rise is described here.

◆   ◆   ◆

THE MARCOS ERA

— by David Joel Steinberg

Magsaysay's immediate successors lacked the vision and political power to maintain the momentum he had built. Carlos Garcia, Magsaysay's vice president, was elected in 1957, and Diosdado Macapagal in 1961. This era, subsequently known as the "Old Order," clearly revealed the structural contradiction of the postindependent, oligarchic society. It was a working democracy, in the sense that people out of office could through the electoral process win power. It was dominated, however, by a single elite, whose members jumped parties with dizzying speed. It was a period of private armies, growing lawlessness, and uneven economic development.

Land reform was much talked about but never implemented. The elite had no intention of abolishing the source of its wealth; and, even had it wanted to, it lacked the economic resources to fund the program. At the same time, it was also an era of substantial business growth. Multinational corporations entered the Philippines in large numbers as world prosperity, fueled by the American economy, sought new markets and opportunities. It was in this era that the modern sector of the society moved out to Makati, the new city built just outside Manila.

Under the entrepreneurial management of the Zobel family, highrise buildings, broad boulevards, shopping centers, and residential subdivisions all sprouted on land previously trampled by carabao. To misquote Marx, if the rich got richer and the poor got children, there was also a sense of optimism, prompting large numbers of youngsters to seek college education as the vehicle for upward mobility to the good life. The free press limited some of the excesses of the system by spotlighting them, and there was a growing sense of national pride, a growing awareness of the Asian-ness of the Philippines.

In 1963, an ambitious senator, Ferdinand Marcos, successfully challenged the prewar oligarch, Eulogio (Amang) Rodriguez, for the presidency of the Senate. Two years later, Marcos jumped parties, became a Nacionalista, and won a landslide presidential victory. In his 1965 inaugural address, he said, "The Filipino, it seems, has lost his soul, his dignity, and his courage. Our people have come to the point of despair. We have ceased to value order." Marcos continued by noting that the "government is gripping the iron hand of venality, its treasury is barren, its resources are wasted, its civil service is slothful and indifferent, its armed forces demoralized, and its councils sterile."

Marcos, the creature of the "Old Order," claimed to be the savior of the nation. In 1969, running on the slogan, "Rice and Roads," and liberally spending money from the public treasury, Marcos was reelected president, the first man ever to win a second full term. His claim to be a distinguished war hero enhanced his glamour, and his flamboyant, beautiful wife Imelda made them seem like Philippine versions of the Kennedys. This was an era of prosperity, fueled in large measure by the growing American presence in Indochina.

Figure 8.3   In August 1971, bombs exploded at an anti-Marcos rally being held at the Plaza Miranda Hotel in Manila. The attack killed nine persons and wounded a hundred others, including some of Marcos' leading opponents. A seminal event in modern Philippine history, the Plaza Miranda bombing triggered a chain of events that led to Marcos's 1972 declaration of martial law. Attributed initially to Marcos, the bombing was actually carried out by Maoist rebels of the Communist Party of the Philippines in an attempt to provoke government repression and push the country toward a people's revolution.

"Constitutional Authoritarianism"

What distinguished Marcos from his immediate predecessors was his interest in a new political ideology for the Philippines. Marcos saw democracy as not only wasteful but licentious, as not only corrupt but paralyzing. In his view, "constitutional authoritarianism" should supplant the "Old Order." The authoritarian instinct had been articulated by Apolinario Mabini at the Malolos Constitutional Convention in the 1890s. During World War II, Jose Laurel, Marcos's mentor, took the presidency in his belief that the Philippines needed a fundamental reorganization in keeping with a worldwide trend in which "totalitarianism [was] gradually supplanting democracy:"

Throughout his career, Ferdinand Marcos was obsessed with constitutions. To his last days in office, he clung to the notion that there had to be a law to justify an action. This made his regime increasingly like that of the Queen of Hearts in Alice in Wonderland.

On September 21, 1972, Marcos proclaimed martial law. Claiming he was exercising his power "to protect the Republic of the Philippines and our democracy," Marcos moved rapidly to end all forms of dissent and opposition. Thousands of persons were arrested, habeas corpus was suspended, the media was drastically curtailed, the courts substantially weakened, and the army strengthened. Marcos justified this declaration by claiming there was a serious threat of a Communist takeover led by a new generation of radical Maoist students, many of whom were upper middle class by birth.

In fact, Marcos was motivated by a broader set of issues. He viewed the constitutional convention that was then debating the future of the government

Figure 8.4   President Lyndon Johnson met with Ferdinand Marcos and his wife, Imelda, in Manila in 1966.

structure as a threat to society. He was in his seventh year as president, constitutionally banned from running for a third term. Moreover, as his power began to slip away, he was being challenged by members of the oligarchy, including the powerful Lopez family, owners of the *Manila Chronicle*, television stations, and the Manila Electric Company. A young Senator Benigno Aquino was the likely next president. The last issue of the *Free Press,* the leading opinion magazine at the time, carried a prophetic cover bearing a picture of Aquino targeted through the crosswires of a rifle sight with the caption, "Senator Benigno S. Aquino: TARGET?"

Marcos's declaration of martial law won the strong support of the modern business community and of U.S. president Richard Nixon. In the first three years, tourism and government revenues tripled, and the economy grew at an average annual rate of 7 percent. The private armies of the oligarchies were disbanded and some 500,000 privately held weapons were confiscated. In those early years, Marcos often was compared to Lee Kuan Yew of Singapore. If he violated human rights with impunity, his was a less brutal dicta-

torship than some others. People indeed were arrested and tortured and murdered. The total story of brutality has yet to be told, and yet, many Filipinos saw these years as a time of progress and seemed willing to surrender liberty for economic development.

Marcos dramatically expanded the army's role in society, tripling its size. The officer corps was given opportunities to acquire great wealth, and the tradition of a nonpolitical military disappeared. Marcos issued a new constitution, replaced Supreme Court justices and changed the court system, created people's organizations at the mass and local level, and built a new political party, the KBL (Kilusang Bagong Lipunan). Manipulating patronage and the power of government effectively, and using referenda, constitutional amendments, and other techniques, Marcos built a dominant political organization which stifled dissent. In 1976, while amending the constitution, Marcos inserted Amendment 6, which gave him transcendent political power no matter what structure might subsequently be put into place.

By 1975, however, the ideological fervor dissipated and it became apparent that the new order was a vehicle for Marcos's personal aggrandizement. Crony capitalism gave close friends of the First Family vast economic opportunity. Sugar and coconut areas were made exempt from the land reform which had begun with such fanfare in 1973. The obvious growing greed of the cronies and of Imelda Marcos substituted profit for ideology. This was the period known as the "Conjugal Dictatorship." With her jewels, her jet-set friends, and her many projects, Mrs. Marcos became the symbol of corruption. Known as Nuestra Señora de Metro Manila because, among many other posts, she was also governor of Metropolitan Manila and minister of human settlements, she chaired no fewer than twenty-three government councils, agencies, and corporations. She controlled hundreds of millions of dollars annually through their budgets, and it was during this period that she built eleven five-star hotels, the Manila Cultural Center, and the five thousand seat International Convention Center, a $21 million Film Center, and a sprawling terminal at the airport. Increasingly, she became the most visible representative of the regime, and speculation centered on her succession to the presidency on her husband's illness or death. The aimless drift of the Marcos government was perfectly summarized during a press conference with Mrs. Marcos in 1982 when she said, "The Philippines is in a strategic position — it is both East and West, right and left, rich and poor." After a pause she went on to note, "We are neither here nor there."[6]

◆   ◆   ◆

THE LEGACY OF "PORK BARREL DEMOCRACY"

The oil shocks of the 1970s were calamitous for the Philippine economy, particularly because they combined a drop in prices for key export commodities with the parasitic greed of Marcos and his close associates, the "crony capitalists." The ambitious plans laid by his technocrats to modernize the economy were overwhelmed by mounting oil bills, the necessity of massive foreign borrowing, and unproductive "glamour" investments by Marcos' wife, Imelda, who exercised considerable power alongside her husband.

PHILIPPINE DEMOCRACY

The traditional clientelistic, opportunistic style of Philippine politics — which views public service as a means for private gain and pursues the struggle for power with violence, fraud, and procedural abandon — has clearly undermined democracy; and yet the widespread popular and elite commitment to democratic participation made it much more difficult to institutionalize an authoritarian regime in the Philippines than in Thailand or Indonesia.

— Larry Diamond, in *Democracy in Developing Countries: Asia*

Unaware of the far-reaching implications of the growing economic crisis, Marcos decreed an end to martial law in early 1981 and permitted free elections in which the only viable opposition candidate to Marcos, former senator Benigno Aquino, was prohibited from running. Following Marcos' victory in an election widely known to have been fraudulent, Vice-President George Bush visited Manila and, in a celebratory toast, announced to Marcos, "We love your adherence to democratic principles — and to the democratic processes."

The Marcos regime was moving steadily toward a political crisis that would be brought about in part by severe economic problems. However, the growing economic crisis alone did not precipitate the Marcos downfall any more or less than it did that of other regimes in East Asia. What it did impose in the case of Ferdinand Marcos was an even greater dependence on those who were most resistant to democratic solutions. On the one hand, the middle class and business elites of Manila were increasingly alienated from Marcos once his personal quest for wealth and political power began to overwhelm the economic interests of the nation. This was a critical loss of support from the core group that could sustain Marcos in power, forcing him to rely further on a handful of extremely powerful oligarchs, such as Eduardo

Cojuango and Roberto Benedicto, to whom he had given national monopolies in coconut and sugar production, respectively.

Philippine foreign indebtedness provides a key indicator of how bad conditions had become by 1983. A debt that totals 20 percent of a nation's the gross national product (GNP) is considered heavy but sustainable. For the Philippines, in that year the figure was 60 percent — more than $25 billion. Yet in spite of these difficulties Marcos refused to break the economy-sapping monopolies held by his powerful friends.

The final push that toppled the Marcos regime was not economic but political: the assassination of his chief political opponent, Senator Aquino. Effectively exiled to the United States following his release from prison in 1981, Aquino had chaffed to reenter Philippine politics and challenge Marcos to a popular electoral showdown. Assuming that Marcos was gravely ill and might soon die, thus permitting his wife Imelda and the security chief General Ver to seize power, Aquino ignored explicit warnings from the Marcos regime and announced that he would return to Manila. On August 21, 1983, as he stepped from his plane at the Manila airport he was shot and killed by a gunman who was, in turn, conveniently killed on the spot by the airport security command.

The Aquino murder galvanized Philippine society and the international community. Many conservatives who had supported Marcos, particularly those in the mainstream Manila business community and the United States, openly declared their revulsion toward the regime and called for him to resign. Although a Commission of Inquiry defied Marcos and accused a military group including General Ver of conspiring in the murder, a military tribunal declared that all the defendants were innocent.

By this time (the early 1980s) the flow of money and people leaving the Philippines for overseas locations was rising. Following the Aquino assassination, it became a full-scale hemorrhage. The peso plunged against the dollar and tens of thousands of people urgently searched for countries to which they could emigrate. Inflation soared and the international banking community fretted over the prospect that the bankrupt country might bring about a global financial crisis by defaulting on its $27 billion debt. Marcos appeared in public less frequently and seemed to be growing seriously ill. In October 1985 Senator Paul Laxalt was sent by President Reagan to urge sternly that Marcos institute a broad range of reforms.

Meanwhile, opposition began to coalesce around Aquino's widow, Corazon, who had become an outspoken advocate of continued democratic competition against Marcos. When in late 1985 Marcos responded to American and public pressure by calling for a snap presidential election, "Cory" Aquino announced that she would run. On the assumption that he could buy and manipulate any election, Marcos allowed his opponents considerable freedom amid widespread international press coverage. Once the influential Chinese mestizo archbishop of Manila, Jaime Cardinal Sin, had persuaded Mrs. Aquino's chief rival, Salvador Laurel, to join her in a political alliance, the opposition was vastly strengthened and gained momentum in the weeks prior to the election.

By election day, February 7, 1986, the international press corps had descended on the Philippines. Their presence increased the pressure on

From Marcos to Ramos

Regimes' Principal Years	Foreign Money Coming In ($billions)	Annual Average	
		GDP(%)	GNP(%)
Marcos I: 1971-80	12.2	5.8	6.1
Marcos II: 1981-85	11.1	-1.1	-1.7
Aquino: 1987-91	24.1	3.9	4.5
Ramos: 1992-96	74.7	3.4	4.1

Table 8.2

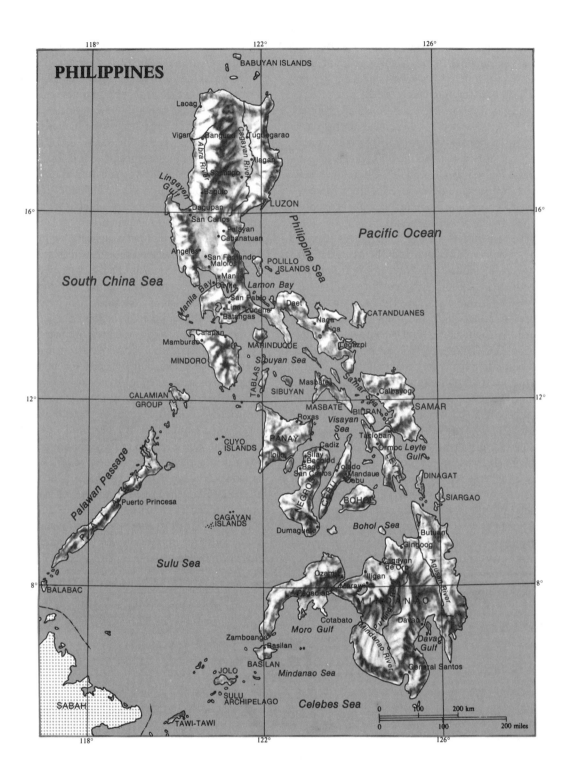

PHILIPPINES

BABUYAN ISLANDS

Laoag

Vigan Banguer Tuguegarao

Abra River Cagayan River Ilagan

Lingayen Gulf

Baguio

LUZON

Dagupan

San Carlos

Palayan

Cabanatuan

Angeles San Fernando

Malolos POLILLO ISLANDS

Manila

Cavite Lamon Bay

Manila Bay

San Pablo Daet

Lipa Lucena

Batangas Naga

Calapan Iriga

Mamburao MARINDUQUE Legazpi

MINDORO Sibuyan Sea

TABLAS

SIBUYAN

Masbate

CALAMIAN GROUP Roxas

Calbayog

MASBATE BILIRAN SAMAR

CUYO ISLANDS PANAY Visayan Sea

Cadiz Tacloban

Iloilo Silay Ormoc Leyte Gulf

Bacolod Toledo

San Carlos Mandaue DINAGAT

Cebu

Puerto Princesa NEGROS CEBU SIARGAO

BOHOL

PALAWAN CAGAYAN ISLANDS

Bohol Sea

Dumaguete Butuan

Gingoog

Cagayan de Oro

Ozamiz

Iligan

Pagadian Marawi MINDANAO Agusan River

Cotabato Davao

Zamboanga Moro Gulf

BALABAC Basilan Davao Gulf

Mindanao River

JOLO BASILAN General Santos

SULU Mindanao Sea

SABAH ARCHIPELAGO Celebes Sea

TAWI-TAWI

Pacific Ocean

South China Sea

Philippine Sea

CATANDUANES

Sulu Sea

0 100 200 km

0 100 200 miles

Marcos to observe fair elections. An independent poll-watching group called NAMFREL had been formed, supported by the United States, to try to ensure the fairness of the vote count. Yet, as the count proceeded, many "irregularities" occurred. These were noticed and amplified by the NAMFREL, the media, and the church to an extent that led them to, in fact, undercount the Marcos vote in areas such as northern Luzon. Nevertheless, it is generally agreed that Aquino probably won by a slender margin. Marcos claimed victory by turning over the final count to a vote-certifying organization that was controlled by his party. Not surprisingly, Aquino and the opposition refused to recognize his claim.

The stalemate that followed seemed like the worst possible outcome. Both candidates planned inaugural ceremonies. The Philippines appeared to be teetering on the brink of chaos. At that point, two key military leaders, Defense Secretary Juan Ponce Enrile and Lieutenant General Fidel Ramos, led a military revolt in support of Mrs. Aquino. Cardinal Sin urged people onto the streets to surround and protect the pro-Aquino troops on their military base. When the rest of the army refused to attack, "people power" had at last triumphed. Marcos was persuaded by the United States to leave the Philippines for Honolulu where he was to die in exile in 1990, but the underlying problems remained.

The same specters of malnutrition and unemployment that had confronted Marcos now faced the new Aquino administration. The bottom 20 percent of the nation received 5.5 percent of the national income — the top 2 percent received 53 percent. The standard of living for the average Filipino had plummeted under Marcos. The nation owed $27 billion.

Mrs. Aquino held out the olive branch to all her real and potential opponents: the NPA, dissidents within the army, and Marcos loyalists. She rewarded the two powerful figures who had helped her at the critical moment, Enrile and General Ramos, with senior posts. Enrile's personal ambition intruded in future political maneuvering, however, and the reformists within the military became were soon disenchanted with the lack of progress toward fundamental change.

The "people power" movement that brought Aquino into office confirmed the Philippines' long-standing popular commitment to democratic processes, but the old patterns of patronage and factionalism quickly reasserted themselves. Aquino proved to be indecisive at key moments and became surrounded by ineffective executives and posturing politicians who habitually blamed a legacy of American colonialism for the country's ills. In response, an embittered faction of young army officers made several coup attempts after 1986. One attempt in late 1989 very nearly succeeded in toppling the Aquino presidency while another in 1990 had to be suppressed with U.S. air support.

Aquino did not seek re-election and in 1992 was succeeded by retired general Fidel Ramos, leader of the military overthrow of Marcos. Ramos succeeded in bringing about changes in the Philippine economy and government that had eluded his predecessors. He supported new trade and investment liberalization measures which stimulated a surge of economic growth and negotiated a peace agreement with the Moros revolutionaries in Mindanao. As a result, the Philippines achieved a measure of stability and its GNP growth rate surged.

In spite of his economic successes, Ramos still had to contend with the political monopoly of a relatively few powerful families in the Philippines. Investigative journalist Eric Gutierrez revealed in his book, *The Ties that Bind*, that of the House of Representative's 199 members, 145 came from families long involved in politics; 64 were children of powerful *trapos* in the provinces that they represented and 30 were third- or fourth-generation politicians. These politicians often had conflicts of interest. In the face of Ramos' appeal to the Ninth Congress to make itself "the instrument to free and democratize our economy," several congressmen filed bills designed to directly benefit their own business interests. One presented a bill providing for tax rebates for tobacco traders; his wife ran a tobacco trading and hauling business. The Mindanao representatives, all landowners, called for a suspension of agrarian reform. Another Representative whose family owned coconut mills sponsored a bill ordering the soap and detergent industry to shift to 100 percent use of coconut-based chemicals. These examples illustrate the extent to which special interests continue to occupy a central place in Philippine politics.

DEMOCRACY IN SOUTHEAST ASIA

The above examples indicate how, in Southeast Asia, the adoption of new democratic institutions must be measured against the special religious, ethnic and historical circumstances of each society. In spite of this, a political transition of sorts is taking place in most countries. By 1991, Singapore had at last seen Lee Kuan Yew pass the premiership to a new generation, albeit under his watchful eye. A healthy, organized opposition had emerged in Malaysia. In Indonesia strong opposition was not permitted during the country's preparations for parliamentary elections, but the government had begun to allow a more outspoken, younger generation of parliamentarians to emerge. The population of the Philippines, struggling under the weight of immense demographic and economic burdens, became increasingly skeptical and cynical about the competence of its government but was no less committed to democratic processes. Thailand, although rocked by another coup, saw no viable future outside the framework of a civilian parliamentary government.

DEMOCRATIZATION IN SOUTH KOREA

South Korea: The Suppression of Democracy, 1948-1987

South Korea's initial experiment with democracy failed as Syngman Rhee (whose return to Korea at the end of World War II was described in chapter 4) assumed increasingly dictatorial powers. Industrial property taken over from the Japanese had been returned to a small handful of people with powerful political connections. Their abusive monopolization of this wealth led to increasing social unrest. At the same time, Rhee's policies rapidly alienated many members of the newly elected National Assembly who, under the constitution, were the ones who selected the president. In 1952, to foreclose the possibility of being turned out of office by the Assembly, Rhee declared martial law and forced the Assembly to change the constitution so as to have the president elected directly by the people. Two years later, he

once again bullied the Assembly into a constitutional change that removed the provision limiting presidents to two terms in office.

There followed a period of blatant, Rhee-inspired interference at the polls during elections. By the time of the elections in 1960, the regime's unpopularity had become so great that a political eruption seemed inevitable. Massive student demonstrations broke out and elicited widespread support (such actions by students are not only tolerated but often esteemed as a kind of societal conscience in most Confucian cultures). After a brief resistance, Rhee had no choice but to step down. The government that followed, led by the democratically elected Chang Myon, was indecisive and badly divided. It fell to a military coup in 1961 led by Major General Park Chung Hee.

For the next twenty-six years, South Korea was ruled by two authoritarian regimes. The first, under Park, ended when he was assassinated by his own chief of intelligence in 1979. By that time, the regime was facing rising public discontent over its intolerance of criticism. Yet an army general, Chun Doo Hwan, stepped in to fill Park's place and forcefully quell any opposition. His authoritarian rule was to last for an additional seven years until democratic forces took over as described later in this chapter. The transition toward democracy in Korea was therefore a slow and painful one, made especially difficult by the profound limitations Park's rule imposed on democratic political evolution. These debilitating circumstances can be summarized as follows:

- **Absence of a workable, legal framework**. Park's tailor-made constitution was unpopular and unsuited to the nation's needs.

- **Lack of viable political parties.** The activities of political parties — even Park's party — were so restricted that they were unable to serve as a means for deciding who his successor would be.

- **A radicalized political opposition.** Strict authoritarianism over a long period alienated much of society and fostered opposition leaders who sought sudden, radical, and, in some cases, violent change.

- **A politicized military leadership.** The Korean military helped place Park in power and was crucial in his holding onto it. Military leaders became accustomed to intervening during political crises. This decreased their own credibility as impartial guarantors of the nation's security.[7]

The role of the military proved crucial on Park's death as the Korean army moved swiftly into the political vacuum. Massive student-led demonstrations followed in an attempt to force the army to allow elections, it being assumed that the events surrounding the downfall of Rhee in 1960 could be repeated. The army's ruthless suppression of a major demonstration in the southern city of Kwangju in 1980 became a political watershed in Korea. Soon, an underground opposition was using the "Kwangju massacre" as a rallying point not only against the newly installed regime of general Chun Doo Hwan but also against the United States which it alleged had supported the killings. All politicians thereafter would be measured, in part, by their positions on assigning guilt and suggesting necessary remedies for the Kwangju killings.

During this period authoritarian rule in the Republic of Korea came to be viewed by many as the unchangeable fate of the nation. Western-style democracy was said to be "inefficient" and "inappropriate" to the special needs and situation of the Korean people who were accustomed to an authoritarian but benevolent government. These assumptions soon began to change in the face of new political turmoil.

Chun's strategy for maintaining power proved to be unworkable. Like his predecessor, Park, he assumed that he could control party politics through the facade of his own dominant political party. The strategy called for a multiparty system, with Chun's party, the Democratic Justice Party (DJP), maintaining an overwhelming majority. Several minor groups would be allowed opposition and some former opposition leaders were freed from jail to demonstrate a measure of open political competition. By the elections of 1985, however, Chun's plans began to unravel when the small parties coalesced into the New Korea Democratic Party. A virtual two-party system had emerged.

The debate now focused on the legitimacy of the Korean government. Chun was under severe pressure from students, religious leaders, intellectuals, and the United States to somehow reaffirm his commitment not only to a peaceful transition of power, but to one based on popularly mandated constitutional powers. In early 1986 the spectacle of "people power" sweeping through the Philippines, resulting in the collapse of the Marcos regime, may have frightened the Chun government into relaxing its stance. In any case, only a few weeks after Marcos fell Chun relented on the issue of constitutional reform. The debate no longer concerned whether the constitution would be revised, but when and how.

1987: The Korean Democratic Revival

The Republic of Korea in 1987 saw some of the largest mass rallies for democracy in world history. On several occasions it was estimated that more than a million people turned out to hear candidates — particularly those for the opposition party — during what became a dramatic struggle for democratic reform.

Looming as a kind of deadline for the Chun government were the "twin hurdles" of 1988: the long-promised government transition and the 1988 Seoul Olympics. The Olympics increasingly placed the government under close scrutiny from an international community whose respect Chun valued highly. His commitment to step down as president at this critical time served as the benchmark against which global opinion would measure Korea's progress as a modern nation. As noted previously, these pressures at first persuaded Chun to agree in principle that there should be a reform of the constitution, but in early 1987 he announced to a stunned nation that he had decided to suspend a revision of the constitution until after the presidential elections. The move was widely and correctly interpreted as a strategy to ensure that he could install a sympathetic and equally authoritarian successor.

Thousands of student demonstrators — joined this time by members of the middle class — took to the streets in violent protest and by June 1987 areas of Seoul resembled war zones. Korea seemed poised on the brink of civil war as the government, still deeply troubled by its vulnerability to invasion from North Korea during a time of such instability, contemplated a massive military suppression of the opposition movement. A compromise was needed, and Chun sought to find one by calling a meeting with opposition leader Kim Young Sam at which he offered to resume negotiations on the previously agreed-to constitutional reforms. Kim immediately sensed a weakness in Chun's position and, instead of fashioning a compromise, stepped up his demands for an immediate national referendum.

With Chun and Kim Young Sam still at loggerheads, it was left to Roh Tae Woo, a former general, leader of Chun's Democratic Justice Party, and his chosen successor as presidential candidate, to accede to the opposition demands. Ironically, one element of this compromise, a political amnesty for the leading opposition figure Kim Dae Jung, led directly to the defeat of the opposition because both Kim Dae Jung and Kim Young Sam insisted on running for president. In the voting that took place in December 1987, the popular protest vote was split between the "two Kims." Together, they accumulated a majority (55 percent) but because they were unable to reconcile their differences, Roh Tae Woo, the DJP candidate, became President.

Opposition parties scored a significant comeback in the National Assembly elections in 1988 but were still divided and thus unable to achieve executive power. Then, in January 1990, a dramatic shift in Korean party alignments took place with the announcement of a "grand conservative alliance" in which President Roh Tae Woo's Democratic Justice Party merged with the opposition groups led by Kim Young Sam and Kim Jong Pil. The aim was to isolate the more radical Kim Dae Jung who, in turn, denounced the realignment as a move from "military dictatorship to one-party dictatorship." The popular reaction was generally skeptical.

Toward an "Asian-Style" Democracy?

Whatever its long-term future, the new party, which was named the Democratic Liberal Party (DLP), was directly inspired by the model of Japan's political juggernaut in the postwar period, the Liberal Democratic Party (LDP, described in chapter 6). As in the case of the LDP, the new Korean party represented an alliance among big business, the bureaucracy, and some of the left-wing opposition. All shared an underlying commitment to policies that supported rapid economic growth. In justifying the move, one South Korean official said, "We tried to import Western-style democracy, from Europe or the United States, and we almost failed. Now we're trying to import it indirectly, through Japan."[8]

Alongside the examples of other Asian countries in which balanced, strong opposition parties have been difficult to establish, does the Korean transition toward one-party rule within a parliamentary system suggest a pattern? The most obvious example is that of the Japan where a dominant party survives alongside several fragmented, weak opposition groups. Several observers have noted that the authoritarian traditions of Pacific Asia, although gradually eroded by the introduction of a controlled process of competitive politics, still often permit a relatively secure dominant party to command the political scene. In the semi-competitive politics that result, the problem often has been that of establishing the rules of the game: the boundaries of the dominant party and the degree of tolerance of an opposition.

The danger of this style of "Asian democracy" is its tendency to breed corruption and self-satisfaction among leaders of the dominant party. This has been the case in Japan's Liberal Democratic Party as revealed by the extraordinary range of bribe-taking in the "Recruit Scandal" of 1989. For their part, however, Korean voters also have demonstrated a strong interest in reform-minded independent candidates drawn from the professional ranks — lawyers, academics, and professional activists. Public interest movements such as environmental protection and women's rights are gathering momentum.

In a sign that the impetus for political reform remains strong in Korea, Kim Young Sam succeeded Roh as president and soon began a major campaign against political corruption. Over 5,000 civil servants, including cabinet members and legislators in the national assembly, were fired or imprisoned. Eventually, Roh himself was swept up in the campaign and confessed publicly to having amassed a secret fund worth hundreds of millions of dollars during his presidency, most of it collected from the big business conglomerates (*chaebol*). His predecessor, Chun Doo Hwan, was also arrested and both men were put on trial for their role in leading a military coup that included the infamous Kwangju massacre. In 1996, Chun was sentenced to death and Roh to more than 20 years in prison, but President Kim commuted their sentences. Several heads of the *chaebol* received sentences for their roles in supporting Roh's slush fund. Meanwhile, as Korea sought to make reforms required for its entry into the Organization for Economic Cooperation and Development (OECD), the group of developed industrial nations, it entered a new period of political turbulence. Meeting in an unannounced session in late 1996, President Kim's New Korea Party passed laws that weakened labor and civil rights in the name of national security and industrial competitiveness. The resulting strikes and protests, although not as sweeping as in the pre-democracy days, once again suggested that Korea's democratic transition remains incomplete. If President Kim once again seemed to have reverted to familiar patterns of authoritarian rule, some observers pointed to the legacy of confrontation with the North as a primary reason.

Impact of the Threat from the North

While relatively isolated communist regimes collapsed in Eastern Europe in 1989, North Korea (the People's Democratic Republic of Korea, or DPRK) stood out for its continued seclusion from the global community. The North was soon to discover, however, that even its extreme isolation would not long protect it from global economic and political changes.

Chapter 9 will examine the events surrounding the initial division of Korea after World War II and the civil war that broke out between the North and South in 1950. This traumatic and massively destructive event, which left thousands of families divided on either side of the demilitarized zone, continues to reverberate at the center of South Korean politics. After the Korean War, the North's leader, Kim Il Sung, managed to eliminate his key political rivals and embark on a policy of economic reorganization using the Stalinist model of farm collectivization and centralized economic management. In inter-

national affairs, he developed the policy of *chuch'e* (self-reliance), which extended to his own Marxist-Leninist ideology and unsuccessful efforts at economic self-sufficiency. During the 1960s and 1970s, his relations with each of his communist neighbors, China and the Soviet Union, alternated between tension and warmth as he attempted a careful balancing act under the rubric of *chuch'e*.

In the early 1970s, encouraged perhaps by the spirit of a more relaxed international political climate, North Korea made large purchases of plants and equipment from Western countries and Japan. In the end, it defaulted on its payments for these goods and remains today at least three billion dollars in debt to foreign countries.

By the early 1990s, the South had scored a string of diplomatic and economic successes (e.g., burgeoning economic growth, the beginnings of democratization, serving as host to the 1988 Olympics, diplomatic relations with the USSR, commercial relations with China), compelling the North to counter with its own initiatives. There followed in 1990 three meetings between the prime ministers of the North and South, as well as sports exchanges. Japan and the North commenced negotiations on the normalization of relations between them. In 1991 the South announced its intention to apply for a seat in the United Nations, a possibility that had long been foreclosed by an assured Security Council veto from either China or the USSR. This time, both China and the USSR quietly informed the North that they would not block the South's request. Left with little alternative, the North chose to apply simultaneously with the South.

Although a more relaxed attitude toward relations with the North began to prevail in Seoul by the early 1990s, both sides remained watchful and suspicious, with large standing armies still facing one another in a state of war. Especially troubling to the South was the assessment by many experts that the North possessed the material and technology to make small, crude, enriched uranium bombs. Amid efforts by the United States to negotiate an agreement which would replace North Korean nuclear reactors (the source of the bombs) with more benign energy sources along with international nuclear proliferation safeguards, Kim Il Sung suddenly died in July 1994. Having sought

Social and Economic Indicators for Korea (1995) and Germany (1989)

	S. Korea	N. Korea	W. Germany	E. Germany
Population	44.9	23.3	62.1	16.6
GDP per person, $	10,067	957	19,283	5,840
Exports, % of GDP	27.7	3.3	28.3	24.5
Imports, % of GDP	29.9	5.9	22.4	24.3
Infant Mortality/1000 births*	12.8	31.3	7.4	7.5
Farm Population (%)+	13.1	37.6	3.7	10.8
Radios per 1000 population	1,003	207	830	990

*1990 for Korea; +1989 for Korea.

Table 8.3   As costly as German unification was, that of Korea will probably be greater.

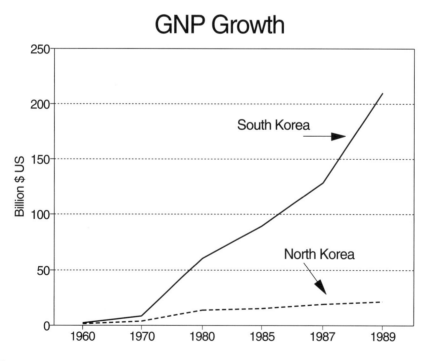

Graph 8.2

to ensure his succession by his son, Kim Jong Il, in hopes of creating a kind of East Asian communist dynasty, his own stature remained, in the hyperbole of his state propagandists, that of the "matchless patriot, national hero, ever-victorious and iron-willed commander, one of the genius leaders of the international Communist movement and workers' movement."

With the death of the elder Kim, whose cultlike stature in the nation was arguably as much a religion as an ideology, North Korea's leadership entered a period of even greater uncertainty. The North Korean economy suffered a series of devastating blows from successive floods, leading to the specter of a full-fledged national famine. Kim Jong Il, seemingly in the leadership role without all the titles once held by his father, remained a remote and enigmatic figure but this did not prevent an eventual agreement on the nuclear issue or his acceptance of international humanitarian aid to feed his starving population.

The reunification of East and West Germany initially prompted speculation about a parallel scenario in Korea, but just as the two Germanys soon discovered how deep a division remained between them after forty years of divergent economic and political evolution, so South Koreans began to realize how difficult the North would be to assimilate. After decades of self-sacrifice to achieve a measure of economic success, many South Koreans are not eager to assume the vast financial burdens that will be required to reconstruct the decrepit economy of the North, even if the opportunity arises.

From the standpoint of the North, the "lesson" of German reunification may be that it is a mistake to permit controlled yet extensive exchanges of personnel and information to pass between the divided peninsula. The East Germans saw clearly the failure of their system after their government allowed such flows to occur from the early 1970s. North Korea is unlikely to commit the same error. Nor is either government going to be willing to share power with the other. Whereas it was once the South that feared the "communizing" influence of the North, now it is the North that fears the "capitalist temptations" of the South and being "absorbed" in the manner of East Germany. The paradoxical situation facing the South, then, is that the more attention and publicity it gives to the issue of reunification, the more threatening it becomes and the more the North is likely to withdraw from contact.

Even if unification remains an uncertain prospect, the North cannot long resist making fundamental changes in the face of the pressures confronting it. At the same time, by its very presence it continues to complicate the process of democratization in the South. Many young students, for whom the Korean War is but a distant trauma in the minds of their parents, hold ideas as ill-informed and idealistic about the North as they are angry and xenophobic toward the United States. Dissidents from the South who contact the North without permission continue to be jailed and become martyrs.

Student protests, at times violent, continued in the 1990s in support of the North and, as noted above, in opposition to restrictive labor laws. Kim Young Sam, once the beneficiary of such demonstrations during the transition to democracy, repressed them forcefully under his presidency. If the result was to underscore the limits of protest in the South, it also served to demonstrate the distance South Korea still must travel in establishing a societal consensus on reunification.

DEMOCRATIZATION IN TAIWAN

After initial upheavals following its 1949 takeover of the island, the Guomindang government on Taiwan reformed and stimulated the island economy, creating one of Asia's most prominent economic success stories. By the early 1980s, however, Taiwan found itself increasingly isolated diplomatically as the People's Republic of China (PRC) continued to score gains at its expense. Even Taiwan's firm supporter, President Ronald Reagan, acceded to a new PRC policy for peaceful unification with Taiwan when, in 1982, he agreed to a joint communique committing the United States to a gradual reduction of its arms sales to Taiwan. Worse, there were growing signs that the ruling party, the Kuomintang (KMT), and the security apparatus were becoming complacent and possibly were out of control. Relatives of a jailed opposition leader were murdered in 1980; a

THE PROCESS OF DEMOCRATIZATION ON TAIWAN

Although Taiwan's democratic transition was not simply engineered from above, it is equally obvious that it did not result from the kind of popular uprising that erupted in the Philippines. The transition in Taiwan is best understood as a tacit or implicit negotiation between the regime and the opposition.

Once the KMT committed itself to some form of political change, it could use that commitment to limit the range of issues open to debate. The KMT's initial tolerance of the DPP was contingent on the opposition meeting three preconditions: no use of violence, no advocacy of separatism, and no support of communism. With these restrictions in place, the KMT could maintain a vague commitment to democratization while stressing the incremental nature of the process and tying the transition to previously scheduled events, such as regular elections.

Yet the opposition had its own means to influence the agenda and to force the pace of change. Once the KMT had committed itself to reform, the opposition gained the advantage of being able to put forward alternative transition paths. The opposition's proposed sequence had a particularly compelling logic. The first step was to demand political liberalization, including repeal of the martial law decrees and the restoration of freedom of speech, press, and assembly. The next step would be reelection of the entire membership of the existing national representative bodies. Only then would the most dramatic change of all take place: direct election of the president and provincial governors. By playing on the KMT's own commitment to democracy, the opposition made it difficult for the regime to maintain the status quo and forced it to act on some important issues.

—Tun-jen Cheng and Stephen Haggard,
"Taiwan in Transition," 1990

visiting Taiwanese-American professor died in police custody in 1981; and, in 1984, a U.S. citizen, Henry Liu, who had written a controversial biography of KMT party chairman Chiang Ching-kuo, was murdered. It was later discovered that the murder was carried out at the order of Taiwan's chief of military intelligence.

In response to these developments and the fact that his society had clearly become much more prosperous, educated, and politically sophisticated, Chiang Ching-kuo embarked on a course of political reform in early 1984. His decision to shift from slow liberalization to more rapid and fundamental democratization responded both to the potential instability that might arise from the increasingly arrogant exercise of power by KMT conservatives and the need to improve his regime's ability to deal with the threats to its international survival. Chiang himself was in precarious health. A diabetic in his seventies, he remained confined most of the time to a wheel-

chair. The possibility of a succession crisis loomed large when his heir-apparent, a popular and able prime minister, suffered a cerebral hemorrhage in 1984. That same year, he chose a native Taiwanese, Lee Teng-hui, to be his vice president and constitutional successor and used his considerable prestige and authority as the son of Chiang Kai-shek to insist publicly that only a constitutional succession would be appropriate.

Ever since the creation of an opposition grouping in the local elections of 1977, dissidents had shown significant electoral capability but had become internally divided even as KMT hardliners moved successfully to repress them. A bloody clash in December 1979 in the industrial city of Kaohsiung resulted in the jailing of most of the leaders of the radical faction, but Chiang's 1984 reforms undermined the KMT hardliners. In 1986 a breakthrough occurred when, amid concerns over the leadership succession, the KMT permitted not only the formation of an opposition party, the Democratic Progressive Party (DPP), but reversed its stand on political change generally and lifted martial law.

Lee Teng-hui benefited enormously from Chiang's endorsement and the increasing "Taiwanization" of politics. On Chiang's death in January 1988, he became the first native Taiwanese president. The KMT benefited as well, for instead of losing the endorsement of the population over which it had ruled in such authoritarian fashion, it found itself performing well in national elections. As in Korea, the "Japanese model" is being attempted in Taiwan. That is, a ruling conservative party, in this case the KMT, continues to dominate overwhelmingly the political scene while the opposition, divided into numerous smaller parties, acquiesces but is consulted regularly. Factionalism within the KMT is a further brake on its potential abuse of power.

Still, Taiwan had not established a new, fully democratic order. Its presidency remained uncontested as did the majority of its legislative seats held by aging, tenured KMT members who were permitted to cling to imaginary constituencies on the mainland. Waning public tolerance of this arrangement and further reforms led to Taiwan's first fully democratic presidential election in 1996, won decisively by the popular Lee Teng-hui. Through this process, a multi-party system has emerged in Taiwan that follows a prevalent pattern in East Asia, i.e., the public supports a strongly dominant party as long as it performs satisfactorily.

The solution to Taiwan's relationship with the Chinese government in Beijing is more illusive. On May 1, 1991, more than four decades of declared civil war between Taiwan and mainland China ended (at least from Taiwan's viewpoint) with the declaration by President Lee terminating the "period of communist rebellion." Still, tensions between Taiwan and the mainland flare up periodically, and are vastly complicated by Taiwan's democratization in sharp contrast to the communist anti-democratic dominance on the mainland. Although Taiwan may have declared the "communist rebellion" at an end, the leaders in Beijing share no such reciprocal view toward the island. Any change on Taiwan that suggests its potential to become an independent state elicits a wrathful response from the mainland. Never-

theless, the pace of interaction with the mainland has quickened. Significantly, it coincides with a relaxation of rules governing Taiwan's domestic political activity.

THE STATUS OF HONG KONG

The extent to which Taiwan and the mainland are able to reconcile their separate systems under a single flag has a special meaning for the people of Hong Kong whose status as a British colony reverted back to full Chinese authority in July, 1997. China has said that it will preserve Hong Kong's extraordinary free market dynamism and its role as a trade and financial center in Asia. In December 1984, during the Sino-British joint declaration on Hong Kong, China's paramount leader, Deng Xiaoping, pledged that China and Hong Kong would be "one country, two systems." Subsequently, China's aging leaders signaled that they valued political control over economic development after Hong Kong residents demonstrated in the streets in support of China's 1989 student-led democracy movement.

The contrast between the Hong Kong and Chinese "systems" makes this transition especially challenging. Prior to the changeover, Hong Kong charged a top corporate tax rate of 15 percent, half the rate across the border in China. Civil servants in Hong Kong have never exercised the extensive controls over business that Chinese officials insist upon. Hong Kong operated under a well-developed common law presided over by barristers and judges of high integrity, but in the new Hong Kong, the Court of Final Appeal is ultimately answerable to China's National People's Congress. Press freedoms in Hong Kong were vastly greater that those granted to indigenous journalists on the mainland as were rights of assembly and other aspects of free speech. Hong Kong's democratic traditions were late in coming, however, and in true colonial fashion Britain always appointed an English, not Chinese, governor over its territory.

At first, emigration by Hong Kong's elite professional class accelerated as concern in the colony grew over the imminent transition, but in the years just prior to the transition, there was a net inflow. Such change in human movement patterns is not unusual in Hong Kong's history, as noted in the description of its "ebbs and flows" on page 101. In any case, the Hong Kong transition is being watched closely throughout the world. For those who have known and enjoyed the bustling, thriving colony in the postwar era, (ironically, it was industrialized in large part by Chinese entrepreneurs fleeing Shanghai after the communist revolution) the future of Hong Kong will be a harbinger of China's ability to adjust to the trials of modernization and global trade liberalization.

MIGRATION AND DEMOCRACY

The historic movement of people in and out of Hong Kong is symptomatic of a larger pattern of Pacific Asian migration that has developed as a result of rapidly rising prosperity and democratization in the Pacific Basin. Whereas Europe was the principal origin of migrants until the 1960s, Asia is fast becoming one of the main "origin" regions of world migration, with large numbers of ethnic Chinese comprising an important part of these flows. Where Asians have emigrated and then returned in response to economic and educational opportunities, they have probably been a factor in favor of democratization in their countries.

As a basic freedom, the freedom to leave one's country for another land is often as constrained by the policies of the destination country as those of the country of origin. With the imposition of new international political boundaries during and after the colonial era, migration became somewhat more restricted, although as before the ethnic Chinese demonstrated remarkable mobility.

DETERMINANTS OF DEMOCRATIC CHANGE IN ASIA

What, then, are the underlying factors that have determined the course of democracy in Pacific Asian countries in the twentieth century? In the examples cited in this chapter, a deterioration in democratic institutions and principles occurred after an initial attempt at their establishment, but there is no simple, broadly applicable explanation for why democratic institutions have evolved or been stifled. There are, however, a variety of important variables to which we can refer for an understanding of future political change in each country.

Political Culture

The first and broadest influence on the prospects for democracy are indigenous cultural traditions and values. These are also the most difficult to measure or assess in terms of their specific impacts on "democratic" behavior. For example, Sukarno's insistence on relying more on traditional village-derived "consensus" approaches to decision-making by the community has been dismissed by some merely as a cynical attempt to undermine the concept of parliamentary democracy, but its continuation in Indonesia also appears to reflect a genuine discomfort with processes that are overly dependent on a formula ("50 percent plus one") rather than a genuine accommodation of everyone's interests.

Is it possible to generalize about a "political culture" shared by most societies in Pacific Asia? Some scholars have suggested that at least there is a paternalistic orientation, shared by the governing authorities and their societies, that has made it difficult for democratic processes to become widespread. Japan, it is noted, has all the institutions that are associated with democracy: a free press, laws that protect individual rights, and opposition parties. Yet only one party, the LDP, has actually ruled Japan during most of the postwar era. As long as its leaders have been seen as "understanding" the needs of the nation, they have been entrusted with power — even in the face of their demonstrable abuses of that power as in the case of bribe-taking and financial scandals.

It is also true that in China's Confucian culture, the high value placed on order, respect, and harmony has reinforced the strict emphasis on ideological uniformity. In a non-Confucian society such as Indonesia, we find similar values, echoed in several other Southeast Asian societies, that support strong authority and control while abhorring the prospect of open conflict and dissent.

Yet open conflict and dissent have occurred in these societies, and such outbreaks, if sufficiently widespread, become watershed events. Political culture by itself is neither determinant of whether a nation will move toward democracy nor is it an absolute, unchanging quality in its own right. Cultural perceptions respond to historical experiences and the spread of new ideas and information. In other words, cultural attributes cannot be said to "support" or "oppose" democracy uniformly.

Historical and Colonial Legacies

Cultural influences have been overlain in many cases by colonialism and the struggle to arrive at an independent national identity. The nature of colonial rule affected the ease with which democratic institutions could subsequently take root. The most extensive effort by a colonial power to foster democratic institutions was that of the United States in the Philippines. After World War II the British attempted to establish parliamentary government in Burma and Malaysia, succeeding in a limited sense in Malaysia but not in Burma. British efforts in Hong Kong have been far less enthusiastic, as attested by their censorship of local films about democracy that might offend Beijing. Hong Kong has essentially been cut adrift from any British-backed democratic moorings to which it might have clung.

The Koreans, Vietnamese, and Indonesians did not fare as well as the Malayans and the people of the Philippines in terms of colonial antecedents. Japanese rule over Korea, for example, was highly authoritarian and centralized. When Japan's control came to a rapid and cataclysmic end, Korea was left not only without the necessary institutions for checks and balances, it also lacked the "input" institutions of political parties and interest groups. As a result, its first president, Syngman Rhee, easily swept aside the fragile structures of democracy that would have checked his power.

The French in Vietnam and the Dutch in Indonesia similarly repressed any indigenous political movements that might have developed in the direction of nonviolent, moderate politics on a broad scale. Instead, they forced opposition parties to become underground movements. Indigenous politics became more radicalized and violent. Amid a determined struggle to overthrow their colonial masters, the Vietnamese had little hope of building the ordinary procedures and institutions of a democracy.

Thailand, on the other hand, was spared from colonial rule. Although like its neighbors it initially lacked parliamentary-style democratic structures, the society escaped the traumas and profound disruptions of the nearby colonies. The monarchy had time to adapt its thinking and encourage a broader base of control through the development of an educated civil elite and a professional military. The latter did come to exercise undo influence in the government, but the absence of a colonialized history left the traditional institution of the monarchy free to evolve as a legitimate, stabilizing, and mediating influence in political affairs.

Ethnic and Regional Rivalries

The success of democratic governance in Pacific Asia has often hinged on the ability of each system to accommodate friction among rival regions or ethnic groups. Malaysia and Indonesia provide the foremost examples as they struggle to maintain stability based on a careful — many would say fragile — balance of ethnic and religious interests. In Malaysia, the emergence of dominant parties within each ethnic group has made it easier to forge a "grand alliance" that contributes to stability while in Indonesia, the secularization of politics has been a key factor.

South Korea, on the other hand, is an ethnically homogenous society where regional rather than ethnic rivalries have slowed the growth of democratic traditions. Each candidate in the 1987 presidential elections drew heavily on a provincial power base. Regional parochialism in Korea surpasses the usual phenomenon of conflicting geographical interests found in most democracies, but this may diminish in importance if the new coalition party is able to accommodate the interests of a sufficient number of regions. At present, regional rivalries seriously impede the process of national consensus-building.

In many countries of Pacific Asia, the need to accommodate the interests of a significant number of minority stake-holders in the system is widely recognized (at least by those that are committed to democratic principles) as the key to successfully overcoming ethnic or regional tensions. This, in effect, means power-sharing with minority or opposition groups or providing them with access to the instruments of power so that the system becomes more acceptable to them.

State and Society

A smoothly functioning democracy requires a balance between a strong, centralized state government, on the one hand, and a dense, pluralistic set of economic, social, and political institutions, on the other. A democracy cannot flourish without formal political parties and party systems. Yet unless the political party system can avoid extreme fragmentation into a mass of individualistic splinter groups, as once threatened to be the case in Indonesia, it cannot establish a coherent, constructive dialogue on important national issues. Also, where credible opposition parties have been discouraged as a matter of "national security," as in the cases of Korea, Taiwan, and Singapore, their legitimate roles have been slow to evolve.

Vigorous, independent legislatures, judiciaries, and the press are important instruments through which popular interests can be expressed and the power of the national executive can be checked. Here again, state security may be viewed as being threatened by persons who would seek to "exploit" the impartiality of an independent judiciary. President Mahathir Mohamad of Malaysia found the authority of that nation's Supreme Court to be so threatening in 1989 that he dismissed the entire bench and replaced it with a more docile set of judges. Similarly, his restrictions on the press after it began reporting heated racial remarks by politicians has left his country with some of the most restrictive press laws in Southeast Asia.

Socioeconomic Development and Economic Performance

Analysts often have debated the possible correlation between a nation's economic performance (especially as reflected in the growth of a middle class) and popular demands for greater participation in political processes. While it is possible to argue that a higher level of socioeconomic development generates social support for democracy (education, media access, mobility, income), economics alone cannot account for the trends toward or away from democratic government. A growing middle class may become

---

DEMOCRACY AND DEVELOPMENT

Most people would agree that no Asian country is likely to modernize successfully if it is ruled by a weak and inefficient government. But it should not therefore be concluded that all countries with strong authoritarian governments can realize rapid development. Indeed, the case that the late-developing countries need strong state structures was first popularized in the late 1930s as a rationalization for the adoption of fascism by Germany, Italy, and Japan. Then after World War II it was thought that Stalin's Russia provided a universal model for rapid industrial development. Many of those who accepted this view either felt that the late-developing states could not afford the "luxury" of democracy or believed that the democracies were on the decline and the technocratic-managerial state was the wave of the future. This was not just Soviet propaganda; it was also the view of many Western intellectuals who held that history was on the side of state planning of basic economic activities. Therefore it is no wonder that many of the Third World leaders were tempted by the "Soviet model." In the 1960s, in fact, it was widely believed that democratic India was severely handicapped in its competition with totalitarian China.

—Lucian Pye, *Asian Power and Politics*

politically conscious and more inclined to support democratization to protect its new-found prosperity, as occurred in Korea in the late 1980s. On the other hand, authoritarian governments such as Singapore — and also the earlier regime of Park Chung Hee in Korea — coopted the middle class by making it believe that its continued well-being depended on the continuation of an authoritarian form of government. In fact, a middle class can be profoundly ambivalent about change toward democracy, depending on the overall circumstances of the nation. Some aspects of economic development may be viewed by the people experiencing them as highly "destabilizing" and threatening to the security of their society. In other instances such as Indonesia, the middle class is so riven by internal differences of class, ethnicity, and religion as to be an unlikely foundation for democratic change.

Social tensions arise from economic change that may require new, more democratically-based solutions if they are to be resolved. Traditional ties of deference to authority break down, new political groups emerge, and demands multiply. People have to adjust, make room for these new entrants, and, in so doing, find their own interests challenged. If authoritarian regimes are unable to adjust to the demands of these new, economically generated constituencies, and if they are unable to find ways to mediate the conflicts between them, their own legitimacy comes under increasing scrutiny.

Economic success is therefore a potential "catch-22" for an authoritarian regime. Although it may help to undergird a government's legitimacy in the short term, over the longer term it multiplies demands for political change in the direction of democratic solutions. A dismal economic performance can always be laid at the feet of the leadership and used to underscore its lack of legitimacy or competence in guiding the national destiny. Yet in the case of Ferdinand Marcos, incompetence in economic affairs was not, by itself, sufficient to bring down his government even if it was a major contributing factor. Nor are brutally repressive regimes likely to topple because of their bumbling, outmoded economic strategies as long as their security apparatuses cooperate, as demonstrated by Burma, China, and North Korea.

International Influences

All regimes are, to some extent, susceptible to influences beyond their borders as regards the prospects for democracy, even when it appears that they totally control internal events. Foreign influences have both promoted and impeded the course of democracy in Asia. Perhaps the most serious and widespread obstacle has been the fear of foreign invasion or subversion. The resulting militarization of a society, accompanied by an authoritarian intolerance of dissent, has had a destructive impact on democratic trends in several countries cited in this chapter. South Korea, for example, may have seemed to outsiders like a paranoid state in matters concerning the North, but events such as the 1983 bombing in Rangoon of the South's cabinet leadership by a North Korean assassination squad confirmed their need to be constantly watchful. Similarly, Taiwan has felt the direct pressure of military invasion from China across the Taiwan Straits. The potential for subversion by enemies whose societies are culturally identical make authoritarian responses to such threats all the more likely.

The influence of powerful allies also has been a factor. During the 1970s and 1980s, the support of the United States government for authoritarian regimes in Asia was used by those governments to legitimize their control. Absent such support, it was argued, those governments would topple and communist forces would seize the advantage. The American role either in maintaining or unseating governments in Asia has perhaps been exaggerated, but there can be little doubt that U.S. influence has been critical at times. It is likely, for example, that the 1963 assassination of President Diem in Vietnam grew directly out of the withdrawal of American support for his regime. By the 1990s, most Pacific nations, including some close American allies, had achieved a level of self-confidence and independence that made their support from or opposition to the United States less a factor in domestic affairs. However, in the Philippines in late 1990, a military rebellion against President Aquino was directly suppressed by American war planes. In a far different way, American support is also deemed critical for Japanese leaders who still take pains to demonstrate to the electorate that they can maintain a strong relationship with the United States.

More diffuse international influences arise from the fact that Pacific Asia is one of the most active trading regions of the world. With increased trade has come a variety of cultural and informational imports that proclaim the advantages of egalitarian lifestyles and social structures. Similarly, televised examples of rapid democratic change have had an impact. Broadcasts of the "people power" movement of the Philippines may have helped inspire Koreans to press for democratic change and to incline their government toward acceptance of it. Internally, the national television broadcast of the Korean presidential elections reinforced the population's perception of its new power. Finally, television presents a "stage" for public demonstrations as will be seen in chapter 10 in reference the 1989 democratization movement in China.

In some cases, examples of democratization abroad may also have encouraged the suppression of democracy in Asia. The spectacle of the violent overthrow of the Ceausescu regime in Romania is said to have deeply shaken the conservative leaders of China and inspired their increasingly repressive measures against any sign of domestic opposition. Nor did the experience of the Burmese military escape China's notice when Burma successfully used a pervasive secret police and ruthless military force to suppress democracy.

Leadership and the Role of the Military

For all that may be said about the importance of culture, history, institutions, economics, and foreign influences, a special place must be accorded outstanding leaders and elites who are committed to democratic change. A broadly based political elite with a deep commitment to democracy can be expected to overcome what may seem at first to be overwhelming resistance to change. The "people power" movement in the Philippines

is again a useful example. At the same time, the Philippines illustrates the extent to which the benefits of democratic reform can be squandered by the political elites when they fall to squabbling over the spoils of victory.

Against the example of self-aggrandizing leaders who refused to allow a succession of power — Marcos, Sukarno, Rhee — the special case of military leaders must also be raised. These are individuals who, like Suharto in Indonesia and Chun in Korea, moved their forces to prevent what, in their view, was a political process fast losing its center, spiraling toward corruption and chaos, or causing a major and intolerable shift to the Left. Although such leaders were reluctant to relinquish power once they seized it, the role of the military in Asia-Pacific democratizing countries has been primarily to guarantee stability rather than to overthrow democratic regimes in a premeditated fashion. However much the militaries of Indonesia and Thailand may have come to pervade domestic political affairs, they see themselves mainly in the capacity of forces that can restrain or remove untrustworthy politicians.

"Democracy" in Pacific Asia

The supporters of democracy in Pacific Asia have had to contend with the same obstacles that have confronted their counterparts in other regions of the world, but the evolution of democracy has departed from its antecedents in the West. Just as Asians reworked Marx's preconceptions about successful communist movements and Weber's notions of capitalist organization, so too they have modified the idea of Euro-American democratic governance to suit their own purposes. The democracies of Pacific Asia are still creating and defining themselves. The outcome in each case is a synthesis of the democratic processes introduced by the West and indigenous traditions of community, leadership, and authority.

NOTES

1. Lucian W. Pye, and Mary W. Pye, *Asian Power and Politics: The Cultural Dimensions of Authority* (Cambridge, MA: Harvard University Press, 1985), pp. 183-84.

2. See Zakaria Haji Ahmad, "Malaysia: Quasi Democracy in a Divided Society," in *Democracy in Developing Countries: Asia*, eds. Larry Diamond, Juan J. Linz, and Seymour Martin Lipset, vol. 3 of 4 vols. (Boulder, Co: Lynne Rienner Publishers, 1989), pp. 368-71 which this section partially summarizes.

3. Ulf Sundhaussen, "Indonesia: Past and Present Encounters with Democracy," in Ibid., pp. 448-49, 462-63, 447-48.

4. The alleged U.S. complicity in the massacres is disputed in an article by H.W. Brands, "The Limits of Manipulation: How the United States Didn't Topple Sukarno," *Journal of American History*, December, 1989.

5. David Joel Steinberg, ed., *In Search of Southeast Asia: A Modern History* (Honolulu: University of Hawaii Press, 1987), pp. 424-25.

6. Ibid., pp. 431-37.

7. Sung-joo Han, "South Korea: Politics in Transition," in *Democracy in Developing Countries: Asia*, Diamond, et. al., pp. 276-77.

8. Fred Hiatt, "Seoul Parties' Merger Shows Influence of Japanese Political Model," *Washington Post*, 27 January 1990, sec. 1, p. A18.

9. Pye, *Asian Power and Politics*, pp. 340-41.

9

Sentimental Imperialists: America in Asia

OVERVIEW

The United States has had an impact on the development of Pacific Asia in the twentieth century greater than any other non-Asian country. This chapter will describe how the scale, scope and significance of American influence has changed over the decades and the extent to which, at century's end, its influence in the region may be waning.[1]

While the emphasis here will be on the post World War II period, it is useful to recall that during the nineteenth century, cultural interchanges, commerce, and shipping — but not military affairs — dominated American-Asian relations. Thousands of American missionaries settled in Asia where their impact and that of their secular counterparts — teachers, engineers, and scientists — was felt profoundly in the modernizing societies of China, Japan, and Korea. The notion of military dominance in any region of the world was alien to Americans of this era. Unlike Europeans who reinforced their national identities in the context of foreign wars, the Americans took pride in their economic prowess, their individual freedom, their restraint of governmental power, and their acceptance of foreigners as potential citizens.

These nineteenth century Americans may have held utopian views about the community of mankind, but many of them had practiced slavery

and they believed in a racial heirarchy of the world's peoples. Yet for the missionaries and educators of the time, it was a heirarchy that could be climbed by the "lowest" people if they were given adequate opportunities for education and advancement. From this vision was born a "sentimental" view of Asia wherein Americans believed that it was their mission to advance other races spiritually, politically, and economically.

The second phase of the encounter with Asia began in 1898 with the Spanish-American War, which suddenly militarized America's Pacific presence after its invasion of the Philippines. Soon, the United States had joined the imperialist club in Asia, taking possession of several additional, small Pacific territories while it built a new, modern navy. It also started construction on the Panama Canal and expanded its trade and investment in the region. American cultural influence in Asia remained strong during this period, with Asians finding much to emulate in American models of education, government, and capitalism.

Until the early twentieth century, America's idealism was expressed only through the individual efforts of missionaries and educators. Then it gained an articulate spokesman in President Woodrow Wilson who established the intellectual framework for a national role in Asia and the world. Wilson's vision combined principles of economic interdependence, collective security, and cultural interchange. If widely adopted, it was hoped, these principles would advance global peace, democracy, and human rights. However much it may have been thwarted by the Versailles Treaty (chapter 4), the Wilsonian vision was initially very beneficial to U.S. relations with the Asia-Pacific region. Naval limitation agreements, a relatively free flow of goods, and cultural exchanges — involving a new generation of American "missionaries" for Christianity, democracy, and modern education — prevailed through the 1920s.

The world economic crisis of the 1930s undermined the Wilsonian world system. National extremists rose to power in Japan, rejecting the notion of global interdependence in favor of Japan's monopoly of resources and markets inside its own Greater East Asia Co-prosperity Sphere. At first, America retreated into isolationism and protectionism, but under the leadership of President Franklin D. Roosevelt, many of the Wilsonian ideals were revived. After World War II, collective security, the expansion of global trade, and the creation of new world institutions marked the next phase of the American-Asian relationship. Roosevelt spoke out as early as 1942 not only for human rights and self determination, the Wilsonian goals, but for social justice and racial equality, principles that held a special importance for Asians.

The wartime conferences of the Allies in Cairo, Yalta, and Potsdam envisioned a world that would be stabilized and made prosperous through close cooperation among the victorious nations. Roosevelt called for a unified Korea and a decolonialized Southeast Asia, among other things, but like the Wilsonian ideals, his hopes were to be compromised by global trends: President Harry S. Truman, his successor, faced a growing military confrontation with the Soviet Union. In the late 1940s, Truman's advisors fashioned what came to be known as the policy of "containment," a strategy to prevent the spread of Soviet expansionism and totalitarianism through economic, political, and military competition.

From its original inception by George F. Kennan, containment policy became focused on security issues as pressures from the Soviet Union and its allies mounted. China fell to the communists, its "loss" to America resulting in a hunt for culprits and subversives that ruined many promising careers and stripped the government of some of its best Asia experts. The Korean War — a civil war that was poorly understood by the United States from the outset — devastated and divided Korea, contributed to the anitcommunist hysteria in the United States, and militarized the concept of containment beyond anything Kennan had envisioned.

The "Truman Doctrine," which was to be supported by successive adminstrations of both political parties, declared that communism would be confronted anywhere in the world and at virtually any cost. The popular American conception of monolithic communism failed to see the growing split between the Soviets and Chinese, nor did it appreciate the significance of nationalist aspirations within communist movements. Thus, Americans naively assumed that "Asia" comprised a homogeneous series of countries that would fall in succession, like dominoes, under the pressure of communism. Such illusions coalesced in Southeast Asia to create a foreign policy disaster, the Vietnam War, whose reverberations still echo in American culture and politics.

This chapter describes these three major events in turn — the "loss" of China, the Korean War, and the Vietnam War. It then examines how, in their wake, an unsentimental strategy of containing communism underwent its own transformations. In the end, a transition toward yet another phase in the Asian-American relationship began in the 1970s with a startling turnaround in U.S.-China relations that incorporated the PRC into America's Asian security system. At the same time, American economic power began to decline relative to that of its allies. The eventual collapse of the Soviet Union altered many of the assumptions upon which American global and regional leadership had been based. The result is yet another period of change and reassessment in the American relationship with Asia. As before, the American cultural impact remains profound even if its economic and strategic roles in the Pacific Basin face new challenges. These challenges have arisen not only from the inherent economic strength and dynamism of the region but also from the successes and failures of American efforts to shape its future.

Figure 9.1 A cartoonist in 1923 was amused by America's insistence, during negotiations with Japan over rights to the island of Yap, that the local population should be subject to U.S. Prohibition laws. His caption: "Bless you, my child."

Figure 9.2 This *New York Herald* cartoon of 1911 typified the optimism with which Americans viewed the Chinese revolution, assuming that a Westernized "New China" would replace the old one. The Manchu's queue, about to be cut, reads "Long ages of graft."

AMERICANS AND THE "LOSS" OF CHINA

— by James C. Thomson

History gives, and history takes away. America's much touted "success" in Japan found its simultaneous antithesis across the Yellow and East China seas in what was widely described as the "failure" of American policy in China.

"Failure" was actually among the gentler terms applied to the triumph of the Chinese Communists and the collapse of the Chinese Nationalists between 1945 and 1949. Instead, the so-called "loss" of China was denounced by many as a "sellout" or "betrayal," the result not merely of incompetence but of conspiracy and even treason among covert American Communists and their liberal "fellow travelers."

The intensity of American reaction to the victory of Mao Tse-tung (Mao Zedong) is difficult to recreate for those of a later generation. Even those who experienced it are sometimes baffled in retrospect.

Yet if you had described to an informed observer, on the eve of Pearl Harbor in late 1941, the shape and condition of Sino-American relations a decade later, in 1951, he would undoubtedly have judged you demented. Recalling the world of 1941 — heroic China struggling for survival against the mighty Japanese empire allied to Hitler's juggernaut — consider the American-East Asian scene ten years later.

In Asia, a strong, reunified China under Communist rule was fighting the United States to a stalemate in Korea. Nationalist China's leaders, their supporters, and some troops — about two million in all — had fled to exile on the island of Taiwan, a hundred miles off the coast. Communist-led insurrections were smoldering in many other parts of Asia, most notably in Malaya and Indochina. And with Japan defeated, occupied, and disarmed, the United States was playing as never before the role of gendarme of the Pacific.

Meanwhile, at home in America, a process of recrimination over China's "loss" and the Cold War — a major Communist scare — was well under way. This was a process that would eventually destroy or maim scores of careers, in and out of government. It would oust the Democratic party from power after twenty years in highest office; and it would make many Americans distrustful of their neighbors and colleagues, "security"-conscious as never before. It was also a process that would lead the American government into an unaccustomed stance of formal Pacific and East Asian militancy in an effort to "contain and isolate Red China."

The question is fairly obvious: How can one explain such a total transformation and the trauma it produced?

The answers lie in the complex tangle of wartime China. Out of that tangle, three general developments seem overriding: the disintegration of the Chinese Nationalists; the simultaneous strengthening of the Chinese Communists; and the new reality of American intervention in Chinese politics, from Pearl Harbor onward.

The Kuomintang's failure is the easiest to diagnose. The central government had been unable in its Nanking (Nanjing) years to cope with the dual problem of internal rebels and external aggressors. It had also failed, moreover, in its hybrid and half hearted efforts to fill the vacuum left by the collapse of Confucianism as an ideology and social cement. During the years of its first united front with the Communists in the 1920s, the KMT had been for a while infused with Marxism-Leninism which meant democratic centralism to increase the party's effectiveness, and a commitment to both social revolution and anti-imperialism. But when Chiang Kai-shek broke with the Communists in 1927, and indeed tried to restore a facade of Confucianism in the 1930s, his regime lost touch with large numbers of the nation's intellectuals and students. It lost further touch with such catalytic groups during its efforts to appease Japan prior to

This section of this chapter is taken from the book *Sentimental Imperialists* by James C. Thomson, Jr., Peter W. Stanley, and John Curtis Perry (New York: Harper & Row. 1981). Their analysis of American involvement in Asia is recommended for an expanded treatment of America's Pacific Century.

1937, since major objectives of Chinese *nationalism*, in all its forms and superheated fervor, were the attainment of national power and the ouster of all foreign imperialists.

Simultaneous with the early and continuing defection of the students and intellectuals was — as we have seen — the KMT government's failure to treat the fundamental causes of acute rural distress, and therefore the eventual defection of vast numbers of peasants once a more promising alternative was available to them. It must be stressed further that this KMT government was initially sustained by its ties with treaty port bankers, merchants, and industrialists on the seacoast — the modern sector of the economy, including a goodly number of American-trained "returned students" who helped staff its bureaucracy. But after the Japanese invasion, Chiang and his colleagues were severed from that more modern, and sometimes progressive, sector as a source of support. And with the retreat to Szechwan (Sichuan) in 1938, the KMT had to rely increasingly on its two other internal sources of support: the landlord class, and several leftover warlords with semi-private armies. In this transition, the Chinese Nationalists became both weaker and much more conservative.

To weakness and conservatism one must add the malaise of creeping demoralization. Although "Free China" rejoiced in the aftermath of Pearl Harbor, now allied to strong friends abroad in a worldwide struggle, its leaders soon discovered that China's role would be largely a holding operation-pinning down Japanese armies of occupation while the "real war" was fought elsewhere. While America's Pacific strategy became a process of island-hopping for the aerial bombardment of Japan, Free China became "the end of the line," with a central minimal purpose of being "kept in the war." Such a role, in the shrouded dankness of Chungking (Chongqing), could only breed corruption, laziness, inflation, and sinking morale.

A simultaneous major development out of the tangle of wartime China was the growth of the Chinese Communists in strength, population, and territory. Survivors of the CCP's several rural redoubts, regrouped after the costly Long March of 1934-35, had settled in a rugged three-province area of Shensi (Shenxi), Kansu (Gansu), and Ninghsia (Ningxia), with headquarters eventually in Yenan. Chiang's kidnapping and Japan's

renewed assault had brought about a new united front in 1937. But this time the partnership was built on intense mutual distrust; and from early 1941 onward, the front was essentially replaced by the renewal of sporadic civil war in the midst of Sino-Japanese stalemate. During these years the Communist troops practiced with considerable success their hard-learned guerrilla tactics. They infiltrated the countryside behind Japanese lines, capturing arms, recruiting troops, and organizing the peasantry. In the regions they held or liberated, they established local regimes, redistributed land, and instituted tax reforms.

Wartime conditions gave the Communists opportunities to expand into territory they had never previously held, and such expansion had major consequences. First, they were able to create "border region" governments, consisting of a pyramid of "people's councils" to administer CCP programs. Second, party membership expanded from about 40,000 in 1937 to 1.2 million in 1945. And finally, party members were given rigorous ideological indoctrination, especially in the writings of Mao Tse-tung (Mao Zedong), who was already emerging as an independent reinterpreter of Marxism-Leninism. By the time of Japan's surrender, the Communists had put together a tightly disciplined party and an army of more than half a million; and they could claim control over an area of nearly 100 million people. All this was accomplished, it should be noted, despite the KMT's relentless efforts to enforce a "blockade" of the Communist territories.

The third key ingredient in the Sino-American transformation, between 1941 and 1951, was American involvement in Chinese politics on a scale heretofore unmatched. Such involvement had a series of phased consequences: initially, extraordinary glorification and glamorization of Nationalist China and its leaders among Americans back home; then, increasing frustration with the realities of Free China, as reported by resident American journalists and officials; and finally, the total collapse of American interventionist efforts to bring about a peaceful compromise resolution of the civil war that erupted in the wake of Japan's defeat.

Before and especially after the shock of Pearl Harbor, glorification came first. It was a welling-up of national sentiment, in the midst of a new world war, sentiment that built upon several decades of sympathies and hopes for the Chinese, but suspicion and competition with Japan. Chiang Kai-shek and his wife had become, through influential media, living symbols of a Christian, anti-Communist, anti-fascist, and pro-American China. The KMT government's impact on the American public reached its zenith during Madame Chiang's triumphal American speech-making tour early in 1943. Her address to a joint session of Congress — her command of English, her passionate rhetoric, her imperious beauty and charisma — produced an extraordinary ovation and ringing pledges of support for Free China. Later she evoked similar adulation from a live audience of 17,000 in Madison Square Garden and a radio audience of millions more.

As A. T. Steele, veteran China reporter for the *New York Herald Tribune* has written of that zenith year, "There was a saying among the cynical that Mme. Chiang was worth ten divisions to the Generalissimo. In terms of her influence on American public opinion this was no exaggeration. It can probably be said, in all truth, that Mme. Chiang at that time commanded more popularity in the U.S. than in her homeland. " Steele nicely summarizes America's love affair with National-ist China in the early and mid-1940s: "This was a fantastic period in Sino-American relations — a period of dreamy unreality, in which the American public seemed prepared to accept and believe anything and everything good and wonderful that was said about the Chinese, their Generalissimo, the Generalissimo's wife, and the heroic Chinese people."

Glorification and glamorization at home in the United States were not, however, paralleled by similar euphoria among American observers in China itself. There something quite different was happening.

For the Chungking government, and for its new American allies in World War II, that partnership was a long and mutual immersion in frustration and ill-concealed anger. First, in the military sphere, Chiang tried but failed to get agreement to a coordinated Allied strategy centered on China. General Joseph W. Stilwell ("Vinegar Joe"), as Chiang's American Chief of Staff, was given the hopeless task of defending Burma, and then, when Burma fell to the Japanese, the grueling three-year

task of reopening a land route to China through northern Burma. Stilwell's arch-rival, General Claire Chennault of "Flying Tigers" fame, even-tually got five big airfields constructed in unoccupied China; but almost at once the main base for the bombing of Japan was shifted to the Mariana Islands, supplied by sea and closer to Tokyo. And Chennault's bases would trigger a deeper Japanese invasion.

So, entering the Pacific war as a prospective Allied base for defeating Japan, Nationalist China found that the job was being done by sea — with China cut off, a low-priority sideshow. The result was the deepening demoralization of Chiang's supporters. As for the generalissimo, he artfully fended off his American advisers, forced the recall of Stilwell, and clung, in haughty isolation, to declining power. The Stilwell-Chennault controversy prefigured a protracted debate about military tactics in Asia, one that would linger into the 1970s.

Frustration and anger on the scene had other sources as well as the exigencies of Allied global military planning. Free China, and especially Chungking as its refugee capital, was a not so happy haven for American diplomats, military officials, journalists, and also private citizens who did not like what they saw. In its state of weakness, corruption, fear of Communism, and psychological depression, KMT China up close was increasingly unattractive to American observers. Economic deterioration and political suppression of KMT critics were compounded by heavy-handed efforts at censorship of negative reporting.

The Chungking regime's unattractiveness was sharply intensified for those Americans who were eventually permitted by Chiang to visit Yenan and the Communist territories. Here the contrasts were astonishing. Morale was extraordinarily high; there was no evidence of any gulf between rich and poor, landowners and the landless; corruption seemed nonexistent; a form of participatory democracy was widely practiced, not just preached (albeit under careful CCP control); the leaders lived simply, mingled easily with the people, and were bluntly and warmly forthcoming in extended conversations with the foreign visitors. Little wonder, then, that the Yenan experience was in almost every case a "persuading encounter" for Americans who had known the other China of

Chungking. Indeed, the Chinese Communists tended to remind American visitors of their own idealized selves.

It was against the backdrop of such divergent views of conditions in wartime China — the outlook from the United States, and the observed realities on the scene — that the American government attempted a major intervention in the Chinese revolution, one destined to failure. That intervention was based on an increasingly strong perception among American officials, from late 1943 onward, that the ongoing struggle between the KMT and the CCP might well result in all-out civil war once Japan had been defeated. To avert such an outcome, American policymakers developed a twofold aim: first, to encourage some form of political settlement between the bitter rivals — a political settlement which even Chiang Kai-shek himself advocated as early as September 1943; and second, to strengthen the Nationalist government's position for such negotiations, partly by building up Chungking's armies, partly by pressing for some basic governmental reforms. In pursuit of these aims, it can be said in retrospect that the KMT's armed forces were in fact much improved in training and equipment, but that all efforts at broadening the government's political base and reducing its multiple abuses (notably, corruption, economic exploitation, and political oppression) were a failure. Chiang and his colleagues remained adroitly resistant.

As for efforts to achieve some form of viable political settlement, talks between the KMT and the CCP were resumed, at American urging, in 1943. Meanwhile, American policymakers sought to move on several levels: internationally, to try to make China a great power in form if not in substance; in Nationalist China, to create a modern army and air force — an effort in which, under Generals Stilwell and Albert C. Wedemeyer, a thousand American instructors and advisers helped train and equip some thirty-nine divisions; and in the Chinese political arena, to resolve the Chungking-Yenan split. In the last of these efforts, high-level American missions came and went, achieving no real results, most notably Vice President Henry Wallace and General Patrick J. Hurley.

Hurley, an Oklahoma Republican and Secretary of War under President Hoover, was dispatched by President Roosevelt as a special emissary and then became U.S. Ambassador to China in 1944-45. A man of mustachioed military handsomeness, much bravado, no knowledge of China, and not a touch of subtlety, Hurley visited Yenan, thought he had negotiated a Chiang-Mao agreement, but was soon undone by the distrust the two leaders had for each other. Chiang especially could not bring himself to cooperate. In the end, Hurley felt betrayed not by the Chinese but rather by the foreign service officers in his Chungking embassy who had deeply doubted — and had reported to Washington their doubts about — his simplistic perception of the KMT-CCP struggle (a struggle much like ones between Republicans and Democrats, he had said more than once). Hurley vented his spleen in two ways. He insisted on the transfer out of his embassy of all who had signed a long and dissenting February 1945 cable to the State Department while he was temporarily in Washington; and, on his resignation in December 1945, he fired a scatter-shot salvo at those American diplomats both in China and in Washington who had allegedly undermined — even sabotaged — his China mission by sympathizing with the Chinese Communists and pushing their cause.

Here, in Hurley's fiery valedictory charges, was the central seedbed of what would eventually become the McCarthy-McCarran investigations five years later, and the hunt for China scapegoats that would follow.

Despite wartime American efforts to avert civil war, Japan's sumbission in August 1945 triggered a China race for territorial control. While the United States used its major air- and sea-lift capacity to move half a million Nationalist forces back to the coastal centers, Communist troops sped overland to expand their domain by accepting Japanese surrenders in northern China. And even as Americans back home began to relax and demobilize, the long foreseen civil war began to erupt. "This was a moment" — in the words of John K. Fairbank — "when the American people were least prepared, emotionally and intellectually, to face a Chinese crisis. We had no intention in the winter of 1945-46 of fighting another war in East Asia."

How, then, to cope with this renewed China upheaval? One response, by President Truman, was the appointment of victory's chief architect, the revered General George C. Marshall, to go on a special mission to negotiate peace between the two civil war contestants. But the mutual distrust ran too deep, and Marshall's heroic efforts, in 1946-47, came to naught. Meanwhile, Washington veered between intervals of attempted neutrality (and brief aid "freezes") and increasing military assistance to the Nationalists — a course pressed upon a very skeptical Democratic administration by a newly elected Republican — controlled Congress in January 1947. But the civil war burgeoned, with initially some three million KMT troops battling Communist forces totalling one million and with American aid to the Nationalists eventually running to over two million dollars in all, between 1945 and 1948.

While the KMT retained control of all the significant cities — including, soon, Yenan — the Communists were highly successful in seizing control of the countryside, especially in Manchuria and northern China. In due course, Mao's armies would skillfully surround and choke off Chiang's urban fortresses one by one. To American military advisers on the scene, KMT military strategy seemed largely "medieval" and grotesquely self-defeating; but American generals, from Stilwell onward, had had a record of non-success in influencing the stubborn generalissimo. Afterward, the last of those advisers, General William Barr, would testify that the Nationalists had never lost a battle through lack of arms or equipment.

The end for the KMT on the mainland, now headquartered back in Nanking, came in massive pitched battles on the North China plain, after the loss of all Manchuria and the peaceful surrender of Peking by its commanding general, in the autumn of 1948 — battles in which the outnumbered Communists regularly prevailed, and the surviving Nationalist troops surrendered, fled southward, or defected in increasing numbers. In the big coastal cities, KMT and "third force" efforts were unavailing; and a final indicator, from September 1948 onward, had been the astronomical inflation rate for Nationalist currency: four new Chinese dollars to U.S. $1 that month, but 60 million to one by the following February. By early 1949, the Chinese civil war was basically all over — except for slow-motion mopping up by the victors, a process that would take all year, up to the "liberation" of Szechwan (Sichuan) late that autumn.

On October 1, 1949, with the KMT remnants removed to Taiwan, and most of China under CCP control, Mao Tse-tung (Mao Zedong) triumphantly proclaimed in Peking's T'ien-an Men (Beijing's Tian'anmen) square the establishment of the People's Republic of China. To the world he announced, "China has stood up!"

Back in Washington, a newly re-elected but distracted Democratic administration, facing a hostile Congress and also mounting problems in other parts of the world, had nonetheless seen clearly the Nationalist debacle — and had tried to cushion the public's learning of the bad news, a Communist victory in China, by preparing a "White Paper" on United States-China relations, a document issued in August 1949. It was a large document that printed selected classified dispatches relating to America's intervention in the Chinese civil war. Its basic message, conveyed by Secretary of State Dean Acheson, was that despite all that the United States could do, China had been lost to the Communist faction by the multiple flaws and errors of the nation's Nationalist leadership. As for the future, Acheson added orally, Washington would "wait for the dust to settle."

Rather than mute or calm the China debate that autumn, that White Paper would enflame it for years to come.

What next happened raises a familiar question: How can one explain the recurrent American obsession with China and the Chinese people? More specifically: How can one explain the effect of China's "loss" to "Communism" on large sectors of American public opinion — and especially the electorate's representatives?

In seeking to understand the American reaction to the Nationalist debacle, one deals with many intangibles. Answers largely lie in the mystery of subterranean forces that shaped the mood of the American people. Yet there is obviously one central ingredient: the very high hopes, building upon deep-rooted sympathy, that Americans had harbored for postimperial China, and, simultaneously, the dashing of those high hopes by a hostile new regime, soon firmly allied to the Soviet menace — a regime that charged Washington with supporting Chiang Kai-shek (while American Republicans, ironically, were charging quite the opposite). To put the matter simply: Here was our ward and tutee and, most recently, ally — and it had been turned against us, had up and bit our helping hand. The key feeling was betrayal; but the key question was, Who had accomplished it, and how?

Beyond China and Asia, however, other factors — a series of alarming events — contributed to the convulsion that China's "loss" caused within the United States. Here are some of them:

In general, Americans knew that fascism had been defeated; but now the nation had an uneasy sense that it had been cheated out of its victory by the sudden new threat of communism. Specifically, the Soviet ally had been sensed increasingly as an adversary in the process of several postwar negotiations, especially regarding Eastern Europe. In 1947, the Democratic administration perceived the danger of a Soviet threat to both Europe and the Middle East; the results were the Truman Doctrine for Greece and Turkey and the Marshall Plan for Europe. But then in 1948 came the Czechoslovakia coup d'etat and the Berlin Blockade — and the Cold War, already begun out of mutual distrust, was a vast glacial reality.

That summer in America came the case of Alger Hiss — the epitome of the Eastern intellectual, a Harvard man, law clerk to Justice Holmes, a lawyer-diplomat who had hovered at the right hand of Franklin Roosevelt at the Yalta great-power conference in early 1945, and then had been a chief functionary at the founding conference of the United Nations in San Francisco later that year. Hiss had been accused of being a Communist agent by Whittaker Chambers, a confessed former Communist and later a Time magazine editor. The Hiss case went through two trials that tore the nation apart. The first produced a hung jury, but the second found him guilty of perjury, in January 1950. The question that many were forced to ponder, both friends and foes, was, If such a paragon of integrity and achievement as Alger Hiss might be a Communist plant, how many others — everywhere — might there be?

In June 1950 came the most alarming development of all: the totally unexpected outbreak of the Korean War. While the administration responded with extraordinary speed — pulling the United Nations along in its wake — Republicans were quick to note that Secretary Acheson, in a major foreign-policy address in January, had not included either South Korea or Taiwan within America's Pacific defense perimeter. Although Acheson's speech had had the unanimous endorsement of the Joint Chiefs of Staff at the time, his critics would argue for years to come that it had been an "open invitation" to Communist aggression. And in that same January, Acheson, a mentor of Alger Hiss, had said at the time of the Hiss conviction quoting the New Testament — that he would not turn his back on his friend. Such times would eventual!y drive even the cold and usually non-demagogic Republican leader Senator Robert A. Taft to assert that "The blood of our boys in Korea is on Dean Acheson's hands."

All these alarming events at home and abroad were contributors — along with the loss of China — to the ensuing convulsion. To sum up their impact: They helped create a nation deeply shaken, even traumatized, by yet another crisis after a global "war to end all wars." They helped create a nation sown with the seeds of mutual suspicion and multiple recriminations, a nation of people unsure of whom to trust anymore. By 1952, it would become a nation with one of its two major political parties out of highest office for nearly twenty years. The left out Republican party was one which had practiced bipartisanship in the European policy sector, but had felt both bypassed in administration planning for the Far East and also acutely in need of a foreign policy issue in order to win the next election. Specifically, some frustrated Republicans — watching American aims thwarted abroad — were willing to run on a very shrill indictment of the Democrats: "Twenty Years of Treason." Others, the "moderates," would settle for "Korea, Communism, Confusion, and Corruption."

Most specifically, the unfolding of the Cold War abroad and the frustrations of the "out-party" at home produced a large group of activists, and their millions of supporters, who were ready to find out once and for all an answer to the cosmic question "Who lost China?" For what had been lost was not merely a valiant wartime ally, not merely 400 to 600 million potential Christians and customers and tutees, but also a very, very big country, the most populous on earth. And it had been lost to communism and, it seemed, to permanent enslavement by Moscow.

Figures 9.3-9.4   Political cartoons reflected an American belief that with the "loss" of China to communism, China would be forever enslaved by the Soviet Union (above) and would magnify Soviet power throughout the Pacific region (below).

What ensued was an extended and relentless search for The Culprits — those responsible for China's alleged loss, the network of conspiracy at home and abroad that had produced this outcome. It was a search heavily fueled by a variegated group of Nationalist China's admirers among Americans, out of both the Nanking and Chungking years. That group — a loose coalition of politicians, businessmen, journalists, missionaries, diplomats, military men, and others — would soon be labeled the "China Lobby," and there would be allegations of covert KMT funding during and after the retreat to Taiwan. But if it was a "lobby," it was more probably held together by shared fears, hopes, and wrath about the China situation than by any secret Nationalist expenditures. No such bribery was needed by a collectivity of true believers in the iniquity of communism and the virtues of Chiang's Nationalists — a collectivity that included, to name a few, publisher Henry R. Luce; China textile importer Alfred Kohlberg; and former medical missionary and by then Minnesota Congressman Walter Judd.

Such longtime China advocates developed powerful allies in the Congress and particularly in the Senate — Republicans looking for an effective issue with which to capture the White House, and also men of both parties (though mainly Republican) who were sincere in their alarm over communism's successes. The men who would shortly rise to most astonishing prominence and power in the search for culprits were first, a rather obscure junior Senator from Wisconsin, Republican Joseph R. McCarthy, and second, the veteran Democratic chairman of the Subcommittee on Internal Security of the Senate Judiciary Committee, Pat McCarran.

That search for culprits seems in retrospect to have gone through three phases. The first was dominated by Senator McCarthy.[2] The second was dominated by Senator McCarran in 1951-52, and it had consequences for some years to come.[3] And the third was dominated by Secretary of State John Foster Dulles and his colleagues, once the Republicans took over the White House in 1953. Meanwhile, in the second Truman administration, the embattled Democrats contributed to the search in a desperate effort to ward off their critics — by setting up a complex new program for the review and enforcement of "loyalty" and "security," a

program that ironically helped legitimize the phenomenon called "McCarthyism."

Perhaps the most poisonous phase of the search for culprits came with the installment of the Eisenhower administration in January 1953 — the first Republican President in twenty years. General Eisenhower had seemed a moderate in the preceding months of partisan fury; and in office he would often be so. But on the subject of China, his internationalist but fiercely dogmatic (and very Presbyterian) Secretary of State, John Foster Dulles, felt and shared the pent-up heat of the congressional witch-hunters. By now, Truman's loyalty-security apparatus had gone to work on scores of China-related diplomats. Most had been "cleared" repeatedly under the Democrats, with the ironic exception of John Stewart Service, who, dismissed by Secretary Acheson, fought for and won reinstatement by the Supreme Court in 1958 (a Pyrrhic victory; he ended his career, under a fearful Kennedy administration, as consul in Liverpool, England).

What Dulles faced, and too easily succumbed to, was the rightwing Republican desire to settle scores finally on the matter of China's "loss." The result was, in simple terms, a wide-ranging purge of all China experts in the bureaucracy (and especially in the State Department) who had shown any signs of sympathy for the Chinese Communist cause. One after another, the most visible ones were dismissed or forced out (Vincent, Davies, and Clubb), despite their proven innocence of all charges. The less visible ones, facing new harassments, departed. And those in between, whose names had been on some interrogator's list but against whom nothing could be proven, were simply sent "to pasture" in places like Latin America, Belgium or the Netherlands. Dulles largely delegated the administering of this housecleaning to his Assistant Secretary of State for the Far East, an archconservative Virginia Democrat named Walter Robertson, and especially to his Director of Security and Consular Affairs, Scott McLeod.

By the end of the Dulles-Robertson-McLeod housecleaning, everyone who had signed the famous cable from Chungking in February 1945 that had so infuriated Ambassador Patrick Hurley (or had supported the contents of that cable) had been removed by one means or another. And in that removal, between 1953 and 1957, an entire generation of America's most carefully developed, and rare, China expertise had been thrown out or banished. With that achievement, and also the severing of ties with the China academic community, America's China policymaking was placed entirely in the hands of people who had little or no experience or understanding of the Chinese revolution, its bifurcation, and the extraordinary complexities of the Chinese civil war.

It would be difficult to overestimate the costs of China's "loss" and the trauma it produced among Americans, from presidents and secretaries of state all the way down to young people looking for vocations and millions of grassroots voters. For nearly a quarter of a century, America's policies in Asia would be skewed by these things. So would American politics, education, and society. Out of that skewing came two perhaps entirely avoidable wars — in Korea and Indochina — at the least, collisions that might have been muted and resolved without massive bloodlettings.

But it was not to be so. Benevolence and sentimentalism toward postimperial China had been transformed into fear and hatred of Communist China, part and parcel of American fear of China's new mentor, Stalin's Soviet Union. Some fear of Stalinist Russia was undoubtedly appropriate. But the extended China trauma exceeded all bounds of reason. Benevolence turned into paranoia, at home and abroad, idealism into grandiosity, a grandiosity newly equipped with the most potent arsenal of weaponry history had ever known. And America's East Asian relations became engulfed by years of blind and lethal zealotry.[4]

◆   ◆   ◆

KOREA: LIBERATION, DIVISION, AND WAR, 1945-1953

— by Carter J. Eckert

August 15, 1945 was a day of jubilation throughout the Korean peninsula. Japan's surrender, unimaginable only a few years earlier, seemed to open the way for Koreans themselves to shape their own destiny for the first time since 1905. Koreans differed, however, in their visions of a postcolonial state and society. While most Koreans welcomed the prospect of independence, forty years of Japanese rule had engendered socioeconomic, political, and ideological cleavages within the country that made national unity problematic. In 1945, as in the late nineteenth century, it was not only Koreans who were interested in Korea. If the Japanese defeat in World War II had brought liberation to the peninsula, it had also created a geopolitical vacuum in northeast Asia that neither of the two great powers of the postwar era, the United States and the Soviet Union, was willing to relinquish to the other, or to the Koreans themselves. In less than five years, the interaction of these forces, internal and external, led to national division and devastating civil war.

The Colonial Legacy and the Transfer of Power

It is impossible to comprehend the events and significance of the period of liberation without reference to the previous four decades of Japanese rule. Colonial policies had shattered the foundations of a remarkably stable nineteenth century bureaucratic agrarian society and unleashed, new forces in conflict with the old and with each other. Korean society in 1945 was a maelstrom of old and new classes, political groups, and ideologies. About eighty percent of the population still lived on the land, but in addition to landlords and tenants, the Korean social scene was now dotted with an assortment of capitalists, white collar professionals, factory wage workers, and hundreds of thousands of landless peasants who had been uprooted from their villages by wartime mobilization policies and were now returning home from other provinces or parts of the crumbling Japanese empire. Colonialism had spawned both an active and passive Korean resistance, including numerous nationalist groups, both in Korea and abroad, each with its own history, personal connections, and political agenda. It had also created a variety of collaborators: Koreans who had openly and enthusiastically supported Japanese rule, those who had unwillingly acquiesced, and a whole range of people in between. Communism in Korea had also developed as a radical response to colonialism, and like other nationalist groups, the

Korean communists were also divided by their experiences and goals.

In this jumble of sometimes overlapping, more often antagonistic, forces and ideas, one can draw a heuristic line between two basic political orientations at the time of liberation — keeping in mind, of course, that there was a whole range of opinions and interests on either side with a grey, possibly even apolitical, area in the center. To the right of the line were the majority of propertied and educated Koreans, many of whom had cooperated in one way or another with the colonial regime and were therefore inclined to be lenient on the issue of collaboration. Most were resistant to fundamental social change such as land reform. Others, including some of the more progressive landlords who had transferred a portion of their assets into industry, regarded change as inevitable, but were anxious to control and contain it so as to preserve their privileged positions in the society. Also on the right were those Koreans with less education and little or no property who had faithfully served the Japanese state, such as the Koreans who comprised about forty percent of the colonial police force.

On the left side of the spectrum were Koreans of varying backgrounds, including students, intellectuals, peasants, and workers who had been politicized by the colonial experience. Some were actual members of the Communist Party or felt an affinity toward communism as a force that had opposed Japanese rule and advocated justice for the poor and oppressed. All were committed first to a thorough purge of collaborators from positions of power and influence. They sought, in addition, some form of redistribution of wealth, such as land reform, that would redress the inequities of the past and transform Korea into a more egalitarian society.

As early as the 1920s the basic antipathy between right and left had already burst forth in the form of an intellectual debate in Korean magazines and newspapers. It had grown in the 1930s as more and more Koreans found themselves participating in the Government-General's economic development programs as junior partners or victims. The wartime mobilization between 1938 and 1945 had sharpened the differences between the two sides and brought the animosity to a new height. By the end of the war, and long before any artificial geographic lines had been drawn at the thirty-eighth parallel, Korea was already an ideologically bifurcated society, held together by the power of the colonial state. The great question of liberation was what would happen once that state was gone.

In August 1945, with the outcome of the Pacific War no longer in doubt, the main concern of the Japanese authorities in Korea was with maintaining order and protecting the lives and property of Japanese citizens until one or more of the Allied victors arrived. For this they needed Korean help.

They turned first to Song Chin-u, a political moderate closely associated with Kim Song-su, his boyhood friend and patron, and with other Korean landlords, businessmen, and "cultural nationalists," many of whom had gradually accommodated themselves to the colonial regime. Like many of his associates, Song had acquired a certain reputation in Korea as a nationalist for his role in the March First Movement of 1919 and its aftermath in the 1920s. Unlike most of them, however, Song had managed to keep a low profile during the war, and by 1945 he was something of a rare commodity in Korea: a politician with elite Korean and Japanese colonial connections who had some relatively untarnished, if modest, nationalist credentials. Between August 9 and 13 the Government-General entreated Song to head up an interim administrative committee to preserve law and order. For reasons that are not entirely clear, but may well have had to do with Song's fear of compromising his already delicate political position, he refused the offer, and the Japanese were forced to consider an alternative candidate.

On the morning of August 15 the Japanese made the same offer to Yo Un-hyong. Yo was a highly respected and popular political figure with impeccable nationalist credentials. A populist at heart, he was politically far to the left of Song and much less attractive in that sense to the Japanese. On the other hand, although he was willing to work with the communists, he had never joined the Communist Party and claimed he could never embrace a materialist view of history. At this point, moreover, the Japanese still expected that the Soviets, who had already attacked the northern port cities of Unggi and Najin on August 10, would be occupying all of the peninsula, and they reasoned that Yo's more radical political stance would give them some leverage with that most dreaded enemy.

The Government-General's hopes that Yo would be a pliable figurehead were immediately shattered. Yo accepted the offer, but only on condition that the Japanese immediately release all political prisoners, guarantee the food supply for the next three months, and absolutely refrain from interference in any Korean peace-keeping, independence, and mobilization activities. The Japanese reluctantly agreed, and Yo quickly set up the Choson Kon'guk Chunbi Wiwonhoe or Committee for the Preparation of Korean Independence (CPKI). From its headquarters in Seoul, the CPKI established contact with a wide range of prominent Koreans throughout the country, and Yo called upon Koreans to act together in unity and to refrain from violence.

The CPKI developed rapidly from a temporary peace-keeping organ as envisioned by the Government-General into a new national government. Branches of the CPKI, called "people's committees" (inmin wiwonhoe), sprang up all over the country almost overnight and assumed control of the local administrative apparatus. All thirteen provinces had provincial committees within a few days after liberation. By the end of August, there were committees in most of the major cities and a total of 145 throughout the peninsula. Within three months, there were committees at all administrative levels down to the smallest villages. At each level the people's committees were supplemented by indigenous workers' and peasant unions, and by peace-keeping, student, youth, and women's groups which affiliated themselves with the local committees. Drawing on this nationwide base, the CPKI convened a representative assembly in Seoul on September 6, and several hundred delegates announced the formation of the Choson Inmin Konghwaguk or Korean People's Republic (KPR) and scheduled future national elections.

Scholars disagree about the political character and legitimacy of the KPR. Standard South Korean and American scholarship has tended to view the KPR as a communist front whose popularity was directly proportional to the degree it was able to camouflage its real intentions, i.e., the establishment of a revolutionary communist state. According to this view, Korea in 1945 lacked the necessary requirements for socialism and Koreans were generally unwilling to espouse the program of the Korean Communist Party. Revisionist studies of the period, on the other hand, have suggested that the KPR represented a genuine attempt at a leftist coalition government and that it had strong popular backing. Scholars of this view do not dispute the fact that Korean communists, many of whom had considerable experience as political organizers in the decade before liberation, played an important role in the formation of the people's committees and the KPR, but they contend that the prevailing mood of the country at the time was revolutionary and that the communists consequently felt confident enough to allow a moderate segment of the right a place in the new government for the sake of national unity.

The KPR's roster of cabinet officers and its platform tend to lend support to the revisionist view. Both suggest an effort toward the establishment of a workable national coalition in which the left, to be sure, would predominate. Cabinet posts went not only to leftists like Yo and Ho Hon, but also to Kim Song-su and to right-leaning nationalist exiles associated with the early independence movement and the Korean Provisional Government in Chongqing (Chungking). Syngman Rhee (Yi Sung-man), a former member of the old Independence Club and onetime president of the Korean Provisional Government when it was in Shanghai, was chosen as the KPR chairman.

A twenty-seven-point platform, announced on September 14, also left a certain niche for the right. The land reform plank called for confiscation without compensation (and redistribution to the peasants who worked it) only of land belonging to the Japanese and to the so-called national traitors who had collaborated with them. Unconfiscated land was to be subject to a tenancy rate reform on a 3-7 basis, by which rent would be capped at 30 percent of the crop. Nationalization was to be applied only to major industries such as mining, large-scale factories, railways, shipping, communications, and banking, most of which were already owned or controlled by the state; small and medium commerce and industry would be allowed to continue and develop, although under state supervision. Labor provisions for an eight-hour day, prohibition of child labor, and a minimum wage were basically reformist and echoed the demands that Korean workers had been making throughout the colonial period. The platform also gave the franchise to all Koreans, both male and female, with the sole exception again of the collaborators, and promised freedom of speech, assembly, and religion.

While the KPR thus strove for coalition, it can hardly be denied that the new government's platform, if carried out, would have constituted a social revolution in the Korean context. The proposed confiscation of land alone would have been a virtual deathblow for the core of Korea's propertied class, because so many in this group were major landowners and collaborators. It is not difficult to imagine, however, that the majority of Koreans, for whom colonialism had been a bitter and degrading experience, would have been supportive of such a measure, and there is, indeed, much evidence of such support. Throughout the country between August and November 1945, Koreans proceeded to dismantle the colonial administration at every level and to expel those judged as collaborators from positions of political power and influence. Although communists played an often significant part in these dramas, they were not invariably the leaders, and observers noted that there was always rapid participation by the local population. The KPR program thus seems to have been a reasonable reflection of popular sentiment.

Soviet-U.S. Rivalry and the Division of the Peninsula

During World War II Americans had gradually become accustomed to hearing their president speak of the "gallant Red Army" and to thinking of the Soviets as allies, but such warm regard for the Soviets was a new phenomenon. Between 1918 and 1920, the United States had sent 9,000 troops to Siberia as part of an allied expeditionary force to crush the Russian Revolution, and it was not until 1933 that the United States had officially recognized the new Soviet state. Hostile foreign policies toward the Soviet Union, moreover, had always tended to find support in longstanding American fears of socialism and communism. The

wartime alliance, in spite of all the rhetoric and seeming goodwill, was for both nations essentially a military marriage of convenience. As the war wound down, the old suspicions, never far below the surface, started to break through again, and one of the first areas to be affected was Korea.

For the Soviet Union, Korea had long been an area of strategic interest. It had all begun in the late nineteenth century as the Czarist empire had expanded east with the Trans-Siberian Railway into its new Maritime Province (between the Ussuri River and the Pacific), acquired from the Chinese in 1860. The concern with Korea was natural, dictated by geography: the two countries shared a common ten-mile border near the mouth of the Tumen River and not far from the new Russian naval port of Vladivostok. Russian concern with Korea, however, had been more than matched by similar Japanese imperialist ambitions and anxieties. After a decade of failed mutual attempts to reach a satisfactory accord on both Korea and Manchuria, including a secret proposal in 1896 to partition the peninsula along the thirty-ninth parallel, the two countries found themselves edging ever closer toward war, finally launched by the Japanese with a surprise attack on Port Arthur in 1904. In the end, the result had been the eclipse of Russian influence in Korea for forty years. At the end of World War II, the imminent collapse of Japan once again made Korea an object of attention in Moscow.

American interest in Korea before the 1940s had been confined for the most part to a few Protestant missions and even fewer businessmen. For that reason, although the United States had been the first Western nation to sign a formal diplomatic treaty with Korea in 1882, it had also been the first foreign embassy to leave in November 1905 after the Japanese had forced the Koreans to sign a protectorate treaty. This policy of acquiescence in the Japanese seizure of Korea had been formalized in the Taft-Katsura Memorandum of 1905, by which Japan had agreed, in turn, to respect America's control of the Philippines. It had remained the basic American policy toward Korea until Pearl Harbor. Thereafter, however, long-range American policy on Korea had undergone a gradual shift. By late 1943 it was clear that Japan's anticipated defeat in the war would make the United States a great new power in East Asia, and former American indifference to Korea was replaced by the same fear of Russian control of the peninsula that had tormented the Japanese at the turn of the century.

While the issue of Korean security was never forgotten, American policy makers in the State Department were temporarily forced by military imperatives to bow to the views of the War Department. Anticipating a long and difficult battle for the Japanese home islands, the United States desperately sought Soviet participation in the war against Japan on the Asian mainland, and U.S. military leaders, including General MacArthur, were willing, if necessary, to pay the price of Soviet control over Manchuria and Korea. An agreement for Soviet participation in the war that left the invasion of these two areas entirely in Soviet military hands was reached at Yalta and Potsdam in 1945.

Subsequent events, however, allowed State policy planers to regain the upper hand. By August 10, after the atomic bombings of Hiroshima and Nagasaki, it was clear that the war was over and that a land invasion of Japan would be unlikely. Concern now centered on the continent, where Soviet armies had already begun to sweep into Manchuria and Korea. At this point there was nothing to stop a complete Soviet occupation of the peninsula; American troops could not be moved quickly enough to prevent it. Nevertheless, at a meeting of the State-War-Navy Coordinating Committee on the evening of August 10-11, a decision was made to divide the peninsula into two occupation zones and hope the Soviets would agree. Dean Rusk, a major at the time, and Colonel Charles H. Bonesteel, later a commander of American forces in South Korea, were given thirty minutes to select an appropriate dividing line. They chose the thirty-eighth parallel, a boundary that gave control of Seoul to the Americans and minimally disturbed the existing administrative divisions. Suggestions were made to rush American troops to Pusan if the Soviets refused to accept the partition, but to everyone's surprise the Soviets agreed, and the Americans did not arrive in Korea until September 8.

Even today a Cold War perspective from the 1950s continues to inform much of the popular perception of the Soviet and American occupations of Korea. A critical reassessment of this perspective is now underway, especially in the United States and South Korea, and the debate will undoubtedly continue as more and more evidence comes to light. In the midst of what can sometimes seem like a quagmire of conflicting interpretations, it is perhaps useful to keep several points in mind. First, both the American and Soviet forces were anxious to insure that whatever political form Korea ultimately took would be friendly, or at least not inimical, to their respective security interests. Second, Americans have often tended to regard communism as a monolithic force centered in the Kremlin rather than as a congeries of localized nationalist and socialist movements with their own historical and cultural roots. Third, Koreans in 1945 were not merely pawns in a great power game: just as Korean actions were affected by the presence of the two foreign armies, so too were the Americans and Soviets influenced and constrained by the Korean milieu.

On arrival in Korea both the Americans and the Soviets were confronted with the existence of the KPR and its people's committees. Their reactions to the fledgling government, however, were very different.

Any discussion of the Soviet occupation must include a caveat about sources. American government and military archives are extraordinarily open and provide an abundance of information about the aims and actions of the U.S. in Korea in 1945. Such access to Soviet files, however, is impossible, at least for now. Nevertheless, a combination of available American and Korean sources suggests the following broad story. The Soviets accepted the Japanese surrender and moved temporarily into the background, allowing the ongoing process of de-Japanization and social revolution to continue at the local levels through the channel of the people's committees. At the same time, they kept a guiding hand on affairs at the top in P'yongyang, although they never set up a formal occupation government. This relatively lighthanded approach to Korea by the Soviets undoubtedly reflected both empathy with the Korean revolution and a pragmatic calculation that the revolution was not contrary in any way to their own strong interest in having a friendly state on the other side of the Tumen River.

The result of Soviet policy was the complete overturn within a few months of the colonial bureaucratic and social structure. Collaborators were thrown out of office, and in March 1946 a sweeping land reform was implemented that destroyed the basis of landed wealth that had existed in Korea for centuries. In addition to the confiscation of Japanese landholdings, about 5,000 Korean landlords lost most of their land in the redistribution process, although those who were not deemed pro-Japanese traitors were given the option of either retaining enough of their land to work themselves (5 *chongbo* or 12.25 acres) or of moving to another district where they would be given a similarly small plot. Atrocities did occur, but in general the reform appears to have been carried out with surprisingly little violence, perhaps because most of the larger landowners were in the south and because many of the northern landlords had already fled by the time the reform was announced.

Other social changes followed in the wake of land reform. Major industries were nationalized, although small and medium businesses were encouraged to remain active. Labor reforms included an eight-hour workday, social security insurance, higher pay, and equal pay for equal work regardless of sex. The equality of women was also protected in a law prohibiting such practices as concubinage and prostitution, female infanticide, and other forms of female exploitation. Such reforms were executed under Soviet auspices, and there is no doubt that Soviet intervention and patronage gave the Korean communists a political edge not only over the right — which they really did not need — but also over the moderate left. Nevertheless, the reforms were led and carried out by Koreans and reflected to a considerable degree the original leftist spirit of the KPR.

The American Occupation

The American thrust in Korea contrasted sharply with the Soviet political push. Playing Iago to an already suspicious Othello, the Japanese authorities in Seoul had passed the word along to the American command in Okinawa in early September that Korean communist and independence agitators were plotting to subvert Korean peace and order and had warned of possible sabotage and mob violence. Thus even before leaving Japan, the Americans were already distrustful of Korean intentions and inclined to regard the anti-colonial revolution taking place there as a Soviet-inspired communist conspiracy antithetical to American interest. Once in Korea, the American occupation force, the XXIV Corps commanded by General John R. Hodge, refused to recognize the KPR (Hodge was, in fact, under orders from Washington not to recognize any Korean government) and eventually outlawed it. Instead, the U.S. set up a formal United States Army Military Government in Korea (USAMGIK) and proceeded to resurrect much of the discredited colonial administrative structure throughout the country. Briefly, at the beginning of the occupation, USAMGIK even attempted to make use of existing Japanese personnel, but this policy was abandoned when it stirred up an inevitable uproar from Koreans. The Americans then began to appoint more Koreans to USAMGIK posts, but many of the most important joint or subordinate positions went to Koreans who only a few weeks earlier had been serving the Government-General before being removed by the people's committees. Such Koreans were often promoted to fill positions formerly held by the departing Japanese and included thousands of Korean colonial policemen who had been in flight or in hiding when the Americans had landed. While the Americans were not unaware of the problem of collaboration, they chose largely to ignore it for the sake of administrative efficiency and because they distrusted the leftist character of the KPR.

Many of the Koreans who came to fill the higher echelons of the military government, including the two top Korean police officials, Cho Pyong-ok and Chang T'aek-sang, were affiliated with the Korean Democratic Party (KDP). The KDP had been founded on September 16 by a group of wealthy landlords and businessmen with close ties to Kim Song-su and Song Chin-u. Some of its more moderate elements, like Kim and Song, had originally gone along with the KPR in the interest of self-preservation when it had still appeared that the Soviets would be occupying most or all of the peninsula. As soon as it had become clear, however, that the Americans would be occupying the southern half, including Seoul, Kim and Song and their associates had set up their own political organization, which eventually became the KDP, and had issued a denunciation of the KPR for its communist activities. With little or no appreciation of the historical context in which they were operating, General Hodge and his officers tended to equate the Koreans in the KDP, who were property-owning and anticommunist — in addition to being well-dressed, educated, and often even English-speaking — with the middle class that formed the political basis for American democracy. Unfortunately, what seemed middle-class and democratic by American standards was more often than not upper class, reactionary, and collaborationist by Korean standards in 1945.

It was one thing to deny recognition to the KPR as a legitimate government; it was another to extirpate the KPR's nationwide structure of people's committees and their supporting organizations, including labor and peasant unions. The process was long and violent, exacerbated by ill-conceived USAMGIK economic policies, and reached a climax in September 1946 with a general strike by railroad workers in Pusan. The strike quickly spread to mass demonstrations in Taegu and eventually turned much of the southern occupation zone into a hotbed of insurrection. Korean rightist forces, including the National Police and a Korean constabulary established by USAMGIK the previous year, put down the rebellions with the support of American troops and material, and by the end of 1946 most of the people's committees in the south were gone. At least one, however, managed to survive into 1949. On Cheju Island that year the people's committee was finally rooted out only after a sustained assault that destroyed three fourths of the island's villages and left tens of thousands dead.

Economic and social reform under American military rule reflected USAMGIK's basic political orientation toward the right. Although the Americans moved quickly to reduce tenancy rates from one-half to one-third of the crop, land reform of any kind was continually postponed at the urging of USAMGIK's conservative Korean advisors in the KDP, many of whom were large landowners. It was thus not until March 1948, in the last months of military rule, that the Americans finally carried out a land reform, but it was limited to those rental lands formerly owned by the Japanese, less than twenty percent of the total. USAMGIK also instituted labor laws banning child labor (children under the age of fourteen) and limiting employment to sixty hours per week (with overtime rates for work in excess of forty hours). From the beginning, however, USAMGIK took a dim view of labor unions and strikes, often incorrectly assuming them to be the work of communists; such an attitude, in turn, encouraged rightist-controlled police and private goon squads to deprive Korean workers of many of the basic rights enjoyed by their counterparts in the United States.

The Emergence of Separate States

Neither the Soviet Union nor the United States had envisioned the formation of two separate Korean states in the summer of 1945. At the Cairo Conference in December 1943, the United States, Great Britain, and China had agreed that Korea should become free and independent "in due course," and Stalin had concurred in this sentiment when Roosevelt told him about the Cairo discussions soon afterwards in Teheran. Koreans who learned of the Cairo declaration took the phrase "in due course" to mean immediately after liberation, but the great powers, at Roosevelt's initiative, were actually thinking in terms of a four-power trusteeship that might last as long as forty or fifty years. The trusteeship question was discussed again at Yalta and Potsdam in 1945 and was finally resolved in December of that year at the Moscow Conference. The Moscow accords stipulated a four-power trusteeship of Korea for up to five years and provided for a Soviet-U.S Joint Commission to work toward the establishment of a unified provisional Korean government.

The Joint Commission met in 1946 and again in 1947, but it was already clear by the end of the first set of meetings that the commission was in trouble. The stumbling block was the question of whether or not Korean political parties and organizations who opposed trusteeship should be consulted in connection with the formation of a

Figures 9.5-9.6 Syngman Rhee proved to be a wily and recalcitrant ally as both General Douglas MacArthur (below) and Secretary of State John Foster Dulles soon discovered.

provisional government. The underlying cause of the trouble, however, was the right-left polarization of Korean politics as a result of Soviet and American occupation policies. At first the opposition to trusteeship had cut across Korean political lines, as one might have expected in a country that had just suffered four decades of foreign rule. The communists, however, suddenly reversed their original anti-trusteeship stance as a result of calculated self-interest and probable urging from the Soviets, and anti-trusteeship subsequently became a rallying point for the right, one of the few genuinely popular rightist issues during the entire liberation period. Although the communists made a point of saying that they supported trusteeship in the context of the entire Moscow agreement, which specifically enjoined the U.S. and the Soviet Union to work toward the establishment of a provisional Korean government, the rightists seized upon the opportunity to denounce the communists as "country-selling Soviet stooges," and USAMGIK added to the confusion and ferment by deliberately implying that trusteeship was solely a Soviet policy.

The fact was that while both the United States and the Soviet Union were committed at the highest levels to an internationalist solution to the Korean problem through trusteeship, their occupation forces on the ground were being allowed to pursue nationalist policies that envisioned a unified Korean government only on terms that excluded, respectively, either the right or the left, a view that was encouraged by Koreans themselves on both extremes of the political spectrum. Such a position naturally inclined each occupation force and its Korean allies to prefer two separate Korean states to a unified state in which power had to be shared. Indeed, even before the first meeting of the Joint Commission in March 1946, both the Soviet and the American occupation forces had already moved in that direction by sponsoring separate Korean advisory and administrative bodies in Seoul and P'yongyang.

The process had begun as early as the fall of 1945, when each occupation command had publicly welcomed back its own favorite Korean patriot-in-exile. In the north the Soviets gave their support to Kim Il Sung, famous to many Koreans — and notorious to the Japanese police — for his guerrilla activities with the Chinese communists

in Manchuria in the 1930s. Kim's history between 1941 and 1945 is obscure, but he appears to have retreated to Soviet military training camps in Khabarovsk and Barabash to wait out the war. There is evidence to suggest that Kim landed at Wonsan on September 25, and on October 14 he was accorded a public welcome by the Soviets as "General Kim Il Sung." Although only 33 years old, Kim's unblemished reputation as an anti-Japanese fighter, the backing of a loyal band of armed partisans, personal charisma, and — not least of all — unequivocal backing of the Soviet occupation force allowed him to gain control of the north's politics over older and more established communist leaders who had stayed in Korea throughout the colonial period. (The southern communists remained largely under the control of Pak Hon-yong, an important communist activist in the country since the 1920s.) In February 1946 a de facto provisional central government, the Interim People's Committee, was inaugurated in P'yongyang with Kim at its helm, and non-communist northern political leaders like Cho Man-sik, who had originally supported Kim, were gradually squeezed out of the political process. In the fall of 1946 a northern army also began to take form.

Almost simultaneously with such centralization in the north, USAMGIK was laying the foundations for a separate rightist provisional government in the south. On October 20, 1945, the American command presented Syngman Rhee to the Korean public with great fanfare. Rhee, who was 70 years old in 1945, had acquired a reputation as a patriot for his work in the Independence Club and the Shanghai Provisional Government and had spent most of his adult life in the United States, where he had received advanced degrees from both Harvard and Princeton. He was a fervent anticommunist and proceeded immediately upon his return to Korea to denounce not only the Soviets and the Korean communists but any Korean group, such as the KPR, that was willing to work with them.

Such rhetoric was too extreme at the time even for General Hodge, who was still under pressure from the State Department to cooperate with the Soviets, but it endeared Rhee to the political right, centered in the KDP, and gave him an advantage over Kim Ku, his main rival for rightist affection:

although both Kim and Rhee possessed the requisite nationalist credentials that the KDP so desperately needed to make a bid for political power, Kim was less tolerant of the KDP for its collaborationist past and willing, if necessary, to strike a deal with the left to insure a unified Korean government. Rhee thus soon became the rightist favorite, and General Hodge, in spite of a growing personal dislike for Rhee, eventually came to acknowledge his importance to those Koreans most favored by the military government. In February 1946, just as Kim Il Sung was forming the Interim People's Committee with Soviet approval and help in the north, Syngman Rhee was in the process of founding the Representative Democratic Council, which USAMGIK seemed to regard as a possible forerunner of a Korean provisional government.

After the breakdown of the first Joint Commission in the summer of 1946, General Hodge, still hoping for an acceptable political alternative to Rhee, and under pressure from the State Department, launched an eleventh hour attempt to put together a centrist political body that would be acceptable to the Soviet Union and thus save the Moscow accords. The idea was to exclude extremes of both the right (Syngman Rhee) and left (Kim Il Sung in the north and Pak Hon-yong in the south) in favor of a coalition of the moderate left (Yo Un-hyong) and moderate right (Kim Kyu-sik). In the polarized Korean political atmosphere that had developed during the first year of foreign occupation, however, there was little support for such a coalition, and it came to nought. Relations between the United States and the Soviet Union, moreover, were beginning to undergo a major change, as Roosevelt's internationalism was gradually replaced by Truman's policy of containment. By the summer of 1947, USAMGIK had moved even closer to a separate southern government with the inauguration of a South Korean Interim Legislative Assembly (December 1946), the Truman Doctrine had been officially proclaimed (March 1947), and the Soviet-U.S. Joint Commission had become moribund.

Given both the Korean and international political climate at this time, it was all but inevitable that two separate Korean regimes would now eventually emerge. The final step in this tragic process was taken in September 1947, when the United States announced its intention to move the Korean question to the newly created United Nations. There, despite Soviet protests, the United States succeeded in obtaining approval in the General Assembly for the establishment of a United Nations Temporary Commission on Korea (UNTCOK) to supervise general elections leading to the formation of an independent Korean government. P'yongyang disputed the UN's authority to undertake such a mission and refused UNTCOK entry to the northern zone. At American insistence, the United Nations then voted to proceed with elections only in the south. In spite of objections from both P'yongyang and from southern nationalists like Kim Ku and Kim Kyu-sik, who feared a permanent division of the country and still hoped for an accommodation with the north, the elections were held in May 1948. Two months later a constitution was adopted by the new National Assembly, and on August 15 the Republic of Korea (ROK) was established with Syngman Rhee as its first president. On the basis of the UN-supervised elections, the ROK claimed legitimacy as the only lawful government in Korea and was promptly recognized by the United States and its allies. P'yongyang responded to these events by holding its own elections on August 25, and the Democratic People's Republic of Korea (DPRK), also claiming to be the only legitimate government on the peninsula, was proclaimed in September with Kim Il Sung as premier. In late 1948 the Soviets withdrew their troops from Korea, and the Americans followed suit in June 1949. The stage had now been set for civil war.

The Korean War, 1950-1953

Each of the two Koreas has consistently blamed the other as the sole aggressor in the Korean War of 1950-53, but expert opinion today suggests a far broader and more complex view of the war's origins rooted in the 1945-50 period described above. While there is little room for doubt that the north actually launched the attack across the thirty-eighth parallel on June 25, 1950, it is also important to place that attack in the

SIGNIFICANCE OF THE KOREAN WAR

Charles Bohlen once remarked that the Korean War rather than World War II made the United States a world military and political power. After 1945, the United States had disarmed, as it had after 1918 and after wars previous. But the Korean War was not followed by American disarmament. For the first time in history, the nation maintained a large standing army. A big share of the national budget would go to support the military establishment. The military emerged as a powerful force in American public life. General MacArthur may have failed to use his military reputation as effective leverage to attain the presidency, but General Eisenhower did not. And, unexpectedly, he warned in his famous valedictory address of the danger to American society of "the military-industrial complex."

The Korean War created great fear in the United States, apprehension lest the war explode into global conflict, but also fear of a world-wide Communist conspiracy fusing all the Communist states and parties into a monolithic force infiltrating and subverting the top circles of power in the "free world" countries, Many Americans were moved by this fear into readiness to accept conspiratorial interpretations of complex historical events. Fear exacerbated tension with the Soviet Union; and with the American tendency to separate the world into "communist" and "free" nations, revolutionary nationalism most often fell into the first category.

The Korean War diverted American attention and resources from domestic reform, interrupting the programs of the New Deal and the Fair Deal, postponing their continuance until the 1960s. War served as a powerful stimulus to an already healthy economy, superbly managed by the Truman administration, which succeeded in keeping both inflation and unemployment low. Few Americans suffered very much from the war. It was not a national trauma; it was not to be compared with World War II. Some 33,000 Americans died, but that was less than one-fourth the number of highway and traffic deaths for the same period.

The power of the President in foreign affairs was greatly increased by the initiative which he had exercised in taking the nation into war. Likewise the prestige of the United Nations and the principle of collective security were greatly enhanced. But the post-Korea search for security carried the United States toward bilateral agreements and regional groupings. The United States furnished massive military aid to Western Europe: weapons, equipment, the building of air bases, ports, and pipelines; and the United States undertook to keep its own troops stationed on European soil. NATO was no longer simply a pious understanding but became a hard and specific alliance, to which the U.S.S.R. replied with a similar regional grouping, the Warsaw Pact nations.

In Asia, America again became entangled with the Chinese revolution by providing support, military and financial, to the Chinese Nationalist government. Between America and the Chinese People's Republic there now seemed no possibility of conciliation. The two nations were firm foes. To Americans for twenty years, China was "lost," until Richard Nixon "found" it in 1972.

Americans had new interests but uncertain goals on the Asian mainland: Korea, where American troops remained, and Vietnam, where, as the French let go, the Americans came in.

—John Curtis Perry, in *Sentimental Imperialists*

context of the increasingly violent political polarization of the peninsula in the previous five years, especially in the two years following the establishment of separate Korean regimes in 1948. Between the end of 1948 and June 1950, South Korea was the scene of a bloody, and ultimately unsuccessful, indigenous leftist guerrilla war that erupted on Cheju Island and in Yosu-Sunch'on in South Cholla and spread throughout much of the country. During this same period military conflicts along the thirty-eighth parallel between northern and southern forces, many of which appear to have been initiated by the south, became increasingly frequent and intense and continued right into the spring of 1950. Both Rhee and his generals, moreover, spoke openly during this period of retaking the north by force. In the end, the crucial factors affecting the DPRK decision to attack in June 1950 were probably the failure of the southern guerrilla movement, the return to North Korea in 1949 of tens of thousands of battle-hardened Korean veterans of the Chinese civil war, and North Korean fears of a major preemptive attack from the south.

Following the blitzkrieg attack on June 25, the well-trained and more experienced DPRK troops, equipped with World War II tanks and fighter planes obtained from the Soviets, soon overwhelmed the ROK army. They took Seoul in three days and continued to sweep south. By early August they had captured all but a small, fifty-by-fifty mile slice of the peninsula extending east from the Naktong River to the port city of Pusan (the so-called Pusan Perimeter). The United States moved quickly to intervene militarily under UN auspices, and the course of the war changed dramatically in September when General MacArthur, commanding the UN and ROK forces, carried out a successful amphibious assault on the port of Inch'on near Seoul, thus cutting the northern army in two. Seoul was retaken on September 28, and within weeks the UN and ROK troops had pushed north to the Yalu River.

In late November, however, the course of the war was abruptly reversed again, when hundreds of thousands of Chinese soldiers who had been gradually crossing into Korea since mid-October, launched a major counter-offensive, pushing the UN and ROK forces back down the peninsula. On January 4, 1951, Seoul fell for the second time. Although UN forces succeeded in recapturing the capital city in March, a stalemate between the two sides subsequently developed around the thirty-eighth parallel. After two years of negotiations a truce was finally signed at P'anmunjom on July 27, 1953. Since then the Chinese have withdrawn their forces (1958), but the United States has continued to maintain about forty thousand or more troops on the peninsula, even down to the present day.

Three years of fighting had solved nothing and brought ruin to both halves of the country. The toll in human lives was staggering. In the south alone, the combined total of military and civilian casualties — Koreans who had been killed, executed, wounded, kidnapped, or gone missing — was about 1.3 million people. Nearly half of the industrial capacity and a third of the housing in the south were destroyed along with much of the public infrastructure. Although precise figures are not available, the human and physical destruction of the war appears to have been even greater in the north. With a population base of about only one-half that of the south, the north suffered military and civilian casualties estimated at 1.5 million people. Intense aerial bombardment of the north throughout the three-year period ravaged the countryside and reduced cities like P'yongyang to ashes and rubble.

Those who experienced the war know that such numbers do not even begin to convey a sense of what it was like. Those who did not can only try to imagine: the terror of alien armies and incendiary bombing; the separation of families, often to be permanent; the frantic flight to refugee camps up and down the peninsula; the subsequent struggle for survival in a swirling mass of similarly displaced and desperate people; the fear of reprisal from one side or the other, or from a neighbor taking advantage of the chaos or politics to settle an old score. The war killed and maimed millions of Koreans, but it also left its scars on an entire generation of survivors, a legacy of fear and insecurity that continues even now to affect the two Koreas both in their internal development and in their relations with each other.[5]

◆   ◆   ◆

VIETNAM AND THE AMERICANS

—by Alexander Woodside

The leader of the new goverment in the southern half of Vietnam, which had evolved in the last five years of the war with France, was Ngo Dinh Diem. Diem was a devout Catholic mandarin whose father had been a court official at Hue. His own political career had included brief service as a cabinet minister to the young Bao Dai emperor in 1933. After 1950, the U.S. government had helped finance the French war in Indochina out of a deep fear of southward expansion by Communist China, whose huge armies had confronted the United States in the Korean War (1950-53) and whose submissive underlings the Vietnamese Communist leaders in Hanoi were thought to be.

Having refused along with South Vietnam to sign the Geneva Agreement that would have permitted nation-wide elections in 1956, the United States hoped to make Diem the Winston Churchill of Southeast Asia (as Vice President Lyndon Johnson publicly hailed him in 1961) and thus work through him to reform those bewildering Vietnamese political habits which most facilitated communism and frustrated the realization of Washington's world-view. In his 1953 inaugural address, President Eisenhower had found that a common anti-Communist faith conferred "a common dignity upon the French soldier who dies in Indochina [and] the American life given in Korea." Eisenhower regarded Vietnam as a land shaped "roughly like a bent dumbbell" whose surrender to "Communist enslavement" would "threaten" Thailand, Burma, and Malaya and would mean the irreparable loss of "valuable deposits of tin and prodigious supplies of rubber and rice." The Kennedy administration continued the Eisenhower policy of regarding the suppression of communism in South Vietnam as geopolitically indispensable. As his secretary of state and his secretary of defense told President Kennedy in November 1961, "the loss of south Vietnam would make pointless any further discussion about the importance of South-east Asia to the free world; we would have to face the near certainty that the remainder of Southeast Asia and Indonesia would move to a complete accommodation with Communism."

Accordingly, American advisers, ranging from political science professors to Central Intelligence Agency paladins (Edward Lansdale) to land reform experts (Wolf Ladejinsky), descended upon Saigon in order to share "the best possible American political thinking" (as Lansdale put it) with Ngo Dinh Diem and to help supply Diem with a decent republican constitution (1956), a bureaucracy, a police force, and schools. It must be kept in mind that the Communists did not challenge such outside efforts to introduce new, American-flavored institutions to the south until the end of 1959, when they finally launched their "synchronized uprisings" against Diem and the Americans in the Mekong delta and in the hill country of central Vietnam. At first, therefore, the results of such efforts looked much better than they were. But the president of South Vietnam, as Diem became by 1955 in a referendum that was rigged more heavily than it needed to be, was difficult to advise. He had intractably Vietnamese cultural values and social class characteristics. At his best, Diem the mandarin saw politics in essentially Confucian rather than American liberal terms as an arena in which any political opposition, no matter how fervently anti-Communist it was, called into question by its very existence the moral authority of the ruler, who supposedly governed through superior virtue. At his worst, and strongly prompted by his more sordid brother who became his real political manager, Diem debased his residual Confucian ideals by resorting to the procedures of a police state, arbitrarily arresting and mistreating tens of thousands of political prisoners, many of whom were not even Communists.

For all these reasons, there was never much chance that Diem would carry out the Americans' wish that South Vietnam be made a nursing ground of vital non-Communist "grass roots political organizations." Diem eliminated provincial and municipal council elections. He tried to relocate grumbling peasants into large fortified villages. And he converted his presidency into a sort of artless informal monarchy, buttressed by a network of brothers and other relatives (a dynastic house being one part of his political heritage) if not by a reliable non-family civil service (another part of that heritage). The old rural social structure in the south, with its rich landlords, remained unscathed by Diem's token 1956 land reform.

Figure 9.7 Reminiscent of World War II propaganda posters that depicted Japan as an octopus reaching out to hold Asian territory, this political cartoon of the 1960's "depersonified" Ho Chi Minh with the same menacing image.

Figure 9.8 Lyndon Johnson's sessions with his advisors to design sophisticated military strategies in Vietnam involved a number of misperceptions, including the notion that bombing strikes against the North would break its people's will to fight.

Diem's politically inept police raids upon Buddhist temples, in the summer of 1963, climaxed his hostility as a Catholic and Confucian ruler to the rise of intermediate organizations, like the General Association of Vietnamese Buddhists (founded in 1951), which he could not control. The raids ended the Americans' romance with him. The U.S. ambassador in Saigon intrigued with dissident Vietnamese military officers who were plotting against Diem and even proposed the island of Saipan as a convenient place for the "removal of key personalities."

The Vietnamese Communists, north and south, had not formally challenged the Diem political machine until 1959, partly because they initially underestimated it. They were restrained as well by Soviet and Chinese pressure upon Hanoi to defer any major uprising in the south and by Hanoi's preoccupation with the restoration and transformation of the north's economy. But they were in a strong position to preach social revolution in the south. Most of the Vietnamese landlord class lived there. During the war against France, the Viet Minh had won adherents by redistributing 630,000 hectares of land to poorer peasants; southern peasants had been major beneficiaries. After 1954, land-owners who supported the Saigon government had reclaimed redistributed lands, angering peasants to a degree dangerous to Diem's survival.

In December 1960 the Communists formally resurrected the southern branch of the Viet Minh, in the form of a new patriotic coalition which called itself the National Liberation Front (NLF). Known to its enemies by the derisively over-simple term "Viet Cong" (an abbreviation of the Vietnamese term for "Vietnamese Communists"), the NLF certainly included implacable veteran Communists but also at least a few liberal intellectuals whom a less autocratic Diem might have been able to win over. Fighting a skillful guerrilla war, the Viet Cong soon created a state within a state in the south. By November 1962 they controlled or influenced, by U.S. estimates at the time, some two-thirds of all the south's villages. The Diem government had centralized decision- making power above the villages and relied for its revenues upon colonial use and consumer taxes (market taxes, sales taxes, fees for the issuance of documents) it had inherited from the French, and

"The reasons why we went into Vietnam . . . are now largely academic. At each decision point we have gambled; at each point, to avoid the damage to our effectiveness of defaulting on our commitment, we have upped the ante. We have not defaulted, and the ante (and commitment) is now very high."

—Memo by Under Secretary of Defense
John McNaughton, January 18, 1966

which most heavily victimized the poor. The NLF in its early years gave considerable decision-making authority to people who actually lived in the villages and pursued tax and property distribution policies which favored the poor. In the towns its satellite organizations, such as the "Committee for the Preservation of the National Culture," appealed to some teachers and students who feared that the progressive "Americanization" of southern institutions, as seen in the penetration of teaching colleges and the National School of Administration by American money and advisers, might eventually turn them into "yellow-skinned Americans." By 1969, although it was past its prime, the NLF formed a "Provisional Revolutionary Government." It had its own schools, newspapers, and broadcasting service.

To respond to this threat, the Americans began their overt military intervention in the south with the development in 1961-62 of a "Military Assistance Command Vietnam" (MACV). The U.S. secretary of defense stated in November 1961 that even if Hanoi and China attacked "overtly," the "maximum U.S. forces required on the ground in Southeast Asia" would not exceed "about 205,000 men." MACV was the nucleus of what was to become, by 1967, an American armed force in South Vietnam of 525,000 men. American-supported Saigon military officers murdered Diem in a successful coup against him in November 1963. After the general who immediately replaced Diem made it clear that he did not want U.S. advisers installed in Vietnamese villages because this would look too much like colonialism — he was removed in another coup (January 1964) that U.S.

officials knew about in advance and did not discourage. By 1965, when Major-General Nguyen Van Thieu became the leader of the Saigon government, the Saigon military elite, less well educated, less steeped in classical traditions, and thus more willing to experiment with Western political and economic techniques than Diem, had seized control of the non-Communist power structure. Armed with a new constitution in 1967, which replaced the Diem constitution and called for American-style presidential elections every four years, General Thieu served as the president of the southern republic from 1967 until its collapse in 1975.

With the murder of Diem, the war expanded. By 1965 its nature had changed and it became a direct confrontation between the conventional military power of the United States and the disciplined and tenacious army of North Vietnam. Advised by the U. S. ambassador in Saigon that U.S. bombing of north Vietnam might "bolster morale and give the population in the south a feeling of unity," President Lyndon Johnson contrived a congressional resolution,[6] which authorized him to use "all necessary measures" in Indochina, and began to bomb Ho Chi Minh's republic systematically from February 1965. General William Westmoreland, the U.S. commander in South Vietnam, was allowed to deploy a large American conscript army which embarked on openended "search and destroy" assaults throughout the southern countryside. Such assaults, when combined with bombs and napalm, drove much of the rural population into the cities as refugees and succeeded by sheer firepower in damaging the

political connection between the Viet Cong and the peasantry. In response, the regular northern Communist army came south, eventually overwhelming the largely southern membership of the NLF. And in February 1968, the Vietnamese Communists, following the precedent of the Taysons' surprise attack upon an invading army from China during the lunar New Year of 1789, launched their "Tet" (New Year's) offensive. They briefly penetrated even the grounds of the U.S. embassy in Saigon and seized the old imperial capital of Hue, from which they were not dislodged for weeks. The Tet offensive, gruesomely televised in millions of American living rooms, was a turningpoint in the war. On the one hand, its dramatic if temporary success exposed the falseness of President Johnson's claims that he was firmly managing, and even winning, what was supposed to be a "limited" American war in Asia. On the other hand, the offensive's failure to trigger large proCommunist uprisings in southern cities, let alone any pro-Communist inclinations in the Saigon army itself, made it clear to leaders in Hanoi that popular support for the revolution they had envisaged in the south was stagnating. Representatives of the Hanoi and Washington governments therefore agreed to meet for peace talks in Paris later in 1968.

The Paris peace talks did not reach a conclusion until January 1973, after four more years of slaughter. President Richard Nixon and his chief foreign policy adviser, Henry Kissinger, even reversed more than two decades of unrelenting U.S. hostility to Mao Tse-tung's [Mao Zedong's] China, in 1971-72, partly to encourage this Communist superpower to press its ally in Hanoi to accept U.S. peace terms. Although this move successfully irritated the historically difficult relations between China and Vietnam, which Washington had belatedly discovered, it did not prevent the 1973 peace treaty from being a triumph for the Vietnamese Communists.

The original American objective in the peace negotiations had been the mutual withdrawal from South Vietnam of "external forces," both North Vietnamese and American. Washington's central ideological proposition had been that American and North Vietnamese soldiers were equally "external" when they fought in the south, that the Vietnamese south was a legitimately separate nation-state. Acceptance of this proposition would have meant the de facto annulment of the Vietnamese Communists' claim to be leading a national revolution. Having more at stake than Washington, the Vietnamese Communists resisted and prevailed.

The 1973 treaty allowed Hanoi to keep its army in the south indefinitely, after American ground forces had been removed. In Saigon, President Thieu had little difficulty in seeing what Nixon and Kissinger refused to acknowledge: that the parallel legitimation of the Viet Cong's "provisional revolutionary government" (which was a partial signatory to the treaty with Thieu); the permanent presence of northern troops in the south; and the withdrawal of American forces all portended his downfall.[7] The United States poured more weaponry into Saigon to enable the humiliated Thieu government and its army, by now one of the world's biggest, to hold their own. This proved to be impossible. In the spring of 1975 a Vietnamese Communist offensive, propelled by the 264,000 fresh combatants Hanoi had sent south since 1973, finally destroyed the non-Communist republic of Vietnam and reunited north and south on the Hanoi government's terms.

Such was the end of a bleak and bloody episode in Vietnamese history. Millions of Vietnamese were killed and wounded; about 58,000 Americans also died. Superficially, it seemed to be a Vietnamese encounter with the operations of an American neocolonialism that ultimately lost both its stamina and the consistency of its worldview. The United States did not perfectly control any Saigon government between 1954 and 1975. But it is also true that no Saigon government ever survived without enormous American economic and military aid. And no Saigon government whose behavior the U.S. government seriously distrusted remained in office for very long.

But there was another side to this story, which explains why the passions aroused by the war did not cool quickly. The south's 1967 constitution had conveyed the hope that a meaningful multiparty democracy might be born in Vietnam, despite the Saigon military elite's often ill-disguised admiration for the manipulative Leninist political methods of its northern adversaries. Although President Thieu rigged elections and ignored the principle of the separation of powers

expressed in this constitution, a complex assortment of Catholic priests, Buddhist monks, religious sect theoreticians, lawyers, teachers, economists, and labor union organizers, based usually in the cities and towns, worked courageously and against very great odds to achieve a real democracy in the south. They were under no illusions about the obstacles. The French colonial police had helped prevent the emergence of large, public, non-conspiratorial political parties in Vietnam. There were twenty-four non-Communist parties in Saigon at the end of 1970. The unsympathetic Thieu government's command of the foreign aid-based economy, and of conscription, denied the parties necessary financial and human assets. Their more enlightened members still persevered in a struggle for political freedom that could somehow tap the instincts of a very ancient Vietnamese humanism.

Saigon between 1954 and 1975 was the home of a subtle and variegated literary culture whose intellectuals stood for a cosmopolitan emancipation of Vietnamese energies. As one example, young women novelists suddenly flourished during this period. They wrote fiction about prostitutes, decaying landlord families, and "dust of life" street people, as if such fiction were a desperate form of "ghost raising" (in the words of one such writer, Tuy Hong). In such a literature-loving nation, the fact that three women won the top literary prizes in South Vietnam in 1970 demonstrated the growth of a significant new female cultural freedom. After 1975, the Communist leaders of the reunified Vietnam were too autocratic and too insecure to accommodate such women, or tireless and versatile Saigon literati like Vo Phien, with their expert knowledge of Camus and Kafka and Stephan Zweig — and of dissident Soviet literature. The repression of this critical middle-class intelligentsia, or their forced flight to the West to become Canadian grain elevator workers or American government clerks or overseas journalists, was a Vietnamese national disaster of incalculable proportions. But although such people lost, the history of modern Vietnam belongs to them as well as to the Hanoi politburo and the Saigon militarists.[8]

◆   ◆   ◆

STRATEGIES OF CONTAINMENT IN ASIA

As noted at the beginning of this chapter, the American-Asian relationship has evolved through several stages that were shaped by a combination of sentimental and imperial motivations. If the sentiments were at times misguided, they also expressed an ideal of what America had to offer Asia and the world. An outpouring of economic assistance and an opening of the U.S. domestic market after World War II confirmed and supported the benevolent aspects of this vision of democracy and capitalism.

In addition, however, U.S. foreign policy treated Asia as an arena for competition with the Soviet Union. The Americans who helped design what would become known as the policy of containment were calculating in their approach to the cold war. As former Secretary of State Henry Kissinger would later write, "Our objective was to purge our foreign policy of all sentimentality."[9]

For some Americans, the relationship with the Philippines could never be reduced to Kissinger's unsentimental terms, in light of the profound U.S. involvement in supporting that country's move toward independence (described in chapters 4 and 5). The successful policies of Ramon Magsaysay marked an important period, but his accomplishments were tragically cut short by his death in a plane crash in 1957. The United States saw in Magsaysay a rare leader who, had he survived, might have succeeded in loosening the brake on social and political reform held by the Filipino elite. The extent of the support he received from the United States, including advice and campaign management from the CIA's Edward Lansdale, does not detract from his own achievement and potential.

The American support for Magsaysay underscores the strategic importance attached by the United States to the Philippines. In Asia, only the Philippines and Japan were listed in a 1948 memo by George Kennan as areas that could not be permitted to fall into "hostile hands." As one of the most influential figures in U.S. postwar diplomacy, Kennan is widely credited with being a key architect of America's policy of "containment." In Kennan's original formulation, this policy called for the coordinated use of political, economic, and military influence to prevent the expansion of Soviet control in vital regions of the world. Kennan placed emphasis on the first two of these three elements whereas subsequent administrations gave increasing weight to military power — a change that was to have dramatic implications for the U.S. economy.[10]

Kennan's idea was to use a combination of deterrents and inducements to re-shape the Soviet Union's approach to international relations. In 1948 he persuaded the Truman Administration that Soviet behavior toward the West was fundamentally determined by forces internal to Soviet society that were not in U.S. interests and could be changed only if America patiently applied "counter-pressures." Arguments alone would not

---

THE "BLANK CHECK"

[Dean] Acheson used an open-ended analogy... in a talk to students at the National War College:

"Collective security is like a bank account. It is kept alive by the resources which are put into it. In Korea the Russians presented a check which was drawn on the bank account of collective security. The Russians thought the check would bounce. . . . But to their great surprise, the teller paid it. The important thing was that the check was paid. The importance will be nothing if the next check is not paid and if the bank account is not kept strong and sufficient to cover all checks which are drawn upon it."

If it occurred to any of the Secretary of State's audience to wonder why the United States should be issuing blank checks to its adversaries in the first place, or how it proposed to keep its account balanced indefinitely in the face of such demands on it, they were too polite to ask.

—John Lewis Gaddis, *Strategies of Containment*

persuade the Soviets to change, he said. Instead, they must be confronted with situations to prove that the use of conflict and force to gain advantage with the outside world was futile and counter productive. Kennan did not want to divide the world into Soviet and American spheres of influence, but to create independent, multiple centers of power in Europe and Asia.

To American officials who had faced Soviet belligerence during the early post-war period, Kennan's formulation of containment seemed idealistic. It suggested that the primary inducement for change in the Soviet Union would be "the integrity and dignity" of the American example. Kennan's vision seems no longer naive but prescient in light of the epochal developments of 1989-91 in the U.S.S.R. and Eastern Europe, but the alternative, predominantly military emphasis given to "containment" strategy from the 1950s onward reflected the reality at the time. In fact, burgeoning Soviet economic growth and military strength, combined with its influence over communist parties in Japan and Europe, initially shook the confidence of U.S. policy makers in the ability of the free world to prevail.

The United States could expect little from its World War II allies who had become exhausted and dispirited. The British, French and Dutch began to lose their holds over their Asian colonies while they struggled to rebuild their nearly bankrupt, war-torn economies. British weakness was especially telling in early 1947 when it announced that it was no longer able to provide military and financial support to Greece and Turkey even when those countries came under severe pressure from Soviet-backed communist insurgencies.

The framework within which American policy responded to these circumstances and the frequent Soviet diatribes in the United Nations was enunciated by President Truman shortly after the British announcement. On March 12, 1947 he proclaimed the "Truman Doctrine" which, although it grew out of a decision to replace the British role in aiding Greece and Turkey, amounted to a commitment by the United States to resist Soviet expansionism wherever it appeared. The key phrase, "it must be the policy of the United States to support free peoples who are resisting attempted subjugation by armed minorities or outside pressures," seemed to imply

that substantial American support could be counted on anywhere. East and Southeast Asia presented an awesome potential for U.S. involvement under these terms, a fact that was all the more troubling to policy-makers like Kennan.

The Philippines became a cornerstone of the U.S. strategy to confront, contain and roll back the surge of communist movements in Southeast Asia. The U.S. shored up the Philippine government with advisors and assistance and upgraded its two bases, Clark Air Force Base and the Subic Naval Base. The Philippine government was in a severely weakened state at the time the agreements on the bases were negotiated in 1946-47 and therefore accepted onerous conditions for their enlargement that have rankled ever since. The bases became the most consistent, visible, and emotional of the issues that troubled U.S.-Philippine relations in the post-war period. By 1990, few Filipino legislators supported the continued presence of the bases but polls often showed a narrow majority of the population still wanted them. Negotiations with the U.S. in 1990 for the renewal of the bases agreements proceeded amid a changed regional security environment in which the Soviet threat had diminished significantly — and with it American willingness to pay a high price for a continuation of the agreement. In 1991, the eruption of the Mount Pinatubo volcano damaged the Clark air base facilities so badly that they were deemed unfit for use. The end of the bases appeared in sight in September when the Philippines Senate voted to reject a renewal of the bases agreement and President Aquino reluctantly concurred.

The rest of Southeast Asia has been far more disinclined than the Philippine politicians to see a significant reduction of the American military presence. Long taken for granted by ASEAN as the primary security umbrella for the region, the United States in return viewed ASEAN as a key component of its containment strategy. Especially during the 1970s and 1980s, when the Soviet military threat seemed most formidable and the Maoist New People's Army in the Philippines began to grow alarmingly, the United States was unable to abandon its support for an increasingly dictatorial and corrupt Marcos regime for fear of destabilizing the entire country. American policy was trapped between its role as a guarantor of

REALITIES OF THE COMMUNIST THREAT IN ASIA

Throughout the 1950s and the early 1960s, most Pacific Asian societies were characterized by the following conditions. First, a high degree of domestic violence prevailed. Crime levels in major cities were extremely high. Banditry was common in rural areas. Warlords dominated many regions of Southeast Asia, and their feuds were frequently violent. Poverty, a sense of injustice, fears of the market economy, outrage over governments' failure to ensure order, endemic violence, and the presence of a communist ideology encouraged the emergence of strong communist guerrilla movements and procommunist forces in virtually every country of Pacific Asia. At one point, the communist Huks had Manila surrounded. The Malayan Emergency was resolved only after years of bloody, bitter fighting. Until early 1966, the Indonesian communist party was the most institutionalized and fastest growing political force in that country, and it was the third largest communist party in the world. Through the early 1960s, poverty and disorder were the norm in South Korea and procommunist sentiments were widespread. Thailand and Burma had important communist parties, and Singapore's communist party seemed very strong as late as 1959. The communist parties were the best organized political forces in Indochina.

Second, revolutionary enthusiasm was widespread in the region. This is analytically distinguishable from the gradual growth of organized communist parties, which in principle could have occurred through solid organization and technocratic calculation without revolutionary fervor. They could, in short, have been more like the Communist Party of the Soviet Union in the 1980s and less like the communist enthusiasm of China during the Cultural Revolution. But, on the contrary, this was an era of revolutionary enthusiasm.

Third, both communist giants — China and the Soviet Union — were actively promoting revolution and revolutionary enthusiasm. Both were seen as revolutionary powers seeking to promote revolutions everywhere. Their principles were admired by broad segments of Asian populations and were considered, even by liberal, pro-Western intellectuals, to be serious alternatives to democratic, liberal Western principles. Fourth, with countries of the region at a common, low level of economic development, communist discipline proved decisive in domestic and international competition. Within countries, the communist parties were disciplined and directed toward relatively coherent goals, while their opponents were loose coalitions practicing fractious indiscipline and pursuing incoherent priorities. Between countries, the noncommunist powers displayed the internecine strife of market economies and of more or less undisciplined coalitions, while the communist countries displayed organization, purposefulness, and the ability to direct both economy and polity toward clear political and military goals. In countries as disparate as Indonesia and South Korea, it was widely assumed by leftists, neutralists, and pro-Western analysts alike that the communist forces possessed a kind of natural and inexorable superiority that could be overcome only by overwhelming external pressure from the United States. The degree to which this perception predominated was so great that it is difficult to communicate to a younger generation that never experienced it. Finally, throughout the region, territorial disputes were the rule rather than the exception. The Philippines claimed Sabah in Malaysia. Indonesia had territorial disputes with Malaysia and the Philippines. For a while Indonesia seemed to claim the right to dominate most of the region. Malaysia and Thailand had serious border disputes, as did Thailand, Burma, Laos, Cambodia, and China, wherever they had common borders. These situations prevailed for most of the first post-World War II generation in Pacific Asia.

—Willam Overholt, "The Moderation of Politics,"
in James W. Morley, ed., *The Pacific Basin*, 1989

regional security and an advocate of basic human freedoms and democracy. Only in 1986, after massive popular discontent with Marcos had spilled into the streets (chapter 8), did the United States finally encourage and facilitate his departure. However, by pressing him to go to Honolulu, the United States left most Filipinos convinced that it is American officials in Washington who exercise ultimate control over their politics and society. This makes it all the more difficult for Filipino leaders to agree on constructive solutions, rather than scapegoats, for their nation's problems.

The Militarization of Containment

McCarthyism drew its initial momentum from memories of 1930s "appeasement" of Hitler, frustration and fear spawned by the "loss" of China, and from 1950 to 1953, the fighting and stalemate in Korea. The most enduring impact of the Korean War on the United States was to shift its strategy of containment firmly in the direction of reliance on military strength, a policy that was to be supported by both Democratic and Republican administrations. In the late 1940s, the Truman Administration had made economic assistance the central pillar of its anti-communist policy, well ahead of defense expenditures, the most notable example being the Marshall Plan to rebuild Western Europe. The early Truman-era officials assumed that the United States would use its technological and economic resources (the "arsenal of democracy") rather than its military manpower to maintain the balance of power overseas. Few Americans objected to the rapid decline of the country's military power immediately after World War II. By 1950 defense expenditures had dropped so low that when the Korean War broke out President Truman had to ask Congress for an immediate increase of 257 percent.

The Korean War did not dissuade Truman and his cabinet from their certainty that Europe would be the front line in competing with the Soviet Union. Policy planners realized that U.S. forces there had been allowed to grow perilously small but they were loath to ask Congress for the funding to support reinforcements. The outbreak of the Korean conflict thus provided them with the opportunity to bolster U.S. defenses in Europe. In the end, permanent U.S. forces stationed in Europe were enlarged far more than those in Asia.

The first and most comprehensive statement of the strategy of containment emerged under Kennan's successor in the office of Director of the State Department Policy Planning Staff, Paul H. Nitze. With his guidance a small committee drew up a document that came to be known by its bureaucratic code name, "NSC-68." In its most significant departure from Kennan's thinking, NSC-68 concluded that no distinction could be made between peripheral and vital interests of the United States when confronting the Soviet challenge around the world. Even in geographical areas that might to any objective observer seem largely removed from vital U.S. interests, a further advance by the Soviet Union would create the *perception* of American weakness and impotence. In other words, it was assumed that the balance of power depended as much on its image as its reality.

This shift in strategic thinking had enormous implications for U.S. policy in Asia. In effect, a strategy had emerged that required the defense of an entire "perimeter" in the Pacific and elsewhere rather than a limited number of well-established, indigenously supported "strongpoints" such as the Philippines and Japan. Little attention was given to alternatives; for example, exploiting differences within the international communist movement, although senior policy makers did acknowledge that such splits might occur.

NSC-68 was drafted just before the Korean War broke out, but it had not yet been approved by President Truman. To some historians, it has seemed more than a coincidence that the war suddenly made it possible to persuade Congress to approve the costly defense policy required by NSC-68 and they have argued that American officials engineered the war. However, testimony

---

"Without superior aggregate military strength, in being and readily mobilizable, a policy of 'containment'. . . is no more than a policy of bluff."

—NSC-68

---

from Soviet officials in the late 1980s supported the much more widely-accepted view that Kim Il Sung launched the attack against the South at Stalin's urging.

Douglas MacArthur was among the more vocal critics of NSC-68, having recognized its authors' biases toward Europe. "This group of Europhiles," he argued in 1950, "just will not recognize that it is Asia which has been selected for the test of Communist power and that if all Asia falls Europe would not have a chance — either with or without American assistance." Ironically, it was precisely the policy enunciated in NSC-68 that guaranteed a profound degree of American involvement in Asia. One of the most astute observers of America's containment policy, John Lewis Gaddis, has noted that the adoption of NSC-68 was equivalent to giving a "blank check" to the Soviet Union and China — one with which they could create costly challenges to the U.S. anywhere in the world. In Asia, that "blank check" came due in Vietnam.

Vietnam and "The Domino Theory"

The sudden massive entry of the Chinese army into the Korean conflict did much to convince leaders in Washington that Mao Zedong was equally capable of expanding southward into Vietnam, if not by direct invasion then by means of what was presumed to be his control over the communists in Hanoi. Seemingly unaware of the complex and often contentious history between China and Vietnam, and determined to prevent further communist expansion, both the Truman and Eisenhower administrations supported France's efforts to hold onto its colony until its final, ignominious defeat in 1954 at the battle of Dien Bien Phu.

The Geneva Agreement in 1954 called for a temporary division of Vietnam along the seventeenth parallel. While China and the Soviet Union continued to support Ho Chi Minh in the north, the United States became the chief patron of the regime in the south which, with U.S. encouragement, refused to sign the Geneva accord. The tenacity with which a succession of administrations clung to a policy of escalating military involvement in Vietnam can best be understood in terms of the legacy of the 1950s, that is, the obsession with the the so-called loss of China, the trauma of the Korean War, and the hard-line East Asia policies of successive adminstrations.

By the early 1960s, East Asian policy in the U.S. was being formulated according to rigid and doctrinaire ideas. The Department of State had been purged of its best senior China expertise, a result of McCarthyism. The more perceptive of those who remained were painfully aware that the fate of their dismissed colleagues could be traced to frank and honest reporting (in particular, the cable sent behind the back of Ambassador Hurley). Also, the new Democratic administration remembered the intensity with which a communist witch hunt had been conducted only a few years earlier and knew that there were still political undercurrents that might be exploited by conservative Republicans.

Paired with these political constraints, United States policymakers faced a growing dilemma during the late 1950s and 1960s while they assessed the growing split in the communist movement. Moscow had hinted at a growing interest in 'detente' in the 50s as both the Soviet Union and the United States became apprehensive over the strident rhetoric and growing nuclear capability of China. When Beijing challenged American policy toward Taiwan and then later threatened to become involved in the Vietnam War, China was perceived in Washington as a more dangerous and volatile adversary than Moscow. During the Kennedy administration, cautious explorations of cooperation were even made with the U.S.S.R. against China, although such initiatives essentially came to nothing.[11]

Equally problematic, however, was the public perception of a monolithic Communist bloc. The simplicity of this viewpoint spilled over into the policy of containment which assumed that if one U.S. ally in Asia fell to communism, all the rest would go down like a row of dominos. This "domino theory," which came to be used to rationalize a massive U.S. military commitment in Asia, was based on a crude assumption that societies and politics in the vast, diverse Asia-Pacific region were essentially all alike.

A rigid, anti-communist ideology eventually obscured all other policy considerations in the U.S. relationship with Vietnam. Escalating military

Figure 9.9   In 1957, Mao Zedong stood alongside Soviet premier Nikita Khruschev in Red Square at the fortieth anniversary of the Bolshevik Revolution. Many in the West thought their alliance would be unbreakable.

commitments were broadly accepted at first not just by leaders in Washington but by the American public — until American casualties reached alarming levels. Initially, attention focused on the action and strategy of the conflict, the underlying policy having been uncritically accepted in terms of its vague, moralist, anti-communist goals.

The growing public disapproval of the war that developed by the early 1970s is assumed by most historians of the conflict to have been the key factor leading to the American withdrawal and, ultimately, the humiliating defeat of its policy in 1975. While it is true that public pressure did affect the course of the Vietnam strategy, the success of the North Vietnamese depended heavily on its ability to draw on its allies for assistance: China, and to a lesser extent the Soviet Union, provided massive assistance. In this respect, the anti-communist rhetoric was on target even if it was unaware of the tensions that existed between Hanoi and its patrons. The Soviets, for example, advised Hanoi to compromise with the South, but once the U.S. began air raids against the North in 1965 the North Vietnamese leaders demanded and received advanced weaponry from both Moscow and Beijing. Subsequently, the Soviets and Chinese competed with one another in their limited influence over the leadership in Hanoi, offering a

wide range of armored vehicles and trucks as well as financial assistance. By 1973, when U.S. diplomacy had successfully lowered tensions with both China and the Soviet Union, such assistance had dropped significantly but not before a massive build-up of materiel had occurred.

REVERSAL OF FORTUNE: U.S.-CHINA RAPPROCHEMENT

The mindset that supported the war in Vietnam can be best be understood in light of the 1950s anti-Communist legacy, but the question remains why policymakers believed far-away Vietnam represented vital U.S. interests. Political scientist John Lewis Gaddis puts the question:

> *What, precisely, was the United States interest in Vietnam? Why was the balance of power at stake there? Walt Rostow had warned that "major losses of territory or of resources would make it harder for the U.S. to create the kind of world environment it desires, . . . generate defeatism among governments and peoples in the non-Communist world, or give rise to frustrations at home."*

But when pressed to explain why the loss of such a small and distant country would produce these drastic consequences, Washington officials generally cited the SEATO treaty obligation,[12] *which, if not honored, would raise doubts about American commitments elsewhere in the world. "The integrity of the U.S. commitment is the principal pillar of peace throughout the world," Rusk wrote in 1965. "If that commitment becomes unreliable, the communist world would draw conclusions that would lead to our ruin and almost certainly to a catastrophic war."*

This was curious reasoning. It required justifying the American commitment to South Vietnam as essential to the maintenance of global stability, but then portraying that stability as endangered by the very vulnerability of Washington's commitment. It involved both deterring aggression and being held hostage to it. The confusion, it would appear, stemmed from the failure of both the Kennedy and Johnson administrations to articulate independently derived conceptions of interest in Southeast Asia; instead, they tended to view the American stake there as determined exclusively by threats and obligations. The security of the United States, indeed of the entire noncommunist world, was thought to be imperiled wherever communist challenges came up against American guarantees. Vietnam might be insignificant in itself, but as a point of intersection between threat and commitment, it was everything.[13]

The Opening to China

Vietnam was arguably the greatest U.S. foreign policy debacle of the twentieth century. Yet the scope of the disaster has tended to obscure a key shift in the strategy of containment that occurred just when the scale of the conflict had reached its height. This shift brought about an eventual reversal of the deteriorating U.S. position in Asia and ultimately inaugurated a new era of lowered tensions in the Pacific Basin. Its architects were Richard Nixon, newly elected President in 1968, and his chief foreign policy adviser, Henry Kissinger.

The first task for the new administration when it took office in 1969 was to bring about an end to the involvement in Vietnam. In this it agreed with previous administrations that capitulation was unthinkable, but by means of the "Vietnamization" of the war, a process begun at the end of the Johnson administration, Thieu's army could be built up to compensate for the reduction of U.S. forces. Within a few months of taking office, Nixon traveled to the western Pacific where, on the U.S. territory of Guam, he announced what came to be known as the Nixon Doctrine. In describing the nature of American commitments to its security treaties, the Doctrine stated that the U.S. would "look to the nation directly threatened [by aggression] to assume the primary responsibility of providing the manpower for its defense." Nixon thus withdrew the implicit "blank check" that had characterized U.S. containment policy or, the way Kissinger later put it, "Our interests must shape our commitments, rather than the other way around."

This decision made, the withdrawal of American troops from Vietnam proceeded at approximately the pace with which they had been sent there. At the same time, Nixon and Kissinger became even more aggressive toward the North Vietnamese, bombing Hanoi with B-52 raids and mining the harbor of Haiphong. Amid assurances that the United States was respecting Cambodia's sovereignty, bombing raids were secretly being conducted against North Vietnamese sanctuaries inside Cambodia from March 1969.

The most striking evidence of the new strategy emerged not in Vietnam, however, but in America's relations with China. The first hints of change came when Beijing remained uncharacteristically quiescent in its public statements about the war even while Nixon covered his strategic withdrawal by bombing Hanoi and Cambodia. The specter of a Chinese intervention — and a possible repeat of the Korean War debacle — had restrained Lyndon Johnson in his military strategies, but Nixon felt a greater freedom of action, having convinced the leaders in Beijing of his intention to pull out of Vietnam.

Unknown to the world and even to their respective bureaucracies, the senior-most leaders of the United States and China had begun to communicate about a normalization of their relations. Only a few years earlier such a possibility had been deemed unthinkable by the fervent anticommunist Secretary of State Dean Rusk. But times had changed and now the antagonism between Moscow and China, which had begun with the abrupt withdrawal of Soviet aid and advisors from China in 1958, was apparent to the world. A change of policy in Washington that could exploit the rift was unlikely, however, until a President emerged who combined strong anticommunist credentials with nonideological flexibility. Nixon was such a person. As he explained to Mao in 1972, "Those on the right can do what those on the left only talk about."

The Moscow-Beijing split had worsened during the 1960s when China accused the Soviets of ideological backsliding and collusion with the "capitalist imperialists." Ominously, their arguments began to erupt in military conflicts along their disputed 4,500 mile-long border. In 1969 the Soviet Union even made a discreet inquiry as to how the United States might react if the U.S.S.R. staged a pre-emptive attack against Chinese nuclear facilities in Xinjiang. In response, Nixon made it clear that the United States would not permit China to be defeated or seriously weakened in a Sino-Soviet war. Suddenly, after two decades in which their internal politics had militated against any rapprochement, the foreign policies of China and the United States were in a rare state of synchronization. With a million Soviet troops on its border and increasingly hawkish statements emanating from Moscow, China responded to the U.S. overture out of a sense of peril. For its part, the United States had become increasingly frustrated by Soviet intransigence in arms negotiations and its support of revolutionary communism in the developing world. By improving its relations with China, the United States suggested the potential for a Washington — Beijing axis that would tip the global balance of power against Moscow, thereby exerting new pressure on the Soviets to be more forthcoming in arms negotiations. In doing so, Nixon and Kissinger reasserted George Kennan's original concept that American interests lay most fundamentally in a global balance of power which, if maintained, would eventually lead to a moderation of the Soviet threat.

By February 1972 the Sino-American chasm had been bridged. Richard Nixon stepped down

the ramp of *Air Force One* at the Beijing airport to shake the hand of Premier Zhou Enlai and then to meet with Mao Zedong. The trip ended a week later with the issuance of the "Shanghai Communique," a document that indicated the desire of the two nations to move toward "normalization" of their relations but left unresolved the question of the status of Taiwan. Notably, however, the U.S. portion of the communique did not disagree with Beijing's assertion that Taiwan was, ultimately, a part of China. The dire warnings that had accompanied suggestions of any such rapprochement with Beijing were shown to be false: China replaced Taiwan in the United Nations Security Council and proved itself not to be a belligerent, destructive force in the organization which had been predicted by its former American opponents. Although Taiwan was finally "de-recognized" by the United States at the time ambassadors were exchanged between Washington and Beijing in December 1978, it did not collapse but went on to become one of the most prosperous economies of Asia, conducting an increasing amount of its trade with the mainland, albeit amid continuing uncertainty as to its future status.

The reversal of American fortunes in Asia was complete. Within the first four years of the Nixon administration the path had been taken out of the self-destructive entanglement in Vietnam and the United States became the pivot in the triangular balance of global power.

SUMMARY AND CONCLUSION

From the time of its first major involvement in Asia, the takeover of the Philippines, American foreign policy has been concerned with the regional balance of power. Persuasive arguments were made by America's allies as early as 1899 that its assumption of authority in the Philippines was obligatory: if it did not control the archipelago, Germany or Japan would.

Initially, a moral certainty underlay this presumption of a overseer's responsibility, but such confidence waxed and waned according to the circumstances in which Americans found themselves. The public abhorence of atrocities committed in the suppression of a revolution in the Philippines presaged the doubts that would grow with an even more aggressive policy decades later and demonstrated the limits of American public tolerance for military engagements that do not directly defend the nation itself. The Korean War tested this tolerance against the backdrop of a global political challenge from the Soviet Union and China, one that was presumed to threaten the American way of life. In the early post-war years the United States engaged in this contest amid a heightened fear of communism, blinded to the differences that divided its adversaries.

The policy of containment, initially defined by George Kennan, was militarized to a degree that obligated the United States to "bear any cost" against incursions by communists anywhere in the world. In Vietnam, a country as far-removed as possible from the United States, the cost became intolerable. Yet from the humiliating defeat in Vietnam there emerged a strategy that at last exploited the rift between the Soviet Union and China. As a result, a "Pax Americana" prevailed in the Pacific, permitting Southeast Asian nations to grow and prosper. As noted in chapters 6 and 7, even the outbreak of wars in Korea and Vietnam served as powerful stimulants to the Japanese and Korean economies, respectively. Emerging from its isolation, China ceased its support of communist insurrections in other Asian countries, contributing to a more relaxed regional political atmosphere.

Vietnam's ambitions for unification and complete political independence were finally realized in 1975 at a vast economic and human cost. Initially an object of international sympathy, it nevertheless remained in an economic backwater and soon found itself mired in the ancient enmities of mainland Southeast Asia. As will be seen in chapter 11, Vietnamese military incursions in Cambodia led Americans to impose an economic embargo that furthered its isolation and dependence on a weakening Soviet Union which, like Vietnam, remained on the periphery of Asia's economic boom.

The cold war served to justify a costly US military umbrella for Asia and an open American market for Asian imports. With the collapse of the Soviet Union, the "glue" that held this framework together began to weaken. Americans began to reassess the costs of a large overseas military presence, particularly in the face of a large trade deficit with Asia, human rights abuses in China, and labor rights disputes with several countries. The challenge for US policy toward the region became one of managing relationships with nations that, having once been dependent "clients," had now become fractious partners.

In other respects the United States realized its postwar vision for the region. A community of relatively peaceful, prosperous, and mostly capitalist nations emerged whose friendly relations with the United States supported its security and economic interests.

Only in one aspect did American ambitions in Asia part like a river around a great, unmoving boulder. China, having endured a century of civil strife, reform, and invasion, "stood up" in the second half of the twentieth century and reasserted its central role in the Asia Pacific. As described in the next chapter, China's rise as a regional power, newly-oriented toward trade and investment with capitalist nations, has brought America's Pacific Century to an ironic close. The sentimental imperialists have won the cold war only to discover that, as triumphant capitalism shapes the global future, "Communist China" is among its most formidable practitioners.

NOTES

1. See Akira Iriye, "The American Experience in Asia," in *The United States and the Pacific Basin: Changing Economic and Security Relationships*, eds., Mary Brown Bullock and Robert S. Litwak (Washington, DC: the Woodrow Wilson Center Press, 1991), pp. 13-29.

2. McCarthy's charges were centrally about the existence of communists in government, and eventually — when party membership or even Communist sympathies could not be proved — about what became known as "guilt by association." The Senator concentrated initially on the State Department. . . . In the end, when he had broadened his focus to the United States Army itself, under a Republican President (and retired general), his heretofore cowed but now embarrassed Senate colleagues cut him off through a vote of censure. [—James C. Thomson]

3. McCarren's subcommittee conducted an intensive investigation of an extended professional club of academics, journalists, businessmen, officials, and many others who shared an interest in Asia: the Institute of Pacific Relations (IPR). In the course of that year of hearings the informal fraternity of East Asianists — and particularly China specialists — was temporarily split, out of fear and malice, suspicions and recriminations. [—James C. Thomson]

4. James C. Thomson, Jr., Peter W. Stanley, and John Curtis Perry, *Sentimental Imperialists: The American Experience in East Asia* (New York: Harper & Row, 1981), pp. 217-34.

5. Carter J. Eckert, "Liberation, Division, and War, 1945-1953," in *Korea Old and New: A History*, Carter J. Eckert, et. al. (Seoul, Korea: Ilchokak Publishers, 1990), pp. 327-46.

6. The so-called Tonkin Gulf resolution was based on a presumed attack by North Vietnamese gunboats against U.S. destroyers. Firm evidence that the attack ever really occurred has been illusive.

7. For their part, however, the communist leaders in Hanoi were seriously troubled by the size and capabilities of Thieu's million-man army as it began to retake key sectors of the South in early 1973. (See Stanley Karnow, *Vietnam: A History* (New York: Viking, 1983), pp.658-59.) [—Ed.]

8. David J. Steinberg, ed., *In Search of Southeast Asia: A Modern History* (Honolulu: University of Hawaii Press, 1987), pp. 361-66.

9. Henry A. Kissinger, *The White House Years* (Boston: Little Brown, 1979), p. 191.

10. Kennan summarized his view to a National War College audience in October 1947: "As things stand today, it is not Russian military power which is threatening us, it is Russian political power. . . . If it is not entirely a military threat, I doubt that it can be effectively met entirely by military means."

11. Evidence presented by Gordon H. Chang in *Friends and Enemies: The United States, China, and the Soviet Union, 1948-1972* (Stanford: Stanford University Press, 1990) suggests that the American adminstrations' perceptions of diversity about the communist movement were more sophisticated than was often indicated in the public, anti-communist statements by officials.

12. Signed by the U.S., Britain, France, Australia, New Zealand, Thailand, and Pakistan in 1954, the Southeast Asia Treaty Organization (SEATO) was one of several treaties created by the U.S. in the 1950s to cement alliances against communist threats around the world. Vietnam was not a SEATO signatory, but a protocol attached to it extended its provisions to cover "Cambodia, Laos, and . . . the State of Vietnam." Although later cancelled, the SEATO treaty continued to apply to U.S. security arrangements with Thailand. Other treaties effecting security relationships in the Pacific were the treaty with Australia and New Zealand (ANZUS 1951), Japan (1951), the Philippines (1951), Korea (1953) and Taiwan (1955). [—Ed.]

13. John Lewis Gaddis, *Strategies of Containment* (New York: Oxford University Press, 1982), p. 240.

10

China's Long March Toward Modernization

OVERVIEW

On the first of October, 1949 Mao Zedong stood looking out over a vast crowd in Beijing's Tian'anmen Square and announced the creation of the People's Republic of China. "We, the 475 million Chinese people have now stood up, and the future of our nation is infinitely bright," he had declared the day previously. It was a period of hope and promise for all who believed that Mao's communist-led revolution would lift up China from its status as the "poor man of Asia."

Forty years later, the Square was again the scene of a great demonstration, only it marked what some have called "the end of the Chinese Revolution." For these young demonstrators, the Chinese Communist Party (the CCP) was a subject of derision, and the "dictatorship of the proletariat," which it had extolled, was repudiated in favor of bourgeois democracy.

During the forty years bracketed by these two events, China's leaders moved from the heady atmosphere of triumph over Chiang Kai-shek to a state of political siege by their own people. Toward the end, the communist ideology had become discredited by policy disasters and the collapse of communist regimes in Eastern Europe. It is too early to know whether the brief but epochal period that has seen the rise of the Chinese Communist Party will begin to evolve toward a government that is more tolerant of organized opposition, but patterns of the past can be discerned in the present. As will be seen in this chapter, China's modern leaders have viewed their mandate to govern and the role of the state in terms that are as old as China itself. Perhaps just as the harsh Qin dynasty of the First Emperor eventually gave way to forces that created the more moderate Han dynasty, so may the Communist Party one day be viewed as a transitional stage in China's search for a stable, modern economic and political system. For the present, however, any such transition is obscured by an immediate concern to maintain stability and authority, requiring an extensive effort to control information and ideas.

What is certain is that any claim the Party leaders might once have made to holding the "Mandate of Heaven" was lost in May, 1989 when one of the largest mass protests in contemporary world history was staged against them. Peaceful, student-led demonstrations sprang up all over China, but most prominently in Beijing where the world press, assembled for the historic visit of Soviet leader Mikhail Gorbachev, found itself reporting an even greater story. Soon after his departure, the demonstrations — which by then had the support of a broad spectrum of China's urban society — were brutally suppressed by the People's Liberation Army at the direction of a small group of the country's elderly officials.

As a result, China's progress in reforming and rejuvenating its economy from troubles brought on by the previous decades of centralized rule was stalled. Key reformers were removed from office and national policy drifted. Pro- and anti-reform factions struggled with one another to assert control. The levers of the propaganda departments were clearly in the hands of the conservatives, however, who sought to wash away the stain of the Tian'anmen murders from any public memory. The tragic effects of this often-repeated process, referred to as "the Chinese amnesia" by one of China's leading dissidents, Fang Lizhi, is described in this chapter. Yet even as history seemed to have been placed "on hold" in China, many of the student protesters turned their energies to the pursuit of careers within a system that tolerates capitalist profits more than dissident politics.

The crisis that arose for Chinese communism in 1989 does not obscure its early achievements. Even the propagandists could claim correctly in the 1950s that the government's first Five Year Plan was a major success. Modeled on the state-controlled industrial production strategies used in the Soviet Union at the time, the Plan succeeded in part because it started from such a low economic base. Nevertheless, it was a daring and radical reorganization of the Chinese economy.

One of the most fundamental changes was a 1950 Land Reform Law that deposed landlords and redistributed their property to the peasants. The primary agents of this change were Communist Party members called *cadres* who moved to the countryside and established the village Peasant Associations that were to become the instru-ments of Party control. Similarly, by 1952 most of the industrial holdings in private hands had been consolidated under government control; the owners of factories were systematically tried and persecuted. This transition was a brutal and traumatic affair for the private owners whose lives and families were thereafter shattered. For their part, the Communists found that the process of breaking up the economic base of the bourgeoisie greatly strengthened their confidence and that of the people in the Party's leadership. By the end of 1952 the Party had allotted membership to 6 million people.

China soon moved from the purely Soviet-inspired model of development to one that distanced itself from Moscow's leadership. Mao's reliance on ideological frameworks, however, led the nation into economic disasters and political upheavals. His death in 1976 resulted in new political struggles for control from which emerged a reformist regime under Deng Xiaoping. Deng's subsequent economic and foreign policies led to a new surge in China's growth and increased cooperation with the Pacific Basin and the world community. At the same time, China's leaders continued to exercise as much control as possible over flows of information and ideas inside China. In spite of this, both the structure of the Chinese economy and the expectations of its populace are being dramatically altered.

China's First Five-year Plan, 1953-1957
Actual Gains as a Percentage of Plan

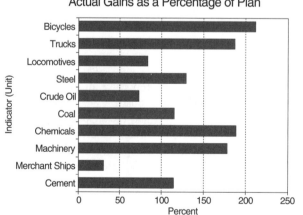

Graph 10.1

Figure 10.1 Mao Zedong declares the founding of the People's Republic of China, Beijing, October 1, 1949.

Four Decades of Chinese Communism: A Chronology

1949

Communist Victory

After defeating major Kuomintang (KMT) forces in Manchuria in late 1948, Communist troops quickly moved to occupy Tianjin and Beijing. After the subsequent decisive Huai-hai battle in central China, KMT resistance collapsed. Red Army units crossed the Yangzi river and began moving south in early 1949. KMT forces under Chiang Kai-shek retreated to Taiwan. Party Chairman Mao Zedong proclaimed the establishment of the People's Republic of China at Tian'anmen Square in Beijing on 1 October.

1950-53

Land Reform Movement

Nearly 40 percent of China's cultivated land changed hands in the course of radical restructuring rural China, a process that had begun in the years 1945-49 in areas under CCP control. Landlords as a class were eliminated and the holdings of rich peasants were greatly reduced. As many as 5 million landlords and other "undesirable elements" were killed, partially in an expression of long-standing local tensions between peasants and landlords.

1950-51

Korean War

China intervened in the Korean war in October 1950 as UN troops reached the Sino-Korean border. By mid-1951, China had pushed the UN forces back to a line near the thirty-eighth Parallel. The conflict led Washington to deploy the U.S. 7th Fleet in the Taiwan Straits in defence of Taiwan, effectively committing both the U.S. and China into postures of mutual hostility that would persist for two decades. China also invaded Tibet during this period.

1954-57

Rural Collectivization and Urban Expropriation

By 1956, more than 90 percent of all rural families had been organized into about 700,000 higher-level agricultural producer cooperatives (APCs). Retaining only houses and small private plots, peasants turned over their land and tools to the collective, receiving pay in the form of work points. Privately owned urban factories, restaurants and shops were converted first into joint state-private ventures, then in 1955 into state-owned enterprises (in most cases paying compensation to former owners).

1956

Eighth Party Congress

With the completion of the state takeover of the urban economy and consolidation of an emerging Stalinist-model socialist system came the rise to political prominence of a group of Party bureaucrats centered around Liu Shaoqi and Deng Xiaoping. Both were named to the newly created politburo Standing Committee at the Eighth Party Congress in September 1956, where Liu announced that the transition to socialism had basically been accomplished and class struggle concluded. Meanwhile, at the Soviet Party Congress in Moscow, premier Nikita Khrushchev made a secret speech denouncing Stalinism and the "cult of personality" that had grown up around him. Mao took the speech as an implied threat to his own standing and stature.

1957-58

"Hundred Flowers Movement" and "Anti-Rightist Campaign"

Despite the skepticism of the Liu-Deng group, Mao moved to relax political control to allow a degree of open public debate. The "Hundred Flowers Movement" quickly got out of hand, however, as university students, journalists and some officials directly attacked the Party and its monopoly of political power. Stung, the Party moved quickly to reimpose limits on debate and

conducted a purge of liberal intellectuals. Nearly half a million people were stigmatized during the "Anti-Rightist Campaign," many banished to labor camps in remote areas of China.

1958-59

The "Great Leap Forward"

Abandoning the Eighth Congress program of sober, planning-based, Soviet-style economic development, Mao decided that China could rapidly develop both industry and agriculture through more extensive rural collectivization and decentralized economic decision-making.

By the end of 1958, almost all of the rural populace had been incorporated into some 25,000 people's communes. The communes were intended to swiftly increase agricultural output by imposing military-like organization and labor-intensive projects such as dams and irrigation systems. Industrial output targets were revised upwards sharply, and localities established many small "backyard" factories to produce steel and other goods. In December, partly in response to the failure of the policy of the Great Leap Forward, Mao withdrew from active participation in day to day decision-making.

1959

Revolt in Tibet

Widespread resistance to China's reimposition of its dominance over Tibet (1950-51) had in turn led to Chinese reprisals and reinforced military presence. Mass demonstrations in Lhasa in March 1959 culminated in open rebellion, which was suppressed by Chinese troops. The Dalai Lama, Tibet's religious and secular leader prior to 1950 escaped to India.

1959

The Dismissal of Peng Dehuai

With extremely favorable weather conditions, China experienced a record harvest in 1958 which initially reinforced Mao's strategy. The extent to which the Great Leap was creating serious dislocations in both agriculture and industry became apparent in 1959. After minister of defence Peng Dehuai sharply attacked Mao's policies at an enlarged politburo session at Lushan in the summer of 1959, Mao responded by threatening to appeal for direct support for his policies from the military, and if necessary even to return to the countryside and lead the peasants in a new revolution.

Unwilling to decisively overturn Mao's leadership, the politburo acquiesced in the purge of Peng and other prominent critics of Mao as members of an "anti-Party clique." At the same time, Mao accepted the necessity of major adjustments to the people's communes.

1960

Sino-Soviet Split

Under the Sino-Soviet treaty signed in 1950, Moscow had extended loans, technical assistance and sales of military equipment to Beijing, which essentially built its governmental, industrial and military systems on the Soviet model. Nikita Khrushchev's de-Stalinization speech in 1956 and the subsequent upheaval in Poland and Hungary shocked the Chinese, who felt Moscow's apparent willingness to compromise with the West undercut their position vis-à-vis the U.S. over Taiwan. Moscow, in turn, was contemptuous of China's abandonment of the Soviet model of economic development in the Great Leap and its claims to co-equal status within the Communist bloc.

Beijing's fears were strengthened by Moscow's only qualified support for China during the Taiwan Straits crisis of 1958. The following year, Khrushchev abrogated an agreement to help China build nuclear weapons. After Beijing launched an open ideological attack on Soviet "revisionism" in 1960, Moscow withdrew its advisers and technical experts.

1960-62

Retreat from Radicalism and "Three Bitter Years"

Extensive drought in 1960-61 and other natural disasters exacerbated the agricultural disasters.

Grain production plummeted from the 1958 record of 200 million tons to only 143.5 million tons. At least 10 million people died in the famine over 1960-62. Industrial production, already suffering from the dislocation of the Great Leap and the withdrawal of Soviet technicians in 1960, was further affected by major shortages of raw materials and lack of sufficient food for urban workers.

1960-62

Sino-Indian War

The Tibetan revolt in 1959 heightened tensions over conflicting territorial claims between India and China. Beijing launched two brief but devastating attacks on Indian positions in late 1962, followed by a unilateral ceasefire and withdrawal to the 1959 line of actual control between the two countries.

1962-65

Emerging Struggle Between Two Lines

The disaster of Mao's Great Leap strengthened the position of the Party bureaucrat group headed by Liu Shaoqi and Deng Xiaoping, who sought to establish a collective leadership to curb Mao's influence. Mao launched a counter-attack at the Tenth Plenum in September 1962, demanding that collectivist policies be strengthened and measures taken against a restoration of capitalism. The result was a stalemate: the Party decided to endorse Mao's principles but Liu and Deng's gradual dismantling of his policy continued.

The clash between "Maoists" and "Liuists" within the leadership intensified in 1963-64, including differences over cultural policy, education, and internal Party organization as well as rival models of economic development. In 1965, the politburo rejected Mao's demand for a rectification campaign against the play Hai Rui's Dismissal from Office (a thinly disguised critical commentary on Mao's 1959 purge of Peng Dehuai). To Mao's dismay, his governmental position was formally eliminated in 1964. Lacking a commanding position at the center, he then left Beijing for Shanghai to launch an attack on his critics from outside the Party leadership.

"Cultural Revolution" I —
Attack on Party Bureaucrats,
Formation of Red Guards

Mao's attack on the orthodox Party bureaucrats who had supplanted his leadership initially focused on purification of cultural and educational policy, but the target of the campaign quickly broadened to encompass "power-holders in the Party who take the capitalist road." A Mao-endorsed critique of the play "Hai Rui's Dismissal" was published in Shanghai which fueled a rectification campaign and launched the Cultural Revolution.

A last-minute attempt by Liu and Deng to ease Mao out of the leadership by convening a special Central Committee Plenum in June 1966 was blocked by military forces under defence minister Lin Biao. With Lin's support, leftists convened their own plenum in August, excluding more than half of the regular central committee membership, which affirmed Mao's Cultural Revolution policies and named Lin Vice-Chairman.

The leftists also mobilized college and secondary school students to attack teachers and local Party leaders. These Red Guard groups were responsible for persecuting and torturing hundreds of thousands of people and the destruction of books, temples, museums, and cultural artifacts. Violent clashes between rival Red Guard groups, some secretly backed by Party leaders under attack by Maoists, occurred all over China.

By early 1967, after Liu, Deng and most of their supporters in the central leadership had been humiliated and purged, the Maoists focused their attention on local Party organizations. In the

Figure 10.2 The Cultural Revolution purged many of China's most senior leaders, including Liu Shaoqi, who at one time was thought to be Mao's natural successor. In this poster, he is denounced as "China's Khruschev" (a reformist) and effectively "erased" by the Red Guards, who clutch their red books of Mao Zedongs's quotations. The caption reads: "Politically, intellectually, and ideologically, thoroughly criticize China's Khruschev."

provinces and countryside, however, there was mass resistance to the Red Guards, including workers organized by local Party leaders, leading to military intervention.

1967-70

"Cultural Revolution" II —
Civil Anarchy and Military Intervention

Mao's January directive to Lin calling on the military to intervene in support of the Left brought into the open the divisions within the People's Liberation Army (PLA) between the central military organization controlled by Lin and the regional commanders. Some local military leaders supported the Maoists, others resisted them, while others attempted to remain neutral. By mid-1967 serious armed clashes had occurred among military units and Red Guard groups all over China.

The threat of civil war led to a realignment among the surviving power centers in 1967 as Lin, regional military commanders and premier Zhou Enlai began to cooperate to contain the Left. Mao acquiesced as joint PLA-worker units suppressed Red Guard organizations, many of whom were sent to the countryside in 1968-70.

By 1969, a new Party leadership had coalesced in the form of a coalition between Maoist leftists, the military under Lin, and the surviving elements of the state bureaucracy under Zhou, which began the reconstruction of Party and civil government organizations.

1971

Death of Lin Biao

Lin died in a plane crash in September 1971 after a failed coup d'état, prompted by his failure to secure his position as Mao's successor. Lin's death and Mao's progressive withdrawal from involvement in domestic affairs strengthened the position of moderates led by Zhou. Despite opposition from radical leftists, Zhou was able to engineer the gradual restoration of rational economic policies and rehabilitation of Party officials purged during the Cultural Revolution, culminating with Deng who resumed his post as Vice Premier in 1973.

1971-72

Rapprochement with the United States

Chinese apprehensions about the mounting Soviet military threat heightened after border clashes along the Ussuri river in 1969, intensifying a debate over strategic realignment within the leadership. Lin Biao, while still defence minister, called for improving relations with the Soviet Union to counter U.S. imperialism, while moderates led by Zhou, with increasing support from Mao, argued for cooperation with the U.S. to check Soviet expansion in Asia. The progressive weakening of Lin's position within the leadership and U.S. moves to wind down its involvement in the Vietnam war facilitated the victory of the

Figure 10.3   Chairman Mao and his "close comrade-in-arms," Lin Biao, in November, 1966.

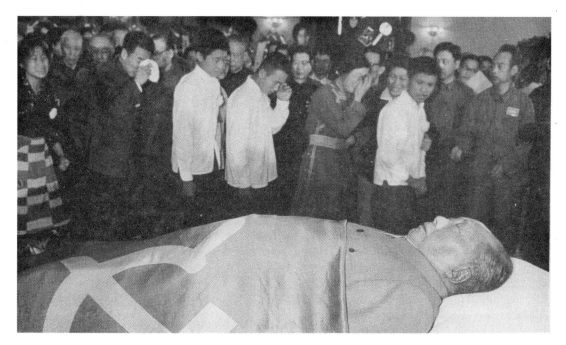

Figure 10.4　The death of Mao Zedong in September 1976 was a turning point in China's postwar era.

moderates, which culminated in U.S. president Richard Nixon's visit to China and the signing of the Shanghai communiqué in February 1972. This fundamentally redefined the politico-military contours of East Asia and laid the basis for China's open door policies of the 1980s. China replaced Taiwan as one of the five permanent members of the United Nations Security Council, providing it with one of the most powerful and influential positions in that world body.

1976

Tian'anmen Riot and Arrest of Gang of Four

Hua Guofeng became premier in February 1976 following Zhou's death, and radical elements in the leadership mounted a new attack on Deng, apparently supported by Mao who was by then seriously ill. The removal of wreaths memorializing Zhou from Tian'anmen Square sparked a massive anti-radical demonstration in April. Deng was blamed for the riot and removed again from posts as Vice-Premier and member of the politburo Standing Committee, retaining only his Party membership.

Shortly after Mao's death in September, Hua arranged for the arrest of Mao's widow, Jiang Qing and other key leftist leaders, later known as the Gang of Four, with the support of senior military leaders. Hua was named Party Chairman in October. Deng was restored to his posts in 1977.

1978

Third Plenum of the Eleventh Central Committee

Contention between Deng and Hua centered on Deng's advocacy of thorough-going economic and educational reforms and his status as senior surviving victim of the Cultural Revolution versus Hua's increasing reliance on Maoist symbols and slogans to buttress his own authority.

The Third Plenum in December 1978 marked the ascendancy of Deng over Hua and a decisive rejection of Maoist Cultural Revolution politics. Economic modernization replaced class struggle as the focus of Party work. New Deng allies replaced Hua supporters on the politburo. The counter-revolutionary verdict on the 1976 Tian'anmen Square riot was officially reversed.

1978-79

Democracy Wall

The successful reversal of the Tian'anmen Square verdict encouraged new and more radical demands for political liberalization and democracy. Activists presented critical ideas in wall posters at Xidan Wall in Beijing and in other cities as well as establishing new unofficial magazines.

Under pressure from other Party leaders, Deng set forth new limits to political reform at a politburo meeting in March 1979 in the form of the Four Basic Principles ("Upholding the socialist road, dictatorship of the proletariat, leadership of the Communist Party and Marxism-Leninism-Mao Zedong Thought"). Democracy Wall was closed and a number of democratic activists (the most prominent of whom was Wei Jingsheng) were arrested and tried. Many remain in detention.

1979

War with Vietnam

Sino-Vietnamese relations, already strained by regional rivalries in the wake of the U.S. defeat and by Hanoi's growing ties to the Soviet Union, ruptured with Vietnam's invasion of Cambodia in late 1978. China initiated a punitive invasion of Vietnam in February 1979, only weeks after Deng Xiaoping's visit to Washington for normalization of Sino-U.S. relations. Chinese forces briefly captured four provincial capitals, with heavy losses, but failed to force Vietnam to withdraw from Cambodia.

1980-81

Leadership Changes and Economic Readjustment

Hua was removed from his top leadership post in 1980, replaced by Deng allies Zhao Ziyang as Premier and Hu Yaobang as acting Party Chairman, while Deng later took the post of Chairman of the central military commission. However a far-reaching program for political reforms to separate the Party and state and establish checks and balances among key state and Party institutions was blocked, and Party conservatives launched a brief campaign against "bourgeois liberalization" in literature and art. Economist Chen Yun sharply attacked Hua's ambitious economic policies, launching readjustment policies to cut investment in heavy industry and deficit spending.

1980-82

Twelfth Congress and the Early Economic Reforms

Rural reforms restoring the production team and eventually the family household as the basic agricultural production unit were pioneered in the late 1970s in Sichuan under Zhao and in Anhui under Wan Li.

The Twelfth Party Congress in September 1982 named Hu as Party General Secretary (abolishing the post of Party Chairman) and approved new reform policies including rural decollectivization, more autonomy for industrial enterprises, expansion of private enterprise and introduction of free urban markets.

1983

Campaign Against Spiritual Pollution

Orthodox Marxists among Deng's political allies including Chen Yun, Deng Liqun, and Wang Zhen spearheaded a campaign to contain cultural influences from the West and to criticize journalists and theoreticians who had begun to explore concepts of alienation and Marxist humanism.

1984

Agreement on Future of Hong Kong

A Sino-British agreement signed in September 1984 provided for Hong Kong to become a special administrative region of China after 1997, continuing as a capitalist enclave and theoretically autonomous except in matters of foreign relations and defence for 50 years.

1985

National Party Conference

Tensions within Deng's coalition of reformists and veteran pre-Cultural Revolution leaders emerged at an extraordinary National Party Conference. It endorsed continuing reforms, but Chen Yun stated his reservations about excessive reliance on market forces, corruption, and relaxation of the Party's political and ideological work.

1987

Downfall of Hu Yaobang and Campaign Against "Bourgeois Liberalization"

Massive pro-democracy student demonstrations in Shanghai, Beijing and other cities elicited a strong conservative backlash. Hu was forced to resign from his post as Party General Secretary, replaced by Zhao, and veteran leaders including Chen, Peng Zhen, and Wang Zhen assert their authority by launching a new ideological campaign targeted against liberal intellectuals in the Party.

1987

Riots in Tibet

Smoldering discontent burst into violent rioting in Lhasa on 1 October. Six Tibetans and as many as four Chinese died in the incident which grew out of a pro-independence demonstration by Tibetan Lamaist monks. This sparked new criticism of China by human-rights activists abroad. Continuing demonstrations and rioting in Tibet led to the declaration of martial law in Lhasa in 1989.

1987

Thirteenth Party Congress — Zhao

Conservative excesses during the campaign against bourgeois liberalization and intrusions into the spheres of economics and cultural affairs ultimately backfired. Fearing a major reversal of reforms and intensified inner-Party struggle, the Party leadership strengthened its support for Zhao's efforts to limit the scope of the campaign. Deng's reaffirmation of support for Zhao in May was a clear signal that the anti-reform tide had been turned.

Deng, Chen, and Li Xiannian stepped down from the politburo Standing Committee at the Congress as originally planned. Zhao, who was confirmed as Party General Secretary, was joined on the Committee by Acting Premier Li Peng, Hu Qili, Qiao Shi and Yao Yilin. Ultra-conservative ideologue Deng Liqun unexpectedly failed to win election to the central committee, and hardline Party propaganda chief Wang Renzhi only barely scraped through.

1988

Economic Retrenchment, Reformists in Retreat

Public concern over steep rising inflation peaked in the summer of 1988 with panic-buying in many major cities after the politburo tabled a resolution to begin comprehensive price reforms — allegedly personally sponsored by Deng. Rice reform plans were shelved and Li Peng and planning chief Yao Yilin enacted a sweeping program of economic retrenchment. Zhao's position appeared weakened as Li and Yao move economic policies back towards Chen Yun-style central planning.

1989

"Beijing Spring," and Downfall of Zhao

Student protests after the death of former Party General Secretary Hu Yaobang in April quickly expanded into huge mass demonstrations in Beijing's Tian'anmen Square. Party and government officials openly participated in protests for democratic reforms, action against official corruption, and called on Li Peng to resign and Deng to step down. More demonstrations erupted in other cities throughout China.

The Party leadership was split between liberals headed by Zhao, who urged that concessions be made to the protesters, and hardliners, headed by Li and state president Yang Shangkun, backed by Deng.

The impasse was broken by the intercession of veteran retired and semi-retired Party leaders including Chen Yun, Li Xiannian, Peng Zhen and Wang Zhen. Li declared marshal law in Beijing on May 20, but demonstrators used trucks and buses to block key intersections on successive nights to keep PLA units from entering the city in force.

Troops supported by armored vehicles finally forced their way into Beijing on the night of June 3, overcoming violent resistance by demonstrators who threw rocks and Molotov cocktails, destroying hundreds of tanks, armored personnel vehicles, trucks and buses. Hundreds of demonstrators and onlookers and dozens of soldiers, were killed. Rui Xingwen and Yan Mingfu were removed from the Party Secretariat. Jiang Zemin replaced Zhao as Party General Secretary. Jiang, Li Ruihuan and Song Ping were named to the politburo standing committee.[1]

1990-91

New 5-Year Plan Reflects On-going Tensions and Dilemmas

Amid plummeting foreign investment, mounting debts by state-owned industries, and resistance to Beijing's economic authority by the wealthier coastal provinces, the Party formulated a new 5-Year Plan that reflected great uncertainty in the economic planning process. Trials and detentions of hundreds of persons connected with the 1989 demonstrations continued.

1992

Deng Revives the Reform Process

Deng Xiaoping made a highly publicized journey to the southern provinces of China where he endorsed the idea of fast growth through economic reforms and private enterprise. His "to get rich is glorious" comment unleashed a new wave of capitalistic enterprise, but many local authorities interpreted the comment as a license to use their offices for private gain. Meanwhile, Deng used his vast weight as "supreme leader" to prevent his old colleague, Yang Shangkun, from unseating Li Peng and Jiang Zemin.

1993-1996

Economic Boom Continues Amid Political Transition

Deng's visibility gradually receded with his terminal illness. He had failed to establish a clear transition to a new leadership. The General Secretary of the Party, Jiang Zemin sought the role of consensus leader and mediator among the Party elite as Zhu Rongji managed the economic boom. China sought membership in the World Trade Organization (WTO) and to be the host of the 2000 Olympics, but was denied both, angrily interpreting these setbacks as a US-led effort to "contain" its growing influence.

◆　　　◆　　　◆

Figure 10.5   Zhao Ziyang spoke to student hunger strikers in May 1989.

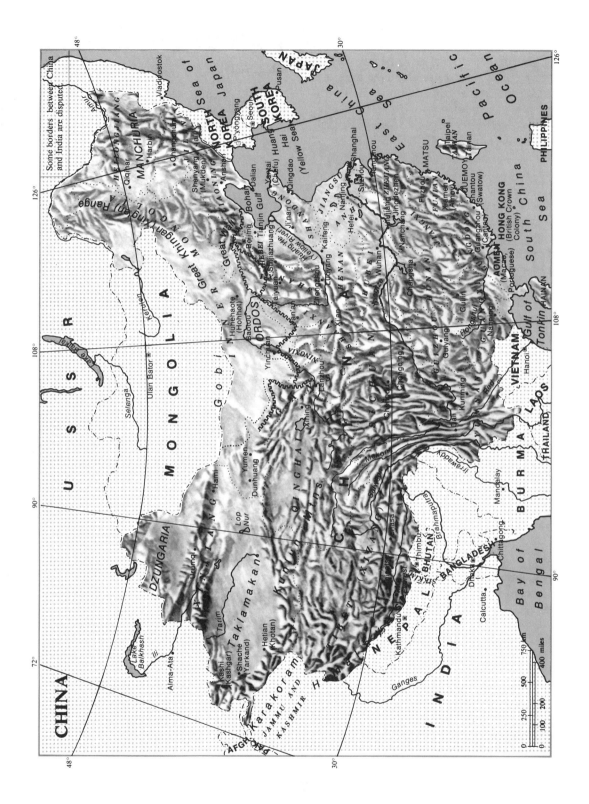

"THE CHINESE AMNESIA"

— by Fang Lizhi

In 1957 Mao Zedong launched an "Anti-Rightist Movement" to purge intellectuals, and 500,000 people were persecuted. Some were killed, some killed themselves, and some were imprisoned or sent for "labor reform." The lightest punishment was to be labeled a "Rightist." This was called "wearing a cap" and meant that one had to bear a powerful stigma. I had just graduated from college that year, and also in that year was purged for the first time.

After the 1957 Anti-Rightist purge, what worried me most was not that I had been punished, or that free thought had been curtailed. At that time I was still a believer, or a semibeliever, in Marxism, and felt that the criticism of free thought, including my own free thought, was not entirely unreasonable. But what worried me, what I just couldn't figure out, was why the Communist party of China would want to use such cruel methods against intellectuals who showed just a tiny bit (and some not even that) of independent thought. I had always assumed that the relationship between the Communist party and intellectuals, including intellectuals who had some independent views, was one of friendship — or at least not one of enmity.

Later I discovered that this worry of mine seemed ridiculous to teachers and friends who were ten or twenty years older than I. They laughed at my ignorance of history. They told me how, as early as 1942, before the Party had wrested control of the whole country, the same cruel methods against intellectuals were already being used at the Communist base in Yan'an. In college I had taken courses in Communist party history, and of course knew that in 1942 at Yan'an there had been a "rectification" movement aimed at "liberalism," "individualism," and other non-Marxist thought. But it was indeed true that I had had no idea that the methods of that "rectification" included "criticism and struggle" — which meant in practice forcing people to commit suicide, and

even execution by beheading. People who had experienced the Yan'an "rectification" paled at the very mention of it. But fifteen years later my generation was completely ignorant of it. We deserved the ridicule we received.

After another thirteen years, in 1970, it became our turn to laugh at a younger generation. This was in the middle stage of the Cultural Revolution that took place between 1966 and 1976. In the early stage of the Cultural Revolution, Mao Zedong had used university students, many of whom supported him fanatically, to bring down his political opponents. But in the early 1970s these same students became the targets of attack. In 1970 all the students and teachers in the physics department of the Chinese University of Science and Technology were sent to a coal mine in Huainan, Anhui Province, for "re-education." I was a lecturer in physics at the time. The movement to "criticize and struggle" against the students' "counterrevolutionary words and deeds" reached its most intense point during the summer. Some students were "struggled"; others were locked up "for investigation;" a good number could not endure the torment of the vile political atmosphere and fell ill. One of my assignments was to pull a plank-cart (like a horse cart, but pulled by a human being) to transport the ill students. Of the group of forty-some students working in the same mine as I did, two were driven to suicide — one by jumping off a building, the other by lying in front of a train.

Most of these students, as innocent as I had been in 1957, never imagined that the Communist government could be so cruel in its treatment of students who had followed them so loyally. Later one of the students, who became my coworker in astrophysical research (and who is now in the U.S.), confided to me that he had had no knowledge whatever of the true history of the Anti-Rightist Movement. It was not until he was himself detained and interrogated that he slowly began to appreciate why some of the older people he knew lived in such fear of the phrase Anti-Rightist. The whole story of the main actors and issues of the Anti-Rightist Movement had, for this generation, become a huge blank.

This was all repeated again in 1989. According to one incomplete survey of students who participated in the Tian'anmen democracy movement, more than half of them had no precise knowledge of what happened in the spring of 1979 when young activists posted independent views on the Democracy Wall in Beijing and were soon arrested for doing so. They did not know about Deng Xiaoping's persecution of the participants of the Democracy Wall Movement, or about the "Fifth Modernization"[2] or that Wei Jingsheng, one of the most outspoken of the activists, was still serving time for what he did. Events of a mere ten years earlier, for this new generation, were already unknown history.

In this manner, about once each decade, the true face of history is thoroughly erased from the memory of Chinese society. This is the objective of the Chinese Communist policy of "Forgetting History." In an effort to coerce all of society into a continuing forgetfulness, the policy requires that any detail of history that is not in the interests of the Chinese Communists cannot be expressed in any speech, book, document, or other medium.

If, inside China, the whole of society has been coerced into forgetfulness by the authorities, in the West the act of forgetting can be observed in the work of a number of influential writers who have consciously ignored history and have willingly complied with the "standardized public opinion" of the Communists' censorial system.

The work of the late Edgar Snow provides one of the most telling examples of this tendency. Snow lived many years in China; we must assume that he understood its society. And yet, in his reports on China after the Communists took power, he strictly observed the regime's propaganda requirements — including the forgetting of history. In *Red China Today* he had this to say about China in the early 1960s:

> *I diligently searched, without success, for starving people or beggars to photograph. Nor did anyone else succeed. . . . I must assert that I saw no starving people in China, nothing that looked like old-time famine, [and] that I do not believe that there is famine in China at this writing.*[3]

The facts, which even the Chinese Communists do not dare to deny publicly, are that the early 1960s saw one of the greatest famines in more than two thousand years of recorded Chinese history. In the three years between 1960 and 1962 approximately twenty-five million people in China died of hunger. As for beggars, not only did they exist, they even had a kind of "culture," with communist characteristics. In 1973 in Anhui I listened to a report by the "advanced" Party Secretary of a peasant village. One of his main "advanced" experiences was to organize his villagers into a beggars' brigade to go begging through the neighboring countryside.

Snow's tomb is located on a quiet and secluded little hillock on the campus of Beijing University. He was respected in China during his lifetime; no one doubted the sincerity of his love for China and the Chinese people. But his writings have not received similar respect. His books have adopted too much of the viewpoint of his old friend Mao Zedong, which is to say the viewpoint of official Communist propaganda. The works of China experts such as Snow have served, in fact, as a "Special Propaganda Department" for the Communists. They have helped the Communists' "Technique of Forgetting History" to become a completed circle, continuous both inside and outside China.

This foreign aid has helped the Chinese Communists, over a long period of time, to carry on their activities beyond the reach of world opinion and exempt from effective scrutiny. The Communists' nefarious record of human rights violations is not only banned from memory and discussion inside China, but has also been largely overlooked by the rest of the world, which never condemned its repression with the urgency and rigor that would have been appropriate.

The events in Tian'anmen Square were the first exception to this pattern — the first time that Chinese Communist brutality was thoroughly recorded and reported, and the first time that virtually the whole world was willing to censure it. In the early 1960s Edgar Snow was invited to stand next to Mao Zedong on top of the wall at Tian'anmen and take part in the grand pomp and ceremony. By 1990, the lot of reporters had come to include beatings by troops at the base of that same wall. This has been one of the extremely significant changes occasioned by the Tian'anmen events.[4]

◆   ◆   ◆

POLITICAL REFORMS

— by Harry Harding

China's post-Mao leaders have been frank, even brutal, in their assessment of the political institutions that they inherited from the Maoist period. In August 1980, in a speech now regarded as the starting point of political reform, Deng Xiaoping admitted that the Chinese political system was "plagued by problems which seriously impede the full realization of the superiority of socialism." Seven years later, at the Thirteenth Party Congress, General Secretary Zhao Ziyang similarly noted that China's "current political structure... is no longer suited to our drive for modernization... or to the development of a socialist commodity economy."

Through most of the 1980s, therefore, China's leaders attempted to reshape the major dimensions of their nation's political life. The political reforms reduced the influence of ideology over intellectual and cultural life, loosened administrative controls over the economy and Chinese society, institutionalized and regularized the political process, and expanded opportunities for political participation. The restructuring of the political system was an integral part of the broader program of modernization and reform that China began undertaking after the death of Mao Zedong in 1976.

As in the economic sphere, however, the effort to reform China's political system was a halting and tortuous process. Chinese leaders sponsored only a limited degree of political liberalization to avoid any challenge to the dominant position of the Chinese Communist Party. They encountered obstacles that have prevented them from accomplishing all their objectives, and many of their political reforms had unintended and unwanted consequences. The huge demonstrations that swept Tian'anmen Square in the spring of 1989 showed just how much political controls on society had been relaxed, and how much more political reform was demanded by residents of urban China.

The Intellectual Imperative

One of Mao's purposes in launching the Cultural Revolution in the mid-1960s was to increase the role of ideology in all aspects of China's political life. As a result of his efforts, China in the mid-1970s had become a highly doctrinal polity in which the symbols of ideological commitment and conformity were virtually omnipresent. Ideological tracts crowded other works off the shelves of China's bookstores. Quotations from Marx, Lenin, and Mao — usually printed in boldface — were sprinkled liberally through the pages of Chinese newspapers and periodicals. Huge red billboards with political exhortations painted in white characters punctuated China's urban landscape.

The ideology of the late Maoist period stressed the need to continue class struggle and exercise "proletarian dictatorship" against alleged enemies both inside and outside China. In the cultural realm, Maoism rejected traditional Chinese literature and art, belittled Western culture, and exalted a banal blend of socialist realism and revolutionary romanticism. It denigrated the role of markets, private ownership, foreign trade, and material incentives in the nation's economic development. Maoism ridiculed intellectuals as the "stinking ninth category" of counterrevolutionaries, condemned administrative officials as "Party persons in authority taking the capitalist road," and called on industrial workers and the poorer peasants to seize power from the Party apparatus.

Any sort of reform in the post-Mao era, whether economic or political, would have been impossible if this ideological straitjacket had not been loosened. Economic modernization, too, would have been severely limited by the constraints that doctrine imposed upon intellectual and scientific activity. Therefore, one of the first elements of political reform since 1976 has been a redefinition of both the role and the content of the ideology of the late Maoist period.

To begin with, there was a critical reassessment of the basic ideological principles of the past and the specific policies and historical episodes that had emerged from them. The key breakthrough in this regard occurred at the end of 1978 when the Party's Central Committee first endorsed Deng Xiaoping's call to "seek truth from facts," rather than mechanically perpetuating whatever policies had been associated with Mao Zedong. Three years later, another plenary meeting of the Central Committee adopted a resolution on Party history that repudiated the Cultural Revolution, the Great Leap Forward, and most of the other programs associated with Mao's later years. Subsequently, leading reformers called for more "ideological breakthroughs" that would create a new body of Marxist ideology, suitable for China's conditions in the latter part of the twentieth century.

That new doctrine, which the Party has variously described as "socialism with Chinese characteristics" or the principles to guide national development during the "primary stage of socialism," a much more liberal version of Marxism than the utopian Maoist vision that it replaced. It stressed economic modernization rather than revolution, national unity rather than class struggle, and socialist democracy rather than proletarian dictatorship. Increasingly during the 1980s, the ideology of reform welcomed material incentives, diverse forms of economic ownership, markets for the allocation of goods and services, and fuller integration of China with the international economy. It valued not only the traditional notions of self-sacrifice, fraternity, and collectivism but also competition, initiative, and risk taking. Signboards that once carried revolutionary messages occasionally bore a new slogan, first popularized in the Shenzhen Special Economic Zone just outside Hong Kong, that neatly summarized the spirit of the new age: "Time is money; efficiency is life."

In addition to changing the content of ideology, China's reformers also reduced its role in economic and political affairs. A wide range of cultural and scientific issues could at last be addressed on their merits, without reference to ideological considerations. Discussions of social and economic policy increasingly accepted the legitimacy, even the desirability, of studying the experience of advanced capitalist countries and adopting whatever policies contribute to the most rapid rates of economic growth.

Chinese leaders were willing to tolerate the reemergence of religion — whether Buddhist, Moslem, or Christian — and some reformers explicitly acknowledged that ideology could not in itself satisfy all the spiritual requirements of the Chinese people. Increasingly, too, the Chinese Communist Party began to base its rule on an appeal to Chinese nationalism while placing less emphasis on securing from non-Party members an active commitment to Marxism. In all these ways, the role of ideology in post-Mao China shrank relative to the role of other bodies of belief.

Although the Chinese Communist Party was willing to purge its ideology of discredited principles, to incorporate new concepts that were once regarded as heretical, and to reduce the scope of activities governed by ideological concerns, it was not prepared to repudiate Marxism. The Party described the redefinition of official doctrine as the "enrichment and development" of its ideological heritage, not as its abandonment. Nor did the Party agree to allow the public presentation of ideological alternatives.

The Party's reluctance to abandon Marxism arose from several considerations. The most fundamental of these was its recognition that the abandonment of Marxism or the acceptance of ideological pluralism would seriously undermine its own legitimacy, which is still rooted largely in its claim to having unique mastery of a scientifically correct body of social and political philosophy. Other factors were at work as well. Many members of the Party appeared to require the reassurance that the reforms of the post-Mao period have been in keeping with Marxist traditions and are still intended to lead toward an ideal communist society. And a sizable number of ordinary citizens, including many intellectuals, also held to the traditional Chinese concept that good governance requires, and the unity of society demands, that the state uphold an official doctrine and educate both officials and ordinary citizens in its basic tenets.

However, the redefinition of official doctrine did not fill the moral and political vacuum created by the discrediting of utopian Maoism. Many intellectuals appeared to prefer the comprehensive and programmatic qualities of ideology to the pragmatic, experimental approaches to policymaking being practiced in post-Mao China. Many peasants wondered whether the liberal rural policies that were described as appropriate to the "primary stage of socialism" would be abandoned when the Party decided China had entered a more advanced phase of development. The alternative belief systems that began to be tolerated or encouraged — nationalism, pragmatism, science, and religion — did not yet create a sense of sacrifice or unity among the

Chinese people comparable to that engendered by Maoism. Indeed, Chinese society seemed to be plagued by apathy, materialism, and moral decay, as reflected in a steady rise of corruption, crime, and other forms of social deviance. As economic reform began to enter a more delicate stage, therefore, the legitimacy of the Chinese political rested on a rather fragile base.

The Political Imperative

The political leadership that emerged from the Chinese Cultural Revolution was, in several respects, ill-suited to a program of sustained economic or political reform. Fully half of the members of the Chinese Communist Party had been recruited when class background and revolutionary zeal, rather than formal education or technical competence, were the principal criteria for membership. The Cultural Revolution had produced a highly factionalized and unstable political system, featuring sharp divisions within the elite, the arbitrary exercise of power by individual political leaders, and abrupt and often violent changes of leadership.

In this context, it was necessary for Deng Xiaoping and the other reformers to reconstitute the national leadership in ways that would support a program of economic and political reform and then to institutionalize the system to maximize the chances that reform would survive Deng's eventual departure from China's political stage. These political imperatives provided a second rationale for restructuring China's political system.

Gradually, Deng was able to remove key conservatives, such as Mao's immediate successor, Hua Guofeng, from the central leadership of the Party, replacing them with officials more enthusiastic toward reform. He then utilized his growing political base in Beijing to restaff the Party and state bureaucracies at lower levels. Between 1978 and 1985, the reformers achieved a massive turnover of state council ministers, provincial first secretaries, and provincial governors — comparable in scale, although not in method, to the great purges of the Cultural Revolution. Fully 89 percent of the cabinet members and 93 percent of the provincial first secretaries and governors who had been in office in 1978 were removed by 1985.

They were replaced, on the average, by officials who were younger, better educated, and who presumably would be more supportive of reform after Deng's death.

Finally, Deng attempted to create a regular system for leadership rotation to avoid the kind of succession crisis or struggle for power that could jeopardize reform. Deng's plan was to specify limited terms of office for top Party and state leaders, to move senior officials into ceremonial positions once they had served their terms, and to establish predictable patterns of promotion from the ministries and provinces into the Party Secretariat, the State Council, and the Politburo. Deng also tried to reestablish the norms of collective leadership, free debate, and Party discipline among the elite that had been so seriously shattered during the Cultural Revolution.

Through these strategies, Deng Xiaoping was able to shift the center of gravity of the Chinese political spectrum rather decisively in the direction of reform. In 1976-77, when Deng began to challenge Hua Guofeng, the reformers were on the fringe of Chinese politics, with the predominant position held by those who wished to restore the efficiency and vitality of a centrally planned economy and a Leninist political order. A little more than a decade later, Chinese politics was dominated by those committed to a sustained program of economic and political reform, with more conservative leaders relegated to subordinate positions.

This is not to say, however, that the national leadership was united, despite the customary Chinese efforts to insist that it was. Although virtually all leaders in Beijing supported some kind of reform, there were still significant differences over how far to go, how fast to proceed, and what strategies to adopt. The degree to which central planning should be completely abandoned in favor of a regulated marketplace, and the extent to which public enterprise should be converted to private ownership, has proved especially controversial. The differences of opinion were even wider at lower levels of the Party and state bureaucracies.

Differences of opinion are normal within any political system and should be expected, and even welcomed, in a country of China's size and complexity. They need not necessarily have a destabilizing impact on the political system. Nonetheless, it soon became clear that these divisions within China's leadership would not be expressed or resolved entirely through institutionalized mechanisms.

Before the Tian'anmen Incident, the best example of the problem was the fate of Hu Yaobang, first the chairman and then the general secretary of the Party from 1981 until early 1987. Hu's apparent disinterest in ideology, alleged tolerance of dissent, and advocacy of a rapid retirement of veteran Party officials made him controversial, as did his reputation for spontaneous and ill-conceived statements that occasionally departed from official Party policy. Ultimately, a nationwide series of student demonstrations in late 1986 and early 1987, which called for greater democracy and accelerated political reform, provided a convenient pretext for Hu's removal. Hu's dismissal in January 1987, disguised as his "resignation" from the post of Party general secretary, was engineered by a group of senior conservative Party leaders (some of whom had formally retired from the Politburo), endorsed by Deng Xiaoping, and then implemented by an irregular meeting of the Politburo. The dismissal took place even though Hu's term of office would have ended at the Thirteenth Party Congress later that same year.

Zhao Ziyang, Hu's successor as general secretary, appeared to be encountering similar political difficulties by the middle of 1988. Where Hu had been controversial for his stand on various political and organizational issues, Zhao came under fire for his management of the economy. Zhao's advocacy of export-processing zones along the Chinese coast, his insistence upon rapid price reform, his support for other radical economic reform measures, and his apparent acceptance of a relatively high rate of inflation aroused the skepticism of more conservative leaders both inside and outside the Politburo. Once again, Deng's support for his heir apparent seemed to waver, as he reportedly declared, "I shall not protect anybody, and whoever fails to give a good account of himself should go." This foreshadowed Zhao's resignation after he refused to support the imposition of martial law to suppress the mass protests of 1989.

The fate of Hu Yaobang in 1987 and that of Zhao Ziyang in 1989 illustrate one of the most striking dilemmas of political reform in post-Mao China. Unlike Mao Zedong, who held on to the chairmanship of the Party until the bitter end, Deng attempted to withdraw gradually from a formal role in Chinese politics to minimize the impact of his eventual death on the political stability of his country. By 1988, he held only one formal institutional position, that of the chairman of the Party's Military Affairs Committee, from which he has since also retired. By his own account, he did not participate in the drafting of the detailed programmatic statements on economic or political reform. And yet, Deng was clearly China's paramount leader throughout the entire decade of reform and intervened decisively when critical questions of direction, pace, or personnel were at stake.

The dilemma was that, in the short run, the success of reform critically depended on Deng's personal prestige and political acumen; and yet, over the long run, the fate of reform rested on his ability to remove himself from politics to ensure a smooth transition of power to his successors. His continued active involvement in politics made it increasingly likely that his eventual departure from the political stage would create a vacuum of power that would prove disruptive.

The contradictions inherent in Deng Xiaoping's ambiguous role in Chinese political life were echoed in the equally ambiguous standing of other senior leaders throughout the Chinese political system. One key element in Deng's succession arrangements was to ease veteran officials into comfortable retirement by offering them positions as advisors to Party and government bodies at various levels. And yet, these older officials, many of whom have little firm commitment to reform, still played an active role in Chinese politics at both the national and local levels. In many provinces and cities, they continued to influence key personnel appointments; in Beijing they apparently formed the core of the opposition to both Hu Yaobang and Zhao Ziyang. The senior officials formed a group of skeptics and critics of the reform program and they managed to actively assert their views.

The Economic Imperative

From an economic perspective, the Chinese political system on the eve of reform combined the worst features of Leninism and Maoism: it intruded heavily into the economy but was poorly designed to support either economic modernization or reform. Government officials were, in many cases, overaged and undereducated. The state bureaucracy comprised a huge array of administrative agencies, whose job it was to exercise close and direct control over every detail of economic activity. At the same time, the Party inserted itself into every other institution in the country — from factories to universities to government agencies — and took as its mandate the maintenance of political loyalty and ideological orthodoxy rather than the promotion of economic development.

As the reformers saw it, therefore, the very structure of the political system was an obstacle to economic reform. It would be difficult to encourage entrepreneurial activity by enterprise managers if their decisions were constantly subject to interference by local Party committees or government agencies. The transition to a regulated market economy would be nearly impossible if the state bureaucracy continued to consist mainly of agencies designed to exercise direct administrative control rather than indirect regulatory oversight. Foreign investors would be reluctant to launch projects in China if they had to deal with unqualified and unimaginative officials and inefficient and hesitant bureaucratic agencies. For all these reasons, successful economic reform required political restructuring as well.

The political reforms that followed from this economic rationale included five principal components. First, there was an effort to reorganize the state bureaucracy to make it more compatible with the needs of economic development and reform. Agencies responsible for central planning and for direct administration of economic activity began to be eliminated, merged, or streamlined. Conversely, government organizations responsible for economic regulation (such as the banks, auditing agencies, statistical bureaus, and taxation agencies) were to be strengthened and expanded. This program was launched on an experimental basis at the municipal level in 1986 and extended to a small number of central ministries prior to the events in 1989.

Second, Chinese reformers announced their intention to rationalize and modernize their nation's civil service. Recruitment to government positions was to be on the basis of open competitive examinations, with young officials drawn increasingly from the nation's pool of college graduates rather than from the ranks of workers and peasants.

Third, discussions of political reform hinted at measures to decentralize administrative power in an effort to grant provincial and municipal governments greater power to adopt their own regulations and legislation, greater freedom to adapt central policy to local circumstances, and greater autonomy over financial affairs. As one measure of decentralization, investments made by local governments and individual enterprises outside the state budget constituted more than 60 percent of the total in 1986, as compared with less than 25 percent during the Fifth Five-Year plan in the late 1970s. This degree of financial decentralization began to threaten both the revenue base of the central government and its control over how the nation's financial resources were invested.

A fourth aspect of political reform was to create a more rational policymaking process, particularly at the national level. Academic specialists, housed in a growing number of research institutes connected with major government and Party agencies, exerted some influence over the content of national policy. Drafts of central documents were circulated for comment to administrators, academic specialists, local officials, and enterprise managers before being formally considered by the Party Politburo, the State Council, or the National People's Congress. Foreign experts, in organizations such as the World Bank, frequently served as consultants and advisors. Although China's policy research institutions remained understaffed and undertrained and policy analysis was rather rudimentary by Western standards, the reforms created the basis for a more objective and pragmatic policymaking process.

Finally, and most important, the political reforms of the 1980s envisioned a distinctively reduced role for the Chinese Communist Party in routine political and economic affairs. The Party was no longer to exercise direct control over administrative matters that were deemed the proper province of government agencies, industrial and commercial enterprises, or public organizations. To that end, the Party's control over government appointments was to be restricted under the civil service law to a top echelon of policymakers at each level of government, with lower-ranking officials governed by civil service procedures. The Party cells in central government agencies were to be abolished, and Party departments in the localities that overlapped with government agencies also eventually eliminated. In grassroots organizations, the director or manager was to exercise day-to-day responsibility, with the Party secretary in a supervisory position.

Of all the political reforms discussed thus far, these five measures were perhaps the least advanced in both design and implementation at the time of the Tian'anmen Square demonstrations in 1989. It was apparent that both the Party apparatus and the government bureaucracy maintained tenacious holds over their previous areas of responsibility, despite every effort to relax them. Tensions rose partly because this suggested to many that economic liberalization required a further, and even deeper, reform of both the political structure and the system of economic ownership — trends which conservative leaders in the Party refuse to accept.

One problem that emerged from incomplete political reform concerned the continuing role of the government in the economy. Despite the steps to increase enterprise autonomy, the state bureaucracy has proven inventive in finding ways to retain considerable power over state enterprises. Even at the height of the reforms, government agencies still had to approve decisions to alter an enterprise's product line, build a new factory, or shut down existing production facilities. The state bureaucracy still appoints enterprise managers, allocates key inputs provided under mandatory planning, and negotiates the contracts for annual production and profit quotas. The proposals to transfer administrative authority from central bureaucratic agencies in Beijing to their counterparts in China's various provinces and municipalities may simply exacerbate the problem, for decentralization is giving even greater power to local agencies that appear eager to interfere in the workings of the marketplace.

The continued control of the state bureaucracy over the industrial economy led some Chinese reformers to propose an even more radical restructuring of the system of ownership of state industry.

The proposals varied widely, but their common denominator was to break the connection between bureaucratic administration and economic management by creating new forms of ownership that would be independent of the state.

Similar problems are apparent with regard to the role of the Party. The Party retains the responsibility for ensuring the implementation of national policies and directives and the authority to nominate or approve the appointments of leading officials in every other organization. Although some Party secretaries supported reform, others used these residual powers to obstruct or distort the implementation of various reform programs. Thus, some scholars and policy analysts suggested even more radical changes in the structure of the Party to further restrict its control over basic-level organizations, including an end to its control over personnel appointments, or an abolition of Party committees in factories, universities, and government offices.

The Societal Imperative

By the time of Mao Zedong's death in 1976, the Chinese political system had become at once increasingly totalitarian and increasingly illegitimate. The totalitarian features of the system — the construction of a Leninist Party, the formation of a vast network of mass organizations under Party control, the promulgation of an official ideology, and the mobilization of popular support for redistributive policies — had been created in the 1950s, during the early years of the new government. But they had been exacerbated during the anti-rightist campaign of 1957, the Great Leap Forward of 1958-59, and particularly during the Cultural Revolution of 1966-76. In all these political movements, Mao had attempted to sustain a high level of popular mobilization for economic development and a high degree of mass struggle against poorly defined class enemies inside and outside the Party.

The result of these campaigns, however, was not popular support but mass alienation, particularly in urban China. Intellectuals were the principal targets of persecution in both the anti-rightist campaign and the Cultural Revolution. Urban workers saw their levels of consumption virtually stagnate after the mid-1960s. Young people, encouraged to join the Red Guards during the Cultural Revolution, were dispatched in the tens of millions to the rural areas in the late 1960s and early 1970s, with little prospect of returning to their homes. By 1980, China's post-Mao leadership acknowledged that, unless remedial measures were taken, China potentially faced a political crisis comparable to the one that Poland was then experiencing.

As the post-Mao economic reforms unfolded, the danger of a crisis of confidence in the Party's leadership took on a new dimension. The leadership was aware of the resentment and concern being created by some of the unintended consequences of reform, particularly inflation, inequality, corruption, and abuses of power. It also recognized that even more painful reforms lay ahead, including price reform, wage reform, housing reform, enterprise bankruptcy, and the like. Although popular support for the general concept of reform appeared to remain fairly strong, there were growing complaints about some of the particular problems associated with the reform program, and even some nostalgia for the economic security and moral commitment of the Maoist era. Increasingly, therefore, political restructuring was aimed at preventing a new crisis of confidence from emerging as a consequence of reform.

One important early measure was the removal of the political and class labels that had been assigned to every Chinese citizen during the Maoist years. In 1977, virtually all those who had been landlords, rich peasants, or capitalists before 1949 were politically rehabilitated. Beginning the following year, similar treatment was extended to approximately three million Chinese who had been tarred as "rightists" or "counterrevolutionaries" during the anti-rightist campaign and the Cultural Revolution. In the subsequent decade, the pre-revolutionary class background of one's family came to have much less influence on the chances for university education, employment, or even Party membership.

A second significant reform was the relaxation of the political controls over most aspects of ordinary life. The individual Chinese came to have more choice than ever before over his occupation, place of living, and life-style. Ordinary Chinese spent much less time in political study and were freer to practice religion. Artists, writers, and scholars had much greater freedom of inquiry and expression. Consumers were able to obtain more fashionable furniture, clothing, and hairstyles, and to enjoy a wider range of hobbies and leisure activities. Attitudes toward premarital sex and divorce became noticeably more relaxed.

There were also efforts to make the remaining political controls more predictable and less arbitrary. China made considerable strides toward the creation of a more complete legal system that specified the substantive and procedural rights of Chinese citizens. A new criminal code and code of legal procedure were adopted in 1979. Laws governing the press, publication, association, assembly, and demonstration were drafted as well as an administrative litigation law, providing citizens with relief against illegal or unjustifiable government actions.

Reforms also involved the establishment of more channels of communication between political leaders and ordinary citizens. The press began to carry somewhat fuller accounts of major government and Party meetings, including unprecedented reportage on plenary sessions of the Politburo. The advantages and disadvantages of various competing policy options, in such areas as price reform and enterprise reform, were more openly debated in both scholarly journals and the popular press. Meanwhile, public opinion on major policy issues was solicited through investigative reporting, contacts with mass organizations and professional associations, attitudinal surveys, and other mechanisms for what was described as "consultation and dialogue."

The revitalization and restructuring of legislative and deliberative bodies, particularly at the national level, was another feature of recent political reform. Competitive elections for delegates to local and county-level people's congresses were authorized in 1982 and made mandatory in 1986. A degree of competition was also introduced into provincial and national government; the Standing Committee of the National People's Congress, the governors of eight provinces, and the vice-governors of 29 provinces were selected by the relevant legislature through competitive elections. The National People's Congress engaged in discussion and debate of various policy issues much more openly and demonstrated its ability to delay or modify important elements of legislation, secure revisions in the state budget, and block a limited number of personnel appointments.

Finally, a small degree of democratization was introduced into the Chinese Communist Party itself. There have been some competitive elections to Party congresses and committees at various levels, and the Thirteenth Party Congress decided that the practice should be made universal in the near future. At the congress itself, more candidates were nominated for membership in the Central Committee than for which there were vacancies, and at least one prominent conservative leader, Deng Liqun, actually went down in embarrassing defeat.

Despite these unmistakable signs of progress, there remained significant limits on the design and implementation of these aspects of political liberalization even before the suppression of the protest in Tian'anmen Square. An intrusive birth control campaign, controls on publications, and periodic criticisms of unorthodox intellectuals and works of art indicated that the hand of the state remained strong. The revised legal system still lacked provisions regarded as essential in much of Western law, including the presumption of innocence, protection against self-incrimination, and the practice of an aggressive courtroom defense. Dissidents and protesters were still subject to arbitrary arrest, lengthy detention without trial, torture and solitary confinement, and severe prison terms for loosely defined offenses. The Party controlled the nominations for contested elections, and legislative bodies lacked the power to introduce their own legislation. Generally, the totalitarian institutions of the Maoist era were deactivated, but not yet dismantled.

Moreover, the representative institutions of the post-Mao era enabled the Chinese Communist Party to seek advice and opinion without forcing it to be accountable or responsive to popular demands. Chinese leaders continued to reject the possibility of an independent press, truly independent interest groups, independent opposition parties, or an independent judiciary and legislature. Although the Party was willing to consult various sectors of society in making its policies, it was not prepared to engage them in a genuine competition for political power.

And yet, even this limited degree of political liberalization produced serious dilemmas for the Chinese Communist Party. Although intended to reinforce reform in other areas, the political relaxation that occurred after 1978 in some ways increased the ability of various sectors of Chinese society to obstruct the aspects of reform to which they objected. The National People's Congress blocked for several years the adoption of a national enterprise law that would have made possible the closing of unprofitable state enterprises. Strikes and slowdowns by workers hampered the implementation of wage and price reform. In all these ways, political liberalization may paradoxically have served not to reinforce, but to hinder, efforts at economic reform.

A further dilemma was that political liberalization and economic reform produced pressures for more pluralism. Even though Western concepts of multi-party democracy, competing ideologies, and independent interest groups are not deeply rooted in Chinese tradition, a key trend by 1989 was the emergence of a small but significant protest movement that called for greater democratization. Ethnic questions, although not as central in Chinese politics as in the Soviet Union, also were the subject of protest, as evidenced by rioting in Tibet. As levels of education continued to rise, as economic reform created a larger class of professionals and entrepreneurs, and as contact with Western societies increased, the pressures for democratization and pluralism grew.

Conclusion

In retrospect, we now see that the partial political reforms undertaken in China in the 1980s constituted a dangerous blend of success and failure.

The reforms were successful in relaxing the administrative and ideological controls over society that has been put in place shortly after the Communist Revolution of 1949, and that had been tightened during the decade of the Cultural Revolution. At the same time, the economic reforms of the post-Mao era reduced the role of the state plan, increased the role of the market, allowed greater room for private and collective enterprises, and produced more housing and consumer goods. Together, these efforts at political and economic restructuring meant that large segments of urban China enjoyed greater freedom of thought, a growing ability to discuss political issues, more access to ideas and information from the outside world, and greater independence from Party cadres and government officials in acquiring scarce goods and services.

On the other hand, the post-Mao reforms failed to create a more rational or responsive political system. Despite some efforts to build a more effective civil service, to recruit more educated and open-minded leaders, to disengage the Party from routine administrative affairs, and to create a more scientific policy-making process, at the end of the 1980s decisions on critical economic issues were still being made arbitrarily and implemented ineffectually. The resulting economic problems — corruption, inflation, and inequality — were thus widely regarded as the result of an incompetent government. Moreover, the remaining restrictions on political participation, especially the impotence of elected legislatures and the absence of independent interest groups, gave Chinese citizens few channels through which they could express their grievances. This made the Chinese government appear insensitive as well as ineffective.

The Chinese experience shows the danger, then, of incomplete political reform, particularly at a time of rapid economic change. The various imperatives outlined above — intellectual, political, economic, and societal — forced the deactivation or dismantling of many of the totalitarian institutions of the past. But the Chinese Communist Party was not prepared to move equally rapidly toward the creation of new institutions that could permit the articulation or aggregation of political demands. Freer to speak, but still unable to be heard, the frustrated citizens of urban China poured into the streets of their cities in unprecedented number in the spring of 1989. Unwilling to respond to this challenge by promising further political reform, China's elderly leadership managed instead to mobilize the necessary military force to suppress it.

The Tian'anmen Incident seriously set back the process of political reform in post-Mao China. The suppression of the demonstrations was followed by the arrest of protest leaders, a resurgence of orthodox ideology, a resumption of political education, and a tightening of controls over the universities and the press. Over the longer term, however, the pressures for renewed political reform are likely to become irresistible. As China continues to modernize, and as the result of East Asia experiments

How Chinese Would Express Grievances

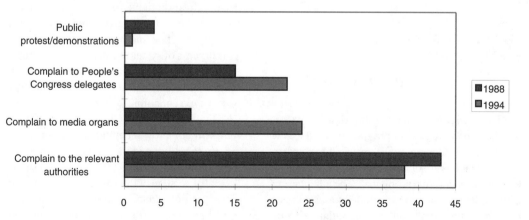

Graph 10.2 Although Chinese can be expected to respond cautiously to surveys, a poll by a well-respected research institution, repeated five years after the 1989 Tiananmen demonstrations, revealed that media and the People's Congress are gaining as outlets for the expression of grievances.

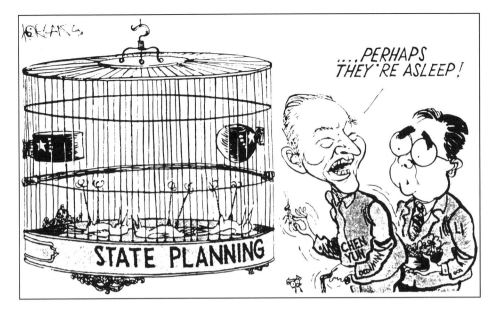

Figure 10.6   Chen Yun, a staunch conservative who engineered China's economic recovery after the Cultural Revolution, gained renewed prominence after the 1989 crackdown, but he could not re-invigorate state industries.

with greater pluralism, demands for more fundamental political change will become a permanent feature of the Chinese political debate. Over the distant future, it is not inconceivable that, if economic reform can be sustained, China will also evolve, if gradually and haltingly, toward a more pluralistic political order.[5]

♦   ♦   ♦

THE CHINESE ECONOMIC SYSTEM TODAY

— by Robert F. Dernberger

Two basic questions remain: To what extent has the economic reform program created a new and different economic system in China and to what extent has it solved some of China's basic, long-term economic problems? The changes in China's basic economic institutions and policies have been too significant and cumulative to be regarded as just temporary deviations from the traditional Soviet-type system. On the other hand, many of the most basic institutions remain in

place with the role they had in the traditional system.

The four types of ownership — individual, private, cooperative, and state — exist in almost every sector of the economy, but the state sector dominates production for most sectors except agriculture. On the other hand, the economic reform program significantly reduced the control of the central planners and enhanced the authority of local officials and cadre. More important, the decentralization movement was accompanied by a serious attempt to remove some economic activity from the state and planned sectors altogether. This process of systemic change has progressed to the point where China's economic system can no longer be described as a centrally planned or Soviet-type economic system.

On the other hand, China's leaders assert that they will not allow a capitalist, market economic system to return, and they appear to be serious in their efforts to seek a truly mixed system — a "socialist system with Chinese characteristics." Their present economic system does represent a mixed system, but one in which state-planned or controlled economic activities still dominate, at least outside the agricultural sector. A rather lengthy period of unstable relations between the remaining elements of the traditional system and the elements of the expanding nonstate sectors may lie ahead.

Much of the reform movement involved the removal of constraints imposed on the economy in the past, not the building of a new economic system. When instability or imbalances occurred as a result of this liberalization, however, constraints and controls were reimposed. Acknowledging that the state-planned sector still dominates the industrial sector, some observers argued that by allowing and encouraging enterprises to engage in activity outside the plan, they would "grow" out of the state-planned system and create a new economic system. Yet, several fundamental reforms remained to be adopted before the economy could achieve that objective.

Necessary Reforms

In the 1980s Chinese leaders agreed that price reform would be needed for the economic reform program to really obtain the results desired. Yet, the existing price system determines the distribution of income for individuals, units of production, and units of government; and any change will redistribute income, creating winners and losers. Thus, the Chinese tried to introduce price reform on a marginal basis with small changes for a few items, giving subsidies to those who would be hurt. Although the Chinese leadership admitted the need to reform the price system, it continually stalled, postponed, temporized, and largely avoided this major step necessary for the creation of a new and efficient economic system. Subsidies may have been useful in cushioning the blows inflicted on certain groups by the economic reforms, but the state can hardly afford to continue them at levels reached by 1990.

A second fundamental reform must come in factor markets (markets for capital, labor, and land). To facilitate the needed restructuring of the economy, it will be necessary to allow a new level of "fluidity" among these factors so that new production facilities can be created in areas where they are needed while other, obsolete ones are close down.

The Chinese authorities must develop the indirect levers they plan to rely on to control and guide the economy: effective monetary and fiscal policies. Again, they are well aware of the need for these indirect controls over the economy and have actively sought advice from those more experienced with them. Nonetheless, monetary and fiscal policy in China remains very poorly developed.

The 1980s witnessed the successful first stage of economic reform which largely consisted of removing constraints and prohibitions on the various economic agents. Yet, at the beginning of the 1990s, the reform of the price system, the creation of factor markets, the significant reduction of subsidies in consumption and production, the closing of unprofitable and inefficient enterprises, and the creation of effective monetary and fiscal policies remain as challenges. These steps, if taken, would require even more political courage and will than did the first stage and would not yield the instant success experienced in the first. Furthermore, they would encounter significant opposition by those who would lose as a result of these reforms, more so than was true during the first stage of the reform program.

Fundamental Economic Problems

No economy is without serious inefficiencies, many due to the ideological and political preferences of the society. Although China faces budget deficits, foreign exchange shortages, inflation, and probably the inability to sustain as high an average growth rate as over the past decade, its short-term growth potential has considerably improved. The Chinese probably can look forward to favorable economic development and growth over the coming decade or two. However, China's fundamental, long-term economic problems remain to be solved.

Future growth will differ from the growth of the past in a very significant way. The economic reform program encouraged the development of growth nodes, areas that are capable of fast growth. The coastal regions will develop more rapidly and engage in foreign trade more than the interior regions, which are being developed as bases for raw material supplies and consumer goods industries. As a result of this change in strategy, coastal areas such as the Liaoning Peninsula, the Beijing-Tianjin region, the lower

Yangzi river basin and Shanghai, and the Pearl River delta in Guangdong have experienced an economic boom. These regions can be expected to sustain fairly high levels of growth. However, this development will not "trickle down" to the approximately one-third of the population and two-thirds of the area of China outside the growth nodes until well into the future.

In the long run the Chinese face several other fundamental economic problems — agricultural development, employment opportunities, urbanization, and production of competitive products. The amount of arable land is limited, and it is being reduced as urban and industrial development spreads and major water control and hydroelectric projects are completed. Some economists believe the Chinese have already lost their comparative advantage in agricultural products and will need to rely on imports of agricultural products as China becomes a developed country. Even so, the Chinese still must make the transition to more productive scientific or modern farming, and this transition will take time, as the land area and agricultural population to undergo this transformation are very large.

As agricultural modernization takes place, it will free workers for noncrop activities. The Chinese already estimate that they have a surplus rural population of more than 100 million peasants. Thus, the nonagricultural and nonrural sectors of the economy must absorb labor on a tremendous scale well into the twenty-first century. Part of this employment problem is that the surplus labor exists in areas where the alternative employment opportunities are the most difficult to provide. Urban centers along the coast will absorb some of the surplus workers, but that increase in employment could easily come from the growing urban population. What would resolve this problem is the development of an extensive network of urban centers of varying sizes, that is, the urbanization of China. The need to rebuild China's existing cities, modernize them, and develop new urban centers to keep pace with China's development will be a major drain on the resources available for development and cannot be accomplished overnight.

Since China opened its economy to acquire modern technology from abroad, the Chinese have needed to promote their exports to earn foreign exchange. To become truly competitive and win markets in the hard currency countries, the Chinese must make up for past mistakes or neglect in product quality, marketing, and product innovation — areas in which they are very weak. Competition among the developing countries in the import markets of the developed countries is intense, and China's current practice is to meet that competition through price cutting, a technique that works best in markets for homogeneous products such as raw materials and textiles. Where the demand is for quality, servicing and new products, this form of competition is not viable in the long run and threatens to give China a reputation as a cheap, but low-quality supplier.

These four major problems — agricultural development, employment creation, urbanization, and production of manufactured commodities competitive on the international market — are typical of the process of modernization and growth. Therefore, there is no reason to believe that China cannot become a major world economic power and developed economy in the long run. However, the question is to what extent has the economic reform program helped solve these problems or made them worse. A detailed analysis addressing this issue cannot be presented here, but it is worth noting that the reform program was specifically designed to address China's short-term economic problems; and in several ways, it worked to worsen China's long-term economic problems or, at least, delay their ultimate solution.[6]

◆　　　◆　　　◆

EDITOR'S POSTSCRIPT

By late 1990, the extent to which economic reform had altered China's economy became apparent in the struggle to develop a new 5-Year Plan for 1991-95. The classic tensions between the provinces and the central government in Beijing, cited in previous chapters, now arose with a new and startling visibility as provincial leaders began to assert the fiscal leverage given to them as a result of the previous decade of reforms. Guangdong province, next to Hong Kong, was

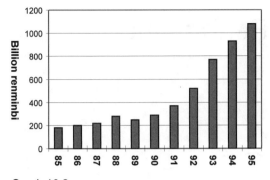

Graph 10.3

State enterprises consume more government investment...

... and employ record numbers of workers...

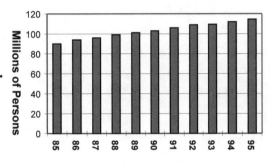

Graph 10.4

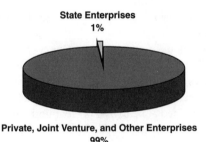

**State Enterprises
1%**

**Private, Joint Venture, and Other Enterprises
99%**

... but generate about 1% of China's industrial profits.

Graph 10.5

perhaps the most brazen in its defiance of the authorities in Beijing, ignoring most of the central-planning directives handed down to it. Other coastal provinces such as Zhejiang, Jiangsu, Liaoning and port cities such as Shanghai and Tianjin demonstrated varying degrees of independence as well.

The source of the provincial authorities' newfound strength was similar to that enjoyed by their historic predecessors in the waning years of the Qing Dynasty: independent revenues. Under Zhao Ziyang's reforms, the provinces were allowed to retain far greater shares of state-enterprise profits

and to control major shares of the raw materials and goods generated locally. Combined with a corrupt tax system that siphoned off and underreported what it owed to the central government, the drop-off in revenues to Beijing was dramatic. In 1978, the year before the economic reforms began, state enterprises contributed fully 75 percent of total state revenues. Raw materials were obtained at fixed low prices and the finished goods sold at fixed high prices, resulting in large "profits" to the enterprises which funded the government. These subsidies to state enterprises in 1978 totaled about 9 percent of government spending.

China: Events and Performance

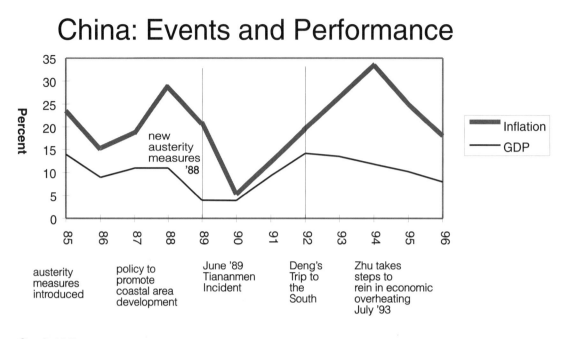

Graph 10.6

By 1990, the costs of supporting the loss-making enterprises had ballooned to nearly 32 percent of total government spending. Meanwhile, the sources of nearly half of Beijing's tax revenues, the wealthy coastal provinces, were effectively in charge of collecting and delivering their own taxes in whatever amounts their very "leaky" systems would bear.

Inter-provincial rivalries also began to crop up, particularly from the poorer interior provinces, and were not easily controlled by the Beijing authorities. Yet all the provinces remained aware of the fact that Beijing could not be defied without considerable political risk nor could its Five-Year Plan, with its decisions about the allocation of resources and major infrastructure projects, be ignored. Backed by the army, the Chinese Communist Party remained a force to contend with at any level of government.

As emphasized by Robert Dernberger in the preceding section, China confronts economic reform in four major areas: agriculture, employment, urbanization, and competitiveness. A fifth area affecting the other four, the environment, will be taken up in a later section of this chapter. Each area impinges directly or indirectly on the status

of state-owned industries which are a drag on China's economy and contribute a steadily declining share of GNP.

It was once assumed that China could "outgrow" the state-owned sector, but that now appears less likely. The share of government investment resources devoted to the state sector has remained at nearly 70 percent throughout the economic reform period. In fact, by the early 1990s employment in the state sector had expanded by 50 percent — an increase of nearly 40 million people. Most of China's urban population remain employed by the state. Before allowing the state industries to declare bankruptcy, China's leaders will need to find employment for the urban workers. The Party recognizes the danger of allowing unemployment to soar in cities where the potential for political volatility is greatest. The state-owned industries are under pressure to become profitable but the sector continues to receive massive subsidies. Most of its industries remain uncompetitive in the global economy. This lack of competitiveness, in turn, underlies China's trade protectionist policies, thus contributing to friction with its major trading partners. Rural areas, by contrast, have seen a rapid expansion of private enterprise. By the year 2000, China's government estimates that 70 million people in China will be working for private enterprise out of a total working population of 800 million.

◆   ◆   ◆

DEMOGRAPHIC AND SOCIAL CHANGE

— by William Lavely

No government in history has more actively intervened in population matters as has China in the past four decades, nor has any population policy been marked by such tremendous swings. Historically hostile to "Malthusian" birth control measures, China has embraced the most radical, yet successful, fertility control policies in the world. At the same time, policies that restricted peasants to the land and successfully slowed the rate of urban growth have given way to the active encouragement of rural-to-urban migration. Together, the current policies of fertility control and rapid urbanization are producing a demographic revolution that has important implications for China's economy and social structure.

China's reversal in birth control policy was in reaction to the legacy of earlier demographic policies and the demands of the current economic restructuring. China has a large, young population with considerable growth "momentum" as a result of the lack of effective birth control policies in the 1950s and 1960s. Even at the current low fertility rate, China's population has a net growth of about 14 million per year. In the decade following the inception in 1979 of the policy that encourages one child per couple, China's population increased by about 130 million, over one-half the population of the United States. In the next two decades, China's population is likely to increase by another 200 million, assuming that the fertility rate continues downward.

These projections are particularly alarming to China's leaders because population growth will

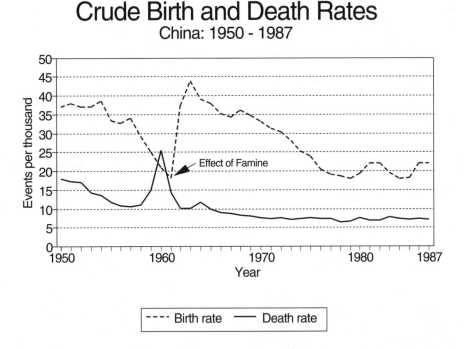

Crude Birth and Death Rates
China: 1950 - 1987

Graph 10.7

China's Total Population
Selected Years

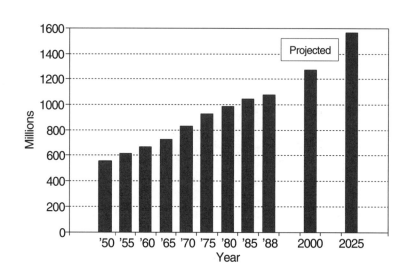

Graph 10.8

seriously complicate the process of their program of economic and political reforms. For a number of reasons, population growth placed few obvious strains on the economic institutions of Maoist China. The rural economy placed little demand on the state budget. The rural collectives absorbed new workers by continuously redividing the income and tasks, thereby providing a social and economic niche for all members. The relative stagnation of the rural economy and the thinly disguised unemployment were tolerable politically because the collective provided essential elements that legitimated Maoist rule: economic equality and a modicum of economic security. In other words, rural population growth could take care of itself, while the government diligently controlled the more burdensome problem of urban population growth. This was accomplished through control of both urban fertility and rural-to-urban migration.

By contrast, the economic structures and political commitments of the reform period are quite unforgiving of population growth. In dismantling the rural collectives and replacing them with family-managed farms, the post-Mao reformers have placed economic growth and efficiency above equality as a prime virtue. The reformers, like other Asian government leaders, are staking their legitimacy on improved living standards and increased income per capita. Slower population growth is a common denominator of these goals.

The harsh one-child policy is a measure of the reformers' determination to limit population growth. Although falling considerably short of the one-child goal, the policy has successfully held the birth rate to low levels. But the policy's consequences can be expected to range far beyond the simple economic outcomes envisioned by its authors. Low fertility is creating a population revolution in China that should eventually alter prospects for employment, family structure, and welfare for the elderly.

The new economic strategy also implies large-scale population mobility. The government estimates that a large part of the rural labor force is underemployed, and this group is being encouraged to take jobs outside the agricultural sector. It is projected that the agricultural labor force will contract gradually and the nonagricultural labor force will nearly double by the year

2000. By then, it is projected that over one-half of China's population will be engaged in nonagricultural occupations.

The movement out of agriculture entails the creation of new jobs and massive movement of workers to cities and towns. Most of these migrants represent a new "third category" of worker, distinguished from urban workers in the state sector and farmers by the fact that they enjoy neither the economic guarantees of state employment nor the security of the family farm. This growing class of the population lacks any guarantee of employment or safety net of social welfare. China's demography thus presents tremendous risks and challenges to those who must implement the new economic strategy.

China's Demographic Transition

China's leaders do not view China's population as a natural force, like the weather, to which they can only react. They are committed to the proposition that population growth and distribution, like economic output, can be planned and influenced by administrative means. This view may be in part a legacy of China's imperial history of state-sponsored migrations and elaborate mechanisms for the enumeration and the control of population. Their confidence in administrative intervention is no doubt reinforced by their success in recent decades in reducing mortality, controlling migration to urban areas, raising literacy levels, and developing policy to plan births.

The effects of government intervention are evident in the vital statistics of the past 35 years. During this period, China experienced a demographic transition from high to low birth and death rates. The death rate fell rapidly in the 1950s, from about twenty per thousand in 1949 to eleven per thousand in 1958. The decline was punctuated by the three-year (1959-61) famine that followed the Great Leap Forward campaign, which caused approximately 30 million deaths. After the famine, mortality resumed its downward trend and levelled off at a low of nine deaths per thousand in the 1970s.

The decline in the death rate is not unprecedented but is nonetheless unusual for such a large and poor population. This decline depended on the same imported public health technologies that have reduced mortality elsewhere in the Third World — improved sanitation and water supplies, pest control, and vaccination programs — but it was only accomplished by unusually high levels of government investment in public health and by harnessing China's vast administrative and organizational resources. Mass health education campaigns, an emphasis on public health and preventive medicine rather than curative medicine, and a large network of semiprofessional midwives and "barefoot doctors" were among the innovations that produced the decline.

It is plausible that a mortality transition would have occurred in China with far less government intervention, but without it, it seems unlikely that the death rate would have declined so far or so fast. In 1981, the Chinese reached a life expectancy of 68 years, a level more typical of countries with three to four times China's per capita gross national product (GNP).

The decline of the death rate was rapid, but the decline of the birth rate has been spectacular. The crude birth rate fell from 33 per thousand in 1970 to 18 per thousand in 1979, down nearly 50 percent in a decade. This is the fastest fertility decline on record for any large population, but it was exceeded by major subpopulations. For example, in rural Sichuan province, in the mid-1970s fertility declined 50 percent in just three years.

The causes of this decline are complex. One explanation points to China's record of rapid social change. In other countries, declines in fertility have often been preceded by reductions in the death rate, increased levels of educational attainment, and other fundamental changes in family and economy. China had achieved all of these prerequisites. Mortality had declined, the rural economy had been reorganized through collectivization, and, in the process, considerable economic risk had been transferred from the family to the community. Moreover, education had moved deep into rural areas, and female illiteracy was on its way to being eradicated.

Although such developmental factors were probably important, the speed and character of the Chinese fertility decline argue strongly for the role of government intervention. Rising educational levels, for example, have had only a minor direct effect on the fertility decline. The fertility of illiterate women has also declined spectacularly and virtually simultaneously with the better educated.

China's unique birth planning policies also suggest the role of government in the fertility decline. In 1970 China launched a policy of "late marriage, child spacing, and fewer children" (*wan, xi, shao*), a program that relied strongly on administrative intervention. Under the program, registrars declined to issue marriage licenses to couples below the government's suggested age for marriage, births in factories and rural communities were allocated annually according to quotas, and a network of birth-planning workers actively discouraged women from having more than two children. These efforts were apparently quite effective.

Fertility Policy in the Post-Mao Era

China's fertility control policy was radical by international standards, even in the early 1970s, the waning years of the Maoist era. In the post-Mao period, birth control became a top priority; and with the launching of the one-child-per couple policy in 1979, China could clearly lay claim to the most radical family planning policy in the world. The policy was prompted by projections that even at two children per couple (replacement level fertility), China's population would continue to grow rapidly into the next century. Due to the high fertility rates of the past, particularly in the 1960s and early 1970s, China's population had considerable growth momentum. About 180 million females were born in China between the end of the great famine and 1975. If each of them gave birth to a single child by age 24, this would add nearly 180 million births by 1999. But, of course, no one expected them to stop at only one. These prospects threatened the reformers' plan to quadruple the per capita GNP by the end of the century. With the goal of holding China's population to 1.2 billion by the year 2000 and achieving zero population growth thereafter, they promulgated a policy in 1979 that could attain that goal: one child per couple.

The implementation of the policy draws on the powerful administrative resources available to the Chinese state. Particularly in cities, where most employees work in state enterprises, government officials use numerous administrative means to reward those who conform to the policy and punish those who do not. In theory, the policy depends on positive incentives to win compliance: couples signing a one-child pledge gain benefits, including longer maternity leave, wage supplements, and special school privileges for their single child. In practice, there is a far broader range of informal sanctions that can be brought to bear on those who resist the policy, involving access to housing, raises, and promotions. As a result, compliance in cities has been high. In the first three years of the program from 1979 to 1981, 83 percent of the births in Chinese cities were first births, compared with 39 percent for rural births.

For a number of reasons, birth planning in rural areas had moved less steadily in the past decade. Most rural Chinese desire at least one son, a preference that makes a one-child family unacceptable to many. For some, this desire is motivated by the religious imperative to carry on the family line, but for others there are economic and social imperatives — a son is needed to manage the family farm and provide support in old age. Daughters are seen as less able to fulfill this role because they generally move to their husband's residence at marriage. The government's means of enforcement are also weaker in rural areas. Under decollectivization, most rural Chinese have become independent farmers and entrepreneurs, relatively impervious to economic sanctions. At the same time, the network of local cadres that formerly linked the central government to the peasant households has largely dissipated.

As a result, implementation of the one-child policy in rural areas has vacillated between draconian enforcement and relaxation. Mass sterilizations, IUD insertions, and coerced abortions have been used during times of rigid enforcement, particularly in 1983. However, there has been a policy shift toward moderation in recent years. National guidelines established in 1984 stressed that coercion must be avoided and set forth a number of exceptions to the one-child rule. Relaxed control of marriage is another hallmark of 1980s policy that has caused fertility to rise. Still, the total fertility rate has remained at or below 2.5 for most of the decade. Some relaxation of the one-child policy has occurred, including, since 1988 in many provinces, a rule permitting rural couples whose first child is a girl to have a second child. At the same time, third and higher-order births have become an increasingly rare phenomenon.

It is difficult to measure the extent of volunteerism in the Chinese birth-planning program. A number of recent surveys suggest that rural Chinese couples have family size preferences ranging between two and three children, low for a poor agrarian society but still above the prescribed limit. To the extent that fertility is held at low levels involuntarily, the task of administering the birth-planning program is complicated. The program has concentrated on passive contraceptive methods. About half of the couples using contraception are sterilized, and another 40 percent use the IUD. Regulations and propaganda against "illegal" IUD removal suggest that not all contraceptive use is voluntary.

Chinese officials have clearly retreated from their ambitious goals of a few years ago. The one-child policy is now largely an urban phenomenon; in most rural areas, the actual policy is to maintain the rate at two children per couple. It now appears that China's population will exceed 1.3 billion by the year 2000, 100 million over target. Still, the achievements of the birth-planning policy must be put in perspective — even the current total fertility rate of 2.5 children per women implies a level far below the norm for a nation of China's income. If fertility can be held at present levels, the Chinese fertility decline must be viewed as an unprecedented feat of social engineering.

Migration and Urbanization

The current movement of population out of agriculture marks one of the most momentous revolutions in China's modern history. Since the mid-1950s until recently, the Chinese government sought to keep the peasants on the land and to keep the urban portion of the total population from

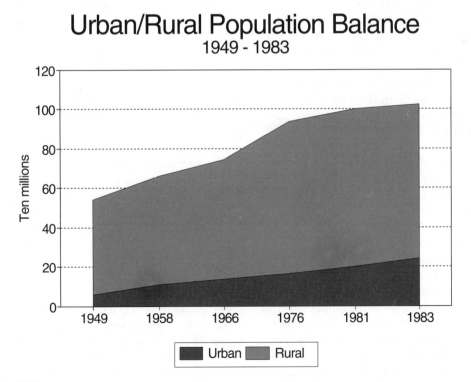

Urban/Rural Population Balance
1949 - 1983

Graph 10.9

growing. The policy was quite successful; the urban population remained at roughly 20 percent of the total between 1960 and 1980. However, the urban population increased rapidly in the past decade, and continued growth is expected through the end of the century.

The term urbanization often conjures up an image of growth in cities, but much of China's "urban" growth is in an intermediate sector that is neither city nor farm. The urbanization trend is largely fueled by peasants who leave the land to ply trades in market centers in rural areas and by the redefinition of many of these centers as towns. While the change may not represent a shift to urban modernity for most, it nonetheless marks a rapid and momentous transition of an agricultural society toward a fundamentally nonagricultural way of life.

The Reformers and Urbanization

In a sharp reversal of Maoist policy, the reformers sought to increase agricultural productivity by encouraging excess labor to leave agriculture. Urbanization was actively promoted and perceived as inevitable. Thousands of new towns were thrown open for rural migrants to pursue industrial and service occupations. The result was a large-scale exodus from agriculture. Village markets and county towns, moribund in the Mao era, now have the most dynamic and volatile populations in China. The number of towns grew from 2,800 in 1982 to nearly 10,000 by 1989 with the aggregate population growing from about 66 million to over 200 million. A large part of this growth is due to the redefinition of towns, but much of it was due to actual migration. Official statistics now put China's urban proportion at over 40 percent, but this figure includes many agricultural workers who are resident in sprawling areas officially designated as "urban." By definitions consistent with past practices, the urban proportion is now approximately 25 percent.

Migration to major cities has clearly grown in recent years. The growth rate of China's major urban centers lags behind that of major Third World cities, but this is largely because of the low birth rate in Chinese cities. City populations are swollen by a substantial "floating population" of temporary migrants who lack permanent urban registration. Recent surveys indicate that the floating population makes up approximately 10 percent of the urban population of Beijing and Shanghai.

China's current urbanization is a large-scale transformation. The shifts of population out of agricultural pursuits means that the world's largest and oldest agrarian state is on its way to becoming a predominately nonagricultural society.

Employment

The rapid fertility decline and the urbanization movement will influence China's demography for decades, affecting employment, schooling, family relations, and old age welfare.

Two demographic facts overshadow the employment situation and imply the need for millions of new jobs. First, the large youthful population, the legacy of past fertility, swells the yearly numbers of first-time job seekers far beyond the numbers retiring. Second, the population is moving out of agricultural occupations.

Under the assumption that urbanization will rise to 50 percent by the end of the century and that current labor force participation rates remain fixed, a recent U.S. Census Bureau study projects that in China between 1985 and 2000, the number of rural workers will decline from 362 million to 333 million, while the urban workforce will rise from 208 to 384 million, an 85 percent increase.

According to this projection, 176 million new urban jobs would need to be created between 1985 and 2000. An economic reversal could slow the rate of urbanization because the movement out of agriculture is partly demand driven. If this demand should slacken, the rate of urbanization is likely to decrease as well. Some decrease in participation rates is also expected; female participation may decline as some women return to the roles of housewife and mother. But should the economic boom falter, high rates of urban unemployment could result.

Unemployment is a particular danger for the self-employed entrepreneurs and tradesmen of the new towns, the third category of workers who lack the basic guarantees of jobs and housing enjoyed by state employees. As yet the new towns can provide little in the way of an economic safety net.

The urbanization transition and the demographically driven demand for jobs thus contain the potential for hardship and unrest should China experience a recession.

The present period is critical because of the large number of people born in the early 1970s who are now reaching employment age. The pressure should diminish as the number of those born in the late 1970s and reaching employment age in the early 1990s is smaller. In 1988 China had about 123 million people in the 15-19-year-old group. By 1995 this fell sharply to around 95 million and is projected to continue to decline gradually until it peaks again in 2010, reflecting projected births in the early 1990s, an "echo" of the high fertility rate of the late 1960s. By the late 1990s, the problem of large annual numbers of first-time jobs seekers should stabilize.

Dependency

A large proportion of China's population is of working age because of the rapid fertility decline.

Therefore, the age structure of China is now quite conducive to economic productivity and should remain so for at least two decades. If fertility remains low, however, China's population will age significantly early in the next century, and by the middle of the next century, China will have to adapt to a large elderly population.

The dependency ratio, defined as the ratio of population 0 to 14-years old and 65 and over to the population that is 15 to 64-years old, has fallen sharply in the past two decades. This ratio fell from 0.78 in 1970 to 0.53 in 1985, owing entirely to a reduction in the population under age 15. A projection, assuming a total fertility rate of 1.75 births per woman beginning in 1990, shows the dependency ratio continuing to decline, from 0.44 in 1990 to a low of 0.36 in 2015, and then rising slightly. The easing of the dependency burden is entirely because of the smaller proportion of children in the population. The proportion of the population age 65 and over rises from 5.6 to 9.1 percent by 2015.

Although the dependency ratio rises toward the middle of the next century, it never attains the

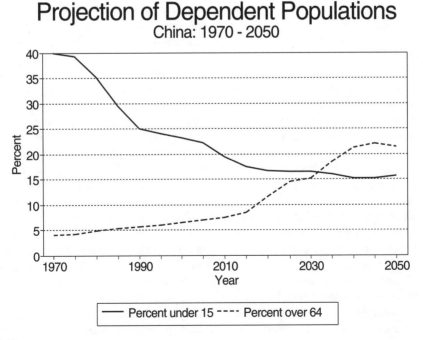

Projection of Dependent Populations
China: 1970 - 2050

Graph 10.10

levels that China experienced in the 1970s. However, the nature of dependency changes radically. Whereas in 1970 the elderly accounted for one-tenth of the dependent population, in 2050 the elderly would account for more than half. By the year 2040, 21 percent of Chinese would be over age 65. To put this in perspective, in the United States currently about 12 percent of the population is over age 65 , and in Sweden, which has the world's highest share of senior citizens, about 18 percent is over age 65.

This shift in China's age structure has a number of implications. By early in the next century, China's population will begin to resemble those of contemporary Europe. The number of people annually seeking jobs will become relatively small, and the labor market can be expected to tighten as the number of annual retirements begins to exceed the number of entrants. But an older age structure also has costs. The support of elderly dependents is far more expensive than for young dependents, and the returns to society are far less. As China's population ages, it can be expected to become more conservative and less adaptive to change. In the coming decades, China will need to develop an extensive welfare apparatus to support and care for the retiring population and devote an increasing proportion of resources to this end.

The Family

China's population policies are having a profound influence on family structure, family relations, and the status of women. Fertility declines change the family. Smaller families are conducive to equality between spouses. Released from many of the child-rearing tasks that formerly occupied most of their married lives, women are free to devote themselves to economically productive pursuits that enhance their status within the family.

It is also plausible that lower fertility alters the relationship between parent and child. Fertility transitions generally mark a divide between a traditional and modern outlook on childbearing. As modernization brings reduced mortality and a more secure environment, children are seen less as an economic asset than as an end in themselves. And as the number of children declines from five or six to one or two, parents become more able and willing to invest time and economic resources in their offspring. Couples who are limited to one or two children are likely to view these children differently than they would a larger brood, and fathers may be more likely to take an active role in their children's upbringing.

Smaller families thus hold the potential for substantial change in socialization and personality. Chinese children growing up in a traditional extended family learn their roles in relation to a hierarchy of siblings, cousins, and other kin; and group-oriented behavior and cooperation is learned early. The urban single child, by contrast, is generally the sole focus of parental attention. The implications for behavior and personality are uncertain. Popular reports in the Chinese press have stressed the negative aspects of one-child socialization, raising the possibility that the next generation of Chinese will be more individualistic and self-centered. But recent studies suggest that personality and academic achievement of single children are at least the equal of children with siblings.

In the long run, low fertility will simplify Chinese family and kinship. In urban China, where the single child family may be the norm for years to come, terms such as *brother* and *sister* will eventually be seldom used except among migrants from rural areas, and other terms for collateral relations, such as cousins and uncles, will also fall into disuse. The decline of collateral kin will paradoxically tend to focus family relations more on vertical, parent-child ties. Although welfare programs could assume the economic burden of the elderly, parents may increasingly look to their single child for emotional sustenance in their old age. Many Chinese couples must adapt to a new vision of the future in which old-age security cannot be guaranteed by their children.

Decollectivization of agriculture has also influenced the family, but the effects are paradoxical. Kinsmen once tied to the same collective soil are now pursuing a variety of occupations far from their native village. At the same time, the reestablishment of the family household as the center of economic management and entrepreneurship is lending new solidarity to the family. These conflicting forces are producing a greater variety of family forms and relationships.

The Prospects for Population Growth

The legacy of the pro-natalism of the 1950s and 1960s poses a difficult dilemma for the Chinese people and their leaders — a classic case of conflict between public and private good. It may be quite rational for individuals to desire three or four children and feel that being limited to one or two is a costly hardship. But according to the macroeconomic calculations of China's leaders, free choice in reproductive matters would bring disaster. China's economic prospects, and, indeed, the shape and tenor of Chinese society in the next century, are crucially dependent on the outcome of current efforts to control fertility.

Should China's fertility control program continue to be successful, China's population could grow to between 1.4 and 1.6 billion in the year 2025. If the program breaks down and Chinese couples return to bearing an average of three to four children, as they did in the early 1970s, China's population could conceivably rise to over 2 billion by the year 2025.

Consistency and continuity in fertility policy is one of the keys to future success. Since China's fertility levels are maintained through administrative pressure, there is the potential for a sudden and possibly disastrous "decompression." A number of recent surveys indicate that Chinese would prefer to have more children then they are now having. If just a quarter of China's women in their reproductive years gave birth in one year — a theoretical possibility despite China's high rates of sterilization — there would be 50 million births.

The economic reforms have complicated the task. By permitting peasants to become independent farmers and entrepreneurs, the reforms have possibly increased the value of children to some. More serious, though, is that the reforms have undermined enforcement of the fertility policy. The central government no longer has the far-reaching administrative apparatus that formerly linked it to the grassroots. Nearly one-third of Chinese villages lack a family-planning worker. Local leaders no longer have the array of administrative sanctions that were available under the collective. The greater mobility of the population is also a problem. The large floating population of people residing away from their legal residence has been able to reproduce with relative impunity.

Birth-planning policies are only just beginning to catch up with these developments. For example, new regulations that require temporary migrants to present family-planning documents when they depart their village and when they take jobs in urban areas are now in place.

Under the reformers, economic and social life was liberalized to a very great degree. Reproduction is the only aspect of life that has actually become more restrictive than it was in the Mao era. One might say that the government purchased cooperation in family planning with other freedoms and affluence. By the same token, a reversal of economic fortunes could be the undoing of the fertility control program on which so much else depends.[7]

♦   ♦   ♦

CHINA'S ENVIRONMENTAL CRISIS

The foregoing discussion of population underlies what has become a matter of spreading concern in China: an environmental crisis of unprecedented scale. Far from having reached a peak during the investment and building boom of the 1990s, the environmental predicament has grown, even if it has not received the national and global attention it warrants. Population growth will add yet another 125 million people to the country in the 1990s. This bow wave of expanding population will place still more pressure on an already strained environment.

Simplistic predictions of future Chinese prosperity, based on patterns of growth, production, and consumption in successful Asian economies such as Korea, have been used to suggest that China will repeat all growth characteristics of the "Asian tigers." As a result, ominous pictures of China's global impact have emerged, such as futurist Lester Brown's suggestion in the early 1990s that, based on straight line projections, China's population will consume most of the global grain production in the next century. This and other doomsday scenarios will continue to be debated as the extent of China's environmental limitations become better known, but the outcomes are more complex than is commonly assumed.

China has not ignored the problem. It enacted several broad environmental laws and has created some new regulatory authorities to enforce them. Whether this will result in reliable, long term enforcement remains to be seen, but in view of the vast scale of the problem, the near term objective will be simply to reduce the momentum of the environmental decline, not halt or reverse it. In *China's Environmental Crisis*, Vaclav Smil, a Canadian geographer with extensive knowledge of China's environmental problems, provides a comprehensive overview of the debacle. While Smil has suggested elsewhere that Lester Brown's alarmist predictions about rising levels of Chinese grain consumption are likely to be exaggerated, he is not so sanguine about the larger trend of environmental degradation in China. The following passage from his path-breaking book describes the nature of the challenge.

REALITIES AND ASPIRATIONS

— by Vaclav Smil

It cannot be, when the root is neglected, that what should spring from it will be well ordered.
— The Great Learning

China's environmental predicament is made much more acute by a restrictive synergy of natural endowment and human action. Intensifying economic production depletes natural resources whose per capita availability would be quite limited even should the country have a stationary population. Progressing ecosystemic degradation affects natural services whose provision, owing both to the country's climatic and geomorphic peculiarities and to its long history of deforestation and intensive farming, would be recurrently impaired even without further onslaughts. Resulting realities are stunning in their magnitudes, effects, and potential implications: a few paragraphs will reiterate the critical weaknesses.

Land, the irreplaceable foundation of China's food production, is degrading in many ways. Soil erosion incompatible with sustainable farming is affecting at least one-third of China's fields; desertification and toxification have much

smaller nationwide impacts but are of growing regional and local importance; the combination of such degradative processes and takeovers for housing and industries is diminishing the arable land by an annual rate of nearly 0.5 percent (yet already among the populous poor nations only Bangladesh and Egypt have less farmland per capita than China); inadequate crop residue and manure recycling and less frequent and simpler crop rotations are depriving the soils of essential organic matter; and unbalanced use of synthetic fertilizers leads to substantial nutrient losses.

Highly unequal distribution of water resources means that densely populated northern China, a territory producing 40 percent of the nation's food and nearly half of all industrial output, receives a mere quarter of all precipitation and can draw on less than 10 percent of all stream runoff. During the 1980s not only countless small reservoirs but even many major storages in the region dried up, as did numerous rivers. Yet the region's inefficient irrigation wastes commonly more than half of the increasingly scarce water, and modernization plans call for enormous volumes of water for thermal electricity generation, further intensification of farming, and urban housing.

The long history of massive deforestation has not been reversed during the past two generations. Instead of moving toward a long-term goal of 20-25 percent forest coverage, the opposite happened, as all of the still relatively richly forested provinces (above all Sichuan, Yunnan, and Hainan) lost between a third and two-thirds of remaining tree cover in just forty years, as the area of mature forests decreased by one-third in just seven years between 1982 and 1989, and as the current wood removal is about $100 \, \text{Mm}^3$ above the sustainable rate. There is a very real chance that the country will have no mature natural forests to cut by the year 2000; neither will it have a sufficient volume of new plantings ready for harvesting.

China's comparative success in achieving adequate average provision of basic nutrition is marred by the realization that much of this food output comes from unsustainable farming. Too much monocropping, too few crop rotations, inadequate cultivation of legumes, drastically reduced organic matter recycling, unbalanced fertilization, and very high levels of nitrogen applications are all major concerns.

Additional Annual Output Required by the Year 2000

	Additional output at 1990 per capita level, and with 2 percent growth per year	Comparable to the 1990 output of:
GNP ($billion 1980)	160	Netherlands
	520	Brazil and Spain
Primary energy	110	Brazil
	360	India and Brazil
Coal mining (Mt)	110	United Kingdom
	360	India and S. Africa
Electricity (TWh)	65	Pakistan and Malaysia
	215	Brazil
Steel (Mt)	7	Australia
	23	Italy
Cement (Mt)	25	Brazil
	80	Japan
Grain (Mt)	45	Canada
	100	Africa
Nitrogen (Mt)	3	Canada
	10	Japan

Table 10.1

Similarly, China's relatively high (in comparison with other populous poor countries) per capita output of fossil fuels and electricity hides the enormous, and environmentally crippling, rural energy shortages and is the source of extensive land losses and pollution, above all the huge emissions of particulate matter and sulphur dioxide, SO_2. Should the anthropogenic planetary warming become an unmistakable reality, rather than a serious potential concern, China's rising generation of CO_2 and other greenhouse gases would make it the world's largest emitter sometime during the second decade of the next century — and so inevitably a prominent target of global pressure.

Assessed against this background, China's modernization plans guarantee further extensive environmental deterioration, destruction, and pollution. Merely to maintain per capita consumption at the 1990 level for the 125 million people born during the 1990s, production of an additional 110 million tons of coal equivalent (Mtce) of primary energy, 110 million tons (Mt) of raw coal, 25 Mt of cement, and nearly 50 Mt of grain would be required by the year 2000.

A modest average per capita consumption increase of 2 percent a year for the whole population would more than treble these totals, and comparisons of required output increment with appropriate existing national totals show the enormity of additional stress to be put on China's resources by the year 2000 (Table 10.1). In most cases, attainment of modernization goals for the year 2000 would require emplacement in just one decade of a variety of productive capacities equivalent to total national outputs of such populous nations as India or Indonesia, or such industrialized economies as Japan or Canada!

The environmental implications of these enormous gains will be far-reaching as the additional demand for living space, water, food, energy, and raw materials will accelerate ecosystemic degradation and inexorably diminish the per capita

Some Environmental Impacts of China's Economic Expansion During the 1990s

	Additional impacts at 1990 per capita output level, and with 2 percent per year growth	Country compared to (1990 totals)
Arable land loss (Mha)	3.4	Malaysia and Nepal
	6.0	Vietnam
Water needs (Gt^3)	60	Egypt
	90	Mexico
Particulate Emissions (Mt)	2.0	Canada
	6.5	United States
SO$_2$ emissions (Mt)	2.2	France
	7.2	Germany

Table 10.2

availability of already strained or restricted resource utilization. Table 10.2 lists some of these losses and degradations and again illustrates the magnitudes of these changes by equating them with some commensurate national totals.

These enormous losses, demands, and waste generation rates do not exclude some local improvements (such as reforestation of barren slopeland or better drinking water supplies) or some notable sectoral advances (for example, widespread installation of high-efficiency particulate emission controls in cement plants), but there is no doubt that the overall state of China's environment will be more precarious by the year 2000 than in 1990, and that this unfavorable trend will continue during the first decades of the new century.

China is obviously not alone in facing a prospect of continuing decline in the quality of its environment, nor is it alone in having to deal with it from a position of relative poverty and limited technical, research, and managerial capabilities. But its relatively limited natural resource endowment, the already dismal state of its environment, its huge and far from stabilized population, and the magnitude of its modernization plans present a uniquely incompatible combination.

There are no solutions within China's economic, technical, and manpower reach that could

halt and reverse these degradative trends, not only during the 1990s but also during the first decade of the new century. An outside observer must find the thought deeply disturbing. The reality for tens of millions of Chinese in the worst-affected areas will be a desperate effort to survive; for the nation as a whole, the continuing decline in environmental quality will mean a steady narrowing of future developmental options and inexorable lowering of possible goals. For the world, China's environmental debacle will be yet another intractable destabilizing factor.

But the rapidity of the future decline will make much individual and collective difference. Here lies the only realistic potential for effective action: future rates of China's environmental impacts can be reduced, often appreciably, by a combination of rational economic strategies, price reforms, technical innovations, managerial innovations, and better law enforcement. The success of these moves will not fundamentally change China's precarious environmental outlook, but it could ease immensely much of the human suffering and start the country on the path to an eventual recovery.[8]

◆   ◆   ◆

MAO'S REVOLUTION AND
CHINESE CULTURE

— by Martin Whyte

It would be oversimplifying things to view the period of Mao's rule as an overall assault on traditional Chinese culture and the reform era as primarily a revival of this long-suppressed traditional culture. The reality is much more complex. Even though the CCP espoused a Western ideology, Marxism-Leninism, the establishment of the People's Republic in 1949 in no way constituted a victory for wholesale Westernization and a repudiation of traditional Chinese values. In certain very basic respects, Maoist rule emphasized fundamental Chinese traditions and defended these against rival Western ideas.

It may not be too far-fetched to argue that Maoism in power represented a last effort to defend traditional Chinese culture against Western cultural influence.

To be sure, the CCP was not simply a traditional dynasty disguised in Marxist-Leninist slogans. A variety of far-reaching institutional changes were made in Chinese society; many traditional customs and cultural practices (such as arranged marriages, burials, spirit mediums, and kowtowing to elders) were discouraged or banned; and new ideas, concepts, and cultural forms were forcefully introduced, in some cases in the face of popular resistance or incomprehension. Spoken dramas with factory workers as heroes, an emphasis on struggle and social class unity rather than on harmony and kinship solidarity, suppression of mercantile instincts, pronouncements that man was descended from apes, encouragement to call nonkin "comrade" and one's spouse "beloved," and many other new things about CCP rule took many, if not most, Chinese a while to become accustomed to. As a result, China became a very different kind of social order. There really was a CCP-led revolution in China.

But in certain respects Maoist rule was not really so iconoclastic and, in fact, was deeply rooted in Chinese tradition. Ancient Chinese assumptions about social order were built upon and reinforced, even though they began to be interpreted in Marxist-Leninist, rather than in

Confucian, terms. Society was conceived of as a vast bureaucratic hierarchy in which every individual was to have a place and be subordinated to the social group (now termed a collective) in which he or she was enmeshed. National unity was to be fostered by developing a coherent set of values (to which the specifically modern term ideology would apply) that would mandate how to behave, rather than by promulgating a national code of laws and administrative procedures. Primary duties of political leaders at every level, as in imperial China, were to maintain the coherence of the official ideology, to indoctrinate the population, and to enforce compliance. Any conception of autonomous subgroups, independent cultural innovation, or a freewheeling competition of ideas was directly contrary to the Maoist ethos, as it was to the traditional imperial doctrines.

So the content of the culture in Maoist China was in many ways new, but the idea that China required a uniform culture to survive as a nation and that the authorities should enforce an orthodoxy to maintain cultural, and thus political, cohesion was very old. Indeed, the vigor with which Mao and those around him imposed their new orthodoxy reflected the fact that their Marxist-Leninist convictions in this instance reinforced traditional Chinese assumptions. Socialism entails central planning and regulation not only of economic production but also of all social life, including culture and values. In contrast to traditional Chinese thought, the prevailing image of society in Marxism-Leninism is a society as a single, well-regulated factory, rather than as a hierarchical chain of human relationships, but the implications are much the same. There is one correct way for society to be organized, and cultural unity and officially imposed ideology play central roles in maintaining societal cohesion. Allowing alternative values and cultural practices would hinder the pursuit of socialism and communism and foster political disunity.

Enforcing a New Cultural Orthodoxy

In spite of the considerable overlap between traditional Chinese and Marxist-Leninist assumptions about cultural unity, there is also a basic difference in practice. The CCP, using modern technology, a huge central bureaucracy, and organizational practices learned from the Soviet Union, had the wherewithal to put these ideas into practice much more thoroughly than its imperial predecessors ever could have dreamed. The result was much tighter central control over schooling, the mass media, literature, the performing arts, social life, and even styles of dress and leisure activities. Even prior to the Cultural Revolution, the CCP had successfully used its increased powers to change traditional Chinese culture. From suppressing secret societies to campaigning against mah-jongg, from reforming Chinese opera plots to purging and standardizing school textbooks, all facets of Chinese cultural life witnessed the activist efforts of China's communist revolutionaries. Still, the goal was to forge a Chinese society united around a common set of values and ideas — a very traditional goal.

The Maoists used the power of the state vigorously to exclude Western cultural influences and, after 1960, even Soviet influence. More was involved than simply expelling foreigners in the 1950s and taking over the factories, schools, churches, hospitals, newspapers, and other property they had owned or controlled. Efforts were also made to restrict and control cultural influences from foreign movies and magazines and foreign travelers. In addition, there were campaigns against Western ideas and values that had gained a foothold in China in the previous century, such as enthusiasm for the rule of law, an autonomous press, and competing political parties, in an effort to stop the process referred to as "creeping Westernization."

The CCP did not exclude all foreign influences entirely (although during the Cultural Revolution it nearly did). Foreign influences penetrated China only in a manner that the government chose and on the government's terms. Western orchestras on tour and Western exchange students were allowed, whereas listening to foreign radio broadcasts and independent travel abroad were not. Special hotels, stores, and travel arrangements were developed in the 1950s under the pretext of shielding foreign visitors from the hardships of Chinese life, but their more basic purpose was to protect most of Chinese society from possible "contamination" by foreign guests. The desire of China's nineteenth century modern-

izing elite to carefully screen foreign influences and selectively admit only those elements deemed practical had eluded them but came much closer to being realized by their post-1949 successors.

Mao used the power of the state in an effort to forge a new cultural orthodoxy that would eliminate large parts of both the traditional inheritance and Western culture. The CCP had a greater ability to impose this new orthodoxy throughout China than any of its imperial predecessors. Yet, for all of the vigor with which this effort was pursued, it is now clear that it was only partially successful. Many values and practices that were attacked in Maoist China were only driven underground and did not disappear. And after Mao's death, as controls were being relaxed, both traditional and Western heterodox (in the Maoist view) influences began to resurface.

The Reforms and Chinese Culture

The death of Mao Zedong in 1976 and the implementation of the reform program by his successors produced a rethinking of all aspects of the Maoist social order. This, in turn, resulted in a reaction against the rigid and impoverished cultural straitjacket that characterized China during Mao's last decade in power. In most respects, the reformers allowed and encouraged a very broad cultural liberalization.

Writers were permitted to explore the dark side of society and to depict themes, such as romantic love and distaste for politics, that Mao's partisans had tried to ban during the Cultural Revolution. Artists were allowed to revive traditional styles and to experiment with a variety of Western forms, including abstract and surrealistic art. Freedom of religious belief and practice was reinstated, and Buddhist temples, Islamic mosques, and Christian churches were revived and refurbished with official approval and were to be staffed by both rehabilitated religious leaders and new graduates of reopened monasteries and seminaries. School curricula were revamped with a renewed emphasis on pure academics and the establishment of formerly proscribed or neglected fields, such as law, sociology, political science, and business management.

The mass media witnessed an explosion; a few tightly controlled and highly politicized publications were replaced by a bewildering variety of new, specialized journals, catering to those interested in calligraphy, classical Western music, the martial arts, weightlifting, and other decidedly nonpolitical realms. The effort to impose a uniform "proletarian drab" style of dress was repudiated, and a variety of clothing styles are now available, ranging from traditional Chinese slit-sided dresses to miniskirts and from "Mao jackets" to Western suits and ties. Formerly suppressed or discouraged hobbies and leisure pursuits ranging from tropical fish raising to stamp collecting and playing mah-jongg were allowed to revive, and specialized markets in birds, fish, spirit incense, funeral supplies, and other products became widely visible.

Official tolerance of differing ideological ideas also increased. Ideas that would have been risky to express a few years ago, such as having officials be bound by laws, recognizing and allowing interest groups to compete in the political arena, or making divorce easier, could now be expressed. Controls over the communications technologies that facilitate the transmission of ideas and cultural products independently of the state were relaxed. Computers and printers, cassette recorders, mimeograph machines, photocopying machines, and videotape recorders were not to be found everywhere, but an increasing number of them came into the hands of private individuals and local organizations who used them in a variety of ways, not all of which pleased the authorities.

Of course, there were clear limits to the reform-era liberalization. Perhaps most important, the ideas and cultural products of the late Mao era were for the most part proscribed, and there was political risk in advocating them. One did not see people quoting Mao's sayings from their "little red books," performing Jiang Qing's model revolutionary operas, or publicly advocating mounting new class struggle campaigns. Periodically the authorities did fulminate against "harmful" cultural influences that arose in the reform era and they purged writers, arrested alleged disseminators of pornography, and published new regulations against unauthorized publications. Still, the growing diversity and liveliness of cultural life in the post-Mao era is indisputable.

Impact on Chinese Traditional Practices

The traditional cultural legacy has been a major beneficiary of the post-Mao liberalization. Signs appeared everywhere in China of a revival of a variety of traditional Chinese practices. A vast amount of new research and publishing on ancient and imperial China got under way. The past no longer had to be portrayed as a simple conflict between heroic but oppressed peasants and evil and cruel landowners and officials. Traditional operas, music and dance, and performance troupes and associations dedicated to the preservation of these arts, were revived. Traditional-style painting, calligraphy, and other fine arts enjoyed a renaissance as well, and there is a new pride emerging in China's artistic heritage. Many tombs, monuments, and temples have been renovated and reopened, and they are less likely now to be accompanied by signs describing the exploitation and misery the common people suffered during their construction.

Confucius has also been "rehabilitated." His ancestral temple and adjacent facilities have been refurbished, new journals and associations devoted to the study of his writings have been established, and international symposia have been convened on the lessons of, Confucian ideas for the modern world. An underlying theme in this "neoneo-Confucianism" is that the great philosopher's values must have played a role in explaining the economic successes of the other East Asian Confucian societies (Japan, Taiwan, South Korea, Hong Kong, and Singapore); therefore, the People's Republic could benefit as well from renewed respect for his legacy. In addition to the possible material benefits, it is argued that greater stress on Confucian values like moderation, benevolence, harmony, and filial piety will help to overcome the social conflicts and frayed nerves that are legacies of the Mao era.

Western Cultural Influences

The relaxation of official controls and the open-door policy fostered a major new infusion of Western cultural influences. The reform policies increased the number of diplomats, foreign businessmen, teachers and tourists in China and have resulted in tens of thousands of Chinese traveling to the West, either on short business trips or for extended periods of study. Contacts intensified with Chinese living abroad who have already made their accommodations with Western cultural practices, and particularly with Chinese from Hong Kong and Macao and those visiting from Taiwan. The number of Taiwanese returning to visit has been increasing since 1987. In some parts of China, and particularly in the coastal areas of Guangdong and Fujian provinces, the primary bearers of Western cultural influence are these overseas Chinese, rather than non-Chinese foreigners.

During the reform era, most foreign broadcasts were no longer banned or jammed,[8] and in fact listening to them was an approved way to help develop valuable foreign language skills. Foreign movies and television series were regularly shown in China, although the selection criteria were obscure. Movies ranged from *The Sound of Music* to *Convoy*, a violent film about American truckers; television shows ranged from "Little House on the Prairie" to "The Man from Atlantis," a series canceled long ago in the United States. American football's Super Bowl and baseball's World Series appeared on Chinese television, to the evident puzzlement of many Chinese viewers. Japanese, European, Latin American, and even Soviet films and television shows were shown in China as well. Stories about movie and music stars from the West, Hong Kong, and Taiwan competed for space in popular magazines with stories about China's own rising celebrities.

Numerous other signs of foreign cultural influence were everywhere in China's cities, and occasionally even in the rural backwaters. A very partial listing includes video parlors, pool halls, amusement parks (complete with bumper cars and corkscrew roller coasters), disco and ballroom dancing, jazz, Pepsi and Coke, cosmetic surgery, Kentucky Fried Chicken, white wedding gowns, bodybuilding and beauty contests, commercial advertising, rock bands, tennis, golf, windsurfing, and motocross racing. And an increasing variety of translated foreign literature was also available to Chinese readers, ranging from classic works available earlier but suppressed during the Cultural Revolution, such as those by Shakespeare, Dickens, and Victor Hugo, to currently popular fiction, James Bond stories, and nonfiction by writers such as Lee Iacocca, Dale Carnegie, Freud, Malinowski, Gorbachev, and various Western popular writers on business management and futurology.

As with the revival of traditional Chinese culture, the authorities are by no means pleased with all of the new forms of Western cultural influence. Considerable debate has surrounded the appearance in China of such things as bodybuilding and beauty contests. Critics cite a long list of harmful influences that have erupted in China at least partly as a result of the open-door policy. Foreign influences are blamed, for instance, for increases in premarital sex, divorce, venereal disease, prostitution, pornography, drug addiction, and even for general increases in crime and juvenile delinquency rates. Of equal or even greater official concern is the alleged foreign effect on popular values, particularly among the young. The open door, it is argued by critics, has fostered doubt about the virtues of socialism, China's institutions, and the leadership of the CCP, and may be creating perceptions that the institutions and values of foreign societies are superior. The same theme was sounded in the early 1950s — Chinese must be dissuaded from the notion that "the American moon shines brighter than the Chinese moon."

Even though there were persistent efforts to monitor and control foreign contacts and to prevent harmful ideas and practices from entering, the increase in foreign influence has been so rapid, and its forms so massive and diverse, that it has proved impossible for the authorities to effectively monitor and control everything. To some extent this inability was inherent in the reform process itself, for the granting of local autonomy that is vital to the economic reforms inevitably leads to activities and influences that are outside of the range of central controls.

Cultural Dilemmas

Critics of recent cultural trends differ on whether the resurgence of traditional practices or the influx of Western influences is more problematic and potentially harmful. Some argue that China's most serious problems arose from the way

Figure 10.7 Following the Tian'anmen Square crackdown in June, 1989, Deng Xiaoping was no longer depicted as a reformer, but rather as someone holding back the tides of change.

centralized state socialism reinforced the worst, feudal tendencies of the traditional legacy, producing "little emperors" ruling over factories, offices, and schools throughout China. For such critics the revival of traditional cultural forms and the new respect given to Confucian ideas is particularly worrisome, since these can only make the effort to eliminate the "feudal remnants" from contemporary China more difficult.

Others argue, however, that Western influences pose more of a threat than the revived traditional practices. In addition to the greater familiarity of the traditional heritage, there is also the comfortable (but probably mistaken) view that harmful traditional practices are the products of backwardness and ignorance; therefore, with time, modernization, and rising educational levels, these will gradually disappear. No such assumption can be made about foreign influences. In addition to their being more alien to begin with, they are found in societies that are more modern and well educated than China. The dilemma for the screeners of such foreign influences, then, is how to identify which elements of Western culture are required by any modern society and thus have to be allowed to develop in China and which

elements are unnecessary for China's modernization effort. Where do neckties, rock music, premarital sex, or for that matter electoral democracy and competitive individualism fit?

As the central authorities have struggled with these problems, they have been unable to come to a consensus. Clearly, the more radical among the reformers have felt that China benefits from most of the new Western cultural infusions and that the resulting changes in Chinese practices to date have been too slow. In other words, the new influences have still only had a partial and superficial effect, mostly among the young and urban intellectuals, but have not yet had much impact on the deep recesses of Chinese organizations, families, and individual psyches. More conservative leaders perceive the infusions of Western influence to date as excessive and undesirable. They see the open door causing both a rising tide of social problems and a loss of national pride and faith in the system. These conservatives argue that the loss of centralized control over cultural innovation and transmission is even more dangerous than the specific kinds of harmful phenomena fostered, for it spells the doom of any serious attempt to forge cultural orthodoxy and will thus lead to political fragmentation and social chaos.

Twice in the 1980s (prior to 1989) these conservatives managed to launch campaigns designed to gain greater control over Chinese cultural life and punish those involved in spreading "unhealthy" Western influences — in the Anti-Spiritual Pollution campaign of 1983-84 and the Anti-Bourgeois Liberalization campaign of 1987. That each of these conservative initiatives faltered after a few months, after claiming a few prominent victims and intimidating many others, did not mean the debate was weakening. It merely indicated that the conservatives had not managed to gain sufficient support within the elite for a more thorough cultural crackdown.

Meanwhile, the ordinary population is confused and uncertain. The Chinese man and woman on the street (and rural lane), while generally appreciative of improved consumption standards and less oppressive political controls, often find the lack of clear consensus on values and cultural forms unsettling. For people who have grown up in a highly didactic and moralistic society, being faced with options and with no clear standards for

TIBET

Once an independent state, Tibet is presently an Autonomous Region of China. Located in southwestern China, it shares borders with Bhutan, Burma, India, Nepal, and Pakistan. Average altitude in Tibet ranges from 10,000 to 15,000 feet above sea level. Most major Asian rivers have their source in Tibet, including the Indus, Ganges, Mekong, Yangzi, and Yellow (Huang He). Both agriculture and nomadism are traditional ways of life.

Although it has suffered periodic setbacks, Buddhism has emerged as an important feature of Tibetan identity. Central to Tibetan Buddhism are the lama and belief in reincarnation. A lama (guru) is a spiritual leader who explains and interprets Buddhism to lay people. The Dalai Lama ("Universal Guru") is the highest-ranked monk of Tibetan Buddhism, and is believed to be an incarnation of Buddha.

Tibet existed peacefully with its neighbors until the Qing encroached upon Tibet in the nineteenth century. Manchu representatives were expelled with the fall of the Qing, and the thirteenth Dalai Lama attempted to modernize his nation.

In 1950, the People's Republic of China invaded Tibet. Tibetan resistance was crushed, and the fourteenth Dalai Lama, Tenzin Gyatso (b. 1935), was forced to accept Chinese rule. The Chinese closed Tibet to the rest of the world; foreigners were not allowed into Tibet until 1983. There were rebellions against the Chinese in the 1950s, and the situation in Tibet worsened. In 1959, the Dalai Lama, with about 100,000 other Tibetans, fled the country to India where he established a government-in-exile. Since then, the Dalai Lama has come to be a respected world figure and in 1989 he was awarded the Nobel Peace Prize.

In the course of consolidating their hold in Tibet, the Chinese have destroyed temples and suppressed Buddhism and other aspects of traditional culture. Since the initial invasion, it has been estimated that 1.2 million Tibetans—about 20% of the pre-1950 population—have been killed by the Chinese, including monks, nuns, women, and children. Entire villages have been sterilized. At the same time, massive migrations of Han Chinese into Tibet have been encouraged, with the result that at present there are more ethnic Chinese in Tibet than Tibetans. The apparent goal of the communists is the destruction of what was once the Tibetan nation and the assimilation of its people into the Chinese "motherland."

—Blaine Erickson

selection is unfamiliar. Should they cultivate an interest in Western classical music, rock, traditional operas, Chinese folk tunes, or perhaps favorite martial tunes from the socialist tradition (or all of the above)? Should they wear the latest Western fashions or retain the proletarian drab of the Mao era? Should they push their children down the "white road" toward academic learning and expertise, the "yellow road" toward business success and financial wealth, or the "red road" toward political activism and party membership? How should they celebrate a family wedding or a funeral? How would they react if a son came home and announced he wanted to leave a state job to go into private business, live together with his girlfriend without benefit of marriage, or go into training to become a Buddhist monk?

This uneasiness of the general population has several sources. It is not simply that people are unfamiliar with being faced by such choices. Nor is it solely a matter of being nervous in the face of the uncharacteristic restraint of the CCP and worried that in the future, if this restraint is abandoned and cultural uniformity is again forcefully imposed, they may be criticized for having made the wrong choices. As much as anything else, this popular uneasiness can be attributed to the fact that both in imperial times and in the Maoist era, Chinese were accustomed to living in a society in which habits and cultural forms were infused with political and moral meanings that flowed from the cultural orthodoxy — a trait still very much alive. Even though China is an avowedly atheistic state, in a certain sense, until the reform era, China was a minimally secularized society. The sort of secularized, pragmatic societies in which Westerners have grown up, in which most spheres of daily life and culture are seen as detached from higher moral battles, has never been part of the Chinese experience. For this reason many Chinese have the gnawing feeling that they are sailing into uncharted seas without a clear moral rudder. Today's situation may then be interpreted not so much in terms of new freedoms and choices, but as a moral vacuum in which, for example, individuals are encouraged to get rich without experiencing the restraints of socialist, traditional Confucian, or Western moral values.

China has struggled for more than a century to cope with the problems involved in adapting Chinese culture to the modern world. Because the Chinese define "being Chinese" in cultural terms and both the elite and the masses believe that forging a unifying cultural orthodoxy is vital, cultural debates have constantly spilled over into the political realm. Similarly, political leaders in imperial, Republican, Maoist, and reform-era China have all had devising and implementing the proper cultural policy high on their political agenda. But in spite of this century of efforts, the debate, particularly in terms of how Chinese culture will accommodate Western influence, is still unresolved, and arguments in this realm remain volatile. It is still very unclear whether a well-defined cultural orthodoxy will emerge from the new round of debates on these issues in the 1990s and what form that orthodoxy might take.[9]

◆   ◆   ◆

THE END OF THE CHINESE REVOLUTION

— by Roderick MacFarquhar

When Deng Xiaoping suppressed the Beijing Spring [of 1989], he thought he was putting down a new Cultural Revolution. Pirated notes from a Party meeting in late April quoted him as telling his colleagues:

This is not an ordinary student movement. It is turmoil. . . . What they are doing now is altogether the same stuff as what the rebels did during the Cultural Revolution. All they want is to create chaos under the heavens.

As the leading living victim of those ten years of terror Deng could not tolerate chaos or a revival of mob rule. What he did not comprehend was that Tian'anmen Square 1989 was virtually the mirror opposite of Tian'anmen Square of 1966.

The million-strong Red Guard demonstrations at the outset of the Cultural Revolution recreated the hysteria of Nazi Nuremberg; the 1989 protest was redolent of an urban Woodstock. The Red Guards were conjured up by the revolutionary incitement of Chairman Mao; the 1989 demonstrations were a genuine grass-roots protest, if one skillfully organized by student activists. The Red Guards worshiped the living Mao; the prodemocracy protesters worshiped nobody, though they sprang into action out of affectionate respect for the dead "liberal," Hu Yaobang. The Red Guards rallied to Mao's drumbeat for proletarian egalitarianism; the 1989 students called for universal freedom, symbolized by their styrofoam goddess of liberty. The cultural revolutionaries, fueled by hate, marched forth from Tian'anmen Square to "drag out," abuse, and frequently murder "capitalist roaders." The would-be democrats of 1989 demanded the resignations of Deng Xiaoping and Li Peng, but showed pacifist solicitude even for troops sent to suppress them.

For all these stark contrasts, both protesters and repressors of 1989 acted within the dark penumbra of the Cultural Revolution. Deng and his accomplices were obsessed with the memory of the disorder and destruction unleashed by the Red Guards in the cities of China a quarter of a century ago. The upheaval exhilarated Mao who initiated it, but still unnerves his surviving colleagues of the Long March generation, most of whom were purged and disgraced, along with virtually the entire upper echelon of the Chinese Communist party (CCP).

Mao's onetime heir apparent, head of state Liu Shaoqi, died in anonymity after a long period of medical neglect. Others were persecuted to death or committed suicide. Deng himself escaped relatively lightly, with public humiliation and exile to a menial job in south China. He was probably saved from a worse fate by three decades of loyalty to Mao as a member of his innermost circle. One of his sons, however, was thrown out of a window and crippled for life. Yang Shangkun, today China's president and Deng's hatchet man, the man who has been calling for harsh treatment of the students, was a key Central Committee official then, and one of the first to be dismissed, followed by Peng Zhen, then the mayor of Beijing, now, at eighty-seven, one of the hardest of the old warriors behind Deng.

Chinese chroniclers of the Cultural Revolution claim that 100 million people were affected by it, though that figure may have been inflated by including the entire populations of cities where the Red Guards were active. Rough estimates by foreign scholars point to a death toll of up to half a million. Whatever the numbers, for China's elite, it was a deeply traumatic experience.

It was also an institutional trauma for the Chinese Communist Party. The evident disarray of China's top leaders during the weeks before the tanks rolled in and the popular disdain for the strictures of martial law were reminders that the Party has never regained the cohesion and authority of its reign before the Cultural Revolution started. Mao, in setting it off, may have wanted simply to rid himself of some senior colleagues and to transform the rest into born-again revolutionaries. But the humiliation of thousands of members of China's "new class" inevitably sapped the respect for the Party itself in the eyes of its subjects. For much of the Cultural Revolution, the Party was an empty shell. In practice, the Party consisted of a set of warring factions: a military clique, headed by Defense Minister Lin Biao; a bureaucratic faction under Premier Zhou Enlai; the radical Gang of Four; and, later, the so-called "whatever faction" of younger Mao loyalists, led by his short-lived heir, Hua Guofeng. Thirty years of unity, forged at the Yenan revolutionary base, had been shattered beyond repair.

The erosion of Party authority had its corollary in an invigoration of people-power. At first, in 1966, students spoke out, as they had in the brief blooming of the Hundred Flowers in 1957, because Mao had licensed and encouraged them.

But eventually they began to act autonomously, if mindlessly. Yesterday's Red Guards are now a generation of thirty-five to forty-five-year-olds who cannot have forgotten the heady experience of challenging authority, taking initiatives, and relying on their own resources. Mao's admonitions to "dare to think, dare to speak, dare to act" because "to rebel is justified" resonated long after 1968 when the Red Guards' internecine warfare led the Chairman to consign them to the countryside. It also produced a redefinition of the relations between subsequent generations of students and the state.

Toward the end of the Cultural Revolution, on April 5, 1976, there was truly spontaneous combustion in Tian'anmen Square when students and citizens exploded in wrath over the removal of the wreaths they had brought there to mourn the recently deceased Premier Zhou Enlai. The demonstrators were severely beaten by police and militia for defying the Gang of Four. Mao was also an implicit target of their anger and Deng Xiaoping was their implicit hero, as the man who had just been deprived of the succession to Zhou and was most likely to have ruled in the same pragmatic style. When Deng returned to power after his second disgrace, he insisted that the Tian'anmen incident of 1976 be redefined as a popular uprising rather than a counterrevolutionary event. Thus he added his imprimatur to Mao's on the legitimacy of mass protest, even in the heart of the capital.

Deng benefited from spontaneous mass action again two years later with the emergence of the Democracy Wall movement. There were few determined dissidents among the activists of 1978. Most simply wanted a more relaxed political atmosphere, and they saw Deng's return to power as the way to ensure that. They created a pro-Deng bandwagon that undoubtedly helped him triumph over the last Maoist holdouts at the decisive meeting of the third plenum of the eleventh Central Committee in December 1978. But three months later, the Democracy Wall was closed down, and a few outspoken activists like Wei Jingsheng were later sentenced to long periods in jail. To this day, it is unclear whether Deng had simply used the movement cynically for his own ends, or whether he was persuaded to suppress it by more conservative gerontocrats as part of the price for their support. What is certain is that every time Deng had to choose between power and democracy he chose power.

Guns and tanks were not required to deal with the young people who put up posters in 1978. But military men were already entrenched in top Party councils at that time as a result of Mao's earlier resort to PLA peacekeepers to subdue the Red Guards. The contradiction between army power and civilian control is an old theme in Chinese Communist history. The military establishment has always wielded more political clout in China, where it won the civil war, than in the Soviet Union, where the Red Army was created only after the Revolution. Mao struggled hard, not wholly successfully, to ensure that the Party commanded the gun. It was one of Deng's greatest achievements over the past ten years that he managed to cut army politicians down to size. His biggest success came in 1985, when he persuaded large numbers of Long March veterans to retire, reducing the proportion of PLA officers on the Central Committee — 50 percent at the height of the Cultural Revolution — to under 20 percent.

Like Mao before him, Deng failed to impose full civilian control on the Party's Military Affairs Commission (MAC), which Mao chaired from 1935 until his death, and which is responsible for issuing orders to the army. The generals refused to allow the PLA to be run by a new body responsible to the National People's Congress, and they also resisted Deng's attempts to hand over his own chairmanship of the MAC to his chosen successors, Hu Yaobang and then Zhao Ziyang. When Deng retired from the Politburo at the Thirteenth Congress in 1987, the army's obduracy forced a change in the Party constitution which entitled him to continue to chair the MAC. Zhao Ziyang was made first vice-chairman, an honor never conceded to his predecessor as Party boss, Hu Yaobang, but it was the old military man Yang Shangkun who was Deng's real deputy as permanent vice-chairman.

In a revealing and hyperbolic passage in a secret speech in June, 1989, Deng underlined how the chairmanship of the MAC was more important even than the nominally top job of Party general secretary. "I have kept an eye on Zhao for quite a few years," said Deng. "He has wild ambitions. Had he become the chairman of the Military Commission, all old comrades like us would have been beheaded."

Deng's inability to bring the military to heel was only the most obvious proof of his failure to revamp China's political system. Yet the economic reform program which he masterminded beginning in 1979 demanded a more flexible political structure, one that could respond to new pressures from the outspoken groups within an increasingly autonomous, self-confident, and compartmentalized society. These included farm families liberated by decollectivization; private entrepreneurs and industrialists providing much-needed services and employment; international traders confronting their foreign opposite numbers with increasing sophistication; and students and intellectuals fired up by access to the new ideas that filtered in through China's newly opened door. Instead of the radical restructuring of the polity which these new interest groups required, the old system was retained but put under unsustainable stresses.

Ideological certainty, already eroded by cultural revolutionary overkill, was further weakened by Deng Xiaoping's marginal interest in ideology, though Marxism-Leninism-Mao Zedong Thought was still enshrined as one of the four sacrosanct national principles. More importantly, Party cadres were told, in Deng's famous motto, that practice was the sole criterion of truth and furthermore that technical competence was to be a condition of employment. For the 19 million Party members recruited during the Cultural Revolution, many for their skills as political agitators, this was a threat to their careers. For the Party as an institution it was delegitimizing. If its claim to power rested on getting the economy right, this was a very shaky foundation indeed.

With their traditional role as guardians of orthodoxy undermined, Party cadres were forced to work in a newly commercial social setting. The old Maoist ideal of "serve the people" had been replaced by the Dengist injunction "to get rich is glorious." For officials sorely tempted by the opportunities of Deng's brave new world, the thin line between indulging in personal corruption and taking shortcuts on behalf of a collective unit became blurred. The blatant misuse of political connections by the "princes' party" — children of top brass and the Party elite — to gain wealth and power encouraged cynicism and emulation lower down. Gradually corruption became endemic, with baksheesh demanded for every official service. A few courageous journalists like Liu Binyan, now in the United States, became national heroes for their muckraking exposés. Contempt for the Party grew, but to no avail.

For all his talk of legality and democratization, Deng took no decisive institutional steps to alter the formal relationships between state and society. Lawyers were trained, but mainly to cut better deals with foreign firms, not to risk their careers fighting for the little man against the state. Democratization meant a few hopeful experiments in multiple-choice candidacies in local elections, and a few negative votes in the National People's Congress, but nobody at the top had Gorbachev's understanding of the potential value for rulers of electoral mandates; let alone a genuine commitment to pluralism.

The result was the worst of all worlds. Deng allowed some relaxation of political controls because he knew it was necessary for the economic reform program. This encouraged intellectuals and students to speak out with increasing boldness, but they felt frustrated because their voices went unheard. Deng was occasionally suborned by the conservatives into cracking the ideological whip, as in the campaign against spiritual pollution at the end of 1983. But when reformists like Zhao Ziyang argued that ideological campaigns were damaging the economy, Deng called a halt. Only when he believed that there was a serious threat to law and order, as in the student demonstrations of 1986 and 1987, did he take a drastic step and dismiss his first chosen heir, the Party general secretary, Hu Yaobang.

Economically too the reform program was running into trouble. In the summer of 1988, after price rises had set off a run on China's shops, Li Peng and his conservative allies emerged victorious from a conflict with Zhao Ziyang's reformers and proclaimed a two-year freeze on price reform and cuts in capital investment. By the beginning of 1989, three out of four million workers in the private construction industry were out of jobs and many of them turned to crime. Another 20 million workers in unprofitable rural industry were potential additions to the ranks of the unemployed. Inflation had hit 30 percent in the towns, perhaps

50 percent for food products. The government had insufficient cash to pay the peasants for their crops and palmed them off with IOUs; some government officials collecting state grain quotas asked to be accompanied by police.

Deng had watched Poland and Hungary struggle through their reforms and did not rule out similar urban unrest in China. He started taking precautions as early as 1983 when he reestablished a 400,000-man national armed police force which gradually took over the internal security functions performed by the PLA during the Cultural Revolution. This force was supervised by Politburo Standing Committee member Qiao Shi. More recently, an anti-riot force was created within the armed police, trained by Poles and Austrians, skilled also in martial arts, and equipped with American helicopters, Yugoslav tear gas, and German electronic gear. But Deng and Qiao Shi were looking in the wrong direction; they anticipated trouble on the streets from strikers and the lumpen unemployed, not from college campuses.

One dissident intellectual was predicting the imposition of martial law as far back as February, 1989. He saw a gathering confrontation between rulers and ruled, with nobody in the leadership capable of defusing it. Well before the first protesters moved into Tian'anmen Square, the credibility of China's self-selected leaders was already in doubt. Even the most committed reformers had failed to create channels for legitimate protest or alternatives to repression. During his six-year tenure as Party boss, Hu Yaobang had pleased intellectuals with his tolerance of dissent, but he never articulated a broad-based program of democratization.

His successor, Zhao, endorsed democracy in order to facilitate economic reform, but did nothing to promote pluralism. Indeed, after his defeat in the reform debate he tried an opposite tack. His braintrusters began to advocate a "new authoritarianism," citing Taiwan and South Korea as proof that China would modernize better and faster with a strong, centralized government and a powerful hand at the tiller. Ironically, Zhao seemed to be hoping for army support, in the belief that martial law might be the only way of forcing through price reforms. Zhao could no longer rely on Deng to defend the reform program and was progressively losing ground to the economic conservatives, Li Peng and Yao Yilin. Instead of redoubling his efforts, Zhao seemed to lose heart and his young Turks began running for cover, seeking other jobs or going abroad.

When the demonstrations began in mid-April, there was no Chinese leader to whom the students could turn and no institutions through which they could channel their frustrations. In this vacuum Deng remained the ultimate arbiter. Both reformers and conservatives had long relied on him as a bulwark against the potential excesses of the other faction. Despite Deng's genuine efforts to avoid playing a Mao-like role, it seemed that the Chinese polity still demanded the linchpin of the maximum leader. But he was showing signs of wear and tear. He had heart trouble and his eyesight and memory were failing. His speech was sometimes difficult to understand and he had taken to communicating with colleagues through an intermediary, alarmingly like Mao in his dying days.

As the critical seventieth anniversary of the patriotic movement of May 4, 1919, approached, the regime worriedly issued plans for commemorations, all of which omitted one of its two original slogans, "democracy," and mentioned only the other, "science." Students were planning their own celebrations. Then Hu Yaobang had his heart attack at a Politburo meeting, reportedly after losing his cool in an argument. His death on April 15 sparked the prairie fire of the student mass movement culminating in the now infamous Tian'anmen massacre.

The indiscriminate slaughter of hundreds, perhaps thousands, of fellow citizens by troops of the PLA in the heart of the capital was a tragic act of monumental folly. The subsequent arrest by Qiao Shi's armed police of thousands of students, intellectuals, and others recalled 1950s campaigns against counterrevolutionaries which Deng had long since proclaimed a thing of the past. In the last analysis Deng and his aged supporters had learned the wrong lessons, both from the Cultural Revolution and from perestroika in the Soviet Union and Eastern Europe.

Divided at the top, the Chinese Communist Party could no longer cope with the multiple pressures upon it and finally cracked. While Premier Li Peng acted as the hard-faced front man,

it is clear that decisions were ultimately taken not by his State Council, or by the Politburo, nor even by its five-man Standing Committee, but by the duumvirate in charge of the Military Affairs Commission, Deng Xiaoping and President Yang Shangkun, cheered on by a fire-eating group of aged revolutionaries. No attempt appears to have been made to summon the Party's supposedly supreme organ, the Central Committee, even though the crisis had lasted six weeks before its bloody denouement; perhaps Deng feared that the 285-member Central Committee included too many softies from Hu Yaobang's stable. When Deng finally reappeared in public to commend the PLA on its repression, he was flanked almost exclusively by octogenarians against a backdrop of generals. As in Poland in 1981 after the crackdown against Solidarity, China had collapsed into military rule.[10]

◆　　　◆　　　◆

A POST-DENG CHINA: THE NEXT PHASE

— by Philip Bowring

The death of Deng Xiaoping was, understandably, followed by ritual promises by all members of China's collective leadership to follow the path he set. That is a political necessity for a Party hierarchy, none of whom has yet to achieve the prestige of the late "paramount leader." It is also comforting to a China fearful of sudden shifts of power and policy that tend to accompany transition from one dynasty to the next.

But promises of adherence to Deng Xiaoping Thought beg the question of what they actually mean in the current context. Deng's philosophy is perhaps best summed up by the adage: "It doesn't matter whether the cat is black or white so long as it catches mice." Policy is to be judged by effectiveness, not theoretical purity. In other words, pragmatism.

However, Deng's pragmatism in economic affairs existed within the context of the importance of the Party as China's unifying force and as machinery for policy implementation. Deng came to power at a time when expectations were very low. His successor, whether it be Jiang Zemin or someone else, faces the difficulty of meeting much increased aspirations at the same time as decisions demanded of the leader are becoming politically more difficult to arrive at.

Deng's Progress

The first phase of Deng's liberalization — the ending of communes and introduction of market incentives in agriculture — was clearly popular with the peasants and quickly yielded huge output returns. The second phase, the opening up to foreign — but in practice mainly Hong Kong and Taiwan — investments in light export industry had catalytic impact on the whole country. The southern coastal provinces, notably Guangdong, where these "experiments" started, were soon growing so fast that other regions wanted to follow their lead. It spurred the development of township and village enterprises, real estate development and a general de-centralization of economic activity.

After a more conservative period following the Tiananmen crackdown of June 1989, Deng relaunched a liberal, de-centralizing economic program with his celebrated tout of the south in 1992. What was to be Deng's last policy legacy almost ended in disaster. His "dash for growth" ushered in a couple of years of unrestrained and often largely speculative investment, leading to inflation which hit almost 30 percent, and general loss of central control over the economy. It was also accompanied by massive corruption and what amounted to private expropriation of better slate assets through corporatization of enterprises.

The process was de-stabilizing, but it unleashed forces which pushed China further towards a market economy, or what Beijing chose to call a "socialist market economy." The past two-and-a-half years have seen the leadership, notably economic czar Vice-Premier Zhu Rongji, try to restore macro-economic stability without bringing growth — so needed to create jobs and satisfy aspirations — to a halt. Broadly, Zhu succeeded, re-establishing central control over money supply and bringing inflation down from 30% to 5%. However, it is hard to imagine that

this could have been achieved without collapsing economic growth had it not been for a huge influx of foreign investment, this time not so much into light export industries as into medium-technology intermediate goods and consumer durable industries aimed primarily at the domestic market. Whatever its problems, however remote the profits, foreigners found the prospect of the supposed billion-consumer market irresistible.

The vital foreign role owed its existence to Deng who appreciated that Chinese nationalism was best served by learning from foreigners. However, Deng-ism had less to say about how to make growth self-sustaining without foreign reliance — in particular, what to do about the state-owned enterprises (SOE), which in most cases were over-manned, losing money and accounted for a dwindling share of exports. (Foreign-invested enterprises account for more than 50% of manufactured exports).

SOEs and Other Challenges

In the immediate post-Deng period, the leadership has promised to press ahead with SOE reforms, cutting costs and losses and, if necessary, jobs. Zhu told the National Peoples Congress that a tight money policy would be continued and that state banks had to reduce their non-performing loans by 2% a year or their managers would face the consequences.

Such tough talks reveals a commitment to continued reform of which Deng would have approved. However, the problem of the SOEs encapsulates the core problems that Deng-ism left unaddressed:

- The difficulty of reforming the SOEs while their managements are so closely linked to Party and state bureaucracies.

- The centrifugal tendencies of China when economic forces are given free rein. There is perceived to he a point where liberal economics threatens national unity as well as the Party's grip on power.

- The problem that the SOE workforces remain a privileged urban elite, not perhaps compared with non-SOE workers in Shanghai and Guangzhou, but certainly compared with the huge and growing informal urban work force, not to mention the rural masses.

- The enclave nature of much of China's recent growth, creating immense income gaps whose social consequences are only partly held in check by controls on labor mobility.

- Lack of any clear distinctions between the roles of private and public property. Share ownership is encouraged, and in many cases cadres get rich quickly through corporatization of state assets. However, genuine privatization of large and medium enterprises is not even a goal.

In other words, Deng has left unresolved the key roles of both the Party and private property. It was easy to liberate peasants and small enterprises from the center's yoke. Even Lenin had done that in the Soviet Union with his New Economic Policy (NEP). But the linkages between the political system and the commanding heights (however inefficient) of the economy are too close to allow any but very gradual change.

Stalin reversed Lenin's NEP to seize the small enterprise surplus for investment in heavy industry. China has not had to do the same because of foreign investment and a high urban household savings rate. However, that could change if the SOEs remain unreformed, foreign investment dries up, or the pressures increase to build long gestation infrastructure in the disadvantaged inland provinces.

It may not matter whether the successful cat in 2000 is black or white. But does it need to be a Party member?

NOTES

1. "40 Years of Chinese Communism," *Far Eastern Economic Review*, 5 October 1989, pp. 51-58.

2. Deng Xiaoping had advocated "Four Modernizations:" of the economy, the military, education, and science & technology. In a famous essay, the Democracy Wall activist Wei Jingsheng advocated that politics be the "Fifth Modernization," meaning democracy.

3. Edgar Snow, *The Other Side of the River: Red China Today* (New York: Random House, 1961), p. 619.

4. Fang Lizhi is a prominent Chinese astrophysicist and dissident. An outspoken supporter of efforts to foster democracy in China, he and his wife were forced to take refuge in the American embassy in Beijing following the Tian'anmen Square massacre in 1989 in order to avoid arrest. They were permitted to leave China the following year. This article is excerpted from: Fang Lizhi, "Chinese Amnesia," trans. Perry Link, *The New York Review of Books* (27 September 1990), pp. 30-31.

5. Excerpted and updated from Harry Harding, "China's Political Reforms," in *Asia Pacific Report, Focus: China in the Reform Era,* eds., Charles E. Morrison and Robert F. Dernberger (Honolulu; East-West Center, 1989), pp. 43-51.

6. Robert F. Dernberger, "China's Economic Reforms," in Ibid., pp. 61-64.

7. William Lavely, "Demographic and Social Change in China," in Ibid., pp. 65-73.

8. Smil, Vaclav. *China's Environmental Crisis.* (Armonk: M.E. Sharpe, 1993). pp. 190-194.

9. Martin Whyte, "Evolutionary Changes in Chinese Culture," in Ibid., pp. 95-101.

10. Roderick MacFarquhar, "The End of the Chinese Revolution," in *The New York Review of Books* (20 July 1989), pp. 8-10.

11. Philip Bowring, "The Next Phase," in *Capital Trends*. Vol.2, No.4. pp. 3-7. Washington DC: Nikko Research Center (America). March 1997.

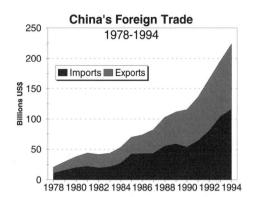

Graph 10.12

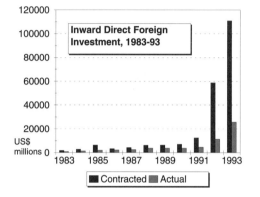

Graph 10.11

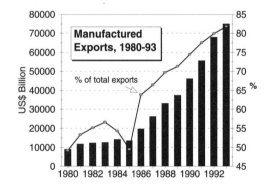

Graph 10.13

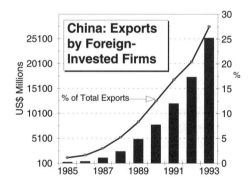

Graph 10.14

11

Beyond the Revolution: Indonesia and Vietnam

by Michael Williams

OVERVIEW

Since the end of the Second World War in 1945, Indonesia and Vietnam have been the two main indigenous political actors in Southeast Asia. Between them, they account for 250 million of the region's 440 million inhabitants, or more than half of the total population of Southeast Asia. It is in the political realm that developments in these two countries have tended to shape the destiny of the region as a whole, as well as relations with outside powers such as the United States, the Soviet Union, Japan, and China. While other Southeast Asian countries, such as Singapore, Malaysia, and Thailand, have enjoyed greater economic success, Indonesia and Vietnam have been the two countries whose policies and activities have had the most important impact on the affairs of the region and the roles of the external powers there.

For two decades after 1945, Indonesia's prominence as a disturber of regional order and as a lightning rod for cold war involvement resulted largely from the abilities of its first head of state, President Sukarno, to exploit extreme nationalism and revolutionary romanticism. Under his successor, President Suharto, Indonesia's continued importance to the region and the world has rested on its enormous size and wealth of resources. By contrast, Vietnam's centrality in the region since

1945 has reflected not its natural advantages but its role in the cold war environment and its rule by a dedicated and cohesive revolutionary group determined to unite the country under communist rule.

Indonesia and Vietnam share a common heritage in that the modern history of both countries was forged in revolutionary wars against the former colonial powers. After independence, they continued to share a common antipathy toward involvement in the region by outside powers which they have maintained to the present day. Although the two countries subsequently pursued very different political paths, leaders in both Hanoi and Jakarta have always felt that an affinity remained between them that was not shared by other countries in Southeast Asia.

While all of Southeast Asia, with the exception of Thailand, was colonized by outside powers before the Second World War, it was only in Indonesia and Vietnam that the fight for independence took a revolutionary form after 1945. Indeed, it is striking that in both countries nationalist leaders took immediate advantage of the Japanese surrender to proclaim their own country's independence. In Indonesia, Sukarno and Mohammed Hatta proclaimed an independent Republic August 17, 1945, while in Vietnam, Ho Chi Minh announced the establishment of the Democratic Republic of Vietnam September 2. While Vietnam's revolution was both national and social at the same time, Indonesia's was largely nationalist. In contrast, in neighboring Malaya, as it was at the time, and in the Philippines, independence was to be achieved by a more gradual process of negotiation, with sovereignty finally being handed over to elites who were closely tied to the former colonial powers, Great Britain and the United States.

If Indonesia and Vietnam were in the vanguard of nationalist development in Southeast Asia in 1945, it was to be a long time before either country achieved full independence. In both countries, the respective colonial powers, the Netherlands and France, fiercely resisted the nationalist seizure of power and in both cases the colonial powers received varying degrees of support from the United States and Great Britain. Thus was born in both Indonesia and Vietnam not only a deep-rooted attachment to nationhood but an abiding fear and hostility to the involvement of external powers in the region, although both countries have occasionally aligned themselves with external powers.

After a protracted guerrilla war, Indonesia finally won its independence from the Dutch in December 1949. In the case of Vietnam, the struggle against the French was to last even longer and to culminate in the humiliating French defeat at Dien Bien Phu in May 1954. Although the Vietnamese forces had appeared victorious on the battlefield, the Geneva conference of that year left the Communist Viet Minh forces, led by Ho Chi Minh, in control of only the northern half of the country. In the South, the Republic of Vietnam was established as a separate pro-American administration.

The success of revolutionary struggles in Indonesia and Vietnam and the withdrawal of the Dutch and the French sounded the death-knell for colonialism in Southeast Asia. The last remaining colonial power, Britain, granted independence to Malaya in 1957 and to Singapore in 1963. Although events in Indonesia and Vietnam had contributed greatly to undermining Britain's position in the region, neither country felt that it had fully freed itself from outside interference. In the case of Vietnam, the country found itself divided after 1954. The Communists in North Vietnam, who had founded the country's Republic back in 1945, regarded the government of South Vietnam

as little more than an American puppet regime. In their view, the United States had simply replaced France as the imperialist enemy.

Although Indonesia had attained full political independence from the Dutch in 1949, the nationalist government led by President Sukarno continued to regard itself as facing a threat from outside. First, much of the economy remained in the hands of Dutch companies, and, second, the Dutch continued to occupy the territory of West New Guinea (now the Indonesian province of Irian Jaya). President Sukarno's desire to have Indonesia be seen as leading anti-imperialist forces not only in the region but in the Third World generally was shown in his convening of the 1955 Bandung Asian-African Conference. This was the first gathering ever of the leaders of the newly independent countries and it played a critical role in the later formation of the Nonaligned Movement. Thus, in both Hanoi and Jakarta in the 1950s, governments continued to regard the revolutionary struggle as incomplete.

After a brief hiatus, the Communists in Vietnam resumed the revolutionary struggle in the South with the founding of the National Liberation Front (NLF) in 1960. Escalation of the war against the regime of Ngo Dinh Diem increasingly brought the communist forces into conflict with the United States, whose involvement in Vietnam deepened after the assassination of Diem in 1963. In Indonesia, too, continuing disputes with the Netherlands over Dutch property and over the disputed territory of West New Guinea increasingly brought President Sukarno's government into confrontation with the West. Nor did the eventual transfer of the territory to Indonesia in 1963 alter Sukarno's distrust of what he perceived as Western imperialism. Covert American involvement in regional revolts in 1957-58 had left Indonesian nationalists with an abiding suspicion that the West hoped to see Indonesia dismembered. In 1963, Sukarno launched a campaign of confrontation, or konfrontasi, against the federation of Malaysia, which had been created in that year by bringing together Malaya, Singapore, and the former British Borneo territories of Sabah and Sarawak. The Indonesian president saw the move as an attempt by Britain, and the West, to shore up its position in Southeast Asia. Sukarno's actions not only brought Indonesia into conflict with the

West, but also led him to ally his country closely with China and North Vietnam.

As well as sharing a common antipathy to the involvement of Western powers in Southeast Asia, Indonesia and Vietnam shared a common platform in rejecting Western concepts of democracy. In North Vietnam after 1954, the Communist Party had established a one-party state closely modeled on its two main allies, the Soviet Union and China. Indonesia, although initially a multiparty democracy, soon rejected this in favor of what, after 1957, Sukarno called "Guided Democracy." Right-wing parties were proscribed, the media became tightly controlled, and the influence of the Indonesian Communist Party (PKI), then the third largest in the world, grew enormously. Increasingly, Sukarno assumed for himself an executive presidency that showed little tolerance of domestic opposition. Both in their external and internal policies, Indonesia and North Vietnam found themselves at odds not only with the West but also with their neighbors in Southeast Asia: Malaysia; the Philippines; and Thailand.

The Watershed Year: 1965

The year 1965 was a watershed in the political evolution of Southeast Asia, and of Vietnam and Indonesia in particular. It was a year of dramatic political upheaval in Indonesia which changed the country's internal and external orientation. At the same time, the war in South Vietnam moved from being an internal conflict between communist and anticommunist forces to a full-scale war between North Vietnam and the United States. In August 1964, on the pretext of a North Vietnamese attack on U.S. naval craft (the so-called Tonkin Gulf Incident), President Lyndon B. Johnson ordered the first air attacks on North Vietnam. In February of the following year, the first regular U.S. combat units arrived in Da Nang. By the summer of 1965, U.S. forces were involved in heavy fighting in the Central Highlands and along the coast. Although heavy casualties were inflicted on the NLF and North Vietnamese forces, the response of the communist leadership in Hanoi was to send further reinforcements south. Their resolve to do so was fortified by massive U.S. bombing of North

Vietnam, which in the next three years was the target of more bombs than were used throughout the Second World War.

From this time on, it was U.S. forces that bore the brunt of some of the heaviest fighting in the South. The United States had become involved militarily not only to strengthen the South Vietnamese regime, then led by Nguyen Van Thieu, but also to demonstrate to the communist leadership in Hanoi and to aspiring communist insurgencies elsewhere U.S. resolve to prevent successful "national liberation" struggles. In so doing, the United States seriously underestimated the extent to which the communist movement and Vietnamese nationalism were almost synonymous. The more the United States became involved in propping up successive South Vietnamese regimes the more the Communists were able to appeal successfully to Vietnamese nationalism. In addition, U.S. strategy, because it concentrated on the physical control of population and territory, ignored the main source of support for the NLF, namely the peasantry.

INDONESIA, 1965-1968

Fall of the Communist Party

Events in Indonesia in 1965 produced one of the most significant political shifts in Asia and the Pacific in the postwar period. As a result, not only did the country undergo a dramatic volte-face in its internal politics, but the whole balance of power in Southeast Asia changed significantly. The September 30 incident (often referred to by its Indonesian acronym, Gestapu), involving an attempted leftist coup and a countercoup led by General Suharto, provided the casus belli for a virtual military offensive against the Indonesian Communist Party and the overseas Chinese as well as a break with China itself. For most senior military figures, these were three elements of the same security problem. The floodgates were now open and the pent-up frustrations and hostilities of two decades burst forth. In the process, Indonesia was the scene of one of the worst bloodbaths in modern Asian history. The political map of the country was effectively redrawn in the eighteen

CONTINUITY IN INDONESIAN POLITICS

It should be understood, however, that the political change inaugurated by Suharto's "New Order" involved a notable reduction in the degree of pluralism within the system and not an assumption to power by new elements. The armed forces, and particularly the army, which assumed command of the political heights of the Republic, had been a factor of political importance from the onset of the national revolution. As an institution, it was imbued with a strong sense of nationalism and a similar view of regional entitlement to that exhibited by Sukarno and his supporters. Moreover, General Suharto employed the same constitutional structure as his predecessor. Indeed, it had been the army which had encouraged Sukarno to introduce "Guided Democracy" based on the 1945 Constitution. That constitution was confirmed as the source of political legitimacy because it suited Suharto's political purpose and also because of his perception of the primary needs of the Indonesian state. Thus, there was not total discontinuity in the structure of the political order in the wake of the abortive coup. Correspondingly, foreign policy was not cast in a totally new mold, especially as the army had shared the experience of national vulnerability which had given rise to deep suspicion of the intent of all extraregional powers.

—Michael Leifer
Indonesia's Foreign Policy

months after October 1965, eliminating the world's third largest communist party and resulting in the eventual replacement of President Sukarno as head of state by General Suharto. A "New Order" was proclaimed and the country's internal and external policies moved significantly to the right.

While evidence existed that PKI leaders were at least apprised of the leftist coup led by Lieutenant-Colonel Untung on September 30, 1965, little or no evidence has been forthcoming of Chinese involvement. In one sense this did not matter. The military was deeply suspicious of local Chinese, whom they considered to be procommunist and loyal to Beijing, and given the PKI's ideological orientation and Sukarno's proclamation of a Beijing-Jakarta axis, it was axiomatic that the military would accuse China of involvement in the coup. China, the PKI, and local Chinese were inextricably linked in the military mind. Moreover, the existence of an externally inspired plot lent credibility for the military's desire for a break in relations with China and helped justify their own dominant position in politics after 1965.

For China, needless to say, the events of September-October 1965 were a debacle. Almost

overnight what had looked like the most spectacular achievement of Chinese foreign policy had turned into a dramatic reversal. So spectacular was this reversal that the Chinese leadership appear to have taken weeks and months to digest it. As late as early 1966, they seem to have clung to the hope that although the PKI had been liquidated, Sukarno might yet be able to pull off some political miracle and contain the right-wing generals. It was only in May 1966 that China withdrew its ambassador from Jakarta.

Following President Sukarno's handover of effective power to General Suharto on March 11, 1966, pressure grew from within the military for a complete break in relations with China. The New Order's Foreign Minister, Adam Malik, anxious that Indonesia should retain a nonaligned profile in its foreign policy, was able for many months to keep these pressures at bay. In April, however, Djawoto, the Indonesian ambassador in Beijing, asked for and was granted political asylum in China. For its part, China, realizing that Sukarno had failed to regain the political initiative, was increasingly critical of the New Order regime. For the most part, its criticisms were directed at the mistreatment of ethnic Chinese rather than concern over the fate of the PKI or the reorientation of Indonesian foreign policy. Beijing's belated defense of its friends and allies in Indonesia played into the army's hands. By early 1967, the military pressure on Malik to break with China had become intense. In April, the Chinese chargé d'affaires in Jakarta was expelled. A renewed outbreak of anti-Chinese rioting in Jakarta coincided with the takeover of the Foreign Ministry in Beijing by an ultra-leftist group. As the Cultural Revolution took hold of China, little seemed to be lost from Beijing's viewpoint in trying to maintain relations with Indonesia. In July, it gave public backing to the now underground PKI and called for a "people's war" against the "Suharto fascist regime." Daily demonstrations took place outside the Indonesian embassy in Beijing and it was clear that it was only a matter of time before a final break would occur. It is a testimony to the influence that Adam Malik exercised over Suharto that even at this stage he was able to avoid a total rupture, declaring instead on October 9, 1967, that relations with China were frozen.

The break in relations with China was one of the most radical symptoms of the changes in Indonesia in 1965-66. The PKI ceased to exist as a political party and tens of thousands of its members were massacred throughout the country. Widespread purges also took place in the armed forces, the professions, the bureaucracy and the Nationalist party, with the military leadership rooting out those they considered to be leftist sympathizers. Although Sukarno's "Guided Democracy" had distinct authoritarian overtones, Suharto's "New Order" did not usher in a more democratic order.

In the months after March 1966, when President Sukarno ceded virtually all his remaining powers to General Suharto, the atmosphere of Jakarta politics underwent a drastic change. Many of the president's principal foreign and economic policies were reversed. Demands grew for a complete break with the past, including the removal of the president himself. Nevertheless, Suharto as army commander continued to move slowly, aware that Sukarno still had enormous support in the country, especially in East and Central Java. The hesitancy of Suharto and his senior generals in taking decisive action to dismiss Sukarno was

---

MILITARY DOMINANCE

"The army's domination of the government machinery at all levels enabled it to set the tone of the entire administration. Even though positions of authority were shared with civilians, the civilians had to fit into a system in which power lay with the military. Control of the administration meant not only that the army had strong influence over government policies at all levels, but also that officers could distribute benefits and dispense patronage to their military colleagues and civilian friends. Appointments throughout the administration became dependent on the approval of army officers, and power over the issuing of licenses, granting of contracts, and determination of projects enabled the army to reward those who accepted military domination and to penalize those who did not."

—Harold Crouch
The Army and Politics in Indonesia

---

reinforced by their traditional Javanese values, which gave them a sense of propriety that inhibited them from completely humiliating the man who was still the founder of the nation. It became clear, however, in the course of 1966, that Sukarno would not be satisfied with the role of a constitutional head of state. The president openly expressed his disapproval of the direction in which the generals were taking the country and, in so doing, he continued to pose a threat to the army's hold on the government. The army countered this by holding show trials of several of Sukarno's ministers in a clear bid to discredit the president. In March 1967, the Indonesian parliament, now dominated by supporters of General Suharto, stripped Sukarno of all his remaining powers and appointed Suharto as acting president. Although Sukarno had lost all the attributes of the presidency, General Suharto was not confirmed in

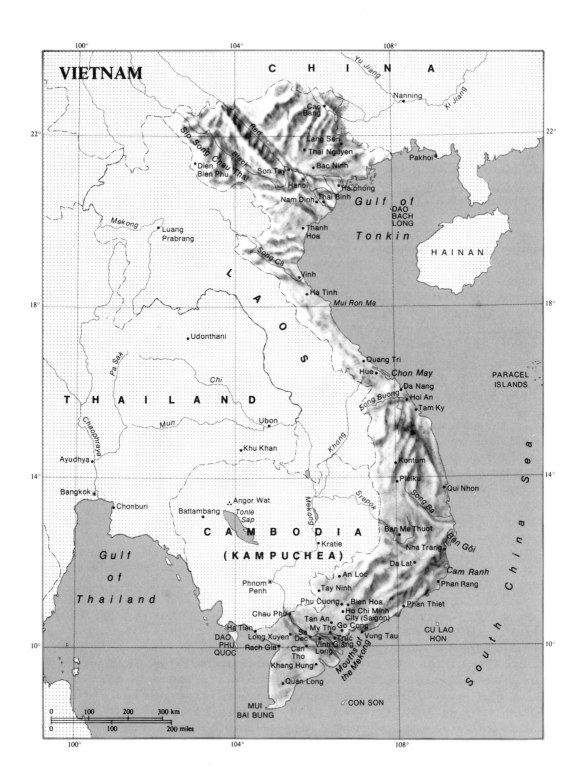

VIETNAM

C H I N A

Yu Jiang

Nanning

Xi Jiang

Cao
Bang

Lang Son
Thai Nguyen

Red

Son Tay
Dien
Bien Phu
Bac Ninh
Pakhoi

Sip Song Chau Thai

Black

Hanoi
Haiphong
Nam Dinh
Thai Binh
Gulf of
DAO
BACH
LONG

Thanh
Hoa
Tonkin

HAINAN

Mekong
Luang
Prabrang

Song Ca

L
A
O
S

Vinh

Ha Tinh

Mui Ron Ma

Udonthani

Pa Sak

Quang Tri
Hue
Chon May

Chi
Da Nang
Hoi An
Song Buong
Tam Ky

PARACEL
ISLANDS

T H A I L A N D

Mun

Ubon

Khong

Khu Khan

Kontum

Chaophraya

Ayudhya

Pleiku

Qui Nhon

Song Ba

Bangkok

Chonburi

Angor Wat

Battambang
Tonle
Sap

Mekong

Srepok

Ban Me Thuot
Bến Gôi

Kratie

Nha Trang

C A M B O D I A
(KAMPUCHEA)

Da Lat
Cam Ranh

Gulf

of

Thailand

An Loc

Phan Rang

Tay Ninh

Phnom
Penh
Phu Cuong
Bien Hoa
Phan Thiet

Chau Phu
Ho Chi Minh
City (Saigon)

Tan An
My Tho
Go Cong
CU LAO
HON

Ha Tien
DAO
PHU
QUOC
Long Xuyen
Sa
Dec
Truc
Vung Tau

Rach Gia
Vinh
Long
Can
Tho
Khang Hung
Mouths of
the Mekong

South China Sea

Quan Long

MUI
BAI BUNG
CON SON

0   100   200   300 km

0   100   200 miles

office as Indonesia's second president until March 1968. Sukarno was by now under effective house arrest and died in ignominy in June 1970.

In the late 1960s, Suharto moved to consolidate his power in Indonesia by neutralizing other potential sources of leadership in the armed forces. Above all, he sought to eliminate the remnants of the PKI, which had been the main political enemy of the army before 1965. An Internal Security Command (Kopkamtib) was established to root out communist sympathizers in all sectors of Indonesian society. In 1966, and again in 1968, in the Blitar area of East Java, there were attempts to revive the PKI but these were quickly and brutally suppressed by the army. As many as half a million alleged PKI supporters were killed in the massacres following the 1965 coup attempt and hundreds of thousands of others were arrested and detained until the late 1970s. Kopkamtib gradually became the government's main instrument of political control, dealing eventually not only with alleged Communists but also with student radicals and fundamentalist Moslem dissidents. Newspapers, too, were brought under Kopkamtib's supervision by requiring its permission to publish.

Although the government was dominated by the army after 1966, it sought the association of Western educated civilian technocrats to create an atmosphere of domestic legitimacy and, above all, to create a favorable image among Western aid donors. Technocratic members of the government lacked any real political power. Like the cabinets led by Sukarno, those led by President Suharto since 1967 have not essentially been decision-making bodies. They have met mainly to hear guidelines from the president and to report to him. For more than twenty years after 1966, the military's preeminent role in government went largely unchallenged.

Inevitably the dramatic political upheaval in Indonesia also had a major impact on Southeast Asia. The confrontation that Sukarno had engineered with Malaysia was, in the course of 1966, formally brought to an end. A radical political realignment now took place in the region with the formation in August 1967 in Bangkok of the Association of Southeast Asian Nations, or ASEAN. The new grouping brought together Indonesia, Singapore, Malaysia, Thailand, and the Philippines in a loose association pledged to uphold

regional stability and encourage economic development. (Brunei was to join in 1984 after it achieved full independence from Britain. In 1995, Vietnam became a seventh member) In the course of the next two decades, ASEAN was acknowledged as one of the most successful regional groupings in the Third World.

VIETNAM, 1965-1975

The End of the War in Vietnam

More than any other conflict after the Second World War, the war in Vietnam seemed to symbolize the struggle of Third World radicalism against the determination of the United States to stem the tide of communism in the developing world. The war was to act as an inspiration to communist movements elsewhere in the Third World and played a key role in the emergence of the New Left in the advanced capitalist countries in the late 1960s. Ironically, the massive involvement of the United States in the conflict in Vietnam only postponed an almost inevitable communist victory and succeeded in contributing to the eventual communist successes in Laos and Cambodia as well.

The Tet Offensive

In late January 1968 communist forces launched a sustained offensive throughout South Vietnam to coincide with the annual New Year's festival, known in Vietnamese as Tet. The most prominent attacks were on Saigon itself and the former imperial capital, Hue. While the losses of the communist forces during the offensive were considerable, the psychological damage inflicted on the United States through the extensive television coverage of the battle amounted to a victory for Hanoi. In Saigon, parts of the U.S. embassy itself were occupied, while in Hue the NLF and North Vietnamese forces succeeded in holding parts of the city for three weeks.

The Tet offensive represented a dramatic turning point in the Vietnam War. It became apparent to the Johnson administration in Washington that despite the commitment of 500,000 troops the war could not be won militarily. Within months of the offensive, President Johnson had suspended the bombing of North Vietnam and opened peace talks in Paris. He also announced that he would not be seeking another term of office. Fighting continued while the Paris talks dragged on, but on a smaller scale if only because of the heavy casualties both sides suffered during the Tet offensive. Under Richard Nixon, who assumed the U.S. presidency in January 1969, the United States pursued a policy of "Vietnamization" of the war, withdrawing some troops and increasingly leaving most counterinsurgency operations to South Vietnamese forces. The last major offensive operation involving U.S. forces was the April 1970 invasion of Cambodia, which succeeded only in contributing to the rise of the Khmer Rouge, Cambodia's indigenous communist insurgency led by Pol Pot, and alienating even larger numbers of Americans from the war.

The Paris Peace Agreement and the Fall of Saigon

After more than four years of talks in Paris, North Vietnam and the United States finally signed an agreement on January 23, 1973, providing for the complete withdrawal of American forces and a cease-fire between South Vietnamese and communist forces.

By the end of March, the last American combat troops had been withdrawn. As with the Geneva Agreement some nineteen years earlier, peace was not restored to Vietnam. In the weeks and months following the cease-fire, negotiations on a future political structure and on a military settlement quickly broke down amid mutual recriminations. Soon communist and South Vietnamese forces were fighting again.

Expectations in Hanoi had been high after the Paris Peace Accords that the Thieu regime could be overthrown without resort to further armed force. The South Vietnamese government, however, remained unwilling to see the NLF, by now called the Provisional Revolutionary Government, accommodated in the political structure of the southern half of Vietnam. Moreover, the revolutionary forces were not strong enough by themselves to engineer Thieu's downfall. In these

circumstances, in the autumn of 1974 the communist leadership in Hanoi decided to launch a major offensive in the South in early 1975.

It has been made clear from subsequent accounts by Vietnamese leaders that the success of the 1975 offensive and the quick demise of the Thieu regime exceeded all expectations in Hanoi. In the first stage of the offensive in January, communist forces captured Tay Ninh Province, northeast of Saigon. Two months later, they seized Ban Me Thuot, the largest city in the Central Highlands, with very little resistance. President Thieu made the fatal mistake of ordering a retreat from the northern part of the country, leaving only the coastal cities defended. Panic now beset the South Vietnamese army and by the end of March Hue, the former imperial capital, was in communist hands.

It was at this stage that the Politburo in Hanoi, flushed with the continuing success of the offensive and convinced that the United States would not intervene to save the beleaguered Thieu regime, decided to press for final victory. Communist forces poured south from the Central Highlands and along the coast and by mid-April were on the outskirts of Saigon. For a brief period they were halted by stiff resistance from South Vietnamese troops at Xuan Loc, less than 100 kilometers east of Saigon. By April 21 thirteen North Vietnamese divisions had surrounded the South Vietnamese capital. The following day, President Thieu resigned and left the country. The presidency was taken over by Duong Van Minh, who vainly sought a negotiated settlement with the Communists. On April 30, with South Vietnamese resistance at an end and helicopters evacuating the remaining Americans from rooftops, North Vietnamese troops stormed into the grounds of the presidential palace in Saigon. The second Indochina war had come to an end.

INDONESIA, 1968-1976

The Consolidation of Suharto's New Order

With the formal inauguration in March 1968 of General Suharto as Indonesia's second president, the old order of Sukarno was finally laid to rest. In its place, President Suharto began the construction of his "New Order." If the military enjoyed a preeminent position in the politics of the New Order, this was not without some popular support after the economic chaos of the last years of the Sukarno regime and the apparent threat of a communist seizure of power.

As events unfolded it became clear that the New Order was as intolerant of political pluralism as President Sukarno's old order. Previously banned parties, such as the modernist Moslem Masyumi and the social-democratic Indonesian Socialist Party, or PSI, remained prohibited. Whereas before 1966 political parties in order to survive had to subscribe to the anti-imperialist rhetoric of Guided Democracy, under the New Order political parties were once again enjoined to abandon their sectional interests in pursuit of the wider goals of modernization and development. In so doing, it was taken for granted that not only would they abandon any hope of forming a government but they would also leave uncontested the army's grip on power.

Establishing its own civilian organization, Golkar (Organization of Functional Groups), to contest elections in 1971, the army ensured that its civilian arm scored an overwhelming victory, which reduced independently organized civilian influence to insignificant proportions. The elections had two aims. First, to give the government a degree of legitimacy domestically and internationally and, second, to give the parties a degree of participation in the political system without threatening the army's hold on actual political power. In the elections held on July 5, 1971, Golkar scored an overwhelming victory, winning almost 63 percent of the votes. Despite its electoral success, Golkar was essentially a creation of the military authorities with little sense of its own identity. It was a federation of organizations mobilized and manipulated by the army with the express purpose of weakening existing political parties. At the beginning of 1973, the old parties "voluntarily" dissolved themselves and formed two new parties under government-endorsed leadership. The old Moslem political parties were replaced by the United Development Party (PPP), while the former nationalist and Christian parties were amalgamated into the Indonesian Democratic Party (PDI).

THE ARMY AND CIVILIANS

"The emergence of the army to a position of unchallenged domination of the government had been welcomed enthusiastically by a small section of civilian political opinion and accepted as an unavoidable reality by most of the rest. In the wake of the turbulence of the preceding period, army rule seemed at least to guarantee a more stable political climate. Further, many civilians hoped that in the new atmosphere the army would feel the need to seek popular acceptance and support by associating civilians with the regime. Political stabilization in the long run, it seemed, would require the setting up of a new political framework within which civilian groups could be accommodated. However, in the accommodation that eventually emerged, popular participation through the political parties had no important place."

—Harold Crouch
The Army and Politics in Indonesia

The success of the political framework of the New Order is succinctly summed up by Lucian Pye:

With the New Order under General Suharto a new triad was created as the basic framework for Indonesian politics: the army as the key element, a rejuvenated civil bureaucracy, and an "official," functionally based "political party" called Golkar. Suharto displayed surprising, and extraordinary, political genius when he decided that the strongest-based political structure would be a coalition of a large number of occupationally, professionally, and socially defined subgroups, each hierarchically organized according to bapakism (literally, father-child, i.e., patron-client relations). This was precisely what the Dutch had discovered much earlier. Golkar insists that it is not really a political party but a higher order of popular participation. To ensure the electoral success of Golkar, General Suharto executed the clever ploy of insisting that the two religious parties should merge into the Muslim United Development Party (PPP) and that the secular opposition parties should become the Indonesian Democratic Party (PDI), a requirement which forced people without bapak ties to work together. As a consequence they could only engage in unseemly feuding, proving to everyone that they lacked the coherence necessary for ruling the country.[1]

The New Order Economy

In the economic realm, as in the political, many characteristics of the Indonesian economy under Sukarno were retained in Suharto's New Order. Indeed, the army had already become extensively involved in the country's economic life following the expropriation of Dutch properties. More often than not these were taken over and run by the military. The Indonesian state oil firm, Pertamina, was established by the military in 1957. The state generally has continued to play an important role in the Indonesian economy under President Suharto with many sectors of the economy continuing to be dominated by state corporations.

There were also important differences. Sukarno had sought legitimacy in the promise of continuing the revolution and struggling against Western imperialism by adhering to the principles of the 1955 Bandung Conference and of the Nonaligned Movement. President Suharto, by contrast, has ruled in the name of stability and development. Thus the military domination of political life could be justified in terms of the country's economic development. As elsewhere in the developing world, the military, it was argued, stood for the national interest rather than the selfish and sectoral interests of the politicians.

It was above all with regard to foreign aid and investment that President Suharto's policies differed sharply from those of his predecessor. A new foreign investment law in 1967 opened the way for a rapid inflow of foreign capital which turned

into a flood in the 1970s. By 1973, more than a billion dollars in foreign investment had poured into Indonesia. The typical arrangement was for the investment to take the form of joint ventures in which the Indonesian side consisted of a partnership between senior military officers and Chinese businessmen. To many observers, such as Harold Crouch, the influx of foreign investment had inevitable effects on the country's social structure.

"The economic policies introduced by the government in 1966 and afterward brought great benefits to the commercial enterprises with which army officers were associated. The government's policies created conditions favorable for foreign investment, which was attracted by price stability, the liberalization of foreign trade, the incentives and guarantees of the 1967 investment law, and, most important, the evidence that the generals were firmly in control. The sharp rise in foreign investment was channeled mainly through joint ventures, in which the Indonesian partner had military connections and often contributed little more than arranging the necessary approval from the government. Basing their economic strength on political influence rather than entrepreneurial skill, members of the Indonesian military elite acquired the characteristics of a comprador class whose interests ran parallel with those of the foreign corporations with which they were associated. Rewarded with a share in the profits that enabled them to live in a style similar to that of their foreign partners, the private interests of the comprador elements in the elite were well served by the new strategy of economic development."[2]

Despite these criticisms, the achievements of President Suharto in turning around the Indonesian economy have been impressive. Much of this has been the result of the considerable foreign aid and investment Indonesia has received since the late 1960s as well as shrewd exploitation of the country's significant gas and oil deposits. In 1967, the United States, Japan, and other Western countries, together with multilateral financial institutions, formed the Inter-Governmental Group on Indonesia (IGGI) to coordinate their aid policies. The large increase in resources now available to the government enabled it to control inflation, correct the balance of payments deficit, and promote the rapid development of the modern sector

Southeast Asia's Labor Force

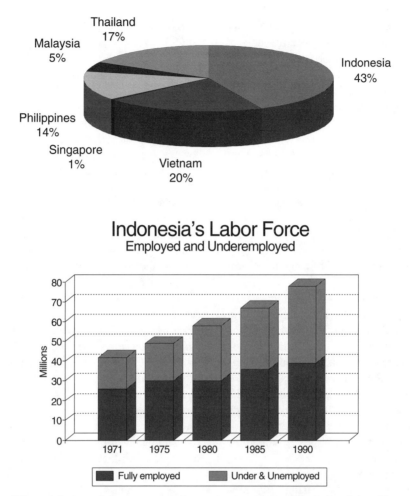

Indonesia's Labor Force
Employed and Underemployed

Graph 11.1 Although Indonesia's economy is becoming gradually more industrial and less agricultural, it faces a serious challenge in generating employment for a still-burgeoning work force.

of the economy. The huge credits granted by Western countries, together with growing private investment, enabled Indonesia to achieve an average annual rate of growth of 7 percent in the decade 1967-76 while industrial production also grew considerably. Exports grew more than sevenfold between 1967 and 1975, rising in value from $595 million in 1967 to $4,700 million by 1975. Agriculture also was not neglected. Rapid increases in rice production were achieved by the 1970s and the country became self-sufficient.

New Order Foreign Policy

As we have seen earlier, the New Order sharply reversed President Sukarno's foreign policy. The key elements of this break were the termination of the conflict with Malaysia and the freezing of diplomatic relations with China. At the same time, the New Order's first foreign minister, Adam Malik, was anxious that the country not become too dependent on the West even though Indonesia had to turn to that quarter for economic assistance. With President Suharto's blessing, he sought to foster regional solidarity in Southeast Asia with the creation of ASEAN in 1967. Malik also resisted moves to make a complete break in relations with communist countries. Thus while diplomatic relations were broken with China, long seen by the military as the main threat to Southeast Asia, Indonesia retained ties with the Soviet Union and with North Vietnam. As evidence of what was termed Indonesia's "independent and active" foreign policy, the country remained a key member of the Nonaligned movement.

After 1965, some army generals were keen to forge closer ties, including security links, with the United States but President Suharto and Malik were determined to maintain Indonesia's traditional policy of avoiding bilateral defense commitments with Washington. Nevertheless, the United States did become a major military supplier to the New Order regime supplanting the Soviet Union which prior to 1965 had been Indonesia's largest arms supplier. U.S. military aid rose from $5.8 million in 1969 to more than $40 million by 1976. The United States also provided about a third of the economic assistance that Indonesia received after 1970. Indonesia was careful not to become too dependent on Washington and balanced this aid with similar commitments from Japan and Western Europe. After the boom in oil prices in 1973, Indonesia's reliance on foreign aid was reduced and its capacity for taking an independent foreign policy stand correspondingly enhanced.

The most contentious issue in foreign policy in the 1970s was Indonesia's invasion and subsequent incorporation of the former Portuguese colony of East Timor. Following the 1974 revolution in Portugal, the authorities in Lisbon ordered a withdrawal from all the country's colonies. In East Timor, a period of political confusion ensued that was utilized by Indonesia to justify its seizure of the territory on December 7, 1975, the day after U.S. President Gerald Ford visited Jakarta. In July 1976, the territory was formally incorporated into Indonesia as the country's twenty-seventh province. The move brought widespread condemnation of Indonesia from the international community. To this day, the United Nations has still not recognized the move and sporadic resistance to Indonesian occupation continues from the leftist nationalist movement, Fretilin (Revolutionary Front for an Independent East Timor).

VIETNAM, 1975-1990

The Strains of Reunification

In the aftermath of the fall of the South Vietnamese regime in April 1975, administration of the southern half of the country was taken over by the Provisional Revolutionary Government, maintaining the fiction of the independence of the revolutionary forces in the south. It was clear, however, that all major decisions regarding the South were now being made by the communist leadership in Hanoi. Despite the fact that the Thieu regime had little support outside the armed forces, the new communist administration met with much passive resistance. Third Force or neutralist elements, who had expected some role in the new southern government, soon found themselves excluded by northern cadres moved south. Thousands of military and civilian officials of the defeated southern regime were later imprisoned for varying periods of time and subjected to "reeducation." Early promises to maintain the capitalist economy in the south were quickly overlooked. In the face of resistance by the dominant ethnic Chinese business to measures of control, the Communist Party Politburo in Hanoi responded by tightening political control of the south. On July 2, 1976, the two halves of the country were formally reunified in the Socialist Republic of Vietnam (SRV).

The absorption of the capitalist south placed enormous strains on Vietnam's already inadequate administrative structure. The huge toll the war had taken of revolutionary cadres and the speed with which reunification took place added to the country's difficulties in the late 1970s. At the Fourth Congress of the Communist Party in December 1976, highly unrealistic plans for industrialization and the socialization of the South's economy were adopted. The alienation of much of the southern population intensified and by 1978 tens of thousands of Vietnamese were leaving the country by boat to seek new lives in the West. The exodus from the South was accelerated by the failure of the ambitious economic plans of 1976, a failure caused in part by the inability to attract foreign aid on any significant scale and the U.S. imposed economic embargo. Hostility toward Chinese business in the south and deteriorating relations with the Chinese-supported Khmer Rouge regime in Cambodia, led China to cut off aid in 1978. The same year, Vietnam aligned itself with the Soviet Union in a Treaty of Friendship and Cooperation and became a member of Comecon (Council for Mutual Economic Assistance), the trade association of communist countries. The Soviet navy was granted base facilities at the former U.S. bases of Da Nang and Cam Ranh Bay. As so often in its history, Vietnam's nationalism was tempered by the need, if only temporarily, for a powerful external patron to meet the perceived threat posed by the Khmer Rouge and China.

The Third Indochina War

By 1978, Vietnam's relations with Cambodia had worsened to the extent that bitter border fighting was taking place. On December 25, 1978, in response to the deteriorating situation, Vietnamese forces invaded "Democratic Kampuchea," as it had been renamed by the Khmer Rouge, and toppled Pol Pot's three and a half year regime.

On January 7, 1979 Vietnam installed a new government in Phnom Penh led by Heng Samrin which adopted the name "People's Republic of Kampuchea." Despite the odious reputation of the Khmer Rouge and the almost universal condemnation of its period in power, the new government was recognized only by Vietnam's communist

allies and, later on, by India. The Khmer Rouge, still led by Pol Pot, fled to the Thai-Cambodian border where they were to be rearmed and resupplied by China, aided and abetted by Thailand. At the United Nations the Khmer Rouge still occupied the Cambodian seat and the U.N. itself condemned Vietnam for its invasion and called for the withdrawal of its forces. The United States moved to tighten its economic boycott of both Vietnam and the new People's Republic of Kampuchea and other Western countries, with the exception of Sweden, followed suit.

The Chinese replied to the Vietnamese invasion of Cambodia by launching a punitive attack along Vietnam's northern borders on February 17, 1979. Vietnam was at war once again and the world was stunned to see the first intercommunist war in history.

The Chinese invasion, however, achieved little. Despite fighting a war on two fronts, on its northern border and in Cambodia, Vietnam's battle-hardened forces had acquitted themselves well, inflicting more than twenty thousand fatalities on the Chinese forces in a six-week campaign. China failed to inflict a decisive lesson on the Vietnamese, and Beijing's hope to use its occupation of the border areas as a bargaining chip to pry the Vietnamese out of Cambodia failed. The failure only reinforced China's resolve to continue to support the Khmer Rouge in order to bleed the Vietnamese in Cambodia. The war had sown deep seeds of enmity between two former allies. For many years to come the peoples of Vietnam and Cambodia were once again to be denied the fruits of peace.

The Chinese attack on Vietnam had little impact on the conflict in Cambodia itself where, in the early months of 1979, the Vietnamese were welcomed as liberators as noted by Nayan Chanda:

In hundreds of Cambodian villages, the Vietnamese invasion was greeted with joy and disbelief. The Khmer Rouge cadres and militia were gone. People were free again to live as families, to go to bed without fearing the next day. Some 300,000 people from the western provinces and from Phnom Penh were forced to join the retreating Khmer Rouge into the forest. But for the rest of Cambodia it was as if salvation had come. Villagers emptied the government granaries and slaughtered pigs and chickens to have their first hearty meals in four years. Hundreds of thousands took to the roads to return to their home-towns.[3]

Reestablishing a functioning government in Cambodia after the years in power of the Khmer Rouge was no easy task. Quite apart from contin-uing resistance from the Khmer Rouge, countless thousands of professional and middle-class peo-ple had been killed in the Cambodian holocaust. Formal education and health care, currency, and even the towns had been all but abolished. Recon-structing Cambodia, the Vietnamese found, could only be achieved by massive infusions of Vietnamese advisers and skilled workers to rebuild the most basic services. This was quite apart from the 100,000 or more Vietnamese troops necessary for the country's security. As time went by, the presence of so many Vietnamese reawakened traditional Cambodian fears that they would become swamped by their stronger neigh-bor to the East.

Vietnam's Vietnam: The War in Cambodia

Few countries had the stomach to support the Khmer Rouge after their eviction from power in 1979. The one exception to this was China, which saw in Vietnam's invasion of Cambodia an attempt by the leadership in Hanoi to impose its hegemony on the whole of Indochina. Moreover, Vietnam was closely allied with the Soviet Union and, for Beijing, the Moscow-Hanoi axis raised the specter of the encirclement of China. The United States, which had by now normalized rela-tions with Beijing, saw the conflict in Indochina increasingly in terms of its own strategic interests, and, for Washington, as then Secretary of State Alexander Haig noted in 1984: "China may be the most important country in the world."

For this reason, and many would argue because of its continuing resentment at losing the war in Vietnam, the United States under President Ronald Reagan tacitly approved of the Chinese efforts to rehabilitate the Khmer Rouge and turn

"I do not understand why some people want to remove Pol Pot. It is true that he made some mistakes in the past but now he is leading the fight against the Vietnamese aggressors."

—Deng Xiaoping, November 1, 1984

them once again into a formidable fighting force. For the noncommunist countries of Southeast Asia grouped in ASEAN, there were still serious misgivings about supporting a movement with such an appalling record in power as the Khmer Rouge. Moreover, some ASEAN members, nota-bly Indonesia and Malaysia, still nurtured suspi-cions of China's long-term intentions in Southeast Asia. Others, especially Thailand, the frontline state, and Singapore, feared Vietnam more, seeing in its invasion of Cambodia a flagrant breach of international law. For them the Vietnamese had become "the Prussians of Asia." Nevertheless, ASEAN did manage to maintain a common policy of opposition to the Vietnamese military presence in Cambodia.

This stance was made much easier by the formation in June 1982 of the Coalition Govern-ment of Democratic Kampuchea (CGDK). The coalition, formed after constant pressure by ASEAN, brought together the Khmer Rouge; a noncommunist group, the Khmer People's National Liberation Front (KPNLF) led by a for-mer Cambodian Prime Minister Son Sann; and forces supporting the former head of state, Prince Sihanouk. The formation of the Coalition Govern-ment and the fact that Sihanouk became its presi-dent, gave some international respectability to the efforts to dislodge the Vietnamese and the Heng Samrin government in Phnom Penh. Henceforth, the United States and ASEAN developed a pro-gram of economic and military assistance for the two noncommunist factions in the Coalition Gov-ernment. This, however, still fell far short of the massive assistance rendered the Khmer Rouge by the Chinese. Although the two noncommunist groups had military forces of their own, the Khmer Rouge remained the single most important group militarily and the most significant threat to the Vietnamese in Cambodia.

While Vietnam was more than able to hold its own against the Khmer Rouge, it was only able to do so at a considerable price. The government it had installed in Phnom Penh was not only denied international recognition but also because of its close ties to the Vietnamese it lacked legitimacy in the eyes of many Cambodians. Moreover, Vietnam could only maintain itself in Cambodia because of the vast amounts of economic and military aid it received from the Soviet Union. Economic aid alone was believed to be worth $1 billion a year by 1980. These considerable sums were a factor in the granting of base facilities to the Soviets at Da Nang and Cam Ranh Bay.

China's border war of attrition against Vietnam drained Vietnamese resources. Denial of Western aid and loans deepened Vietnam's economic difficulties further. By the mid-1980s more than a million Vietnamese had fled the country since the communist takeover in 1975. Vietnam, once a hero of the Third World as a giant-killer, had become an international pariah condemned by the United Nations. By the beginning of 1986, Vietnam's foreign debt had risen to $6.7 billion and, because of their default in repayment, all international lending institutions, such as the World Bank and the IMF, had closed their doors. The country's economy was racked by a lack of capital, gross economic mismanagement, and a rapidly growing population.

The Slow Road to Reform: The 1986 Party Congress

Although the scale of conflict in Cambodia and along the Chinese border declined after 1981, it continued to contribute to a garrison state atmosphere within Vietnam. This and the imposition of the U.S.-led economic embargo against the country delayed considerably the onset of reform in Vietnam and have continued until the present day to place constraints on the reform process in Vietnam. With the possible exceptions of North Korea and Cuba, no other communist country has had to endure such an enforced and prolonged economic and political isolation from the international community. Even within the communist bloc, Vietnam became isolated as, first, the Eastern European states and, then, the Soviet Union moved to improve their relations with China.

Although half-hearted attempts were made at economic reform in the early 1980s by reducing the level of economic subsidies and by granting a greater level of responsibility to enterprises, these only succeeded in worsening the country's economic problems. Indeed, as a result of price, wage, and currency reforms, inflation soared in 1985 to a staggering annual rate of 700 percent. In May 1986 Le Duc Tho, one of the most senior communist leaders, openly attacked the party's shortcomings which he said had led to demoralization, sycophancy, and opportunism. Tho spoke of corruption "tainting every level of the party." What made his criticism all the more damning was the fact that he had been at the center of Vietnamese politics for four decades.

Pressure for reform grew as the crisis in Vietnamese society increased. In December 1986 at the Sixth Congress of the Vietnamese Communist Party, the country's three most senior leaders, Prime Minister Pham Van Dong, General Secretary Truong Chinh and senior Politburo member Le Duc Tho, all resigned from office and a new reforming party leader, Nguyen Van Linh, was elected. It was openly acknowledged that the main reason for the dramatic resignations was the fundamental failure of the country's economic and political policies. The new politburo elected at the Congress confirmed a definite bias toward economic reformers.

The Sixth Congress heralded a decisive move in the direction of economic reform. Most significantly the leadership began to give greater emphasis to light rather than heavy industry and provided greater incentives for private industry. Past policies were criticized for attaching excessive importance to the state sector and discriminating against the collective and private sector, upholding an inefficient system of centralized allocation of resources in the state sector, failing to rectify the serious sectoral imbalances, and ignoring agriculture. By 1988, the economic reforms had gathered pace and increasingly aimed at fundamentally changing the faltering economic system rather than "perfecting" it. Agriculture was effectively decollectivized and wide-ranging financial reforms were enacted. The latter brought inflation under control and, by devaluing the

Vietnamese currency, the dong, it cut back on the black market for foreign currency.

The reform program adopted by the Vietnamese Communist Party in December 1986 was accompanied the following year by a clean-up campaign within the party itself. The campaign, launched in September 1987, was designed to rid party and government ranks of all those deemed to be "corrupt and degraded." At the time, the party newspaper, *Nhan Dan* (People's Daily) acknowledged that never before had "morale been so eroded, confidence been so low, or justice been so abused." Even by the standards of "glasnost" or greater openness, adopted since 1986, the editorial was striking in its indictment of party and government shortcomings.

The Sixth Party Congress accelerated the pace of economic reform in Vietnam which was also clearly influenced by Mr. Gorbachev's policy of perestroika in the Soviet Union. For its part, the Soviet Union put increasing pressure on Vietnam to undertake wide-ranging economic reforms. In December 1986, a senior Soviet Politburo member, Yegor Ligachev, revealed during a visit to Hanoi that Soviet economic aid to Vietnam had reached U.S. $2.5 billion a year. Criticism of the use of Soviet aid in Vietnam now appeared frequently in the Soviet press. In May 1987, when Vietnamese leader Nguyen Van Linh visited Moscow, Mr. Gorbachev complained about what he called the "weak economic bonds" between the two countries.

The New Openness

Reform in the economy was accompanied by a greater general openness in Vietnamese society. "Glasnost" had arrived in Vietnam. The launching of the reform program, known in Vietnamese as *doi moi*, or renovation, at the Sixth Party Congress in December 1986 led to a greater tolerance and pluralism in the arts, media, and religion. One of the first signs of this was the appearance of articles in the party newspaper, *Nhan Dan*, under the byline N.V.L., the initials of course of party leader, Nguyen Van Linh. The articles pressed the need for economic reform, urged greater democracy in party life, and strongly criticized middle-level bureaucrats who were resisting the tide of reform.

It remains unclear whether the articles were written from a position of political strength or weakness. In many ways they had a Gorbachevian ring to them of appealing to the people against the conservative hierarchy. Linh himself acknowledged authorship of the articles in October 1987, telling one interviewer that the initials stood for noi van lam, or speak and act. The important point, however, was that the appearance of the "NVL" articles gave journalists and the media generally an apparently high level endorsement to be more critical of the established order. The "NVL" articles underlined the commitment of Linh to the reform program and led to the adoption of a more open press policy. The first article appeared in *Nhan Dan* on May 25, 1987. For several months the articles urging the public to act against bureaucratic tyrants and bullies produced only a deafening silence. By August 1987, the party daily was receiving six hundred letters a month denouncing various government agencies and officials. The fight initiated by "NVL" against corruption and abuse of power encouraged private and public criticism of public policy that fuelled a more liberal governing trend. The press was particularly affected and became a more aggressive critic of government policy. In some cases it was instrumental in removing local party bosses who had flagrantly abused power and obstructed reforms. In the first six months of 1988, no fewer than 1,100 party cadres were tried for corruption, often after they had been exposed in the press. The openness with which many of Vietnam's leaders addressed their shortcomings in the press in 1987-88 was unparalleled. Journalists and the media generally were encouraged to expose failings at all levels. A party directive from the Central Committee in September 1987 emphasized that not only journalists but every party member and citizen had the right to criticize officials guilty of wrongdoing. It also warned officials against attempting to harass or punish those who documented their shortcomings in the press. In August 1987, an editorial in *Nhan Dan* described the struggle for economic reform and renovation as a matter of life and death for Vietnamese society. In December of the same year, a communique following a ten-day meeting of the Communist Party Central Committee painted a gloomy picture of economic hardship and political mismanagement. The press talked of a serious slump in grain production and

Vietnam: Resource Gap & External Debt

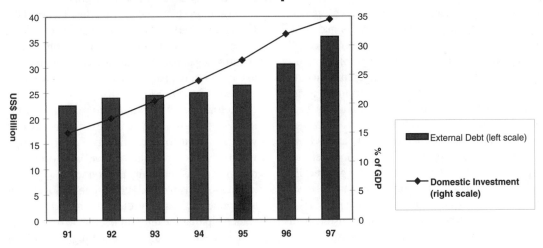

Graph 11.2

constant shortages, of falling industrial growth, and declining standards of living. In an extraordinary condemnation of its own failures, the party communique, which received wider attention in the media than usual, held the leadership responsible for the crisis in Vietnam, accusing itself of bureaucratic, incompetent, and undisciplined centralism. Additionally, in a quite remarkable call for any ruling Communist Party to make, it appealed for a struggle against the state of the bureaucracy and its oppression of the masses.

The initial openness in the press came from *Nhan Dan* but the trend to a more critical press soon spread to Ho Chi Minh City (as Saigon was renamed), with *Saigon Giai Phong* (*Saigon Liberation*) running a column written by its own readers entitled "Speaking Frankly and Truthfully." Another Saigon newspaper, *Tuoi Tre* (*Youth*) opened a complaints department with reporters assigned to investigate readers' problems. Issues such as drug addiction, prostitution, and draft evasion, which were simply not discussed in the press before 1987, now became subjects of heated debate. Western culture, previously covered only in a critical fashion, was now

written about in a more dispassionate manner. Even beauty contests became the subject of a column in *Nhan Dan*.

The greater freedom accorded the press from 1987 was also extended to the arts. Western music and videos, previously vigorously suppressed, were now openly tolerated. For years Western pop music and culture had been decried by the authorities. Even ballroom dancing was banned, much to the resentment of many Vietnamese and particularly those in the south of the country. The ageing northern leadership seemed to be imbued not just with the Leninist concept of creating a "new socialist man" but also the Confucian ethic of self-restraint. After 1987 the authorities showed a far greater tolerance toward Western culture in both its popular and elitist variants. One of the most important factors in contributing to the more relaxed attitude by the authorities was the growing realization that most young Vietnamese were deeply disillusioned by the austere regime hitherto imposed by the Communist Party. It increasingly seemed to be counterproductive to repress Western culture. Soon rock music was heard as frequently on the streets of Vietnamese cities as in other parts of Southeast Asia. "Video-cafes" also became part of the scene in Hanoi and Ho Chi Minh City.

Books by Western writers became more generally available, and Vietnamese writers and filmmakers gathered confidence and soon challenged the country's social and economic problems. Similar changes began to take place in cinema, theatre, and art with a greater willingness to move away from the previous norms of socialist realism. Typical of the new mood was the film *Decent Stories*. Made in 1985, the film was shown in late 1987 on Hanoi television, apparently after an intervention by Nguyen Van Linh himself. The film graphically depicts homeless beggars on the streets of Hanoi and then switches to scenes of a lavish party.

The post-1986 reform movement also had an impact on religion. This was most noticeable in the more relaxed official attitude towards the Catholic Church. Unlike North Korea or China, the Catholic Church has never been banned in Vietnam, although it has found its activities subject to many constraints. After the Communist Party's Sixth Congress in December 1986, Vietnam's four million Roman Catholics began to

enjoy far greater official tolerance. In May 1987 the party leader, Nguyen Van Linh, held an unprecedented meeting with the country's Catholic bishops in Hanoi, where he assured them of the Communist Party's "unswerving policy of respect for freedom of religion." Linh went on to acknowledge that there had been shortcomings and errors in the past by many cadres toward the Catholic Church.

Reform had its limitations, as events in 1989 in Vietnam and elsewhere in the communist world were to indicate only too clearly. Political reform was to be called into question and even economic reform was hampered by the country's punishing international isolation. By the late 1980s, it was becoming increasingly clear to the Vietnamese leadership that meaningful economic reconstruction in Vietnam and in its allied regimes in Laos and Cambodia depended on ending Indochina's economic isolation. That in turn depended on terminating the continuing conflict in Cambodia. The first step in this direction was taken in December 1987 when talks opened in Paris between Prince Sihanouk, the leader of the Cambodian resistance, and Hun Sen, the Prime Minister of the

Vietnam: Foreign Direct Investment

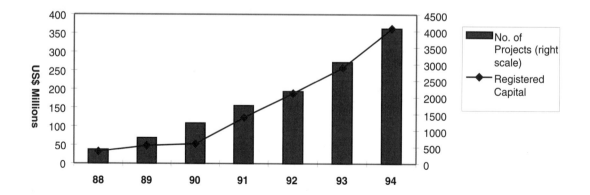

Graph 11.3

Vietnamese-backed government in Cambodia. In May 1988, Vietnam announced that it was withdrawing 50,000 of its estimated 120,000 troops from Cambodia because of what it described as the improving security situation in the country. At the end of the year, Laos also reported that all of the estimated 40,000 Vietnamese troops in the country had been withdrawn.

These measures drew a cautious response from the West and from the noncommunist countries of Southeast Asia. Vietnam announced that it would withdraw all its forces from Cambodia by September 30, 1989. The announcement was followed by the convening of a new international peace conference in Paris on July 30. A gradual rapprochement between China and Vietnam, both under pressure as surviving but beleaguered communist states, accelerated the progress toward peace, especially in 1991. On October 23, 1991, an historic peace agreement was signed. Under the treaty, the four factions agreed to temporarily share power on a Supreme National Council during an 18-month transition period. Prince Sihanouk was to serve as the nominal head

of the interim Cambodian government. The most unusual aspect of the agreement was the creation of a large military and civilian force, the United Nations Transitional Authority in Cambodia (UNTAC), to disarm the combatants, administer the country, and organize free elections.

Amid fears that the agreement might permit the dreaded Khmer Rouge to return to power, the United States also signed the agreement and simultaneously announced that it was prepared to begin a process aimed at normalizing relations with Vietnam, based on cooperation in a full accounting for American servicemen missing since the Vietnam War. At long last, the two countries began to bury the trauma of their past relationship.

Rice Production

By 1991, Vietnam had also made progress in the fundamental problem of feeding its people, having become an exporter of rice in 1989. Most of the exports came from the fertile southern

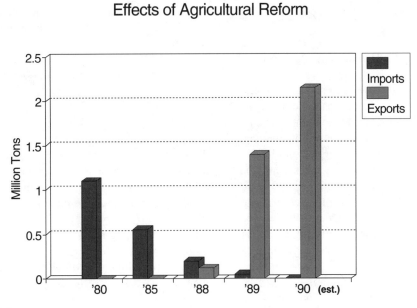

Vietnam's Rice Trade
Effects of Agricultural Reform

Graph 11.4

Mekong River delta, but the more densely populated northern regions contributed as well by becoming self-sufficient in their own food grains.

The turnaround came about as a result of several factors. First, Vietnam's economic reformers made massive investments in the improvement of irrigation systems in the delta. Second, they granted farmers long-term tenure on their land and relaxed many controls over them. At the same time, they provided sufficient price incentives to the farmers to improve their standard of living. Such measures stood in stark contrast to earlier ideological dictates of collective agriculture after 1975 that resulted in a fall in rice production in the Mekong and eventually threatened the nation with famine.

Whether Vietnam will achieve permanent status as a major Southeast Asian rice exporter remains to be seen. A rapidly growing population, limited availability of arable land, and sharp cutbacks in Soviet-supplied fertilizer are among the obstacles that will make it difficult for Vietnam to remain more than just self-sufficient in the years ahead. But if the nation were able to sustain its rice exports at a significant level, the resulting inflow of foreign exchange would provide a critical support for Vietnam's long term economic development.

INDONESIA IN TRANSITION

Economic Growth, Democratic Decline

By the end of the 1970s, President Suharto seemed to be in a position to maintain his "New Order" regime indefinitely. His skills at balancing the country's vested interests seemed, if anything, to grow as time passed. Foreign aid and investment, together with rising revenues from the country's oil and gas exports after the 1973 oil price hike, provided him with the resources to satisfy rival groups in the army and the growing middle class. Rivalries still continued within the military elite, but those who lost out in the struggle were rewarded with lucrative company directorships or foreign diplomatic postings.

The military's position as the dominant force in Indonesian politics continued to be justified on

THE POLITICAL ARMY

The Indonesian army differs from most armies that have seized political power in that it had never previously regarded itself as an apolitical organization. From the army's beginnings in 1945 as a guerrilla force to combat the return of Dutch colonial rule until the consolidation of its political power under the New Order, Indonesian army officers have always concerned themselves with political issues and for most of the period actively played important political roles. Having participated fully in the nationalist struggle against Dutch rule, most officers continued to feel that their voices should be heard in postindependence political affairs. After the imposition of martial law in 1957, their right to participate was given formal recognition through appointments to the cabinet, parliament, and the administration. During the Guided Democracy era, the army became one of the two major organized political forces, which, with President Sukarno, dominated the politics of the period. Finally, the army's drive against the PKI in 1965 and its success in easing President Sukarno out of office left it as the dominant force in Indonesian politics.

—Harold Crouch
The Army and Politics in Indonesia

the grounds that civilians still needed the strong leadership that only the army could provide. This role was justified by the doctrine of Dwi Fungsi (dual function) which the armed forces claimed gave it both military and social-political duties. The historical origins of this went back to the Indonesian revolution of 1945.

After the elimination of the Indonesian Communist Party (PKI) and the dismissal of Sukarno, the army's domination of politics was unchallenged and, as we have seen earlier, the remaining centers of independent power in the political parties and other civilian organizations were completely subordinated. Political activity on university campuses was banned and the press remained one of the most tightly controlled in Asia. The complete ascendancy of the military leadership meant that the most important struggles for influence took place within the military elite among generals whose power rested on their capacity to win the confidence of their fellow generals rather than on their ability to mobilize organized support outside the elite. Contenders for power did not challenge either the army's continued domination of politics or President Suharto's own leadership but concerned themselves largely with key appointments and the division of the spoils of power. The emasculation of the political parties, already evident in the general elections of 1971, remained a constant feature of Indonesian politics as the military-backed Golkar organization further increased it. In the elections of 1977, its share of the poll was, as in 1971, 62 percent but by the elections of 1982 this had risen to 64.5 percent and by the 1987 elections to 73.2 percent. The main competition to Golkar continued to come from the Moslem-based United Development Party (PPP) but even its share of the poll fell from 29 percent in 1977 to 16 percent in 1987. Moreover, in the eighties the government tightened further restrictions on Moslem organizations.

This did not mean that there was not at times acute civilian frustration with the regime. Substantial economic growth and the seeming impossibility of removing the military from governmental control, however, exercised a fatalistic grip over Indonesian society. Military power had become institutionalized in Indonesia to a degree almost unparalleled elsewhere in the Third World. The vigilance of the country's security apparatus ensured that no significant revolutionary opposition to the government emerged. Occasionally, as in Jakarta's port of Tanjung Priok in September 1984, there were major riots. These were inevitably followed by security clampdowns which stopped the unrest from spreading elsewhere in the country.

Undoubtedly, the country's economic good fortunes contributed greatly to social and political stability. With its plentiful oil and gas deposits,

Indonesia benefited greatly from its membership in OPEC (Organization of Petroleum Exporting Countries). By the early 1980s, oil and gas accounted for more than 65 percent of Indonesia's exports, and the same percentage of government revenues was derived from corporate oil taxes. These considerable funds enabled the government to embark on a far-reaching program of industrialization in fields as diverse as steel, aircraft production, petrochemicals, and shipbuilding. Foreign and domestic investment in textiles and consumer goods industries underwent considerable expansion. Government infrastructure projects in rural areas provided increased employment opportunities and substantial food reserves were built up that enabled the government to prevent sudden increases in food prices and social unrest. Indonesia became self-sufficient in its rice production for the first time in 1984. There also have been significant improvements in health and education under President Suharto's New Order. In the field of family planning, Indonesia's achievements were recognized by the United Nations in 1989 when it made a special award to President Suharto.

Indonesia's Regional Context

Indonesian foreign policy in the 1980s remained concerned, above all, with regional order in Southeast Asia. The Suharto administration inherited from President Sukarno's government a longstanding suspicion of all external powers. Under Suharto's leadership, however, this has been tempered by an evident pragmatism with regard to the United States and Japan. On the other hand, there has been a continuing hostility until recently toward China. Ideally, Indonesia would prefer that none of the great powers had a military presence in Southeast Asia but President Suharto's government has been realistic enough to recognize that an American presence is a necessary counterweight in the region to the Soviet Union and China.

Indonesia's ambivalence toward the United States has been more than matched by its relationship with Japan which has played an increasingly important role in the country's economy. By the 1980s, Japan had become the single most

Indonesia: Changing Patterns of Foreign Direct Investment, 1980–1994

Graph 11.5

important provider of aid and investment to Indonesia and was also a major market for its oil and natural gas. At the same time, suspicions of Japan's growing economic might and even downright hostility at a popular level remained intense.

The main focus of Indonesian foreign policy for maintaining regional order in Southeast Asia remained ASEAN. The Vietnamese invasion of Cambodia in 1978 was a major challenge for the organization and especially for its one frontline member, Thailand. Indonesia shared Thailand's concern at the violation of national sovereignty. For Indonesia, Vietnam's military undertaking did not replace China as the principal, if long-term threat to Southeast Asia, a view not shared by the government in Bangkok. Even after three of Indonesia's ASEAN partners — Malaysia, Thailand, and the Philippines — had recognized China in the mid-1970s, President Suharto showed no inclination to join the flock of pilgrims

to Beijing in the wake of China's new "Open-Door" policy. Indeed, the outbreak of hostilities between China and Vietnam in 1979, preceded by Beijing's intervention on behalf of ethnic Chinese in Vietnam, reawakened for Indonesia old fears about China's role in Southeast Asia. The fact that by the early 1980s China and ASEAN were making common cause in backing the anti-Vietnamese resistance in Cambodia did little to persuade Indonesia that its best interests were served by restoring ties with the People's Republic. Almost alone in ASEAN, Indonesia insisted on the need to maintain an open dialogue with Vietnam which was not confined to diplomatic channels. Indeed in 1984, General Benny Murdani became the first noncommunist military commander to be welcomed in Hanoi. That visit served to underline not only the foreign policy role played by the Indonesian military but also its continuing suspicion and hostility toward China.

> *"The economic relationship with Japan is endured because it serves the requirements of political elites committed to development policies which rest on Indonesian participation in the international capitalist economy. However, despite the measure of dependence which this might appear to entail, there has been no inclination to endorse America's encouragement of Japan to assume a military role in Asia. Japan is tolerated as a necessary economic partner but is not regarded with any enthusiasm as a prospective regional one."*
>
> —Michael Leifer
> *Indonesia's Foreign Policy*

Despite some faltering initiatives in the 1970s, the outlook for Sino-Indonesian relations in the early eighties hardly looked any better than it had a decade or so earlier. Fundamental distrust of China, especially by the military, remained as deeply entrenched as ever. Nor was this picture changed by Vietnam's 1978 invasion of Cambodia and apparent attempt to establish political hegemony over Indochina. Even the establishment of a Soviet military presence at the former American bases at Da Nang and Cam Ranh Bay did not ring the alarm bells in Jakarta that it did in Bangkok and Singapore. On the contrary, Vietnam was seen as a strong bulwark to Chinese encroachment in the region, and the long-term military perception of China as the main threat to stability in Southeast Asia remained unchanged. This point was driven home in a dramatic fashion in February 1984 when, as noted above, to the delight of Vietnam, General Benny Murdani, the commander-in-chief of the Indonesian armed forces, visited Hanoi. Not only was Murdani the most senior ASEAN official to visit Hanoi since its invasion of Cambodia but he was the first noncommunist military commander to hold extensive military consultations with the Vietnamese. Moreover, a new irritant in Sino-Indonesian relations had arisen following Jakarta's annexation of the Portuguese colony of East Timor, an action that was described by Beijing as "a naked act of aggression." At the United

Nations, China backed up its condemnation by voting until 1982 for a resolution calling on Indonesia to withdraw its forces from East Timor and allow its people to decide their own fate.

Indonesia's ambitions to play a greater role within the Nonaligned Movement and even to chair the movement, as well as its efforts to find a solution to the Cambodian conflict through the Jakarta Informal Meetings (JIMS), were all hampered by the absence of diplomatic relations with China. The two meetings that Indonesia hosted on Cambodia in 1988 and 1989 were handicapped by the noninclusion of China, the principal diplomatic and military backer of the Cambodian resistance and gave Vietnam a greater opportunity to dominate the proceedings. Growing indications that the two superpowers were disengaging from Southeast Asia also made Indonesia feel that it had to position itself to take a more active part in the processes of détente. Rapprochement between the Soviet Union and China showed only too clearly that the balance of power in Asia was undergoing radical change. Indonesia could no longer afford to be isolated from one of the key players in East Asia.

The final breakthrough came on February 23, 1989, in the Imperial Hotel in Tokyo when President Suharto met with the Chinese Foreign Minister Qian Qichen. In a move that took observers by surprise, the two countries reached agreement to move toward normalizing their relations at an early date. Within eighteen months of the Tokyo meeting, the Indonesian Foreign Minister Ali Alatas had visited Beijing, and the Chinese Prime Minister Li Peng had visited Jakarta. Diplomatic relations were officially restored on July 8, 1990. President Suharto himself paid an official visit to China in November 1990, the first by an Indonesian head of state since 1964.

VIETNAM: SETBACK TO REFORM

Paralysis of Leadership

By the middle of 1990, Vietnam, which had in the mid-1980s begun a serious engagement with the processes of reform, appeared to have been left far behind by the sweeping transformation of Eastern Europe. Indeed, Vietnam had fallen so far behind the curve of socialist reform that it appeared to occupy a Stalinist bunker with China, North Korea, and Cuba. For the beleaguered Vietnamese leadership, the experiences, different though they were of China and Eastern Europe in 1989, reinforced a fear that the process of reform could easily spin out of control and threaten the very basis of the communist regime. By the end of that year, reform in Vietnam itself was paralyzed by the inability of the leadership to confront the dilemma of how to achieve change within the framework of socialism without eroding the bases of socialism itself.

In the course of 1989, the considerable gains that the reform process, *doi moi*, had brought Vietnam since the Sixth Party Congress in 1986 came under threat. The crisis of international communism in China, the Soviet Union, and Eastern Europe inevitably had an enormous impact on the party leadership in Hanoi which had long prided itself on its "internationalism." Domestic factors, too, contributed to a rigorous application of the brakes to the whole reform process. The results were severe, especially in the realm of social and political reform.

A foretaste of the hardening mood was already evident in February 1989 when Nguyen Van Linh addressed newspaper editors and journalists in Ho Chi Minh City. He warned the country's media against publishing reports that caused a loss of confidence in the Communist Party or the government. At the same time, Linh delivered the first of several warnings that there could be no question of political pluralism developing in Vietnam. The press, Linh argued, had to remain a tool of the Communist Party even while reflecting the views of the people. Significantly, articles by Comrade "NVL" stopped appearing in *Nhan Dan* several months earlier. Two months before Linh's warning to the press, an article had appeared in the party theoretical journal, *Tap Chi Cong San* (*Communist Review*), by Interior Minister Mai Chi Tho, accusing the press of ideological laxity and commercialization. The limits of reform in Vietnam had already been reached. Henceforth, although while there was faltering endorsement of "perestroika," the previous period of "glasnost" was brought to an end.

In August 1989, the Communist Party's Central Committee met in Ho Chi Minh City to tackle what were called "urgent ideological problems." In a communique published at the end of the meeting, the party strongly attacked bourgeois liberalism and accused the United States of

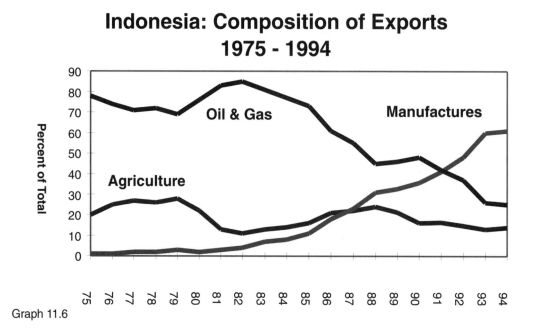

**Indonesia: Composition of Exports
1975 - 1994**

Graph 11.6

> *"There is but one alternative: capitalist dictatorship or proletarian dictatorship. There is no middle-of-the-road path."*
> —Nguyen Van Linh

attempting to undermine socialism worldwide. It went on to rule out any prospect of political reform and denounced such measures in other socialist societies as being little more than attempts to restore capitalism. In a closing speech at the conference, Nguyen Van Linh went out of his way to threaten severe punishment for those who organized or incited civil unrest. He also admitted that there had been widespread ideological confusion within the ranks of the party as a result of the events in Eastern Europe.

The Seventh Plenum was followed by a further tightening of restrictions on the press. Some journals were closed and the editors of others were replaced. Before the opening of the Journalists' Association Congress on October 15, *Nhan Dan* warned of what it called the press's shortcomings. At the Congress itself, Prime Minister Do Muoi spoke of the duty of journalists to "struggle against reactionary forces and thoughts that sabotage the revolutionary gains of the country." In December, a motion at the National Assembly to allow private individuals to publish newspapers was heavily defeated. The publications of the Ho Chi Minh City-based dissident group, the Club of Former Resistance Fighters, were also banned.

At the same time, attempts by hardline conservatives to consolidate their hold on the party leadership still met with resistance. In a speech in December, 1989 Politburo member Tran Xuan Bach called for greater openness, stating openly that the turbulent events that had shaken Eastern Europe would also affect Asia. His apparent advocacy of greater political reform lost Bach his positions on both the Politburo and the Central Committee at the Eighth Party Plenum in March 1990. Attacks on the concept of political pluralism increased in the party press.

It may well be that for Vietnam there is no stable halfway house between the system it has known to date and the free-market system that inspires some of its reforms. The dilemmas it faces are numerous and the political strategies and conceptual outlines of reform contain many ambiguities and contradictions. To date, the evidence in Vietnam, as perhaps in other communist states, suggests that partial reform cannot succeed and carries a momentum that will one day fundamentally alter the political structure of the country. Yet Vietnam's leadership, while not willing to go all the way, seems already to have gone too far to turn back. Whether this will result in a prolonged and inconclusive political stalemate and an economy that suffers from the worst of both worlds remains to be seen but it is now a distinct possibility. However, the demise of the Soviet Union as a source of support, the competition for investment from the West, and rising expectations internally may yet put the reform movement back on the road.

CONCLUDING REMARKS

Both Indonesia and Vietnam had fought long and hard to achieve independence and regional security in Southeast Asia. In no other Southeast Asian countries, with the possible exception of Cambodia, was the nationalist spirit so strong. Their struggles for independence propelled them on different political courses, yet each nation retained an affinity and a respect for the other. Moreover, while Vietnam was a communist state and Indonesia noncommunist, the political systems of the two countries shared many common characteristics. In both, there was a rejection of the Western concept of democracy in favor of an authoritarian and highly centralized polity. In Vietnam, after reunification in 1976, a one-party state prevailed, while Indonesia was far from being a true multiparty democracy. In both countries, the military enjoyed a privileged position, although in Vietnam it was subordinate to the ruling Communist Party. Even in the economy, although Vietnam had become a socialist state and Indonesia nonsocialist, there were similarities. The state and planning mechanisms also play a great role in Indonesia and moves toward deregulation and privatization are more hesitant than in any other nonsocialist state in Southeast Asia. There the similarities end.

> *"We want to build socialism quickly, we want to transform our country quickly, we want our people to be glorious quickly. This is especially to prevent the enemy from harming us."*
>
> —*Tung Padevat* (Revolutionary Flag),
> June 1976

Revolution had brought both countries the cherished goal of independence. However, Vietnam's longer experience of war, economic mismanagement, and international isolation wreaked havoc on its economic development. By the 1990s, Indonesia had proceeded much further along the road to economic development, had successfully brought about agricultural self-sufficiency, and had implemented family planning. Vietnam must still engage these problems in a meaningful way. If Indonesia's economic and social development had outpaced Vietnam, its political system, like Vietnam's, showed signs of strain especially as Indonesians began to think of their future in the post-Suharto era. In both countries, there were growing indications of popular demands for greater openness in government.

In foreign policy, the two countries remain the most important political actors in Southeast Asia. Their predominant position in the region is assured by virtue of their physical size, population, geopolitical situation, and military strength. Moreover, they continue to share an active distrust of powers external to the region. The advent of what appears to be a more peaceful era in Cambodia may be the harbinger of new political and economic opportunities for these countries at the end of the century.

APPENDIX

Cambodia: The Khmer Rouge in Power

The victory of the Khmer Rouge in April 1975 surprised outside observers when it did not lead to the public emergence of the Cambodian Communist Party. Instead, the Khmer Rouge referred only to the shadowy Angkar Loeu or "Organization in High," as playing the most important political role in the country. The country was renamed Democratic Kampuchea, and Pol Pot became prime minister. Prince Sihanouk, who had long harbored deep misgivings about the Khmer Rouge, returned from exile in China to live out the next few years under virtual house arrest in his own palace. The tone of the new regime was set in its first three days in power when it ordered the mass evacuation of the capital, Phnom Penh. The city, whose population had swollen to more than two million as a result of the American bombing and the civil war, was abandoned by its inhabitants on pain of death.

The period in which the Khmer Rouge were in power, from April 1975 to January 1979, was marked by one of the most savage experiments in social engineering the modern world has ever witnessed. The country's new rulers embarked on a policy of self-reliance and isolation from the outside world. The towns were effectively abandoned except for Khmer Rouge personnel and all formal education was abolished. In the countryside, the population was gathered in collectives and all vestiges of individualism, even family life, were strongly discouraged. The population of the evacuated cities and towns, known as the "new people" as distinct from the "base people" (the peasantry), was moved to agricultural sites where the people were forced to work on vast irrigation sites under strict discipline.

As a matter of policy, the Khmer Rouge, from the very beginning, used terror against their real and perceived enemies. Personnel of the former Lon Nol regime, members of the old bourgeoisie, and Western-educated intellectuals were slaughtered by the thousands. In many cases, wives and children were also executed to prevent them from becoming future opponents of the Khmer Rouge. Intellectuals, often described by the Khmer Rouge as "the worthless ones," were also systematically killed. All religious activity was ruthlessly suppressed and ethnic minorities, such as the Chinese, Vietnamese, and the Cham, a Muslim people, suffered numerous mass executions. Ordinary Cambodian people were not spared either. Behavior the regime regarded as offensive, such as illicit sexual relations, resistance to communal eating, or even alleged laziness, was often punished by death. Conservative estimates put the number of those killed by the Khmer Rouge when they were in power at approximately a million, out of a total population of only six million.

The Khmer Rouge had few friends in the outside world. The Soviet Union refused to recognize the regime and its only real ally was China. Relations with the Vietnamese Communists, which had been poor since well before 1975, deteriorated after the Khmer Rouge took power. Cambodians who had enjoyed close relations with the Vietnamese were killed and the Khmer Rouge laid claim to considerable swathes of territory in Vietnam. By 1977, several serious border clashes had occurred between the two countries and, in December of that year, diplomatic relations between Hanoi and Phnom Penh were severed. Throughout 1978, tension between the two countries remained high and in December Vietnam launched a massive invasion of Cambodia, toppling the Khmer Rouge from power. On January 7, 1979, a new government was installed in Phnom Penh led by Heng Samrin, a former Khmer Rouge cadre, and the country was renamed the People's Republic of Kampuchea. The Khmer Rouge retreated to the Thai border where, rearmed by China, they continued to resist the Vietnamese and their Cambodian allies.

Of all the mass killings carried out during the period the Khmer Rouge were in power, the most clearly documented are those that took place at Tuol Sleng, also known as S21. Tuol Sleng was a former school in Phnom Penh, used by the Khmer

---

Tuol Sleng

Evil microbes inside the party will emerge, pushed out by the true nature of socialist revolution.

—Khmer Rouge internal party document

Rouge as a center for torture and execution. Careful records that were kept of prisoners and the prison archives which have survived virtually intact, show that nearly fifteen thousand people were liquidated between April 1975 and January 1979. Many of those executed were themselves members of the Khmer Rouge.

At any one time, the prison held a minimum of a thousand prisoners. Most were held for a short time, tortured, and forced into writing confessions before being killed. The names of alleged co-conspirators, elicited through confessions, were recorded and elaborate charts were drawn up showing lines of "contacts" in colored inks. The rate of executions increased after October 1977. On October 15, 1977, the prison record books show 418 killed; on October 18, 179 were killed; on October 20, 88; and on October 23, 148. The highest single figure was 582 recorded executions on May 27, 1978. In many cases, as with the veteran Communist and former Khmer Rouge Minister of Information, Hu Nim, the cause of death was recorded as "crushed to bits."

NOTES

1. Lucian W. Pye, *Asian Power and Politics: The Cultural Dimensions of Authority* (Cambridge: The Bellknap Press of Harvard University Press, 1985), p. 304.

2. Harold Crouch, *The Army and Politics in Indonesia* (Ithaca: Cornell University Press, 1988), p. 299.

3. Nayan Chanda, *Brother Enemy* (San Diego: Harcourt Brace Jovanovich, 1986), p. 370.

Indonesia, Vietnam, and Cambodia: A Post-War Chronology

Date	Indonesia	Vietnam	Cambodia
1941	Japan captures Indonesia from Dutch.	Japan takes Vietnam from France. Ho Chih Minh forms the Viet Minh resistance.	Japan takes over Cambodia. Permits French to administer it with new king, Norodom Sihanouk.
1945	Japanese occupation ends. Sukarno and Hatta proclaim independent Indonesia. War with Dutch ensues.	Japanese occupation ends. Emperor Bao Dai abdicates. Ho declares Vietnam's independence from France.	Japanese occupation ends. Sihanouk cooperates with France.
1949	Dutch agree to political independence for Indonesia.	Viet Minh battle French forces from 1947 on.	Guerrilla forces, allied with Vietnam, combat French.
1953		French launch decisive battle of Dien Bien Phu but are surrounded by General Giap's army.	France grants Cambodia independence under Sihanouk.
1954		French defeated. Geneva agreement partitions Vietnam.	Geneva agreement calls for independent Laos and Cambodia.
1955	Indonesia hosts Bandung Conference of non-aligned nations. Indonesian communists gain in elections.		Sihanouk launches new political movement; attempts neutrality in cold war.
1957	Sukarno abandons parliamentary rule in favor of "guided democracy."		
1960		Ho forms new front to fight against South.	Pol Pot named to Central Committee of CPK.
1963	Dutch transfer West New Guinea to Indonesia. Sukarno launches "confrontation" with Malaysia.	Assassination of President Diem. War between north and south escalates.	
1965	Attempted leftist coup crushed by Suharto who launches purge of communists and massacre of indigenous Chinese.	First US combat units arrive in Vietnam, heavy bombing of north begins.	Pro-Vietnamese Cambodian guerrillas make gains against Sihanouk's forces.
1967	Suharto becomes acting president. Changes foreign investment law to permit inflow of foreign capital.	US increases forces in Vietnam to 500,000. Korea, Australia send troops as well. Fighting escalates.	
1968	Formal inauguration of Suharto.	Tet offensive launched by Viet Minh. Ho Chi Minh dies the following year.	

1970	US, Europe, Japan establish financial aid packages for Indonesia.		US-supported military coup topples Sihanouk. US Forces bomb, invade Cambodia. Pol Pot takes over guerrilla leadership.
1973	Boom in oil prices reduces reliance on foreign aid.	Paris accords provide for US, allies withdrawal. Fighting resumes.	
1975	Indonesia seizes East Timor from Portugal.	North Vietnam conquers South. War ends.	Khmer Rouge victory in Cambodia. Terror campaign launched. Millions of Cambodians killed.
1978	Indonesia's support for Vietnam divides ASEAN over issue of Vietnam's Cambodian invasion.	Vietnam invades Cambodia, topples Pol Pot. Relations with China sour as Vietnam joins Soviet bloc.	New Kampuchea government set up by Vietnam. Khmer Rouge resumes guerrilla war in countryside.
1979		China launches border war of attrition against Vietnam.	100,000 Vietnamese troops occupy Cambodia.
1982			Coalition government formed in Kampuchea to oust Vietnam's occupying army.
1986		New policy of *doi moi* launched.	
1989	Indonesia and China agree to normalize relations (officially restored, 1990).	Conservative reaction in opposition to *doi moi* policy.	Vietnam troops withdraw from Kampuchea.
1991		Former premier Do Muoi becomes General Secretary. Relations with China normalized. Inflation reaches 83 %.	Cambodian peace agreement among factions. China stops backing Khmer Rouge.
1993		Inflation at 8%, GDP 8%, foreign investment soars.	Cambodian national elections, supervised by UN, support Sihanouk, undercut Khmer Rouge.
1995		Vietnam becomes member of ASEAN, normalizes relations with US.	Coalition government rules amid growing corruption.
1997	Suharto suppresses dissent, revives hunt for communists as new presidential election looms.		Khmer Rouge forces split in deadly factional dispute. Pol Pot deposed. Coalition partner Hun Sen takes over in military coup.

12

Siberian Salient: Russia in Pacific Asia

by John J. Stephan

EDITOR'S INTRODUCTION

Russia has figured only marginally in Western thoughts about the Pacific. "Pacific Islands" conjure up Micronesia and Polynesia rather than Sakhalin, the Kuriles, or the Aleutians. "East Asia" brings to mind China, Japan, and Korea but not the enormous expanse of territory between these countries and the Arctic. Such blinkered vision is changing, however, as Russia's eastern periphery plays a more active role in the Pacific Basin.

Historically, what came to be known as the Soviet Far East has been anything but isolated from the Pacific. Asia and America were linked for millennia by a land bridge, and migration between these continents have continued for at least thirty-five thousand years. For two thousand years, seminomadic inhabitants of forests and steppes periodically penetrated the northern borders of China and established new dynasties.

Russia began to make its presence felt in Northeast Asia during the seventeenth century when Cossacks and others moved across Siberia from the Urals to the Pacific in quest of furs. During the 1640s and 1650s, small bands of Cossacks led by Poyarkov and Khabarov (namesake of a major Soviet Far Eastern city) pushed southward into the fertile Amur Valley in search of an agricultural base to provision Eastern Siberia.

Alarmed by encroachment on their homeland, China's Manchu rulers resorted to a combination of diplomacy and force, culminating in the Treaty of Nerchinsk (1689) which expelled Russians from the Amur Valley.

Blocked in the south, Russia expanded during the next 120 years toward North America and Japan. Implemented by both officials and entrepreneurs, this movement was fiercely resisted by Amerasian aborigines (Koryaks and Chukchi in Northeastern Siberia, Tlingits in Alaska) and was perceived by the Japanese as a "northern threat." At the initiative of Czar Peter the Great, a series of expeditions were carried out in the North Pacific between 1725 and 1750. From the port of Petropavlovsk, established in 1740 on the eastern coast of Kamchatka, the Dane Vitus Bering and others surveyed the coasts of Siberia, Alaska, and Japan three decades before the voyages of Captain James Cook (cf. chapter 2). In 1799, St. Petersburg granted the Russian-American Company a fur trading monopoly along the entire North Pacific rim from the Kurile Islands to Vancouver Island. Lacking provisions, Russia's Pacific settlements were supplied fitfully by agricultural bases in California and Hawaii, by Bostonian merchants operating in the Pacific Northwest, and by Russian naval vessels sailing halfway round the world from the Baltic.

During the mid-nineteenth century, Russia's attention shifted from North America back to East

Asia. Alaska was sold to the United States (1867), and the Amur Valley was detached from China (1858-60). Taking advantage of China's defeat in the Sino-Japanese War (1894-95), Russia extracted from Beijing during 1896-98 the right to build a railroad across Manchuria to Vladivostok with a southern spur to Port Arthur, which became Russia's principal administrative and military base in the Far East. Russian penetration of Manchuria and Korea triggered resistance from Japan which, having first secured an alliance with Great Britain (1902), launched an attack on Port Arthur in 1904.

Defeat in war with Japan (1904-05) checked Russian expansion in Asia and catalyzed political upheaval at home. Strikes erupted throughout the country in 1905, paralyzing the Trans-Siberian Railroad and preventing the expeditious demobilization of troops concentrated in Manchuria and the Russian Far East. Rebellious soldiers and sailors even seized Vladivostok for a few days early in 1906.

Although St. Petersburg reasserted a degree of control during 1907-14, military setbacks, poor leadership, and diminishing morale in the rear eroded governmental authority. A breakdown in transportation leading to bread shortages triggered demonstrations in Petrograd (St. Petersburg) that quickly escalated into the overthrow of the czarist regime in the "February Revolution" (March 1917). A provisional government was formed but it could not cope with mounting political and economic crises. After eight months, the provisional government was overthrown by an alliance of revolutionaries led by the Bolsheviks under Vladimir Lenin (the "October Revolution"). Lenin's separate peace with Germany in March 1918 set the stage for intervention by England, France, Italy, the United States, and Japan, as well as for civil war between "Reds" and "Whites" (an unstable and mutually suspicious aggregation of czarist officers, Cossacks, Siberian autonomists, and anti-Bolshevik socialists), delaying the establishment of Soviet power on the Pacific until 1922.

The events of 1917-22 both weakened and enhanced Russian influence in Asia. Dissolution of the Empire and the subsequent failure of the "White" counterrevolutionary movement undermined Russian military and economic power in Asia, as well as in Europe. At the same time, the emotional and intellectual appeal of the October Revolution among some Asian nationalists was harnessed for strategic purposes in the Moscow-controlled Communist International, or Comintern. Vladivostok served as an important base for Comintern operations in the Pacific region between 1923 and 1941.

Japanese expansion on the Asian continent after 1928, coinciding with the victory of Stalinism within the USSR, had ambivalent consequences for the Soviet position on the Pacific. A massive arms buildup in the Far East helped the Soviet Union to deter Japan in 1931-41, and giant industrial projects in Siberia ensured survival and eventually victory over Germany in 1941-45. On the other hand, forced collectivization and mass terror annihilated some of the most gifted and productive elements of Soviet society.

This chapter suggests that various obstacles have prevented realization of a Soviet or Russian "Pacific Century." Distance and climate posed barriers to communication and development. An obsession with security constricted international contacts and alarmed neighbors. A centralized command economy discouraged regional initiatives and placed a low premium on individual responsibility. Nepotism and corruption amid lofty rhetoric about "socialist construction" for a "radiant future" nurtured widespread cynicism. Designed to revitalize the Soviet system, perestroika instead catalyzed a crisis of authority between the USSR, the Russian Republic, and several local administrations between Vladivostok and the Bering Straits.

Historian John J. Stephan assesses Russia's "Pacific Destiny" on the basis of study of the USSR since 1959 and regular visits to the Russian Far East since 1966. His sardonic treatment of conventional wisdom and bureaucratic optimism should not detract from the fact that Russia, richly endowed with natural resources, has a significant economic potential in the Pacific region. Yet in the wake of the collapse of the communist party a failed conservative coup, leaders in both Moscow and the Far Eastern periphery still have not formulated coherent strategies to achieve this potential.

◆   ◆   ◆

1. Muscovy in 1500

2. Russia in 1650: Conquest of Western Siberia, penetration of Eastern Siberia and Amur Valley.

3. Russia in 1820: Retreat from the Amur Valley (1689), Conquest of Kamchatka and Chukotka (1697-1750), advance into North America

4. Russia in 1900: Acquisition of Amur and Maritime Regions (1858-1860), sale of Alaska (1867), penetration of Manchuria (1896-1900).

5. Soviet Union in 1945: Penetration of Mongolia (1921), Penetration of Manchuria and Northern Korea (1945).

6. Soviet Union in July, 1991

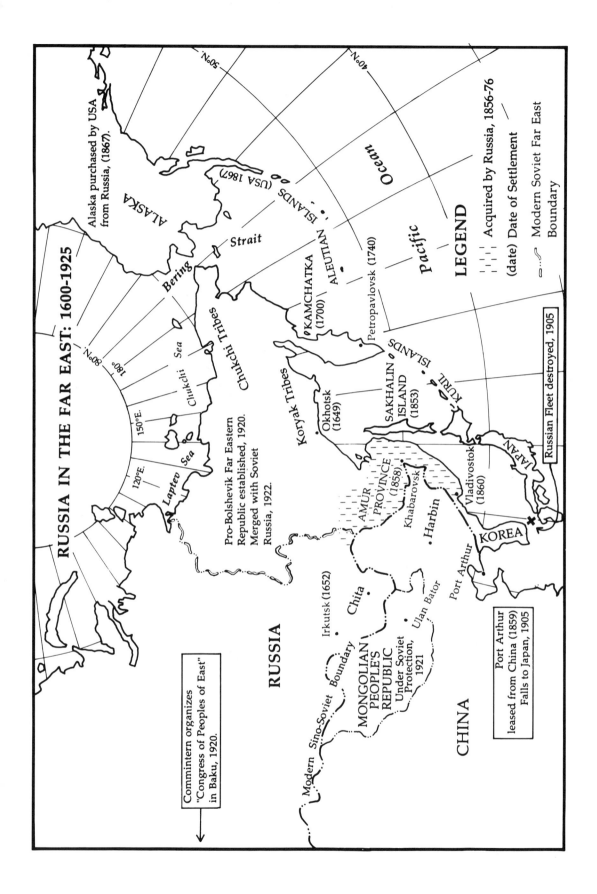

RUSSIA IN THE FAR EAST: 1600-1925

Alaska purchased by USA from Russia, (1867).

ALASKA

ALEUTIAN ISLANDS (USA 1867)

Bering Strait

Pacific Ocean

LEGEND

Acquired by Russia, 1856-76

(date) Date of Settlement

Modern Soviet Far East Boundary

Chukchi Sea

Chukchi Tribes

Chukchi

Laptev Sea

80°N.

180°

150°E.

120°E.

KAMCHATKA (1700)

Petropavlovsk (1740)

Koryak Tribes

Okhotsk (1649)

SAKHALIN ISLAND (1853)

KURIL ISLANDS

JAPAN

Russian Fleet destroyed, 1905

Pro-Bolshevik Far Eastern Republic established, 1920. Merged with Soviet Russia, 1922.

AMUR PROVINCE (1858)

Khabarovsk

Harbin

Vladivostok (1860)

KOREA

Port Arthur

RUSSIA

Irkutsk (1652)

Chita

MONGOLIAN PEOPLE'S REPUBLIC

Under Soviet Protection, 1921

Ulan Bator

Modern Sino-Soviet Boundary

CHINA

Comintern organizes "Congress of Peoples of East" in Baku, 1920.

Port Arthur leased from China (1859) Falls to Japan, 1905

RUSSIA IN PACIFIC ASIA

Prologue: The Vladivostok Initiative

On July 28, 1986, at Vladivostok, Mikhail Gorbachev delivered a speech that seemed to usher the USSR into the Pacific Century. This "Vladivostok Initiative" held out shimmering prospects of a historic shift from cold war confrontation to regional cooperation, from military intimidation to economic engagement, from Brezhnevian heavy-handedness to Gorbachevian sophistication. Some observers professed to see Gorbachev orchestrating bold departures from the "era of stagnation," animating Soviet-Pacific relations with the spirit of perestroika. All this was quite exhilarating, particularly if one took the rhetoric at face value.

Hopes raised by the "Vladivostok Initiative" were partly fulfilled in the international arena. Political and economic relations with China, Japan, and the United States improved. Moscow and Seoul established diplomatic ties. Pacific Rim market economies boosted trade with and investment in the USSR. Domestically, however, the Vladivostok Initiative soon foundered on managerial inexperience, budget deficits, and bureaucratic resistance. By 1991, Gorbachev's historic visit to Japan and South Korea was overshadowed by rampant separatism, economic sclerosis, social fragmentation, and the specter of a military crackdown.

Any attempt to characterize Russia in Pacific Asia during the current "time of troubles" risks falling victim to instant obsolescence. Yet even fugitive symptoms are anchored in geography and history. Consequently, the subject will be approached by looking at the changing roles of what has been known as "the Soviet Far East," by challenging some popular myths, and by exploring the sources of contemporary sensibilities.

A Siberian Salient

The Far East of the Russian Republic (henceforth "Far East") offers a key to understanding Russian ties with the Pacific, because the Far East is Russia on the Pacific. Yet one would not think so, reading the bulk of relevant Western commentary. Geographers excepted, commentators are wont to divorce foreign affairs from their spatial milieu. Moscow's policies toward China, Japan, Korea, Southeast Asia, and Oceania have been conventionally treated in abstraction from the USSR's physical presence in Northeast Asia. The Far East commonly figures in analyses as a prop: a repository of natural wealth, an arena for military deployments, a receptacle for prisoners and exiles, a platform for Gorbachev.

Although popularly subsumed into Siberia, the Far East has a distinct geography, history, economy, and society. Embracing 2.4 million square miles between the Arctic Ocean and China, between the Lena Basin and the Pacific, the Far East accounts for 28 percent of the USSR and 36 percent of the Russian Republic, an area comparable to 60 percent of China, 70 percent of the United States, two Indias, or sixteen Japans. The Far East encompasses five time zones and several climates. Lying on roughly the same latitude as Venice, Vladivostok defies popular stereotypes about "Siberian" inclemency. Washed by the warm kuroshio current, the southern Kurile Islands shelter a "Riviera" of warm beaches, bamboo, and magnolia.

Historically, the Far East has played a role in Russian relations with Pacific neighbors akin to that of Texas in American relations with Mexico. More than just a distant province, the Far East has participated in Russian and Soviet policies toward China, Japan, Korea, North America, and Oceania. Until just over a half-century ago, Far Eastern officials enjoyed a status approaching that of satraps. In the mid-nineteenth century, one governor-general took unauthorized initiatives on Chinese territory and negotiated a treaty with Manchu officials expanding Imperial Russia's eastern frontiers. After the October Revolution, Far Easterners were slow in recognizing Soviet power. Even local Communists did not always follow orders from Moscow. Between 1920 and 1922, the Far East assumed the form of an independent state with diplomatic missions in China, Japan, and the United States. During the 1930s, Far Eastern leaders wielded military and economic power unparalleled in any part of the USSR. If Siberian regionalism troubled czarist authorities, the specter of Far Eastern secession haunted Stalin.

Recent Soviet initiatives in the Pacific have created a powerful magnetic field for academic and journalistic entrepreneurship. Anyone seeking to understand USSR-Pacific relations cannot afford to overlook the Far East, which hovers on the periphery of the Western imagination but for centuries has formed the meeting ground of Europe, Asia, and America.

Geographical Myths

Physical as well as conceptual obstacles litter approaches to an understanding of Russia on the Pacific. In the initial years of perestroika, the Far East remains one of the least accessible regions of the USSR, with foreign tourists shunted through Nakhodka and Khabarovsk. Invited foreigners could glimpse Provid..eniya, Magadan, Vladivostok, and Yuzhno-Sakhalinsk, but as a rule neither tourists nor guests were encouraged to tarry. Diplomats, businessmen, scholars, and exchange students still cluster west of the Urals.

One does not have to go to the Far East to see from a map that Russia and the Pacific are contiguous. Their contact zone extends 3,100 miles from Korea to the Bering Strait, about the distance from New York to Los Angeles. One would think that this spatial relationship is straightforward enough, yet we frequently hear about the USSR being "landlocked." Siberia enters our imagination as a continental cul-de-sac somewhere east of Moscow. A number of intelligent people would be surprised to learn that the USSR not only has a Pacific coastline, the nation is in fact "waterbound." Three quarters (30,000 out of 40,000 miles) of Soviet frontiers are maritime. Over half of maritime frontiers (16,700 miles) are in the Far East. The Soviet Far Eastern coastline — 12,000 miles — is the longest of any nation in the Pacific Basin.

If Russia and the Pacific are contiguous, Russia and Asia overlap, spatially and ethnically. Three quarters of the USSR is in Asia. A third of Asia is in the USSR. Fifty million Soviet citizens, the most rapidly growing element of the population, are Asians. Eighty million Soviet citizens, nearly one of every three, live in Asian parts of the USSR. Although the Far East lies entirely within Asia, its population is overwhelmingly Slavic as a result of immigration. Excluding Yakutia, about 90 percent of the population consists of Russians, Ukrainians, and Belorussians.[1]

Conventional notions of Far Eastern geography can be quite imaginative. When Chinese and Soviet border guards fought over an Ussuri River island (called Damansky or Zhenbao, depending on one's semantic politics) on March 2, 1969, a map on the front page of the London Times placed the battleground in the suburbs of Vladivostok. A 1985 United Press International report transmogrified Yuzhno-Sakhalinsk, administrative capital of the Sakhalin District, into a peninsula on the Bering Strait. A Honolulu newspaper put Petropavlovsk-Kamchatskii on the southern tip of Sakhalin. An American Universities Field Staff report on the Soviet Far East concocted a "Yakut Azerbaijan Soviet Socialist Republic."[2] A brochure for the 1990 Goodwill Games in Seattle listed a Far Eastern "Jewish Autonomous Republic."[3] Recently, a Vladivostok-bound American official, on learning that flights from Japan landed at Khabarovsk,[4] told an aide that he would catch a cab from the airport to his destination.

The "Northern Territories," former Japanese islands occupied by Soviet forces in 1945, have been the subject of considerable confusion in the West. "Northern Territories" is an elastic term, stretching or contracting according to political party and irredentist organization. The Japanese government defines the Northern Territories as Etorofu (Iturup), Kunashiri (Kunashir), Shikotan, and Habomai. Western commentators sometimes referred to these as "four islands," although Habomai is not an island but an island group.[5] They also are wont to describe the Northern Territories as "small" or even "tiny." Perhaps they are, compared with Russia, but seen in a Japanese context they assume a more impressive magnitude. The "four islands" are about the size of Delaware. Etorofu alone is double the size of Okinawa. The opposition parties (including the Socialists and the Communists) define the Northern Territories as the entire Kurile arc between Hokkaido and Kamchatka, an area larger than Connecticut. Ultra-rightist groups throw in southern Sakhalin,[6] which together with the Kuriles is somewhat larger than the combined area of New Hampshire and Vermont.

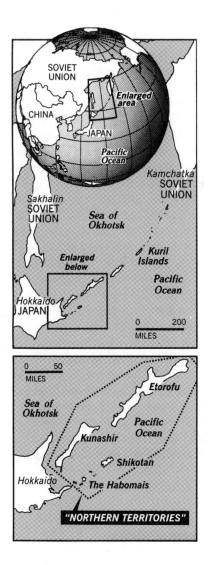

SOVIET UNION

Enlarged area

CHINA

JAPAN

Pacific Ocean

Kamchatka
SOVIET UNION

Sakhalin
SOVIET UNION

Sea of Okhotsk

Enlarged below

Kuril Islands

Pacific Ocean

Hokkaido
JAPAN

0   200
MILES

0   50
MILES

Sea of Okhotsk

Etorofu

Pacific Ocean

Kunashir

Shikotan

Hokkaido

The Habomais

"NORTHERN TERRITORIES"

Historical Myths

Geographical errors are easier to spot than historical myths. Take, for example, the question of who has the earliest historical ties with the Amur, Sakhalin, and the Kuriles. Chinese writers, whether governed by Beijing or Taipei, categorically insist that the Amur was part of China from antiquity. Japanese writers tend to stress the primacy of Nippon's ties with Sakhalin and the Kuriles. Soviet writers call Chinese and Japanese pretensions "chauvinist" and "revanchist," respectively, and chorus that Russians discovered all three territories and saved their aboriginal populations from extinction. To drive the point home,

Moscow eliminated Japanese place names from southern Sakhalin and the Kuriles in 1947 and Chinese place names from the Maritime Province in 1973.

Chinese, Japanese, and Americans alike subscribe to the notion of Soviet territorial expansion in the Asia-Pacific region. Russia's frontiers in Asia have expanded and ebbed, as have the frontiers of China and Japan. The USSR today is smaller than the Russian Empire 150 years ago. The sale of Russian America (Alaska and the Aleutian Islands) in 1867 dramatically reduced Russia's possessions in the North Pacific. In seizing southern Sakhalin and the Kurile Islands in 1945, Moscow regained (with the arguable exception of the southernmost Kuriles) territories lost or bartered away by czarist authorities. Soviet extraterritorial concessions in Manchuria (northeastern China), traceable to Imperial Russian diplomacy between 1895 and 1900, were surrendered after the Chinese Communists came to power in 1949.

Those who ingest the myth of Soviet expansion on the Pacific are also likely to equate territory with power. On a map, particularly one with a Mercator projection, Siberia and the Far East dwarf China, Korea, and Japan. It is easy to interpolate portentous elements into such a spatial configuration. Having lots of room did help the Red Army withstand the German juggernaut in 1941-43. Yet in Northeast Asia, bigness has been more of a liability than an asset, because it translates into distance and isolation. As early as 1888, Priamur Governor-General Korf pointed out that the Far East's sprawling size made the region strategically vulnerable. Events have repeatedly confirmed his insight. Distance hobbled Russian operations against Japan in the war of 1904-5. Distance prevented Bolsheviks from gaining control over Kolyma, Kamchatka, and Chukotka until seven years after the October Revolution. Today, guarding the far-flung Far Eastern perimeter drains precious human and material resources from a weak economic base.

The growing size, sophistication, and range of the Soviet Pacific Fleet since the 1960s have provided Western commentators with opportunities to exercise their short-term memories. In 1984, a senior American military officer asserted that Russians were breaking with their historical role as a land power to confront the United States on "our turf," the high seas. In fact, Russia had a naval facility on the Pacific thirty-six years before the United States came into existence. The Russian navy made important contributions to Pacific exploration during the eighteenth and nineteenth centuries. Consider, for example, place names in Micronesia (Kutuzov and Suvorov islands) and Polynesia (Spiridov and Krusenstern islands). The Hawaiian Chain, home of the U.S. Seventh Fleet, contains an island named after a Russian naval officer (Lisiansky). Russia's superior knowledge of North Pacific geography confounded the British and French during the Crimean War (1854-56).

Cold war preoccupation with superpower rivalry obscured a tradition of Russian-American naval cooperation. American merchant ships ran the British blockade during the Crimean War to supply Russia's Pacific settlements. Visits by the Russian Fleet to San Francisco and New York during the American Civil War boosted the Union's morale at a time when England and France openly favored the Confederacy. When full-scale Sino-Japanese War hostilities erupted in 1937, the U.S. Asiatic Squadron called at Vladivostok in a demonstration of Soviet-American concern. During World War II, the United States trained fifteen thousand Soviet officers and sailors in the use of 138 surface craft handed over to the USSR under the Lend-Lease Act. The United States contributed more to Soviet naval power in the Pacific than any country except Weimar Germany and Mussolini's Italy which supplied the Pacific Fleet with submarines.

Such episodes notwithstanding, foreign intervention after the October Revolution make it logical for Soviet observers to assume that President Woodrow Wilson sent an American Expeditionary Forces (AEF) to Siberia in 1918 to crush the young Soviet state and turn Siberia into an American colony. In fact, the commander of the AEF had a higher regard for Bolsheviks than he did for the Japanese and their White (i.e., anti-Soviet) protégés. In his memoirs, a celebrated Red commander asserted that Japan withdrew from Siberia in 1922 largely thanks to American pressure. Under Stalin, such testimony was suppressed and the authors — repressed.

Soviet-Japanese relations offer fertile soil for myths. Even under glasnost, Soviet historians

assume that Soviet policies toward Japan have always been peace-loving. In Japan, meanwhile, the perennial "Russian threat" bogey still enjoys wide currency. American complacency has been fed by the notion of Russo-Japanese "historical enmity." Hooked on public opinion polls and blinkered by selective amnesia, American commentators are for the most part unaware that Russia/USSR and Japan have worked quite handily together when each felt it was in its interests to do so. Russia's Pacific Fleet wintered in Nagasaki during the 1880s and 1890s. St. Petersburg and Tokyo cooperated in demarcating their spheres of influence in Manchuria and Mongolia at the expense of China and the United States during 1907-12. The Russo-Japanese military alliance of 1916 and Soviet-Japanese Pact of 1941 had serious consequences for Germany and the United States, respectively.

While underestimating the resilience of Russo-Japanese relations, Americans have a habit of indulging in fashionably optimistic prognoses about the problem of the Northern Territories. For more than twenty years, State Department officials, scholars, and journalists have forecast a "solution," sometimes venturing a date. Such predictions, conventional journalistic-academic wisdom in the Gorbachev era, may simply be farsighted, for they have yet to come true.

New Myths

Gorbachev's "Vladivostok Initiative" spawned a new crop of myths about Russia on the Pacific. To minds unencumbered by memory, the general-secretary's rhetoric sounded innovative. In fact, Kalinin (1923), Zhdanov (1939), Mikoyan (1945), Khrushchev (1954 and 1959), and Brezhnev (1966 and 1978) delivered speeches at Vladivostok proclaiming the importance of regional development and peace. Gorbachev's highly touted "concession" to China on the river frontiers was merely an unacknowledged reversion to an earlier Soviet position recognizing the main channel as the international boundary. As to the "newness" of special economic zones, the Far East enjoyed more autonomy and more scope for interaction with Asia-Pacific nations in 1900 or 1920 than it did in 1990.

As a symbol of the Far East's "new" accessibility, the city of Vladivostok personifies Western illusions. Paraphrasing the great Russian poet Pushkin, Gorbachev predicted in 1986 that Vladivostok will be a window on the Pacific as St. Petersburg was a window on Europe. Carried away by the "window" metaphor, *The Christian Science Monitor* asserted that Vladivostok had been closed since 1862. In fact, from 1862 until 1909, with a brief interruption, Vladivostok was a free port with a foreign community that constituted up to half of the population. It continued to be a cosmopolitan emporium through revolution and civil war into the 1920s. Chinese, British, Swiss, American, and Japanese enterprises conducted business there until 1932. Chinese and Japanese consulates functioned there throughout World War II. The United States and the Third Reich opened consulates-general there in 1940. Although the Germans closed up shop in 1941, the Americans stayed on until 1948. During the 1950s, Chinese and North Korean delegations frequented the city. Indonesian, Peruvian, and Chilean naval squadrons sailed into the Golden Horn[7] during the 1960s and 1970s. President Ford met Brezhnev there in 1974.

A Shared Pacific Destiny?

More than a hundred years ago, Walt Whitman and Alexander Herzen declared that Russia and America shared a Pacific destiny. The poet and the revolutionary both saw two waves of raw energy converging across vast continents toward a great ocean. Their common vision was not entirely whimsical. A certain symmetry can be detected in forces drawing Russians and Americans to the Pacific: restlessness with metropolitan constraints, hunger for free land, the lure of gold, the search for routes to China and Japan, and evangelism.

Yet differences overshadow commonalities. The Pacific has become a major part of American life. The U.S. Pacific Coast has a diversified economy with its own capital base, extensive domestic and international trade, and a developed infrastructure. More than forty million Americans, one of every six, live in the Pacific region.

The Pacific figures modestly in Russian life. The Far East's economy is based on extraction of raw materials and depends on capital inputs from the Center. For all its massive physical presence in the Basin, Russia has relatively few economic and cultural ties in the region. Russia accounts for only 4 percent of Pacific Basin trade. The Far East has barely eight million inhabitants (less than 3 percent of the Russian population). Fewer people live on the Russian Pacific littoral than on Japan's northernmost island of Hokkaido.

Russians have never moved voluntarily to the Pacific in large numbers. "Go East, young man!" reverberates feebly in Soviet folklore. Of those who went East during the Stalin years (1929-52), millions (how many millions is a subject of debate) did so under the auspices of the security organs. Incentives proved less efficacious than coercion in keeping people in the Far East. A third of skilled laborers leave within three years of arrival. Turnover rates among scientists and managers are only slightly less volatile.

Geographical, historical, social, cultural, and political conditions underlie the gulf between Russian and American experiences on the Pacific. These conditions assume sharp focus in contrasting attitudes toward frontiers.

Russian Frontier Spirit

Traditionally, the American frontier has been a horizon beckoning with promise, an outlet, a safety valve, an arena to test oneself and pursue ideals or riches. In the nineteenth century, the frontier receded from Appalachia to the Pacific as the United States purchased or took land from France, Spain, Mexico, American Indians, Russia, and the Hawaiian Kingdom. This process evolved without major setbacks and left scars principally on native Americans and Hawaiians. U.S. continental frontiers have an uncomplicated geopolitical configuration. Canada and Mexico pose no military threat. Neither nurtures territorial claims on the United States. Proximity to the USSR has led to disputes about sovereignty over continental shelf resources and some arctic islands, but these issues remain relatively minor. Drug running and illegal immigration have raised public awareness about frontiers. Yet after being beefed up in the late 1980s to address these problems, the U.S. Border Patrol still employs fewer than six thousand men and women.

Figure 12.1   Goldi tribesmen photographed in the Far East in the 1890s.

Russian frontier consciousness springs from less benign circumstances. Russia is located on the Eurasian Plain across which peoples have migrated for millennia. Invasions have buffeted Russia in every century since 1200. Some of these invasions came out of the East, leaving Russians with complex attitudes about Asia. The Mongol conquest destroyed the Kievan state and traumatized survivors. When Russian eastward expansion began in the sixteenth century, defeat at the hands of Asians was still fresh in the collective memory. Tartar raiders burned Moscow in 1571, barely a dozen years before Cossack bands breached the Urals. Cossacks moving across Siberia met more resistance than did pioneers moving across North America. Remnants of the Mongol Empire barred approaches to the Kazakh Steppe and Altai. The Manchus expelled Russians from the Amur Valley in 1689. Japan rebuffed Russian

attempts to open trade between 1739 and 1813. The United States nudged Russia out of North America in 1867. During the war of 1904-5, Japan invaded Sakhalin and secured control of the island's southern half. The Imperial Japanese Army deployed 300,000 men in the Amur and Maritime provinces between 1918 and 1922, occupied northern Sakhalin from 1920 to 1925, and maintained a military presence in Manchuria (northeastern China) from 1905 until 1945. China, Japan, the United States, and even North Korea have articulated territorial claims on the Far East. U.S. planes, warships, and satellites have girdled — and penetrated — the Far Eastern perimeter.

Foreign power within the Far East also shaped Russian frontier consciousness. Far Eastern commerce between the 1850s and 1920s was largely in the hands of Americans, Germans, British, Canadians, Scandinavians Japanese, Chinese,

Koreans, and Russian Jews with American passports. Czech, American, British, French, Italian, Chinese, Polish, Canadian, and Japanese troops bestrode the Transbaikalian, Amur, and Maritime region cities and towns during the Allied Intervention in the Russian Civil War (1918-22). Japanese commanders in Vladivostok and Khabarovsk issued military script, put up Japanese signs, forcing Russians to bow in the presence of Imperial Army officers, and "pacifying" villages suspected of harboring partisans.

Throughout the nineteenth century, foreigners enjoyed unobstructed access to the Far East. Czarist authorities regarded space as sufficient security and were loathe to dip into the imperial treasury to garrison remote outposts. American and British whalers, traders, and poachers exploited Far Eastern marine life, forests, and aborigines. Vladivostok, Imperatorskaya Gavan, Nikolaevsk, Okhotsk, and Petropavlovsk-Kamchatskii were open (duty-free) ports. Chinese and Korean laborers commuted in and out of the Amur and Maritime regions, smuggling half of Amur gold production out of the country.

Efforts to establish a modicum of control over the Far Eastern perimeter were belated and half-hearted. In 1880, the Ministry of Finance created small frontier guard forces which operated only in the ports. In 1897, Amur-Ussuri river patrols were inaugurated. By 1914, two boats covered twelve thousand miles of Pacific coastline.

Frontiers ceased to exist during the Civil War (1918-22) when foreign expeditionary forces came and went at will, and White (anti-Bolshevik) units moved in and out of Manchuria. Japanese fished at will in Far Eastern waters. An American geodetic survey team landed on Chukotka and left a bronze plaque warning: "$250 fine or prison term for removal."

The establishment of Soviet rule in the Far East in 1922 had little affect on frontier porosity. Chinese smugglers continued to take out gold and bring in consumer goods. Chukchi[8] sent their children to school in Alaska. Anticommunist Cossacks and religious sectarians received support from émigré groups in Manchuria. Japanese agents infiltrated at will between Mongolia and Kamchatka.

Bolshevik leaders disagreed on how to deal with state frontiers. Lenin and Stalin insisted that borders be closed in the interests of security.

Others, such as Bukharin, Zinoviev, and Kamenev, argued for keeping frontiers open to expedite economic reconstruction. Lenin and Stalin carried the day, and in late 1917 Soviet frontiers were closed — on paper. The following year, a force of border guards (pogranichniki) was created and placed under the Cheka[9] which designated Lenin an "honorary border guard." A Decree on Soviet Frontiers (1923) set up restricted and free-fire zones.

Such measures proved unenforceable in the Far East, where frontiers were too extended. Some remote settlements adapted to the October Revolution by setting up cosmetic "soviets" and continuing to do business as usual. When a Soviet gunboat sailed into Chukotka's Providenya Bay in 1924, a local constable dressed in czarist uniform came out in a skiff to place the captain and crew under arrest for flying a red flag.

After Japan seized Manchuria in 1931-32, Stalin took drastic measures to seal Far Eastern frontiers, measures that have continued and been refined by his successors. A national campaign mobilized citizens to put USSR frontiers "under lock and key." A revised border control law gave pogranichniki latitude to shoot violators of the control zone (several miles in width) and the "KSP,"[10] a strip of regularly ploughed earth on which telltale footprints could readily be detected. Today about a quarter of the KGB's 175,000 uniformed border guards serve east of Lake Baikal, assisted by guard dogs, helicopters, electronic surveillance devices, a volunteer militia (to plough the KSP), and a network of reservists and youth organizations, such as the Young Friends of Border Guards. Accoutrements of a cult abound: songs ("March of Pacific Border Guards"), operas ("Frontier Under Lock and Key"), place names, monuments to KGB martyrs, and ubiquitous slogans ("Every Soviet citizen is a border guard!").

Far Eastern frontier consciousness has shown itself resistant to perestroika. Notwithstanding a former Alaska governor's 1988 assertion that "Russian institutional paranoia about their border is gone," neither "friendship flights" across the Bering Straits nor poignant speeches about a North Pacific ecumene have diluted frontier vigilance. In 1990, as Foreign Minister Shevarnadze apologized for the destruction of a Korean airliner seven years earlier,[11] a KGB Border Guard Museum opened in Vladivostok. The main exhibit celebrates Colonel Nikita Karatsupa, a thirty-year veteran pogranichnik who intercepted 467 and shot 297 border violators in the Maritime Region. Perestroika notwithstanding, there are still plenty of minds "under lock and key" finding release in socialist realist haiku:

Frontier love
Dizzy from fragrance
Of a freshly ploughed KSP

Center versus Periphery

Regionalism in Imperial Russia and the USSR has primarily an ethnic basis. Balts, Ukrainians, Georgians, Armenians, and Central Asians have their own cultures, as well as memories of political independence. Although regional consciousness is less developed in Siberia and the Far East where Russians form a majority of the population, these areas have not been exempt from centrifugal forces.

Until the late nineteenth century, the Center (Moscow and St. Petersburg) viewed Siberia and the Far East as a colony. At the same time, the Center knew that these vast, remote lands offered a potential base for ambitious, unmanageable officials and took measures to preclude the emergence of a political challenge from the region. During the seventeenth century, Moscow deliberately fragmented power among mutually competing military commanders. Periodic administrative reorganizations during the next two hundred years reflected St. Petersburg's search for a balance between central control and efficiency.

As a result of distance and poor communication, St. Petersburg could not prevent unauthorized initiatives in the Far East and the Pacific. Raids on Japanese settlements in Sakhalin and the southern Kuriles in 1806-7 and an abortive attempt to take over the Hawaiian Islands in 1815-17 had to be disavowed by the Center Governor-General of Eastern Siberia N.N. Muraviev acted largely on his own initiative to acquire the Amur region during 1849-60. He was supported by, among others, political exiles and young officers who flirted with the notion of detaching Siberia from orthodox Russia and forming with the Republic across the Pacific a United States of Siberia and America.

Muraviev's opponents in St. Petersburg wanted to keep Siberia as a cul-de-sac and warned that the Amur would act as an escape artery and as an avenue for subversive foreign contacts. Muraviev carried the day by deftly encroaching on China while its Manchu rulers were preoccupied by the Taiping Rebellion. After incorporation of the Amur and Maritime regions into the Russian Empire in 1858 and 1860, Muraviev was made a count, but rumors that he aspired to be a "Siberian czar" hastened his political eclipse.

Siberian regionalism found articulate spokesmen in two Tomsk intellectuals, Nikolai Yadrintsev (1842-1894) and Dmitry Potanin (1835-1920). Both men called Siberia a "colony" abused by the Center as a dumping ground and milch cow. They argued that autonomy would serve Siberia's social, economic, and cultural interests. For their temerity, both men were imprisoned and exiled for allegedly plotting to detach Siberia from Russia. After their release, they continued to champion Siberian autonomy within a reformist rather than revolutionary or secessionist political context, winning supporters among the region's commercial and professional classes.

Birth of a Far Eastern Identity

Far Eastern regional consciousness surfaced later and, while sharing some characteristics with its Siberian cousin, had different constituencies and priorities. Cossacks and religious sectarians figured prominently in Far Eastern regionalism before 1920. Contacts with Pacific neighbors gave it a cosmopolitan complexion. Chukchi spoke English rather than Russian (the word "Russian" to them meant "criminal"), prompting the future Czar Alexander III to complain in 1879 that "unless something is done, they'll forget they belong to us." When the free-port status of Vladivostok was debated in the Duma (principal czarist legislative assembly) during 1909, a Moscow editor warned that if St. Petersburg imposed imperial tariffs on Far Eastern ports, it would reap the same consequences that overtook the British Empire when London imposed imperial tariffs on the American colonies.

Revolution and civil war reified the bogey of Siberian regionalism. Bolsheviks enjoyed little

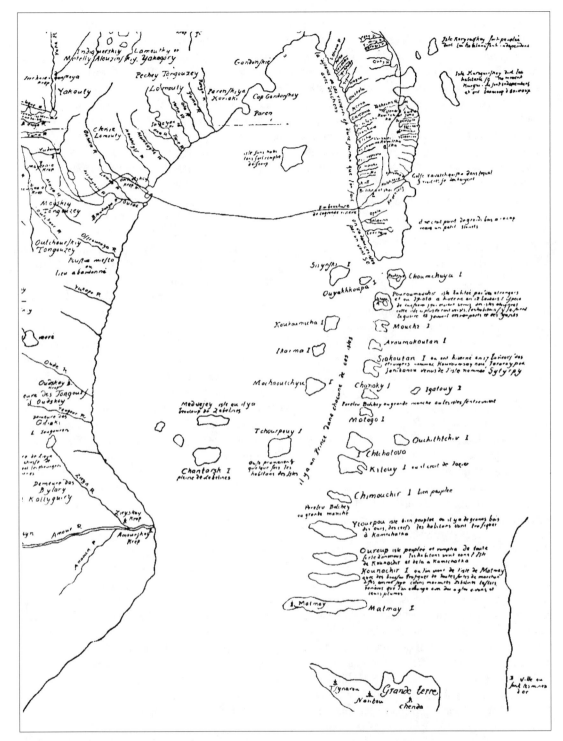

This French language map illustrates the crude level of geographical knowledge of Siberia in 1727 when it was presented to the Russian Senate as part of an effort by the Cossack, Afanase Shestakof, to gain approval for a new expedition of conquest against the natives of Northeastern Siberia. The map indicates Russian interest in the Kurile Islands (lower right) and recognizes the "great land" to the south as Japan. It was not known at the time that the Amur River (lower left) turns northward to empty into the sea.

support in Siberia and the Far East, where the proletariat was smaller than the middle classes and where peasants were too independent and prosperous (Lenin called them "sated") to respond to Bolshevik propaganda. Socialist Revolutionaries (SRs) commanded a greater following in the radical intelligentsia. Siberia and the Far East bristled with anti-Bolsheviks of all varieties (monarchists, Cossacks, Kadets, Siberian autonomists, right SRs) in 1918 when armed Czech POWs seized the Trans-Siberian Railroad, and several foreign military contingents disembarked at Vladivostok.

A Republic and Cohort

Moscow's response to counterrevolution beyond the Urals reinforced Far Eastern regionalism. To induce Japanese expeditionary forces to withdraw from the Amur and Maritime regions, Lenin devised the strategy of creating a Far Eastern buffer state called the Far Eastern Republic (FER) in 1920. Stretching from Lake Baikal to Kamchatka, the FER had the trappings of sovereignty: a flag, a legislative assembly, a constitution, and an army. FER officials included Bolsheviks, Mensheviks, SRs, Kadets, and even monarchists. Democratic in form, the FER was supposed to be under communist control. However, some FER officials took independence seriously, including two putative Bolshevik repatriates from the United States, President Alexander Krasnoshchekov (University of Chicago, class of 1912) and Foreign Minister Vladimir ("Bill") Shatov.

Although the FER was liquidated on the departure of Japanese troops in 1922, Moscow had little choice but to tolerate de facto Far Eastern autonomy throughout the decade. The Center had neither capital nor cadres to manage its most distant province. The Far East supported itself; by trading with Pacific neighbors and by selling concessions to foreign investors. Spared "war communism," the Far East leapt directly into the "New Economic Policy" (NEP), which persisted on the Pacific for years after NEP had been discarded in European Russia.

From 1923 until 1937, Far Eastern political leadership revolved around a cohort of former partisans, party underground activists, and ex-

FER officials who occupied key positions in regional party, soviet, and military organs. The Far Eastern cohort was held together by two able civil war veterans: Vasily Blücher, former FER war minister and commander of the Special Far Eastern Army, and Yan Gamarnik, chairman of Far Eastern soviets and first secretary of the Far Eastern party organization.

Victorious against Trotsky, Kamenev, Zinoviev, Bukharin, and other "oppositionists," Stalin could neither penetrate nor manipulate the Far Eastern cohort. Central policies were not always implemented if the cohort did not consider them appropriate to Far Eastern needs. Faced with the forced collectivization campaign, Blücher warned Moscow that unless the Far East were exempted he could not accept responsibility for regional security. Japanese continental advance gave Blücher's warning teeth, and Moscow backed down — but did not forget.

The Far Eastern cohort reached its apogee in the early 1930s when it controlled nearly a quarter of the USSR with its own party, army, navy, and security organ members. Blücher's Special Far Eastern army was the strongest military unit in the USSR. As Chief of the Red Army's Main Political Administration, Gamarnik appointed political commissars throughout the country and spent six months of every year in the Far East. Far Eastern troops, unlike counterparts in other units, brought their families with them to the Far East. Some worked on farms while in military service.

At the time, the Far East had both the manpower and resources to defy the Center. With direct access to Manchukuo, Japan, and the United States, it could not be blockaded or sealed off by Moscow. Stalin's attempts to dismantle the cohort by nonviolent administrative means, such as personnel shifts and party purges, foundered on a tactic well known to provincial officials: Propitiate higher authorities with a show of zeal.

The Burden of Memory

By 1937, Stalin and the Yezhovian NKVD[12] suspected that the Far Eastern cohort was involved in a plot centering around ranking Red Army officers. Acting on his suspicions, Stalin decapitated Far Eastern party, army, managerial, security organ, and educational cadres. The Far Eastern army was disbanded. Teachers, journalists, scientists, and scholars disappeared into GULAG.[13] Journals and schools ceased to exist. The Far Eastern State University in Vladivostok closed in 1939 and did not reopen until well after Stalin's death. Not a single Far Eastern delegate to the seventeenth Party Congress (1934) showed up at the eighteenth Party Congress five years later. The Far East never again formed a single administrative unit with its own party organization. Moscow balkanized it between 1938 and 1956, leaving half a dozen districts each accountable to Moscow.

For more than fifty years, Far Easterners have borne a heavy burden of unutterable memories. Khrushchev rehabilitated (posthumously) Blücher and Gamarnik and partially dismantled the labor camps. Yet no public inquest into the full consequences of the "cult of personality" followed. The moral costs of massive complicity in systematic terror were never addressed.

Glasnost made a belated début in Far Eastern media, surfacing in 1988; but by 1990, it was making up for lost time. Traditionally conservative Far Eastern journals and newspapers followed the lead of central publications such as the magazine *Ogonyok* in filling in "blank spots" from the Stalinist and Brezhnevian past. New, independent newspapers in Magadan, Petropavlovsk-Kamchatskii, and Yuzhno-Sakhalinsk published accounts of recently discovered mass graves, lists of local victims, testimonies of survivors, and portraits of beneficiaries.

According to a Yakut legend, words uttered outdoors in winter freeze into soundlessness but recover their resonance in the spring thaw. As Far Easterners heard voices from the past, they began to recover their collective memory. Whether greeted by sorrow, anger, shame, or indifference, the revelations are restoring credibility to public discourse.

Pacific Wallflower

Until the mid-1980s, the Soviet Union hardly figured in Western discussions about a Pacific Community. The omission was deliberate and reflected a reluctance to deal with the USSR as a regional partner. Conventional metaphors for Soviet international behavior oscillated between "hungry bear" to "loose cannon." During the "age of stagnation" (1964-85), Moscow demonstrated a genius for mistiming and insensitivity. It built up a formidable military presence in Northeast Asia and the Pacific, only to witness that displays of raw power isolated the USSR internationally and impoverished it domestically. Leonid Brezhnev managed to broach an Asian Collective Security Proposal in 1969 amid Moscow-inspired rumors that the USSR was contemplating a surgical strike against Chinese nuclear installations. By deploying a division in the southern Kuriles during Sino-Japanese negotiations in 1978, Moscow ensured that an antihegemony clause could be incorporated into the Sino-Japanese peace treaty. By supporting Vietnam's invasion of Kampuchea (1979), by invading Afghanistan (1979), and by shooting down a Korean airliner (1983), Moscow confirmed the characterizations of its harshest critics.

Negative images of the USSR in the Pacific were reinforced by defectors, few of whom had much good to say about their homeland. Japan attracted a steady trickle, including KGB Major Levchenko whose revelations provided grist for "northern menace" mills. Clumsy efforts at damage control did little to improve public relations. When Lieutenant Belenko decided to act on the Aeroflot jingle "One mig ["instant"] and you're in Japan!" and flew a MIG-25 to Hakodate, Moscow evoked hilarity by claiming that the errant pilot had lost his geographical, but not his ideological, bearings.

The party and ministerial bureaucracy rarely missed an opportunity to damage Soviet interests by assigning *apparatchiki*[14] of inspired tactlessness to deal with Asia-Pacific countries. Between 1970 and 1985, Soviet diplomats were expelled from Japan, China, Indonesia, Thailand, Malaysia, Singapore, the Philippines, Australia, and New Zealand. Former Red Army interpreter-interrogator Ivan Kovalenko, durable fixture of the Central Committee's Information Department, addressed senior Japanese parliamentarians, diplomats, and businessmen as if they were POWs. Ambassador Dmitry Polyansky went about cultivating Japanese goodwill as a blacksmith would repair a woman's watch. When a Foreign Ministry protocol officer politely asked about his hobbies,

Dmitry Stepanovich looked sharply at the questioner and cautiously countered: "I'll consult Moscow first." Polyansky won applause — in Washington — after telling a Japanese audience that he could win election to the Supreme Soviet by running on an "annex Kyushu" platform.

Soviet officials, sent abroad by connections rather than qualifications, stumbled on unfamiliar Asia-Pacific terrain. "Is Thailand still a British colony?" inquired one envoy to his appalled hosts. Celebrating Khabarovsk-Niigata sister city ties, a Khabarovsk bureaucrat announced that Niigata was the first city in the world to have been obliterated by an atomic bomb.

"New Thinking" on the Pacific

Following Gorbachev's "Vladivostok Initiative" in 1986, Soviet policies toward the Asia-Pacific region attracted wide and, in some quarters, rapt attention. Gorbachev tried for a couple of years to maintain PR momentum by making highly publicized pronouncements on Asia and the Pacific in an Indonesian newspaper (1987) and at Krasnoyarsk (1988), both of which basically elaborated what had already been said at Vladivostok. The initiatives of 1986-88 yielded tangible dividends for the USSR. Partial fulfillment of China's three preconditions for normalization (withdrawal from Afghanistan and reduction of troop levels in Mongolia, Transbaikalia, and the Far East) was rewarded by trade, scientific exchanges, and the first Sino-Soviet summit in thirty years on the eve of the Tiananmen Square massacre. Trade with and investment from Japan has grown, although not as much as Moscow would like because of the Northern Territories problem. Relations have been normalized with Seoul, opening vistas of South Korean assistance in modernizing the Far East's anemic infrastructure. Economic and cultural ties have proliferated with Thailand, Singapore, Australia, New Zealand, and the Philippines.

Gorbachevian initiatives did not change Soviet-American relations in the Pacific region to

Figure 12.2   In September, 1990, Eduard Shevardnadze, then Minister of Foreign Affairs of the USSR, addressed a regional meeting of Asia-Pacific experts in Vladivostok during which he called for greater integration of the Soviet Union with the Asia-Pacific economies.

the degree that they did in Europe or the Middle East. Strategic rivalry persists despite reductions of troop levels and Pacific Fleet operations. On close examination, concessions look like unilateral cutbacks mandated by a crumbling economy. Efforts to revitalize the Far Eastern economy with infusions of American capital and technology have produced more sound than substance. Dozens of conferences and symposia have been held in Vladivostok to advertise the city's new "openness." Reams of protocols have been initialled calling for scientific and economic cooperation. Seattle, Portland, and Anchorage have exchanged delegations with Vladivostok, Khabarovsk, and Magadan. "Friendship flights" shuttle bureaucrats, entrepreneurs, and tourists across the Bering Straits. Student exchanges have been set up on paper, and some have been implemented.

"New thinking" about the Pacific has been expressed intellectually, professionally, and institutionally within the USSR since 1986. Denounced in 1985 as a "threat to peace," the Pacific Community idea has won fulsome endorsement. Moscow is assiduously seeking membership in regional organizations. Newly promoted apparatchiki are setting peripatetic records networking around the Basin. The word "Pacific" adorns a gaggle of new sectors, departments, agencies, divisions, and committees. At the center of all this activity is a younger generation of facilitators, suave, sophisticated, better informed, and socially more presentable than their predecessors. Some are also more ready to emigrate.

Bitter Fruits of Glasnost

Glasnost revealed to millions of Soviet citizens their country's actual, rather than idealized, international stature. This awareness eroded cherished assumptions that sustained people through seventy years of sacrifices in the name of "proletarian internationalism," the "radiant future," and the "socialist community."

Many ordinary people came to realize that the Soviet Union wielded modest moral authority. Until recently, the mass of citizens assumed that the Great October Socialist Revolution inspired all the oppressed peoples of Asia. They believed implicitly that the Red Army and Pacific Fleet liberated China, Korea, and Southeast Asia from colonialism and imperialism by defeating Imperial Japan, giving Chinese communists a "revolutionary base" in Manchuria, and protecting the Korean Democratic Republic and Vietnam from American aggression.

The expectation of gratitude, often stronger than the emotion of gratitude itself, is notoriously susceptible to disappointment. *Glasnost* revealed that gratitude to Russia for real and imagined services is in short supply throughout East Asia. Chinese write ironically about the Red Army Manchurian campaign of 1945. The late "Beloved Leader" Kim Il-sung could hardly be expected to share credit for Korea's liberation with a suitor for Seoul's economic favors. Hanoi is likewise frugal in assessing the Soviet contribution to victory in South Vietnam. Even Mongolia has stopped catering to past Soviet self-images

More and more Russian citizens have a sinking feeling of having been left behind by dynamic Asia-Pacific economies. Anyone who has gotten hold of an American fashion magazine or electronic gadgets from Japan, South Korea, Hong Kong, Taiwan, or Singapore is forcefully reminded of his or her deprivation.

For decades, Far Easterners have been told that socialist construction put them in the Pacific avant-garde. As late as 1984, Soviet pundits were calling Siberia and the Far East "symbols of all that is new and progressive." Construction of the Baikal-Amur Railroad or BAM (1974-84) was hailed as the "project of the century." There was heady talk of building giant hydroelectric and nuclear power plants, of damming the Tartary and Bering straits, of rerouting Siberian rivers to Central Asia. By 1990, the Siberia rivers project had been scrapped. BAM was being described as a monument to waste. Accessible deposits of coal, oil, gas, and ore were approaching exhaustion. Forests had been cut down with little thought of renewal. Lake Baikal was polluted, and the Amur was dying. Chernobyl cast a shadow over the Bilibino nuclear power plant, built on Chukotka permafrost.

Enduring dependence on imported foodstuffs, notably grain, has become a symbol of the emptiness of slogans. Every five-year plan since 1928 proclaimed that the Far East will achieve self-sufficiency in grain. In 1991, the Far East still imported half of its grain. Ironically, the Far East filled its own grain needs in 1890, and in 1907 produced a surplus. Thanks to an energetic peasantry and extensive use of imported agricultural machinery, the Amur Province grew enough wheat to feed the entire region. Such productivity probably underlay the prediction in 1909 by a senior Russian official that a hundred million people would inhabit the Far East by the year 2000 (less than eight million did in 1991). In 1909, such a prediction did not seem whimsical, for between 1900 and 1914, regional economic growth rates exceeded those of California, Canada, Australia, and New Zealand.

What happened to this momentum, this promise? Revolution, civil war, and foreign intervention dealt the region heavy blows. Forced collectivization and repression destroyed the Far East's most productive class (independent peasants), crippled its educational and research institutions, and removed or liquidated its most gifted inhabitants (party secretaries, soviet chairmen, military commanders, factory managers, engineers, agronomists, teachers, journalists, writers, Koreans, Chinese). In annihilating the Far Eastern

cohort and balkanizing the Far East, Stalin turned the Pacific periphery into an appendage of a centralized command economy. His victory proved costly not only in human lives but in long-term economic performance. For more than fifty years, Russia's Far East has depended on the Center for supplies, plans, investments, and vision. The habit of subservience left regional leaders reluctant to take initiatives or assume responsibilities.

Notwithstanding all the talk of accelerated development, engagement with the Pacific Basin, foreign investment, joint ventures, and special economic zones, Russia's Far East is one of the most backward provinces of a Third World country. An ambitious regional development plan, announced with much fanfare in 1987, was scrapped after two years because of budget deficits. Living standards fall below the national average. Housing and health care are notoriously substandard. A maritime region drenched by monsoon rains cannot provide its inhabitants with decent drinking water. Vladivostok pours raw sewage into Peter the Great Bay. Khabarovsk reputedly leads the country in per capita kidney stones. Yuzhno-Sakhalinsk air has the highest concentration of soot of any city in the USSR.

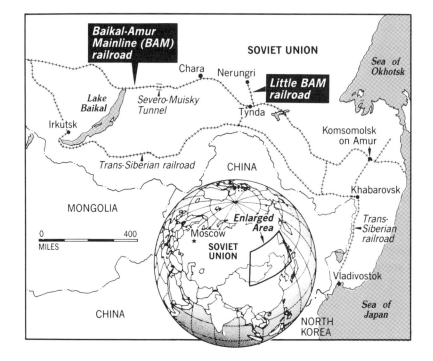

Among aborigines, life expectancy is about twenty years shorter than the USSR average, suicide rates are three to four times the USSR average, and infant mortality two to three times that of the country as a whole. Nuclear tests on Novaya Zemlya have caused radiation disease among people living along the arctic coast. Higher wages and quicker promotions do not keep most immigrants from leaving within five years.

Balkanized Regionalism

In 1986, Gorbachev saw engagement with the Pacific Basin as a catalyst for development of the Soviet Far East. Five years later, that engagement instead helped catalyze regional challenges to the Center.

Long kept in check by the party-state apparatus and by fear inherited from generations that lived (and died) under Stalin, popular anger was exacerbated rather than exorcized by *perestroika*. Open repugnance at official rhetoric, cronyism, and empty promises cropped up as early as 1986 when Gorbachev toured Vladivostok, Khabarovsk, and Komsomolsk. Few Far Easterners welcomed the bureaucrats sent by Gorbachev to replace Brezhnevian holdovers. During 1988 and 1989, ad hoc political groups sprang up in each Far Eastern city and successfully challenged party and state incumbents. In June 1988, a minirevolution overthrew the Gorbachevian secretary of the Sakhalin party organization. In the 1989 elections for the Congress of People's Deputies, five out of seven Far Eastern regional party secretaries (all Gorbachev appointees) were defeated, including the commanders of the Pacific Fleet and the Far Eastern military district.

Meanwhile, open distrust of Moscow party and ministerial bureaucrats legitimized the once treasonable idea of regional autonomy. Favorable references to a Far Eastern Republic (FER), audible in 1989, reverberated as political slogans in 1990. The FER was openly called a "model." Reprints of the FER constitution quickly sold out. A "Far Eastern Republic Freedom Party" held a "constituent assembly" in Vladivostok; independent newspapers call for a Far Eastern Union Republic.

Some officials are already acting as if the Far East had achieved economic autonomy. Each regional and district executive committee has set up a section to manage local relations with Japan, China, North and South Korea, Canada, Australia, and the United States. Far Eastern delegates to the Supreme Soviet hold caucuses in Khabarovsk. The chairman of the Sakhalin executive committee favors turning the island into a special market economy zone, taking control of local production from central ministries, paying taxes only to local authorities, and keeping foreign currency in Sakhalin banks.

Far Eastern regionalist aspirations which once collided with an entrenched Soviet bureaucracy must now cope with a resurgent Russian Republic. By assuming broad powers following the failed coup of August, 1991, Boris Yeltsin signaled his intention of asserting control over Russia's Pacific periphery.

Divisive forces *within* the Far East undermine regional cohesiveness. Vladivostok and Khabarovsk vie for leadership. Sakhalin, politically and economically the most radical district, goes its own way. Magadan and Kamchatka compete for primacy in the U.S. Pacific Northwest. Leaders of the Chukchi and Koryak national areas, seeking autonomy from Magadan and Kamchatka districts, respectively, are allying themselves with the Center in the hope of being granted the status of autonomous republics. Far Eastern regionalism reflects the fragmentation of Soviet society.

"Illusion of Stormy Activity"

Whether heartening or discouraging, a hefty portion of what seems to be transpiring in the Far East today falls into a rich tradition of Russian and Soviet theatrics. Anyone who has read the classics of Gogol, Saltykov-Shchedrin, and Zoshchenko, or who has "worked" in a Soviet *kollektiv*, knows that the gulf between words and action widens in direct proportion to the proximity of officials. Far Easterners have perfected this technique under the roguish rubric IBD[15] or "illusion of stormy activity."

IBD is alive and well on the Pacific. Gorbachev, Yeltsin, and local pundits issue plans, directives, and declarations, but administrative measures are more likely to disguise than to change hard realities. The Vladivostok executive committee might rename the city "Vladivostopol"[16] to convey a meridional ambiance and attract tourists, but come winter the harbor's famous inlet, the Golden Horn, will still freeze over.

NOTES

1. Slightly more than half of Yakutia's population is Slavic.

2. A Yakut Autonomous Soviet Socialist Republic has existed since 1922. Yakuts are Turkic-speaking peoples inhabiting the Lena Basin in Northeastern Siberia. The Azerbaijan Soveit Socialist Republic is located more that three thousand miles to the southeast and borders on Iran.

3. It is a Jewish Autonomous District.

4. Khabarovsh is located 487 miles north of Vladivostok.

5. There is no island by the name "Habomai." Calling Habomai an "island" is like calling the Philippines an "island".

6. Japanese links with Sakhalin can be traced to the seventeenth century. Japan renounced all claims to Sakhalin in favor of Russia in 1875 in exchange for the central and northern Kurile Islands, but seized the island during the Russo-Japanese War. Awarded sourthern Sakhalin at the Portsmouth Peace Treaty (1905), Japan ruled it until August 1945 when the Red Army occupied southern Sakhalin and the Kuriles.

7. A long narrow inlet forming Vladivostok's inner harbor. Named after the Golden Horn of Constantinople.

8. Aboriginal people inhabiting Chukotka, the northeastern extremity of the Soviet Far East.

9. Acronym for security police; subsequently: GPU, OGPU, NKVD, MVD, and KGB.

10. Acronym for *kontrol'no-sledovaya polosa* (control-tracking strip).

11. During the night of August 31 - September 1, 1983, a Soviet Far Eastern Air Defense fighter shot down a KAL Boeing 747 (Flight 007) carrying 269 passengers and crew off the southwestern coast of Sakhalin after it had strayed deeply into Soviet air space en route between Anchorage and Seoul. There were no survivors.

12. Nikolai Yezhov headed the secret police (NKVD) during the height of the Great Terror (1936-38).

13. Acronym for State Administration of Corrective Labor Camps.

14. From the word *apparat* (apparatus); bureaucrats in central party and state organs.

15. Acronym for *illiuziia burnoi deiatel'nosti*.

16. A play on the Black Sea port Sevastopol. "Vladivostopol" cropped up as a colloquialism among Russian sailors in the nineteenth century.

13

Pacific Century: Regional and Global Perspectives

OVERVIEW

The term "Pacific Rim" when used in reference to the diverse societies, political systems, cultures, and general geography of the Western Pacific is among the more vague of many imprecise terms used for this region. As noted at the beginning of this book, even the word "Asia" has had various meanings since the time of Alexander. Yet the concept of Pacific Asia as a region has developed in the last few centuries, having become especially strong in recent decades. In fields as diverse as national security, communications, logistics, and marketing, the challenge is to understand the dynamics of this regionalism and its strengthening during Asia's modernizing interaction with the West.

As described in Chapter Two, the 19th century wave of Western incursions from the sea accelerated the pace of change in Pacific Asian societies. These were by no means the first such interactions with the West, but the scope of their combined impacts was unprecedented. By the twentieth century, rising education and the printed media brought Asians into new patterns of contact with one another. Amid revolution and upheaval, a sense of regional identity began to develop. Rising levels of economic interdependence and cooperation helped to solidify this process, redefining the region to itself and the global community.

This chapter examines the contemporary dynamics of that change in regional terms, looking as well to interactions between Pacific Asia and the rest of the world. Economic, demographic, political, and natural resource trends are our principle references, allowing us to trace the outlines of what may be viewed as a new Pacific "age of commerce."

BACKGROUND

The Pacific and the World Economy in the Post-War Era

Asia's large population has made it a major contributor to the global economy for centuries, albeit at a lower per capita rate in comparison to most other regions. At the beginning of the 20th century, Asia accounted for about a third of world output according to economic historian Angus Madison, with North America and Europe producing over half. Asian production was then largely agricultural but this soon began to change and accelerated after World War II. Several Asian economies underwent an industrial transformation that dramatically altered the structure of Asian production and significantly increased Asia's share of global GNP. But their rapid rise from poverty, the so-called Asian Miracle, could not have taken place without fundamental changes in the rules of global trade following the War.

Prior to World War II, massive distortions in the global economy had dampened Pacific commercial growth. These distortions arose from such factors as high trade barriers, state-to-state trading arrangements, and the widespread cartelization of domestic and international industries. By the late 1930s world trade had fallen to half its previous peak. International capital flows, which were of fundamental importance in the earlier years of growth, were so constrained by private and public controls that they dropped to one fifth their turn of the century levels.

Reconstruction policies in the aftermath of World War II reversed this trend. Through institutions and funding led by the United States, developed nations started afresh and reduced most of their trade and investment barriers. The so-called Bretton Woods institutions were created (i.e., the World Bank, the International Monetary Fund) and, of particular importance for global economic recovery, the General Agreement on Tariffs and Trade (GATT) succeeded through a series of global negotiating rounds to greatly reduce tariff barriers. The European Economic Community was established, eventually to become the world's largest common market. All these initiatives generally stimulated market opening measures in many regions of the world.

The result was a period of strong economic growth for the developed nations that lasted from the late 1940s to the early 1970s. These multilateral initiatives helped create economic conditions that prevented a repeat of the doldrums of the 1930s. Instead, the era of strong growth continued until people began to believe it might last indefinitely. From around 1950, real GDP among the developed countries[1] increased by an average of nearly 5 percent a year. This was two and a half times more rapid than growth in the four preceding decades and twice as rapid as would occur later in the 1970s.

In spite of this impressive expansion, several factors were building prior to 1973 that undermined the "golden age" of post-war growth. Wages began to accelerate in Europe, especially after the politically tumultuous year of 1968. Gains in worker productivity, vital for sustaining growth without inflation, began to slow. Finally, the so-called Bretton Woods system of fixed international exchange rates broke down in the early 1970s when the United States went off the gold standard.

The end came dramatically when the international oil crisis broke out in 1973 accompanied by the first oil price shock. The long-lasting effects of the crisis came not so much from the initial reduction of oil supplies as the crippling increase in prices. Inflation soared throughout the economies

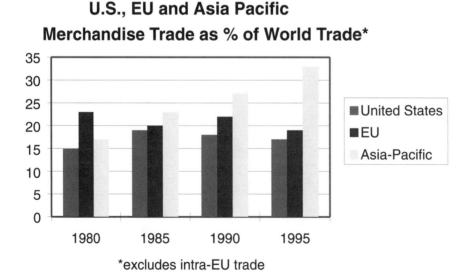

U.S., EU and Asia Pacific
Merchandise Trade as % of World Trade*

*excludes intra-EU trade

Graph 13.1

of developed and developing nations alike and all of them struggled to find ways to adjust to the losses of their real incomes and deteriorating terms of trade. Most slipped into serious recessions. The blow fell especially hard on energy-dependent Asian economies, including Japan. Then, in 1979, wage-price increases assumed newly destructive proportions with a second oil shock and in its wake much of the world endured another serious recession in 1980-81 and in some areas for a longer period.

By the early 1980s, however, the Asian capitalist economies were moving aggressively, wherever possible, to increase the energy efficiency of their industries and to reduce their overall dependence on imported energy. The Newly Industrialized Economies (NIEs) and Japan, in particular, responded to the income-reducing blows of the oil shocks with belt-tightening measures that enabled them to emerge with their economies in relatively strong competitive positions. The European countries, by contrast, remained in the doldrums and in the early 1980s their policy-makers became increasingly concerned about their capacity to compete economically with the Pacific Basin nations. This was to be an important element in motivating "regionalist" responses in both Europe and the Pacific in the 1980s.

Early Stimulus of the U.S. Market

A striking aspect of Asian post-war growth has been its heavy reliance on regional markets. By far the most important market has been that of the United States, since World War II one of the most open in the world. East Asian export-led strategies have depended on this openness even though in the initial post-war period they were themselves inward-looking and protectionist. Indonesia, the Philippines, and Korea rationalized their trade barriers by citing a need for greater self-sufficiency and the protection of fragile, new domestic industries. By the late 1960s, however, political transitions had taken place that permitted these and other countries to pursue new, somewhat more liberal trade policies that were designed by a new generation of U.S.-educated "technocrats." Their main thrust was to encourage exports rather than imports. Trade and investment barriers, by

U.S. standards, remained relatively high. In the 1980s, when the U.S. trade deficit with Asia grew at an unprecedented rate, these barriers became a source of serious tension.

Asymmetry thus became the dominant feature of Asia-Pacific trade in the later post-war period. The swift resurgence of Japan, described in chapter 6, not only failed to correct this imbalance but added to it. Between 1980 and 1984 the United States absorbed an estimated 71 percent of the growth in manufactured exports from East and Southeast Asia and the Pacific while Japan took only 9 percent. This asymmetry was reflected in general trade patterns during much of the 1980s.

The size and openness of the U.S. market became a vital underlying growth factor for the region. By 1984 seven of the United States' major trading partners were in the Pacific Basin. The growth and imbalance in the flows were especially striking in the case of the NIEs. Their exports to the United States accelerated until in the late 1980s they reached more than $60 billion annually, rising by 60 percent between 1985 and 1989. U.S. exports to the NIEs, on the other hand, amounted to only $38 billion in 1989, more than double the amount of 1985 but leaving a yawning deficit with the NIEs of over $20 billion (plus some $45 billion with Japan).

The negative effects of the NIE export-oriented strategies became obvious with swings in the relative values of the yen and dollar. These shifts — which effectively changed the prices of their goods in foreign markets — were completely beyond their control. Still, as will be seen, these economies were able to enjoy a ride up the currency roller coaster (when demand for their lower-priced products surged) before starting down.

The Impact of Currency Values

By the early 1980s, Japan's mounting trade surplus with the United States created even greater political frictions than with the NIEs. One American explanation for the imbalance assumed that Japan's trade barriers and predatory marketing practices (chapter 6) were to blame. Another explanation ascribed it to Japan's undervalued currency. The currency exchange rate explanation gained wide official acceptance on both sides of

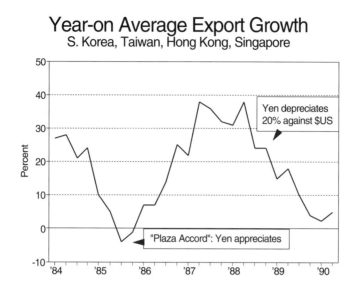

Year-on Average Export Growth
S. Korea, Taiwan, Hong Kong, Singapore

Yen depreciates
20% against $US

"Plaza Accord": Yen appreciates

Graph 13.2

the Pacific, and by 1985 it became the subject of the so-called "Plaza Accord" among the Group of Seven industrialized nations. It was, in effect, an informal agreement among the key nations' central banks to allow the yen to appreciate relative to the dollar.

Early hopes that the Plaza Accord would sharply reduce Japan - U.S. trade frictions were soon dampened. A sufficiently strong Japanese currency, it was said, would lower and perhaps even eliminate America's trade deficit with Japan because Japanese goods would become much more expensive in U.S. markets (Americans would buy less of them) while sales of the less-expensive American goods would rise in Japan. During the next two years the dollar lost over 50 percent of its value against the yen — twice the amount that was estimated to be necessary — yet at the end of 1990 Japan's trade surplus with the United States still stood at $38 billion and with the world it was $ 52 billion.

Even if the trade imbalances did not respond as sharply as hoped, the change in currency exchange rates did have an impact. During the five years that followed the Plaza Accord, America's global trade deficit dropped by more than 50 percent in dollar terms, even more in volume terms, and its trade with the European Community moved into surplus. The dramatic change in

currency exchange rates had an equal if not greater impact on the NIEs. As Figure 13.2 illustrates, the Plaza Accord provided an initial boost to NIE exports because initially the values of their currencies moved only slightly. With currencies that were undervalued relative to the yen as well as the dollar, goods from these economies became all the more competitive in foreign markets. Then, in 1989 the trends began to run against them. Not only did the NIEs come under increasing U.S. pressure to appreciate their currencies (in line with the same rationale that had been applied to Japan) but a slide in the value of the yen further dampened their export growth.

Exchange rates alone did not cause the current account fluctuations, however. (The current account is the broadest measure of a nation's trade in goods and services.) Another factor was the rising and falling level of consumption in different countries. When a country consumes less relative to its trading partners, it imports relatively less from them and they buy relatively more from it. Because America's domestic demand grew more slowly than that of Japan or Europe, its exports soared and helped improve its current account. Conversely, Japan's rising demand at home reduced the size of its current account surplus.

Still, policy-makers had hoped that these shifts would be even greater in view of the

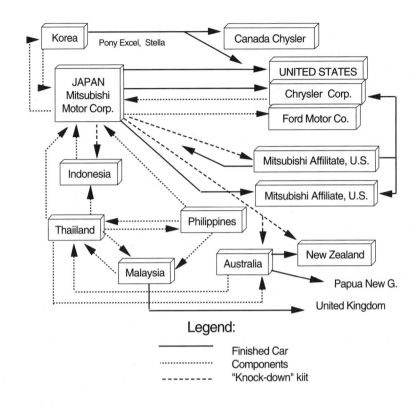

Graph 13.3   The Mitsubishi Motor Corporation's manufacturing network in the Pacific Basin.

extreme change in the value of the Japanese yen. A countervailing factor was the globalization of large private firms. Major multinationals now base their production facilities within a broad global network. Trade accounts do not accurately reflect the movement of components, services and finished products within these networks even though, as the globalization of industries broadens and deepens, an ever-greater proportion of trade will take place inside them. An example of how such a network looks from the perspective of a single company's automobile manufacturing in the Pacific Basin is illustrated by Graph 13.3. Japan has become preeminent in building these linkages throughout the Asia-Pacific region and the world. Because such firms now position much of their production overseas they are themselves less sensitive to exchange rate swings.

We can draw at least three conclusions from this: first, if traditional statistical measures such as the current account are to be used, the national deficits and surpluses will always be less responsive to currency shifts than was once hoped. Second, trade figures alone are less relevant than they used to be in associating the "competitiveness" of a large multinational company with conditions in its host nation. Third, these changing conditions are causing major Asian economies such as Japan and Taiwan, possessing surplus capital, strengthening currencies, and extensive trade networks, to spread their base of production throughout the region.

REGIONAL DYNAMICS

Trade and Investment Trends

The strong economic expansion and integration of the East Asia economies, described in Chapter 7, has been underlain by rising levels of international trade and, since the mid-1980s, direct foreign investment. East Asia's share of world trade rose from around 14 percent in 1980 to a little over 19 percent in 1990. The share of world trade of the regional Asia Pacific Economic Cooperation (APEC) economies, described later in this chapter, rose from 30 percent to 37 percent over the same period. The share of East Asia in world trade will increase to 33 percent by the year 2000 while the share of the APEC group is expected to rise to almost 40 percent.

Most of the growth in East Asian and APEC trade has been with other countries in the Asia-Pacific region. Intra-East Asian trade increased from around 24 percent of total East Asian trade in 1970 to 36 percent by 1992. Intra-APEC trade rose less dramatically, but from a higher level, from around 63 percent of the Asia-Pacific total in 1970 to around 68 percent in 1992.

The growth in intra-regional trade in East Asia has not been encouraged by discriminatory trading blocs as was the case in Western Europe. In fact, there has been no economically significant action by East Asian economies to collectively discriminate against outsiders in order to expand their common trade. To the extent that there have been trade preferences within the region their impact has been negligible, although the commitment by ASEAN governments towards the ASEAN Free Trade Agreement (AFTA) may become an exception. Trade discrimination under the Australia-New Zealand Closer Economic Relations Agreement has also affected a relatively small proportion of regional trade. Meanwhile, the two most rapidly expanding intra East-Asian bilateral trading relationships over the past few years, between China and Taiwan, and between China and Korea, have developed in spite of discriminatory trade restrictions.

Does rapid growth of intra-Asia trade nonetheless "divert" commerce that would otherwise benefit a larger world community? Apparently not, according to the Asian Development Bank which finds by means of a complex measure that, if anything, there has been a slight drop-off in the "intensity" of trade in the region, regardless of its growth rate.[2] In other words, given its economic status, Pacific Asia is actually trading more than might be expected with the larger world community than with itself.

The Role of Foreign Investment

In addition to strong growth in regional trade there has been, more recently, very strong growth in direct foreign investment. While trade expansion is important in promoting economic growth in the region, foreign direct investment plays a key role as well. In fact, foreign direct investment may provide an even stronger stimulus to economic development than increased trade. It transfers not only financial resources for production but also technology and management know-how which improve technical and managerial efficiency. Foreign direct investment also expands marketing and information networks and stimulates the competitiveness of domestic markets. Even the efficiency of local industries supplying foreign firms is benefited because foreign firms that demand high quality services, timeliness etc. invest in improving the efficiency of their local suppliers.

In the second half of the 1980s the East Asian newly industrializing economies and the ASEAN economies experienced a 430 percent and 570 percent increase, respectively, in direct foreign investment. The rate of increase in direct foreign investment worldwide was less, although still dramatic, at 330 percent over the same period. The flow of direct foreign investment to China, in particular, surged in the 1990s.

JAPAN'S ROLE IN THE ASIA-PACIFIC ECONOMY

Regional Expansion in the 1980s

During the 1980s Japan decisively supplanted the United States as the leading source of manufactured goods, new business investment, technology and economic aid in an area stretching from South Asia to the Pacific islands.[3] Although this trend was widely anticipated, Japanese economic dominance in Asia accelerated faster than expected in the late 1980s in response to the currency realignments created by the Plaza Accord. Suddenly, Japanese companies found themselves confronting production costs at home that were far higher than those of their competitors in the NIEs. In order to remain competitive, they moved rapidly to locate new production off-shore. A major share of their investment went to the NIEs and Southeast Asia — increasing six fold between 1985 and 1989 — where the objective was not just to enlarge market share within the host country but to use the location as an export platform and thus maintain market share in third countries such as the United States (Figure 13.4). As a result, private Japanese business investment began to fuel growth in the NIEs and countries such as Thailand and Malaysia. Japan began to distinguish much less between itself and the rest of Pacific Asia in planning its marketing and manufacturing strategies. In many cases, Japanese manufacturers have found partners in the overseas Chinese business communities (described in chapter 7) whose contacts in local trade and finance are renowned. By some estimates, nearly half of all Japanese exports will be bound for the region in the first decade of the 21st century while the U.S. will absorb less than one-fourth, a reversal of the relationship in the late 1980s.

Throughout the region, the tide of Japanese investment became visible in the form of new Japanese business offices, hotels and manufacturing plants. Consumer merchandise from Sony, Panasonic and Canon began to appear in Korea and Thailand not as imported items but locally-produced products. The most far-reaching change was in the regional production base itself: Japanese companies began to manufacture components in different parts of Asia according to each country's comparative advantages in resources, infrastructure and labor (Figure 13.3).

While benefiting from the surge of Japanese investment, the NIEs did not stand still. They enhanced their competitive position against Japanese multinationals in the lower technology areas of consumer markets and, like Japan, became major investors in Southeast Asia. Taiwanese and Korean companies moved offshore for reasons of their surplus capital and strong currencies. Singapore and Hong Kong were driven by a search for skilled workers. Singapore reached into nearby Malaysia with its first large investments while Hong Kong invested in the neighboring Guangdong province of China. In the latter case, significant flows of money were being channeled from Taiwan since Taiwanese investment in China was officially impermissible.

Japan's Offshore Production, 1987

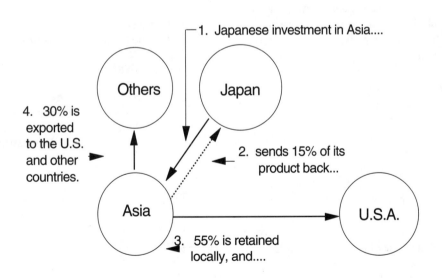

Graph 13.4

The Structure of Japanese Economic Relations with Asia

Japan has become the dominant foreign economic presence in three of the developing countries of the Association of Southeast Asian Nations (ASEAN), Indonesia, Malaysia and Thailand, and it approximately balances the overall U.S. trade, aid, and investment presence in the Philippines. It is by far the largest investor in ASEAN as a result of the cost-of-production pressures to move plants overseas. Japan's rush to build in Thailand, for example, has contributed to an almost chaotic state of development in the Bangkok area where transportation and communication bottlenecks have hindered the efficient use of many new investments. These are temporary problems and are underlain by an overall strengthening of economic ties between Japan and ASEAN. Japan's imports from ASEAN are primarily raw or lightly processed materials and low-priced consumer products. As noted above, its foreign manufacturing investments in ASEAN are intended to serve local markets to a substantial degree as well as to create export bases to Japan and third country markets.

After decades of direct investment, Japan's corporations have established a massive presence in ASEAN. By 1994, Japanese affiliates employed an estimated 800,000 people in ASEAN and the number has grown since then. As an example of how some companies have come to play a key role in these economies, Matsushita Electric Industrial Company is estimated to account for more than 4 percent of Malaysia's gross domestic product. Japanese manufacturers control about 90 percent of the automotive market in most ASEAN countries.

The apparent dominance of Japanese networks in Southeast Asia has led some analysts to suggest that Japanese companies are replicating the *keiretsu* structure on an international scale. The parent industries appear to "embrace" their subcontractors — small Japanese or host-country firms — in long-term, exclusive relationships that may benefit their smaller partners in the short term but place them in a state of perpetual dependence. Non-Japanese companies are said to be effectively shut out of these dominant, regional supply networks which appear to replicate the *keiretsu*

pattern so prevalent in Japan. It is uncertain, however, that such exclusionary networks are an advantage in an increasingly open and dynamic market system, nor have the networks faced serious competition from Koreans, Europeans, and Americans until recently. Japanese executives clearly believe that their own influence in Asian capitals is waning.[4]

Moreover, the weight of Japanese investment should be viewed in the context of the total gross capital formation in each country. Although flows from Japan are significant, they still comprise but a small part of existing stocks (Table 13.1).

China is another important arena for Japanese trade and investment not only because of China's efforts to modernize but because its size and military potential have always meant that Japan must pay close attention to developments there. In the late 1970s, once it became clear that Deng Xiaoping's reforms were truly underway, Japan accelerated its aid loans to China. By 1982 China had become Japan's largest aid recipient, displacing Indonesia. The United States began to invest in China's manufacturing production; Japan invested heavily in real estate ventures. Meanwhile, China's liberalized import policy permitted Japanese consumer products to flood the country. By 2025, China is expected to overtake the U.S. as the largest market for Japanese products. The implications for

Japanese Foreign Direct Investment (FDI) to Selected Asian Nations as a Percentage of Total FDI Flows to These Nations, 1987-1991

	As % of Total FDI Received	As % of Total Gross Domestic Fixed Capital Formation
S. Korea	49	0.60
China	10.4	NA
Indonesia	69	2.5
Malaysia	25	6
Philippines	28	2
Singapore	19	8
Thailand	44	6
Average %	25	3

Table 13.1

Japan's Direct Investment

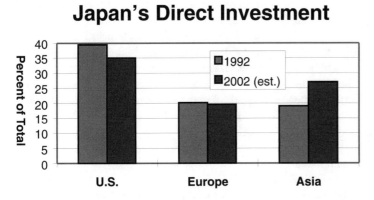

Graph 13.5   **Japan's investments in Asia will continue to rise . . .**

Manufacturing Subsidiaries in Developing Asia   1987-1992

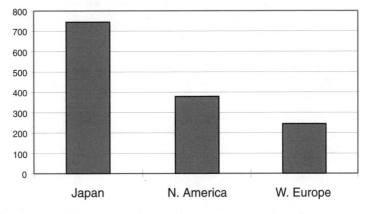

Graph 13.6   **. . . along with a large manufacturing base . . .**

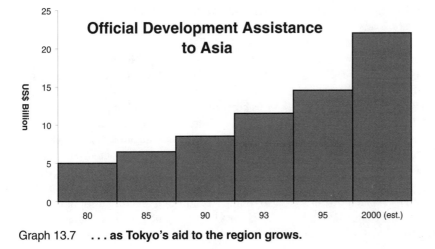

Official Development Assistance to Asia

Graph 13.7   **. . . as Tokyo's aid to the region grows.**

Japan are profound: the decisive factor in the health of its economy will be China, much less so the United States.

Japan's relationship with the NIEs is more complex inasmuch as its competition with them has risen. It is the largest supplier to the NIEs of foreign technology and capital, but until the late 1980s it was an insignificant export market for the NIEs. The latter shipped a large part of their finished production to the United States while maintaining a chronic trade imbalance with Japan and competing with it for market shares in the United States. As wage rates rose in Korea and Taiwan, they were forced to develop higher value products in more advanced technological fields. Korea, for example, became a major producer of computer memory chips in the late 1980s.

Japan is the largest aid donor in Asia, a trend that was magnified by the appreciation of the yen. By 1988 Japan's official development assistance (ODA) to the Asia-Pacific region, about $4 billion, had already nearly doubled that of the United States total. Of that amount, $984 million was sent to Indonesia, $360 million to Thailand, and $534 million to the Philippines, representing more than 20 times U.S. aid to Indonesia, 15 times the U.S. aid to Thailand, and about double the U.S. aid to the Philippines. In the early 1990s, Japanese ODA for Asia rose above $6 billion while assistance from other industrial countries fell. But Japan's economic slowdown and growing fiscal problems have put further growth of such aid on hold.

Japan sees aid as an element of "economic cooperation" rather than merely a means of assisting the poor. It channels more than 80 percent of its bilateral loans to relatively well off Asian neighbors, most of which are loans for major infrastructure projects in which Japanese engineering, construction and trading companies are prime contractors. This assistance reached such levels by the early 1990s that at least one expert estimated Japan's aid to be equal to 15 percent to 20 percent of the official government budget expenditures of many Asian countries.[5] Even if this were true, the fast pace of economic growth in these economies suggests that the proportion is rapidly receding.

Although it was replaced by Japan as the primary exporter of capital to Asia, the United States remains Asia's location of choice for overseas training and education. No other country, including Japan, provides as much advanced education and work experience in its industries. Technology transfers from the United States to Asia also have been massive throughout the post war period. In the late 1980s, for example, even as Japan's exports of high technology goods to Asia began to double those of the United States, America still received three times more in royalty payments for licensed technology than Japan.

The Regional Division of Labor

When Japan's direct investment in Asia accelerated in the late 1980s, its leaders and intellectuals began to promote the idea of a new "division of labor" in the region, one that would be centered on Japan and based on the Japanese production system. Their analogy for the relationship was that of a formation of flying geese. In the lead position were said to be countries with the most advanced levels of technology sophistication, Japan and the United States. Ranked behind them in a spreading "V" of decreasing levels of technical sophistication would be the developing economies. The "geese" further back, it was argued, would learn from the progress of those up ahead, move into their positions, and eventually close the technological gap.

Asians outside Japan viewed this concept skeptically. The formation of geese seemed to them unlikely to close ranks any time in the near future. To them, the image was a rationalization for why Japan should always be in a position to determine what they, with less access to advanced technology and information, would be allowed to learn. The "flying geese" paradigm revealed, in any case, Japan's view of itself as the leader and mentor of economic development in Asia, even if other Asians are ambivalent about the relationship this implies. Some, such as Singapore's Lee Kuan Yew, are forthright in stating that they would prefer to see an economic order in Asia that is not dominated by Japan, but most other Asian leaders have muted their concerns in public.

These concerns have increased in proportion to rising technological competition between Japan and its neighbors. Korea has gained a major share of the semiconductor market, for example, but the immense scale of Japanese investment in new product development and R&D dwarfs that of Korea or any other Asian country. Japanese companies' strict control over key aspects of their advanced technologies has long rankled Asian leaders, even if the dispersal of technology production and research in Asia is closing the gap in some areas. This issue will dominate debates about future economic growth in the NIEs in particular as an overall structural slowdown forces them to seek new, higher value-added areas of growth.

Asia's New Engines of Growth

To the surprise of many, the Japanese recession of the early 1990s did not slow the pace of growth for many of its neighbors. Instead of lagging in step with Japan's slowdown, the developing economies took over the role of driving the Asian economic expansion with a new wave of investments and exports. The NIEs were well-prepared for this role, having passed through the crisis of the strengthening yen in the late 1980s with rising wages and revalued currencies. Theirs was a dual transformation: shifting toward domestic demand-driven growth and moving their labor intensive industries to the poorer Asian economies. As a result, the NIEs continued on, relatively unchecked by the Japanese recession. By the early 1990s, they had surpassed

Japan in importance as importers from and investors in ASEAN and China. Similarly, a third or more of ASEAN's exports were bound for the NIEs while only a fourth went to Japan. At the same time, China's exports to the NIEs soared to over 40 percent of its total exports. Between 1990 and 1993, trade in the region (including with the United States) rose $228 billion. Of this growth, the East Asian NIEs, ASEAN, and China absorbed nearly 70 percent, $156 billion. Thus, although by their sheer size, Japanese trade flows will continue to be a major factor in the region, and although the NIEs' trade deficit with Japan has increased, the relationship between the NIEs and the rest of Asia outside Japan represents an important new axis of economic interaction (Tables 13.2, 13.3).

Foreign investment trends mirror patterns found in the trade sphere. After 1990, the four East Asian NIEs carried out more investment in ASEAN than either Japan or the United States, even without counting the massive, unrecorded flows of capital from the Chinese networks that dominate investment by three of the NIEs. By the mid-1990s, Barings estimated that the combined investments of multinational Asian companies outside Japan was ten times that of Japanese corporations. Regardless of whether this trend will continue to the end of the century, it reflects the extraordinary growth in output and demand that these new Asian centers of commerce represent. Nor does their emergence necessarily

	Exports			**Imports**		
	1970	1980	1992	1970	1980	1992
North America	31.1	24.9	26.9	27.4	20.6	19.3
United States	28.6	23.3	25.1	23.9	18.2	17.4
Pacific Asia	29.6	33.8	39.8	27.7	32.5	45.1
Asia except Japan	22.3	23.0	31.7	13.9	19.8	29.1
APEC	64.1	61.4	68.8	62.0	57.6	68.1
Europe	17.2	17.8	17.1	15.3	10.7	13.1
EU-12	14.2	15.3	14.8	12.8	8.8	10.4
Rest of World	18.8	20.8	14.1	22.7	31.8	18.8

Shares (%) of Various Regions in the Total Trade of Pacific Asia

United Nations and OECD trade data from SIE World Trade Data base. cf. Stephen S. Cohen and Paolo Guerieri, "The Variable Geometry of Asian Trade," In *Japanese Investment in Asia: International Production Strategies in a Rapidly Changing World.* Eileen M. Doherty, Ed. San Francisco: The Asia Foundation. 1995.

Table 13.2

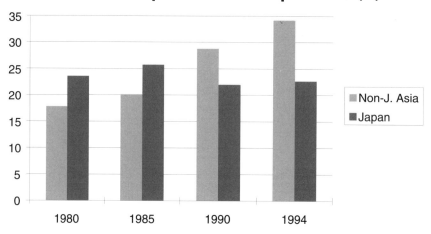

Shares of Exports to Non-Japan Asia (%)

Graph 13.8   By 1990, Japan's neighbors had begun to trade more with one another than with Japan.

reflect negatively on Japan since, in many respects, they are the beneficiaries of Japan's own structural transformation.

The Global Geometry of Asia's Trade

Pacific Asia is heavily dependent on exports and runs large trade surpluses with the rest of the world. This trade surplus began in the late 1970s and has accumulated rapidly since the 1980s. In manufactured goods it reached $1.36 trillion between 1986 and 1992, most of which was accounted for by Japan (Table 13.4).

The widespread notion of an evenly distributed "lattice-work" of trade among various world economies is misleading. Instead, the pattern is strikingly triangular between 1) Japan, 2) the rest

of Asia, and 3) North American and Europe. As shown in Table 13.5, these world regions have either maintained or increased their growth of internal trade. However, the import/export vectors that link the "corners" of this triangle are notably asymmetrical. Japan exports heavily in all directions while, in comparison to its relative wealth, it imports much less. The rest of Asia imports heavily from Japan, but like the rest of the world it is unable to penetrate Japan's markets except in specific, permitted areas. As a result, the Asian economies offset their Japan trade deficit with a large trade surplus with Europe and North America. This pattern, sustained over two decades, has brought about major problems of industrial adjustment in the West where some industries have found it nearly impossible to compete against the flood of lower cost imports.

Cumulative Trade Balance in Manufactures of Pacific Asia, Japan and the NIEs, 1986-1992 (US$ millions)

Exporter	World	Asia	Japan	NIEs	ASEAN	N. America	Europe
				Importer			
Pacific Asia	1,360,781	-	-343,444	271,528	104,591	806,536	263,460
Japan	1,296,817	343,444	-	232.823	87,687	484,332	223,077
Asian NIEs	189,479	-271,528	-232,823	-	15,919	300,030	75,883

Table 13.3

Intraregional Export Shares in Regions of the World

	1984	1994
Asia*	27	39
Middle East	8	10
European Union	54	57
Latin America	14	20
North America	42	48
Africa	5	7

* excluding Japan

Table 13.4

Japan's Diplomatic and Political Role

The above pattern of trade and financial flows reflect important shifts in regional power relationships. Although the Gulf War in early 1991 demonstrated convincingly that military power remains a critical element of national influence, in most of Pacific Asia, economic strength is as high a priority as military strength. Not only is it well understood that domestic stability and growth are closely intertwined, but a sound economy is essential in a competitive global economy. By this measure, in spite of its economic slowdown, Japan is the foremost Pacific regional economic power.

In matters affecting regional stability and security, on the other hand, Japan has traditionally deferred to American leadership. Japan recognizes the lingering suspicions left over from the Pacific War with which other Asian countries view Japan's future military role. It thus tends to focus its attention on regional and global economic activities. The President of the Asian Development Bank, an institution created in 1965 to support regional economic development, customarily has been Japanese. Without Japan to provide grants and loans, a major debtor country such as the Philippines would face an uncertain future.

By the early 1990s Japan seemed ready to embark on a new era of regional political activism. Thailand encouraged Japan in this role, but other Asian countries did not and they watched with some dismay as an effort by Japan to mediate talks between the warring factions in Cambodia unraveled amid vague pronouncements by

Japanese Prime Minister Kaifu. Undaunted, Kaifu traveled to ASEAN the following year to state that Japan intended to play a larger role in regional affairs. His foreign ministry's suggestion in 1991 that there be an expansion of the regional dialogue with ASEAN to include security matters was seen in many Asian capitals as another historical benchmark in the gradual evolution of the region away from the traumas of World War II and toward a new era of military-security cooperation that would include Japan.

From time to time, the United States has pressured Japan to assume a greater regional security role and thereby relieve the United States of the burden, something that Japan's neighbors have not welcomed. Japan responded to the American "burden-sharing" pressure in the mid-1970s with a major buildup of its self-defense forces which continued to be upgraded. During the cold war between the United States and the Soviet Union, Japan was seen as a key component in the defense of Western Pacific sea lanes. With the collapse of the Soviet Union and a lowered profile for Russian military forces, Japan's military capabilities are now relevant mainly with respect to Korea and China. Pacifism remains a powerful current in Japanese domestic politics, confirmed in 1990 by the massive disapproval of the Prime Minister's efforts to send Japanese Self Defense Force personnel to the Persian Gulf for non-combat purposes. In spite of this public resistance, pressure for a more flexible and assertive military posture is building from the United States and from Japan's own strategic vulnerability vis-a-vis China and Korea.

Japan in Asia: Alliance and Hegemony

In its entire history, Japan has had only three alliances and all of them were made in this century. The first, in 1902, was with Great Britain, an island people whose dominance over a global trading empire brought them wealth and international prestige. The British symbolized all that the Japanese hoped to achieve. The alliance was an enormous asset to Japan until 1923 when Britain terminated it under pressure from its allies (chapter 4). Animosity and distrust toward Japan mounted in the West, particularly when Japan pursued an aggressive export drive during a period of increasing protectionism. Within two decades Japan responded to the growing political hostility from Britain and America by forming a new alliance with the Axis powers, Germany and Italy, which lasted only briefly and ended in national ruin in 1945.

The third alliance, the Mutual Security Treaty, was forged in 1951 with the United States under circumstances very different from today.[6] As in the previous two alliances, Japan offered its geographical position to be a counterweight to Russia. The Americans stipulated no obligations for Japan either in terms of market-opening or war-making, for in neither respect did it appear to offer much to support U.S. interests. As a secure point in the Asian network to contain communism, Japan played its role dutifully if somewhat circumspectly in the United States shadow.

The use of "alliances" as an instrument of foreign policy is more prevalent in the West. Asian dynasties and empires traditionally used alliances in a temporary strategic sense, preferring to build influence through hegemony, then requiring submission. Hegemony remains a salient idea today in the Western Pacific, with the United States viewed as the ideal hegemonic military power in the region since, with the end of communist-led revolutions, America's domination is relatively benign and the nation is geographically distant. From an American perspective, however, the incentive to maintain a large and costly force structure in the region began to diminish after 1989.

The prospect of U.S. force reductions troubles leaders of many smaller Asian countries who cannot envision an alternative power that would reliably provide the region's security umbrella. A history of previous invasions and internal meddling by the two other Asia-Pacific giants, Japan and China, means that neither would be acceptable in such a role. This partly explains the steady military build-up in many individual countries in spite of a steady lessening in regional tensions. Defense policy-makers in Asia believe that their security environments will remain unstable, not only because of potential flare ups in "hot spots" such as Cambodia and the Korean peninsula, but because they know that the pattern of conflict in Asian countries has often developed from within

through civil wars rather than from without through external invasions.

Meanwhile, China's military is being modernized in the direction of rapid deployment in relatively limited engagements, suggesting a concern with border relations and domestic stability. (As noted in chapter 10, the People's Liberation Army temporarily reverted to the role of an internal security force in 1989-1990.) Instability in China sends ripples of concern throughout the Asia-Pacific region, most of all in Hong Kong and Taiwan, but also in Japan and elsewhere because of China's immense population and economic weight.

Japan maintains a potent defense force. It keeps a low-key military profile with an eye toward the modernizing Chinese army and Japan's old foe in Asia, Russia. Prospects for a Russian-Japanese rapprochement may improve but Japan remains concerned with Russia's long term military potential. For its part, China does not pose a current military threat to Japan, but its influence over events all across the Asian mainland give it special importance in the eyes of military and diplomatic strategists in Tokyo. Japan did not condemn China as much as did the West for the events of June, 1989, but neither has China been an object of Japanese adulation.

Asia-Pacific countries are increasingly willing to discuss their regional security concerns with one another. An unstated message in Japanese Prime Minister Kaifu's proposal for a regional security dialogue was the widely shared view that such concerns should be addressed within a broader framework than one imposed by fiat through U.S. bilateral security treaties. An annual regional security meeting now occurs under the ASEAN Regional Forum (ARF). While only a "talk shop," it supports a trend toward consultations and new cooperative linkages to meet the changed security environment in Asia.

A Yen Bloc?

Japan's Asian neighbors have gradually reconciled themselves to its growing economic presence in their countries and they acknowledge the significant economic contribution to the region that has come with widespread Japanese investment and manufacturing activities. At the same time, they are concerned over what appears to be a master plan for regional production owned by and centered on Tokyo. This will come about, it is said, because Japan's influence will eventually create a so-called "yen bloc," i.e., an area in which the yen will be the primary currency of trade and investment. Trade within the Western Pacific continues to grow faster than trade with North America and has begun to surpass it, fueling speculation that Japan, as the powerhouse of that commerce, will soon establish the yen — not the U.S. dollar — as the preferred currency of transaction.

The yen is still a minor, albeit growing, part of the official currency reserves held by Asia's central banks. For this reason alone, a "Western Pacific Monetary Union" on the order of the union contemplated by the European Community is not in the offing. However, in the 21st century a *de facto* yen bloc could emerge, driven by the need to transact more trade in that currency. If so, the implications of a newly dominant international currency, one that would challenge the U.S. dollar as a standard, may reach far beyond the Pacific

Basin to the global financial system whose modern, electronically activated markets have never known anything but the relative stability of a single reserve currency.

The trade and investment dominance of Japan in the Western Pacific provides the geographical outline for such a bloc and the rationale for its existence. First, it would simplify the payment mechanisms. Southeast Asian shippers to Japan or a third country could price their products in yen and be certain of the price several months later. Second, yen transactions would dampen inflation in the region as long as inflation stayed low in Japan, which is highly likely. This is a further incentive for nations in the region to move their economies into alignment with Japan. However, there will be little incentive to shift toward the yen as long as transactions with the United States remain a major part of the Pacific economy.

The Impact of Travel and Tourism

Regional integration in the Pacific is being driven not only by trade and investment but by

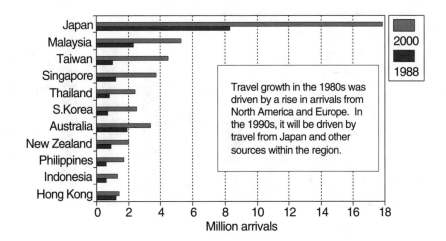

Travel to Destinations in Pacific Asia
By Country of ORIGIN

Graph 13.9

travel and tourism. The travel industry in Asia is growing more rapidly than in any other world region with the possible exception of Eastern Europe (where volumes are generally lower). In several Asia-Pacific countries, tourism alone now ranks second or third as a contributor to GNP growth and a source of foreign exchange. Thailand in particular has enjoyed an extraordinary boom of tourism. Visitor arrivals in the Western Pacific are projected to grow at an annual rate of 7 percent through the year 2000, twice the rate projected for North America and Western Europe.

Initially, the increase in travel came from sources outside the region, but the volume of intra-Asian travel has begun to accelerate. Japan is the major factor underlying this trend. When the increased buying power of the yen became evident in the aftermath of the 1985 Plaza Accord, Japanese tourists surged into the Asia-Pacific region. In 1988, 8.3 million arrivals from Japan were registered. By the year 2000, the number is expected to swell to nearly 18 million. Other newly prosperous Asians are following a pattern of travel growth similar to that of Japan. Their

movements, often linked to new investments from their countries, add both to the level of inter-regional commerce and a growing frequency of person-to-person interactions across national borders.

CHINA'S REGIONAL IMPACT

China's great size looms large in the future of Pacific Asia. Some 300 million people will be added to its nearly 1.3 billion population by the year 2025 and recent years of high growth have increased its economic impact in the region. Like the NIEs, China was instrumental in taking up the slack during Japan's economic stagnation in the early 1990s. The Pacific region (including North America) accounts for three-fourths of China's foreign trade and two-thirds of its invested foreign capital.

Hong Kong, now a part of China, has been its largest investor. With Macao, Hong Kong accounted for nearly two-thirds of all foreign investment in China in the early 1990s, rivaled

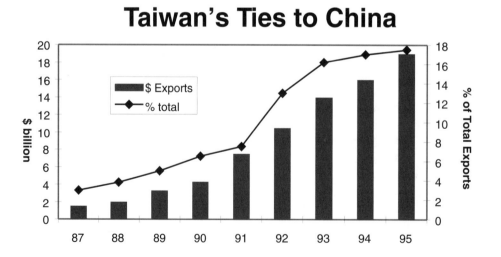

Graph 13.10

The "Push and Pull" of Foreign Investment

The forces driving investment in the Asia Pacific region have occurred in a sequence of "waves." In the 1970s, the motivation was to secure resources and to capitalize on the low cost advantages in the East Asian NIEs as well as to some extent in Southeast Asia. The main investors were Japan and the US. In the 1980s, the relocation motive was still important, especially in the post-Plaza Accord period, but in the 1990s, the surge in foreign direct investment (FDI) was by and large market-driven due to a number of interrelated factors. "Push factors" included appreciation of currencies, rising labor costs, high land prices, graduation by developing economies from the generalized system of preferences (GSP), and relocation to reduce trade friction with markets of developed economies such as the US and European Union. Japanese corporations and, most recently, those from Asian NIEs were more international and globalized. Their investments in the region accordingly led to the creation of production networks linking different parts of the Asia-Pacific.

"Pull" factors have also been important in facilitating the surge of FDI in the region. The investment climate of developing host economies improved vastly in the 1980s due in part to unilateral actions that deregulated foreign investment. This, plus resource endowments that included low cost labor and growing technological capabilities, served to allocate production processes across much of the region.

An additional "pull" factor has been a growing recognition that the Asia-Pacific contains the fastest growing markets in the world. For example, manufacturing investments in China and to a lesser extent Indonesia clearly have been motivated by the potential size of the domestic markets. As purchasing power increased in conjunction with a relaxation of rules governing foreign investors, investments for products aimed at the wider Asia-Pacific marketplace have become more important. Foreign investment has also been driven by the creation of new strategic alliances in which wealthy Asian companies carried an unprecedented weight. Thus, while low labor costs and the availability of raw materials remain factors for investment, locational advantages based on technological capabilities, domestic partners, and domestic markets are also important bases for such decisions.

---

only by Taiwan whose investments began to move above twelve percent of China's total. The "overseas Chinese" communities have begun once again to play their distinctive regional investment role, this time serving to transform the economy of China.

The coastal regions of China are the primary beneficiaries of this capital inflow. Their close partners in growth, Hong Kong and Taiwan, have strong linguistic and ethnic bonds with two nearby coastal provinces, Guangdong and Fujian, respectively, which are also the beneficiaries of the economic liberalization that Beijing permitted to occur early-on in China's coastal zones.

The extraordinary volume of trade and investment linking China, Hong Kong (treated here as a separate economic unit of China) and Taiwan has given rise to speculation about a looming Chinese "economic superpower" or "Chinese economic sphere" that will emerge in East Asia to rival the size of Japan, the United States and Europe. The World Bank has contributed to this view by suggesting that in terms of 1991 exchange rates, the area represents a $600 billion market. Although this would be substantially less than the Japanese market ($3.4 trillion) and United States ($5.5 trillion), the Bank went on to utilize a new measure, purchasing power parity (PPP), for its estimates. Using this alternative measure, the Chinese economic sphere swells to $2.5 trillion, while Japan shrinks to $2.1 trillion and the U.S. remains roughly the same at $5.7 trillion. Most

Global Direct Investment into Developing Pacific Asia, '89-'94

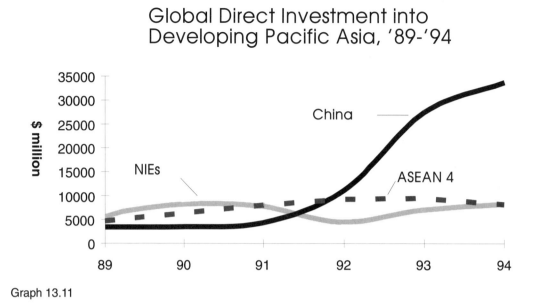

Graph 13.11

dramatically, the Bank projected the growth of the three in PPP terms and concluded that China would reach $9.8 trillion by the year 2002, surpassing the United States and becoming twice the size of the Japanese market ($4.9 trillion). Combined with forecasts of China's growing population, military power, and extravagant predictions by some observers of a high per capita food/energy consumption level, the World Bank projection led to a new, more problematic assessment of China's future in the region and the world.

PPP measures, however, can be misleading. In fact, the World Bank later revised downward its PPP estimates for China in recognition of this fact. Intended primarily to compare the living standards of different countries, the revised PPP may still exaggerate China's economic size because, by international standards, the prices of most domestic items are quite low (which increases the "purchasing power" of its population). Especially when used in a trade-related comparison, the measure is problematic. Many foreign products cannot be artificially reduced in price to fit a hypothetical, low-cost PPP market in China; hence, the need to use standard exchange rate values.

Comparisons using official exchange rates produce a reverse picture: that of a China whose absolute economic size, while expanding rapidly,

still remains at a low per capita level. The Bank's calculation for Hong Kong's GNP is twice that of Guangdong; Taiwan's GNP is 16 times that of Fujian. In 1994, the combined GNPs of Hong Kong and Taiwan were nearly 60 percent of China's *total* GNP, a proportion that can be expected to decline only gradually. If linkages between these two Chinese provinces continue to develop with their counterpart economies in Hong Kong and Taiwan, China's coastal provinces will effectively become part of the NIEs. This lends a new perspective to the idea of a "Chinese economic area." If one indeed emerges, it is an open question whether China would economically "absorb" Taiwan and Hong Kong or whether the reverse would occur.

China's Competition with ASEAN

The Asian NIEs have invested heavily in ASEAN, but their focus shifted to China in the early 1990s as part of the broad shift of international interest toward China investments. The NIEs maintained a level of capital-intensive investment in ASEAN, such as cement in Indonesia and the Philippines and petrochemicals in Malaysia, but China represented a new frontier for their labor-intensive investments.

In 1994, China announced guidelines for new industrial investment, giving priority to electronics, machinery, automobiles, and petrochemicals. These are the same industries that need to be developed in ASEAN and, like ASEAN, China expects to finance a great part of the expansion with foreign capital. Whether or not there is sufficient private capital to serve both areas, it is likely that many investors will seek to serve burgeoning local markets in each. Within the region, only ASEAN members like Vietnam and Indonesia will be able to compete against low-cost Chinese labor. Moreover, ASEAN will increasingly find itself in competition with China not only for foreign capital but to maintain shares of specific Japanese, European, and American export markets.

ASEAN's declining comparative advantage over competitors such as China worries its members and they have begun to search for ways to strengthen their economic positions. One strategy is to form an ASEAN Free Trade Area (AFTA) which will expand the scale of the ASEAN market. Special attention is being given as well to the idea of "growth triangles" and corridors, leading to special joint planning among some members.

The potential competition between China and ASEAN extends to natural resources, particularly in the waters of the South China Sea where there are many conflicting territorial claims. These disputes are especially sensitive in view of the potential undersea oil and gas deposits that the parties wish to exploit. A focal point for conflict remains the Spratley and Paracel Islands, generally unhabitable by all but small garrisons, but strategic for purposes of defending claims. Notwithstanding an occasional military thrust in these islands, China has pledged to settle the issue peacefully. A possible venue for such a settlement may begin in the regional security dialogue, the ASEAN Regional Forum (ARF).

POLITICAL FOUNDATIONS OF REGIONALISM

Fundamentally, Pacific integration is driven by economic forces, but it is undergirded by a long history of other interactions. Subregional influences such as Confucianism, Buddhism, Chinese language, invasions, migrations, and international commerce were divisive or unifying, depending on circumstances, but each contributed to linkages that serve as an historical undercurrent linking East Asia and Southeast Asia. With prosperity growing in most economies through intra-regional commerce, political obstacles to cooperation have diminished, giving rise to "regionalist" perspectives in national capitals throughout Pacific Asia.

At its modern inception, Pacific regionalism fed on the trauma of the Western incursions in the nineteenth and early twentieth centuries. As a rallying point, the shared experience of colonial oppression found little more than rhetorical use until the 1930s and early 1940s when Japan tried to make it the rationale for a Greater East Asia Co-Prosperity Sphere. In the postwar era, "Pan-Asian" sensibility has been occasionally invoked as in the address by Zhou Enlai to the Bandung Conference in 1955, and in the early 1990s, Malaysian Prime Minister once again called for Pan-Asian solidarity under the aegis of an East Asian Economic Caucus (EAEC).

In spite of these entreaties, the response in Asian regional capitals has been more circumspect and subtle. Appeals to Pan-Asian solidarity, are largely in the background rather than the foreground to what might be termed the "regionalist" political and economic strategies of governments. Contemporary regionalism is manifested in the frequent caucuses of the ASEAN states in international fora where they often vote as a bloc. ASEAN continues to occupy center stage in all efforts to forge Pacific cooperation. Its members have used their unity at various times to obstruct, retard, or set clear limits to any Pacific initiatives outside their own arena.

A diffuse, inchoate, Pan-Asian regionalist perspective first emerged when Asian leaders and intellectuals converged on Tokyo at the beginning of the century to learn from the Meiji experience. Later, a "Pan-Pacific" regionalism between Pacific Asia and North America was encouraged by the non-governmental Institute of Pacific Relations (IPR) in which many outstanding scholars and public figures from both sides of the Pacific participated prior to World War II.

Both strains of regionalism, Pan-Asian and Pan-Pacific, are in evidence today. The Pan-Asian sensibilities that are invoked by Mahathir suggest uniquely "Asian" aspirations and sensibilities, but the fact of Asia's dependence on global markets has persuaded most countries to respond coolly. Nevertheless, Japan is clearly impressed that, for the first time since World War II, a leading Southeast Asian voice had called for its participation — in fact, its implicit leadership — in an exclusive, Western Pacific economic group.

Pan-Pacific regionalism is similarly vague if still viable. The barriers that once seemed to hinder formal political discussions of Pacific regional interests have largely disappeared. Leaders are more relaxed about the their political and economic diversity and their fear of dominance by the major economic powers, Japan and the United States, is counterbalanced by a growing self-confidence. The sea change of attitudes is especially

---

Geographical Concentrations of Economic Activity

The attractive investment environment of the Asia-Pacific economies becomes more evident when they are identified within emerging regional subgroups. Hong Kong has been the major entrepôt for China and Singapore is a pivotal city-state in Southeast Asia, extending trade ties to Australia and India. Mexico benefits from its proximity to the United States. This blurring of national borders is based on the establishment of export processing zones (EPZ), growth triangles, and free trade areas in the region that are linking economies to their regional neighbors.

Industrial estates, special economic zones (SEZ), bonded areas, and export processing zones (EPZ) are designated areas within PECC economies offering international corporations a combination of fiscal incentives and infrastructure facilities. A growth triangle is based on agreements among neighboring countries to combine their respective comparative advantages in resources, labor and socio-economic infrastructure to mutual economic benefit. The flow of trade among Hong Kong, Chinese Taipei and southern China is an early example, and the development of Batam Island, which brings together Singapore, Johore (Malaysia), and Riau Province (Indonesia), is a recent example. A free trade agreement (FTA) is another type of regional subgroup, easing the flow of goods, people, money, and information across national borders. The coalescence of economies under the Australia-New Zealand Closer Economic Relations Trade Agreement (ANZCERTA), ASEAN Free Trade Agreement (AFTA), and the North America Free Trade Agreement (NAFTA), are major examples.

The mix of EPZ, growth triangles, and FTA spread across the region tempers the individual country risks. For instance, Japanese car makers are increasing their investments in Southeast Asia in anticipation of the implementation of the AFTA; and Indochina becomes an attractive production base as it becomes integrated with its ASEAN neighbors. Consequently, as corporations pursue emerging business opportunities in these regional sub groups, individual economies are losing their salience as an unit of investment.

By examining the distribution of foreign direct investment in the region, the outlines of larger regional subgroups emerge. There are three major investment corridors in the Pacific Basin, one located in Northeast Asia, anchored at one end by Japan, running along the coastal areas of South Korea, Chinese Taipei, and China, and anchored at the other end by Hong Kong. A second corridor is located in Southeast Asia, extending from Chiang Mai (Thailand), through the Malay peninsula, and down to Surabaya (Indonesia). The third corridor connects North America with northern Mexico. A majority of the transnational corporation subsidiaries are concentrated in these three investment corridors.

—by Dennis Tachiki
Sakura Research Institute

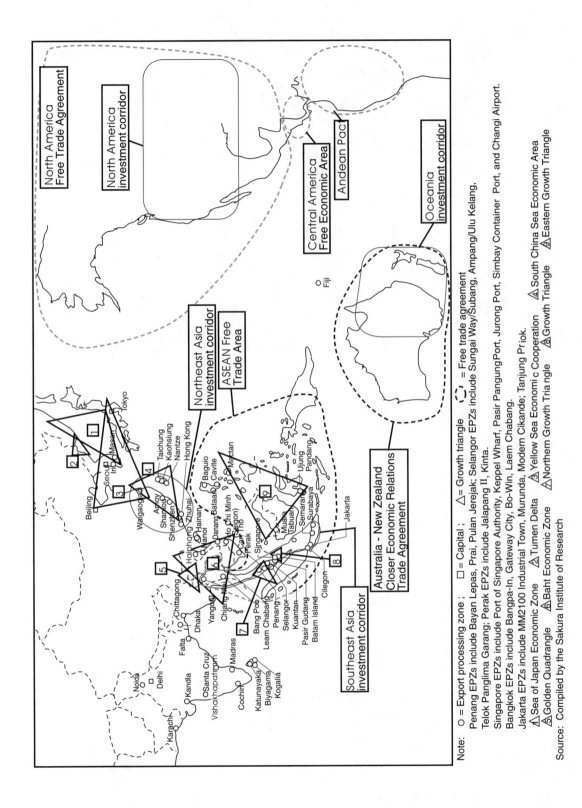

Note: O = Export processing zone ;   □ = Capital ;   △ = Growth triangle   = Free trade agreement
Penang EPZs include Bayan Lepas, Prai, Pulan Jerejak; Selangor EPZs include Sungai Way/Subang, Ampang/Ulu Kelang,
Telok Panglima Garang; Perak EPZs include Jalapang II, Kinta.
Singapore EPZs include Port of Singapore Authority, Keppel Wharf, Pasir PangungPort, Jurong Port, Simbay Container Port, and Changi Airport.
Bangkok EPZs include Bangpa-In, Gateway City, Bo-Win, Laem Chabang.
Jakarta EPZs include MM2100 Industrial Town, Murunda, Modern Cikande; Tanjung Priok.
△Sea of Japan Economic Zone   △Tumen Delta   △Yellow Sea Economic Cooperation   △South China Sea Economic Area
△Golden Quadrangle   △Baht Economic Zone   △Northern Growth Zone   △Growth Triangle   △Eastern Growth Triangle
Source: Compiled by the Sakura Institute of Research

Figure 13.1   In 1980, the prime ministers of Australia and Japan, Malcolm Fraser (seated, third from right) and Masayoshi Ohira (standing), advocated the formation of a non-governmental, regional body that became the Pacific Economic Cooperation Council (PECC), based in Singapore.

evident in ASEAN capitals where, as late as 1981, leaders made strident remarks against any Pacific cooperation wider than ASEAN. The extent of the shift derives from a gradual, if partial, acceptance of Japan's regional economic role and from changes that took place in the global economy during the 1980s — particularly with respect to European regionalism.

"Europessimism" and the EU Response

The confidence of the European Community was badly shaken by the economic shocks of the 1970s and early 1980s. High unemployment seemed to be endemic in Europe. The GNP growth, which for countries like France and Germany had been 3-4 percent in the 1960s and 1970s, fell to half that rate by the early 1980s. Meanwhile, Japan, the United States, and the industrializing nations of Asia emerged from the two recessions with stronger growth rates than Europe. Particularly alarming to the Europeans

was the continued strong growth of manufacturing in North America and Asia. Manufacturing is usually the most dynamic part of a nation's industrial sector, but in Europe its growth slowed to a virtual standstill in the 1980s even while it surged ahead in the Pacific Basin. Driven by an accelerating pace of innovation and industrial adjustment to international competition, several Pacific nations (especially Japan and the United States) provided a striking contrast to stagnation in Europe. One continental diplomat, in the depths of what came to be known as "Europessimism" or "Euroschlerosis," called Europe a quaint "museum" for visiting Americans and Asians.

By the end of the 1980s, the outlook in Western Europe began to improve along with plans to make the region more competitive globally. A major impetus for Europe's newly found resolve was the challenge it recognized in the North American/Western Pacific commercial axis. Private industries in Europe realized that unless action was taken by their governments to create a large, integrated market they would become

"Euro-pessimism" in the Early 1980s
Growth Rates, 1980 - 1985

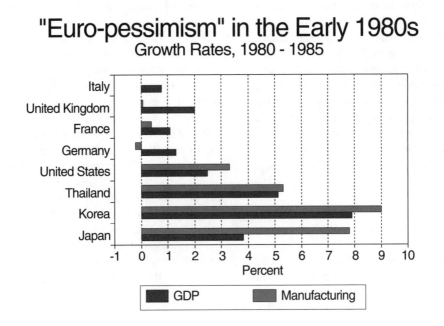

Graph 13.12

Inflation and Employment, 1979 - 85

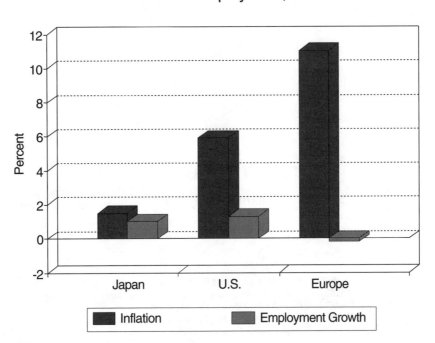

Graph 13.13

permanently inferior to and dependent upon giant Asian and North American companies. Effective international competition in newer, high technology fields requires greater economies of scale and even a unified currency that a more integrated Europe might provide. Thus, implementation of the Maastrich Treaty outlining European monetary reform, rationalizations of technical standards, and market integration measures constituted a significant European response. This, in turn, further stimulated Pacific Basin interest in its own level of regional cooperation.

The United States, Asia, and Europe

Chapter 2 described how, in the nineteenth century, Great Britain and European countries dominated China. Somewhat ambivalently, the United States sought to act on behalf of China with the "Open Door" policy but the relationship with Asia was encumbered by the war in the Philippines and other setbacks. Even so, U.S.-Pacific friendships, alliances, and interdependencies gradually expanded.

The aftermath of World War II shifted the focus of the US-Asian relationship from China to Japan and the United States began to assert a more vigorous international leadership role. It viewed itself as the principal guarantor of regional security and economic growth in the Pacific Basin and as a major factor in Pacific Asia's economic resurgence.

Many parts of the region prospered under this security umbrella and trade with the United States flourished. By the early 1980s, trans-Pacific trade

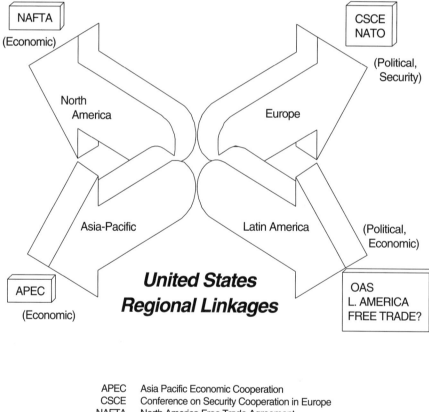

United States
Regional Linkages

APEC	Asia Pacific Economic Cooperation
CSCE	Conference on Security Cooperation in Europe
NAFTA	North America Free Trade Agreement
NATO	North Atlantic Treaty Organization
OAS	Organization of American States

Graph 13.14

began to rise dramatically above the levels of trans-Atlantic trade. North America became more firmly linked than ever to the Pacific Basin community. As a result, the United States has developed an economic relationship with Pacific Asia that is analogous to that of Germany to Europe. Both Germany and the United States now conduct more than half of their total trade within their respective regions, up from around a third two decades ago (German trade with France and U.S. trade with Canada are treated as comparable situations within these regions). Germany is much more dependent than the United States on trade for its total GNP, but both nations will rely on the expansion of their international markets for future growth.[7]

In other respects the U.S. regional role is unique. Western Europe forged its regional pact with strong U.S. backing and encouragement. Pacific Asia, however haltingly, is doing likewise — but here the Atlantic and Pacific paths diverge. In the Pacific, regional integration has been led by the private sector whose joint venture and investment activities have created a multitude of cross border linkages. In Europe, the private sector's international role was more likely to follow rather than lead initiatives by governments. A further contrast with Europe is evident in the Asian view of the American role. Both Europe and Pacific Asia have viewed the United States as an anchor for regional security, but in Asia there is a greater inclination to deal with the United States as a member of a Pacific economic region. The American orientation is similarly turning — slowly and with limited planning — in the Pacific Basin direction. In terms of formal participation in regional economic arrangements, U.S./Canadian opportunities lie to the south and across the Pacific — but not across the Atlantic, a fact that may become decisive in shaping the two countries' global economic agendas. A significant counterforce to a U.S./Canadian bias toward Asia is the legacy of these countries' origins and cultural roots in Europe.

In the wake of its initial efforts to achieve greater integration, the European Union has sought to improve its ties to Pacific Asia. As it is for most other Western countries, the relationship is complicated by differences with Asia's developing economies over policies affecting trade and investment, the environment, and human rights. Nevertheless, an initiative to improve and consolidate EU-Asian ties, focused around summits of the heads of governments, began with the first such meeting in Bangkok in 1996. Although Europe has taken a smaller share of imports from the developing countries of Pacific Asia than North America, its industries have, as noted earlier, come under similar heavy pressure from the flood of manufactured goods from Asia and, like North America, its interdependence with Asia is growing.

Regional Interdependencies

It was noted earlier that three world regions —Pacific Asia, North America, and Europe — have increased their interdependence with one another while having also increased their trade within their respective regions. As reflected in Table 13.6, the twin increases in intra-regional and interregional interdependence have caused the relative levels of interdependence with other regions of the world to decline, but interdependence in all directions remains significant. This suggests that a Japan-centered trade bloc in Asia will not emerge. The global interdependencies and the high global exports from Asia guarantee that a triangulation of world trade and investment will remain the dominant pattern well into the next century.

Regionalism in the 1980s

Even if a global trade is paramount for Asia, the growing levels of intra-Asian trade and investment raise the question of how far the region might move in the direction of formal economic cooperation. Regionalism is often a response to outside threats, yet there is no widely perceived, external threat that would compel Asia-Pacific countries to respond jointly in the way that invigorated the regional organization of ASEAN after the fall of Saigon in 1975. Then, Southeast Asian countries were galvanized into self-defensive action which led to one of the strongest regional institutions of the developing world.

As opposed to security threats, external *economic* challenges by themselves are usually less

Changing Patterns of Intra-Regional and Inter-Regional Trade (percent)

Trading Regions		East Asia	North America	European Community	Others
East Asia	1980	34	21	11	43
	1990	40	23	14	22
North America	1980	20	29	18	37
	1990	27	31	19	23
European Community	1980	4	7	52	36
	1990	7	8	63	22

The formula used in the computation is as follows: for intra-regional trade, (intra-regional trade x 2)/(total exports + total imports). For inter-regional trade (exports + imports) with a particular region/(total exports + total imports).

Table 13.5

influential in activating a strong movement toward regional organization. The exception occurred in Asia in the 1930s with the catastrophic effort by Japan to form an economic and political bloc — partially a result of protectionism in the West and its boycott of vital resources to Japan. This same historic sensitivity in Japan to the prospect of trade alliances being formed against it arose once again in the 1960s after the European Economic Community began to grow stronger. Japanese leaders and analysts responded with a cautious proposal for an institutional counterweight to the EC in the Pacific Basin.

The idea of a Pacific trading regime held little appeal for the rest of the region at that time. It had long been recognized that Asia's political and economic differences would prevent the creation of an economic bloc similar to the European Community, and Pacific Asian nations had grown accustomed to resolve their trade frictions with the West bilaterally, in a low-key and inconspicuous way. In their negotiations with the United States and Europe, Asians succeeded in part by appearing to be acquiescent and passive. Regional responses were unappealing because they might incite alarm and further protectionism in the West. Suggestions that the Pacific Asia should be "organized" to improve both its economic growth and assert its interests in global fora thus received limited attention.

By the late 1980s conditions had changed. The European Community had demonstrated the potency of regional cooperation in both its trade-creating and trade-restricting aspects. The Europeans became increasingly obdurate in trade negotiations, refusing at first to even consider a new global round of trade liberalization. When their intransigence eventually caused a stalemate in the Uruguay Round talks in 1990, leaders in Pacific Asia began to consider the lessons of the EC example. At the same time, Europe had long been viewed in Asia as an example of what *not* to do in terms of its state-supported "welfare capitalism" which, in Asia's view, made industries uncompetitive. Instead, Pacific nations, including the United States, Canada, and Mexico, began to consider how they should prepare in case a "fortress Europe" were to turn inward and discriminate against them economically. Europe had shown that concrete advantages do arise from regional cooperation, even if North Americans and Asians might dislike how it is practiced. The question was simply how to respond.

Another factor conducive to Pacific regionalism has been the growing confidence of Asian nations in their own economic viability. The mounting size of the total Asia-Pacific economy, its increasing interdependence, the lowering of political tensions following the U.S. withdrawal from Vietnam, and the normalization of Sino-American diplomatic relations all served to create a more congenial atmosphere for cooperation in the 1980s. The creation of a government-supported private body in 1980, the Pacific Economic

Cooperation Council (PECC),[8] encouraged this trend but initially there was little enthusiasm in ASEAN for a more formal institutional framework. ASEAN saw alternative institutions in the region as potentially undermining its own integrity and solidarity.

As PECC and other nongovernmental bodies advocated the creation of a formal mechanism for regional cooperation, the difference between the Pacific and European versions of this process became apparent. No regional leader of the stature of a Robert Schuman or Jean Monnet in Europe stepped forward to lead the Pacific. The most powerful nations, Japan and the United States, were restrained by the sense that such action would be seen as an effort to consolidate their nations' regional hegemony. At the same time, it was recognized that no serious regional movement could occur without the participation and leadership of the two countries. To move beyond this impasse, a bridge was needed between the assertive dominance of the largest developed countries and the suspicions of ASEAN. Australia, although it is a member of the developed club, provided this critical role. In recent years, Australia and its neighbor New Zealand have reoriented their economies toward the Western Pacific. For both, but particularly New Zealand, this became a matter of vital necessity when in 1973 the United Kingdom joined the European Common Market, thus restricting access to what had been a major market for agricultural exports. The two countries rapidly diversified and expanded their export markets in Asia.

This growing stake in the Asia-Pacific future prompted the Australian Prime Minister, Bob Hawke, to propose in 1989 the formation of an intergovernmental forum on "Asia-Pacific Economic Cooperation" (APEC). His initial soundings on the proposal were limited to Western Pacific countries, but Canadian and U.S. interest in the concept, combined with support from several Asian nations, led to the eventual formation of a 12-nation group comprising the (then) six ASEAN countries plus Australia, Canada, Japan, Korea, New Zealand, and the United States. In 1991 it was announced that the APEC forum would be enlarged to include China, Hong Kong and Taiwan under a formula like the one used for their membership in the PECC. In 1993, APEC added Chile, Mexico, and Papua New Guinea as members. Meanwhile, numerous working groups began to develop information and analysis on areas of potential regional cooperation.

After establishing its Secretariat in Singapore, APEC grew to become the largest and most active economic policy body in the Asia-Pacific. Initially bolstered by regular meetings of its foreign ministers and trade ministers, the early growth of APEC marked the beginning of a new phase in regional institution-building.[9] When President Clinton hosted a meeting of his counterparts from APEC (referred to as "Pacific Leaders") in 1993 in Seattle, the pressure on APEC to develop substantive initiatives grew. A year later, a meeting of the Leaders hosted by President Suharto in Indonesia declared a goal of "free and open trade" in the APEC region by the year 2010 for developed economies and 2020 for developing economies. As a distant goal, the so-called "Bogor Declaration" left much to be resolved, particularly in key areas such as:

- Which economies would be considered "developed" or "developing" by the year 2010.

- Specific steps and schedules of liberalization.

- Whether new liberalization would occur on a most-favored nation (MFN) basis.

- How asymmetrical "free trade" for developed but not the developing countries would be implemented during the 2010-2020 decade.

A resolution of these issues will profoundly affect the nature of APEC as an institution, particularly as regards its role in the global trading regime. In 1997 APEC members announced a set of "individual action plans" by which they volunteered to liberalize sectors of their own choosing according to their own, separate schedules. In many cases, this constituted little more than the liberalization measures that most members had already committed to achieve under the World Trade Organization (WTO). The APEC Leaders also agreed to lower tariffs on information technologies and software, a consensus that broke the logjam for such an agreement among most WTO members. This suggests that the liberalization potential of APEC lies in its role as a lever for global rather than Asia-Pacific regional trade actions.

Unweighted Average Tariffs of APEC Economies, 1988-1996

	1988	1993	1996
Australia	15.6	9.0	6.1
Brunei	3.9	3.9	2.0
Canada	9.1	8.8	6.7
Chile	19.9	14.9	10.9
China	40.3	37.5	23.0
Hong Kong	0.0	0.0	0.0
Indonesia	20.3	17.0	13.1
Japan	7.2	6.5	9.0
Korea	19.2	11.6	7.9
Malaysia	13.0	12.8	9.0
Mexico	10.6	12.8	12.5
New Zealand	15.0	8.0	7.0
Philippines	27.9	23.5	15.6
Singapore	0.4	0.4	0.0
Taiwan	12.6	8.9	8.6
Thailand	40.8	37.8	17.0
USA	6.6	6.6	6.4
AVERAGE	15.4	12.9	9.1

Table 13.6

The United States Role

It is significant that the Hawke proposal to create APEC was viewed by many as inviable without American participation — but only after considerable hesitation by some Asian countries such as Thailand and Malaysia. Earlier in the 1980s, American participation might have been taken for granted, but by the end of the decade U.S. belligerence on trade matters toward Japan and other Asian nations had created new tensions with the region. From the standpoint of these countries, American participation was desirable only if it moderated U.S. militancy.

A paramount concern has been to prevent the rise of competing blocs in global trade, an issue in which the United States plays a pivotal role with its strong trade ties across both the Atlantic and Pacific oceans. Although uniquely situated, the United States has not been consistent in its views and practices regarding trade groups. For example, while berating Malaysian President Mahathir for proposing an East Asia Economic Caucus

(EAEC) that excludes the United States, the US moved to establish its own regional economic group, the North American Free Trade Agreement (NAFTA), with Mexico and Canada.

Few areas of trade policy evoke such broad concern as the formation of regional trading blocs. In the strictest sense, they constitute a common market and tariffs against nonmembers, with free internal mobility of capital and labor. APEC does not constitute such a group, but the potential for it to develop certain discriminatory practices against nonmembers continues to loom in the perceptions of European observers, a concern that the United States has exploited from time to time in its negotiations with Europe.

Asian Influence in World Affairs

Pacific Asian countries have found that their economic ascendance does not translate into a parallel rise in global political influence. Japan has attempted to be more active in global issues, but its influence remains disproportionately small alongside its economic strength. As the second largest economy in the world and a financial superpower, Japan has long felt that it should be granted a permanent seat on the United Nations Security Council. Yet the fact remains that its generally pacifist population remains uncomfortable with the possibility of new responsibilities for Japan in the UN Security Council, particularly if forced to vote on the application of military power. The only permanent member of the Security Council from Asia, China, cannot be said to broadly represent Asian interests in global fora, particularly in economic institutions such as the WTO. These inherent handicaps for China and Japan have limited Asia's global political impact.

The Gulf crisis provided a telling indication of Pacific Asia's dependence on outside powers and its peripheral political influence. Virtually the entire Pacific Asian region — recipient of more than half of all the Middle East's oil — remained a spectator to the land and sea actions of Western nations in the Gulf. Many in Asia viewed the Western military retaliation against Iraq's invasion of Kuwait as unnecessary. For pacifist Japanese citizens the crisis was a remote issue that ought to have been resolved through a search for "international harmony." Southeast Asia's vast Moslem population saw it as an uncomfortable reminder of Western cultural and economic dominance. China abstained in the UN Security Council vote that permitted military force to be used against Iraq. These are telling indicators of the kinds of gaps in political and cultural perceptions that remain between Asia and the West.

OVERVIEW:
THE STATE OF THE PACIFIC

The modern transformation of Pacific Asia promises to bring with it a range of economic and environmental challenges whose impacts may eventually equal the political and military upheavals of previous eras. Throughout the region there is a growing recognition that changes in demography, technology and the environment increasingly exert major influences on national stability and growth — influences that can spread across borders. In areas as diverse as energy, food, and high technology manufactures, the message of globalization and interdependence is being brought home. If these changes have become disruptive in many societies, fostering an undercurrent of insecurity, is useful to remind ourselves of the underlying fundamental trend: the gradual if limited enrichment of many hundreds of thousands of lives as described in a recent World Bank survey, summarized in the following sections.

The Reduction of Absolute Poverty[10]

From a level of 400 million in 1970, the number of absolute poor in East Asia is estimated to have fallen to 300 million in 1980, and to 180 million in 1990, reductions all the more remarkable as the East Asian population grew by some 425 million persons over the two decades. Not only were 220 million poor lifted out of poverty, but another 425 million people were added above poverty standards. East Asia's poverty reduction to a tenth of the population today is in sharp contrast to other regions. In 1990 the absolute poor remained at around half the population in South Asia and Africa and a fourth in Latin America.

Poverty was and remains predominantly a rural problem: with almost 90% of East Asia's poor in rural areas today, even though most of the reduction in the number of poor took place in rural areas. Cities more than doubled their populations in the past two decades as they absorbed rural emigrants who would otherwise have added a third to the rural population. They nevertheless managed to reduce their number of poor slightly from about 25 to 20 million.

The two most populous countries, China and Indonesia, made the most progress. Since 1970, China has lifted an estimated 175 million out of poverty and added some 300 million more people above the poverty line. It virtually eliminated poverty in urban areas. In its rural areas, China started with 275 million absolute poor in 1970, or one person in every three. Progress accelerated in the late 1970s and continued at a high pace until the mid-1980s, such that only one person in 10 has been poor since then. With China's population of more than a billion, however, that still left 100 million poor in 1990, more than half the East Asian total. Indonesia lifted over 40 million out of poverty and added 60 million above the poverty line. Indonesia started the 1970s with more than half its people in poverty, some 70 million, but by 1990 the incidence came down to 15% and the number of poor, to about 27 million, 15% of East Asia's poor.

Korea and Malaysia, having accomplished considerable progress by 1970, reached out to the marginal poor, many of them bypassed by overall economic growth. They ended the 1980s with fewer than 5% of their people in poverty, only slightly more than 1% of East Asia's poor.

By contrast, Thailand and the Philippines were unable to shrink the *number* of poor in the 1980s — Thailand despite rapid economic growth, and the Philippines without much economic growth. Through the 1980s Thailand had some 9 million absolute poor, and the Philippines 13 million — together about 12% of East Asia's poor in 1990. The Philippines reduced the incidence of absolute poverty by about a third in the 1980s, to 20% of the population. Thailand's incidence was about 16% in the 1980s. This represented a substantial reduction from the previous decade, but it was as high as Indonesia's, even though Thailand's average GNP per capita was 2.5 times higher.

The countries of Indochina — Myanmar (Burma), Laos, Vietnam, and Cambodia — are estimated (less reliably) to have some 25 million poor, or 15% of East Asia's total. Vietnam would

have the most, around 15 million. Some evidence points to a poverty reduction over the 1980s, but insufficient data precluded estimates.

Poverty in East Asia has become more and more localized, increasing with the remoteness from main cities. Remote areas tend to be resource-poor, unable to sustain dense agricultural populations, and afflicted by scarce water. The poor were generally younger families, with more children and higher dependency ratios than the nonpoor — extracting a basic living from small farms, often too small for subsistence, and from seasonal, informal off-farm jobs. They tended to have less formal education and often were ethnic minorities. The simple fact that poor have more children made children over-represented among the poor. Even though women tend to receive less education than men and less health care than desirable, they were not over-represented among poor, based on income.

Social Indicators

Social indicators — reflecting improvements more for the many in lower and middle-income brackets than for the few in high-income brackets — are a broader gauge of progress than absolute poverty. In East Asia, social conditions greatly improved, even in the countries where economic growth faltered. Actual data for recent years are often missing, but some broad generalizations are possible for the 1980s:

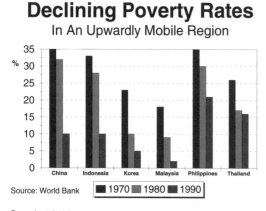

Declining Poverty Rates
In An Upwardly Mobile Region

Source: World Bank   ■ 1970 ■ 1980 ■ 1990

Graph 13.15

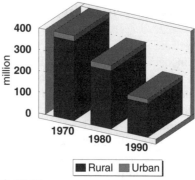

Rural & Urban Poverty

■ Rural ■ Urban

Graph 13.16

- Average per capita food intakes increased by more than 10% — both in calories and in the more costly and nutritive proteins.
- Life expectancy at birth increased in all countries, by three to four years, to an average of 63 years.
- Infant mortality declined substantially, falling by almost one-third.
- The use of contraceptives became widespread, and the age at childbearing increased, reducing fertility rates. On the other hand, death rates fell faster than fertility rates, so the population continued to increase but at a slower pace, 2.1% a year.
- The average illiteracy rate was reduced by a third, with the percentage of adults considered literate increasing by some 16%. Most East Asian countries achieved the objective of universal primary education, with full enrolment at least in lower grades.
- The share of the population in cities rose from a fourth to a third, absorbing two-thirds of the population increase in the decade and easing pressures on rural economies.
- The proportion of people served with safe drinking water and sanitation increased.
- The increases in GNPs per capita were even more outstanding, almost doubling in China and Korea, and rising by two-thirds in Thailand, half in Indonesia, and two-fifths in Malaysia. In the Philippines, growth was elusive, with GNP per capita (and food intakes) decreasing (until the early 1990s).

Demographic Change in the 1990s

As suggested by the above data, the demographic structure of Pacific Asia is changing rapidly. The major elements of this change are (1) declining fertility rates — as women become wealthier and better-educated, they bear fewer children, (2) the emergence of new, independent households — a "baby boomer" phenomenon, and (3) aging populations — more elderly dependents, fewer children, and middle range age group with higher living standards.

Fertility declines often occur when incomes and education increase. Parents recognize that children are more likely to survive to support them

in their old age, cultural attitudes toward family size and childbearing change, contraceptives become more widely used, and more women postpone child rearing in order to join the industrial labor force. Japan was the first to embark on this transition, but since the 1960s South Korea, China, Singapore, Thailand, Malaysia and Indonesia have followed. In Thailand and Indonesia women now average around three births each. In Korea and Taiwan the rate has dropped below two births per woman. The fertility decline in China also has been dramatic.

Households are becoming increasingly affluent. In 1988, with a population of less than 6 million, Hong Kong could already boast 245,000 households with annual incomes greater than $24,000. Yet this is only a fraction of the number of relatively wealthy households that will emerge by the year 2000 in Korea and Taiwan. The pattern is similar for per capita GDPs. Hong Kong's lead among developing economies is being overtaken by Singapore while South Korea and Taiwan will substantially narrow the gap by the year 2000.

Life expectancy, too, is having a pervasive influence on the region's economy. In 1960, Japanese life expectancy was the shortest of any industrial market economy. Today it is the longest (78 years). Other Pacific Asian nations are following the Japanese pattern. Yet even if population growth in these countries has slowed as a result of declining birth rates, the overall growth continues because of lengthening life spans and the present concentration of couples at the childbearing ages. Of all age groups, the elderly are the fastest growing age group in Asia, partly because they began from such a small base. Their swelling ranks will pose a challenge to traditional, family-centered patterns of caring for the elderly.

Urbanization

In spite of having achieved major reductions in overall poverty levels, many of Asia's developing economies have fallen further behind in addressing urban poverty. The cities of Manila, Kuala Lumpur, Bangkok and Jakarta have more than one third of their residents living in slums. These are families that have little or no access to clean water, sewage systems, health care or education. In the past, some

Asia's Urban Population
(Includes South Asia)

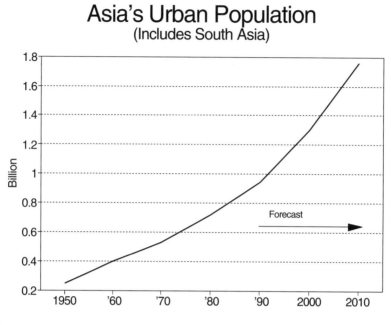

Graph 13.17

Demographic Profiles in Pacific Asia

	Most Demographically Advanced	Rapidly Advancing	Advancing	Less Demographically Advanced
	Japan Hong Kong Singapore South Korea Taiwan	China Indonesia Thailand	North Korea Philippines Vietnam Malaysia	Burma Cambodia Laos
Total Fertility Rate	1.4 - 2.1	2.4 - 3.5	3.9 - 4.7	4.4 - 6.7
Life Expectancy at Birth	68 - 78	58 - 70	54 - 68	39 - 54
Rate of Nat. Increase	0.5 - 1.3	1.4 - 2.1	2.0 - 2.8	2.1 - 2.9
% Population under 15	21 - 30	29 - 40	37 - 40	35 - 46
% Population over 65	4 - 11	3 - 6	3 - 4	3 - 4

"Advanced" refers here to reduced rates of fertility and population growth, and older populations.

Table 13.7

Population in Capital City
As Percent of Total Population

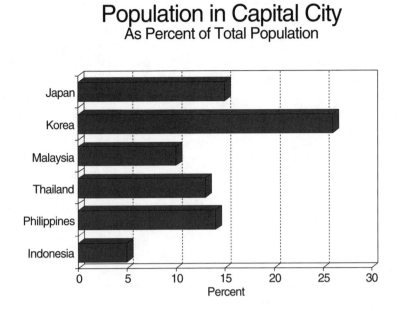

Graph 13.18

A Tale of Two Cities
Urban Growth in Bangkok and Jakarta

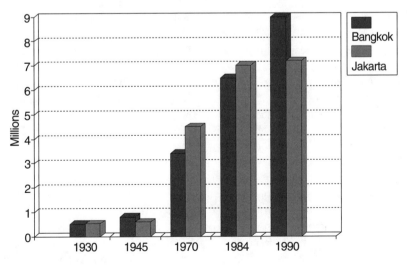

Graph 13.19

leaders have been more interested in hiding such problems than solving them. In their heyday, Ferdinand and Imelda Marcos ordered high walls to be built around Manila's worst slums so that important visitors would not see them, but the pollution and degradation can no longer be ignored.

The problem is exacerbated by a massive movement of people from the countryside to the cities. As governments struggle to provide the expensive infrastructure required by urban areas, they drain much-needed services and assistance away from the rural areas where most of the Asian population still lives. Notable exceptions to this imbalance of investment are found in South Korea and Taiwan, both of which are 70 percent urbanized. In Southeast Asia, the urban population is climbing rapidly. By the year 2000, 37 percent of Indonesia's population will be urban as compared with 29 percent in 1990. Half of Malaysia's people will live in urban areas by then.

The settlement patterns of many cities in Pacific Asia follow ethnic lines but, unlike western cities, communities based solely on economic and class groupings are less common. Asian cities can boast a greater mixture of the residential and work-related environments as well. A number of cities have evolved not from a central growing core but through the blending of smaller, local cities into one giant megapolis. The great cities of Asia now dominate the culture and politics of their respective nations as never before, often at the expense of the rural areas.

When young people leave the land and the remaining population grows older, the poverty afflicting the rural areas becomes all the more acute. This worldwide phenomenon varies considerably within Asia. As noted above, progress continues to be made in reducing both urban and rural poverty at a rate that generally outstrips other areas of the developing world, but significant levels of poverty persist. The most successful policies provide a range of employment possibilities either through investments in infrastructure and agriculture or through training and education for manufacturing jobs. Both strategies depend on healthy international trade. Thus, a prolonged global economic downturn, brought about by trade protectionism or other factors, would be devastating to Asia's developing economies.

Migration

Internal migration has been relatively free in some parts of Asia, but international migration has been far more restricted. Illegal immigration is an especially sensitive issue in some countries. In Japan, for example, labor costs are driving employers to search for immigrant labor, but there is strong governmental resistance to the intrusion of foreign workers. Illegal migration from the Chinese mainland into the crown colony of Hong Kong was long a sensitive subject until it was overshadowed by the arrival of boat loads of people fleeing the oppression and poverty of Vietnam. Between 1980 and 1985, refugees streamed out of Vietnam into Southeast Asia at a rate of 49,000 per year, often falling prey to ruthless pirates and eventually landing in squalid camps created by reluctant host governments in neighboring economies.

In the 1970s and 1980s, some of the largest international flows of workers were from Pacific Asia into the Middle East where the labor required for large infrastructure projects was contracted by Asian companies that used both low and high skilled workers. Remittances to their families back home provided an important part of the foreign exchange earnings of Korea and the Philippines. When these workers were driven out of Iraq and Kuwait in 1990 with the onset of the Persian Gulf crisis, the risk of national dependence on such returns became painfully apparent. In the case of the Philippines, the loss of income and influx of returnees, many of whose consumption patterns and expectations had been lifted during their Middle East experience, placed new strains on the shaky finances and political stability of the government.

Today, tight restrictions on immigration in nearly all Pacific Asian economies create a growing number of illegal migrants in the region. These are people who are willing to work in occupations that local residents shun. Legal admissions tend to favor foreigners with desired technical skills that will help boost local industries up the economy ladder.

Infrastructure

Population growth has placed enormous pressures on national infrastructures. Housing, schools, roads, and communications in many cases are woefully behind the swelling curve of demand. Burgeoning car ownership has created massive traffic problems in capital cities; Seoul, Taipei and Bangkok suffering the most congestion. Housing is an even more serious problem in these and other cities, mainly because it is an explosive social and political issue. In terms of both traffic and housing, Singapore is among the better off. Its tiny population and efficient public administration have enabled it to restrict traffic growth and to place 85 percent of its people in public housing.

Based on current growth forecasts, the whole of Pacific Asia could account for nearly half the world's energy consumption by the year 2010. Supplying such a massive amount of energy will require large scale infrastructure investment, raising special issues within each economy concerning the role of the private sector in financing, building and managing the infrastructure required.

Transportation infrastructure needs are as acute as those of the energy sector. If Bangkok has become legendary for its traffic jams, it is but one of many Asian capitals in which road and bridge-building have not kept pace with the burgeoning use of vehicles. China faces perhaps the most critical national transportation infrastructure problems. These will be exacerbated by its announced "family car" program. In 1984, China had only 5,600 privately owned vehicles; that number exploded to about 600,000 by 1993. By early in the next century, 180 million Chinese households could own cars, making China the biggest auto market in the world. The country plans to build 200,000 km of highways by the early 21st century at an estimated cost of up to $52 billion. These and similar infrastructure needs throughout Asia in energy, transportation, tele-communications, housing, and water systems leave governments with little choice but to seek financing through privatization and open, well-regulated capital markets. The latter, in particular, are needed to support long term debt instruments that developed countries often use to finance major infrastructure projects.

Most of the capitalist Asia-Pacific countries are planning ambitious public infrastructure projects. South Korea is building 2 million new housing units and doubling the length of the Seoul subway. A massive industrial infrastructure costing $31 billion has been proposed for the west coast of the nation. Korean and Japanese construction companies are fanning out across the region to take advantage of other major infrastructure projects in Southeast Asia. The result will be yet a further physical transformation of Pacific Asia when these projects move toward completion.

Technology Competition

Productivity growth remains one of the most important means by which to improve living standards without inflation or burdensome debt. Pacific Asia has only begun to address the problem of sustaining productivity gains, having previously enjoyed major productivity boosts through massive and relatively inexpensive technological upgrading.

Japan led the way in this process. Its early adaptation of technology enhanced its global competitive position and brought its productivity level more in line with that of other industrial countries. The NIEs have begun to follow the same path, investing heavily in advanced technologies, acquiring them from abroad, and creating research centers at home.

Not only has productivity become the subject of a new debate in Asia (Chapter 7), but the need to advance up the technology ladder is increasingly pictured as a competitive race. New technologies provide the critical edge that enables specialized companies to stay ahead of their competition. Technology acquisition thus has become a source of growing friction between developed and developing nations in the region. The less developed nations search eagerly for ways to advance their own capabilities in science and technology, a goal that requires expensive investments in technical training and education for their work forces.

Korea and Taiwan have made major investments in key technology sectors such as computers and electronics. Taiwan's growth in this area — involving more than one in every five of the top 500 Taiwanese firms — derives largely from its own, not foreign, investments. Most of its technical cooperation agreements are with Japan. Korea similarly has licensed a great deal of Japanese technology. Both Korea and Taiwan decided to enter into the world semiconductor race in the 1980s. Korea now ranks first in world

Asia in the Global Semiconductor Market

As a vital component of most advanced electronic technologies, semiconductors have become a core commodity for technology growth and are an important factor in the development plans of several Asian economies. Significantly, the region dominates global semiconductor production, accounting for around 90 percent of all semiconductors made, with Europe accounting for only 10 percent. Similarly, the region dominates consumption of semiconductors, the three largest consumer categories being the United States, Japan, and the Asian developing economies, respectively, with the EU in fourth place.

In 1994, the United States resumed leadership of world semiconductor production and it also passed the Japanese as the largest seller of chips to non-Japan Asia. The largest chip consumer in the latter group is Chinese Taipei.

Of particular note is the explosive growth of production and investment in semiconductors in China, Korea, Chinese Taipei, and Singapore in the 1990s. In spite of this, consumption in the region has climbed so steeply that it has usually matched or exceeded production. Among the developing economies, Korea has expended the most total capital on semiconductors, having become a powerhouse global exporter of DRAM semiconductors. While it consumes less than half its production, it has become dangerously dependent on global markets for this price-volatile commodity. Taiwan has taken a somewhat different route by developing one of the world's fastest growing and most innovative industries to use semiconductors: personal computers.

---

production of DRAMs (memory chips) while Taiwan continues to move up the ranks of producer economies. In the other two NIEs, Singapore and Hong Kong, high technology centers began to appear in the late 1980s. In an effort to constantly upgrade their technologies and remain competitive, corporations based in the NIEs have begun making direct investments in small but strategically important technology companies in the United States.

The lesson being learned by Asia's NIEs is that in order to attract new technology, they must already possess technology. Having entered the technology race at a critical time, they are able to just keep pace with industrial giants in selected areas. This challenge becomes ever more daunting. The vast size of investment required in plant and equipment continues to favor the largest companies, but even they must now enter into international strategic alliances.

The less developed nations, while supporting an increasingly educated and experienced work force, are in danger of falling behind unless they are able to join these alliances or make their own. China could be the exception if it is able to successfully marshall its massive body of science and technology workers while continuing to attract foreign investments in information technologies. Recognizing this trend, Japanese, Taiwanese, and Hong Kong companies have begun to utilize China's large supply of software engineers with on-site facilities.

Japan towers over the rest of Asia in the overall size and sophistication of its scientific and technological base, exemplified by its ambitious plans in outer space. In Asia, only China has been launching satellites into orbit longer than Japan (but in the throw weight of its launch vehicles it is falling behind.) In March, 1990, Japan became the third nation to send a craft into lunar orbit and it began plans for an unmanned lunar mission and a Venus probe. Japanese high technology and capital is now sought by American and European companies in alliances aimed at megaprojects such as advanced microprocessors and supersonic passenger aircraft.

Education and Human Resources

Broad contrasts in national technology capabilities serve to highlight the need for Asian countries to maintain and improve their educational resources. Education has been one of the most important wellsprings of change in Asia just as it has in the West. Access to educational opportunities stimulated new ideas about government and progress early in this century and later it enabled Asians to acquire and use industrial technologies. The Confucian emphasis on education helped to vitalize the growth of a more educated populace. South Korea provides the leading example, spending on education proportionally as much or more than any other Asian country outside Japan. Yet, like Japan, Korea is saddled with an education system that relies heavily on the university entrance examination system and in both countries the desperate competition among students ("examination hell") has become a major social headache.

One effect of Asian governments strong emphasis on human resource development has been the emergence of what might be called a regional market for people with advanced technical training. Japanese companies show an increasing willingness to hire university graduates from other Asian countries. In one survey, Japanese executives indicated that they expected educational quality in the NIEs to surpass Japan by the year 2000. Japanese investment in Pacific Asia seems to follow this view: It now extends to specialized research and development facilities such as the Matsushita Institute of Technology (MIT) on Taiwan.

Environmental Degradation

Science and technology will play an important role in addressing environmental problems in Pacific Asia, but the solutions continue to lag far behind the need. Much of the burgeoning pollution in Asia is a direct result of industrial growth. Traffic fumes choke Bangkok, Jakarta, and Taipei; Manila's five rivers, which provide drinking water to hundreds of thousands, are teeming with dangerous effluents. The sugar mills of the Philippines, the palm oil plants of Malaysia, and the tapioca industry of Thailand and Indonesia each dump tons of contaminants into rivers.

China presents the greatest single environmental dilemma in Asia, one that threatens to severely hobble the nation's economic growth. By the government's own estimates, a fifth of China's rivers and lakes are polluted. Thick smog hangs over many cities as a result of the massive and inefficient use of low-grade coal — 900 million tons annually. By 1988, the city of Benxi in northeast China had become so dirty that it rendered the city invisible on satellite photographs. Meanwhile, the quality of soil is degrading and the amount of farmland decreasing in the face of erosion and advancing deserts. While in some areas a cleanup effort appears to be making progress, the general trend in environmental quality in China, as noted in Chapter 10, is decidedly downward.

As early as 1956, an industrially-caused environmental disaster occurred in Asia when chemical wastes from the Nippon Chiso Hiryo company poisoned first the fish and then the people of Minamata in southern Japan. At the time, Japan's income per capita was little better than that of the Philippines today. Not only did the Minamata disaster begin to awaken Japan to its deteriorating environment, its subsequent rapid climb in wealth enabled it to begin to address the worst of its problems. Elsewhere in Pacific Asia, societies have only recently begun to acquire the levels of income that encourage governments to impose such controls over pollution. In the less developed economies, environmental investments are perceived to be either a luxury or a low priority in economic growth, but pressure from indigenous "green" movements is growing.

The destruction of tropical forests continues to be an especially controversial environmental issue. From the Asian point of view, the cutting of the rain forests merely follows the pattern established in the once heavily forested continents of Europe and North America. Governments see an urgent need to exploit their forest resources for immediate profit rather than balance their moderate, sustainable use for the longer term. The pace of the harvest has been especially rapid in Southeast Asia where Thailand, for example, has gone from being an exporter to an importer of timber. In 1900, there were two and a half million square kilometers of virgin forest in the region outside of Papua New Guinea. By 1990 there were around 600,000 square kilometers. At present rates of destruction, nearly all of it will be gone by the year 2010.

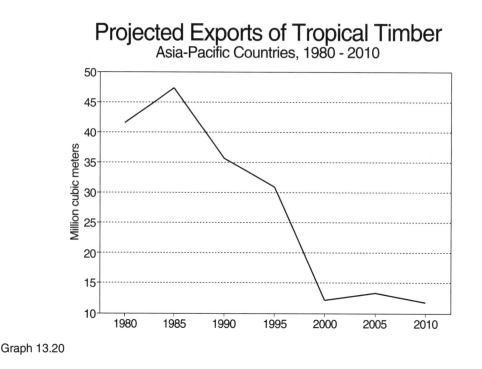

Projected Exports of Tropical Timber
Asia-Pacific Countries, 1980 - 2010

Graph 13.20

Communications

The combination of modern transportation, telecommunications and new information technologies exerts a powerful force for change throughout Asia. Radio and television have succeeded in reaching mass audiences, even in remote rural areas and, as elsewhere, the telephone has become the key instrument of communication. International telephone traffic within the Western Pacific soared in the 1980s as a result of growing commerce, new facilities, the spread of telephone-linked facsimile machines. In the 1990s, the expansion of the Internet added to this momentum. Satellite broadcasts of television programs have leapfrogged inadequate, land-based infrastructures, enabling governments to extend their messages into remote areas.

Government control over communications remains one of the most sensitive aspects of change in Asia. The importance attached by authoritarian governments to managing and supervising information is brought home from time to time during national crises such as the Tiananmen Square demonstrations in China in

1989 (Chapter 10). In the aftermath of that event, the government demonstrated its ability to censor most forms of communication including television, radio and newspapers. It jammed Voice of America broadcasts into the country and closely monitored facsimile machines. The authorities were able to restrict information flows from the larger world into China, preventing by some estimates all but about 75 million party cadre and a few million others in urban areas from learning details of the upheavals in the European communist systems. More recently, China has sought to prevent its citizens from gaining access to Internet World Wide Web sites of which it does not approve. Meanwhile, China's communist neighbor, North Korea, has elevated information control to an obsession, creating an Orwellian world in which the government's radio voice is permanently switched on in most dwellings. The capitalist government of Singapore under Lee Kwan Yew, while not carrying matters to such extremes, was nevertheless vigilant over the content of press and television reports about itself and waged bitter court battles with such independent media giants as Dow Jones & Company.

"This is a crucial moment in Asia's history. Every country in AsiaSat's footprint is thinking about what to do. There is no precedent in the world for television from AsiaSat ..."

—Anonymous Japanese official,
Far Eastern Economic Review,
June 14, 1990

A collision between the need to utilize new technology while restricting the flow of information that is released thereby is exemplified in China's dilemma. In 1989 China, eager for foreign exchange, contracted to use its Long March III rocket to place a potentially revolutionary communications satellite into stationary orbit over Asia. Christened AsiaSat I, the instrument is capable of broadcasting 24-hour television to anyone with a small, relatively inexpensive dish antenna. The satellite broadcast "footprints" that cover the region stretch from Malaysia to Iraq and from Japan to India. China, centered within these broadcast areas, finds itself unable to jam broadcasts emanating from overhead. Not only China, but several other governments are concerned at the prospect of uncontrolled broadcasts. While the owners of communications satellites are unlikely to risk the wrath of a powerful governments by broadcasting inflammatory programming, the entry of uncensored information into Asian societies is becoming increasingly difficult to prevent.

The Pacific in the 21st Century

The emergence of China as a regional economic power alongside Japan has created a new political and commercial dynamic in Pacific Asia, one that promises to revive ancient patterns of competition and cooperation. As China returns to its historical regional role, commensurate with its size and influence, Japan weighs the opportunities of a vast new market alongside the liabilities of a nearby, modernizing military giant. Similarly, China's other Asian neighbors must calibrate their future relationships with Japan and the United States — two mature and largely predictable industrial economies — against their relations with a less predictable China. The situation contrasts sharply with the cold war framework when two outside powers competed within the region for allegiances. Today, China and Japan must coexist and compete for influence — almost mirror images of one another in politics, demography, and economics — while a third, more distant power insists that its own values and interests have a place in their affairs.

If this seems to present a variety of scenarios for open conflict, stable relationships are equally possible. The ability to project power militarily occupies a low priority in most Asian nations today, including China. International economic competition is the foremost concern even if it too leads to acrimonious international disputes. Innumerable transnational business alliances in Asia may succeed in fostering an era in the Pacific that might have evolved in Europe early in this century had not World War I intruded to prevent it. But just as the Great War occurred in spite of the presence of intensive cross border trade, so may Asian regional stability depend less on economics than on the ability of respected international institutions and mechanisms to resolve conflict.

Much has been said of the role of United States in promoting stability for the region, but Japan plays an equally important, complementary role. Having destabilized the region in mid-century, Japan has since become Asia's greatest builder and investor. To the extent that the U.S.-led Occupation contributed to this role reversal, the legacy presents a paradox that will challenge leaders of the next generation: a powerful yet dependent Japan whose security is defined in terms set by an American-made constitution and an American-dominated bilateral Security Treaty. These have been the bedrock of postwar expectations for regional stability and they remain anchor points for regional security arrangements. At the same time, there is a growing assumption in Pacific Asia that U.S. military power must be augmented by a more complex mix of mutual responsibilities involving Japan and other nations.

A changing perception of the balance of power in Asia has enabled Japan, slowly but surely, to build the confidence of its Asian neighbors in Japan's trustworthiness and good intentions. By the early 1990s, ASEAN had begun to admit a greater political and diplomatic role for Japan in the western Pacific.[11] At the same time, China's looming presence made ASEAN reluctant to encourage a more direct security role for Japan lest ASEAN be seen by China as encouraging an "alliance" against it.

Any transition toward a larger security and diplomatic role for Japan will be fraught with tensions and potential misunderstandings between Japan, China, and the United States. Not only does China tend to interpret security cooperation between Japan and the US as an attempt to "contain" China in the mold of the cold war strategy, but it also requires Japan and the United States to adjust to one another's changing economic and political roles in the region, a prospect that both countries find troubling. From the Japanese viewpoint, Americans masked their own societal and policy failures in the 1980s with bullying and complaints against Japan. In 1991, a $13 billion contribution from Japan to the cost of the Persian Gulf War received scant praise from the United States where attention seemed to focus instead on Japan's lukewarm enthusiasm for the war. Trade frictions, discussed in previous chapters, have fueled resentment on both sides. For a time, a new Japanese word even became popular: *kenbei*, meaning "dislike of the United States."[12] Equally irritating to Japan has been what seems an American tendency to view it as a banker and passive partner in funding U.S. foreign policy initiatives. Americans, for their part, often see Japan as a remote, enigmatic, self-centered, almost impenetrable nation that lacks a moral vision or purpose and seeks purely economic goals. There are elements of truth in the perceptions on both sides.

Many centuries ago, an anonymous Japanese cartographer drew a map of Asia that showed his country wrapped in the coils of a great dragon, its body curled like a fortress to hide and isolate Japan from the rest of the known world. Modern Japan may have been transformed since that time, but at its cultural core there remains a desire to be insulated by a powerful, even divine, force. As Japan seeks a larger world role, this cultural legacy will retain its influence.

Yet it is China's resurgence rather than Japan's cultural insularity that poses the central questions for the coming Pacific Century. Alarmists in the West have sought to emphasize China's potential for military and political dominance over the region. They view China as a monolithic force, overlooking its chronic internal problems. In keeping with its history and population, China aspires to a major regional and global role but it will also adapt to the pressures that a globalized economy impose.

These problems are generally well-recognized in the region. The Korean peninsula alone will exact an immense cost in the reconstruction of the North, either through peaceful redevelopment or a wrenching finale that demands the attention and resources of many nations. China's population continues to expand by the tens of millions, testing the region's carrying capacity with all its implications for global resource demand. Still another kind of "demand" has grown in parts of Asia: the demand for greater human liberty, equality of opportunity, and governmental accountability.

The challenge for countries outside the region will be to address and adjust to these changes in all their complexity, for they are part of an ongoing integration of the world economic system that tests the adaptability of individuals, communities and nations.

ISOLATION, INTEGRATION, AND CHANGE

A Clash of Values?

In the Introduction to this book, it was noted that a "modern" nation is one that can self-confidently "join others on equal terms in the quest for new markets, new technologies, new ideas." By this measure, the emergence of modern Pacific Asia is still incomplete. Efforts to control access to ideas and technology, as noted above, remain a focus for some governing authorities. Their strategy is to try to selectively acquire the latest technologies and attract needed foreign investment while blocking the cultural and political "pollution" that such influences bring. In the communist nations, this phenomenon waxes and wanes according to shifts in the ideological winds. We cannot say how North Korea, Vietnam and China will come to terms with the pressures that are being imposed by an increasingly integrated world, but their solutions will be conditioned more by their own internal histories and dynamics than by external forces, however inexorable the latter may seem.

The fact that these governments cling to the outward forms of a failed Marxist-Leninist ideology should not obscure the contribution their countries have made to the modernization process in Pacific Asia. Millions of people responded to visionary leaders who inspired them to take control of their national destinies. Zhou Enlai's youthful battle cry in 1919, "There must be struggle; there must be method; there must be sacrifice," was repeated, in a sense, all across Pacific Asia in capitalist and communist nations alike. The results, on the whole, have been spectacular.

In an age in which cultural conflict seems to be the norm, it is easy to overlook the commonalities that the modernization process engendered in many parts of the world from the eighteenth century onward. Notwithstanding the mistaken notions that Western scholars once harbored about an Asia in which modernization was blocked by "Oriental despotism," the idea of a civil society in which a neutral legal code ensures human rights, due process, and political pluralism is gaining ground in the region. Chapter 8 examined the experiments with democracy and the difficult transitions that are being attempted by governments as they adapt to the demands of increasingly prosperous and assertive citizenries. Pressures toward this transition are reinforced by the decentralized nature of capitalist economic organization and new communications technologies. Together, the ideas of capitalism and democracy have accelerated the modernization process in the Pacific even if, in their assimilation, "capitalism" and "democracy" are transformed in ways that now set them apart from their Western origins.

This does not discount the very clear differences that exist between East and West, particularly with respect to many Western nations' long-standing conviction that Asia must be "opened" to participate fully and fairly in a competitive global economy. If this has seemed to many Asians to be the ultimate Western conceit, following centuries of colonial occupation, it has also presented an opportunity to develop and articulate an "Asian" point of view in the face of Western pressure for change.

For this reason, the meaning and purpose of "openness" itself continues to reflect fundamental issues that divide Pacific Asia and the West — openness on trade, information, human rights, and democratization to name but a few issues. This tension reinforces the inclination of some Asian governments to limit and control the intrusion of foreign sources of communications within their societies. An objective indicator of how far such controls are being relaxed (or are no longer effective) may be the number of small satellite broadcast receives that are sold without restriction to individuals, permitting them to receive foreign television or unimpeded, unmonitored access to the Internet.

The post cold war world has brought these tensions into greater focus, giving rise to the suggestion that "Asian values" are fundamentally different from those in the West. Advocates of this view go so far as to note that a political/cultural gap between East and West can only widen as each side becomes more assertive of its views. They postulate a "clash of civilizations," inaccurately applying the word "civilization" to conflicts that derive from more localized sources. The difference has been noted most explicitly by the playwright Masakazu Yamazaki who argues that:

> The peoples of East Asia today can be said to partake of modern Western civilization at the topmost stratum of their world, to retain their national civilizations and nation-states in the middle stratum, and to preserve their traditional cultures in their day-to-day lives...
>
> Failure to distinguish clearly between culture and civilization marks the thought of the prophets of the clash of civilizations. The thesis is predicated on the mistaken notions that a civilization can be as predetermined a property of an ethnic group as its culture and that a culture can be as universal and expansive as a civilization...
>
> The rule of culture extends at most from the family, village, or circle of social acquaintances to the tribe or nation. Civilization, in contrast, encompasses different tribes and nations and creates a world.[13]

The unbridgeable East and West of Kipling's famous phrase find a growing if tentative common ground along the Pacific Rim in spite of its differentiated geography and cultures. Yamazaki has suggested that aspects of design, theater, fashion, and art are emerging that define a "Pacific International Style." If so, its origins are found in the history of the Pacific Century, from the shores of Indonesia to the California coast. Its crucible has been the modernization experience in Pacific Asia, its elemental carriers the jet airplane, telecommunications, and computer chips, its defining quality an interpretation of Asian forms and traditions defined also by Western influences.

An outgrowth of the new technologies of communication and travel, this aspect of a "Pacific" identity is as yet ambiguous and difficult to define. But just as a century ago there emerged a generation of Asians with broad visions of their societies' common future and potential, so there appears today a similar groundswell of self confidence and expectation in the region. It is testimony to the qualities of those earlier generations that, as we conclude this momentous Pacific century in a period of peace and prosperity, their legacy remains the subject of endless fascination and debate.

NOTES

1. The developed countries referred to in this chapter comprise the members of the OECD, the Paris-based Organization for Economic Cooperation and Development.

2. Trade intensity in this context refers to a measure of the ratio of an observed bilateral flow to its expected value. cf. Asian Development Bank, *Asian Development Outlook, 1996 and 1997.* Hong Kong: Oxford University Press. 1996. p. 191.

3. Conclusions and data from this section are derived partly from Richard P. Cronin, *Japan's Expanding Role and Influence in the Asia-Pacific Region: Implications for U.S. Interests and Policy* (Washington, DC: Congressional Research Service, 7 September 1990).

4. Yamamura, Kozo and Walter Hatch, "A Looming Entry Barrier: Japan's Production Networks in Asia," *NBR Analysis.* Seattle, Washington: The National Bureau of Asian Research. VIII, No. 1, February 1997.

   A counter view is summarized in Johnston, Christopher B. and Atsushi Yamokoshi, "Strength Without Dominance: Japanese Investment in Southeast Asia." *JEI Report.* No. 19A. May 16, 1997. Washington, D.C.: Japan Economic Institute.

5. Orr, Robert M., Jr., "The Rising Sum: What Makes Japan Give?" *The International Economy*, September/October 1989, p. 83.

6. An overview of U.S.-Japan relations in the light of Japan's historical alliances is to be found in Murray Sayle, "Broke New World," *Far Eastern Economic Review*, 31 May 1990, pp. 32-36.

7. See Lawrence Krause, "Pacific Economic Regionalism and the United States," in *Impact of Recent Economic Development on US-Korean Relations and the Pacific Basin* (Washington, DC: Korea Economic Institute, 1991).

8. By 1986 the PECC membership included the ASEAN nations, the Pacific Islands (represented through the Forum Secretariat, Fiji), both China and Taiwan, Korea, and the five OECD nations (Australia, Canada, Japan, New Zealand, and the United States). Over the following ten years were added Chile, Colombia, Mexico, Hong Kong, Peru, Russia, and Vietnam were added for a total of 22 economies. The body changed the final word in its name from Conference to "Council" in 1992.

9. The APEC working groups have been assigned areas such as technology transfer, transportation, tourism, trade promotion, telecommunications, ocean pollution, and improvements in economic data. In this sense, they begin to serve functions similar to the Organization for Economic Cooperation and Development (OECD) whose members are industrialized nations. Developing economies in Asia do not belong to the OECD which suggests that APEC may eventually begin to serve OECD-like functions in the Pacific Basin.

10. This section derived from Johansen, Frida. World Bank Discussion Paper No. 203. Washington DC: The World Bank. 1993.

11. Joint statement of the ASEAN Institutes of Strategic and International Studies. *A Time for Initiative: Proposals for the Consideration of the Fourth ASEAN Summit.* ASEAN-ISIS, Jakarta, June 4, 1991. p. 21. The Institutes, while nominally independent from their respective governments, often serve to reflect or help influence official policy views.

12. The nuance of the term *kenbei* is to permit an expression of disapproval while permitting one to hold a fundamental pro-American stance, as opposed to the stronger and more rarely used *hanbei* which is redolent of cold war anti-Americanism.

13. Yamazaki, Masakazu "Asia, A Civilization in the Making," In *Foreign Affairs*, July/August 1996. pp. 106-118.

Representation of Foreign Words and Names

All foreign names in this text are given in the "native" order. Unlike most other cultures, the family name comes first in Chinese, Japanese, Korean, and Vietnamese. After the family name comes the personal name(s). Many Chinese, Japanese, and Koreans are known by their surname alone, and referred to in that way. However, when called by just one name, the Vietnamese practice is to use the given name. Initial appearance in the text uses the full name. In subsequent reference, certain individuals may be referred to by just one name. Thus, the Japanese leader Ito Hirobumi is referred to as Ito, the Chinese Zhou Enlai is Zhou, and so forth.

Burmese names usually have two syllables. The first letter of a name is determined by the day of the week of the person's birth. There are no family names and names do not change for marriage. The order for Filipino names is the same as English. Due to the long presence of the Spanish in the Philippines, many people have Hispanic given names, and even Hispanic family names (such as Ramon Magsaysay and Ferdinand Marcos). In Indonesia, some individuals use only a single name (such as Sukarno).

ROMANIZATION

Chinese

Romanization is in Pinyin, a system developed in China in the 1950s to represent Mandarin Chinese. Pinyin, with the addition of four simple diacritics, is an accurate guide to the pronunciation of modern Mandarin. However, the diacritics which indicate tone are not included in this text.

All Chinese words in this text appear in Pinyin. Exceptions are made for those terms better known in the West in other forms, such as "Hong Kong" (instead of Pinyin "Xianggang"). All such exceptions are noted in the text.

There are several Chinese regionalects, such as Cantonese, Fujianese, and Hakka, in addition to the national standard of Mandarin. These languages are all related but mutually unintelligible, like French and Italian share Romance roots but are different languages. Hong Kong, Sun Yat-sen, and Chiang Kai-shek are three names that did not come from Mandarin. Accordingly, they are presented in this text as they appear here, and not in their Pinyin equivalents (which are "Xianggang," "Sun Zhongshan," and "Jiang Jieshi," respectively).

Wade-Giles is a system of romanization initially developed by Thomas Francis Wade in the mid-nineteenth century. His system was refined by Herbert Giles in the early twentieth century. Older (pre-1980) works usually employ Wade-Giles. In this text, the first appearance of a word in Pinyin is usually accompanied by its Wade-Giles equivalent in parenthesis in order to avoid confusion with earlier texts.

It should also be noted that due to the deep political rift between Taiwan and mainland China, Taiwanese publications do not employ Pinyin (which is a PRC innovation).

Japanese

The Hepburn system is universally employed. Developed by American James Hepburn in the nineteenth century, this system is regarded as easiest for readers of English to pronounce correctly. However, macrons indicating long vowels have been omitted.

Korean

The McCune-Reischauer system is employed. George McCune and Edwin O. Reischauer completed this system in 1939. It has since been designated by the South Korean government as the standard. However, the diacritics of the system are not used, due to typographic limitations.

Malay

As the official language of Brunei, Indonesia, and Malaysia, Malay is the only international language of Southeast Asia. Although once written with a variation of the Arabic script, it is now written with the familiar Latin alphabet. Malay words appear in this text as they would in Brunei, Indonesia, and Malaysia.

Thai

The Royal Thai General System, the romanization scheme approved by the Thai government, is used. Thai, like Chinese, is a tonal language. However, the diacritics which indicate tones are not included.

Vietnamese

The Quoc Ngu (literally "National Language") system is used. It has several diacritics, which indicate either tone for the syllable or a different sound value for the letter. However, the diacritics are not employed in this text. The Quoc Ngu script was developed by seventeenth-century European missionaries, particularly one Alexandre de Rhodes. It was adopted as the Vietnamese standard in 1945.

PRONUNCIATION GUIDE TO CHINESE NAMES

Most foreign languages have sounds which are not found in English, or sounds that are similar but not quite the same. Romanizations allow for representation in the Latin alphabet and help English speakers to approximate these foreign sounds. For full explanations of romanization and phonology, please refer to any good language textbook. Pinyin, however, presents a special challenge in pronunciation because although it uses the Latin alphabet, certain letters are used in ways that do not correspond to standard usage in English. Most of the Chinese words and names used in the text appear in the following guide.

An Lushan:	ahn loo shahn
Baihua:	bai hwa
Beijing:	bay jing
Cao Xueqin:	tsaow shüeh chin
Changcheng:	chahng chung
Changjiang:	chahng jyahng
Cai Yuanpei:	tsai yuahn pay
Chen Duxiu:	chen doo shyoh
Cixi:	tsi shee
Dao:	daow
Daode jing:	daow duh jing
De:	duh
Deng Xiaoping:	dung sheeaow ping
Dong Zhongshu:	dohng johng shoo
Du Yuesheng:	doo yüeh sheng
Du Yushang:	doo yü shahng
Fang Lizhi:	fahng lee jr
Fu Sinian:	foo si nien
Fuzhou:	foo joh
Gemingdang:	guh ming dahng
Guangdong:	gwahng dohng
Guangxu:	gwahng shü
Guangzhou:	gwahng joh
Gu Jiegang:	goo jyeh gahng
Guo Huaiyi:	gwaw hwy ee
Guomindang:	gwaw min dahng
Haifeng:	hai fung
Han:	hahn
Hankou:	hahn koh
Hong Xiuquan:	hohng shyoh chwahn
Huangpu:	huahng poo
Hua Guofeng:	hwa gwaw fung
Hubei:	hoo bay
Humen:	hoo mun

Hu Shi:	hoo shir	**Qing:**	ching
Hu Yaobang:	hoo yaow bahng	**Qingdao:**	ching daow
Hu Yuan:	hoo ywahn	**Qin Shihuangdi:**	chin shir hwahng dee
Jian:	jyen	**Qiu Jin:**	chyoh jin
Jiang Jieshi:	jyahng jyeh shir	**Jiang Qing:**	jyahng ching
Jiang Qing:	jyahng ching	**Quanzhou:**	chwahn joh
Jianguo fanglue:	jyen gwaw fahng lüeh	**Sanmin zhuyi:**	sahn min joo ee
Jiangxi:	jyahng shee	**Shaanxi:**	shahn shee
Jiazhou:	jyah joh	**Shanxi:**	shahn shee
Kang Youwei:	kahng yoh way	**Shanghai:**	shahng hai
Kangxi:	kahng shee	**Sichuan:**	si chwahn
ketou:	kuh toh	**Song:**	sohng
Kong:	kohng	**Song Jiaoren:**	sohng jyaow ren
lai hua:	lai hwa	**Sui:**	sway
Laozi:	laow dz	**Sun Yixian;**	soon ee shee-en
Liang Qichao:	lyahng chee chaow	**Sun Zhongshan:**	soon johng shahn
Li Dazhao:	lee dah jaow	**Tai Zong:**	tai dzohng
Li Hongzhang:	lee hohng jahng	**Tang:**	tahng
Lin Biao:	lin beeaow	**Tian:**	tien
Lin Xiangqian:	lin sheeahng chien	**Tian'anmen:**	tien ahn mun
Lin Zexu:	lin dze shü	**Tianjin:**	tien jin
Li Ruzhen:	lee roo jen	**Tongmenghui:**	tohng mung hway
Liu Shaoqi:	lyoh shaow chee	**Wei Zheng:**	way jung
Li Zhi:	lee jr	**Wenyan:**	wen yen
Lufeng:	loo fung	**Wudi:**	woo dee
Lu Xun:	loo shün	**Wuhan:**	woo hahn
Mao Zedong:	maow dze dung	**Wu Zhihui:**	woo jr hway
Nanjing:	nahn jing	**Xi'an:**	shee ahn
Nanyang:	nahn yahng	**Xianfeng:**	shee-en fung
Ningpo:	ning paw	**Xiang Jingyu:**	sheeahng jing yü
Peng Dehuai:	pung duh hwy	**Xingzhonghui:**	shing johng hway
Pin Zhun:	pin jun	**Xinhai:**	sheen hai
Puyi:	poo ee	**Xiongnu:**	sheeohng noo
Qi:	chee	**Xu Guangjin:**	shü guahng jin
Qian Long:	chien lohng	**Xun Zi:**	shün dz
Qian Xuantong:	chien shuahn tohng	**Yan:**	yen
Qin:	chin	**Yang Jian:**	yahng jyen
		Yangzi:	yahng dz

Ye Mingchen:	yeh ming chen
Yuan Mei:	yuahn may
Yuan Shikai:	yuahn shir kai
Zeng Guofan:	dzung gwaw fahn
Zhao Ziyang:	jaow dz yahng
Zhejiang:	juh jyahng
Zheng:	jung
Zheng He:	jung huh
Zhongguo:	johng gwaw
Zhong Ke:	johng kuh
Zhou:	joh
Zhou Enlai:	joh en lai
Zhou Shuren:	joh shoo ren
Zhuangzi:	jwahng dz
Zhu De:	joo duh
Zhu Xi:	joo shee

Zhu Yuanzhang:	joo ywahn jahng
Zi:	dz
Zongli Yamen:	dzohng lee yah mun
Zuo si:	dzwaw si

Notes on Sounds:

1. The Chinese combination "_ai" should be pronounced as "I."

2. "j" is like the "j" in "job," not like the "j" sound in "rouge."

3. "shir" is like the "shir" in "shirt."

4. "si" alone or in the unit "tsi" is like the "si" in "sit."

5. Hyphenated sounds above are said as one word.

Contributors:

The Introduction to this section was supplied by Blaine Erikson, along with pronunciation guides for the Faculty Manual and Study Guide. Christopher Ragonese contributed the above Guide to Chinese Pronunciation.

Sources For Graphs

1.1 DeFrancis, John, *The Chinese Language: Fact and Fantasy*. Honolulu: University of Hawaii Press, 1986.

2.1 Reid, Anthony, "An 'Age of Commerce' in Southeast Asian History," *Modern Asian Studies*, vol. 24, no. 1., February, 1990, p. 7.

2.2 Reid, Anthony, "An 'Age of Commerce.'" p. 16.

2.3 Reid, Anthony, "An 'Age of Commerce.'" p. 20.

2.4 Spence, Jonathan, *The Search for Modern China*. New York: Norton, 1990. p. 129.

2.5 Eastman, Lloyd E., *Family, Field and Ancestors*. London: Oxford University Press. 1988. p. 129.

3.1 Fairbank, John, K., et. al., *East Asia: Tradition and Transformation*. Boston: Houghton Mifflin, 1978, p. 545.

3.2 *The Times Concise Atlas of World History*. London: Times Books Ltd., 1982. p. 127.

3.3 The Times Concise Atlas of World History. p. 127.

4.1 Lee, Ki-baik, Trans. by Edward W. Wagner with Edward J. Shultz, *A New History of Korea*. Cambridge: Harvard University Press, 1984. p. 348.

4.2 Robinson, Michael, *Korea Old and New: A History*. Carter J. Eckert, et.al, Seoul: Ilchokak, 1991. p. 311.

6.1 Organization for Economic Cooperation and Development (OECD), *Structural Adjustment and Economic Performance*. Paris: OECD, 1987. p. 54.

6.2 Bank of Japan, 1989. c.f. *Far Eastern Economic Review*. 21 June 1990. p. 40.

6.3 Japan Defense Agency

6.4 Japan Economic Institute, *JEI Report*. No. 22A. 14 June 1991. p. 11.

6.5 Ibid. p. 10.

6.6 *Japan Fair Trade Commission, The Second Survey on the General Trading Company. Tokyo, 1975*, pp. 17-18; *Far Eastern Economic Review* graph, 27 December 1990, p. 44.

6.7 OECD. *Structural Adjustment*. p. 19.

6.8 *Business Week*, August 26, 1991. p. 36.

6.9 *Look Japan*. September, 1990. p. 9.

6.10 Japan Economic Institute, Washington, DC.

7.1 *Far Eastern Economic Review*. 9 August 1990, p. 52.

7.2 *World Development Report 1979*. New York: Oxford University Press, 1979.

7.3 *Far Eastern Economic Review*. 18 April 1991. p. 44.

7.5 Asian Development Bank

7.6 *Asian Development Bank Outlook, 1989*. p. 83.

7.7 *World Development Report 1991*. New York: Oxford University Press, 1991. p. 137.

7.8 *Far Eastern Economic Review*. 11 April 1991. p. 50; General Agreement on Tariffs and Trade.

7.9 Morgan Guaranty Trust, IMF, Nomura Research, *The Economist*, 23 February 1991, p. 32.

7.9 Federation of Korea Trade Unions; Bank of Korea; *Far Eastern Economic Review*, 19 April 1990. p. 74.

7.11 *Far Eastern Economic Review*. June 27 1996 p. 58; Pacific Economic Cooperation Council

8.1 (Graph) Esposito, John L., *Islam in Asia: Religion, Politics, and Society*, (New York: Oxford University Press, 1987).

8.1 (Table) Ulf Sundhaussen, "Indonesia: Past and Present Encounters with Democracy," in, *Democracy in Developing Countries: Asia*, Larry Diamond, Juan J. Linz, and Seymour Martin Lipset, eds., vol. 3 of 4 vols. (Boulder, Co: Lynne Rienner Publishers, 1989)

8.2 (Table) Philippine central bank, National Statistical Coordination Board, the Philippines; c.f. *Far Eastern Economic Review*, June 19, 1997. p. 42.

8.3 (Table) Dresden Bank.

8.3 (Graph) Korea Institute for International Economic Policy

10.1 Spence. *The Search for Modern China*. p. 543.

10.2 Chinese Academy of Social Sciences; Beijing Market Research Consultancy; c.f. *Far Eastern Economic Review*, December 7, 1995.

10.3-5 State Statistical Bureau of China; c.f. *Far Eastern Economic Review*, September 12, 1996 pp. 62-63.

10.6 DBS Bank, Singapore

10.7 Lavely, William, "Demographic and Social Change in China," In *Asia-Pacific Report*, Charles E. Morrison and Robert F. Dernberger, eds., Honolulu: East-West Center, 1989. p. 67.

10.8 East-West Center, World Bank.
Spence. *The Search for Modern China*. p. 689.

10.9-10 Lavely. "Demographic and Social Change in China." p. 71.

10.11-14 Lardy, Nicholas. *China in the World Economy*. Institute for International Economics, 1994.

11.1 *Asia-Pacific Report 1989*. Honolulu: East-West Center, 1989. p. 117; *World Development Report 1995*. Washington,DC: World Bank, page 144, Table A1.
Far Eastern Economic Review. 5 July 90, p. 44.

11.5-11.6 Pacific Economic Cooperation Council. Pacific Economic Outlook, Structure. *Capital Flows in the Pacific Region, Past Trends and Future Prospects*. Background Papers. Osaka, Japan: Kansai Economic Research Center. p. 176.

13.1 *IMF Direction of Trade Statistics Yearbook 1986, 1992, 1996* cf. Report of the Commission on United States-Pacific Trade and Investment Policy. Washington DC: USTR 1997. page 3.
(Chart) Asia-Pacific Economic Cooperation. Second APEC Working Group Meeting on Expansion of Investment and Technology Transfer, Bali, Indonesia, 13-14 June, 1991. Annex 6. p. 5, and *UN Direction of Trade Statistics*. March 1991.

13.2 *Far Eastern Economic Review*. 5 July 1990. p.54.

13.2 (Table) Cohen, Stephen and Paolo Guerrieri. "The Variable Geometry of Asian Trade," In Doherty, Eileen M., ed. *Japanese Investment in Asia*. San Francisco: The Asia Foundation and BRIE. 1995. Table 6C.

13.3 Pacific Economic Cooperation Conference (PECC). Triple T Task Force.

13.4 Cronin, Richard P., *Japan's Expanding Role and Influence in the Asia-Pacific Region: Implications for U.S. Interests and Policy*. Washington, DC: Congressional Research Service, September 7, 1990. p. 2.

13.5, 13.7 Bloomberg Financial Markets, Deutsche Bank Capital Markets Asia), OECD, cf. *Business Week*, April 10, 1995, p. 110.

13.5 (Table) Urata, Shujiro, "Globalization and Regionalization in the Asia-Pacific Region," In Doherty, Eileen M., ed. *Japanese Investment in Asia*. San Francisco: The Asia Foundation and BRIE. 1995. p. 185.

13.6 Oba, Tomomitsu. "Japan's Role in East Asian Investment and Finance," *Japan Review of International Affairs*,p Vol 9. No. 3. Summer 95 p. 247.

13.7 (Table) Population Reference Bureau; *Far Eastern Economic Review*, 17 May 1990, p.30.

13.8 Asian Development Bank. *Asian Development Outlook 1996-1997*. p. 187.

13.9 *Far Eastern Economic Review*. 31 May 90, p. 43.

13.10 Mainland Affairs Council, Taipei.

13.11 Asian Development Bank. *Asian Development Outlook 1996-1997*. p. 20.

13.12 OECD. *Structural Adjustment*. p. 54.

13.13 World Development Report 1987. New York: Oxford University Press, 1987.

13.15-13.16 World Bank data.

13.17 United Nations, "Prospects of World Urbanization," 1989; *The Economist*. 6 October 1990. p. 19.

13.18 *World Development Report 1991*. New York: Oxford University Press, 1991. p. 137.

13.19 Ibid.; United Nations.

13.20 *Far Eastern Economic Review*. 12 January 1989. p. 38.

Credits

Maps

Encyclopedia of Asian History. Copyright © 1988 The Asia Society. (New York: Charles Scribner's Sons, 1988), reprinted by permission of the publisher.

Informational Graphics Laboratory, Department of Geography, University of Oregon, by David Cutting, Cartographer.

Page 63; Milton Osborne, *Southeast Asia* (Sydney: George Allen & Unwin, Ltd., 1985), pp. 19. Copyright © 1985 by Milton Osborne. Reprinted by permission of the publisher George Allen & Unwin, Ltd.

Page 107; John K. Fairbank, et.al., *East Asia: Tradition and Transformation*, (Boston: Houghton Mifflin Co., 1978). p. 481. Copyright © Houghton Mifflin Co., reprinted by permission of the publisher.

Pages 493, 504; Copyright © *The Washington Post.*

Text

Text boxes in which the names of authors are followed by *EAH* are taken from Ainslie T. Embree, Robin J. Lewis, Richard W. Bulliet, Edward L. Farmer, Marius B. Jansen, David S. Lelyveld, and David K. Wyatt, eds., *Encyclopedia of Asian History*, (New York: Charles Scribner's Sons, 1988), Copyright © 1988 The Asia Society. These, and other cited excerpts from the *Encyclopedia*, have been reprinted by permission of Charles Scribner's Sons.

Chapter 1

Caroline Blunden and Mark Elvin, *Cultural Atlas of China*, (New York: Facts on File, 1983).

Abridged from: Anthony Reid, *Southeast Asia in the Age of Commerce 1450-1680: The Lands Below the Winds*, vol. 1 (New Haven: Yale University Press, 1988), pp. 3-10, by permission of the publisher.

Abridged from: Milton Osborne, *Southeast Asia* (Sydney: George Allen & Unwin, Ltd., 1985), pp. 18-35. Copyright © 1985 by Milton Osborne. Reprinted by permission of the publisher.

Esposito, John L., *Islam in Asia: Religion, Politics, and Society*, (New York: Oxford University Press, 1987). pp. 14-15. Copyright © 1987 by the Asia Society. Reprinted by permission.

Abridged from: Anthony Reid, "An 'Age of Commerce' in Southeast Asian History," *Modern Asian Studies*, vol. 24, no. 1, February 1990, pp. 3-7. Copyright

© 1990 by Cambridge University Press. Reprinted by permission of the publisher.

Chapter 2

Page 88. David Joel Steinberg, ed., *In Search of Southeast Asia: A Modern History.* Honolulu: University of Hawaii Press, 1987. p. 146-7. Copyright © 1987 by University of Hawaii Press. Reprinted by permission of the publisher.

Chapter 3

Mikiso Hane, *Modern Japan: A Historical Survey* (Boulder: Westview Press, 1986), pp. 185-90. Copyright© 1986 by Westview Press, Inc. Reprinted by permission of the publisher.

Chapter 4

David Joel Steinberg, ed., *In Search of Southeast Asia: A Modern History.* Part 3. Honolulu: University of Hawaii Press, 1987. pp. 273-81. Copyright © 1987 by University of Hawaii Press. Reprinted by permission of the publisher.

Excerpted from Jonathan Spence, *The Search for Modern China* (New York: W.W. Norton & Co., 1990), pp. 318-19. Copyright © 1990 by Jonathan Spence. Reprinted by permission of the publisher.

Caroline Blunden and Mark Elvin, *Cultural Atlas of China*, (New York: Facts on File, 1983). Reprinted by permission of the publisher.

Chapter 5

James C. Thomson, Jr., Peter W. Stanley, and John Curtis Perry, *Sentimental Imperialists* (New York: Harper & Row, 1981), pp. 190-98, 201-02, 211-16. Copyright © 1981 by James C. Thomson, Jr., Peter W. Stanley, and John Curtis Perry. Reprinted with the permission of the publisher.

David Joel Steinberg, ed., *In Search of Southeast Asia: A Modern History* (Honolulu: University of Hawaii Press, 1987), pp. 356-61, 418-22, 431-34. Copyright © 1987 by University of Hawaii Press. Reprinted by permission of the publisher.

Chapter 6

Chalmers Johnson, "The People Who Invented the Mechanical Nightingale," *Daedalus*, Summer 1990, pp. 79-88. Copyright © 1990 by the American Academy of

Arts and Sciences. Reprinted by permission of the publisher.

Chapter 7

William Overholt, "The Moderation of Politics," in *The Pacific Basin: New Challenges for the United States*, ed., James W. Morley (New York: Academy of Political Science, 1986), p. 39. Copyright © 1986 by the Academy of Political Science. Reprinted by permission of the publisher.

East West Center, *Asia-Pacific Report: Trends, Issues, Challenges*. (Honolulu: East-West Center, 1986), pp 17-26. Copyright © 1986 by the East-West Center. Adapted, updated, and reprinted by permission of the publisher.

Nigel Holloway, "The New NICs," *Far Eastern Economic Review*, February 28, 1991. p. 72. Reprinted by permission of the publisher.

Carter J. Eckert, "Korea's Economic Development in Historical Perspective, 1945-1990," in *Korea Old and New: A History*, Carter J. Eckert, et. al. (Seoul: Ilchokak Publishers, 1990), pp. 388-418. Copyright © 1990 by the Korea Institute, Harvard University. Reprinted by permission.

Chapter 8

Ulf Sundhaussen, "Indonesia: Past and Present Encounters with Democracy," in, *Democracy in Developing Countries: Asia*, Larry Diamond, Juan J. Linz, and Seymour Martin Lipset, eds., vol. 3 of 4 vols. (Boulder, Co: Lynne Rienner Publishers, 1989) pp. 448-49, 462-63, 447-48. Copyright © 1989 by Lynne Rienner Publishers, Inc. and the National Endowment for Democracy. Reprinted by permission of the publisher.

David Joel Steinberg, ed., *In Search of Southeast Asia: A Modern History* (Honolulu: University of Hawaii Press, 1987), pp. 424-25, 431-37. Copyright © 1987 by University of Hawaii Press. Reprinted by permission of the publisher.

Tun-jen Cheng and Stephen Haggard, "Taiwan in Transition," *Journal of Democracy*, Vol. 2, No. 4., Spring 1990. p. 62. Reprinted by permission.

Chapter 9

James C. Thomson, Jr., Peter W. Stanley, and John Curtis Perry, *Sentimental Imperialists: The American Experience in East Asia* (New York: Harper & Row, 1981), pp. 217-34. Copyright © 1981 by James C. Thomson, Jr., Peter W. Stanley, and John Curtis Perry. Reprinted with the permission of HarperCollins.

Carter J. Eckert, "Liberation, Division, and War, 1945-1953," in *Korea Old and New: A History*, Carter J. Eckert, et. al. (Seoul, Korea: Ilchokak Publishers, 1990), pp. 327-46. Copyright © 1990 by the Korea Institute, Harvard University. Reprinted by permission.

David J. Steinberg, ed., *In Search of Southeast Asia: A Modern History* (Honolulu: University of Hawaii Press, 1987), pp. 361-66. Copyright © 1987 by University of Hawaii Press. Reprinted by permission of the publisher.

William Overholt, "The Moderation of Politics," in *The Pacific Basin: New Challenges for the United States*, ed., James W. Morley (New York: Academy of Political Science, 1986), p. 36-7. Copyright © 1986 by the Academy of Political Science. Reprinted by permission of the publisher.

Chapter 10

Fang Lizhi, "The Chinese Amnesia," trans. Perry Link, *The New York Review of Books* (27 September 1990), pp. 30-31. *Copyright* © 1990 by the New York Review of Books. Excerpted and reprinted by permission of the publisher.

Asia Pacific Report, Focus: China in the Reform Era, eds., Charles E. Morrison and Robert F. Dernberger (Honolulu; East-West Center, 1989). Copyright © 1989 by the East West Center. Updated, excerpted and reprinted by permission of the publisher:

Harry Harding, "China's Political Reforms," pp. 43-51.

Robert F. Dernberger, "China's Economic Reforms," pp. 61-64.

William Lavely, "Demographic and Social Change in China," pp. 65-73.

Martin Whyte, "Mao's Revolution and Chinese Culture," pp. 93-101.

Roderick MacFarquhar, "The End of the Chinese Revolution," in *The New York Review of Books* (20 July 1989), pp. 8-10. Copyright © 1989 by *The New York Review of Books*. Reprinted by permission of the publisher.

Vaclav Smil. *China's Environmental Crisis*. (Armonk: M.E. Sharpe, 1993). pp. 190-194.

"Tibet," p. 451, was researched and written by Blaine Erickson.

Philip Bowring, "The Next Phase," in *Capital Trends*. Vol.2, No.4. pp. 3-7. Washington DC: Nikko Research Center (America). March 1997.

Chapter 13

Frida Johansen, World Bank Discussion Paper No. 203. Washington DC: The World Bank. 1993.

Nigel Holloway, *Far Eastern Economic Review*, Volume 150, Number 41. p. 73. Reprinted by permission of the publisher.

Masakazu Yamazaki, "Asia, A Civilization in the Making," In *Foreign Affairs*, July/August 1996. pp. 106-118.

Photograph and Graphic Credits

Andromeda Oxford Ltd., 1.2, 1.4; AP/Wide World, 8.1, 8.3, 10.5; Archives Nationales de France, 14.10; Buffalo & Erie County Historical Society and SUCB Library, 9.5; California State Historical Society, 2.10; *Chicago Tribune*, 5.6; *Dallas Morning News*, 5.1; Review Publishing Company, 7.5, 10.6-7, 13.25; *Graphic* (Sept.3, 1894) 7.2; Japan Ministry of Foreign Affairs, 3.4; Japan National Committee for Pacific Economic Cooperation, 13.1; Kansas State Historical Society, 4.1, 4.3; Library of Congress 2.1, 2.3, 2.4, 2.7, 3.1-3.3, 3.5-13, 4.2, 4.4, 4.8-9, 4.11-14, 5.9, 5.11-12, 5.14, 6.1, 7.1, 9.1, 9.2, 9.6, 12.1; Lyndon B. Johnson Library, 8.4, 9.8; Mainichi Newspaper Company, 5.5, 5.10, 5.7; Malaysia National Archives, 8.2; Mansell Collection 2.6; National Archives, 5.4, 5.8; *New York Times*, 9.4; Popperfoto, 9.9; Soviet National Committee for Pacific Economic Cooperation, 12.2; *Peking Review,* 10.3; *St. Louis Post Dispatch*, 9.3; U.S. Naval Historical Center, p. 83, 2.6; *Washington Star*, 5.2. 9.7; Xinhua, 4.5-7, 10.1-2.

About the Book and Author

The Asia-Pacific is rapidly emerging as a global economic and political powerhouse. Looking at both Southeast and East Asia, this richly illustrated volume stresses broad, cross-cutting themes of regional history, with an emphasis on the interactions between cultures and nations. Mark Borthwick begins his discussion with an overview of political evolution and cultural and economic trends from ancient times through the eighteenth century. He then considers more recent developments in Asia in their historical context, balancing national and international factors that underlie Asia-Pacific economic growth and political change. Special chapters are devoted to the dilemmas confronting modern China and to the history of the Russian Far East. The conclusion weighs the key domestic and international issues facing the nations of Pacific Asia and the probable interactions these nations will have with the global economy.

This book stands alone as an interdisciplinary introduction to Asia and the Pacific. It is also the companion text to a PBS college-level telecourse and television series. The original telecourse consists of ten one-hour television programs, this text, a study guide and faculty manual. *The Pacific Century* telecourse was developed by the Pacific Basin Institute and is part of the Annenberg/CPB Collection.

For information about purchasing video-cassettes, taping off-air, and licensing the telecourse, call 1-800-LEARNER in the United States.

Mark Borthwick is the U.S. Executive Director of the Pacific Economic Cooperation Council (PECC), an organization of twenty-two Pacific Rim economies comprising businesses, research institutions, and government agencies. A veteran of the Vietnam War, 1969-1970, he joined the sociology and anthropology faculty at Iowa State University in 1977 after receiving a Ph.D. in social anthropology from the University of Iowa. In 1978 he became a Fellow of the Duke University Roundtable on Science, Technology and Public Affairs; he moved to Washington, D.C. in 1979 as a AAAS Congressional Fellow to serve on the staff of the House Subcommittee on Asian and Pacific Affairs. Since 1992 he has served as Chairman of the PECC International Coordinating Group, the organization's policy research body.

INDEX

China (continued)
  women's movement, 189
  worldview, 30
Chinese amnesia, 415–416
Chinese Communist Party (CCP), 177, 178, 179,
  180, 181(figs.), 182, 183, 184, 188, 418–424*pas-
  sim,* 450, 453
  culture and, 443–449
Chinese revolution, end, 449–453
*Chinese Women's Journal, ,*189
Cho Chung-hun, 294
Chola Dynasty, 76(n10)
Cho Man-sik, 384
Chong Chu-yong, 295
Cho Pyong-ik, 381
Choshu, 122, 123, 125, 129, 131, 134
Choson Dynasty, 297, 299, 301
Chou Ta-kuan, 61
Christianity, 32, 52, 69, 72, 80, 81, 132, 142, 146,
  300
  missionaries, 150, 157, 365, 366
  see also Catholicism
Chuang Chi-yon, 196
Chuch'e, 353
Chukchi, 487, 497, 498
Chulalongkorn, 110(fig.), 111
Chulalongkorn, 325–326
Chun Doo Hwan, 291, 350, 351–352, 353
Chungking (Chongqing), 369, 370
Churchill, Winston, 217, 226
Citizen armies, 137
City planning, 292
Civil service, 35, 421
Cixi, 104, 144–145, 150, 173, 174
Cleveland, Grover, 114
Clive, Robert, 84, 92
Cloth, 83–84, 86, 199
  see also Silks; Textiles
Cloves, 74, 78(graph), 88
Clowns, 342
Coal, 113, 128, 243
Coalition Government of Democratic Kampuchea
  (CGDK), 470
Cochinchina, 111, 237
Cock-fighting, 57
Coffee, 77, 88, 109
Cojuango, Eduardo, 346–347
Cold war, 235, 238, 243, 244, 368, 373, 401
Collectivization, 406, 432
Colonialism, 77, 309, 525
  democratic change and, 359
  Korea, 289–290, 295, 376–379
Comintern, 179, 180, 182, 193, 488
Committee for the Preparation of Korean Indepen-
  dence (CPKI), 378

Communes, 182, 185, 406
Communications, 113, 544–545
  see also Media, the
Communism, 180–185, 395
  China, 368–372*passim,* 372–376*passim,* 374(fig.),
    403, 404, 415, 416, 418. *see also* Chinese Com-
    munist Party
  China, chronology, 405–413
  Confucianism and, 311
  Indonesia, 336, 340, 458–461, 463
  Japan, 250–251, 252
  Korea, 353–355, 376–385*passim*
  Philippines, 344(fig.)
  US and, 388
  US view, 366, 373, 374(fig.), 380, 397, 402(n11)
  Vietnam, 388–392*passim,* 479–480
  Vietnam War and, 463
Compasses, 36, 45
Competition, Pacific Asia, 324–325
Computer chips, 248–249
Confucianism, 19–21, 25–26, 30, 32, 42, 63, 97,
  98, 142, 157, 173, 177, 190, 196, 324–325, 350
  academies, 27, 53
  attacks on, 186, 188, 192
  business and, 310
  capitalism and, 308–317
  China, 312, 368
  democracy and, 358
  economic growth and, 307–308
  family business and, 312–313
  Japan, 28, 33–34, 49, 121, 151, 158, 312
  Korea, 27, 47, 146, 312
  merchants and, 25, 36
  Neo-Confucianism and, 38, 48, 49, 72
  South Korea, 299–301
  Vietnam, 388, 473
Confucius, 307(fig.), 311–312, 445
Consensus politics, 33, 34
Constantinople, 77
Constitutions
  Japan, 33–34, 137, 138, 208, 225, 229, 252–253
  Malaysia, 332–333
  Philippines, 344–345
  South Korea, 350, 351
  Thailand, 329
  Vietnam, 392
Containment, 401
Cook, James, 87, 487
Coolies, 97, 117
Corruption, 142, 196, 203, 235
  Vietnam, 471, 472
Cossacks, 487, 496, 497
Cotton, 5, 87, 137, 210
Coups, 127–128, 147, 148, 174, 194, 208

Industrial Revolution, 78, 87, 211
Industry, 284, 294, 313, 406, 429(graph)
Inflation, 243, 247, 248, 528(graph)
Influence of Sea Power on History, The, 202
Infrastructure, 540–541
Inner Asia, 4–5
Inner Mongolia, 4
Inoue Junnosuke, 205
Inoue Kaoru, 125, 158
Intellectuals, China, 25, 406, 415, 417, 422, 423,
    452, 453
Inter-Governmental Group on Indonesia (IGGI),
    466
Interest rates, 248
Intermarriage, 53
International influences, democratic change and,
    361–362
Inukai Tsuyoshi, 205
Investment. *See* Foreign investment
Iran, 248
Iran–Iraq War, 248
Irrigation, 61
    see also Water
Islam, 32, 67, 68, 71, 72, 73, 88, 330, 336, 342
    see also Muslims
Isolationism, 2, 50, 146
Isuzu, 244
Italo–Ethiopean war, 216
Italy, 162, 173, 211, 216
Ito Hirobumi, 123, 125, 129, 131, 132, 135, 136,
    138, 142, 149, 150, 155, 158
Ivory, 79
Iwakura Mission, 129, 134
Iwakura Tomomi, 125, 158
Iwasaki Yataro, 145, 158

Jaisohn, Philip, 194–196
Jakarta, 231
Jansen, Marius B., 27
Japan, 11, 38, 47–48, 75, 76(n7), 78, 84, 101, 114,
    119–160, 124(map), 141(map), 161, 201–211,
    204(map), 239–240, 241–272, 242(map)
    agriculture, 130
    alliance, 519–520
    ancient, 27–28
    Asia–Pacific economy and, 512–522, 513(graph),
        514(table), 515(graphs), 517(tables)
    balance of power, 545–546
    bureaucracy, 257, 262, 263(graph), 268, 269, 270,
        294
    business, 262, 263(graph)
    capital, 259
    cartels, 243, 245
    character, 254
    China and, 156–158, 314

commerce, 314
conscription, 132, 136, 137
consensus, 254
constitutions, 33–34, 137, 138, 208, 225, 229, 252–
    253
contradictions, 159
daimyo, 129, 131
defense, 251(fig.), 255, 520
democracy, 159, 203, 205, 207, 210, 213, 227,
    228, 262–265
diplomacy, 519
diplomatic identity, 250–252
domains, 123, 128, 129
earthquakes, 203, 224
economy, 49–50, 128, 130, 137, 147, 157, 201,
    202–203, 207, 224, 229–230, 241–272, 252–
    261, 265–270, 272, 274, 310, 366, 545
education, 132, 133, 151, 156, 228–229
elections, 205
electoral system, 267
elites, 265
emperor's role, 205, 207, 225
environment, 543
executives, 258
expansion, 488
exports, 255, 266, 518(graph)
family businesses, 309, 312, 315
farmers, 129, 131, 132, 137
Finance Ministry, 134
fishing, 148–149
foreign policy, 128, 134, 136, 252–253
GDP, 265–266(graph), 269
geography, 5
GNP(graph), 255, 263
Great Britain and, 125, 134, 135, 140, 150, 152,
    173, 202, 519–520
hegemony, 519–520
Hong Kong and, 314
imports, 246, 256(graph), 260–261(graph)
income-doubling plan, 247, 249
individual, the, 254, 258
Indonesia and, 477–478
industrial policies, 245–246
industries, 250, 257
investments, 246–247
isolation, 27, 50, 51, 81
Korea and, 28, 40, 47, 50, 131, 134, 135, 145–
    148*passim,* 151, 288–294, 314
Koreans in, 203
Korean War boom, 243–244
labor, 243, 244–245(graph)
labor-management, 254–255
land reform, 229, 243
living standards, 250
local self-government, 132

Japan (continued)
    management, 314
    manufacturing, 249(graph)
    military, 138, 140, 149, 156–159*passim,* 203–
        211*passim,* 214, 224, 229, 244, 251–252
    modernization, 98, 123, 128, 130, 131, 156–157,
        158, 160
    Namamugi incident, 125
    national studies schools, 50–51
    nationalism, 252–253
    navy, 125, 149, 202, 205, 209, 218, 227
    Netherlands and, 50, 81, 121, 122
    NIEs and, 283
    obedience tradition, 157
    Occupation period, 214, 225, 227–230, 241, 243
    opening of, 114, 159
    pacifism, 244, 250
    political system, 137, 138(graph), 261–265,
        263(graph)
    politics, 519
    power, 325
    propaganda, 389(fig.)
    regionalism, 526
    research and development, 269–270
    rice riots, 202
    role, 250, 252
    Russia and, 487, 488
    sanctions against, 216, 217, 218
    savings system, 254
    security, post-occupation, 251, 252
    self-perception, 250
    silver exports, 86(graph)
    standard of living, 250, 258
    stereotype, 258
    Taiwan, 314
    technology, 255, 266, 541, 542
    textile experts, 210–211
    trade, 2, 139(graph), 147, 248–250, 254, 258–261,
        518(table)
    treaty ports, 125
    US and, 153, 202, 216, 217, 241, 248–250, 251,
        255–259, 510, 519–520
    US view, 367(fig.)
    USSR and, 213, 494
    values, 254
    Vietnam and, 235
    women, 133, 156, 205, 228, 229, 244, 264(graph)
    world affairs, 535
Japan Development Bank, 245
Jardine Matheson, 93
Jardine, William, 93
Java, 58, 64, 67, 68, 73, 75, 79, 88, 106, 108, 170,
    210, 231, 232, 233, 336, 340, 342, 461
Java War, 106, 109, 170
Jesuits, 80

Jian family, 189–190
Jiang Qing, 190, 410, 445
Jiang Zemin, 413
Jiazhou territory, 178
Jiji Press, 133
Joffe, Adolph A., 179
Johnson, Chalmers, 254, 255, 257, 262–265, 268,
    317
Johnson, Lyndon, 293, 388, 389(fig.), 391, 399,
    459, 463, 464
Johor sultanate, 108
Jones Act, 168
Judaism, 32
Judd, Walter, 375
Junks, 74
Jurchen tribes, 36, 38, 51
Jusen, 266, 267

Kabayan, 342
Kabo Reform, 151, 194
Kagan, Richard C., 277
Kagoshima, 125, 134
Kaifeng, 55
Kaifu, Prime Minister, 519, 520
Kampuchea. *See* Cambodia
Kanagawa, Treaty of, 120, 121, 147
Kanghwa Island, 146
Kang Youwei, 145, 154, 174, 177
Kanrin Maru, 123, 125, 133
Kanto earthquake, 203, 224
Kapsin coup, 148, 151, 194
Kartini, Raden Adjeng, 170
Katipunan, 163
Kato Komei, 140
Katsu Kaishu, 121, 125, 128
Katsura Taro, 152
Kawasaki Steel, 246
Keio University, 133, 192
Keiretsu, 259–261, 260(graph), 271
Kelantan, 111
Kenbai, 546, 549(n13)
Kennan, George F., 366, 393–394, 396, 401,
    402(n10)
Kennedy, John F., 388
Keppel, Henry, 108
Khabarov, 487
Khmer Empire, 59, 61–62, 68
    see also Cambodia
Khmer People's National Liberation Front
    (KPNLF), 470
Khmer Rouge, 464, 469–470, 482–483
    China and, 470, 483
    USSR and, 483
Khruschev, Nikita, 398(fig.)
Kido Koin, 123

Laozi, 21, 33
  see also Daoism
La Solidaridad, 163
Last Emperor, The, 174
Latin America, 69, 108, 113
Laurel, Jose, 235, 344
Laurel, Salvador, 347
Lavely, William, 431–439
Laxalt, Paul, 347
Lay, Horatio N., 104
Leadership, democratic change and, 362
League of Nations, 202, 203
Le Duc Tho, 471
Lee Deng-hui, 277
Lee Kuan Yew, 278, 315, 316(fig.), 335, 350, 544
Lee Teng-hui, 356, 357
Legalists, 19, 21, 25–26
Legge, John D., 172
Leifer, Michael, 460, 479
Lenin, Vladimir, 112, 179–180, 488
Letters of a Javanese Princess, 170
Liaodong Peninsula, 149, 203
Liberal Democratic Party (LDP), 252, 261–267*passim,* 352
Li Dazhao, 182, 185, 186, 188
Life expectancy, 537
Ligachev, Yegor, 472
Li Hongzhang, 98, 104, 142–150*passim*
Li–Lobanov Treaty, 149–150
Lin Biao, 408, 409(fig.), 450
Linh, Nguyen Van. *See* Nguyen Van Linh
Lin Xiangqian, 182
Lin Zexu, 94, 97
Li Peng, 412, 413, 452, 453, 479
Li Ruihuan, 413
Li Si, 22–23
Literacy, 51, 52, 114, 128, 132, 158, 237
Literature, 32, 51, 78, 99, 171, 187, 191, 197, 232, 474
  China, 444, 445, 446
Liu, Henry, 356
Liu Shaoqi, 406, 407, 408(fig.), 449
Li Xiannian, 412, 413
Lon Nol, 482
Long March, 185
Lopez family, 345
Louis XIV of France, 81
Low-income economies, 287
Lu Xun, 187, 188
Luang Phibun Songkhram, 326
Lubis, Mochtar, 318
Luce, Henry R., 184, 375
Lucky, 295
Luna, Antonio, 166

Mabini, Apolinario, 164–165, 166, 344
Macao, 80, 81, 83, 105, 522
Macapagal, Diosdado, 343
MacArthur, Douglas, 214, 220, 223, 225, 229, 243, 383(fig.), 386, 387, 397
Macartney, Lord, 90–91, 101
Mace, 74, 78(graph), 80
MacFarquhar, Roderick, 314, 449–453
MacMurray, John V.A., 215
Madison, Angus, 507
Madrid, 180
Magellan, 81, 87
Magsaysay, Ramon, 235, 343, 393
Mahan, Alfred Thayer, 165, 202
Mahathir Mohamad, 318, 333, 334, 335, 360, 526
Mai Chi Tho, 480
Makassar, 72, 73, 74, 83, 107
Malacca, 64, 68, 79, 105
Malacca Straits, 43, 63(fig.), 88, 107
Malaria, 92
Malay, 278
Malaya, 278, 280, 458
Malayan Chinese Association (MCA), 332
Malayan Indian Congress (MIC), 332
Malaysia, 62, 64, 74, 86, 88, 105–109*passim,* 217, 239, 280–283*passim,* 331(map), 350
  democracy and, 359
  economic policy, 334
  economy, 536
  ethnic Chinese, 318(graph)
  ethnic groups, 330(graph)
  exports, 284(graph), 285
  geography, 6–7
  Great Britain and, 332
  Japan and, 330, 332
  language, 71, 88, 172
  parliamentary democracy, 330–336
  political evolution, 330, 332–333
  religion, 330
  riots, 333, 334
Malik. *See* Adam Malik
Mamlukes, 74
Management, 313–315
Manchu Dynasty, 4, 5, 487, 496
Manchukuo, 184, 203
Manchuria, 4, 11, 48, 54, 114, 149, 150, 153, 184, 185, 201, 203, 205, 219, 226, 493, 497
Mandalay, 100
Mandarin, 54, 76(n1)
Mandate of Heaven, 18–19, 28, 30, 403
Manifest Destiny, 119
Manila Galleon, 84, 86, 87
Manufacturing, NIEs, 284

Mukden, 152, 198, 203, 205
Munholland, J. Kim, 113
Muoi, Do, 481
Murasaki Shikibu, Lady, 28
Muraviev, N.N., 498
Murdani, Benny, 478, 479
Muruyama, Tomiichi, 267
Music, 57, 100, 197
Muslims, 79, 80, 86, 88, 108, 109, 231, 477
   see also Islam
Mussolini, Benito, 162
Musyawarhara, 339
Mutsu Munemitsu, 135
Mutsuhito, 129
Mutual Security Treaty, 520
Myanmar. *See* Burma

Nagasaki, 214, 226, 380
Nakasone Yasuhiro, 252–253
Nam Phong, 191
Namamugi incident, 125
NAMFREL, 349
Nanjing, 47, 55, 80, 95
   Massacre, 209–210
   Treaty of, 96, 101, 103
Nanyang Brothers Tobacco Company, 190
Napier, Lord, 93–94, 101
Nara period, 28
Nasser, Gamal Abdel, 238
Nasution, 336, 339
National Liberation Front (NLF), 390, 458
National liberation movements, 239
National Party Conference, 412
Nationalism, 155, 161, 162–163, 179, 220, 223, 230
   China, 369, 370
   Indonesia, 457, 458
   Korea, 378, 381
   South Korea, 298–299, 303
   Vietnam, 458
   See also particular country
Nationalist Party, 192
Nationalistas, 168, 169, 343
Natsume Soseki, 137, 159
Natural resources, 388
   see also Environment
Navies, 53, 56
   see also Armadas; Japan; Soviet Union
Navigation, 36, 45, 62, 77
Ne Win, 329
Nehru, 238
Nemesis, 106(fig.)
Neo-Confucianism, 300
Nestorians, 80

Netherlands Indies, 170, 217
   see also Indonesia
Netherlands, 48, 77, 81–88*passim,* 92, 106, 107, 121, 170, 210, 231, 233, 458
New Culture Movement, 173, 185–188
New Era in Asia, The, 162
New Guinea. *See* Papua New Guinea
New Order in Asia concept, 213
New World, 86
New Youth, 185, 187
New Zealand, 87
Newly industrialized economies, 274, 276–280, 279(graph), 509–510, 513, 516
   growth, 276(graph)
   Japan and, 517(tables)
   manufacturing, 278, 283
   technology, 542
Ng Lun Ngai-Hai, 101
Ngo Dinh Diem, 361, 388, 390, 458
Nguyen Dynasty, 102
Nguyen Truong To, 190–191
Nguyen Van Linh, 471–474*passim,* 480, 481
Nguyen Van Thieu, 391, 392, 399, 459, 464
Nhan Dan, 472, 473, 480, 481
Nihon Yusen Kaisha, 145
Nimitz, Chester, 220, 223
Nitze, Paul H., 396
Nixon, Richard, 247, 257, 345, 386, 391, 392, 399, 400, 410, 464
Nixon Doctrine, 399
Nogi Maresuke, 152, 159
Nonaligned Movement, 238–239, 458, 466, 479
Norodom Sihanouk, 67, 102, 470, 474, 475
North America, 89
   Pacific coast, 7–8, 487
North Korea, 292, 353, 355, 378–382*passim*
   democracy and, 359
   economy, 354(graph), 355
   Japan and, 353
   United States and, 353
North Vietnam, 236, 237, 402(n7), 459
   China and, 391, 398
   Soviet Union and, 398
   see also South Vietnam
Northern Territories, 492
NSC-68, 396, 397
Nuclear weapons, 214, 226, 238, 353
Nurhachi, 51
Nutmeg, 74, 78(graph), 80, 88

Occupation period, Japan, 214, 225, 227–230, 241, 243
Oceania, 7, 87
Oda Nobunaga, 48
Oe Kenzaburo, 208

Rifles, 48
Rights, 196
Riots, Tibet, 412
    see also Demonstrations
Rizal, Jose, 154, 163, 164(fig.), 318
Robertson, Walter, 375
Robinson, Ronald, 113
Roches, Leon, 125
Rodriguez, Eulogio (Amang), 343
Rogers, John, 145
Roh Tae Woo, 352, 353
Rohlen, Thomas P., 312
Roman Empire, 25, 29
Romulo, Carlos P. 234
Roosevelt, Franklin, 169, 217, 218, 366, 371, 373, 385
Roosevelt, Theodore, 153, 160, 174
Roxas, Manuel, 169, 234, 235
Rozhdestvensky, Zinovi, 152
Rozman, Gilbert, 308–317
Rubber, 77, 109, 111, 217
Rui Xingwen, 413
Rural economy, 282
Rusk, Dean, 380, 399
Russia, 112, 114, 121, 140, 149–150, 179, 360, 487–506, 489(maps), 490(map)
    frontier spirit, 495–498
    geography, 493–494
    Japan and, 488, 496
    US and, 402(n10), 495
Russian–American Fur Company, 89
Russian Revolution, 179, 488
Russo–Japanese War, 140, 150, 152–153, 154
Ryukyu Islands, 11, 50, 75, 120, 145

Sahul Shelf, 7
Saigon Giai Phong, 473
Saigon, Treaty of, 109, 111
Saigo Takamori, 128, 131, 136, 147, 158
Saito Makoto, 198, 199
Sakamoto Ryoma, 127
Sakhalin Island, 153, 200, 226, 506(nn6, 11)
Sakuma Shozan, 146
Samsung, 295, 296
Samurai, 41, 49, 51, 121, 122, 127–131*passim,* 137, 158, 310, 314
San Francisco, 117
San Francisco Peace Treaty, 214, 245
Sandalwood, 88
Sanjo Sanetomi, 125
Sappanwood, 74
Saracens, 41
Sarekat Islam movement, 172
Satow, Ernest, 125

Satsuma han, 122–131*passim,* 134, 136
Satsuma Rebellion, 131, 136
Savings and investment, 272
Scholar-bureaucrats, 310
Schumpeter, Joseph, 112
Schurman, Jacob, 165, 166
Science, 105, 143, 146, 157, 158, 171, 186
Search for Modern China, The, 2
Seiyukai party, 135
Sejong, 47
Sekigahara, Battle of, 48, 49
Self-determination, 168, 179, 193, 215
Self-Strengthening Movement, 98, 103, 144
Semar, 342
Semiconductor market, 542
Sentimental Imperialists, 368
Seoul Textile Company, 199
Seppuku, 131
Service, John Stewart, 375
Seven Years' War, 84
Seventeen Article Constitution, 33–34
Shamanism, 300
Shandong Province, 114, 149, 173, 201, 203
Shang, 19
Shanghai, 97, 107, 125, 160, 183, 184, 189, 190, 200
Shanghai Communique, 400
Shatov, Vladimir ("Bill"), 500
Sherman, 146
Shestakof, Afanase, 499(map)
Shevardnadze, Eduard, 502(fig.)
Shibusawa, 158
Shimabara revolt, 50
Shimoda, 119, 120
Shimonoseki, Treaty of, 145, 149
Shinto, 28, 33, 51, 158, 199
Shipbuilding, 45, 74, 246
Shizoku, 130
    see also Samurai
Shotoku of Japan, 33
Siam, 73, 75, 79, 86, 111
    see also Thailand
Siberia, 487
    geography, 5–6
Sihanouk. *See* Norodom Sihanouk
Silk Road, 4, 9, 25, 33
Silks, 36, 51, 62, 79, 90, 92, 93, 207
    see also Textiles
Silla kingdom, 27, 28, 29, 34
Silver, 50, 51, 84, 85(map), 86(graph), 89, 90, 96(graph), 163, 189
Sin'ganhoe, 201

United States (continued)
  Declaration of Independence, 236
  democracy, 361–362
  expansionism, 115(map), 119, 159
  immigration, 174, 202
  in Asia, 365–402, 367(fig.)
  manufacturing, 249(graph)
  Marines, 120
  market and, 509
  Navy, 145–146, 220, 223 , 114, 116, 149, 153
  Philippines and, 161, 165–166, 168–169, 214,
    234–235
  productivity, 245(graph)
  reforms, 249–250
  Russia and, 488, 495
  Taiwan and, 239
  trade, 534
  Vietnam and, 235–236
  see also Pacific coast
United States Army Military Government in
  Korea (USAMGIK), 381–385*passim*
Untung, 460
U Nu, 238
Urban areas, 72, 117, 169, 247, 250
Urban expropriation, 406
Urbanization, 537, 540
  China, 428, 435–436

Values, 546–548
Van den Bosch, Johannes, 106
Van Gogh, Vincent, 100
van Wolferin, Karel, 268
Vasco da Gama, 75, 77, 78
Vatican, 80
Venice, 74
Ver, General, 347
Versailles Peace Conference and Treaty, 161, 162,
  168, 172, 179, 193, 201, 208, 366
Victoria of England, 93
Video-cassette recorders, 248
Viet Cong, 390, 391, 392
  see also National Liberation Front
Viet Minh, 193, 235–236, 237, 390, 458
Vietnam, 24, 33, 57–58, 62, 63, 66, 69–72*passim,*
  80, 86, 103, 161, 190–193, 212(nn11, 12), 214,
  235–237, 280, 287, 401
  agriculture, 471–472, 475–476
  Cambodia and, 469–471, 474–475, 479
  China and, 64–65, 411, 469, 475, 470, 471
  corruption, 471, 472
  debt, 471, 473(graph)
  democracy and, 359
  economy, 390, 468–473*passim,* 473(graph), 476
  elections, 237, 386
  foreign investment, 474(graph)

foreign policy, 482
France and, 109, 111, 145, 162, 180, 190, 192,
  235, 236–237, 388, 390, 458
geography, 6
ideology, 480–481
industry, 471
Laos and, 474, 475
nationalism, 190–191, 192
openness, 472–475
politics, 481
post-World War II, 462(map), 457, 463–464
reform, 471–472, 479–481
reunification, 468–476, 479–482, 484–485(chronology)
trade, 475(graph)
US and, 388–392, 389(fig.), 458, 459, 470, 471, 475
USSR and, 469, 470, 471, 472
Western influence, 473–474
Vietnam War, 296, 390–392
  end, 463–464
  public opinion, 398
  South Korea and, 293–294, 301
Vladivostok, 149, 180, 200, 506
Vladivostok Initiative, 491, 494–495
"Vladivostopiol," 506(n16)
Voitinsky, Gregor, 179
Vo Nguyen Giap, 235, 236, 237
Vo Phien, 392

Wa, 27
Waldron, Arthur N., 42
Wallace, Henry, 371
Wallis, Samuel, 87
Wanghia, Treaty of, 96, 114
Wang Kon, 34
Wang Renzhi, 412
Wang Zhen, 411, 412, 413
Wan Li, 411
War of 1812, 88
Ward, F.T., 143
Warfare, 36
  see also particular war
Warren, S., 94
Warring States Period, 20(map)
Washington Conference, 202, 214
Water, 59, 61, 440
Weather forecasting, 45
Weber, Max, 300, 313
Wedemeyer, Albert C., 371
Wei Jingsheng, 411, 416, 450, 455(n2)
Wei Yuan, 143, 146
Wei Zheng, 32
West Germany, 249(graph)
  see also Germany

West New Guinea, 340
West River, 4
Western cultural influence
    China, 443, 445–449
    Vietnam, 473–474
Western Learning, 153, 157
Westmoreland, William, 391
Whaling, 87–88, 119
Whampoa Military Academy, 177, 179
White Lotus Rebellion, 53
Whyte, Martin, 443–449
Wilhelm II of Germany, 153
Williams, Michael, 457–485
Wilson, Woodrow, 162, 168, 174, 365–366, 494
Wi Man, 27
Wing On, 190
Women, 28, 56, 57, 65, 264(graph), 286, 315, 381, 392
Won'gwang, 34
Wood, Leonard, 169
Woodside, Alexander, 388–392
World affairs, Asian influence, 534–535
World Peace Conference, 155
World Trade Organization (WTO), 533
World War I, 117, 140, 161, 178, 192, 201
World War II, 201, 211, 238, 366, 369
    air power, 219, 220, 223, 240(n3)
    see also Pacific War
Wright, Frank Lloyd, 100
Wudi, 24, 25
Wu Zhihui, 187

Xianfeng, 103
Xiang Jingyu, 189
Xijian, 4
Xinjiang, geography, 5
Xiongnu, 18, 24
Xu Guangjin, 103
Xunzi, 26

Yadrintsev, Nikolai, 498
Yakutia, 506(nn1, 2)
Yalta Conference, 226
Yamagata Aritomo, 123, 129–132*passim*, 136, 140, 152, 158
Yamato, 28
Yamazaki, Masakazu, 547, 548
Yan'an rectification, 415
Yang Jian, 32
Yang Shangkun, 413, 450–453*passim*
Yangzi River, 4, 11, 107, 114, 149, 175

Yan Mingfu, 413
Yao Yilin, 412, 453
Yasakazu Yamazaki, 1, 2
Yasuda, 132
Yasukuni Shrine, 252
"Yellow Peril," 153, 223(fig.)
Yellow River, 11, 54, 55
    see also Huanghe River
Ye Mingchen, 103
Yen, 243, 247, 248
Yen bloc, 520–521
Yen Zhi Tui, 325
Yezhov, Nikolai, 506(n12)
Yi Dynasty, 43, 47, 147, 312
Ying–Yang, 25(fig.)
Yi Pyong-ch'ol, 295
Yi Song-gye, 43
Yi Sung-man, 378
Yi Yong-hwi, 200
Yo Un-hyong, 377–378, 385
Yokohama, 121
Yong La, 74
Yoshida Doctrine, 250, 252
Yoshida Shigeru, 227, 250–252
Yoshida Shoin, 122–123
Youth, 228, 232
Yuan Dynasty. *See* Mongols
Yuan Shikai, 147, 148, 175, 176, 177, 178
Yun Ch'i-ho, 195, 196

Zaibatsu, 132, 156, 203, 210, 228, 243, 279(n1)
Zaiton, 74
Zeng Guofan, 98, 143
Zhao Ziyang, 411, 412, 413(fig.), 417, 420, 429, 451, 452
Zheng, 17–23*passim*, 42
Zheng Chenggong, 52
Zheng He, 43, 56, 75
Zhong Ke, 17
Zhou Enlai, 179, 181(fig.), 184, 226, 238, 239, 240, 400, 409, 450, 525, 547
Zhou kingdoms, 17, 18, 19
Zhou Shuren. *See* Lu Xun
Zhu De, 184
Zhu Rongji, 413, 454
Zhu Yuanzhang, 42
Zhuangzi, 21
Zhuxi, 38, 48
Zobel family, 343
Zoku giin, 262, 263
Zongli Yamen, 98, 104, 105